Second Edition

Drugs, Crime, & Justice

Contemporary Perspectives

Larry K. Gaines
California State University, San Bernardino

Peter B. Kraska
Eastern Kentucky University

WAVELAND
PRESS, INC.
Prospect Heights, Illinois

For information about this book, contact:
Waveland Press, Inc.
4180 IL Route 83, Suite 101
Long Grove, IL 60047-9580
(847) 634-0081
info@waveland.com
www.waveland.com

Preface

Why should breaking drug laws hold any more importance for study than breaking burglary laws, family violence laws, or homicide laws—topics that are rarely included on permanent curriculums? The personal experiences of the editors offer one justification for the importance of a reader like this one on drugs, crime, and justice. Despite having taught and researched the drug issue for seven years, we perceived the full impact of its importance while teaching a seminar. No matter which direction our focus turned—social inequality, media coverage of crime, criminal justice as industry, racism, crime causation, prison overcrowding, or expanding police powers—we bumped into substance abuse and drug wars as an influential dimension for each. It became clear that understanding crime and justice issues requires a sound understanding of the nature of substance abuse and our society's reaction to it.

As the first section in this collection illustrates, the rhetoric and ideology of "war" has dominated the response of politicians and bureaucrats to the problem of substance abuse. The war analogy frames all discussion; drugs are an evil enemy to be eradicated in order to save society. Government officials, with help from the media, have linked punishment-oriented drug control efforts with the never-ending "war on crime." Contrary to the rhetoric, the act of altering one's state of consciousness using a chemical or organic substance differs substantively from stealing a car, killing someone, or sexually abusing a child. Yet the government orchestrates coordinated efforts against drug use and distribution, using federal agencies (including the armed forces), state and local departments, and special task forces. In some instances separate court and correctional facilities are enlisted to address the problem of drugs. These efforts yield tremendous "results" in the form of massive numbers of drug arrests, drug convictions, and drug incarcerations.

The numbers alone, combined with issues of civil liberties, make this a vital area of study.

Section two addresses one of the most misunderstood dimensions of drugs. The misguided, simplistic belief—"drugs cause crime"—is a foundation of the drug war. Again, there is nothing intrinsically criminal about using mind-altering substances; what justifies its criminalization is the perceived criminogenic consequences stemming from its use. Research and logic tell us that although drug use itself (especially alcohol use) may contribute to crime, the crime associated with drugs may be better explained as (1) caused by drug *laws* themselves and/or (2) the result of a third variable such as inequality. Understanding the complexities of the drug/crime connection is critical for understanding crime and justice issues in general.

The sources and markets for drugs (section three) and the enforcement of drug laws (section four) are integral issues in the day-to-day operations of each component of the criminal justice system. Even if these substances were not illegal (alcohol provides a prime illustration), they still pose significant health, psychological, and criminal justice related problems for the police officer, juvenile justice practitioner, corrections officer, probation officer, and substance abuse counselor. Criminalization superimposes a sticky moral and legal dimension that most practitioners confront daily. Section six provides several perspectives on important issues of drug use. This book attempts to provide readers with factual, theoretical, and philosophical information about a multifaceted topic.

Contents

Section IV   Policing Drugs

Section V   Treating the Drug Offender

Section VI   Perspectives on the Drug Problem

Introduction

Without some background for the genesis of criminal justice responses to the use of illegal substances, it is difficult to judge whether those responses are adequate, effective, and proportional to the harm. The "war" on drugs is based on the belief that the criminal justice system and punishment are the key ingredients in solving the problems linked with drugs. The goal is a drug-free society; zero tolerance is the rallying cry. The same strategies are pursued repeatedly: interdicting drugs at the border, intense law enforcement, and harsh mandatory sentences. As David Musto points out in the first article, campaigns for abstinence have often been fueled by fantasies. We need a factual record of previous experiences that is not colored by fears, prejudice, and exaggerated accounts about the effects of mind-altering substances. In this introduction we touch on a number of issues to keep in mind as you read the articles in this book.

Defining Drugs

Imprecise terminology obscures precise analysis. Most people do not question that the United States has a drug problem or that drug abuse can destroy people and communities. Mention our "drug problem" to the average person and notice how the immediate link is to *illicit* drugs—not to alcohol, cigarettes, or prescription medications. Using the term "drug" as a generic descriptor provides no information about the properties and effects of individual drugs. The typical citizen may well assume that all illegal drugs have either lethal or highly damaging health consequences, that all illicit drug use constitutes abuse, and that all illicit drugs lead to addiction. Legal drugs are viewed as different—less harmful and dangerous (aside from their legal sta-

1

tus)—than their illegal counterparts. Being "high" on a fifth of bourbon versus being "high" from ingesting multiple lines of cocaine is assumed to be radically different. Emotionally, politically, and socially the differences may seem obvious. Behaviorally, few differences exist, except that the bourbon drinker would probably be more physically impaired.

Dictionaries define drugs as a substance used in medication, but the medical aspects of drugs have been overshadowed by the link to illegality. In the transition, we have learned to personify the substance. Drugs are criminalized as if the substances themselves were little demons committing crimes. Drugs are inert substances; they do not invade people's bodies uninvited, and they do not cause specific, identical behavior. Waging wars on drugs allows us to overlook the underlying reasons why people abuse these substances. We can place blame on the seductive powers of an object—avoiding responsibility for ourselves and for the society that we have created. This would be equivalent to waging war on food, versus discovering psychological, sociological, or genetic reasons for overeating. The language of the ideology fools us into thinking that we're waging war against substances, not real people—many of whom have no more drug addiction than the social drinker who frequents "happy hour" after work.

DRUG USE VERSUS ABUSE

At what point does drug use constitute abuse? Under the prevailing philosophy, drug abuse is redundant; any *use* of an illegal drug constitutes *abuse* and leads to dependence. In actuality, abuse varies with the individual. Abuse occurs when the use of the drug—whether aspirin, beer, caffeine, cigarettes, marijuana, diet pills, or heroin—becomes a psychological, social, or physical dependency. Contrary to commonly accepted opinion, most people avoid *abusing* marijuana, amphetamines, cocaine, and even heroin, just as most people avoid the abuse of beer or wine.

Applying the label "drug abuse" reinforces the distinction between sanctioned and illegal drugs. Prescriptions grant positive connotations to drugs. Therapeutic value is acceptable; recreational is not. John Gilmore, who has contributed money to drug education and research (including DanceSafe, a harm reduction organization providing drug information and pill testing for the electronic dance community), offers this opinion on U.S. attitudes toward drugs.

> You and I can disagree about whether marijuana is useful, but that's not a reason to lock others up. We need to stop conflating use with abuse, the choice to use the drug with addiction. The idea that people who use recreational drugs need treatment is false. I've known hundreds of people over the years who've used recreational drugs—teachers, parents, scientists—and who function normally. They're not rolling around on the ground tearing up the yard, yet if they're caught, they'll be kicked out of their jobs and their lives will be ruined. That's a crime. . . . The largest danger is from adulterated substances, not pure drugs. In a legal market, you'd be able to buy MDMA and know it's pure. . . . The only way for

adults or teens to make responsible choices is to understand the drugs'
long-term effects and addictive qualities, and then make an educated
choice. (Wenner, 2001)

This society, in general, rejects the use of intoxicants for pleasure—with the
exception of alcohol. Why, one columnist asked, are we "so obsessed with
preventing people from ingesting recreational substances that may not be
optimal for their health? We don't send cops out to arrest alcoholics because
they abuse liquor, or imprison smokers because they have a tobacco habit.
Why, then, is the use of marijuana or cocaine a law enforcement matter?"
(Chapman, 2001b). Someone dependent on illegal substances is not granted
the same tolerance or assistance as the alcoholic. Groups have worked dili-
gently to link alcoholism with disease, whereas other interests have ada-
mantly rejected a therapeutic approach to the use of illegal drugs.

SOCIAL AND CULTURAL INFLUENCES

All the rhetoric for more than a century has created a specific vocabulary that
limits discussion of drugs to prohibition and zero tolerance. We need to construct a wider context for analyzing the psychological, sociological, and cultural factors that affect decisions to ingest drugs and to evaluate policies to
determine if the laws and the punishment for breaking them help solve problems or create new ones.

> The drug war rhetoric and scare stories of politicians and the media have
> consistently attributed devastating consequences to crack, as if these con-
> sequences flowed directly from its molecular structure. Such rhetoric
> squeezes out of public discourse any serious consideration of the social,
> cultural, economic, and psychological variables that are essential for
> understanding drug use and its behavioral consequences. If we are to
> forge more effective and humane responses to our drug problems, then
> we must move beyond demonization and pharmacological determinism.
> (Reinarman & Levine, 1997)

Drugs are physical substances with pharmacological effects as well as cultural icons with values and behaviors attached to them by the society in which
they are found. The values and beliefs taught to members of society affect perceptions and expectations. Placing drug use in its social context helps us
understand how some societies have moderate levels of drug use, with low
rates of drug abuse. Careful analysis of issues requires a consideration of multiple factors—and a healthy suspicion of simplistic linear causality.

Drug war ideology glosses over the differing consequences of various
drugs and treats all illegal drugs as uniformly dangerous for the user and for
society. The fact is that the health consequences of smoking marijuana differ
from those of injecting heroin. Gary Johnson, governor of New Mexico,
describes the difficulty of trying to correct misperceptions.

> The two major criticisms of legalizing marijuana are: You're sending the
> wrong message to kids, and, use will go up. My problem is, we're mea-

suring success on use. We should toss that out. If you or I read tomorrow that alcohol use was up by three percent, we wouldn't care. We understand that use goes up or down. What we care about is, is DWI up or down? Is incidence of violence up or down? Are alcohol-related diseases up or down? Those same rules ought to apply to drugs. We ought to be concerned about violent crime, hepatitis C, HIV, turf warfare among drug gangs and nonviolent users behind bars. Those are all distinct harms caused by drugs under our current policy. (Wenner, 2001)

How We Got Here

Harry Anslinger skillfully orchestrated the rapid growth of the Federal Bureau of Narcotics (precursor to the Drug Enforcement Administration) through exaggerated claims about the evils of certain drugs and the minorities who used them. The pattern became entrenched. The belief that evil enemies—from the Chinese to Mexicans to Colombian drug lords to gang members—are robbing our nation of its best qualities has been behind every campaign against drugs. There is steadfast refusal to acknowledge that individuals decide to use drugs. Demand for drugs emanates from the tastes and preferences of millions of individuals; those aspects of life are largely beyond the control of government (White & Gorman, 2000). Drugs function perfectly as an all-purpose scapegoat for social problems. A cluster of social, demographic, economic, and political special interest groups profit from public fear of drugs. Politicians, the media, police, correction and parole officer's associations, the military, prison builders, drug-testing companies, antidrug educators, and numerous others pursue growth relentlessly, mutually reinforcing their importance to the battle against drugs.

WHAT DO THE NUMBERS MEAN?

The United States spends billions of dollars ($74 billion budgeted from 2000–2003) fighting drugs. It also collects a wealth of statistics related to drug use. The intended purpose of these statistics is to expose the pervasiveness of the criminogenic practice of large numbers of people altering their states of consciousness. But what do these numbers reveal? Do the number of arrests and the number of prison inmates convicted of drug offenses reflect the reality of drug use? Or do they tell us about more about the laws that were passed and the consequences of breaking those laws? It is far easier to track the results of law enforcement efforts than to quantify illegal practices. As Joel Best (2001) explains,

> It is difficult to count users of illicit drugs (who of course try to conceal their drug use), but government agencies charged with enforcing drug laws face demands for such statistics. Many of the numbers they present—estimates for the number of addicts, the amounts addicts steal, the volume of illicit drugs produced in different countries, and so on—cannot bear close inspection. They are basically guesses and, because having a big drug problem makes the agencies' work seem more important, the officials' guesses tend to exaggerate the problem's size. (p. 38)

There is no shortage of numbers when it comes to drugs. As we will discuss later, sentencing has also been quantified. The sentence for 5 grams of crack is 5 years. The sentence for 50 grams of methamphetamine or 100 grams of heroin is the same 5 years. The profit on 5 grams of crack might be $600; the profit on the 100 grams of heroin could be $100,000. Which of those various numbers should be more important? Because drugs are illegal, numbers cannot be confirmed as indisputable. Numbers can be found to support any political or institutional agenda. When crime and drug use decline, proponents of prohibition take credit; when either or both increase, those same groups argue that more funding is necessary for law-enforcement policies to be effective (White & Gorman, 2000).

Setting goals to reduce drug consumption is another numbers game. It weights all drug users equally.

> Measuring the extent of a nation's drug problems requires more than estimating the number of persons using illicit drugs. Drug use differs in the damage it does to individuals and in the damage those individuals do to the rest of society. (Reuter, 1999)

It is easier to persuade a light user to abstain than to persuade an addict to quit. Company drug testing might be an incentive for light users to avoid using drugs but would have no effect on unemployed addicts. Similarly, media campaigns, tough rhetoric, and symbolic actions that stigmatize drug use might be effective with some recreational users, but others would be unaffected (Caulkins, 2000).

WHAT EVENTS SHAPE POLICY?

The history of marijuana and crack in the United States reveals how attitudes are formed and laws are passed. Harry Anslinger funded an agency by demonizing a substance. *Reefer Madness* (1936) is the video evidence of his excesses about marijuana. In direct contrast, the government briefly lifted its ban on growing hemp because the products that could be made from it were needed for World War II. *Hemp for Victory* (1942) is the video evidence of the utility of the plant. But the government reversed course once the war ended and declared hemp a prohibited substance without any practical use (J. Gray, 2001).

"Anslinger was a policeman first and last, and he had absolutely no faith in any approach other than law enforcement. His response was always to tighten the screws" (M. Gray, 2000, pp. 85–86). Fiorello La Guardia, mayor of New York, was the first to challenge Anslinger's tendency to invent drug statistics. La Guardia put together a panel of physicians, psychiatrists, chemists, public health officials, police, and medical staff from Rikers Island prison hospital in 1939. The panel produced the most comprehensive study ever conducted on marijuana. Their research over five years concluded that the publicity concerning the catastrophic effects of marijuana in New York City was unfounded. Smoking marijuana did not lead to addiction; it was not a gateway drug; there was no evidence of use by children or in schools; smokers were the opposite of aggressive and belligerent; there was no relationship between marijuana and delinquency; and no major crimes were committed as the result of smoking marijuana. When details of the research began to surface three years before the report was released in 1945, Anslinger began attacking members of the committee as "dangerous" and "strange" people. His public attacks included no evidence. Anslinger was an expert in public campaigns: "If the issue is complex, you don't have to win the debate, you just have to raise enough dust" (p. 83). The scientists, jurists, and academics on the committee were looking for accuracy and justice; Anslinger was protecting his territory.

The Controlled Substances Act of 1970 classified marijuana as a schedule I drug with no medical utility. There were immediate challenges. In 1979 the U.S. Court of Appeals ordered the DEA to hold public hearings on marijuana. In 1986 the hearings began; two years later the record consisted of testimony from doctors, patients, academics, and law enforcement personnel (M. Gray, 2000, p. 175). In 1988, the administrative law judge for the DEA ruled:

> Marijuana in its natural form is one of the safest therapeutically active substances known to man. . . . One must reasonably conclude that there is accepted safety for use of marijuana under medical supervision. To conclude otherwise, on the record, would be unreasonable, arbitrary, and capricious. (p. 176)

The administrator for the DEA simply dismissed the ruling.

In 1995, *High Times* magazine and Jon Gettman petitioned the DEA to remove the classification of marijuana as a schedule I substance. When the petition was denied, the plaintiffs appealed. The United States Court of Appeals for the District of Columbia Circuit upheld the DEA's determination in May 2002. In stark contrast, the FDA granted approval in July 2002 for a medical use of GHB, a date-rape drug (see article 2). The approved pharmacy will send the drug to the homes of registered users who have certified that they understand how to use it and the penalties for abuse (Neergaard, 2002).

Schedule I controlled substances have only one exception to the prohibitions on manufacturing and distribution—government-approved research projects. Under current law, no one can disprove the contention that there is no medical utility for marijuana without obtaining government permission to research the effects of marijuana. The American Public Health Association, the *New England Journal of Medicine*, and about 80 state and national health-care organizations support legalizing access to marijuana for treatment (Page, 2002). One commentator refers to policies demonizing marijuana as an attack on reason.

> Marijuana's benefits are so wide-ranging and its damage so miniscule, the federal government would avidly be proclaiming the drug's virtue were science and rationality the motivating factor. Instead, we are held captive by a fundamentalist mindset that refuses to acknowledge data that threatens its dogma . . . As a society, we remain oddly addicted to

> prohibitionist drug policies. Despite the wealth of information detailing the folly of our ways, we trudge ahead helter-skelter, spoiling thousands of lives and extending the miseries of the gravely ill. (Muwakkil, 2002a)

Crack cocaine provides another instructive glimpse into the evolution of drug laws. In *Crack in Context*, Craig Reinarman and Harry Levine (1997) use the term "drug scare" to describe periods of time when national attention is riveted by crusades against drugs (see article 3). One of the most harmful drug scares began in 1986. After linking a particular substance to a threatening subordinate group, drug scares attribute multiple social problems to the consumption of that substance. Crack did not have universal appeal; the same population that used heroin heavily—the poorest, most marginalized people in society—used crack heavily. Crack was a derivative product. Expensive cocaine powder was reformulated and marketed in an inexpensive form to increase the number of potential purchasers. Crack cocaine is made by taking cocaine powder and cooking it with baking soda and water until it forms a hard substance. These "rocks" are broken into pieces and sold in small quantities. Each gram of powder produces approximately .89 grams of crack.

Reinarman and Levine (1997) detail the "single-minded and simple-minded" demonization of all illicit drug use and the cyclone of press coverage about crack. As they point out, the intense focus did not provide the public with facts. "By and large, the media and politicians' pronouncements about drugs spread exaggerations, misinformation, and simplistic theories of cause and effect. They taught bad pharmacology, bad sociology, bad criminology, bad urban anthropology, and even bad history." False generalizations and frightening sound bites from "experts" about the horrors of drugs formed the basis for media stories rather than investigative journalism intent on finding the truth behind the claims. The *New York Times* and *Newsweek* were among the first to proclaim an epidemic of instant addiction to crack. Reinarman and Levine quote this June 1986 editorial in *Newsweek*:

> An epidemic is abroad in America, as pervasive and dangerous in its way as the plagues of medieval times. Its source is the large and growing traffic in illegal drugs . . . a whole pharmacopoeia of poisons . . . has taken lives, wrecked careers, broken homes, invaded schools, incited crimes, tainted businesses, toppled heroes, corrupted policemen and politicians.

The editorial went on to say that the United States seemed powerless to stop this national scandal. In 1990, *Newsweek* published a decidedly different analysis: "as with most other drugs, a lot of people use it [crack] without getting addicted. In their zeal to shield young people from the plague of drugs, the media and many drug educators have hyped instant and total addiction." There was no mention of their earlier contribution to the drug scare.

Fear is a primal instinct, and fears about children arouse the need for an instant response. Crack was portrayed as so dangerous that pre-natal exposure to the drug doomed babies to a lifetime of disorders (see article 19). Fears about "crack baby syndrome" contributed to the passage of two federal sentencing laws in 1986 and 1988. The mandatory sentence for possession of 5 grams of crack (10–50 doses) is five years in prison. Crack is the only drug that carries a mandatory prison sentence for first offense possession. The maximum sentence for simple possession of any drug other than crack cocaine is 1 year in jail. If you were arrested with 5 grams of powder cocaine, you would probably receive probation; it would require possession of 500 grams (2,500–5,000 doses) to receive a 5-year sentence. A dealer charged with trafficking 400 grams of powder, worth approximately $40,000, would receive a shorter sentence than a user caught with crack valued at $500. In addition to the federal mandatory minimum sentences, 14 states differentiate between crack and powder cocaine. However, none have a ratio as large as the 100:1 federal disparity.

The ramifications of these laws were soon apparent. There were significant increases in the prison population—especially in the number of African Americans in prison. In 1995 and again in 1997 the U.S. Sentencing Commission recommended the elimination of the sentencing disparity between crack and powder cocaine, arguing that the policy had not accomplished its goal of reducing crack use but had resulted in significant unintended consequences. No action was taken. The Commission again presented its case in May 2002. In its report, it included research from Deborah A. Frank, professor of pediatrics at Boston University School of Medicine, and Glen Hanson, acting director of the National Institute of Drug Abuse (NIDA). Judge Diana Murphy, chair of the Commission, summarized the findings in her statement before the Senate Subcommittee on Crime and Drugs:

> Recent research shows that the negative effects of prenatal crack cocaine exposure are identical to the negative effects of prenatal powder cocaine exposure and significantly less devastating than previously believed. The negative effects associated with prenatal cocaine exposure are in fact similar to those associated with prenatal exposure to other illegal and legal substances, such as tobacco and alcohol. Since recent research reports no difference between the negative effects from prenatal crack cocaine and powder cocaine exposure, no differential based on this particular heightened harm appears to be warranted. Congress also set heightened penalties for crack cocaine offenses because it feared that the drug's potency, low cost per dose, and ease with which it is manufactured and administered were leading to its widespread use, particularly by youth. Recent data indicate that the feared epidemic of crack cocaine use by youth never materialized. Crack cocaine use among 18 to 25 year old adults has historically been low. (U.S. Sentencing Commission, p. 10)

Symbols are useful for an audience that prefers simplification and cannot tolerate ambiguity. Symbolism reassures and induces feelings of well being. Legal and political institutions are permeated with rituals that promote conformity and reaffirm beliefs in the rationality of the system. The influence of symbolism on regulatory policy is to reassure the public that a problem is under control. Success is measured by the public's response to the ideal of the policy—not the actual consequences. For example, in order for countries to qualify for U.S. aid, the president must certify that they are cooperating fully with combating illicit narcotics trafficking. There is an inherent hypocrisy in the certification process. Not only would the United States fail its own test, but no country other than Colombia has ever been decertified. Decertification is a hollow symbol.

The choice of drug policy mirrors public views about what constitutes a drug problem and the role of government in solving such problems. The 1960s fostered an antiauthoritarian view and celebration of individualistic lifestyles. In the 1970s people continued to reject law enforcement as the chief tool against drug use. Beginning in 1980, the trend shifted to a more paternalistic view: more government involvement and the belief that punishment would deter drug use. Illegal drugs were viewed primarily as a crime problem. The goal of abstinence replaced treatment. "But a society that deliberately averts its eyes from an honest assessment of a massive and frequently cruel intervention that sacrifices so many other goals for the one desideratum of drug abstinence can scarcely expect to find a well-grounded alternative" (Reuter, 1997, p. 38).

Where We Are

A fundamental factor in the criminalization of any drug is creating the perception that it is directly connected to crime (see article 4). With drug-using behavior and crime behavior so closely associated, both industries flourish. Although many individuals convicted of crime do have a history of previous use of illegal drugs, correlation does not equal causation. There are often equally high correlations of illiteracy, extreme poverty, lack of health care, child abuse, failure in school, smoking, gambling, unhealthy diets, poor employment history, and many other variables in criminal populations. Singling out drug use as the cause of criminal behavior is no more persuasive than singling out any of the other characteristics. Research shows, for example, that rates of violent crime and delinquency are high in neighborhoods that are poor, densely populated, ethnically segregated, and composed of a transient population. Social disorganization and lack of social capital appear to be the crucial mechanisms linking these structural characteristics to crime.

The common cause model rejects a direct causal link between substance use and crime. One behavior does not cause the other; rather, people who use drugs and commit crime share common factors (such as genetic or temperamental traits, antisocial personality disorder, or parental alcoholism). For example, young males account for a disproportionate share of crime and are also the heaviest drinkers and drug users; being male is the common link. In addition to individual-level and interpersonal-level influences, drug use and crime may have common environmental and situational causes. The routine activities perspective argues that bars are crime hot spots because motivated offenders encounter victims in a situation lacking effective guardianship. Situational factors such as location, access, and type of clientele must be considered when looking for causes. Research on trends in drug use and crime supported a common cause model. "The data on trends across cities indicate that there is no uniform association between any type of drug use and any type of crime" (White & Gorman, 2000, p. 170).

Frequently ignored but receiving more attention in the last decade are the criminogenic effects of drug laws. Not only does aggressive law enforcement threaten to undermine communities, but it also, under certain conditions, could contribute to an increase in drug-related violence. Some researchers have found a displacement effect. When drug arrests increased in one community, the violent crime rate went up in a neighboring community. Dealers moved from the targeted community to the neighboring one and used whatever means necessary to establish and protect their new territory. Another result of aggressive enforcement is a correctional system overburdened with nonviolent drug offenders serving mandatory sentences (see discussion below). Police tactics designed to reduce the supply of drugs may not be the most effective means of reducing social harm. The illicit status of drugs could be responsible for some criminogenic effects, including forbidden-fruit effects, labeling, and "stigma swamping." Jon Caulkins suggested the last term to describe the idea that the stigma associated with arrest and incarceration is reduced by the sheer volume of those sanctions (MacCoun, Kilmer, & Reuter, 2002).

Narcotics legislation has a history of turning the screws of criminal machinery: detection, prosecution, and punishment. The unintended consequences of this approach are that it creates additional intractable problems. Prison populations have skyrocketed because of the crackdown on illegal drugs, not because the drug problem has worsened.

> More than ten million Americans—maybe double that—have been convicted of drug offenses ranging from marijuana possession to sale of one illicit drug or another. The 1996 welfare reform act revokes welfare benefits for anyone convicted of a felony drug offense—for life. Under federal law, innocent family members of people who have used drugs can be evicted from public housing—even if the family members do not even know about the drug use. Otherwise law-abiding students are targeted as well: the federal Higher Education Act delays or denies eligibility for federal financial aid to any student convicted of any drug offense, no matter how minor. And in the wake of September 11, as private companies step up their background checks of current and potential employees, more and more people with minor drug offenses in their (often distant) past are finding themselves without a job. (Nadelmann, 2002)

UNEVEN APPLICATION OF LAWS

There is hypocrisy and irony woven through the tapestry of drug issues. Those who can afford to visit a psychiatrist can obtain prescriptions; those who can't risk the criminal label for self-medication. Former police chief

Joseph McNamara (2000b) discusses the irrational aspects of criminalizing one substance but not others.

> Even today, 85 years after the federal government first outlawed narcotics, public and police attitudes toward the dangerousness of drugs are shaped by ignorance of their impact and by mistaken prejudices regarding their users. These are the same irrationalities that led to the criminal prohibition of certain drugs. Individuals taking Prozac (fluoxetine), Valium (diazepam) or other psychoactive prescription drugs are regarded as patients. Yet millions of our own citizens using heroin, cocaine or marijuana have been and are still regarded as dangerous enough to be caged in brutal prisons, frequently under mandatory sentences more characteristic of a totalitarian society than a democracy.

Enforcement of drug laws varies with location and participants. According to Ric Curtis, who has studied the New York's illicit drug trade, couriers routinely deliver marijuana to exclusive Manhattan residences via bikes or limousines. "Rank-and-file officers often wink and look the other way when it comes to a segment of the population. It's not worth the time and effort to go after the more upscale people" (Haynes, 2002b, p. 14).

The consequences of the war on drugs have been devastating for the African-American community. A study by Human Rights Watch in 2000 found that the rate for black men sentenced to state prison for drug offenses is 13 times the rate for white men.

> According to studies of the U.S. Commission on Civil Rights, African Americans constitute 15 percent of the national drug users, but comprise about one-third of all those arrested on drug charges and 57 percent of those convicted on drug charges. (Muwakkil, 2002b, p. 21)

Approximately 1.4 million black men—13% of adult black males—have lost the right to vote as a result of felony convictions (J. Gray, 2001). State troopers in New Jersey testified that Drug Enforcement Administration agents originated racial profiling to catch drug couriers (Casriel, 2001). The rapid expansion of incarceration for drug offenses has implications for everything from family structure to labor force participation (Caulkins, 2000). A study by the Justice Policy Institute released in August 2002 found that in the last two decades the population of black male inmates grew three times as fast as the number of black men enrolled in higher education.

> The jailing of so many young men (and increasingly young women) at the primary age of family formation stunts the vitality of the black community and contributes to family dissolution, single-parent households, increased incidence of HIV/AIDS, reduced job prospects and political participation (due to state-based disenfranchisement laws) and other debilitating effects. (Muwakkil, 2002b)

The enormous gap between sentences for crack and powder cocaine reinforces concerns about racial bias in our justice system. It is one more factor contributing to suspicions and distrust of law enforcement officers in minority communities.

The rapid growth in incarceration has exacted a much higher toll from some communities than others. Ironically, mandatory sentencing purported to treat everyone equally harshly. The Boggs Act created mandatory sentencing for drug offenses in 1951, and the Narcotics Control Act of 1956 doubled the penalties. The belief that severe sentences would deter drug use has its own collateral damage. As James P. Gray (2001), a California Superior Court justice, notes:

> Another little-known result of prison overcrowding is that wardens throughout the country are routinely forced to grant an early release to violent offenders so that nonviolent drug offenders can serve their sentences in full. This is true because, for the most part, federal law requires that even nonviolent drug offenders must serve their entire sentences; however, there is no such law for bank robbers, kidnappers, or other violent offenders. (p. 36)

Melody Heaps, president of Treatment Alternatives for Safe Communities said misguided sentencing practices have sent thousands of nonviolent drug abusers to jails and prisons rather than to treatment programs. "We've had a policy of get tough on drugs and we're seeing that didn't work. It's not only a law-enforcement issue, but a public health issue as well" (Trice, 2002).

The law enforcement net gathers thousands of nonviolent, sometimes unwitting suspects. "Many of the people in federal prison are low-level couriers who carried a package of drugs for friends or romantic partners. They don't know any details, so they usually can't bargain with prosecutors for reduced sentences" ("Double standard," 2000). Between 1986 and 1996, the number of women incarcerated for drug offenses increased by 888 percent, compared to an increase of 129 percent for non-drug offenses. Seventy-five percent of women prisoners are also single parents of young children (J. Gray, 2001). As Judge Myron H. Bright of the U.S. Court of Appeals warns:

> These unwise sentencing policies which put men and women in prison for years, not only ruin lives of prisoners and often their family members, but also drain the American taxpayers of funds which can be measured in billions of dollars. . . . This is the time to call a halt to the unnecessary and expensive cost of putting people in prison for a long time based on the mistaken notion that such an effort will win "The War on Drugs." If it is a war, society seems not to be winning, but losing. We must turn to other methods of deterring drug distribution and use. (p. 36)

INTERDICTION AND PROHIBITION

The Regional Andean Initiative and Plan Colombia were implemented to stop the flow of cocaine and other illegal drugs to the United States from South America, but they have mired U.S. funds and personnel in compromising situations. The military is restricted to lending equipment and assistance to foreign countries to fight drugs. The Amazon is dotted with U.S. radar systems, air bases, and special-operations training units. One of the first concerns of U.S. personnel in the region was to disrupt the "air bridge"—the delivery of Andean coca crops by air to Colombia laboratories. However, shooting down small planes would violate a fundamental precept of U.S. law enforcement. Deadly force is justified only if lives are in danger. The Supreme Court has ruled that it is unconstitutional to use lethal force against fleeing felons. On what basis could U.S. planes justify shooting unarmed planes out of foreign skies? The solution was for U.S. radar installations to detect suspicious planes; a U.S. surveillance plane would investigate, and a local military plane would force down suspected couriers.

In April 2001, Roni Bowers and her 7-month-old daughter were flying back to their home base after a missionary trip. The Cessna in which they were flying had been detected and tracked. Miscommunication between the surveillance team and the Peruvian fighter pilot caused the deaths of Bowers and her baby when the plane was shot down about 140 miles east of Iquitos, Peru (Ramo, 2001).

> Interdiction is dangerous and expensive—and it doesn't reduce the flow of drugs. The impact on coca exports has been invisible. Drug runners have simply shifted where they grow and how they transport coca, moving from the air to the sea and rivers. The success in reducing production in Bolivia and Peru has been offset by the doubling of production in Colombia. In drug-enforcement circles, this is called the balloon effect: the air moves, but the balloon never pops. Shoot down planes and smugglers start using speedboats. Eradicate crops in Peru and growers move to Colombia. (p. 42)

The air bridge is no longer a primary focus. Most cocaine is now grown, processed, and packaged in the Colombia jungle. The distribution mechanisms have changed from those of the Cali and Medellín cartels to more than 100 small operations, each aligned with a faction in Colombia's civil war. U.S. dollars pay for programs to spray herbicides to destroy coca in the fields. However, the spraying sometimes destroys the legal crops farmers plant for food, leading the United Nations to denounce the program as inhumane.

Columnist Stephen Chapman (2001a) explains the problems of interdiction caused by the economics of supply and demand.

> Choking off the supply of illicit drugs is an old fantasy that stubbornly resists being translated into reality. Time and again, the U.S. government and its allies have launched massive campaigns to eradicate crops or stamp out smuggling. Many of them have succeeded at their direct purpose—but none has actually made it hard for Americans to keep snorting, smoking, or shooting up. . . . The problem lies in the law of supply and demand, which no government can repeal. The flow of drugs will continue as long as there are Americans willing to pay handsomely to get high. So maybe we should stop expecting the rest of the world to save us from ourselves. (p. 19)

James P. Gray (2001), California Superior Court justice, also answers the question of whether interdiction has made drugs more difficult to obtain.

> No. Even though ever increasing amounts of tax monies are being spent on the eradication of various drugs both in our country and abroad, and even though virtually all of these efforts are increasingly successful, with more seizures, arrests, and convictions than ever, the price of illicit drugs like cocaine has declined considerably over the past decade. This, of course, means that the supply has *increased*. What we in essence have attempted to do with our drug policy is to repeal the law of supply and demand. Not surprisingly, we have failed completely. (p. 46)

Drug trafficking is so lucrative, couriers constantly devise new plans for smuggling narcotics. Thirty-five people were indicted in connection with a smuggling operation in which infants were rented as a cover for smuggling cocaine in baby formula cans. Drug couriers took one infant on six trips overseas, the first occurring when she was 3 weeks old. Parents who rented their babies were paid several hundred dollars and some narcotics for each trip (O'Connor, 2001). An editorial in the *Chicago Tribune* remarked that interdiction efforts have been "like sprinkling water on an oil fire"; they have only spread the flames. The money expended "could have been much more profitably invested at home in drug treatment and education programs to reduce narcotics consumption" ("Mired," 2002, p. 26).

As discussed in article 14, the Posse Comitatus Act of 1878 barred the military from participating in arrests, searches, seizure of evidence, and other police activity in the United States. The act has been amended to allow the military to assist in drug interdiction and to lend equipment to domestic authorities. The drug exception was used in 1992 in Waco, Texas. In order to enlist military hardware and personnel, federal law-enforcement authorities claimed the Branch Davidians were trafficking in methamphetamine. The U.S. Army Delta Force advised the tank assault, which resulted in the deaths of 80 people. In 2002 the director of homeland security called for a study of using the armed services for domestic law enforcement because "the threat of catastrophic terrorism requires a thorough review of the laws." However, as Gene Healy (2002) cautions:

> The Army is a blunt instrument: effective for destroying enemy troops en masse, but ill-suited to the fight on the home front, which requires subtler investigative and preventative skills. . . . More widespread use of military personnel to do police work would do little to protect us from Al Qaeda; but it would increase the chances of collateral damage: innocent American citizens harmed by those who are supposed to protect them. . . . Normalization of military law enforcement would have grave consequences for our political culture. We do not want to become a society where armed soldiers patrolling the streets are part of everyday life. (p. 17)

We haven't learned much about the economic effects of prohibition in fifty years. Rufus King, chairman of the American Bar Association's committee on narcotics, made these comments in 1953:

> Drugs are a commodity of trifling intrinsic value. All the billions our
> society has spent enforcing criminal measures against the addict have
> had the sole practical result of protecting the peddler's market, artificially
> inflating his prices, and keeping his profits fantastically high. No other
> nation hounds its addicts as we do, and no other nation faces anything
> remotely resembling our problem. (J. Gray, 2001, p. 22)

The laws that make substances illegal increase the cost of those drugs
exponentially. The enormous profits in the drug trade have multiple effects.
Dealing drugs may be the only well-paying option for the undereducated living in poverty (see article 8). To protect their lucrative markets, dealers offer
payoffs. Corruption threatens police forces, court systems, the customs service, and the military. Most of the violence associated with drugs is drug-law
related. There are no legal means to protect illegal markets.

Prohibition creates problems for domestic law enforcement. Since most
drug use involves willing participants, there are rarely complaining witnesses.
Attempting to police consensual transactions has contributed to militarizing
the police. Evidence for drug offenses is obtained only through "police-state
tactics: promiscuous wiretaps, intrusive searches, racial profiling, confisca-
tory property forfeitures, propaganda-laced television shows, militarized law
enforcement, and mindless mandatory minimum sentences" (Bandow, 2000).
Joseph McNamara (1999) was a police officer for thirty-five years. "I have
come to believe that jailing people simply because they put certain chemicals
into their bloodstream is a gross misuse of the police and criminal law."

Current drug policies have damaged the credibility of the criminal justice
system. Although Mark Moore favors laws against cocaine and heroin and is
willing to commit the authority and resources of the criminal justice system
to reduce the availability of those drugs in communities, he states:

> Having said that, I want to acknowledge that this is a very, very expensive
> use of the criminal justice system in the sense that it chews up a great
> deal of authority and money as a means of preventing an increase in the
> rate of drug use and abuse. We have a particular responsibility in this area
> to use the authority of the state, which I think of as a scarce and valuable
> commodity, with effect and fairly. I think we have been a bit indiscrimi-
> nate in the way that we have used authority in the drug war. I don't want
> to eliminate our efforts altogether, but I would like to see us make a more
> sustained effort to focus on the places where it would do a lot of good
> and not cost us so much—and where we can be relatively sure, not only
> in our eyes but in the eyes of the citizenry, that the laws are being brought
> to bear with effect and fairness. (Moore, 1997, p. 66)

FORFEITURE

In 1984, Congress added an inventive and profitable connection of drugs to
crime. The Comprehensive Forfeiture Act of 1984 allows law enforcement
agencies to seize personal assets (cash, residences, vehicles, businesses, etc.)
used in connection with illegal drug activity and to use the proceeds for their

budgets, even if the owner is never convicted of a crime (see article 13). This contributes to a law enforcement agenda that targets property instead of crime and creates opportunities for abuse and corruption. The burden of proof falls on the property owner to prove that the property is "innocent," rather than on the law enforcement agency to prove that the property is actually drug-related. The process can be lengthy and costly for the property owner and brings into question Fourth Amendment rights against unreasonable searches and seizures and Eighth Amendment guarantees against excessive fines. Forfeiture distorts policing by providing an incentive to focus on seizing property to maintain drug enforcement budgets, often at the expense of enforcement of laws against violent crimes like robbery, rape, and murder. Federal, state and local "equitable sharing" agreements, which give state and local agencies most of the seized assets, have resulted in a major shift toward federal jurisdiction over local law enforcement.

TREATMENT

Recently the government has increased its rhetoric about treatment. However, the emphasis is on a criminal justice solution.

> Reduced to its barest essentials, drug control policy has just two elements: modifying individual behavior to discourage and reduce drug use and addiction, and disrupting the market for illegal drugs. Those two elements are mutually reinforcing. Drug treatment, for instance, is demonstrably effective in reducing crime. Law enforcement helps "divert" users into treatment and makes the treatment system work more efficiently by giving treatment providers needed leverage over the clients they serve. Treatment programs narrow the problem for law enforcement by shrinking the market for illegal drugs. A clearer example of symbiosis is hard to find in public policy. Similarly, prevention programs are perennially appealing because they stop drug use before it starts and, in so doing, they reduce the load on the treatment system and, ultimately, the criminal justice system. Prevention programs work best in a climate where law breaking is punished and young people are discouraged from trying illegal drugs in the first place. These different elements of our drug control program are really two sides of the same coin. In some areas, as in the law enforcement and drug treatment systems, the connection is exceptionally strong and should be exploited. (ONDCP, p. 4)

The government language emphasizes coerced abstinence. Critics point to the dangers hidden in the type of treatment the government advocates.

> But the popularity of drug courts and the increasing entanglement of criminal justice with treatment can come at a high price—the sacrifice of confidentiality between patient and caregiver; the diversion of government funding from voluntary and community-based treatment into coerced treatment programs, often behind bars; the propagation of a myth that treatment doesn't work unless it's backed by the state's coercive powers; the de facto criminalization of relapse; the need to treat non-

problematic marijuana use as a basis for revocation of probation or parole; and so on. (Nadelmann, 2002)

Studies have shown that people addicted to heroin who are placed in methadone treatment programs commit less crime, are less likely to contract AIDS, and pose less of a danger to themselves and others. However, methadone may only be dispensed at special clinics; the addict must visit the clinic daily to obtain the treatment. The treatment is so regulated that it costs more than is necessary, and many addicts, burdened by the restrictions, give up on the process. People in the program are subject to stricter supervision than convicted parolees. In Australia, doctors are permitted to dispense methadone. In the United States, because of attitudes that don't approve of trading one opiate addiction for another, the prohibitive restrictions often override what would otherwise be a workable solution.

Joseph McNamara cautions that coerced abstinence is a continuation of the demonization of certain drugs and the dehumanization of their users. Past behavior, including the use of certain chemicals, does not accurately predict the future behavior of a particular individual. The assumption that the presence of a particular chemical in a person's bloodstream is cause for imprisonment closely resembles a police-state mentality of assumed guilt. Writing in response to a *Wall Street Journal* editorial supporting coerced drug abstinence for probationers, McNamara (2000b) said the editorial

> makes the common error of attributing criminality to the use of certain chemicals. This plan assumes that those with dirty urine should be jailed because they will commit robberies, burglaries, and other crimes. This supposition trifles with our most precious right, the presumption of innocence.

STATES' RIGHTS

The Harrison Narcotic Act of 1914 was a radical departure from the separation of federal and state jurisdictions. To avoid questions of constitutionality, Congress had labeled the act a revenue measure, but the Supreme Court in 1925 interpreted it as a penal statute. Since that time there has been a steady increase in federal control over drug issues. The clash between federal and states' rights has heated up considerably, particularly on the issue of medical use of marijuana.

People smoke marijuana to ease the nausea of chemotherapy, to reduce the pain of multiple sclerosis, and to alleviate the symptoms of glaucoma.

> We allow adults to buy cigarettes and alcohol, even though both are highly addictive and kill thousands every year. Experts may disagree, depending on definitions, over whether marijuana smoke is "addictive" or merely "habit-forming" but both sides are hard-pressed to find anyone who has died of a marijuana overdose. Doctors treat the ill with numerous prescription drugs that are more dangerous and addictive than marijuana. But physicians are not allowed to treat the ill with marijuana. (Page, 2002, p. 25)

A Pew Research Center Gallup poll in 2001 found that 73 percent of Americans favored the medical use of marijuana with a doctor's prescription (Muwakkil, 2002a). States that have passed medical marijuana laws are in direct conflict with federal law. By ballot initiative or by legislation, nine states (Alaska, California, Colorado, Hawaii, Maine, Nevada, Oregon, and Washington) and Washington, D.C. have legalized the use of marijuana for medical purposes. Vermont may become the tenth state in 2003. The DEA has raided and shut down medical marijuana dispensaries in California, equating them to drug traffickers. The U.S. Supreme Court ruled in May 2001 that the United States could prohibit the Oakland Cannabis Buyers' Cooperative from dispensing marijuana, rejecting any claims of medical necessity. The reasoning given was that Congress had classified marijuana as a schedule I drug.

In response to the federal government's concerted effort to close marijuana clubs, the Board of Supervisors in San Francisco voted in July 2002 to put a measure on the November ballot that would ask city officials to explore growing marijuana on public land and distributing it to patients ("City," 2002). California state supreme court justices recently decided that users are protected from prosecution in state courts (Haynes, 2002b). In September 2002, the mayor and six city council memebrs in Santa Cruz watched workers from the Women's Alliance for Medical Marijuana dispense the drug outside City Hall after the DEA raided a medical marijuana collective, arrested three people, and confiscated 130 plants twelve days earler (*Los Angeles Times*, 2002). Congressman Barney Frank introduced the States' Rights to Medical Marijuana Act in July 2002 to address the problem of jurisdiction. It would allow states that pass medical marijuana laws to be free from the threat of a federal crackdown; the bill would also move marijuana from a schedule I to a schedule II substance, allowing states to decide whether it should be available by prescription. Whether the bill will gain enough support to make it out of the judiciary committee is debatable. "What's [Frank] been smoking?" was the reaction of another member of the committee. Frank thinks the measure should gain bipartisan support: "This bill does offer a challenge to conservatives who often profess their support for states' rights" (Vlahos, 2002).

CIVIL RIGHTS

The Supreme Court had ruled in 1995 (*Vernonia v. Acton*) that schools confronted with serious drug problems could randomly test student athletes in junior high and high school for illegal drug use. After that ruling, the board of education in Tecumseh, Oklahoma began random, suspicionless testing of all students participating in any extracurricular competitive activities. Two students sued and the issue reached the Supreme Court in 2002. An attorney for the American Civil Liberties Union argued that Tecumseh violated the Fourth Amendment's provision against unreasonable searches and seizures, stating that the 1995 case was a narrow exception to the rule that schools must have a suspicion of wrongdoing before searching students. The attorney for Tecumseh argued that the testing was a "natural, logical and rational application" of the 1995 ruling.

Between 1998 and 2000, the Tecumseh school district tested 480 students; there were 4 positive results. During the oral arguments, Chief Justice William Rehnquist said the few number of positive tests did not necessarily mean there was no problem; rather, the results could mean the school's drug testing program was a successful deterrent (Chapman, 2002).

In June 2002 (*Board of Education v. Earls et al.*) the Supreme Court upheld Tecumseh's policy, stating that it was a reasonable means of furthering the school district's "important interest" in preventing and deterring drug use and did not violate the Fourth Amendment. "Given the nationwide epidemic of drug use, and the evidence of increased drug use in Tecumseh schools, it was entirely reasonable for the School District to enact this particular drug testing policy." In her dissent, Justice Ginsburg discussed the difference between projecting an image or a symbolic need versus demonstrating a concrete danger or evidence of a particular problem. She said Tecumseh's drug policy was designed to "heighten awareness of its abhorrence of, and strong stand against drug abuse. But the desire to augment communication of this message does not trump the right of persons even of children within the schoolhouse gate to be secure in their persons against unreasonable searches and seizures." She concluded her dissent by stating that schools have an obligation to teach by example and to avoid symbolic measures that diminish constitutional protections. "Educating the young for citizenship is reason for scrupulous protection of Constitutional freedoms of the individual, if we are not to strangle the free mind at its source and teach youth to discount important principles of our government as mere platitudes."

Fifty percent of major U.S. firms test their employees for drug use, and more than 500 school districts have screening programs. "The tests are often heralded as infallible, . . . but reliably picking up drug traces that linger days after a user's last high, while ignoring contaminants and similar-looking compounds in medicine and food, is a tall order for even the best technology" (Hawkins, 2002, p. 46). False positives cause dismissal, ruining reputations and livelihoods. In many companies, the initial screening is part of the job interview. If the test results are positive, the process ends. There are no requirements for a second, confirming test. As companies move to on-site urine testing which is cheaper and gives results in minutes, the risk of false positives increases. The tests may be accurate in only one of three cases. With any method of drug testing, there can be problems with the test itself or human error in the chain of custody of the sample.

Arrests decades earlier can affect employment. With background checks pursued more stringently after the terrorist attack in September 2001, companies now search arrest records and prohibit access to their property by anyone with a criminal record. Eli Lilly, a pharmaceutical maker, began conducting criminal background checks on everyone with access to its Indianapolis facilities in 2001. Lilly barred a sheet metal worker from its property because he had been arrested in 1993 for buying a bag of marijuana—for which he spent six hours in jail and paid a $1000 fine—and reported his history to the construction company that employed him. The company then fired the man, who was unemployed for four months and blamed the breakup of his marriage on financial pressures.

I served about 18 of my 35 years in policing as police chief of two of America's largest cities, San Jose and Kansas City, Mo. As chief, it became even more apparent to me that an overwhelming percentage of drug arrests disrupted school careers, caused defendants to lose their jobs, exposed them to brutal incarceration experiences and often led many to become career criminals and addicts. On the other hand, a large number of people who used illegal drugs seem to have grown out of their youthful drug experiments and led productive lives. In fact, most of the police applicants I hired had admitted to some drug use in their youth. If we had automatically disqualified them, we would have severely damaged their lives and lost many fine police officers. (McNamara, 2000c)

In 1997, the Oakland Housing Authority started eviction proceedings against four elderly tenants. The grandsons of William Lee (71) and Barbara Hill (63) had been caught smoking marijuana in the parking lot. Both Lee and Hill had lived in public housing more than 25 years. The mentally disabled daughter of Pearlie Rucker (63) was found with cocaine three blocks from their apartment. The caregiver for a disabled man, Herman Walker (75), was found with cocaine in his apartment for the third time. The Supreme Court ruled unanimously in March 2002 (*HUD v. Rucker et al.*) that local housing authorities can evict tenants if household members or guests use drugs, citing an Act passed in 1988.

With drug dealers increasingly imposing a reign of terror on public and other federally assisted low-income housing tenants, Congress passed the Anti-Drug Abuse Act of 1988. . . . And, of course, there is an obvious reason why Congress would have permitted local public housing authorities to conduct no-fault evictions: Regardless of knowledge, a tenant who cannot control drug crime, or other criminal activities by a household member which threaten health or safety of other residents, is a threat to other residents and the project. With drugs leading to murders, muggings, and other forms of violence against tenants, and to the deterioration of the physical environment that requires substantial government expenditures, it was reasonable for Congress to permit no-fault evictions in order to provide public and other federally assisted low-income housing that is decent, safe, and free from illegal drugs. (Greenburg, 2002)

The Fourth Amendment has been battered by the frenzy to save society from drugs; "the drug exception" is invoked if civil rights interfere with enforcement. Children and employees are required to submit urine samples for the safety of schools and workplaces; elderly people are evicted from public housing because relatives/acquaintances are drug users. Section 115 of the Welfare Reform Act of 1996 provides that persons convicted of a state or federal felony offense for using or selling drugs are subject to a lifetime ban on receiving cash assistance and food stamps. No other offenses, including murder, result in losing benefits. Pretrial release is denied under most drug laws. The criteria for search warrants are relaxed. The Supreme Court allows search warrants to be issued based on anonymous tips or tips from informants and permits warrantless searches of fields or barns.

> For roughly the first 130 years of our republic, Americans' right to life, liberty, and the pursuit of happiness included the right to ingest whatever chemicals one desired. Lest there be any doubt about this, we should remember that Thomas Jefferson, who penned those words in the Declaration of Independence, subsequently ridiculed France for imposing laws on diet and prescription drugs. Jefferson said that a government that controls what its citizens eat and the kind of medicine they take will soon try to control what its citizens think. (McNamara, 2000a)

In 2002, dance and electronic music came under attack in the zeal to squash a perceived threat. The popularity of all-night dance parties and fears about links to drugs resulted in proposed legislation that ignores standard burdens of proof. Politicians may exhibit little creativity in their approach to the use of drugs, but their naming of legislation displays a flair for acronyms. The Reducing Americans' Vulnerability to Ecstasy (RAVE) Act of 2002 was introduced to the Senate (S.2633) in June 2002. The bill extends the federal crack house law (Title 21 U.S.C. Section 856, which makes it a felony to provide a space for the purpose of illegal drug use) to cover promoters of raves and other events (Montgomery, 2002). The RAVE act would make it a federal crime to sponsor an event at which drugs are used. The bill also makes it a federal crime to rent property to medical marijuana patients and their caregivers. A bill introduced in the House of Representatives (H.R. 3782) had the more cumbersome title "Clean, Learn, Educate, Abolish, Neutralize and Undermine Production (CLEAN-UP) Methamphetamine Act of 2002. It would hold promoters liable if they "reasonably ought to know" that someone would use an illegal drug during an event.

The Congressional findings attached to the bill claimed: "Each year tens of thousands of young people are initiated into the drug culture at rave parties or events"; and "the trafficking and use of club drugs is deeply embedded in the rave culture." The ACLU claims that these findings would become part of the legislative history of the bill and could support a prosecutor's claim that any rave would be subject to the penalties. An attorney for the ACLU asserted that music and dance are forms of expression protected by the First Amendment. Ravers collected almost 10,000 signatures over the Internet in five days. "They contend that police, politicians and media have exaggerated the amount of criminal activity in rave culture since it began more than a decade ago" (Montgomery, 2002). They question why no senator has proposed a ROCK act, since drugs are also present at rock concerts. A remark by an aid to one of the bill's sponsors is revealing. When the petitions were delivered, the staff was surprised. "We thought this would be an innocuous bill that everybody would rally in support of." The history of drug legislation is marked by the same tendency to pass legislation based on unfounded, unreflective assumptions.

Prohibition has militarized the police, eroded civil liberties, distorted the justice system, made selling drugs enormously profitable, created opportunities for corruption here and abroad, incarcerated millions of nonviolent offenders, expanded the number of prisons exponentially, increased taxes, decreased precautionary health practices, and diverted resources from other problems both in law enforcement agencies and in the nation. These problems are ignored because federal agencies are addicted to their portion of drug war funds. Drugs can be dangerous, but making them illegal doesn't erase the danger—it creates other harms. The cost to society of an individual using drugs is miniscule compared to the harm to the community caused by making drugs illegal. The juggernaut of punishment fueled by public fear flattens the contours and nuances of issues.

Where Do We Go from Here?

Antidrug and anticrime policies and programs have been developed and have received public funding, political endorsement, and popular support in the absence of any scientific evidence demonstrating their efficacy. Other policies and interventions that offer health benefits or relief for those addicted to drugs are rejected if aspects of the programs conflict with currently accepted views, making the alternate choices unpopular with politicians who fear public reaction. Examples are methadone and needle exchange programs. Programs that fit the ideological agenda will survive regardless of the scientific evidence, as the crack laws illustrate. Research can help us make informed decisions among the choices available, but, more often than not, policy decisions concerning crime and drugs are determined by influences other than empirical evidence (White & Gorman, 2000).

CHANGE OF FOCUS

In 2002, government-sponsored media campaigns against the use of drugs shifted focus dramatically. The "Just Say No" campaign of the 1980s and the "This Is Your Brain on Drugs" campaign in the 1990s emphasized how drugs harm the individual user. The National Youth Anti-Drug Media Campaign launched by the Office of National Drug Control Policy (ONDCP) purported to show how drugs harm the country as a whole by helping bankroll terrorists. The $10 million campaign includes print and broadcast advertising, in-school programming, lesson plans for teachers, and on-line information (antidrug.com for parents; teachersguide.org for educators; and drugstory.org for media). Two 30-second ads were televised February 3, 2002 during the Super Bowl. After the initial telecasts, ads appeared in 200 newspapers and on television. Among the full-page newspaper ads were close-ups of young people proclaiming, variously:

- Yesterday afternoon, I did my laundry, went for a run, and helped torture someone's dad.
- Last weekend, I washed my car, hung out with a few friends, and helped murder a family in Colombia.
- On Wednesday, I played tennis, went shoe shopping, and helped smuggle a load of AK-47s into Colombia.

President George W. Bush declared: "If you quit drugs, you join the fight against terror in America." Asa Hutchinson, administrator of the DEA stated: "The illegal drug trade is linked to the support of terror groups across the globe. Buying and using illegal drugs is not a victimless crime—it has negative consequences that can touch the lives of people around the world." And John Walters, director of ONDCP, claimed:

> One of the reasons these ads are so potent is that they appeal to the ideal-ism of young people. Where previous anti-drug ads have focused on the devastating toll that drugs take on individuals, these ads speak to young people's desire to make the world a better place. We know that proceeds from drug purchases are used to bribe, kidnap, torture, and murder peo-ple around the world, and that many of the most dangerous criminal and terrorist organizations rely on drug trafficking to finance their vicious actions. These ads put to rest once and for all the cynical lie that drug use "doesn't hurt anybody else."

The DEA announced plans for "Target America"—an exhibit about the con-temporary and historic connections between drug trafficking and terrorism around the world.

Not everyone supported the government link of drugs to terror. Ethan Nadelmann, executive director of the Drug Policy Alliance countered:

> It's despicable and dangerous. When you start labeling tens of millions of Americans as accomplices to terrorists or de facto murderers, you are cre-ating and stirring an atmosphere of intolerance and hate-mongering that ends up being destructive and dangerous to the broader society. (Ben-david, 2002, p. 1)

And Eric Sterling, president of the Criminal Justice Policy Foundation, com-mented: "At a time when many are talking about the importance of drug treatment, this rhetoric sends the message that drug users are not people with chemical dependencies, they are aiding and abetting terrorists and need to be locked up" (p. 17).

One of the ironies of linking drugs with terror is that drug enforcement laws have actually aided terrorists. Despite eventually forbidding farmers to grow poppies, the opium trade was a major source of funding for the Taliban during the time it ruled Afghanistan. The illegality of opiates increased Tali-ban profits. Poppy fields eradicated in Mexico, Peru, or Colombia enriched the supplier who still had drugs to market (Chapman, 2001b).

An Alternative Approach

The harm-reduction approach emerged in the Netherlands and Great Britain during the 1970s and 1980s. Advocates of this perspective in the United States view the primary goal of U.S. drug policy—total prohibition of use or zero tolerance—as unrealistic and unattainable. Prohibition policies create unintended negative consequences including neighborhood destabilization and dealer violence. They have failed to lower demand and reduce health and social costs of drug use. Removing criminal penalties for drug use and instituting a regulated, prescription-based model would limit the harm created by the illicit drug market and current drug laws.

There should be far less emphasis on casual users, and resources should target those who create the most harm and have the most intractable problems. Harm reductionists see chronic users as the core issue in the debate over drugs. Drug laws are least effective in stopping addicts.

> In all, there are an estimated 4 million hard-core drug users in the United States. Though making up only 20 percent of all drug users nationwide (the rest being occasional users), this group accounts for two-thirds to three-quarters of all the drugs consumed here. They also account for most of the crime, medical emergencies, and other harmful consequences associated with drugs. (Massing, 1999)

General population surveys (see chapter 2) show a decline in drug use since the late 1980s yet measures of hospital visits (DAWN) show increases. Although general use has declined, the severity of drug-related problems has not. "DAWN has shown that drug problems can increase even as the rate of drug use in the population stabilizes and has provided compelling evidence that drug problems are disproportionately borne by poor and urban minority populations" (Reuter, 1999).

Based on the assumption that not all users can be persuaded to quit, harm reduction involves a redefinition of presumed solutions to the use of drugs. Do the methods chosen help to reduce death, disease, violence, and crime?

> Harm reduction makes the most sense for those who are unconcerned about drug use per se, but who are worried about the social costs associated with use and abuse, including violence and property crime. This is a fundamentally different mindset than the one that has dominated U.S. drug control policy since the Harrison Act. (White & Gorman, 2000, p. 158)

The goal should be policies that reduce the harm caused by drug use rather than the elimination of all drug use. Harm reductionists see the problem as a public-health issue rather than a law-enforcement problem. For those who can't or won't stop using drugs, safe practices are encouraged. Harm reductionists support needle-exchange programs, safe-injection rooms for heroin users, and maintenance programs such as methadone or buprenorphine, which had been under study by the FDA for four years. Thirty thousand people use buprenorphine in France; approved in the United States in October 2002, it is safe to be prescribed as a take-home medication (Keilman, 2002).

Dr. Frank Vocci, director of NIDA's Division of Treatment Research and Development., discussed new treatments for opiate users.

> The results of this research thus open the door to medical mainstreaming—treatment in doctors' offices and private facilities, rather than only in narcotic treatment programs—for individuals addicted to heroin. Heroin addiction is a chronic brain disease, and we can treat it like any other chronic medical condition—considering alternatives for treatment and planning that treatment based on individual patient needs. (Thomas, 2001)

MEDICAL PROBLEM

Most people can use drugs without harming themselves or others. A few million Americans do have a serious problem. Do current policies help those people and society? Alcohol and tobacco are responsible for tremendous social costs, but society treats abuse of those substances as a health problem not a crime. Soldiers steel themselves for war by dehumanizing the enemy. Does demonizing drugs and the people who use them address the right problem?

Ten thousand people contract HIV from dirty needles every year, but syringe possession is illegal in most states. The federal government refuses to fund needle exchange. Teddy Shaw of the NAACP Legal Defense Fund says this is "tantamount to murder by social policy." David Lewis, founder of Physician Leadership on National Drug Policy, thinks doctors have stayed on the sidelines because they "have been more or less driven out by the overwhelming presence of criminal-justice interests—and by the stigma associated with drug and alcohol addition" (Casriel, 2001).

A RAND study in 1994 found that treatment was 7 times more cost-effective than law enforcement (arresting and imprisoning buyers and sellers); ten times more effective than interdiction (stopping drugs at the border) and 23 times more effective than source-control programs (attacking the drug trade abroad).

> Treatment is so inexpensive that it more than pays for itself while an individual is actually in a program, in the form of reduced crime, medical costs and the like; all gains that occur after an individual leaves a program are a bonus. And it doesn't matter what form of treatment one considers: methadone maintenance, long-term residential, intensive outpatient and twelve-step programs all produce impressive outcomes (though some programs work better for certain addicts than for others). (Massing, 1999)

Drug Courts and other diversion programs (see articles 16 and 17) have been instituted in a number of communities, but Arizona and California are the first states to take a comprehensive approach in making treatment available to drug offenders. The number of drug offenders in California dropped to 16,000 from 20,000 after Proposition 36 (a 10-month intensive program open to all non-violent, first- and second-time drug offenders who agree to plead guilty) passed. The state spends $25,607 a year to house an inmate versus $4,000 for treatment. Lonny Shavelson, a physician and treatment advocate, comments: "The best substance abuse programs deal with homelessness, illiteracy, family problems and mental health. If you don't deal with those problems, [the offenders] don't get off drugs" (Haynes, 2002a, p. 11). Proposition 36 has brought together diverse agencies for the first time; courts, treatment centers, probation departments, and social service agencies coordinate services to help offenders. Voters in Michigan, Ohio, and Washington, D.C. will find similar programs on the ballot in November 2002, and Florida is considering an initiative for drug treatment.

DEA Director Asa Hutchinson, after observing a drug court program in Illinois, took a more sympathetic tone than much of the government rhetoric about drugs:

> Seventy-five percent of drug users today are employed. There's not the down-and-out person, the street bum that you always think about. It's the person who is working or perhaps supporting two jobs who needs an extra boost and all of a sudden they're addicted. We see all walks of life. It's not just a criminal element. It's also people that we think of as more normal that become addicted. (Presecky, 2002, p. 2).

The criminal justice system handles the most drug offenses at the state level. New Mexico Governor Gary Johnson predicts states will be the engines of reform. Overburdened states are seeking more effective solutions. They have passed 17 of 19 ballot initiatives to make drug laws more lenient. There are about 700 drug courts that attempt to substitute treatment for prison. Utah and Oregon have restricted forfeiture seizures. As Rocky Anderson, mayor of Salt Lake City, states: "Punitive policies at tremendous taxpayer expense are an unmitigated failure."

The scare tactics of exaggeration and false linkages promoted by the government, media, and others have worked for more than a century. There is some evidence that public opinion may be shifting. Persistent overstatements or misleading information about the impact of drugs may have finally surpassed the public's willingness to find the claims credible.

Although drug war ideology is marked by misinformation and illogic, it is by no means dysfunctional. When the criminal justice system was enlisted to solve the problem of drug use, the answer was predictable: more laws and incarceration for those who break them. The system has a very effective means of continuing current policy. Any criticism is characterized as proof of the necessity to increase efforts. Opposition to the drug war enterprise, no matter how reasonable or factually based the specific arguments, is quickly labelled as an attempt to legalize drugs—a solution assumed by the ideology to be so reprehensible that it can be rejected immediately.

In June 1998 the United Nations held a special session to discuss drugs. Over 500 public figures from around the world signed a letter (sponsored by the Lindesmith Centre) to Kofi Annan. The letter appeared in the *New York Times* and included this passage:

> Persisting in our current policies will only result in more drug abuse, more empowerment of drug markets and criminals, and more disease and suffering. Too often those who call for open debate, rigorous analysis of current policies, and serious consideration of alternatives are accused of "surrendering." But the true surrender is when fear and inertia combine to shut off debate, suppress critical analysis, and dismiss all alternatives to current policies. (Lindesmith Centre, 1998)

There are no simple solutions. The abuse of mind-altering substances is a major concern in the mosaic of social problems. However, the powerful, taken-for-granted ideology masks a complex mixture of beliefs, morals, and assumptions about drugs in the United States. Whether trying to resolve peer pressure to belong, the fears of parents about their children, the concerns of politicians who don't want to appear soft, or the damage drug trafficking does to communities, we cannot reduce the issue of drugs to a simplistic view of deviant behavior to be punished. Is zero tolerance a realistic goal? The rhetoric feeds the zealousness of proponents and stymies the search for a more workable solution. Untangling the web of facts and fiction is a requisite foundation for understanding why the criminal justice system is the front line of attack for an intractable social problem and how current policy might be altered to ameliorate rather than exacerbate that problem.

There are unquestionably harmful effects from some drug usage: physical impairments, criminal acts to pay for drugs, unsafe streets, health endangerment, and possible overdoses. There are also harmful effects from the drug war: imprisoning people does not improve the chances that they will lead productive lives; families are separated; the enormous expenditures on punishment leave few resources for treatment. What price are we willing to pay for what benefits? Is the harm balanced by the efforts to suppress?

If the punishment model isn't the answer, what is? As with any intractable problem, there is no panacea. What will be the costs and benefits of new policies to which groups? How do we balance economic costs and human casualties? Will the moral stance change to accommodate workable approaches? Will the country accept the European approach that drugs are essentially a health and social problem? Can we change our focus to treatment and to reducing the disease and crime that accompany the illegal trade in drugs? Sorting through alternatives requires the ability to look past conditioned responses. If we don't find a way to reframe the discussion of substance abuse, our children will find the twenty-first century repeating the same mistakes as the twentieth. We hope you develop your own antennae to tune in to the information presented. Is there a hidden agenda? Are the evidence and arguments presented based on a solid foundation, or do they rest on assumed but unproven assumptions? The issue of drugs, crime, and justice is important and complex. It requires discerning analysis and synthesis. We hope this collection inspires you to be a well-informed participant in the debate.

REFERENCES

Bandow, D. (2000, December 11). The Robert Downey Jr. problem. *Christian Science Monitor.*

Bendavid, N. (2002, March 24). Critics decry ads linking drugs, terror. *Chicago Tribune,* pp. 1, 17.

Best, J. (2001). *Damned lies and statistics: Untangling numbers from the media, politicians, and activists.* Berkeley: University of California Press.

Casriel, E. (2001, August 2). The new coalition against the drug war. *Rolling Stone Online* (RS 874).

Caulkins, J. (2000). Measurement and analysis of drug problems and drug control efforts. In *Criminal justice 2000, Vol. 4. Measurement and analysis of crime and justice* (pp. 391–449). Washington, DC: U.S. Department of Justice.

Chapman, S. (2001a, August 26). Latin America's drug problem is our own creation. *Chicago Tribune,* p. 19.

Chapman, S. (2001b, December 13). The drug war vs. the war on terror. *Chicago Tribune,* p. 31.

Chapman, S. (2002, February 21). Step up: Mass drug testing for the guilty and the innocent. *Chicago Tribune,* p. 25.

City mulls growing medical marijuana. (2002, July 24). *Chicago Tribune,* p. 16.

Double standard on cocaine. (2000, January 23). *Chicago Tribune,* p. 16.

Geller, A. (2002, July 17). A closer look. *Chicago Tribune,* sec. 6, pp. 1, 4.

Gray, J. (2001). *Why our drug laws have failed and what we can do about it: A judicial indictment of the war on drugs.* Philadelphia: Temple University Press.

Gray, M. (2000). *Drug crazy: How we got into this mess and how we can get out.* New York: Routledge.

Greenburg, J. (2002, March 27). Court oks hard line on drug-use evictions. *Chicago Tribune,* pp. 1, 18.

Hawkins, D. (2002, August 12). Tests on trial: Jobs and reputations ride on unproven drug screens. *U.S. News & World Report,* pp. 46–48.

Haynes, V. (2002a, July 2). Jury out on treatment program. *Chicago Tribune,* p. 11.

Haynes, V. (2002b, August 9). Nevada blazes trail for legal marijuana. *Chicago Tribune,* pp. 1, 14.

Healy, G. (2002, July 22). Use of military for civilian policing is dangerous. *Chicago Tribune,* p. 17.

Hoge, W. (2002, July 11). Britain mellows its marijuana laws. *Chicago Tribune,* p. 3.

Keilman, J. (2002, September 16). Alternative to methadone hits snags. *Chicago Tribune,* pp. 1, 16.

Lindesmith Centre (1998). *Public letter to Kofi Annan* [Electronic version]. http://www.lindesmith.org/news/un.html

Los Angeles Times (2002, September 18). Defiant group gives marijuana to patients. *Chicago Tribune,* p. 14.

MacCoun, R., Kilmer, B., & Reuter, P. (2002). Research on drugs-crime linkages: The next generation. In *Toward a drugs and crime research agenda for the twenty-first century.* Washington, DC: National Institute of Justice.

Massing, M. (1999, September 20). It's time for realism. Beyond legalization: New ideas for ending the war on drugs: A forum. *The Nation.* http://past.the nation.com/issue/990920/0920massing.shtml

McBride, D., VanderWaal, C., & Terry-McElrath, Y. (2002). The drugs-crime wars: Past, present, and future directions in theory, policy, and program interventions. In *Toward a drugs and crime research agenda for the 21st century.* Washington, DC: National Institute of Justice. (NCJ 194616)

McNamara, J. (1999, October 5). The war the police didn't declare and can't win. http://www.cato.org/realaudio/drugwar/papers/mcnamara.html

McNamara, J. (2000a, May 15). Return to true liberty, end drug war. *Wall Street Journal.*

McNamara, J. (2000b, September 1). Commentary: Criminalization of drug use. *Psychiatric Times.* http://www.psychiatrictimes.com/p000903.html

McNamara, J. (2000c, November 26). Citizens quietly rebel against drug war. *San Jose Mercury News.* http://www.commondreams.org/share.htm

Mired in Colombia. (2002, January 19). *Chicago Tribune,* p. 26.

Montgomery, D. (2002, July 18). Ravers against the machine: Partiers and ACLU take on "ecstasy" legislation. *Washington Post*, p. A01.

Moore, M. (1997). Lecture 3: The legitimation of criminal justice policies and practices. In *Perspectives on crime and justice: 1996–1997 lecture series* (Vol. 1, pp. 47–74). Washington, DC: National Institute of Justice.

Muwakkil, S. (2002a, January 28). Drug warriors: U.S.'s internal Taliban. *Chicago Tribune*, p. 15.

Muwakkil, S. (2002b, September 2). Why is prison becoming the norm for black males? *Chicago Tribune*, p. 21.

Nadelmann, E. (2002, August). No longer hope for progress. *Counselor Magazine*, Vol. 3, No. 4. http://www.drugpolicy.org/news/DailyNews/07_23_02Nadelmann _Counselor.html

Neergaard, L. (2002, July 17). FDA oks GHB for narcolepsy. http://stacks.msnbc.com/ news/781978

O'Connor, M. (December 15, 2001). U.S. says parents let smugglers rent babies. *Chicago Tribune*, p. 1.

Office of National Drug Control Policy (ONDCP) (2002). *National drug control strategy: 2002 annual report*. Washington, DC: U.S. Government Printing Office. (NCJ 192260)

Page, C. (2002, May 22). Pushing drug myths with our taxes. *Chicago Tribune*, p. 25.

Presecky, W. (2002, June 25). DEA chief praises Kane's drug court. *Chicago Tribune*, sec. 2, p. 2.

Ramo, J. (2001, May 7). America's shadow drug war. *Time*, 36–44.

Reinarman, C. & Levine, H. (1997) *Crack in context*. Berkeley: University of California Press.

Reuter, P. (1997) Lecture 2: Why can't we make prohibition work better: Some consequences of ignoring the unattractive. In *Perspectives on crime and justice: 1996–1997 lecture series* (Vol. 1, pp. 23–45). Washington, DC: National Institute of Justice.

Reuter, P. (1999). Drug use measures: What are they really telling us? *NIJ Journal 239*, April.

Roosevelt, M. (2001, May 7). The war against the war on drugs. *Time*, 46–47.

Thomas, J. (2001). Buprenorphine proves effective, expands options for treatment of heroin addiction. http://www.nida.nih.gov/NIDA_Notes/NNVol16N2/ Buprenorphine.html

Trice, D. T. (February 20, 2002). New ads hit at change in war on drugs. *Chicago Tribune*, sec. 2, p. 1.

United States Sentencing Commission (2002, May 22). Statement of Diana E. Murphy, chair of the United States Sentencing Commission, before the Senate Subcommittee on Crime and Drugs. http://www.ussc.gov/hearings/test52202.pdf

United States Sentencing Commission (2002, May). Report to the Congress: Cocaine and federal sentencing policy. http://www.ussc.gov/r_congress/02crack/ 2002crackrpt.htm

Vlahos, K. (2002, July 25). Odd bedfellows join fight for medical marijuana. http:// www.foxnews.com/story/0,2933,58666,00.html

Wenner, J. (2001, August 16). America's war on drugs. *Rolling Stone Online* (RS 875). http://www.rollingstone.com/news/newsarticle.asp?nid=14338

White, H. & Gorman, D. (2000). Dynamics of the drug-crime relationship. In *Criminal justice 2000, Vol. 1. The nature of crime: Continuity and change* (pp. 151–218). Washington, DC: U.S. Department of Justice.

Section

I

DRUGS IN CONTEXT

1

The American Experience with Stimulants and Opiates

David F. Musto

The history of drugs in America is a large subject. To make it more manageable I would like to look first at shifting attitudes toward—and consumption of— alcohol. Following the same pattern of looking at attitudes and consumption, I'll also discuss opiates and stimulants, including cocaine and amphetamines.

Alcohol is a drug that has been used throughout the entire history of the United States. We have experienced cycles of high as well as low consumption. These swings in alcohol consumption roughly reflect the use of other drugs such as cocaine and opiates. Although most of these drugs were not familiar products early in the 19th century when the first great temperance movement swept America, they figured in the second temperance movement, which culminated in national Prohibition from 1920 through 1933. We may well be in the first stage of a third temperance movement, which began about 1980. The changing pattern of alcohol use reflects not just a fundamental change in our attitude toward alcohol, but also changes in our attitudes toward food, exercise, the protection of our bodies, the purification of our environment, and the role of government in the creation of a healthier society.

Alcohol: Attitudes and Consumption from 1790 to 1995

The past 200 years have seen three distinct eras of alcohol consumption. In the early Republic, an extremely high level of alcohol consumption (chiefly, distilled spirits) peaked in the 1830s at more than 7 gallons per adult. A rapid

From *Perspectives on Crime and Justice*, vol. II (1998, pp. 51–78). National Institute of Justice, Rockville, MD: National Criminal Justice Reference Service (NCJ 172851).

decline followed and reached a low in the 1850s, coinciding with the first temperance movement and widespread state prohibition in the mid-1850s. We have never again come close to the high levels of consumption of the early 19th century. Consumption rose again until about 1910 to 2.8 gallons per adult, when a second decline began. The level of alcohol use at the end of Prohibition was the lowest in American history. Another rise began in 1934 and reached its peak in 1980 at 2.8 gallons per adult. It took 50 years after Prohibition for alcohol consumption to rise again to its previous high levels. We now are, once again, in a time of declining alcohol consumption.[1]

These declines in alcohol consumption and parallel changes in attitude toward alcohol eventually have been expressed in legal restrictions. The first change in attitude is a transformation from viewing alcohol as a valuable tool and an instrument of health, healing, inspiration, or cheer, to viewing it as a poison. This radical shift has occurred more than once in American history. The concept of a safe upper limit of use is erased gradually. As this process continues, the harm done by alcohol increasingly dominates discussion and finally outweighs its claims as a medicine or a tonic. Moderation evolves to abstinence. Two examples illustrate the beginning and end of this evolution. Dr. Benjamin Rush, signer of the Declaration of Independence, surgeon in the Revolutionary War, and professor at the nation's first medical school in Pennsylvania, saw life differently from most of his contemporaries. He fought for education of African Americans, abolition of slavery, education of women, prison reform, an end to capital punishment—and abstinence from distilled spirits. His reform ideas, however, were far better than his medical theories, which implied that the only effective remedies were strong laxatives and bleeding. Rush blamed high-proof alcohol for causing illness, moral degeneration, poverty, and crime.

Rush approved of beer and wine in moderation but believed that distilled spirits started a person on the downhill path. He likened dependence on alcohol to a disease, and some say he was the first to do so. Rush typified the early days of a temperance movement. He had a vision that few shared in his own time, but it became one of the great reform movements in American history a generation after his death. Interestingly, Rush's antialcohol position was staked out as the nation started on an extraordinary binge that did not peak until 1830.

Rush invoked two powerful forces that are typically American: scientific research and voluntary organization. By encouraging the public to cooperate with what he saw as medical insights into the dangers of distilled spirits, he hoped to improve society. He espoused another very American trait—"logical reformism," in which the dangers of alcohol from distilled spirits were gradually extended to their logical conclusion, the dangers of alcohol from all alcoholic beverages. Compare this with the British experience: In Britain during the gin epidemic of the 18th century, reformers attacked distilled spirits. Gin drinkers were urged to return to the traditional British ale and beer; they were not urged to give up alcohol. But the American approach was different.

If distilled spirits were dangerous because they contained alcohol, then all alcoholic beverages were dangerous. Although some, like beer, were considered mild, they nevertheless could lead to addiction and a desire for stronger drinks. There was no safe threshold of alcohol use.

Lyman Beecher, perhaps the most popular preacher in pre-Civil War America, insisted on this final formulation of the first temperance movement. About a decade after Rush's death, Beecher demanded total abstinence from all alcohol—beer as well as rum and wine as well as whiskey. His only concession was to grant that beer "enables the victim to come down to his grave, by a course somewhat more dilatory, and with more of the good-natured stupidity of the idiot and less of the demoniac fury of the madman." He had no sympathy for what is now called "responsible drinking" and what in his day was called "prudent use." "It is not enough," he wrote, "to erect the flag ahead, to mark the spot where the drunkard dies. It must be planted at the entrance of his course, proclaiming in waving capitals: this is the way to death!! Over the whole territory of 'prudent use' it must wave and warn."[2]

By 1855 about a third of the United States and all of New England were under state prohibition laws, with a number of other states close to approving this ultimate control as well.[3] What had happened since the freely flowing spirits of 1830 when alcohol consumption was three times the current per adult rate? A deep, tenacious new conviction had slowly gripped Americans and reversed their image of alcohol. Abraham Lincoln expressed it best in a temperance lecture he gave in Springfield, Illinois, in 1842. Back when alcohol was seen positively, Lincoln said, the damage done was thought to arise "from the abuse of a very good thing," but now, he said, we know that "the injury arose from the use of a bad thing."[4]

Alcohol's altered image is all the more remarkable because for many Americans alcohol was, and is, an everyday consumable and a part of religious ceremonies. These factors contributed to the failure to sustain Prohibition indefinitely. When Prohibition lost, it lost so completely that the opposing side simply swept away the other point of view. Both sides were fueled by emotions and had few facts to back up their positions. People did not want to hear that liver cirrhosis deaths were cut in half during Prohibition because they could not believe that anything good came from Prohibition.[5] That kind of censorship can be seen with drugs and alcohol. The peaks of Prohibition in the 1850s and 1920s ended in frustration for the antialcohol forces. The backlash to Prohibition added to their regrets; for decades any realistic discussion of alcohol and its problems was nearly impossible.

The prohibition of alcohol was not integrated into our society because too large a fraction of the public did not regard alcohol as a poison. In addition, Prohibition was viewed as an anti-Catholic, anti-immigrant measure.[6] The only two states not to ratify the 18th Amendment were Connecticut and Rhode Island, the two states with the highest Catholic voting populations. At the peak of hostility to alcohol, the prohibition forces did not have more than 60 percent of the public on their side. In contrast, cocaine and opiates came under similar control with almost no opposition: I estimate popular hostility to cocaine and heroin at 95 percent or higher. Alcohol prohibition illustrates that in some of these crusades for health or temperance, reform may go further than can be sustained.

The target of reform during the first temperance movement was not restricted to alcohol; poor health and poor eating habits were attacked as well during this and all other reform movements throughout American history. In that first temperance movement, Sylvester Graham, who advocated fresh vegetables, whole-grain flour (graham flour), water (not alcohol), exercise, and no fried foods, was representative. (His memory lives today in the graham cracker.)[7] The second temperance movement, led by the Anti-Saloon League and the Woman's Christian Temperance Union, also saw a revival of health campaigns out of which came corn flakes and yogurt. Accompanying the current temperance movement is a new health campaign: jogging, whole grains, no red meat, and lots of tofu.

Opiates: Opium, Morphine, and Heroin

In addition to the rise and fall of alcohol consumption and its resulting political and social movements, consider opium and its derivatives. Customs records of the then-legal product reveal the pattern of use from 1840 until 1915, when the Harrison Narcotic Act brought opium and opiates under control and the amount smuggled had to be estimated.

Opioid consumption rose until the 1890s and then declined. By 1914 when the Harrison Act was passed, per capita consumption had fallen to that of 1870. The smoking of opium slowly increased throughout the period; data on it end with the Smoking Opium Exclusion Act of 1909. The decline in the use of opioids coincided with the public's growing fear of addiction and the rise of state laws restricting their availability to a physician's prescription.[8]

During the 19th century and before these state controls, the United States was the only major Western nation to allow unlimited distribution, sale, and promotion of narcotics. The result was not surprising: the use of opium and morphine and, later, cocaine and heroin was extensive. (Heroin was introduced by the Bayer Company in 1898 as a powerful cough suppressant. The firm's ads read, "Aspirin for joint pains. Heroin for coughs.") In the 1890s consumption of opium and its active ingredient, morphine, peaked with an estimated one-quarter of a million addicts. Since the U.S. population in 1890 was 60 million—about a quarter of the current population—a million people would be addicted to opiates now if the same rate applied. Although both past and current numbers are estimates, it is reasonable to assume that the last opiate epidemic at its height was fairly extensive.

The late 19th-century opioid epidemic lasted several decades and continued with many years of easy availability. Eventually, although more slowly than concerned Americans wished, it went away. The broad outline of the earlier wave of drug use and its eventual decline raises questions. Was the decline a result of a shutoff of the drug supply or of Americans' disgust with and fear of drugs? As with the alcohol epidemics, our loss of memory for the earlier drug epidemic contributed to even greater similarities between the two waves of drug use, then and now. In each instance, drugs entered American society surrounded by fantasies that would only gradually be replaced by the reality of drug use.

Antidrug laws were in place when the current drug wave hit the United States in the 1960s. Why were there no laws against drug availability in the 19th century? To understand why a free market existed, it is helpful to look at circumstances unrelated to drugs. First, unlike European nations, the United States did not have strong national organizations of pharmacists and physicians until this century. Organizations with names suggesting such breadth did exist (for example, the American Medical Association, established in 1847), but only a fraction of practicing health professionals were members. Furthermore, licensing of professionals was rare in the mid-19th century; anyone could claim to be a physician or pharmacist. Without a national organization or licensing, control over the practice of the health professions was practically nonexistent.

An early obstacle to national control was separation of federal from state power in the U.S. Constitution. Strictly interpreted separation between federal and state powers prevailed during the 19th century. Therefore, police powers over the regulation of medical practice were reserved for the states. Few people today question the Drug Enforcement Administration's right to register physicians and pharmacists and control what drugs they can prescribe and dispense. In the 19th century, this would have been an unthinkable federal invasion of states' rights. Nineteenth-century America permitted an open market in narcotics. Some current advocates of legalizing drugs have not considered that both our fear of drugs and our first antidrug laws were consequences of unrestricted drug use. Easy access to drugs did not create a peaceful integration of morphine and cocaine into American habits; rather, widespread use of drugs led to the fear of their effects on the individual, the family, and society. History also shows that extensive use of a drug at one time does not mean that such a high rate will continue indefinitely; the drug may fade in esteem and usage, even to the vanishing point. Reasonable national drug policies must take into account the long-term perspective. We should neither hastily surrender in defeat at a time of extensive use nor declare final victory after a long and deep decline in drug use.

The rising use of opium and morphine in the late 19th century prompted some states to enact laws restricting access to opiates to a physician's prescription—unless the opiates were contained in patent medicines. The major difficulty for proponents of a national antinarcotic law—the constitutional separation of powers—was resolved only with great effort. The Pure Food and Drug Act of 1906 required that makers of patent medicines state on the label the amount of any narcotic ingredient they contained, but the law set no ceiling on how much the product could contain. Later, the Harrison Act, in contrast, severely limited the amount of opioids in any remedy sold without a prescription. Although the Harrison Act became law in 1914, the Supreme Court did not interpret it to restrict the reasons for which a physician could provide addicting drugs to patients until 1919.

These laws reflected a nationwide consensus that had been growing for several decades against drugs, particularly opiates and cocaine. Although attitudes toward alcohol were more divided, national Prohibition was achieved through the elaborate process of adopting the 18th Amendment to the Constitution. Opiates and cocaine, however, were so despised and feared by the early years of this century that a similar prohibition was instituted much more simply by a statute and Supreme Court interpretation. This fear of narcotics is painfully portrayed in Eugene O'Neill's *Long Day's Journey into Night*, set in August 1912. Arguably the greatest drama by an American, the play centers on the impact of morphine addiction on a family.

Although the nation's drug use rises and falls, human physiology remains the same. For many, the initial encounter with drugs is attractive; the negative attitude toward drugs is learned from experience.

Another trend often accompanying the nation's rejection of drug use is less constructive—the increasing fear of and anger at the drug user. Anger and fear more and more characterize American attitudes after several decades of watching drugs ravage families, the social order, and personal health.

The American Medical Association had originally supported the Harrison Act: Health workers were as upset about the drug problem as the public. One target of the national laws in the early 20th century was the mercenary physician or pharmacist who irresponsibly prescribed or dispensed narcotics. At times this campaign against health professionals, supported so strongly by the public and government officials, went too far, creating an atmosphere that made health professionals extremely wary of prescribing or dispensing narcotics for pain control, although only a minority had been irresponsible. The effect of their extra caution, however, sometimes led to inadequate pain management, and many patients had to endure unnecessary discomfort. Among health professionals and patients, the fear of addiction reached extreme levels in the decline phase of the earlier opiate and cocaine epidemic. This concern and hesitation over pain medication can still be seen among physicians and patients today.[9]

Although U.S. drug policy is powerfully affected by domestic issues, several foreign influences also bear on narcotic-control measures: the great amount of drugs coming from abroad, the study by Americans of other nations' experiences with drug control, and the prevailing national mood regarding the presence or absence of threats from abroad. Prior to World War I, the United States had faith in international treaties and promoted many having to do with arbitration of disputes and other matters. The Hague Opium Treaty of 1912 was only one of America's efforts to gain international cooperation. All this optimism changed after the war, when the United States distrusted attempts at international cooperation, marked most notably by

U.S. refusal to join the League of Nations. Officials no longer spoke of the inordinate American demand for drugs but instead of the evil intentions of countries that supplied them. These very different attitudes regarding drugs and foreign nations in the decades before and after World War I had an enormous impact on drug policies.[10]

As the epidemic declined, both government and the larger society espoused strategies familiar to any parent worried about a child's decision to risk a dangerous action. Parents do not wish their children to take a chance on their lives even once. They cannot approve "experimenting" with drunken driving or any other dangerous activity available to young people. One method of restraining people from taking unwise actions had been put in place by government: the threat of severe punishment. Two other strategies also were developed.

One strategy was well-intentioned exaggeration. For example, Captain Richmond Pearson Hobson, an American naval hero and an active leader against alcohol, opiates, cocaine, and marijuana, declared in the mid-1920s that one ingestion of heroin on, for example, an ice cream cone, could addict a child. He warned that heroin might have been incorporated into face powder and that heroin not only addicted users but positively drove them to commit crimes whether they needed money or not.[11] In the 1930s marijuana likewise was luridly described with the hope, narcotics commissioner Harry Anslinger explained, that no child would be tempted to try it once.[12]

The other strategy was silence. Under strong pressure from major religious groups, the motion picture industry adopted a policy of never showing narcotic drug use. Enforcement of this policy was approved in 1934 by the Motion Picture Association of America, which comprised the major studios. In addition, the National Board of Film Review could not give its seal of approval to a motion picture that showed narcotic trafficking. Without this approval, a picture would have its viewing opportunities severely restricted and be unprofitable. Until a slight loosening in 1946 to permit showing antidrug activities, this prohibition remained effective until the 1950s.

The radio networks were equally cooperative. On the other hand, the print media published sensational stories about drug arrests. Public fear was large, but the number of people impaired by cocaine, heroin, or marijuana in the 1930s and 1940s was small when compared with today's problem or that evident around 1910.

Paradoxically, success in reducing drug use may have been an obstacle in the long run to maintaining an accurate and effective antidrug campaign. During the 1920s requirements to teach about narcotics in schools spread throughout the states. By 1933, for example, Massachusetts had developed a syllabus for teaching about alcohol, stimulants, and narcotics for grades 1 through 12.[13] Importantly, information about drugs was presented as an integral part of health education, not just as a program against narcotics. As the problem declined, however, silence itself was assumed to be a good policy. By the 1960s, fewer than half the states retained a requirement that the effects of narcotics be taught; by then the information was conveyed by teachers who had little practical knowledge and who allotted little time for the subject. With only a small drug problem confronting American schools in the 1940s and 1950s, resources went elsewhere.

The long-range result in the 1960s was a generation with no protective knowledge about the seductive claims and physiological effects of dangerous drugs or with exaggerated expectations for immediate and dire consequences of drug use. When the generation of the 1960s began to experiment with drugs, the contrast between the truth of their own experience and what they heard from authorities caused them to utterly discount the warnings.

Scientific research on the effects and mechanisms of drug use is easy to overlook in the great contest between users and those combating them. Research into the biological mechanisms of addiction appears to rise and fall depending on the public's anxiety level over drugs and whether the medical/therapeutic approach is in vogue. In the first epidemic, medical treatment approaches eventually gave way to an almost exclusive reliance on law enforcement, and sustained scientific research fell steeply. Once a strict anti-drug policy had been established, both the public's and policymakers' curiosity about the details of a drug's biological effects faded. Federal scientists also feared their research findings might conflict with official policies, so they avoided some areas of investigation.

Stimulants: Cocaine and Amphetamines

For more than a century, Americans have alternately praised stimulants and condemned them as the most fearful of all dangerous drugs. Stimulants are popular initially because they offer a shortcut to goals that are admired as typically American: the ability to work without tiring, the alertness to solve problems, and cheerfulness regardless of the situation. A person can stay up later to follow the international markets or drive farther to cover more miles in one stretch without sleepiness. Faster, more, and longer are promised by stimulants. Energy and efficiency are available simply by taking a substance, a substance that can be cheap as well as energizing.

Alexis de Tocqueville noted this American trait in the 1830s, decades before cocaine was developed as the first powerful stimulant. "It is odd to watch," he wrote, "with what feverish ardor the Americans pursue prosperity and how they are ever tormented by the shadowy suspicion that they may not have chosen the shortest route to get it."[14] For some Americans the shortest route has meant using stimulants, and this helps explain why at the beginning of a stimulant epidemic the drugs are favored by so many of those who are goal oriented—those who are trying to do their job better or working toward some achievement. When a new product promises to give them an edge, they are tempted to improve their chances with the help of chemical engineering.

The current concern over methamphetamine and cocaine might lead some to conclude that this epidemic is America's first wave of stimulant abuse. It is the second. Although during the first epidemic cocaine was widely used and legal at the beginning, the epidemic did come to an end. Its closure was so complete that when Americans witnessed the rise of cocaine in the 1970s, they thought it was a new phenomenon, and as it flourished they despaired of it ever ending.

The isolation of cocaine from coca leaves took place in the 1860s. But it was not until the 1880s that substantial quantities of cocaine were produced. This allowed the first widespread use of powerful stimulants with the introduction of pure cocaine to the American market.[15]

Coca leaf extracts that contained varying amounts of cocaine and were taken by mouth prepared the way for pure cocaine. The most famous of these was Vin Mariani, a combination of French red wine and coca leaf extract. Angelo Mariani's wine was popular as a tonic and stimulant in Europe and America. Mariani offered a discount to the clergy—Pope Leo XIII gave Mariani a gold medal—and he offered a further discount to orphanages. Famous people on both sides of the Atlantic allowed their names and faces to be used for Mariani's publicity—quite famous people, including Jules Verne, Charles Gounod, Frederic Bartholdi (the sculptor of the Statue of Liberty), cardinals, cabinet officers, explorers, and even Thomas Edison. Coca wine was touted as an antidote for melancholy and also as an invigorating stimulant for the healthy.[16]

In what is now the *New England Journal of Medicine*, Dr. Archie Stockwell wrote in 1877:

> Coca causes increased arterial action, stimulates the alimentary secretions and peristaltic action, diminishes weariness, strengthens the pulse, calms nervous excitement, retards waste, facilitates repair, alleviates spasms, and increases mental activity; in fact, it is an economizer of vital energy and an effective aid to nutrition. It invariably contributes to mental cheerfulness, and withal not infrequently causes unequivocal aphrodisia.[17]

An American competitor to Vin Mariani, Metcalf's Coca Wine, advertised in the 1880s that it was a valuable tonic for "public speakers, singers, and actors." Furthermore, "Athletes . . . and baseball players have found by practical experience that a steady course of coca taken both before and after any trial of strength or endurance will impart energy to every movement."[18] This use of coca as a tonic was so popular that J. S. Pemberton of Atlanta, Georgia, concocted what he called a French Coca Wine in 1885. In 1886 he brought forth another coca drink, took out the controversial drug alcohol, and called it Coca-Cola. In its early years (before the cocaine was eliminated), Coca-Cola was described as "the ideal brain tonic."[19] Thus "the pause that refreshes" has an interesting ancestry that testifies to the public's high regard for coca drinks.

If Coca-Cola and Vin Mariani had been the full extent of the public's exposure to coca, we might never have had the intense furor over cocaine that erupted in the decades after 1890 or recurred during our present drug epidemic. Credit—or blame—must be given to organic chemistry, which first produced cocaine, and also to the pharmaceutical industry, which was able to manufacture and distribute the drug in large amounts. As in the 1970s, cocaine a century earlier was initially expensive and restricted to the wealthy; later, it became much cheaper and more widely used.[20]

Also paralleling the current wave of cocaine use were the initial descriptions of the substance as harmless and nonaddicting. Sigmund Freud first wrote about and promoted cocaine with enthusiasm.[21] Even the wise Sherlock Holmes used cocaine in the first years after its introduction, although later he abandoned the practice.[22] Within a year of its American introduction, Parke, Davis & Company offered cocaine in 15 different forms. Describing its remarkable new technology in 1885, the firm claimed cocaine to be a drug which, through its stimulant properties, can supply the place of food, make the coward brave, the silent eloquent, free the victims of the alcohol and opium habits from their bondage, and, as an anesthetic, render the sufferer insensitive to pain.[23]

Several years later the U.S. Hay Fever Association announced that it had chosen cocaine to be its official remedy.[24] Although by then some physicians had issued serious warnings about cocaine's dangers, the power of its attraction submerged criticism as its use spread to everything from soda pop to headache remedies. After all, how bad can something be if it makes you feel good?

In the early stages of a stimulant epidemic, even experts can be misled. Dr. William A. Hammond, one of the nation's leading neurologists and a professor at medical schools, wrote extensively about the brain in the 1880s. His expert opinion on cocaine was very positive: He liked it, he recommended it, and he took it. He even made his own wine-cocaine mixture, which he boasted was stronger and more reliable than Vin Mariani. He rejected fearful stories about cocaine that had appeared in newspapers and medical journals. Dr. Hammond "did not believe there was a single instance of a well-pronounced cocaine habit, the patient being able to stop it at any time, if he chose to do so." Even when presented with detailed accounts of cocaine's disastrous effects, he did not waiver in his belief that cocaine addiction was no more than the equivalent of a coffee or tea habit. Dr. Hammond illustrates that experts can become uncritical in their enthusiasm for a drug, especially if they like the effects of the drug on themselves.[25]

This benign view of cocaine could not last. Within 15 years the positive image of cocaine evolved into a very negative image, as threatening as the earlier was hopeful. Another parallel with the current cocaine problem can be seen when comparing cocaine's portrayal in 1970 as a safe and benign stimulant with its aura of extreme danger in the mid-1980s.

There are, however, differences between the first and second stimulant epidemics. Cocaine entered the marketplace in 1884 as a fully available substance with no restrictions. The laws and regulations did not come about until the public demanded them. Only as a drug came to be seen as a menace were restrictions enacted—initially at the state or local level. As a result, we have experienced whatever advantages a free economy in drugs might offer during much of the [nineteenth] century. Eventually, the fear of drugs grew so great that the traditional separation of federal from state powers was breached to allow, for the first time, federal control of prescribing practices over cocaine and opiates.

As a first step toward controlling cocaine, its distribution was put into the hands of the health professions. For example, in 1902 the state of Georgia made it illegal to provide cocaine in any amount or in any form without a doctor's prescription. In 1906 Al Smith introduced a bill in the New York State Assembly to limit cocaine availability to a doctor's prescription. As with opioids, when local control fell short, Congress enacted the 1914 Harrison antinarcotic law.[26] The measure imposed rules and regulations on the health professions that made the use of an opiate or cocaine a serious matter requiring a tax stamp and careful recordkeeping.

There was a reason behind the laws' increasing restraints. Cocaine started out as an all-American drug, useful to everyone who wanted to gain a step in the race of life—from athletes to clergy to orphans. By 1900, however, it had been transformed into the very image of evil and failure. Propelling this transformation was the appearance and behavior of those who had become hooked. In contrast to the opiate user—dulled and nodding—the heavy cocaine user was often paranoid, violent, and irresponsible. Fear of cocaine intensified. In 1910, President Taft sent to Congress a message in which cocaine was described as "more appalling in its effects than any other habit-forming drug used in the United States" and as "the most threatening of the drug habits that have ever appeared in this country."[27]

The important difference between addiction to a stimulant and addiction to an opiate such as morphine can be seen in the heroic life of the father of American surgery, Dr. William Stewart Halsted. Dr. Halsted was among those investigators who worked with the early batches of cocaine in the 1880s. Not knowing about the mental derangement that cocaine could cause, Halsted, who had repeatedly injected himself to learn about cocaine's ability to block pain, became addicted. His mind was confused, and he felt a constant craving for more and more. When he was sought to be the first surgeon-in-chief at the new Johns Hopkins Hospital, his friends helped him get off cocaine through close observation, sea voyages, and even admission to a mental hospital. Finally, apparently cured, he became the head of surgery at Hopkins.[28]

Only when his own doctor's secret diary was opened in the 1960s was it discovered that after he stopped using cocaine, Halsted took morphine and was addicted to it for the rest of his life. Halsted had a difficult time with morphine but still was able to achieve a great deal, something he could never have done if he had remained on a stimulant.[29] It is important to keep in mind this distinction between stimulants and opioids. Maintenance is possible, although difficult, with morphine, but giving more stimulant to a person with a stimulant problem only makes him more anxious and hyperactive. This is why stimulants are more feared than opiates and why stimulant users seek another substance, like heroin or methadone, to lessen their nervousness.

The mental distortion caused by stimulants probably accounts for another difference from opioids. Opioid epidemics tend to decline less and be longer compared with stimulant epidemics, which tend to fall further and be relatively brief. The last cocaine epidemic almost disappeared, but the number of opiate users never declined to such an extent. The first cocaine epidemic lasted about 40 years—from 1890 to 1930. The current cocaine epidemic began in the 1970s; therefore, if history is a guide, more than an additional decade of changing attitudes may help to reduce cocaine's use. A broad public consensus existed against drugs in the decline phase of the previous epidemic—broader, I believe, than is evident today. The rise and fall of a drug epidemic is not an independent phenomenon like the return of a comet. Citizens' attitudes toward drug use are crucial in determining consumption or rejection. An uninformed public eagerly searching for shortcuts sets the stage for a rise in drug use; a public that has seen the unfortunate consequences of drug use is more protected against the extravagant claims for a new drug.

In America the cocaine problem tends to be enmeshed with other social fears of the time. Around 1900 the fear of cocaine became linked with blacks living chiefly in the South. Blacks were accused of heavy cocaine use that led to violence. Because this era marked the peak of lynchings and the disenfranchisement of blacks, it is easy to see how these accusations could serve other purposes. At one point the U.S. Opium Commissioner was encouraging newspapers in the South to repeat these accusations as a way of obtaining Southern support for a national anticocaine law.[30] The attachment of drugs to other social fears arises from the enormous symbolic power that drugs possess in this society. Too often drugs are cited as the whole explanation for social problems, obscuring other and deeper causes. They can be cited as a reason for not helping inner cities because so many people falsely believe that the inner cities are populated predominantly by drug users. The history of drugs in America illustrates these repeated misperceptions. The question remains: Does knowing the history help curb these flights of fear and accusation?

As cocaine use declined in the 1930s, a new stimulant, amphetamine, appeared. Although it had been synthesized long before, only in 1932 was it introduced to the United States as Benzedrine. By the end of the 1930s, Benzedrine was promoted as a treatment for hay fever, melancholy, and lack of energy. Amphetamines got off to a slow start in the 1930s, but their use became common around World War II, when they were prescribed for fighter pilots and others who had to stay awake and alert. (Again, note the use of stimulants in the role of technology for the mind.) After the war, however, amphetamine use by long-haul drivers was implicated in trucking accidents. Amphetamines also played a role in an infamous kidnaping and murder case in the Midwest in 1953. The explosion in use, however, occurred in the 1960s, when amphetamine and methamphetamine ("speed") became popular among some youths, most notoriously in the Haight-Ashbury district of San Francisco. Methamphetamine use has remained popular on the West Coast and recently spread to the Midwest.[31]

The history of stimulants in America reveals that the past wave of use faded under broad popular condemnation, and it is hoped that the current one will do so also. The saddest impact of a stimulant epidemic is the damage done to users who sought chemical help with life's problems and soon found themselves in a morass of anxiety, hyperstimulation, and paranoia. However, a substantial learning process must take place before we reject a drug that promises joy and accomplishment.

By the time drug use had ceased being a major problem in 1940, society's anger and fear had become so overwhelming that the story of the past use of drugs was simply repressed. Policies were developed that increased punishment rather than treatment, preferred silence to education, and described drugs in extreme terms that bore little relation to reality. This strategy was not a problem when drugs were declining in use and their effects were fresh in memory, but the long-term impact was to leave the nation ignorant of drugs. By the time the 1960s arrived, the negative conditions that had been established in the 19th century were re-created. A struggle with drugs lasting more than 50 years and the practical wisdom painfully gained over those years had been erased from public memory.

The extensive history of drugs in America is not fodder for a simple party platform for one side or another; it is embedded in the broad and complex life of the nation, domestically and internationally. It is a frustrating history because it does not confirm the belief that there is a simple answer to this social problem. These observations can be drawn from the past: First, the timeline of a wave of drug use is quite long, well more than half an average lifespan. Second, at the beginning phase of a drug epidemic, we are filled with hopeful fantasies about drugs; in the decline phase, we are caught up in anger, scapegoating, and excessive punishment. Finally, it is likely that neither the hopeful nor the angry partisans will be persuaded by contrary information from a historian.

Question-and-Answer Session

James Boden, Policy Analyst, Office of Management and Budget, Executive Office of the President, Washington, D.C.: It seems that one of your contentions is that as drug use declines, the problem goes away. In today's case, where we have such an institutionalized process and infrastructure for dealing with this problem, is it likely that you would see the same level of decrease in the response?

David Musto: Institutional momentum is very real and can persist even when the initial justification for it has declined. It is also a relatively new feature of federal antinarcotic endeavors. In the 1920s the U.S. Public Health Service (PHS) had one principal drug expert, Dr. Lawrence Kolb, Sr., who employed one secretary and one half-time clerical assistant. In the 1930s, PHS opened two combination prison/treatment centers—one in Lexington, Kentucky, and the other in Fort Worth, Texas. The Bureau of Narcotics' annual budget from 1930 to 1960 ranged between $2 and $4 million per year.

Since about 1970, the federal drug-abuse control apparatus has become huge and its tendency toward self-perpetuation is a legitimate concern. In order to counteract this tendency, it is very important to have an independent control mechanism. The Drug Use Forecasting (DUF) program, now called the Arrestee Drug Abuse Monitoring (ADAM) program, contributes significantly to that control function. Under this system, booked arrestees participate in interviews and voluntarily provide urine samples for testing. In this way, ADAM provides a valuable independent measure that can serve as a counterweight to the vested interests that exist on all sides of the drug issue.

George Kanuck, Public Health Analyst, Center for Substance Abuse Treatment, U.S. Department of Health and Human Services, Washington, D.C.: Despite all the studies, controversy continues over the use of methadone for opiate addiction. There is currently a movement to simplify regulations governing the use of methadone and place more decisionmaking power in the hands of the physician. There continue to be significant concerns about that in the criminal justice community. Are we approaching a new phase that will permit methadone or other types of pharmacotherapies to be used in the future if they continue to be useful?

D.M.: I think that is a very good question that addresses two somewhat contradictory forces. One is a growing desire for drug-free treatment. Some states have made it illegal for a patient to use methadone for more than a year or so. Those sorts of restrictions put methadone maintenance in jeopardy. I think methadone can be very useful in some cases, but certainly not for people who are not addicted to opiates—for example, cocaine users who believe that methadone will relieve the discomfort of "coming down" from a cocaine high. It is a complicated issue; while there is good use for methadone, I think many people would prefer therapy that did not involve substituting one addictive substance for another.

I have seen a lot of antagonism toward methadone. As you know, the idea of maintaining dependence on an addictive substance runs contrary to our historical antidrug position as established in 1919 by the Supreme Court. In this country, abstinence has always been the goal of treatment, and it was discovered that many people who were maintained on heroin or morphine did not achieve that goal. This appears to be just as true of methadone maintenance—which casts doubt on the future of methadone programs, especially at the state level. This is unfortunate because methadone is an effective long-term treatment for some people.

On the other hand, the impact of AIDS has legitimized a number of measures that appear to be the contrary of drug-free therapy—for example, the distribution of syringes and needles to intravenous drug users. In this spirit of employing any measure that keeps drug users away from dirty needles, there have been efforts to make oral methadone more accessible, and I don't know how this is going to turn out. To me, the success or failure of this sort of approach will be an indication of the strength of this point of view, as opposed to drug-free methods.

Ted Gest, Senior Editor, *U.S. News & World Report*, Washington, D.C.: Given that it is difficult to single out the effectiveness of one particular antidrug measure, can you give us your view of the effectiveness of the Drug Abuse Resistance Education (D.A.R.E.) program or similar in-school programs in recent years? Also, how do you rate the effectiveness of the broadcast advertisements urging young people not to use drugs—either the "Just Say No" campaign of the 1980s or the current one?

D.M.: The D.A.R.E. program and other school-based programs are time-bound classroom experiences that are only one of many influences on a young person's life—and rather brief ones at that. Although the D.A.R.E. program has the great advantage of bringing police officers into direct contact with young people in a positive way, its long-term effects have been difficult to establish. Richard Clayton of the University of Kentucky (someone I greatly respect) has studied the D.A.R.E. program and has not been able to find much significant change in youthful behavior several years after program completion. The D.A.R.E. people reply that they have changed their syllabus, and the new program has not been measured. The fact remains that D.A.R.E. is in 70 percent of the school districts in the United States, and when you see it in action, it is hard to believe that it does not help at all.

Project STAR (Students Taught Awareness and Resistance), a nationwide program begun in Kansas City and aimed at seventh and eighth graders, also has been studied, and there is some evidence that it works better than the D.A.R.E. program.

With regard to your second question, I think advertising has become very sophisticated. The first modern attempts at antidrug advertising began around 1971, when the Nixon administration undertook major drug abuse control initiatives under the direction of Dr. Jerome Jaffe and Egil Krogh, a special assistant to the President. Initial media efforts were so unsuccessful that in 1973, a 6-month moratorium on dissemination of new materials was declared during which federal drug information materials were reevaluated. More recent efforts, such as those of the Partnership for a Drug-Free America, are very well thought out and are largely directed at supporting younger children who live in difficult situations. I am very impressed with some of the things they have done. Of course, the one that everyone remembers is the egg in the frying pan. I guess any campaign that people remember 10 years later must be successful.

Peter Eide, Manager of Labor Law Policy, U.S. Chamber of Commerce, Washington, D.C.: You have the historical perspective and the medical perspective, and you know what's going on today. In 25 words or less, what's the "fix" to the drug problem?

D.M.: The drug problem has deep roots in our society, and its tenacity is very upsetting to us. Americans have great difficulty tolerating ambiguity; things have to be either this way or they have to be that way. There's tremendous pressure for us to direct all our energies toward one pole or the other. The two extremes in the current debate about possible solutions to the drug problem are legalization and wholesale incarceration of drug offenders. Legalization is politically unworkable because a great majority of Americans are frightened by the prospect of making psychoactive substances easily and widely available. On the other hand, there is no way we can put many more people in jail than are already there.

We have to understand that waves of drug use subside gradually. There is no quick fix. At present we are witnessing a gradual decline (except among 12- to 17-year-olds) that is mostly driven by changes in people's minds and hearts. Many of the things we are doing now are the best we can do.

Certainly there are some changes that can be made for the better, particularly in the way antidrug laws are administered. The disparity between sentences for offenses involving crack cocaine versus those involving powder cocaine—estimated at 100 to 1—are a case in point. It has been difficult to modify that ratio because of the symbolic power of the issue and the concern among some members of Congress that a vote for modification would be interpreted as capitulation in the "war on drugs." The political symbolism of the issue makes any change slow and difficult. The only realistic approach is to recognize that any solutions will be the result of patient and incremental efforts over 10 or 20 years.

Mary Bernstein, Director, Office of Drug and Alcohol Policy and Compliance, U.S. Department of Transportation, Washington, D.C.: Given what you have said, particularly about waiting out the problem, what do you see as a good use of federal resources during this time?

D.M.: Scientific research on addiction is one very important focus of federal funding—and such research is being supported. It is amazing how much has been learned in the past 10 years. For example, we know that addiction changes something in the brain, but we don't know what the mechanism is. Since it appears that we are now in a decline phase of drug use when people are more likely to make up their minds about the issue and become less curious, there is some danger that funding for research will come under hostile scrutiny just as we close in on the answers to some very significant questions. If there is to be any hope of research contributing to a long-term resolution of the problem of drug abuse, funding support must also be for the long term.

Law enforcement has an important role to play, too. The late law professor Alex Bickel thought that many professionals had become so sophisticated that they "knew" that laws didn't make a difference. But I think laws do make a difference to the extent that they codify and make understandable the ethical underpinnings of society. To some extent the law tells us what we want our society to be and provides us with an organizing principle for our civic life. It is essential that laws be shaped by rationality and reason.

NOTES

[1] Lender, Mark Edward, and James Kirby Martin, *Drinking in America: A History* (New York: The Free Press, 1987), 205–206.

[2] Beecher, Lyman, *Six Sermons on the Nature, Occasions, Sins, Evils and Remedy of Intemperance* (Boston: T. R. Marvin, 1828).

[3] Lender and Martin, *Drinking in America*, 84.

[4] Lincoln, Abraham, "Speeches and Writings 1832–1858" in *Speeches, Letters, and Miscellaneous Writings: The Lincoln–Douglas Debates*, ed. Don E. Fehrenbacher (New York: Library of America, 1989), 84.

[5] Gusfield, Joseph R., *Symbolic Crusade: Status, Politics and the American Temperance Movement* (Urbana: University of Illinois Press, 1986), 176–177. Gusfield writes, "Temperance issues have served as symbols around which groups of divergent morals and values have opposed each other. On the side of Temperance there has been the rural, orthodox Protestant, agricultural, native American. On the side of drinking there has been the immigrant, the Catholic, the industrial worker and the secularized middle class. In more recent years the clash has pitted the modernist and the urbanized cosmopolitans against the traditionalists and the localities, the new middle class against the old. When Temperance forces were culturally dominant, the confrontation was that of the social superior. He sought to convert the weaker members of the society through persuasion backed by his dominance of the major institutions. Where the dominance of the society is in doubt, then the need for positive governmental and institutional action is greater. The need for symbolic vindication and deference is channeled into political action. What is at stake is not so much the action of men, whether or not they drink, but their ideals, the moralities to which they owe public allegiance."

[6] Lender and Martin, *Drinking in America*, 138.

[7] Rorabaugh, W. J., *The Alcoholic Republic: An American Tradition* (Oxford: Oxford University Press, 1979), 120–121.

[8] Musto, David F., "Opium, Cocaine and Marijuana in American History," *Scientific American* 265 (July 1991): 42. See the graph depicting the volume of American opiate imports from 1855 to 1915.

[9] Musto, David F., *The American Disease: Origins of Narcotic Control* (New York: Oxford University Press, 1987), Chapters 1–8. Opiates in 19th-century America and the origins of the Harrison Act are discussed at great length.

[10] Musto, David F., "American Reaction to the International Narcotic Traffic," *Pharmacy in History* 16 (1974): 115–122.

[11] Musto, *The American Disease*, 350–351 and fn. 33.

[12] Personal communication to the author, 1972.

[13] Massachusetts Board of Education, "The Effects of Alcohol, Stimulants, and Narcotics Upon the Human Body," *Bulletin of the [Massachusetts] Board of Education* 11 (269) (1933).

[14] de Tocqueville, Alexis, *Democracy in America*, trans. George Lawrence, ed. Max Lerner and J. P. Meyer (New York: Harper & Row, 1966), vol. II: 536.

[15] Musto, David F., "Cocaine's History, Especially the American Experience," in *Cocaine: Scientific and Social Dimensions*, ed. Gregory R. Bock and Julie Whelan (Ciba Foundation Symposium 166) (Chichester, United Kingdom: John Wiley and Sons, 1992), 7–19.

[16] Helfand, W. H., "Mariani et le vin de coca," *Psychotropes* 4 (3) (1988): 13–18.

[17] Stockwell, G. Archie, "Erythroxylon Coca," *Boston Medical and Surgical Journal* 96 (1877): 402.

[18] *New York Medical Times* 17 (April 1889): xxi.

[19] Munsey, Cecil, *The Illustrated Guide to the Collectibles of Coca-Cola* (New York: Hawthorn Books, 1972), 315–316.

[20] Musto, David F., "Illicit Price of Cocaine in Two Eras: 1908–1914 and 1982–1989," *Connecticut Medicine* 54 (June 1990): 321–326.

[21] Byck, Robert, ed., *The Cocaine Papers by Sigmund Freud* (New York: Stonehill, 1974).

[22] Musto, David F., "A Study in Cocaine: Sherlock Holmes and Sigmund Freud," *Journal of the American Medical Association* 206 (1968): 125–130.

[23] Parke, Davis & Company, "Coca Erythroxylon and Its Derivatives, 1885," in *The Cocaine Papers by Sigmund Freud*, ed. Robert Byck (New York: Stonehill, 1974), 127–150.

[24] Hammond, W. A., "Coca: Its Preparations and Their Therapeutical Qualities," *Transactions of the Medical Society of Virginia* (1887): 212–213.

[25] Hammond, W. A., "Coca: Its Preparations and Their Therapeutical Qualities, with Some Remarks on the So-Called Cocaine Habit," *Virginia Medical Monthly* (1887): 598–610.

[26] "An Act to Prescribe the Manner of Selling or Otherwise Dispensing Cocaine, to Provide a Penalty for a Violation of the Provisions of this Act, and for Other Purposes, Dec. 5, 1902," Acts and Resolutions of the General Assembly of the State of Georgia, 1902, Atlanta: State of Georgia, 1903: 100, Part 1, Title 5; Musto, "Illicit Price of Cocaine in Two Eras": 321.

[27] Musto, *The American Disease*, 242 and fn. 40.

[28] Olch, Peter D., "William S. Halsted and Local Anesthesia: Contributions and Complications," *Anesthesiology* 42 (April 1975): 480–481.

[29] Penfield, Wilder, "W. S. Halsted of Johns Hopkins," *Journal of the American Medical Association* 201 (12) (Dec. 22, 1969): 2214–2218.

[30] Musto, *The American Disease*, 282–283 and note 15.

[31] Jackson, Charles O., "Before the Drug Culture: Barbiturate/Amphetamine Abuse in American Society," *Clio Medica* 11 (1) (1976): 47–58.

2

The Psychopharmacology and Prevalence of Drugs

Larry K. Gaines

In this article we will look at the psychopharmacology of drugs—the effects of drugs on the mind and behavior. By understanding some of the effects of drugs, we gain insight into why people use drugs and the consequences of those choices. We will also look at various measures of the numbers of people who use both licit and illicit substances to gain an understanding of the extent of drug use in the United States. We begin our discussion with a brief look at what people mean when they use the words *drug* and *abuse*.

As discussed in the introduction, most people immediately think of illegal drugs when the word *drug* is mentioned. However, illegal drugs constitute only a portion of the drugs consumed in our society. Many people consume substances that physically or psychologically affect them, but they don't think of those substances as drugs. For example, some people routinely start the day with a cup of coffee or tea. The caffeine in the drink is a stimulant, but people do not think of themselves as physically dependent on a drug every morning. Because caffeine is a physically addicting substance, a person can experience the withdrawal symptoms of tension headaches and irritability if their intake of caffeine stops.

Other commonly consumed drugs in our society are nicotine (the addicting agent in tobacco products) and alcohol. Each year physicians write approximately 1.6 billion prescriptions (Wivell & Wilson, 1994). The Centers for Disease Control and Prevention (CDC) found that the number of written prescriptions per office visit increased 34% between 1985 (1.09) and 2000 (1.49). Prescription and nonprescription drugs pervade the marketplace. In the last two years, pharmaceutical companies have added more than 100 new

Written for *Drugs, Crime, and Justice*, 2/E.

drugs; more than 1,000 medicines are in development (Deardorff, 2002). Drug companies spend more than $3 billion a year (triple the amount spent in 1997 when the FDA eased restrictions on what prescription drugs could be advertised on television) on direct consumer ads, "which often lead consumers to demand the latest treatments from their doctors, whether they need the medicines or not" (Japsen, 2002). A study released in March 2002 by the U.S. Geological Survey found trace amounts of painkillers, antibiotics, caffeine, antidepressants, and other pharmaceuticals in rivers and streams in 30 states tested. These chemicals passed through people or animals, then through sewage plants, and eventually into the environment. Although the amount of pharmaceutical residue was very small, the research raises concerns about the impact on the ecosystem—and illustrates the extent to which drugs, legal or illegal, are consumed.

The common perception of drugs as either illegal or as prescribed treatment for a disease misses the fact that many drugs are taken for recreational purposes. Lyman and Potter (1998) provide a more appropriate definition: "a drug is any substance that causes or creates significant psychological and/or physiological changes in the body" (p. 60). Physiological changes can include the remedy of some physical ailment. For example, a physician may prescribe antibiotics to cure an infection or steroids to reduce the inflammation in a joint. Physicians may also prescribe psychoactive drugs to treat depression or to sedate someone in an agitated state. Most illicit drug use involves psychoactive drugs, although a few drugs with physiological effects are also abused. Athletes sometimes abuse steroids to increase muscle mass. Viagra, introduced in the United States in 1998 to treat erectile dysfunction, is used recreationally at raves and by gay men to enhance the effects of street drugs such as speed, ecstasy, and amyl nitrate (Breslau, 2002).

Why do people use illegal drugs or use legal drugs illegally? Leading criminologists have applied a variety of theories—including social disorganization, cultural transmission, anomie, opportunity, and differential association—to explain this behavior (see Abadinsky, 2001; Lyman & Potter, 1998). In the early 1980s, the National Institute of Drug Abuse published a monograph, *Theories of Drug Abuse*, which included 40 different theories explaining aberrant drug usage. Perhaps the most basic explanation of why people take drugs is to feel better. People visit doctors and take prescription drugs to relieve pain, eliminate a disease, and generally to improve their well-being. People who take drugs illegally may also want to feel better or even euphoric. There may be a natural tendency for some people to take drugs to change their mood.

There is a continuum of drug use (Abadinsky, 2001). The first phase is *experimental use*, trying a substance to see what happens. In the second phase, *culturally endorsed use*, members of the user's culture accept or encourage continued drug use. Large numbers of people in a given subculture use a preferred drug or drugs. For example, ecstasy is now a popular drug at teen parties, while cocaine is more popular with adults. *Recreational use* is the third phase; drugs are consumed more frequently. People begin to seek opportunities or excuses to use their drugs of choice. For example, many people routinely consume alcoholic beverages after work. The final phase is *compulsive use*. People abuse drugs and develop a physiological or psychological dependency on them. At this point, they become preoccupied with drugs to the exclusion of possible consequences or other activities.

The introduction touched on the topic of when use becomes abuse, which is a value-laden term. Some might conceptualize abuse as the compulsive phase. Others consider *any* use of drugs as abuse, believing that drug experimenters will automatically become compulsive users. Abuse does not have a precise definition or meaning relative to the amount of drugs consumed or the subsequent problems drug consumption might cause. It has become a political term used to solicit support in the war on drugs. There are millions of drug users in the United States who pose no threat or harm to themselves or others. We should be concerned primarily with compulsive use when considering the drug problem. Miller (1995) notes that our concern should rest with those who are addicted, for they cause the most harm to themselves and to others in society.

Surveys and Statistics on Drug Use

Like most aspects of drug use, measurements of its extent and analysis of the data are complicated. There are a number of measures whose statistics are often cited in media stories on drugs. We will introduce the major surveys with a brief explanation and will include some of the relevant data on individual drugs in the sections below. We urge readers to visit the Web sites where these surveys are published to become familiar with the terms used, the size of the samples, who is surveyed, and the procedures followed. Readers then will have some contextual background to help analyze the significance of statistics cited by the media and interest groups.

The U.S. Department of Health and Human Services has a number of agencies that provide statistics on the use of drugs. The federal government has conducted the National Household Survey on Drug Abuse (NHSDA) since 1971 (periodically until 1990; annually since then) through face-to-face interviews in the residences of civilians aged 12 years or older. The Substance Abuse and Mental Health Services Administration (SAMHSA) sponsors the survey, and the Research Triangle Institute collects the data. NHSDA collects information on nine categories of illicit drug use; in 2000, the size of the population sampled was almost 72,000. The survey reports "lifetime," "past year," and "past month" use. The terms are defined differently than an intuitive grasp of their meaning: "lifetime prevalence" means *any* use of *any* illicit substance at some time in the life of the respondent. So, for example, a 50-year-old respondent who tried marijuana once at age 18 would be included in the data for "lifetime prevalence." Similarly, *one* use of *any* substance over the past year is recorded on the "Past Year Prevalence" table and any use in the past month is recorded as current use. In 2000, the survey estimated that 6.3% of the population 12 years and older had used an illicit drug during the month prior to the interview; adolescent drug use (ages 12–17) was 9.7% of the population (SAMHSA, 2001b).

The Institute for Social Research at the University of Michigan conducts the Monitoring the Future (MTF) study, sponsored by the National Institute on Drug Abuse (one of the National Institutes of Health in the Department of Health and Human Services). Students in the 8th, 10th, and 12th grades complete annual, self-administered, machine-readable questionnaires in their classrooms in the first four months of each year. Approximately 50,000 students in 420 public and private schools participate. The survey began in 1975 with high school seniors and was expanded in 1991 to include the two younger groups. The survey includes questions about current and past use of licit and illicit drugs, drug availability, and attitudes toward drug use. In 2001, 11.7% of the 8th graders surveyed had used an illicit drug in the last month; 22.7% of the 10th graders and 25.7% of the 12th graders reported the use of an illicit drug in the last 30 days (Johnston, O'Malley, & Bachman, 2002). MTF publishes a second volume on college students and young adults. Beginning with the class of 1976, follow-up questionnaires are mailed annually to a randomly selected sample of previous participants through age 32; surveys are then mailed at five-year intervals beginning at age 35. The follow-up questionnaires allow researchers to track changes across age groups, changing environments, and role transitions. In 2000, 15.9% of the respondents aged 19–32 had tried an illicit drug in the last 30 days (Johnston, O'Malley, & Bachman, 2001).

The third statistical survey, Drug Abuse Warning Network (DAWN) collects data on drug-related emergency department (ED) visits from about 460 hospitals. Cases are reported to DAWN if there is evidence of drug abuse, drug dependence, recreational use, or attempted suicide. In 2000 DAWN reported an estimated 601,776 visits. The number of visits does not equate to the number of users because one person may make repeated visits. Chronic health conditions from habitual drug use are reportable. Up to five drugs can be recorded per visit; therefore, drug mentions are more numerous than episodes. Alcohol in combination with another drug accounted for 34% of the episodes in 2000. Cocaine was mentioned in 29% of the episodes, heroin in 16%, and marijuana in 16%; the next most frequent mention was acetaminophen (Tylenol) at almost 6%. The majority (56%) of the episodes involve more than one drug (SAMHSA, 2002). The most common reason for a visit was overdose (44%); the most common motives for taking substances were dependence (36%) and suicide (32%).

The Centers for Disease Control is another source for statistical information on drug use. The Youth Risk Behavior Surveillance System (YRBSS) is conducted every two years to assess the prevalence of health risk behaviors among high school students. In 2001, approximately 16,000 questionnaires were collected from 199 schools in 34 states (CDC, 2002). The data from the various surveys do not always coincide. For example, in 2001 YRBSS reported that 47% of the students drank alcohol in the last month and 30% reported episodic heavy drinking during the past month. NHSDA percentages were 16.4% and 10.4%. One explanation for the differences could be that NHSDA data is collected in homes (where parents are in the next room), while YRBSS data is collected in schools.

Interpretations of data sometimes account for conflicting information. The National Center on Addiction and Substance Abuse (CASA) at Columbia University issued a report, "Teen Tipplers," in February 2002 that was disputed by the Department of Health and Human Services. Using NHSDA data, CASA estimated that underage drinkers were responsible for one-quarter of the alcohol consumed in the United States. The government analysis of the same data resulted in a total of 11.4%. CASA issued an explanation stating that although they had not adjusted for oversampling, they believed the government's estimate was too low because no one under age 12 was included, the self-reported data was collected in households where parents were in the next room, and the NHSDA number was based on a typical day's drinks and did not include binge drinking. This example illustrates the need for specific knowledge about what each study measures in order to reach informed decisions about the extent of drug use in the United States.

The National Institute of Justice also provides statistics about drug use. In late 1997, it expanded and enhanced the Drug Use Forecasting (DUF) program, which had been created in 1987 to provide baseline statistics for detecting trends in drug use through urine tests and interviews of urban arrestees in custody. The Arrestee Drug Abuse Monitoring (ADAM) program provides estimates of drug use in 38 communities (NIJ, 2001). The program identifies levels of drug use among booked arrestees, tracks changes in patterns of drug use, and alerts officials to trends in drug use and the availability of new drugs. All sites in the ADAM program test for the drugs named by the National Institute on Drug Abuse (NIDA). The "NIDA-5" are: cocaine, marijuana, methamphetamines, opiates, and phencyclidine (PCP). Specific locations can also test for methadone, benzodiazepines, methaqualone, propoxyphene, and barbiturates.

The Federal Bureau of Investigation publishes information on the number of arrests for drug abuse violations. In 2000, 10.9% of all arrests (1,580,000) were for drug violations. Arrests for drug abuse violations in 2000 increased 0.5% over 1999, 7.5% over 1996, and 49.4% over the 1991 total (FBI, 2001). According to the Bureau of Justice Statistics Bulletin, 61% (82,500) of federal and 21% of state prisoners (253,900) in 1999 were drug offenders (BJS, 2000).

Drugs and Their Effects

For centuries people have used various substances for psychological effects. In South America, people chewed coca leaves for energy, endurance, and pleasure. Alcohol became a fixture in European celebrations. Psychopharmacologists classify psychoactive drugs by their effect on *consciousness* (do they make us sleepy or more alert?), *perception* (do they cause or reduce hallucinations?), and *mood* (do they induce relaxation or euphoria?). Drugs whose chemical compositions differ greatly can be classified together because the psychic effects produced are similar (Doyle, 1987).

To facilitate our discussion of the psychopharmacology of drugs, we have chosen several general categories: depressants, narcotics, stimulants, hallucinogens, cannabis, and inhalants. This classification includes all drugs, legal or illegal. While these classifications are useful in providing a context, it is important to remember that they are not comprehensive. They may illuminate one aspect of the topic but they ignore others. As Erich Goode (1999) notes, the category to which a drug is assigned "depends on what is of interest to a given observer" (p. 41). Our classification, based on the effects of drugs on the central nervous system, differs from that of the federal government. In the 1970 Comprehensive Drug Abuse Prevention and Control Act, the federal government established five "schedules" of drugs (see appendix at end of article) based on the government's findings of medical utility and potential for abuse. For example, the government considers schedule I drugs as having a high potential for abuse or addiction and no medical use; heroin, ecstasy, LSD, and marijuana are all schedule I drugs. The classification was not the result of high levels of illicit usage or public outcry; rather, it was part of the process of criminalizing a number of drugs in an effort to reduce future usage. There is no one-to-one correspondence between a category presented in this article and a schedule established by the government. For example, stimulants appear in each of the five government schedules, with punishments for federal trafficking ranging from one to 20 years for a first offense.

Norman Zinberg (1984) proposed three determinants to understand why someone uses an illicit drug and how that drug affects the user: *drug*—the pharmacologic action of the substance itself (the interaction between the chemical substance ingested and the cells of the body); *set*—the expectations, health, mood, and personality of the person at the time of use (the mindset and characteristics of an individual); and *setting*—the influence of the physical and social environment in which the use occurs, including the historical and cultural meanings attached to particular drugs. As an example, consider the possible differences in effects of two drinks after the football team defeats its archrival versus two drinks after being fired versus two drinks after the death of a spouse. Zinberg also highlighted dosage, method of administration, and pattern of use (including frequency) as important factors. An identical dose for a first-time user will probably produce different results than for a long-time user. If a drug is smoked rather than injected, the reaction is more intense (Goode, 1999). When, where, and with whom a drug is used combined with frequency of use, quantity used, and how the drug is administered affect both behavior and experience.

The new field of pharmacogenomics studies variations in human genetic makeup to determine which legal drugs will or will not be effective for specific individuals. "Scientists have long known that many drugs don't work for 30% to 60% of the people for whom they are prescribed—or may even harm them" (Sherrid, 2001, p. 30). Some people respond to prescribed drugs, others don't. Some people experience the same "effects" if given a placebo if they believe the pill has curative powers. If individual differences alter the effectiveness of prescribed drugs, the probability is that those differences will result in varying experiences of illegal drugs as well.

How do drugs that change consciousness change the brain patterns that affect behavior? Neurotransmitters (a tiny amount of a chemical released into the synapse between neurons when a neuron activates) carry nerve impulses from the end of one nerve cell to another. The neurotransmitter can excite or inhibit reactions (presynaptic or postsynaptic) depending on the specific transmitter and on the membrane with which it combines. Central neurotransmitters include: dopamine, serotonin, norephinephrine, and endorphin. When dopamine is released in the brain, a chemical reaction occurs that affects the drug taker's mood. Volkow et al., (1999) found that drug use increases the amount of dopamine in the brain, which creates mood changes and euphoria. For example, when a person uses cocaine, the dopamine released in the brain causes pleasurable feelings. The chemical formulas of psilocybin and LSD include structures similar to that of serotonin. Serotonin modulates a number of brain states, including mood, sleep, pain, emotion, and appetite. Antidepressants, amphetamine, and cocaine increase the amounts of norepinephrine and dopamine in synapses. Endorphins are the body's morphine-like substances that relieve pain and stress.

Prozac is the best known of a class of antidepressants called selective serotonin reuptake inhibitors. SSRIs prevent the brain from reabsorbing too much of the neurotransmitter serotonin; they improve mood by leaving more serotonin in nerve synapses. Different formulations of SSRIs target subclasses of serotonin. Serotonin-norepinephrine reuptake inhibitors (SNRIs) have been formulated to target the neurotransmitter norepinephrine, secreted in the adrenal gland. Norepinephrine helps control emotion and stabilize mood (Gorman, 2002).

Repeated attempts to recreate the feelings created by drugs ingested can cause physical or psychological dependence on drugs. Physical dependence occurs when the cells in human tissue acclimate to a certain level of a drug's active ingredients. The body changes physically, requiring regular doses of the drug to maintain that chemical balance. Psychological dependence occurs when a person believes he or she requires the drug for mental and emotional stability.

Metabolites are the chemical products that result when a drug reacts with human tissue. The body metabolizes various drugs differently. Some are absorbed immediately and eliminated fairly quickly. ADAM reports detection periods of 2–3 days for cocaine and opiates and 2–4 days for amphetamines. In contrast, the detection period for an infrequent marijuana user is 7 days and up to 30 days for a chronic user (NIJ, 2000). The body metabolizes heroin to morphine. Depending on the toxicology protocols used, heroin and morphine may not be distinguishable. Similarly, when urinalysis detects amphetamine (a substance present in several cold medications), an additional test must be conducted to test for methamphetamine. With some drugs even laboratory tests cannot easily identify the specific drug ingested.

In the sections below we will describe the various categories of drugs and some of their possible effects; the purpose is to provide some context for understanding the multiple facets of drug effects. Again, the physical and psychological effects of drugs depend on the dosage consumed, the method of consumption, and tolerance to the drug; the health, weight (including whether or not there is food in the stomach), sex, mood, and expectations of the user; and the setting in which the drug is taken. It is also important to remember as mentioned above, that many people consume more than one drug—often with dangerously unpredictable results.

Depressants

With the exception of alcohol, most depressants used in our society are prescription drugs. Depressants have a calming, moderating, tranquilizing, or relaxing effect. They slow down the signals passing through the central nervous system and are used to treat a variety of medical or psychological problems, including insomnia, tension, and anxiety. Depressants are commonly abused; those who take them can develop a tolerance and physical dependence.

ALCOHOL

Ethyl alcohol (ethanol) is the intoxicating agent in fermented and distilled liquors. Although some religious groups condemn its consumption, alcohol is almost universally accepted. It has been widely used in most societies for thousands of years. The federal government and the states regulate three classes of alcoholic beverages: beer, wine, and liquor. Fermenting grains and barley malt flavored with hops produces beer. The alcoholic content of American beer is usually 5% or less; some foreign beers have an alcoholic content of 6–7%; malt liquor contains 8% alcohol. Wine is fermented from grapes and generally has an alcoholic content of 5–8%. Liquor is distilled from a variety of grains and vegetables, including corn, wheat, potatoes, and malt. Alcoholic content ranges from 40% to over 50% (liquor labels use "proof" to indicate the percentage of alcohol; the proof of a liquor is double the amount of pure alcohol; a whiskey that is 100 proof is 50% alcohol).

Ethyl alcohol is a psychoactive drug and toxin that depresses the central nervous system, affecting the body similarly to opiates, barbiturates, and tranquilizers. When people drink, endorphins are released in the brain. This results in a rewarding sensation, often resulting in a desire to consume additional amounts of alcohol. Alcohol rapidly produces a tolerance, which decreases if consumption is discontinued for a time. Small amounts of alcohol have a stimulating or euphoric effect, while large amounts have a sedative effect. The drinker's personality and the social setting mediate the effects of the alcohol. Drinkers who have an outgoing, happy personality become even more social when they drink; drinking at parties usually elevates feelings of euphoria. Drinking alone often leads to depression; people who are depressed and aggressive exhibit more tendencies in those directions when they are drinking.

Alcohol is absorbed directly into the bloodstream through the stomach and small intestine. For every shot of liquor, five-ounce glass of wine, or 12-ounce beer, the liver takes approximately one hour to detoxify and remove the alcohol from the body. The drug is removed from the system through perspiration, respiration, and urination. As a depressant, alcohol slows physical responses, reduces the ability to process multiple stimuli, and impairs muscular coordination, including speech. Alcohol increases blood flow to the skin, resulting in feelings of warmth while the body is actually losing heat. A hangover is the body's reaction to mild alcohol poisoning, marked by dehydration, headaches, and nausea.

Genetic factors increase vulnerability to alcoholism, but environmental, cultural, and psychological factors also influence susceptibility. The inability to curb alcohol intake is a common sign of alcoholism, as are blackouts (Center, 2002). Alcoholism is a significant problem in our society. Schuckit (1985) notes that alcoholism is defined by four criteria: (1) amount and frequency of consumption, (2) psychological dependence, (3) physical dependence, and (4) subsequent life style problems, especially in the home or at work. Regular, moderate use of alcohol can lead to psychological dependence, while chronic use can lead to physical dependence or alcoholism. Psychological effects of alcoholism can include lapses of memory (blackouts), hallucinations, and neuritis. Physical withdrawal from alcohol generally results in delirium tremens (DTs), accompanied by confusion, hallucinations, hyperactivity, and cardiovascular problems. Alcoholics can develop a variety of ailments including ulcers, cirrhosis of the liver, cancer, and inflammation of the pancreas. Problem drinkers often lose their jobs and become divorced.

The 2001 MTF study found that four out of every five (79.7%) students have consumed alcohol by the end of high school and two-thirds (63.9%) of 12th graders have been drunk at least once in their life (Johnston et al., 2002). NHSDA reports current alcohol use by 46% (104 million) respondents; binge drinking by 20.6%, and heavy alcohol use (5 or more drinks on each of 5 or more days in the last month) 5.6% (SAMHSA, 2001b).

A study by Henry Wechsler of the Harvard School of Public Health found that binge drinking (four or more drinks in a row, three or more times in a two-week period) at colleges for women had increased 125% from 1993 to 2001 (Morse, 2002). The study found only a slightly higher increase in binge drinking by women compared to men on all college campuses. Since 1999, 16,000 men and 19,000 women have requested screening for alcohol abuse at federally funded clinics held each spring at about 400 colleges. A Syracuse university senior told an interviewer from *Time* magazine, "You don't want to be that dumb girly girl who looks wasted and can't hold her liquor" (p. 57). At Syracuse, twice as many women as men (one or two each weekend) were hospitalized for acute intoxication in 2001. Because women's bodies have a higher ratio of fat to water, alcohol is less diluted when it enters the bloodstream. In addition, women have lower levels of an enzyme (dehydrogenase) that helps break down alcohol. Even if women consume only a fraction of the daily alcohol intake of men, they tend to develop liver disease 10 to 15 years earlier.

The National Institute on Alcohol Abuse and Alcoholism completed a three-year review of existing studies in 2002. It found that drinking by college students contributes to 1,400 deaths, a half-million injuries, and 70,000 sexual assaults a year. One-fourth of college students aged 18 to 24 (2.1 million students) drove under the influence of alcohol during the last year. The study's lead author, Ralph Hingson, commented: "The harm that college students do to themselves and others as a result of excessive drinking exceeds what many would have expected" (Neuman, 2002, p. 10). The Institute's Task Force on College Drinking (formed after an 18-year-old freshman at the Massachusetts Institute of Technology died after a weekend of drinking) brought together researchers who have studied problem drinking and university presidents who must address the aftermath of campus drinking to develop suggestions for reducing the problem. Mark Goldman, co-chairman of the task force, commented on the findings. "Our society has always dealt with this with a wink and a nod, as a rite of passage. But the statistics . . . are stunning to all of us, even the most seasoned researchers" (p. 10).

Alcohol, more than any other drug, is associated with violent crime. A high percentage of rapes, robberies, assaults, and murders are associated with alcohol. In 2000, there were 16,653 alcohol-related highway fatalities (Chapman, 2002). Of the 14 million arrests for all criminal infractions, 2.8 were alcohol related; 1.5 million arrests were for driving under the influence, 637,500 for drunkenness, and 683,000 for violation of liquor laws (FBI, 2001). Alcohol is more costly to our society than any other drug except nicotine.

BARBITURATES

The first barbiturate, Barbital, was developed in 1903. Originally believed to be relatively safe substances, barbiturates have a high potential for abuse and overdose. Barbiturates are the most frequently prescribed depressants; they are effective in treating sleep disorders, anxiety, tension, high blood pressure, and seizures. There are over 2,000 different derivatives of barbituric acid, but only 50 are approved for medical use and only 12 are widely used. The most common are Amytal (blue heavens), Nembutal (yellow jackets), Seconal (red birds), Sombulex, and Tuinal (rainbows or reds and blues). There is a sizeable black market for "downers."

Barbiturates are classified by the speed with which they are absorbed by the body. Choices range from short-acting (those listed above) to long-lasting (Phenobarbital), with the duration of effects ranging from 6 to 16 hours. Barbiturates impede the postsynaptic action of neurotransmitters. They slow heart and breathing rates and lower blood pressure and are most commonly prescribed to induce sleep. A small dose will relieve tension and anxiety, while a larger dose will result in sleep. The effects of sedatives on behavior are very similar to alcohol: slurred speech, loss of inhibition, lack of coordination, and drowsiness. In 2000, MTF found that 1.1% of the respondents aged 19–32 had used barbiturates illegally in the last 30 days (Johnston et al., 2001). The corresponding number for 12th graders in 2001 was 2.8% (Johnston et al., 2002).

Users rapidly develop a tolerance to these sedatives, and withdrawal symptoms can be severe. They range from tremors, weakness, dizziness, nausea, vomiting, and insomnia to delirium, convulsions, and possibly death. In 2000, there were 7,253 emergency department mentions of barbiturate sedatives, 1.2% of all episodes (SAMHSA, 2001a). Barbiturates are particularly dangerous when taken with alcohol. The effects are synergistic; the total impact from the interaction of the drugs is greater than simply adding the effect of one drug to the other. Lack of knowledge about the dangers of ingesting multiple drugs has resulted in a number of accidental deaths.

METHAQUALONE

Methaqualone (quaalude) was a widely used depressant in the 1970s. It was first synthesized in India in 1951 and was thought to be effective in treating malaria. In the 1970s, it was uncontrolled and quickly became a favorite in the drug culture. Called "sopers" or "ludes," methaqualone was believed to be an aphrodisiac. In addition to being a nonbarbiturate sedative, it was also a muscle relaxant, which allowed some people to become more relaxed and enjoy sex. Users rapidly developed addiction to the drug, and an overdose was commonly fatal. For example, popular rock singer Jimi Hendrix died of asphyxiation after taking the drug. Today, it is manufactured in Colombia and smuggled into the United States. However, it is infrequently used (0% of DAWN episodes in 1999 and 2000).

TRANQUILIZERS

Tranquilizers (including benzodiazepines) were developed in the 1930s; they include antianxiety and antipsychotic substances. Antianxiety tranquilizers are weaker but are more frequently abused. Over 70 million prescriptions are written each year in the United States to treat muscle spasms, insomnia, and panic attacks. In general, tranquilizers slow heart rate and breathing, lower blood pressure, and foster relaxation. Antianxiety tranquilizers include alprazolam (Xanax), chlordiazepoxide (Librium), and diazepam (Valium). These tranquilizers can produce sedation, sleep, and muscle relaxation; they also reduce seizures and anxiety. There were 91,000 mentions of benzodiazepines, 8% of total episodes reported to DAWN in 2000. Mentions of the drugs increased 22% from 1994 to 1997 in the DAWN survey and then remained stable through 2000 (SAMHSA, 2002).

The 24-year-old daughter of the governor of Florida provides one high-profile example of illegal use of prescription medications. She was arrested in January 2002 at a pharmacy drive-through window when she tried to buy the anti-anxiety drug Xanax with a fraudulent prescription (Royse, 2002). In 2001, MTF reported that 1.6% of 8th graders, 2.9% of 10th graders, and 3.0% of 12th graders had used tranquilizers illegally in the last month (Johnston et al., 2002). In 2000, the corresponding numbers for respondents aged 19–32 was 1.5% (Johnston et al., 2001). The NHSDA combines four categories of prescription drugs (pain relievers, tranquilizers, sedatives, and stimulants) into a category called "any psychotherapeutics"; 3.8 million people (1.7% of the population aged 12 and older) used psychotherapeutics nonmedically (SAMHSA 2001b).

Date rape drugs, Rohypnol and GHB, have received considerable attention, especially by the news media. They are relatively new on the drug scene and are two of the six "club drugs" popular in dance clubs and raves—high-energy, all-night dance parties that take place in large buildings such as warehouses and feature loud, rapid-tempo music choreographed with laser light shows, smoke, or fog. These events attract large crowds and have been linked with illicit drug sales and sexual assaults.

Rohypnol (flunitrazepam hydrochloride) is a benzodiazepine sedative up to 10 times stronger than Valium. Manufactured and marketed in 80 countries as an anti-seizure drug, its street names are roofies, rope, or roach-2s. Most Rohypnol is smuggled into the United States from Mexico and Colombia. It has been a schedule IV drug since 1984. Effects include deep sedation, muscle relaxation, and reduced anxiety. The effects begin within 15–20 minutes of administration and last up to 12 hours. High doses produce unconsciousness and memory loss.

The drug is a tasteless, odorless, colorless substance that dissolves in liquids. Because of these properties and its sedative effects, Rohypnol has been used to diminish resistance to sexual assault. The drug incapacitates the victim, particularly when used in combination with alcohol. Its effects can last from six to eight hours. A particularly dangerous effect is anterograde amnesia; the victim has no recollection of what occurred while under the drug's influence, complicating any investigation of rape (Fitzgerald & Riley, 2000). The principal commercial manufacturer of Rohypnol recently added a blue dye that appears if the drug is dissolved in liquid.

The availability appears to be declining; only six Drug Enforcement Administration (DEA) divisions reported the drug in their areas—Atlanta, El Paso, Houston, New Orleans, San Diego, and Washington, D.C. (NDIC, 2001b). MTF reported 0.4% of 8th graders had used Rohypnol in the last month, 0.2% of 10th graders, and 0.3% of 12th graders. NHSDA does not track Rohypnol. There were 469 mentions reported by DAWN in 2000 (SAMHSA, 2001a).

GHB (gamma-hydroxybutyrate), another benzodiazepine sedative, was first developed in the 1920s and resurfaced in the 1960s as an anesthetic. Until it was banned by the FDA in 1990 GHB and its precursor GBL (gamma-butyrolactone) were widely available in health food stores, which promoted the drugs as inducing sleep, building muscles, and enhancing sexual performance. Street names for GHB include grievous bodily harm, liquid ecstasy, and Georgia home boy. Effects include a sense of euphoria, hallucinations, drowsiness, increased heart rate, depressed respiration, visual distortions, seizures, unconsciousness, and coma. At higher doses, it can slow breathing and heart rate to dangerous levels. Intoxicating effects begin 10–20 minutes after ingestion and typically last up to 4 hours. On February 18, 2001, the Hillory J. Farias and Samantha Reid Date-Rape Prevention Act of 2000 became law, and GBL became a list I chemical. On March 13, 2000, GHB was classified as a schedule I controlled substance. DAWN reported 4,969 mentions of GHB in 2000 (SAMHSA, 2001a). As of January 2000, 60 deaths had been documented (DEA, 2000). In September 2002, authorities broke up four Internet drug trafficing rings operating in the United States and Canada, seizing enough chemicals for 25 million doses of GHB and similar substances (Yost, 2002).

Narcotics

In the United States, the term "narcotics" has been used historically (and inaccurately) to refer to all illegal drugs. Technically, the term refers to opiates (drugs derived from the opium poppy) or to opioids (synthetically produced opiates). Opiates are analgesics—painkillers. Ancient ceramic pots dating as far back as 1,400 B.C. have been found throughout the Middle East. When turned upside down, the thin-necked vessels with round bases resemble pods of opium poppies. The bases have designs that mimic knife cuts made on poppy bulbs (see below). Gas chromatography has revealed traces of opium on these Mycenaean ceramics. The drug was probably used as medicine to ease pain and disease. Researchers have found Egyptian writings from the third millennium B.C. that indicate opium was used for surgery and to treat pain (Keyser, 2002).

In 1806, a German pharmacist refined morphine from opium. During the Civil War, morphine was used so extensively by military hospitals for wounded Union soldiers that a number of them became addicted. In fact, drug addiction during this period was referred to as the "soldiers' disease." In the late nineteenth and early twentieth centuries, patent medicines, also known as "snake oils" or elixirs, contained large does of cocaine or morphine and were sold over the counter with no restrictions. From 1886 until 1900, cocaine was an ingredient in Coca-Cola. In 1898, one year before they marketed aspirin, the Bayer Company introduced heroin as a powerful cough suppressant (Gray, 2001). Another refinement of opium, codeine, also suppresses coughs and relieves pain. It is the most frequently used legal opiate and the most abused prescription drug today (Center, 2002).

Opium is a natural drug that is derived from the opium poppy plant *(papaver somniferum)* grown primarily in Laos, Burma, and Thailand (the Golden Triangle); Afghanistan, Pakistan, and Iran (the Golden Crescent); and Mexico. To harvest opium, the seedpod produced by the poppy is lanced with a knife to extract the white milky substance. The harvesting of raw opium is labor intensive, which is why it is grown in regions were labor is plentiful and inexpensive. In some regions, the economics of the drug trade is compelling: a pound of wheat might earn three cents, while a pound of raw opium brings fifteen dollars. After the fall of the Taliban in 2001, a farmer in Afghanistan remarked, "It is good to be growing poppies again. At least my family will be able to eat" (Salopek, 2001, p. 17).

HEROIN

Heroin, first synthesized from morphine in 1874, is the fastest acting opiate. Through the 1950s, heroin defined drug abuse and addiction in this country. Other than alcohol, it was the only drug consumed in quantity. In the 1960s, there was a surge of interest in marijuana and LSD; in the 1970s, cocaine use dominated public concern. Throughout the cycles of changes in drug preference, heroin has remained the most consistent drug problem.

Today, Colombia and Mexico produce most of the heroin available in the United States. Small, independent, loosely structured criminal groups are the primary distributors (NDIC, 2001b). Pure heroin is a white powder with a bitter taste. Street heroin is diluted (usually with lactose, starch, and quinine) and is sold 2 to 3% pure. Most available heroin varies in color from white to dark brown; the differences are the result of impurities from the manufacturing process or the presence of additives. In recent years, the purity of heroin has increased because of black tar heroin, produced in Mexico. The name comes from the gooey nature of the substance. It is often sticky like roofing tar or hard like coal, varying in color from dark brown to black because of crude processing. Street names include tootsie roll and goma; it is frequently sold at a purity level of 60 to 70%. Mexican-based heroin dominates the market in the western half of the U.S.

Heroin is a schedule I drug that acts on the central and autonomic nervous systems, relieving both physical pain and mental anguish. The short-term effects of heroin appear soon after taking the drug. Intravenous injection provides the greatest intensity and most rapid onset of the initial rush—7 to 8 seconds after the injection. Intramuscular injection produces a relatively slow onset of euphoric feeling, taking 5 to 8 minutes. Some addicts use "skin popping" where the drug is injected just under the skin. The more experimental smoke it alone or in combination with marijuana. When heroin is sniffed or smoked, the peak effects of the drug are usually felt within 10 to 15 minutes. In addition to a feeling of euphoria, the short-term effects of heroin include a warm flushing of the skin, a dry mouth, and heavy extremities. After the initial euphoric feeling, the user experiences an alternately wakeful and drowsy state, often feeling drowsy for several hours. Due to the depression of the central nervous system, mental functioning becomes clouded.

Heroin is highly addictive; once users develop a tolerance, they require higher doses to produce the same effects. During withdrawal, large amounts of dopamine are reintroduced, which stimulates the brain. Withdrawal symptoms reverse the effects of the drug. Insomnia and hyperactivity replace drowsiness; anxiety and depression replace feelings of well-being; breathing is very rapid rather than slowed, and there is an oversensitivity to pain rather than relief. The longer a person has used heroin, the more difficult the withdrawal. Symptoms can last up to a week and often motivate the user to seek more drugs. Chronic users may develop collapsed veins, liver disease, pulmonary complications, and infection of the heart lining and valves.

Despite its longevity, heroin is not a popular drug. Surveys such as NHSDA consistently show a very small number of heroin users, less than 0.1% in the last month by respondents over the age of 12 in 2000 (SAMHSA 2001b). The rate for college students was 0.2%, and 0.1% of young adults reported using heroin in the 30 days prior to being surveyed (Johnston et al., 2001). Results from the 2001 MTF study showed that 0.6% of 8th graders, 0.3% of 10th graders, and 0.4% of 12th graders reported using heroin in the 30 days prior to being surveyed (Johnston et al., 2002). Opiate positives among adult arrestees are low relative to cocaine and marijuana. The median for female adult arrestees was 8% in 1999 compared to 6% for adult male arrestees (NIJ, 2000b).

The difficulty for heroin users is that there is little difference between a normal dosage and an overdose. Overdoses often result from the inconsistent purity levels of the drug. An overdose may cause slow and shallow breathing, convulsions, coma, and possibly death. Heroin/morphine was the second most frequently mentioned drug in the DAWN survey, 94,400 mentions (SAMHSA, 2002). Heroin mentions have increased 50% since 1994 (SAMHSA, 2001a). For the small number of users, there are a large number of overdoses. Because of the high rates of overdose, death, and lifelong physiological dependency, one federal agency considers heroin the second (after cocaine) greatest drug threat in the United States (NDIC, 2001b).

METHADONE

When morphine was in short supply during World War II, German scientists developed methadone. The schedule II, synthetic substance was used in the United States beginning in 1964 to treat heroin addicts. Methadone is administered orally as a substitute for heroin; it reduces the cravings associated with heroin use without the euphoric rush. Its effects last up to 24 hours versus two to three hours duration for heroin. As a legal medication, methadone is produced by pharmaceutical companies under strict quality control standards. It does not impair cognitive functions and has no adverse effects on mental capability or employability. The methadone maintenance programs were targeted at hardcore heroin addicts, and it was hoped that the program would lead to a reduction of crime. Critics of methadone programs dislike substituting one addictive drug for another; they believe the primary goal of any drug treatment program should be abstinence. Eight states (Idaho, Mississippi, Montana, New Hampshire, North Dakota, South Dakota, Vermont, and West Virginia) prohibit the use of methadone (Abadinsky, 2001). About

20% of the estimated 810,000 heroin addicts in the United States receive methadone treatments (ONDCP, 2000).

OTHER SYNTHETIC NARCOTICS

Fentanyl citrate, used in surgery as a painkiller, is far more potent than morphine. Sold on the street as China White, fentanyl is easily manufactured by someone with a knowledge of chemistry. When not cut properly, it often leads to overdosing. Although emergency department mentions have increased since 1994, fentanyl is mentioned much less frequently (576 mentions in 2000) than other narcotic analgesics (SAMHSA, 2002).

Other analogs or synthetic opiates include hydrocodone (Vicodin, Lorcet, Lortab), hydromorphone (Dilaudid), meperidine (Demerol), oxycodone (OxyContin, Percodan, and Percocet), propoxyphene (Darvon), and codeine. Most are schedule II drugs; codeine is schedule V. The synthetic opiates are commonly used as painkillers in medicine and dentistry, and they frequently are diverted and sold on the street. From 1994 to 2000, mentions of narcotic analgesics rose 85%. In 2000, the most frequently mentioned were: hydrocodone (20,100 mentions), oxycodone (10,800), methadone (7,800), propoxyphene (5,500), and codeine (5,300), which has been decreasing since 1994 (SAMHSA, 2002).

Recently, OxyContin, a synthetic opiate with a very high concentration of oxycodone, has received substantial media attention. It has been dubbed "hillbilly heroin" because it initially surfaced as a diverted pharmaceutical in rural areas such as Appalachia. Approved for treating severe and chronic pain in 1995, the drug is one of the most effective prescription pain relievers on the market. The manufacturer heavily promoted OxyContin as safer than other narcotics because of its time-release mechanism. Unfortunately, the chemical formulation that makes OxyContin such an effective pain treatment also makes it a prime candidate for abuse (Brink, 2002). In fact, abuse of OxyContin has grown faster than abuse of any other prescription drug in decades (Meier, 2001).

Drug abusers quickly learned that if the tablets are crushed and the drug inhaled or injected, the high is similar to that of heroin. Unscrupulous doctors recognized the market for illicit use of OxyContin. Dr. James Graves, 55, was a top prescriber of the drug in Florida. He was convicted on four counts of manslaughter when four of his patients died after overdosing on the painkiller, one count of racketeering, and five of unlawful delivery of a controlled substance. Media reports of abuse and overdose helped create a backlash against the drug. Physicians are now concerned that restrictions will harm the roughly one million legitimate patients who need the pain relief OxyContin offers. Richard Weiner, executive director of the American Academy of Pain Management states "The big question here is what should drive medical care policy—police concerns or clinical concerns" (Kleiner, 2001, p. 42). Another pain specialist points out that patients properly treated with opiates have about a 1% chance of becoming addicted: "They don't get goofy, high, or giddy, and there's no euphoria—the pain is simply gone" (p. 43).

Stimulants

Stimulants increase the electrical and neurotransmitter activity of the central nervous system. They heighten a person's sense of arousal, alleviate fatigue, and increase overall body functions and activity. Thus, they have both psychological and physiological effects. Most stimulants rapidly produce a high tolerance. The two most common forms of stimulants in our society are caffeine (present in coffee, tea, and a large number of soft drinks) and nicotine (consumed through tobacco products). Although most people do not view them as drugs, they cause physiological changes, such as heightened alertness. These are perhaps the two most popular drugs in the world, consumed in many countries and cultures.

AMPHETAMINE

Amphetamine is a synthetic drug that was first developed in 1887. The powerful stimulant was used to treat asthma in the 1930s and to increase the alertness of soldiers suffering from fatigue during World War II. Today amphetamine is generally found in the form of a tablet or capsule, often as an over-the-counter (OTC) drug. Stronger doses are available as prescription drugs. Dieters use amphetamines to curb appetite; long-haul truck drivers use them to stay awake, as do college students cramming for exams; and athletes use amphetamines to increase their athletic prowess and stamina during sporting events. The impact of amphetamines on the central nervous system resembles cocaine but usually lasts longer. Users experience loss of appetite, accelerated breathing, increased heart rate, higher blood pressure, and dilated pupils. Most users become talkative, restless, and excited. Regular use of large amounts of amphetamine can lead to tension, agitation, malnutrition, sleeplessness, and delusions of persecution.

In 2001, the MTF survey found that 3.2% of 8th graders reported use of amphetamines in the past month, compared to 5.6% of 10th and 12th graders (Johnston et al., 2002). The percentage for respondents aged 19–32 in 2000 was 1.9 (Johnston et al., 2001). For the same year, NHSDA reported 0.4% of respondents aged 12 or older had used amphetamines in the last month. DAWN mentions of amphetamines increased 37% from 1999 to 2000 (SAMHSA, 2002).

METHAMPHETAMINE

Today, the most common form of amphetamine is methamphetamine. It was used in World War II to reduce battle fatigue and has been used as a treatment for narcolepsy. Today this extremely powerful drug (also known as speed, crank, jet fuel, lemon drops, or ice) is another "club drug." It is also described as a "designer drug"—a synthetically produced street drug with attributes similar to naturally occurring, mind-altering substances. Designer drugs are created to produce the high of other drugs, often at a lower cost. Meth is chemically similar to adrenaline, a hormone produced by the adrenal gland. It stimulates both the sympathetic and central nervous systems, alleviates fatigue, and produces feelings of mental alertness and well-being. When used in moderate doses, it elevates mood and makes the user more alert, enhancing concentration. Methamphetamine users often display signs of agitation, excited speech, decreased appetite, and increased physical activity levels. This schedule II drug is readily available throughout the western half of the country and appears to be making inroads elsewhere.

Meth can be consumed through smoking, injection, or snorting, which is the most common. Snorting affects the user in approximately 5 minutes versus 20 minutes for oral ingestion; effects can last up to 8 hours. The high is the result of elevated levels of dopamine. About one-quarter of the users report using the drug four times in a typical day. Another pattern is a "run"— daily consumption over a period of 10 to 14 days. The patterns of use are very similar to the patterns for cocaine users. Over time, the amount consumed increases, leading to a number of medical and psychological problems. Meth restricts the diameter of the blood vessels; the user's blood pressure elevates because the heart rate must increase to maintain the blood supply to the body, increasing the risk of hypertension or a stroke. It is also neurotoxic, significantly reducing dopamine transporters. Long-term usage can result in violent tendencies and extreme psychological conditions such as delusions, confusion, extreme paranoia, drastic mood swings, and hallucinations. The behavior of heavy users sometimes resembles that of a paranoid schizophrenic (Pennell et al., 1999).

In 2001, MTF reported that 1.3% of 8th graders and 1.5% of both 10th and 12th graders had used methamphetamine in the past month (Johnston et al., 2002). NHSDA reported past month use by 387,000 people (0.2% of the respondents age 12 and older) in 2000 (SAMHSA, 2001b). As mentioned earlier, meth is one of the NIDA-5 drugs; the median percentage of arrestees who tested positive for methamphetamine in 2000 was 5 (NIJ, 2001). Methamphetamine is the most frequently mentioned "club drug" in the DAWN survey— 13,500 ED mentions, an increase of 29% from 1999 to 2000 (SAMHSA, 2002). There were 2,601 deaths reported between 1994 and 1998 (SAMHSA, 2000).

Methamphetamine use now rivals cocaine use in some areas of the country. A study by Herz (2000) examined drug use in rural Nebraska. She found that only the use of marijuana surpassed meth. In 1995, 10% of all arrestees in her study tested positive for methamphetamine. She found that arrestees in urban areas were more likely to test positive for cocaine, while those from rural counties were more likely to test positive for meth. The majority of meth users were white, and they typically had a substantial criminal record during and prior to their arrest. One-fourth to one-half of the users also engaged in meth trafficking. In an extensive study, Pennell and her colleagues (1999) found that initiation to meth use comes as a result of family members or friends using the drug. Of those questioned, 64% preferred meth to cocaine. Reasons for the preference were: the high lasts longer and is better, meth is cheaper; and it has no side effects (an erroneous conclusion).

Two reasons for increased use of meth are its low cost and easy availability. A lab and chemicals costing as little as $500 can easily produce ("cook") several thousand dollars worth of the drug. According to McCrea and Kolbye (1995), there are 32 different chemicals that can be used in the production of the drug. About one-third are extremely hazardous, and all of them can be obtained through commercial sources. The chemicals involved are extremely volatile. Meth can be produced anywhere, including motel rooms, garages, utility buildings, trailers, and cars. The clandestine labs pose a number of dangers to citizens and to the police. The police often discover a clandestine lab as the result of a fire or explosion, and there have been a few instances where the lab exploded or caught fire during the police raid. The disposal of spent chemicals presents significant problems. Methamphetamine laboratories produce poisonous gas and five to seven pounds of toxic waste for every pound of meth produced. Cookers often dump the chemicals in isolated areas, down storm drains, or in open fields. These deposits are highly toxic and dangerous to anyone who comes in contact with them.

Many labs developed in Mexico, and motorcycle gangs historically were the primary suppliers of meth. Today most supplies of the drug come from Mexico and California. The first meth lab seizure was in 1963 in Santa Cruz County, California. By 1999, the DEA had participated in the seizure of 1,948 clandestine labs. DEA arrests for methamphetamine-related offenses rose 85% from 1996 to 2000. Meth offenses accounted for 14% of all federal sentences in 2000 (NDIC, 2001b). California is the epicenter of meth production. Police in Riverside and San Bernardino counties in California locate from 800 to 1,000 labs annually. Officials from those counties characterize labs as either organized (making large amounts of meth for large trafficking organizations) or "Beavis and Butthead" labs (small operations making meth for themselves and their friends).

One federal agency classifies meth as the third greatest drug threat in the country because of its availability and the involvement of drug trafficking organizations in its distribution (NDIC, 2001b). If meth continues its spike in popularity, the addictive nature of the drug, the violent behavior associated with prolonged use, the dangers inherent in the production process, and the expense of cleaning up the clandestine dumps could exceed the problems presented by cocaine use in earlier decades.

COCAINE

The coca plant grows in the Andes Mountains of South America; natives have used it for thousands of years to combat fatigue and hunger. Europeans took coca leaves back to Europe and began extracting cocaine around 1860. In the 1880s cocaine was used as a local anesthetic in eye, nose, and throat surgeries because it provides relief from pain and constricts blood vessels, thus limiting bleeding.

Three-quarters of the coca cultivated for processing into cocaine is now grown in Colombia. When cocaine was first introduced, many believed it was a wonder drug, an effective treatment for a host of illnesses including narcotic addiction, alcoholism, asthma, depression, and digestive disorders. Until the passage of the Harrison Act in 1914, it was a legal drug and a common ingredient in a number of patent medicines (Musto, 1999). Cocaine became a schedule II substance, approved only as a local anesthetic in eye, nose, and throat surgeries.

Cocaine use was relatively limited through the 1960s. Marijuana and LSD were much more prevalent. In the 1970s cocaine rapidly became the most popular illicit drug in the United States. The explosion in popularity had its roots in the drug's effects (the most potent natural stimulant, believed to have no side effects) and in the ability of Colombian drug cartels to smuggle, market, and distribute their product. Because of its cost, cocaine became the drug of the upper class.

The psychoactive effects of cocaine begin a few seconds after ingestion and diminish in 10 to 40 minutes. Many users feel the drug enhances their capacity to work, their artistic abilities, and their levels of energy. People can be involved in mental or physical activities for longer periods of time when using cocaine. Because it induces pleasurable feelings, cocaine elevates mood and leads to feelings of confidence and mastery. Its effects, much like those experienced when using amphetamine, have widespread appeal to a variety of potential users.

Initially, it was believed that cocaine was not addictive and did not result in health problems. Indeed, there is no evidence that cocaine is physically addicting like nicotine, alcohol, or opiates. However, long-term users can develop a psychological dependence. Because cocaine can overstimulate the brain's fright center, chronic users can experience anxiety and paranoia. Cocaine also stimulates the heart, raises blood pressure, and causes rapid breathing. Discontinued or reduced use of cocaine does not lead to physical withdrawal symptoms. Lyman and Potter (1998) note that the National Institute of Drug Use estimates that only about 3% of cocaine users become problem abusers. Erich Goode (1999) reviewed the research on cocaine usage and found that only a small number of users become problem abusers.

The number of current cocaine users reached its peak in 1985 with 5.7 million Americans. This number represented 3% of the population at that time. In 2000, the numbers were 0.5%, 1.2 million users (SAMHSA, 2001b). MTF reported past month use of cocaine in 2001 by 1.2% of 8th graders, 1.3% of 10th graders, and 2.1% of 12th graders; YRBSS reported past month usage by 4% of students. During 2000, 1.4% of college students and 1.7% of young adults reported past month cocaine use (Johnston et al., 2001). In 2000, 29% of drug episodes in emergency departments involved cocaine mentions (174,881). Those numbers have remained stable since 1994, but cocaine remains the most frequently mentioned illicit substance (SAMHSA, 2001a). Similarly, it was the most frequently mentioned drug by medical examiners in 1999, linked with 4,864 deaths. According to preliminary data for 2000, approximately 30% of adult male arrestees tested positive for cocaine at the time of their arrests (NIJ, 2001). The average sentence for defendants convicted of a federal offense involving powder cocaine in 1999 was 77 months.

In the 1980s, the United States faced a new epidemic. Cocaine could be cooked with baking soda, producing "rocks" of crack cocaine that could be smoked in a pipe. Crack was extremely inexpensive, selling on the street for five and ten dollars a rock. This form of the drug made cocaine affordable for a much larger audience, and they used it in large quantities. Organized youth gangs, such as the Jamaican Posse, Bloods, and Crips, began marketing the drug, inundating larger urban areas with the drug. States and the federal government enacted new laws to combat cocaine as public fear rose in the wake of the epidemic; crack became the focal point for the police.

Smoking crack delivers large quantities of the drug to the lungs, producing effects comparable to intravenous injection. Smoking crack results in an intense, immediate, short-lived high (30 to 90 seconds), with an "afterglow" of about 10 minutes. Compulsive cocaine use seems to develop more rapidly when the substance is smoked rather than snorted. Users develop a tolerance and fail to achieve the same pleasure as their initial exposure to the drug. The number of crack users has declined substantially since its surge two decades ago. NHSDA reported 0.1% of the population (265,000) aged 12 or older had used crack in the past month down from 0.3% (604,000) in 1997 (SAMHSA, 2000b). MTF figures for 2001 were 0.8 for 8th graders in the past month, 0.7% for 10th graders, and 1.1% for 12th graders. The percentage of DAWN mentions of cocaine attributed to crack is 22; there has been no significant change in the statistics since 1994. Approximately 13% of adult male arrestees in 2000 reported using crack in the seven days prior to their arrests (NIJ, 2001). Approximately 22% of defendants convicted of a drug offense in federal court were involved with crack cocaine; the average sentence was 114 months in prison.

Colombian transporters control the smuggling routes for shipment of cocaine through Central America, Mexico, and the Caribbean. About two-thirds of the 645 tons of cocaine exported from South America passes through Mexico/Central America. After reaching Mexico by sea or air, Mexican transporters control the movement of wholesale quantities of cocaine into the western half of the United States. Dominican traffickers control much of the transportation of cocaine in the eastern half of the country. Various transporters, including gangs, move smaller quantities of cocaine, but they are usually supplied by Mexican, Colombian, Jamaican, or Dominican trafficking organizations. Crack cocaine is usually not transported in large quantities or over long distances because of the severe mandatory sentences for possession and distribution of crack. Retail distributors convert cocaine powder into crack in the actual market area (NDIC, 2001b).

MDMA OR ECSTASY

Methylenedioxymethamphetamine (MDMA) was developed in 1914 by a German pharmaceutical firm as an appetite suppressant. In the 1970s it was accepted in Europe as a psychotherapeutic drug, but it never gained wide-spread acceptance in the United States. A number of psychiatrists experimented with the drug as an adjunct to therapy, particularly as a means of engendering trust, and marriage counselors prescribed it for its ability to create warm feelings. Because it was believed to induce a strong euphoric state without any negative side effects, there was some recreational use in the 1980s. As recreational use increased, the DEA temporarily classified MDMA as a schedule I drug in 1985; they made the classification permanent in 1988.

MDMA is a synthetic analog of amphetamine. It has a number of street names including: ecstasy, XTC, Adam, scooby snacks, and disco biscuit. It is taken orally and is usually packaged as a white powder or an off-white tablet. Prices range from $20 to $40 per tablet on the street (Lighty, 2002). Most (90%) ecstasy comes from the Netherlands and Belgium (where the drug is also illegal), with Romania and Poland increasing their market share. Tablets are often manufactured in temporary, often mobile, labs such as semitrailers or barges. Egyptian, Syrian, Israeli, Korean, and Russian organized crime syndicates have been linked with marketing ecstasy (Ragavan, 2001).

Ecstasy is sometimes classified with hallucinogens because some of its effects are similar to those of LSD. However, its most measurable effects (heart rate, blood pressure, sweating, and chills) match those of stimulants. The DEA describes ecstasy as the "hug drug" or "feel good" drug because it lowers inhibitions, reduces anxiety, and produces a feeling of empathy. Its effects last approximately 3 to 6 hours.

MDMA increases the activity of three neurotransmitters: serotonin, dopamine, and norephinephrine. When MDMA causes the release of the neurotransmitters, brain activity increases, similar to the effect of amphetamines. Compared to methamphetamine, MDMA causes greater release of serotonin and somewhat lesser dopamine release. Because it depletes the supply of serotonin, ecstasy suppresses the need to eat, drink, or sleep. It can also lead to dehydration and hypothermia. The impact of MDMA on dopamine production can lead to motor coordination disturbances.

Opinions differ as to whether MDMA is a dangerous drug. Goode (1999) presents both sides of the debate. He includes the opinions of psychiatrists who argue the potential benefits of the drug and note that it is far safer than other drugs that have been assigned less restrictive schedules by the federal government. He also includes discussions by drug researchers who note that cocaine was believed to be safe when first introduced but has now been determined to be very destructive. MDMA may very well be like cocaine, and its harmful effects will not be evidenced until there has been large-scale usage. MDMA can cause heart arrhythmia in some people, but no other physical side effects have been found. Others note that the drug, especially used over long periods, can cause flashbacks, hallucinations, disorientation, and psychotic episodes. Defenders of MDMA note that these problems occur only in certain people, and medical screening can eliminate most problems.

Pedersen and Skrondal (1999) found that MDMA was an element in the culture of raves, adding pressure on adolescents to use the drug to become an accepted member of the subculture. Beck and Rosenbaum (1994) conducted a study of ecstasy users in the San Francisco area and identified three distinct groups of users. *New Age Seekers* used the drug to achieve self-knowledge and to develop better relationships with others. *Dancers* attended raves to follow bands. The final category, *Yuppie Hedonists*, consisted of resourceful young people in independent or well-to-do occupations.

Although MDMA use is not as extensive as amphetamines or marijuana, its popularity has increased over the past several years, especially among young people. The MTF survey reported that ecstasy was the primary drug showing an increase in 2001. Annual use of ecstasy was reported by 3.5% of 8th graders, by 6.2% of 10th graders, and by 9.2% of 12th graders. The numbers for 30-day use were 1.8, 2.6, and 2.8 respectively (Johnston et al., 2002). In 2000, the total 30-day prevalence for respondents aged 19 to 32 was 1.5, similar to cocaine, which was 1.4%. However, there was more use of ecstasy among younger respondents: 3.2% of those 19–20 reported MDMA use versus 1.7% for cocaine; 2.7% of those 21–22 used MDMA compared to 2.1 for cocaine; by age 23–24, MDMA use declined to 1.3%, while cocaine remained at 2.1 (Johnston et al., 2001). In 2000, DAWN reported 4,511 MDMA emergency department mentions (SAMHSA, 2001a). U.S. Customs seizures increased from 400,000 tablets in 1997 to more than 9 million in 2000 (Ragavan, 2001).

The popularity of ecstasy has led to counterfeit pills containing PMA (paramethoxyamphetamine) being sold as a substitute. The counterfeit pills are cheaper to make, increasing profits. PMA is a synthetic hallucinogen with stimulant effects, which has been a schedule I drug since 1973. Sold in tablet, capsule, and powder form, PMA appears similar to MDMA in appearance and cost but is more toxic. Since May 2000, PMA has been associated with three deaths in Illinois and seven in central Florida (DEA, 2000). Street names include death and Mitsubishi double-stack. The most harmful effect is increased body temperature, as high as 108 degrees in the reported deaths.

A product containing ephedrine, extracted from the herb ma huang, is marketed as a substitute for MDMA at nutrition stores. Herbal ecstacy (note the substitute of "c" for "s" in the last syllable) is promoted as a "legal" high. Street names for the drug, which may also contain caffeine, include cloud 9, herbal bliss, ritual spirit, and liquid X. Ephedra is also used for weight loss and bodybuilding. Like all stimulants, effects include increased blood pressure, heart rate, respiration, and body temperature. Sold as a dietary supplement, there are no quality controls or government oversight for the tablets; types and amounts of ingredients vary widely. Federal law limits regulation unless the supplements are proven dangerous by the FDA. Consumer advocates and doctors have lobbied to ban the supplement, which has been linked to 100 deaths and about 1,000 reports of complications since the mid-1990s (Neergaard). In June 2002, the Rand Corporation was hired to review all scientific reports on ephedra and report the results to the National Institutes of Health in the fall. In August 2002, the justice department began a criminal investigation into Metabolife (a company that sells supplements containing ephedra) to determine if the company had lied about the safety of its products.

NICOTINE

Although nicotine is a legal stimulant, many fear its addictive qualities and the health risks associated with its most popular delivery system, cigarettes. Researchers at the University of Chicago looked at how the brain processes dopamine to discover why nicotine is so addictive. One to two milligrams of the ten milligrams of nicotine in a cigarette enter the blood stream and the brain's reward center within 10 seconds after inhalation. The researchers discovered that nicotine also affects regulatory cells that would ordinarily curb the dopamine high. As a result, nicotine causes the reward system to continue to operate for almost an hour (Kotulak, 2002). The brain memorizes the feel-good sensations and craves more. According to John Dani, a neuroscientist who was one of the first to show nicotine's effect on dopamine, "It would be hard to design a drug that acts on the reward center that would be more effective than nicotine" (p. 21). The findings of the new study explain why the 66.5 million people in the United States who use tobacco products find it so difficult to quit. More than 30 million Americans try to quit smoking each year; the American Lung Association says about 2.5% succeed (Yates, 2002).

Some opponents of cigarette use argue that the FDA should regulate all nicotine-delivery systems. Despite age restrictions on the sale of cigarettes, 5.5% of 8th graders and 12.2% of 10th graders reported daily use of cigarettes, compared to 19% of 12th graders (Johnston et al., 2002). NHSDA reports 13.4% of youths 12–17 and 29.3% of the population 12 and over are current smokers (SAMHSA, 2000). YRBSS reported current tobacco use by 33.9% of students surveyed (CDC, 2002). Tobacco use is linked to more than 400,000 deaths annually from cancer, heart attacks, stokes, and emphysema. "It is the nation's most preventable cause of death" (Kotulak, 2002, p. 21).

Nicotine substitutes such as patches and chewing gums have been sold without prescription since 1996. Pharmacists who custom mix drugs for patients (compounding pharmacists) are regulated by state boards of pharmacy and operate under a 1997 FDA law that allows them to combine legal drugs. In 1998 in Augusta, Georgia, a pharmacist developed a lollipop containing nicotine salicylate. The nicotine-substitute lollipops, with names like Nicostop and Likatine, surfaced in hundreds of pharmacies. Available in flavors ranging from berry, lemon-lime, grape, and watermelon to eggnog and tequila sunrise, the pops contained from 2 to 4 milligrams of nicotine salicylate and sold for about $3 apiece. The instructions were to use the pop when the urge to smoke became overpowering. When the craving passed, the lollipop could be returned to its reusable container. Aggressive Internet marketing resulted in an increase of sales of the pops at one supply house from 19,500 in 2000 to 335,000 in 2001—without a prescription or an inquiry about age (Gorman, 2002). The FDA declared the nicotine pops illegal in April 2002 because they contained an untested form of nicotine and were a potential threat to children. Some pharmacists planned to use FDA-approved nicotine such as nicotine polacrilex, the chemical used in Nicorette gum.

RITALIN

Methylphenidate (trade name Ritalin) is produced commercially in 5-, 10-, and 20-milligram tablets. It is often prescribed to treat attention disorders. Studies suggest that people with attention deficit hyperactivity disorder (ADHD) have reduced frontal-lobe activity, possibly caused by decreased activity in the basal ganglia, where dopamine and norepinephrine are generated. Abnormally low levels of these neurotransmitters have been linked with inattention. The theory behind administering stimulants to children with ADHD is that the drugs will adhere to and activate the deficient neurotransmitters (Szegedy-Maszak, 2002). ADHD has become the most commonly diagnosed child psychiatric disorder in the United States. As prescriptions for ADHD have increased, so has diversion for recreational use.

Ritalin is used recreationally to increase alertness and to lose weight; the drug produces many of the same effects as cocaine or amphetamines. At higher doses, there can be euphoric effects. A 20-milligram tablet can bring $2 to $20 on the street. Elizabeth Wurtzel (who also authored *Prozac Nation*) wrote a memoir of her drug abuse, entitled *More, Now, Again*. The abuse began when her doctor prescribed Ritalin to enhance the effects of mood stabilizers, such as Prozac, to which she had developed a tolerance. Wurtzel makes the point that the sanctioned use of methylphenidate by her doctor lulled her into ignoring the signs of addiction and abuse.

Athletes search for whatever advantage they can find. Many believe they must use steroids, human growth hormone, or Ritalin (to improve concentration), whether they are legal or not. As Tom House, former major-league pitcher with a doctorate in psychology, states, "The philosophy in sports nowadays is you don't get beat, you get outmilligrammed" (Rogers, 2002, p. 1).

Cannabis or Marijuana

Marijuana is derived from the leaves and flowers of the hemp plant, *Cannabis sativa*, a very hearty weed that grows easily in both tropical and temperate climates. It was used in China and Assyria for both intoxication and medical purposes as far back as 2700 B.C. In the 1800s, U.S. citizens raised hemp as a popular cash crop. Rumors of marijuana triggering violent sexual behavior led to the Federal Marijuana Tax Act of 1937, which made any use of the drug illegal. Marijuana is one of the most controversial drugs in our society. Although classified as a schedule I drug, many argue that it is relatively safe and less of a problem than alcohol and tobacco.

The Academy of Sciences' Institute of Medicine conducted a study in 1999 that found no deaths associated with marijuana versus 8,000 deaths from nonsteroidal anti-inflammatory drugs like aspirin. Allison Mack and Janet Joy, authors of *Marijuana as Medicine: The Science beyond the Controversy*, report the benefits of marijuana for relief from pain, nausea, spasticity, glaucoma, and movement disorders like multiple sclerosis (Muwakkil, 2002). A Pew Research Center Gallup poll in March 2001 found that 73% of Americans favored the medical use of marijuana with a doctor's prescription. As mentioned in the introduction, nine states and the District of Columbia allow the possession and use of marijuana for medical purposes.

Marijuana is grown in large quantities in countries such as Colombia, Mexico, Jamaica, and the United States. In this country, the leading marijuana-producing states are California, Kentucky, and Hawaii. The profit potential is large; dried marijuana sells for $4000 per pound. In 1998, the National Organization for the Reform of Marijuana Laws concluded that the market value of the California marijuana crop exceeded 3.8 billion dollars— more than grapes and almonds combined (Brandon, 2001). It is the most available illicit drug throughout the United States.

The mood-altering agent in marijuana is delta-9-tetrahydrocannabiol (THC). In 2002 government officials began warning that today's marijuana differs from that of a generation ago, alleging potency levels 10 to 20 times stronger. However, the claims are difficult to substantiate, particularly since the potency studies in the 1960s and 1970s were from small samples. The latest quarterly report by the University of Mississippi's Potency Monitoring Project, which examined 46,000 samples, found an average potency of 6.68 (Page, 2002). There are a number of sources for marijuana, and the THC content varies significantly. Uncultivated marijuana, "ditch weed," has a THC content of approximately 0.5 to 4%. Commercial grade marijuana from the leaves, stems, and seeds of the cannabis plant generally has a THC content of 4.25 to 4.92%. A number of marijuana producers grow sinsemilla, which contains only the leaves and buds of unpollinated female plants. "BC bud" originally referred to sinsemella from British Columbia but now refers to any higher-grade marijuana from Canada. Sinsemilla has a THC content from 11.62 to 13.20%. Hashish is the resinous material from the flowering tops of the female plant; its potency averages 6%.

Marijuana is consumed using a variety of methods. The most common method is to smoke it in a rolled marijuana cigarette. It is also smoked in hollowed-out commercial cigars called blunts, which are often laced with other illicit drugs such as small rocks of crack or PCP. It is sometimes eaten in food such as brownies. Hashish oil, a liquefied concentration of the drug, is usually added to tobacco cigarettes and smoked. When smoked, the effects last two to three hours. When ingested in foods, the effects may last up to 24 hours. Because THC is stored in fatty tissue, it can be detected in the body up to 30 days after use.

THC can act as both a stimulant and a depressant; some first-time users claim to experience no effects at all. The effects of consuming marijuana are rather benign. Low to moderate doses produce feelings of well-being, relaxation, drowsiness, exhilaration and arousal. Consuming marijuana causes redness of eyes, a dry mouth, and an increased heart rate. It is not addicting, and no health risks are associated with the moderate consumption of marijuana. In fact, it is probably much safer than alcohol.

Marijuana is without question the most commonly used illegal drug in U.S. society. In 2000, NHSDA reported 10.7 million users (4.8% of the population) in the last month (SAMHSA, 2001b). In 2001, MTF reported 9.2% of 8th graders, 19.8% of 10th graders, and 22.4% of 12th graders had used marijuana in the last month (Johnston et al., 2002); YRBSS reported 24% of the students surveyed had used marijuana in the past month (CDC, 2002). Daily use of marijuana was reported by 3.7% of respondents aged 19–32 in 2000, versus 14.2% reporting use in the last 30 days (Johnston et al., 2001). Corresponding figures for alcohol for the same group were 4.1% and 66.6%.

Unlike the benign effects of the drug, the legal ramifications can be extremely hazardous. Uniform Crime Reports lists 735,000 people arrested for marijuana trafficking and possession in 2000. "A marijuana arrest can result in imprisonment and a criminal record that could mean a loss of employment or welfare benefits, denial of student financial aid, suspension of driving privileges, and expulsion from school or public housing" (Muwakkil, 2002, p. 15). Some states are addressing the severe penalties. California and Arizona have passed voter referendums that require first- and second-time offenders charged with minor drug violations involving marijuana to be given treatment rather than processed through the criminal justice system. Most state and local law enforcement agencies that responded to the National Drug Threat Survey 2001 identified marijuana availability and use as high but the threat to public safety and health as medium to low and stable (NDIC, 2001b). Many Americans question the severe treatment of marijuana by the government and the DEA. Government officials in the past attempted to portray marijuana as a "gateway drug" that led to other more dangerous drugs. However, there is no evidence to support this assertion. Indeed, there are literally millions of marijuana smokers who have used only marijuana.

Hallucinogens

Ancient Greeks, Romans, Egyptians, and Native Americans all used hallucinogenic plants for spiritual and medical purposes. Recreational use of hallucinogens in the United States became popular and problematic in the decades of the 1960s and 1970s. In contrast to antidepressants that make the neurotransmitter serotonin linger in the gaps between brain cells, hallucinogens are serotonin agonists. Their molecules are very similar to natural serotonin. When ingested in a sufficiently large dose, they push the serotonin system into overdrive (Blakeslee, 2001). Hallucinogens amplify signals from a person's sensory perception, distorting form and size. Users often talk about "seeing sounds," or "hearing visual stimuli."

Arthur Heffter was the first person to identify a hallucinogenic molecule. He extracted mescaline from peyote. In 1993, a professor of pharmacology and medicinal chemistry at Purdue University, David Nichols, founded the

Heffter Research Institute. The institute finances clinical trials with hallucinogens as possible treatment for phobias, depression, obsessive-compulsive disorders, and substance abuse. Some research has shown that psilocybin helps lessen compulsions such as washing one's hands dozens of times a day and alleviates depression; other research has found that peyote helps alcoholics stay sober. The medical director summarized the efforts of the institute: "If hallucinogens ever find their way into mainstream medicine—and I am convinced they will—they will never be handed out like Prozac. . . . These are not drugs you administer every day" (Blakeslee, 2001).

2C-B

There is little information about this potent club drug, which is still relatively rare in the United States. The street names of 2C-B (technically 4-bromo-2, 5-dimethoxyphenethylamine) are nexus and venus. It is classified as a schedule I hallucinogen. Effects are reported as a cross between the touchy-feely mood enhancement of ecstasy and the hallucinogenic experiences of LSD (Stein, 2001). Popular in Germany and Switzerland, its effects are reported to include enhancement of visual and auditory perception, increased sexual desire, and heightened senses of taste and touch. It is 10 times more powerful than MDMA in doses ranging from 5 to 10 milligrams. At lower doses (4 milligrams), users become passive and relaxed. With 8 to 10 milligrams, the stimulating effects increase, producing an intoxicated state with mild hallucinations. Higher doses produce stronger hallucinations and delusions.

LSD

Lysergic acid was first synthesized by a chemist in 1938 in Switzerland from ergot, a fungus that grows on rye and other grains. It was developed as a circulatory and respiratory stimulant. Later, it was investigated as a possible treatment for schizophrenia. In the 1960s, a subculture developed around recreational use of the drug. Lysergic acid diethylamide (LSD) is a clear, odorless substance with a slightly bitter taste. Its street name is acid, and it is marketed in a variety of forms. Windowpanes are small squares of gelatin that contain a drop of LSD. It is also available on small sheets of absorbent paper impregnated with a drop of the drug or as microdots, extremely small tablets. A typical dosage of LSD today ranges from 20 to 80 micrograms (versus 100 to 300 milligrams in the sixties).

This schedule I drug is produced domestically in clandestine labs. The procedure is complex and time-consuming, requiring a high degree of chemical expertise. Distribution of LSD is primarily through mail-order sales. Sellers can remain anonymous, providing some protection from law enforcement operations. The majority of LSD users are youths and young adults attracted to the drug by its relatively low price. Rock concerts and raves are popular venues. It is often used in combination with ecstasy, referred to as "candy flipping" or "trolling."

The effects of LSD are unpredictable. They depend on the dosage; the users' personality, mood, and expectations; and the surroundings in which the drug is used. The first effects of the drug are generally experienced within 30 to 90 minutes and can last up to 12 hours. LSD affects auditory and visual stimulation; higher doses can produce delusions and hallucinations. Perception of time can be distorted, out-of-body experiences may occur, or there may be a perception that one's body has merged with another person or object. These disorienting feelings can cause panic. The physical effects include dilated pupils, higher body temperature, rapid heart rate, profuse perspiration, loss of appetite, sleeplessness, dry mouth, and tremors. Some LSD users experience flashbacks to the LSD "trip" within a few days or up to a year without taking another dose of the drug.

NHSDA reported 0.2% (403,000) of the population aged 12 and older had used LSD in the past month in 2000 (SAMHSA, 2001b). For the same year, MTF reported 0.6% of respondents aged 19–32 had used the drug in the last month (Johnston et al., 2001). The figures in 2001 for 8th, 10th, and 12th graders were 1.0, 1.5, and 2.3, respectively. There were only 4,000 (0.7%) mentions of LSD in emergency department visits in 2000 (SAMHSA, 2001a). LSD does not produce the compulsive drug-seeking behaviors associated with heroin, alcohol, and nicotine. Most users voluntarily decrease or stop its use. However, it does produce tolerance if users take the drug repeatedly. Death as a direct effect of LSD on the body is virtually impossible. However, the panic reactions, delusions, and paranoia experienced by some users can put them at risk.

PEYOTE AND MESCALINE

Mescaline is a natural psychoactive ingredient of the peyote cactus. The "buttons" (fleshy part of the cactus) are removed, dried, and ground into a powder that is usually smoked but can be taken orally. A dose of approximately 400 milligrams produces colorful visions and hallucinations that last up to 12 hours. There appear to be no negative side effects from the drug. Members of the Native American Church have been using peyote for religious rituals for hundreds of years. The rituals involve the use of peyote in a group setting; members of the church use no other drugs (Blakeslee, 2001). This religious use is exempted from the provisions of the 1970 Controlled Substance Act, which classified peyote as a schedule I drug.

PSILOCYBIN MUSHROOMS

Psilocybin is a hallucinogen found in several species of mushrooms. In the sixteenth century, a Spanish priest wrote about the use of mushrooms and peyote by the Aztecs. Central and South American Native Americans have included mushrooms in their rites for thousands of years, and shamans used them to treat illnesses. Since 1968 psilocybin mushrooms have been illegal in the United States; it is also a schedule I drug.

A single dried mushroom contains approximately 0.2 to 0.4% psilocybin. The effective dose is between 4 and 8 milligrams, requiring the user to ingest a minimum of 2 grams of mushrooms to experience any psychoactive effects. Psilocybin is chemically similar to LSD, and the effects are similar, although less intense and of shorter duration (up to six hours). After eating a sufficient dose, the user feels the effects in about 20 minutes. Colors appear brighter and there are similar blends of audio, visual, and tactile senses as with LSD, such as "hearing a color." Users report a sense of detachment from their body and a feeling of unity with their surroundings. Larger doses produce hallucinations, anxiety, panic, paranoia, stomach cramps, and nausea. Psilocybin is not physically addicting.

DISSOCIATIVE ANESTHETICS

Phencyclidine or PCP is a synthetic hallucinogen that was developed as a general anesthetic. It is a dissociative anesthetic, meaning it relieves pain as well as making the user unaware of the environment. It proved to have a number of side effects including agitation, confusion, disorientation, and delirium. Patients sometimes became violent. It was not used widely on humans, but in the 1960s it was marketed for use in veterinary medicine and was classified as a schedule III drug. A substantial amount of PCP was diverted into the black market. When it was reclassified as a schedule II drug in 1978, legal manufacturing was discontinued. It is a white powder with hundreds of analogs or variations that can be cheaply produced in clandestine labs (Center, 2002). Street names are angel dust, rocket fuel, and jet fuel. Injected, snorted, or smoked, the effects of PCP range from auditory hallucinations, image distortion, mood disorders, and amnesia. Users may feel detached and anxious or experience a sense of strength and invulnerability. Larger doses can produce psychoses very similar to schizophrenia. The range between a dose resulting in mild sensory distortions and one with toxic effects is minimal. Compounding the problem is the fact that street sales of PCP often include added impurities such as baking soda or bleach, making it difficult to measure the dose accurately. Because PCP affects the central nervous, cardiovascular, and respiratory systems, an overdose requires immediate medical attention. Although DAWN mentions of PCP are infrequent, they increased to 5,404 in 2000—48% higher than in 1999 (SAMHSA, 2001a). There is a belief among law enforcement officials that individuals on PCP possess extraordinary strength, making them extremely dangerous to subdue. However, there is no evidence to support this contention (Kinlock, 1991).

Ketamine hydrochloride, another club drug, is manufactured outside the United States as a general anesthetic or preoperative sedative for veterinary use. It is available as a powder and a liquid. When diverted for human use, the powder is smoked or snorted. It gained popularity in the 1980s for physical effects similar to PCP and the visual effects of LSD, including dream-like states and hallucinations. At higher doses, ketamine can cause delirium, amnesia, depression, impaired motor function, high blood pressure, and potentially fatal respiratory problems. Since 1999, it has been a schedule III drug. Seizures of the drug have increased from 4,551 dosage units in 1999 to 1,154,463 units in 2000. It is available across the United States, as is GHB (NDIC, 2001b). DAWN reported 46 deaths from 1994 to 1999 from ketamine (SAMHSA, 2000).

Inhalants

The chemical vapors of more than a thousand household and commercial products can be inhaled for intoxicating effect. The ready availability and low cost of these products make them one of the first substances abused. Inhalants were the fourth most cited substance in the MTF survey (after alcohol, cigarettes, and marijuana). In 2001, 4% of 8th graders, 2.4% of 10th graders, and 2.2% of 12th graders had used inhalants in the past month (Johnston et al., 2002). YRBSS reported 4.7% of students surveyed used inhalants in the previous month (CDC, 2002). Inhalant use decreases with age. Only .4% of respondents aged 19–32 reported using inhalants in the past month (Johnston et al., 2001).

There are four classes of inhaled chemicals: *volatile solvents*, such as paint thinner, gasoline, glue, correction fluid, nail polish, and felt-tip markers, vaporize at room temperature if left in unsealed containers; *aerosols*, such as hair spray, spray paint, and fabric protector, contain propellants and solvents such as toluene; *gases* are inhaled from butane lighters, propane tanks, or air conditioning units and include medical anesthetics such as ether, chloroform, and nitrous oxide (used in cans of whipping cream or balloons); and *nitrites* (cyclohexyl nitrite found in room deodorizers; amyl nitrite, a prescription drug, and butyl nitrite) sold in adult bookstores and over the Internet (NDIC, 2001a). The first three classes depress the central nervous system, while nitrites are stimulants and are used more frequently by adults than by adolescents. Anesthetic gases such as ether or nitrous oxide were used for medical/dental procedures. Because ether is highly flammable, it is no longer used for those purposes. Nitrous oxide, "laughing gas," was one of the first inhalants to be abused and is now popular at raves where it is sold in small, sealed vials called whippets. Nitrites are used to enhance sexual experiences rather than for euphoric effects.

Initial effects resemble those of inebriation from alcohol. The inhaled chemical fumes replace oxygen in the lungs, forcing the heart to beat more rapidly and enlarging blood vessels to increase the flow of blood to the brain. The user initially feels uninhibited, excited, and lightheaded. After a few minutes, the user feels lethargic and drowsy as the body attempts to restabilize. Visible effects include slurred speech, clumsiness, drowsiness, impaired thinking, and decreased reflexes. Inhaled nitrates dilate blood vessels, increase heart rate, and produce a sensation of heat and excitement that lasts for several minutes.

There is considerable debate over the effects of inhalants. The effects of huffing have been somewhat exaggerated by the media. Nonetheless, the practice is extremely dangerous. All inhalants produce a variety of physical symptoms including sneezing, coughing, nose and mouth sores, heavy salivation, nosebleeds, bloodshot eyes, nausea, and bad breath. Long-term use can result in a number of physical problems including damage to the liver, kidney, lungs, heart, and central nervous system. Particles like lead in gasoline or metal in spray paint can accumulate in the body and reach dangerously high concentrations. Aerosols are often extremely cold when released and can freeze the lungs or voice box. There were 1,522 emergency department mentions of inhalants in 2000 (SAMHSA, 2001a).

Anabolic Steroids

Performance enhancing drugs are used by athletes at all levels in a variety of sports to obtain a competitive advantage. In 1991, Congress classified 27 anabolic steroids as schedule III substances because of a growing illicit market, abuse by teenagers, and the possible harmful long-term effects of steroid use. Anabolic steroids are synthetic substances chemically related to androgen that promote muscle growth.

A limited number of anabolic steroids have been approved for medical and veterinary use. The primary legitimate use for humans is as replacement therapy for inadequate levels of hormones. In veterinary practice, anabolic steroids are used to improve weight gain, vigor, and hair coat. Most illicit anabolic steroids are sold at fitness clubs, competitions, and through mail operations, after being smuggled into the United States from Mexico or Europe. When used in combination with exercise training and a high protein diet, anabolic steroids promote increased size and strength of muscles, improve endurance, and decrease recovery time between workouts.

The drugs are taken orally or by intramuscular injection. Users generally "cycle" the use of steroids, taking the drugs for 6 to 14 weeks followed by a discontinuation or reduction in use. Often, users "stack" the drugs, using multiple drugs concurrently. Users who "pyramid" gradually increase the dose and frequency of one or more steroids to a peak at mid-cycle and then gradually reduce the dose to the end of the cycle. Escalation of steroid use varies with different types of training. Body builders and weight lifters tend to escalate their dose to a much higher level than do long-distance runners or swimmers.

Although the long-term health effects are not known, there are indications of serious health problems associated with steroid use, including cardiovascular damage, cerebrovascular toxicity, kidney cancer, and liver cysts and cancer. Side effects include elevated cholesterol levels, hypertension, severe acne, and reduced sexual function. Men may experience prostate cancer, reduced sperm production, shrunken testicles. Anabolic steroids have a masculinizing effect on women, resulting in menstrual irregularities, more body hair, and a deeper voice. In adolescents, there may be a premature stoppage of the lengthening of bones, resulting in stunted growth. Feelings of anger or hostility, aggression, and violent behavior are other possible effects.

An NCAA survey conducted in August 2001 reported that 58.4% of the 21,000 male and female college athletes who responded had used a nutritional supplement (non-steroid) other than multi-vitamins during the previous year (see the previous discussion of ephedra); 15.5% of the athletes reported that the source of the supplements was a coach, trainer, team physician or

other school representative. Division 1 athletes used steroids far less frequently (1.6%), but some users also attributed distribution to school personnel. MTF reported a significant increase in steroid use among twelfth-graders
in 2001 (1.3 percent used steroids in the last 30 days versus .8 in 2001).

In May 2002, *Sports Illustrated* printed a story on the prevalence of steroids in baseball. The National Football League, National Basketball Association, and most major amateur sporting associations ban performance-
enhancing drugs and conduct random tests of athletes, but baseball tested
only minor-league players at that time. One current player, Ken Caminiti, said
he used steroids when he won the 1996 National League Most Valuable
Player award. He claimed more than half of major-leaguers use steroids. A
former player, Jose Canseco, claimed the total was closer to 85 percent. Tom
House used steroids during his 13-year career as a relief pitcher and increased
his weight to 225 pounds, despite being less than six feet in height. "This is a
10-year-old story. The only thing is it has gone from the guys who could
afford it to everybody thinking they can't afford not to" (Rogers, 2002, p. 3).
Mark McGwire, who broke the home-run record in 1998, admitted to using
androstenedione that year. Lyle Alzado acknowledged heavy steroid use
throughout his football career; he died of brain cancer. House refers to the
risk-reward ratio of steroid use. Although steroids improve performance, "the
only thing that grows faster than muscle tissue is cancer tissue."

Summary

To some degree, each drug discussed above appeals to a particular demographic. Older Americans, especially in the cities, abuse narcotics. Stimulants, such as cocaine, have several sets of adherents, including professionals,
inner-city minorities, and young people. Women are more likely to abuse
depressants, and marijuana is used primarily by young people and a number
of older Americans who started using it in the 1960s and 1970s. It is important to note that our society does not have "a" drug problem, it has several
drug problems.

From a policy perspective, we must realistically examine each drug and
its effects. This means avoiding hyperbole and political rhetoric. There is no
"one size fits all" problem—or solution. We must develop workable prevention, enforcement, and treatment strategies based on specifics. Our response
to methamphetamine must be different than our response to marijuana. We
must identify the drugs that pose the greatest threat to society and strive for
workable solutions.

REFERENCES

Abadinsky, H. (2001). *Drugs: An introduction* (4th ed.). Belmont, CA: Wadsworth.
Agar, M. (1973). *Ripping and running: A formal ethnography of urban heroin addicts.* New
     York: Seminar Press.
Beck, J. & Rosenbaum, M. (1994). *Pursuit of ecstasy: The MDMA experience.* New York:
     State University of New York Press.

Blakeslee, S. (2001, March 13). Scientists test hallucinogens for mental ills. *The New York Times,* Sec. F., p. 1.

Brandon, K. (2001, September 3). Marijuana farming booms in California. *Chicago Tribune,* p. 1.

Breslau, K. (2002, June 3). The "sextasy" craze. *Newsweek, cxxxix,* 30.

Brink, S. (2002, April 29). More blame and praise for a pain drug. *U.S. News & World Report,* 57.

Bureau of Justice Statistics (2000). *Prisoners in 1999.* Washington, DC: U.S. Dept. of Justice.

Center for Counseling and Student Development (2002). Northeastern University: Alcohol and Other Drug Education Office; http://www.counselingcenter.neu.edu/aod.html

Centers for Disease Control and Prevention (2002). *Youth Risk Behavior Surveillance 2001.* 51(SS04); 1-64 U.S. Government Printing Office (GPO), Washington, DC 20402-9371; http://www.cdc.gov/mmwr/preview/mmwrhtml/ss5104a1.htm

Chapman, S. (2002, January 10). Homegrown killer on rise. *Chicago Tribune,* p. 15.

Deardorff, J. (2002, March 14). Common drugs cloud rivers. *Chicago Tribune,* sec. 2, pp. 1, 8.

Doyle, C. (1987). *Explorations in psychology.* Monterey, CA: Brooks/Cole.

Drug Enforcement Administration (2000). Drug intelligence brief. Washington, DC: Office of Domestic Intelligence.

Federal Bureau of Investigation (2001). *Crime in the United States 2000: Uniform Crime Reports.* Washington, DC: U.S. Dept. of Justice.

Fitzgerald, N. & Riley, K. (2000). Drug-facilitated rape: Looking for the missing pieces. *National Institute of Justice Journal,* (April), 9–15.

Goode, E. (1998). Strange bedfellows: Ideology, politics, and drug legalization. *Society, 35*(4), 18–28.

Goode, E. (1999). *Drugs in American society* (4th ed.). New York: McGraw-Hill.

Gorman, C. (2002, April 15). Licking the habit. *Time,* 62.

Gorman, C. (2002, June 10). The science of anxiety. *Time,* 52.

Gray, J. P. (2001). *Why our drug laws have failed and what we can do about it: A judicial indictment of the war on drugs.* Philadelphia: Temple University Press.

Herz, D. (2000). Drugs in the heartland: Methamphetamine use in rural Nebraska. *Research in Brief,* (April), Washington, DC: National Institute of Justice.

Japsen, B. (2002, July 18). Bill would eliminate tax breaks for drugmakers' ads. *Chicago Tribune,* sec. 3, p. 3.

Johnston, L., O'Malley, P., & Bachman, J. (2002). *Monitoring the future national survey results on adolescent drug use: Overview of key findings, 2001.* Bethesda, MD: National Institute on Drug Abuse; http://www.monitoringthefuture.org/

Johnston, L., O'Malley, P., & Bachman, J. (2001). *Monitoring the future national survey results on drug use, 1975–2000. Volume II: College students and adults ages 19–40.* Bethesda, MD: National Institute on Drug Abuse.

Keyser, J. (2002, August 8). Bronze Age pots reveal narcotic medicines. *Chicago Tribune,* p. 6.

Kinlock, T. (1991). Does phencyclidine (PCP) use increase violence? *Journal of Drug Issues, 21*(4), 795–816.

Kleiner, C. (2001, August 6). A curse and a cure. *U.S. News & World Report,* 42–43.

Kotulak, R. (2002, March 14). Experts say love of nicotine is all in mind. *Chicago Tribune,* pp. 1, 21.

Lewin, T. (2002, February 27). Teen girls' alcohol use catching up with boys'. *Chicago Tribune*, p. 7.

Lighty, T. (2002, February 18). Mistakes cost U.S. ecstasy drug case. *Chicago Tribune*, pp. 1, 2.

Lyman, M. & Potter, G. (1998). *Drugs in society: Causes, concepts, and control* (3rd ed.). Cincinnati: Anderson Publishing Co.

Meadows, S. (2002, January 14). Sister, can you spare a line? *Newsweek*, 63.

McCrea, B. & Kolbye, K. (1995). *Hazards of d-methamphetamine production: Baseline assessment*. Washington, DC: U.S. Dept. of Justice, National Drug Intelligence Center. (NDIC Pub. No. 95-C0109-002)

Meier, B. (2001, October 28). Drug suspected in 282 deaths. *Chicago Tribune*, p. 16.

Miller, N. (1995). *Addiction psychiatry: Current diagnosis and treatment*. New York: Wiley.

Morse, J. (2002, April 1). Women on a binge. *Time*, 56–61.

Musto, D. F. (1999). *The American disease: Origins of narcotic control* (3rd ed.). New York: Oxford University Press.

Muwakkil, S. (2002, January 28). Drug warriors: U.S.'s internal Taliban. *Chicago Tribune*, p. 15.

National Center on Addiction and Substance Abuse (2002). Statement. New York: Columbia University; http://www.casacolumbia.org/

National Drug Intelligence Center (2001a). *Huffing: The abuse of inhalants*. Johnstown, PA: U.S. Dept. of Justice.

National Drug Intelligence Center (2001b). *National drug threat assessment 2002*. Johnstown, PA: U.S. Dept. of Justice.

National Institute of Justice (2001). *ADAM preliminary 2000 findings on drug use and drug markets—adult male arrestees*. Washington, DC: U.S. Dept. of Justice; http://www.adam-nij.net/

National Institute of Justice (2000a). *ADAM 1999 annual report*. Washington, DC: U.S. Dept. of Justice.

National Institute of Justice (2000b). *Annual report on drug use among adult and juvenile arrestees*. Washington, DC: U.S. Dept. of Justice.

Neergaard, L. (2002, June 15). Herb cited in deaths gets further safety check. *Chicago Tribune*, p. 8.

Neuman, J. (2002, April 10). 1,400 deaths blamed on college drinking. *Chicago Tribune*, p. 10.

Office of National Drug Control Policy (2000). *Methadone fact sheet*. Washington, DC: Drug Policy Information Clearinghouse.

Page, C. (2002, September *). The myth of "superweed." *Chicago Tribune*, Sec. 2, p. 11.

Pedersen, W. & Skrondal, A. (1999). Ecstasy and new patterns of drug use: A normal population study. *Addiction*, *94*(11), 1695–1707.

Pennell, S., Ellett, J., Rienick, C., & Grimes, J. (1999). *Meth matters: Report on methamphetamine users in five western cities*. Washington, DC: National Institute of Justice.

Ragavan, C. (2001, February 5). Cracking down on ecstasy. *U.S. News & World Report*, 14–17.

Rogers, P. (2002, June 4). Ritalin use worries ex-ballplayer. *Chicago Tribune*, Sec. 4, pp. 1, 17.

Roosevelt, M. (2002, March 18). Puffing up a storm. *Time*, 79.

Royse, D. (2002, July 18). Jeb Bush's daughter fails rehab, is jailed. *Chicago Tribune*, p. 11.

Salopek, P. (2001, December 26). With Taliban gone, poppy crops return. *Chicago Tribune*, pp. 1, 3.

Schuckit, M. (1985). *Alcohol patterns and problems.* New Brunswick, NJ: Rutgers University Press.

Sherrid, P. (August 13, 2001). Designer drugs: What's best for patients isn't always what's best for profits. *U.S. News & World Report,* 30–32.

Stares, P. (1996). Drug legalization. *Brookings Review, 14*(2), 18–21.

Stein, L. (2001, October 29). Police warn of new drug in club scene. *Chicago Tribune,* p. 3.

Substance Abuse and Mental Health Services Administration (2002). *Emergency department trends from the drug abuse warning network, preliminary estimates January–June 2001 with revised estimates 1994–2000.* Rockville, MD: Office of Applied Studies; http://www.drugabusestatistics.samhsa.gov

Substance Abuse and Mental Health Services Administration (2001a). *Drug abuse warning network detailed emergency department (ED) tables 2000.* Rockville, MD: Office of Applied Studies.

Substance Abuse and Mental Health Services Administration (2001b). *Summary of findings from the 2000 national household survey on drug abuse.* Rockville, MD: Office of Applied Studies; http://www.samhsa.gov/

Substance Abuse and Mental Health Services Administration (2000). *The DAWN report.* Rockville, MD: Office of Applied Studies.

Szegedy-Maszak, M. (2002, May 6). The mind maze: Can "distraction" be found in the brain's biochemistry? *U.S. News & World Report,* 52–53.

Volkow, N., Wang, G., Fowler, J., Logan, J., Gatley, S., Gifford, A., Hitzemann, R., Ding, Y., & Pappas, N. (1999). Prediction of reinforcing responses to psychostimulants in humans by brain dopamine receptor levels. *American Journal of Psychiatry, 156,* 1440–1443.

Wivell, M. & Wilson, G. (1994). Prescription for harm: Pharmacist liability. *Trial, 30*(5), 36–39.

Yates, J. (2002, April 11). Nicotine pops illegal, FDA says. *Chicago Tribune,* Sec. 2, pp. 1, 6.

Yost, P. (2002, September 20). Online federal sweep targets "date rape" drug; 100 arrested. *Chicago Tribune,* p. 14.

Zinberg, N. (1984) *Drug set and setting: The basis for controlled intoxicant use.* New Haven: Yale University Press.

APPENDIX

In 1970, Congress enacted the Controlled Substances Act (21 U.S.C. 812 b). Since then, approximately 160 substances have been added, removed, or transferred from one schedule to another (visit http://www.deadiversion.usdoj.gov/21cfr/cfr/2108cfrt.htm for section 1308 of the most recent issue of Title 21 of the Code of Federal Regulations Part 1300). An alphabetical list of substances classified according to schedule is available at http://www.deadiversion.usdoj.gov/schedules/alpha/index.html. The list describes the parent chemical but does not include all derivatives that could also be controlled substances. As the disclaimer on the site notes, a substance need not be listed as a controlled substance to be treated as a schedule I substance for criminal prosecution. A controlled substance analog is a substance intended for human consumption that is structurally or pharmacologically similar (or represented to be similar) to a schedule I or schedule II substance, which is not an approved medication in the United States.

Schedule I (includes heroin, LSD, and marijuana)

- Drug has a high potential for abuse.
- Drug has no currently accepted medical use in treatment in the United States.
- There is a lack of accepted safety for use of the drug under medical supervision.

Schedule II (includes morphine, used as a pain-killer, and cocaine, used as a topical anesthetic)

- Drug has a high potential for abuse.
- Drug has a currently accepted medical use in treatment in the United States or a currently accepted medical use with severe restrictions.
- Abuse of the drug may lead to severe psychological or physical dependence.

Schedule III (includes anabolic steroids and Marinol)

- Drug has a potential for abuse less than the drugs in schedules I and II.
- Drug has a currently accepted medical use in treatment in the United States.
- Abuse of the drug may lead to moderate or low physical dependence or high psychological dependence.

Schedule IV (includes Valium and other tranquilizers)

- Drug has a low potential for abuse relative to the drugs or other substances in schedule III.
- Drug has a currently accepted medical use in treatment in the United States.
- Abuse of the drug may lead to limited physical dependence or psychological dependence relative to the drugs or other substances in schedule III.

Schedule V (includes codeine-containing analgesics)

- Drug has a low potential for abuse relative to the drugs or other substances in schedule IV.
- Drug has a currently accepted medical use in treatment in the United States.
- Abuse of the drug may lead to limited physical dependence or psychological dependence relative to the drugs or other substances in schedule IV.

3

The Next Panic

Philip Jenkins

That humanity at large will ever be able to dispense with Artificial Paradises seems very unlikely.

—Aldous Huxley, 1954

Since the mid-1970s, synthetic panics have erupted with striking regularity in the United States, and they have generally followed very similar patterns and been based on extremely dubious claims. Similar assertions will unquestionably be heard in the near future, perhaps concerning substances presently unknown outside academic departments of chemistry. With so many precedents at hand, it should be possible to frame a typical model of the panic cycle in operation, with the goal of encouraging both the media and policymakers to acquire greater caution and skepticism in such matters, lest the spurious quest for the next crack cocaine become an endlessly recurring process. The importance of such a defensive effort becomes all the more pressing when we consider the impact of successive panics and drug wars on the wider society: controversies over synthetics raise in an acute form the whole rationale of drug prohibition and its distressing effects. The cumulative effects of anti-drug campaigns are so damaging that they can only be justified if they prevent worse alternatives, and it is far from clear that they do so. The unbending approach that has characterized anti-drug prohibitionism in recent years is a manifestation of a narrowly puritanical view of drugs and medicines that severely limits their potential usefulness for human well-being. The emphasis of drug policy urgently needs to shift from policing to medicine, from zero tolerance to harm reduction.

From *Synthetic Panics: The Symbolic Politics of Designer Drugs*, 183–197. Copyright © 1999 by New York University. Used with permission.

In order to understand how to defuse a prospective panic, we first need to know how such events are constructed in the first place and the means by which a drug is demonized. Let us imagine the administrator of an agency with a vested interest in drug regulation, one who has to report to an investigative or official body about some newly popular synthetic substance: perhaps we might call it Ultra. How might that person go about convincing an audience that the issue was worthy of concern and that the agency in question deserved resources to research and confront it?

Several obvious rhetorical tactics come to mind.[1] The administrator would want to present the problem in terms that would be readily familiar to that audience, to assert that new drug X is closely comparable to established drug Y and would have roughly the same effects. He or she would try to make the substance seem as dangerous as possible, ideally by a catchy label that would lend itself to imaginative permutations in news headlines. The account would emphasize the notorious features of drug abuse already well cultivated in the public consciousness—aspects such as a high potential for addiction, toxicity, devastating effects on families and communities and enhanced personal aggression. These images would be substantiated by impressive statistics illustrating rapid and uncontrollable growth. Throughout, the problems said to be posed by the drug would be illustrated by horrifying case studies of extreme violence or personal devastation, tailored as closely as possible to strictly contemporary concerns: whether the hot social issue of the time involves sex crime or illegal immigration, cults or terrorism, the new drug would somehow be implicated as a player in this wider problem. In short, the rhetorical indictment would be much like that constructed against PCP in the 1970s, designer drugs and Ecstasy in the 1980s, Methamphetamine and CAT in the 1990s.

Past experience suggests that such an account would be accepted quite uncritically by the media, which views its role in such matters as essentially stenographic—recording the fact that a new drug epidemic is in progress and seeking to enhance the charges without critically examining whether they have the slightest validity. But if they ever did choose to apply a skeptical approach, critical observers would find grave flaws at every stage of the presentation.

LAW ENFORCEMENT EXPERTS CLAIM . . .

The first question must apply to the source from which claims arise. By definition, agencies whose primary mission is the control or suppression of illegal drugs have a vested interest in portraying those substances as threatening and ubiquitous. This is true for the DEA especially; its *raison d'être* depends on finding and combating drug abuse, preferably with a regular infusion of issues that are sufficiently new and distinctive to grab the attention of media and political leaders, who face many rival demands for resources. Any statement from such a body must be taken with that agenda in mind. Given the nature of bureaucracies, no drug-enforcement agency is ever likely to present Congress with a statement asserting that the illegal drug menace is under control or largely defeated, as this would invite either a dismantling of the agency or a large reduction of its resources. The same is true for state agencies, like California's BNE.

An English Victorian statesman once bemoaned the self-serving nature of expert advice: "If you believe the doctors, nothing is wholesome. If you believe the theologians, nothing is innocent. If you believe the soldiers, nothing is safe."[2] And as he might have added, if you believe the drug warriors, the nation is always suffering from a drug epidemic or about to face a new one. When approaching such claims, it is always helpful to bear in mind the question, *Cui bono?* Who benefits?

THE SERIAL KILLER OF DRUGS . . .

A presentation intended for a mass audience will frame the new problem through the use of threatening metaphors and other rhetorical devices. Rape drugs, the serial killer of drugs, zombie drug users, the crack of the nineties: all are wonderful grabbers for media stories, but in what sense, if any, do these phrases correspond with reality? It is dangerous to assume that the metaphors developed to tout a given drug are accurate reflections of its destructive qualities—for example, that CAT is clawing up a region, that ice is chilling officials or that methamphetamine is preparing to speed across the nation. And even if a substance is dubbed a rape drug, we cannot presume that everyone possessing it has rape in mind. A little historical perspective permits us to see a term like "the new drug of choice" as the empty cliché it is.

EPIDEMIC . . .

The concept of an epidemic is one such metaphor, however often it seems to be employed in an objective medical or scientific sense. In fact, the term begs several key questions, not least the harmful effects of the substance concerned. To speak of an epidemic of drug X automatically assumes that the substance is a health menace comparable to an infectious disease. Medical analogies ipso facto presume that the subject under discussion is pathological, an impression reinforced by the use of pseudomedical language like "latency periods."

And the word epidemic poses other difficulties. In Western society, the most familiar epidemic of recent times is the AIDS outbreak that began in the early 1980s; in the aftermath of this experience, to speak of a drug epidemic suggests that the behavior observed is likewise a brand new phenomenon that has seemingly come from nowhere. Claims of a drug epidemic are often made without adequate evidence that the behavior in question has really grown: if we know accurately neither how many people were using a drug ten years ago nor how many are using it today, we can make no accurate statement concerning growth or decline of usage.

To speak of an epidemic further assumes that growth in drug usage can be measured accurately, with the model familiar from infectious diseases, but in reality, usage itself is effectively invisible. All we can measure is behavior that is either reported or observed, and it is difficult to extrapolate from that to judge the actual scale of a drug phenomenon. Because illegal drug use is a private behavior that can attract severe sanctions, its scale cannot be determined by the usual means devised to judge the popularity of a television program or a type of margarine. That statement may seem obvious, but its implications are easily ignored when we confront claims about the alleged popularity of a given drug. People often fail to respond accurately to surveys, and that difficulty is all the greater when dealing with illegal conduct, so that agencies must resort to techniques of extrapolation that are controversial at best, ludicrous at worst. Estimates of, say, the number of habitual cocaine users in the United States at any given time in the mid-1990s were variously put at 582,000 and 2.2 million, and in fact one government report presented each of these wildly divergent figures within a few pages of each other.[3] There are no plausible grounds for believing that any of these figures reflects objective reality, any more than we can find grounds to believe the stratospheric, multibillion-dollar figures occasionally hazarded for the financial damage caused by drugs to the national economy.

Drug usage can be quantified in terms of persons arrested, amounts of drugs seized or numbers of laboratories raided, but in all of these cases, what we are measuring is the intensity of official reaction and not the changing volume of drug usage. If a state believes that it has a problem with drug X, its police forces will go looking for it, prosecutors will be more likely to press charges concerning it and medical examiners will tend to look keenly for its role in violent incidents: all of the leading indicators will therefore soar, regardless of whether actual usage is rising or falling. Furthermore, a society that grows less tolerant of drugs will have more arrests and seizures, so that higher statistics for official action may in fact coincide with declining drug usage, as occurred nationwide during the late 1980s.

SOON TO SWEEP THE NATION . . .

It is tempting for the mass media to illustrate a looming drug crisis by taking one area in which a drug is indeed very popular and suggesting that these conditions will soon become generalized, so that the whole nation will soon share the experience of San Jose with PCP, northern Michigan with CAT, Hawaii with ice or Arizona with methamphetamine. The only difficulty is that these extrapolations are virtually never justified by events. If the problem is at present strictly localized, are there any plausible signs of usage spreading, absent the massive free publicity provided by media and legislators?

MORE ADDICTIVE THAN CRACK COCAINE . . .

No less than "epidemic," other standard terms in the law-enforcement lexicon concerning drugs are deceptive in suggesting an objective scientific quality. Yet, in fact, these terms are malleable and unreliable, owing more to rhetoric than to objective science. "Designer drugs" itself is such a phrase, as is the distinction between so-called "hard" and "soft" drugs. In the case of designer drugs, the term is used to cover both potent substances like fentanyl and far milder ones like Ecstasy, both of which have been subjected to equal official stigma.

"Addiction" is another of these flexible words. As long ago as 1946, the famous medical writer Paul De Kruif denounced the FBN's tendency to conclude that a given drug was addictive or damaging based only on anecdotal evidence, on "the unscientific, uncontrolled reports that flow into the files of governmental bureaus dabbling in science."[4] Matters have changed little in the last half-century, and most of the so-called science remains mere dabbling. Police forces and drug-enforcement agencies like to use scientific-sounding rhetoric concerning drugs (as in "epidemiologists . . . have stated that it is South Florida's fastest growing drug problem"), but we should never forget that these statements are taken from political documents that would not conceivably pass muster if reviewed by neutral medical or social scientific observers. As used by politicians and law-enforcement agencies today, the term "addict" often becomes synonymous with "user," or even with a person who has had only one or two contacts with the substance in question and is not addicted by any medical criterion. Whenever claims are made that a given substance is severely addictive, it is crucial to ask how addiction is being defined. The nature and severity of chemical dependency is subject to great debate among professionals, and any claim that a substance produces addiction after a single use should be viewed skeptically: such a claim is so bizarre and improbable that it should raise doubts about other statements made by the same source.

Over the last decade, too, highly questionable charges about the nature of addiction have been made in the context of possible drug effects on babies born to users—the infamous crack-baby phenomenon and its later imitators. As in the case of instant addiction, stories of babies born addicted to any given substance should be treated with great skepticism, especially when all possible pathologies and symptoms suffered by the child are attributed to the influence of that drug.

THE ADDICT WILL KILL YOU IN A HEARTBEAT . . .

Claims about new drugs have a dreadful track record in matters of accuracy and credibility. A century of anti-drug rhetoric has regularly drawn on a rather limited repertoire of images, which have successively been applied to many different drugs bearing no obvious connection. One familiar script suggests that a drug transforms a user into a soulless, drug-lubricated killing machine, a model variously applied over the years to cocaine, marijuana, PCP and methamphetamine. This concept is illustrated by tales of savage murders, sex attacks and mutilation, which acquire an urban legend quality as they are repeatedly retold in successive drug panics. If these earlier scripts are now known to have been thoroughly inaccurate regarding well-known substances like marijuana, is there any reason to suppose that they are likely to be truthful when applied to new or emerging menaces? A hypothetical substance might indeed have a devastating effect on an individual, but as in the case of stories about instant addiction and addict babies, a long record of bogus claims has necessarily shifted the burden of credibility firmly onto the claim-makers themselves.

DRUG-RELATED DEATHS . . .

One yardstick used to substantiate the seriousness of a drug problem is the number of deaths associated with a given substance. As a rhetorical tactic, this is an obvious means of both attracting public attention and contradicting the view that drugs are a harmless, individual vice. But what is a drug-related death? In a particular case, can the given death plausibly be shown to result from the usage of the drug itself, as opposed to, say, a conflict between traffickers? The fact that an individual died while showing traces of a drug in his or her body does not of itself establish causation. The notion of a drug-related death is not implausible in itself, as alcohol, heroin, nicotine and other drugs can certainly cause or contribute to fatalities, but this does not mean that claims about the volume of damage should be accepted without further evaluation.

RUINED LIVES . . .

Claim-makers illustrate the harmful nature of a given phenomenon by giving it a human face, providing case studies of individuals whose lives were devastated by a particular drug. These stories have to be used with caution, especially if, as is so often the case, they portray desperate users in treatment programs and imply that this self-selected sample is representative of every individual who has tried the drug. Such accounts fail to acknowledge that users in such programs are often there under court mandate as an alternative to lengthy prison terms, so they have a powerful incentive to present the starkest possible contrast between their previous drug abuse and their recent progress towards sobriety. The drug users whose lives we can observe are not necessarily representative of nonaddicted consumers. We must beware what Reinarman and Levine term "the routinization of caricature—worst cases framed as typical cases, the episodic rhetorically recrafted into the epidemic."[5] The use of illegal drugs can ruin lives, but often the harm arises less from qualities intrinsic to the drug itself than from its legal consequences.

. . . ROADS NOT TAKEN

Those promoting concern over drug problems frame issues in particular ways, so that for instance the methamphetamine problem of the nineties was chiefly seen in terms of rural and suburban white users, while the rave-drug phenomenon was portrayed as a subset of the sexual endangerment of women. Each of these issues could, however, be viewed with equal plausibility in quite a different way; the topics omitted from official statements and media coverage are as significant as those included. Though new synthetics have often been popularized within the gay clubs, especially the gay dance circuit, no media exposé has ever discussed the problem as one of "gay drugs." Presumably, journalists and editors reasonably feel that such coverage would tend to increase the existing stigma on homosexuality by associating gays with irresponsible and illegal behavior. Whatever the reason, the decision to select one area of an issue rather than another must always be recognized as a subjective one, reflecting political and cultural concerns of the moment. Why does a particular problem acquire the shape it does? How is it made to mean what it does?

The need for such a critical and even debunking approach becomes apparent when we consider the harm wrought by past drug wars and the certainty that they will recur. Much has been written since the early 1980s about the grim social effects of the drug war in terms of mass incarceration, the increasingly militarized ethos of law enforcement, and the disproportionate burden placed upon minority communities.[6] The drug war must take much of the blame for the abysmal state of police-community relations during the 1980s and 1990s and the depths of mutual hatred that became apparent during the wave of urban violence in Los Angeles and elsewhere in 1992. Drug-related prosecutions are largely responsible for the fact that several million Americans now find themselves under the supervision of the state, if not through institutional confinement then through the mechanisms of probation and parole. Meanwhile, the reach of the penal system has expanded to affect ever-new categories, from the youngest to the oldest, women as well as men. The drug war went far in reversing the gains in civil liberties made during the due process revolution of the Warren Court years, and a host of new drug-related cases provided judges with the opportunity to roll back the rights of suspects and prisoners.

Perhaps most troubling is the fact that these trends have no logical or predictable end, in the sense of being a period of unfortunate travail that must be endured before the drug problem is somehow solved and social peace reigns once more, at however great a cost. To adapt the famous saying, even creating a desert will not bring peace. Deterrence can have some effect—the number of people using illegal drugs has fallen since the late 1970s—but the fact that so many millions continue to run the appalling legal risks of the drug-war era suggests that they constitute an irreducible core population. The vision of a drug-free America is a chimera. Even if we imagine that, by some miracle, foreign supplies of illegal drugs had been altogether suppressed and no byproduct of the poppy or the coca leaf ever crossed the American frontier (a ludicrous supposition), the drug war would not abate. The appearance of successive new panic waves in the 1990s shows that the emphasis would shift instead to the synthetic products of domestic laboratories. The anti-drug bureaucracy will continue to wage its destructive campaigns ad infinitum, or at least until some administration acquires the political will to order a halt.

The drug war is a perfect example of what criminologist Jeffrey Reiman once termed a Pyrrhic defeat.[7] The familiar concept of Pyrrhic victory refers to a struggle in which the winner suffers such appalling damage that, in practice, he loses the war. In contrast, a Pyrrhic defeat refers to a battle in which one wins by losing, in the sense that the perpetual failure to eliminate drugs brings a never-ending stream of new resources to law enforcement, which is extolled at length for its heroic struggles against the vast menace. When it appears, however briefly, that a victory might be gained, as in the struggles against heroin and cocaine in the early 1990s, new and still more fearsome foes must be found or concocted.

Though most Americans may not consider themselves directly affected by these events, successive anti-drug movements have in fact had a widespread impact, causing serious harm to millions of mainstream individuals whose direct exposure to illegal narcotics has been slim or nonexistent. Among other things, the fear of abuse has resulted in the removal from the medical arsenal of some highly effective pharmaceuticals, especially those that control pain.[8] In illnesses like terminal cancer, drugs such as heroin are by far the most effective for relieving pain and are commonly used for this purpose in most other advanced countries. In the United States, by contrast, patients are notoriously undermedicated, ostensibly because doctors fear the effects of addiction, as if that were a realistic concern for the terminally ill. In reality, heroin and its analogues are underused because of the overwhelming campaign against them by the anti-drug bureaucracies. A sophisticated health care system thus expects patients to endure excruciating pain, to a degree that would be utterly unacceptable in a less nervous and more humane environment.

The issue recalls another pressing controversy in which the ideological purity of anti-drug politics came into conflict with medical necessity: the matter of needle exchange programs. As the AIDS problem grew worse in the 1980s, activists proposed to offer drug addicts clean needles to prevent the danger of transmitting this and other diseases, including hepatitis, and thereby to save several thousand lives each year. While drug users themselves might conceivably be seen as morally culpable, this would not be true of their spouses and sexual partners, who would also be protected from deadly diseases. Yet, in 1989, the federal government prohibited financing for such programs on the grounds that they might be seen as supporting or acquiescing in drug use. This prohibition was renewed in 1998, despite furious lobbying by public-health experts and AIDS activists. During the 1998 controversy, the argument that proved decisive in influencing the Clinton White House was made by drug czar Barry McCaffrey, who declared that clean needle programs would send the wrong message to children about drugs: the symbolic facade of absolute prohibition must be maintained, even when it kills.[9]

Legislatures over the years have granted sizable resources to the anti-drug bureaucracies, not realizing that in so doing, they were entrusting to these police agencies a de facto supervision over the American medical profession. The right to regulate drugs is in large measure the right to shape medical policy. The resulting overextension of police powers became apparent in the mid-nineties, when several states debated the legalization of physician-assisted suicide and a law allowing it was passed in Oregon. The Oregon measure was swiftly put on hold when DEA chief Thomas Constantine warned that any doctor using drugs for this purpose would be prosecuted for violations of controlled substances laws, as his agency had determined (under pressure from conservative politicians) that assisted suicide did not constitute a "legitimate medical purpose." In this instance, an embarrassed Justice Department overruled the DEA, but the agency's ham-fisted intrusion into delicate ethical debates is still startling.[10]

Apart from such extreme cases, sporadic panics have removed a number of effective drugs from general access. While the classification of drugs into the various CSA schedules is ostensibly based on a rational scientific evaluation of their costs and benefits, this is in reality a highly politicized process in which symbolic and cultural factors play a major part: the result is a systematic tendency towards over-restrictive classification. Contrary to the polemics of recent years, drugs like Rohypnol do have purposes other than merely facilitating rape, as they are effective sedatives when used in pre-anaesthesia situations. When the drug was used for criminal purposes, the manufacturer responded promptly by adding safeguards, so that when slipped into a drink it would color the resulting mixture, thereby alerting a potential victim. However, the anti-rape-drug campaign had become so intense and uncompromising that yet another valuable pharmaceutical was placed off limits. This same process not only removed marijuana from the legitimate pharmacopoeia, but even prevented its return in individual states that democratically expressed their support for such a move in repeated referenda. As in the assisted suicide controversy, drug-enforcement policy implies a substantial shift towards federal authority over social issues.

The campaign against useful medicaments had its widest effects on everyday life when major retailers cooperated with the DEA to remove from store shelves any substance that might conceivably be used in making methamphetamine or methcathinone. The policy initially affected asthma sufferers, but soon had an impact on virtually everyone with a need for an over-the-counter cough and cold medication. In many regions, the ban was extended from ephedrine to bulk sales of pseudephedrine, which is found in many familiar brand-name products.[11] By this standard, it will perhaps not be long before the whole category of over-the-counter medicines ceases to exist, all as part of the desperate endeavor to prevent the unauthorized manufacture of chemicals that someone, somewhere, has labeled a designer drug. The movement to prohibit supposedly harmful substances leads inexorably to a spreading net of proscription, which increasingly takes in harmless and even beneficial drugs and medicines.

Apart from the evidence of collateral damage and social harm, a powerful philosophical argument can be made that the state should not limit an individual's right to consume substances that might harm him or her. The classic text of libertarian thought is John Stuart Mill's *On Liberty*, published in 1859 in direct response to the American movement to prohibit alcohol. Mill argued for a right for individuals to undertake potentially self-destructive behaviors so long as those did not harm other people, a criterion that certainly extended to substance abuse. There are, of course, cases in which drug abuse ceases to be merely victimless crime, and an argument for regulation can be justified in terms of the potential of harm to nonconsenting individuals, as with the so-called rape drugs. Indeed, Mill specifically took account of the question of poisons, which were freely available in Victorian England, and even this arch-libertarian had no difficulty with the prospect of controlling or registering the sale of poisons to prevent crimes. By analogy, the restriction or registration of potential rape drugs is a legitimate role for government, though active suppression is more questionable, and the element of public protection should not altogether overwhelm individual rights. But where there is no threat to innocent parties, a libertarian position should oppose any unnecessary restrictions upon the behavior of responsible adult citizens.

Such an approach is far removed from the moral and political assumptions of contemporary drug policy, in which the idea of individual rights is countered by claims about the interests of children or by varieties of communitarian rhetoric. Regardless of the scientific rhetoric with which decisions are buttressed, the absolutist principles of prohibitionism are based on a distinctive kind of conservative morality, with a traditional, even archaic, puritanical hatred of anything smacking of hedonism. Ecstasy, for instance, was tolerated while it had a limited therapeutic use, but suppressed when it acquired a reputation as a party drug; it was condemned as much by this social context as by the studies suggesting that it might pose health risks.

The example of Ecstasy also raises crucial questions about the criteria employed to prohibit any drug. Even assuming that the scientific evidence for brain damage from Ecstasy is widely agreed to be credible (which it is not), we should recall that all drugs and medicines, even those in most common nonprescription use, can have harmful effects on some individuals in some circumstances: we have already noted that adverse reactions to legal drugs administered in hospitals kill perhaps a hundred thousand Americans each year. The use of legal drugs and medicines is permitted because their benefits vastly outweigh the marginal possibility of harm to a few. To put this in non-drug terms, Americans who travel by air are well aware that hundreds of people die each year as a result of aviation-related fatalities, but they accept the risk because it is tiny in comparison to the possible advantages. Moreover, it is a risk that they consciously, voluntarily, choose to accept. Why should the same principle not apply to synthetic drugs? Why should a drug like Ecstasy not be permitted, despite its possible risks, in view of the mental and spiritual elevation so widely reported by willing users? Why should a chemical not be used for recreational purposes?

The answer, regrettably, is self-evident. None of the regulating agencies accepts that a drug should have as its primary goal the elevation of mood, the giving of pleasure, the enhancement of sexual feeling or the refining of consciousness, at least for normally functioning people (as opposed to the clinically depressed). If none of these features is accepted as desirable or even tolerable, then the slightest evidence of harm automatically outweighs the (supposedly nonexistent) benefits of a given chemical, and it falls under a legal taboo as stringent as that imposed by any religion. It sounds eminently reasonable to say that the benefits of a given drug should outweigh its possible costs, but if one category of benefits is always counted as worthless, if one side of the equation is always set at zero it will always be countermanded by the costs. In this severe view, any use of the given substance constitutes abuse.

To be permissible, then, chemicals can have, must have, no association with pleasure, and still less with ecstasy. The central dilemma here, of course, is that throughout recorded history, humanity has used drugs to alter mind and mood, and the principle of such experimentation is deeply rooted in human cultures. To quote Aldous Huxley once more, "The universal and ever-present urge to self-transcendence is not to be abolished by slamming the currently popular Doors in the Wall." Or as Dr. Ronald Siegel has observed, "Unless you want to defoliate the entire planet and pave it over, and outlaw the science of chemistry and cooking, you'll probably never stop the use of synthetic drugs or natural drugs in the search for ecstasy and altered states."[12] In the last quarter-century, science has evolved a sophisticated understanding of the human brain that should in theory open the doors to any number of new drugs with enormous potential to enhance pleasure and expand consciousness. Yet all are certain to meet diehard opposition from the inflexible doorkeepers of drug enforcement.

In chemistry, as in computing, creativity is usually several steps ahead of the capacity of legislators and policymakers to comprehend the challenge they face in seeking to enforce orthodoxy, much less to present effective countermeasures. Like generals throughout history, they are usually fighting the last war, or even the one before that. The battle to suppress ecstasy in all its forms has always been an unequal one, but now the balance of forces has shifted dramatically to the side of experimentation, which can only be suppressed by increasingly rigid laws and ever more intrusive police supported by a willfully obscurantist media. As neurochemistry and chemical technologies advance, the stage is set for persistent confrontations between an entrenched antidrug bureaucracy and the demonized phantom chemists, the evil scientific masterminds. The outcome, in short, will be recurrent synthetic panics.

NOTES

[1] Compare Joel Best, *Threatened Children* (Chicago: Univ. Chicago Press, 1990).

[2] The quote is from Lord Salisbury.

[3] Jeff Leen, "A Shot in the Dark on Drug Use," *WP*, January 12, 1998, 32–33, weekly edition.

[4] Paul De Kruif, "Demerol," in *JAMA*, September 7, 1946, 43. Among other achievements, De Kruif was the technical adviser for Sinclair Lewis' novel *Arrowsmith*.

[5] Craig Reinarman and Harry G. Levine, eds., *Crack in America* (Berkeley: Univ. of California Press, 1997), 24.

[6] Eric L. Jensen and Jurg Gerber, eds., *The New War on Drugs* (Cincinnati: Anderson, 1998); Michael Massing, *The Fix* (New York: Simon and Schuster 1998); Mike Gray, *Drug Crazy*

(New York: Random House, 1998); Dan Baum, *Smoke and Mirrors* (Boston: Little Brown, 1996); Richard Lawrence Miller, *Drug Warriors and Their Prey* (Westport, CT: Praeger, 1996); Alfred W. McCoy and Alan A. Block, eds., *War on Drugs* (Boulder, CO: Westview, 1992); Sam Staley, *Drug Policy and the Decline of American Cities* (New Brunswick, NJ: Transaction, 1992). For the massive disproportion between the harmfulness of a substance and the official reaction, see also Lynn Zimmer and John P. Morgan, *Marijuana Myths, Marijuana Facts* (New York: Lindesmith Center, 1997).

[7] Jeffrey Reiman, *The Rich Get Richer and the Poor Get Prison*, 5th ed. (Boston: Allyn and Bacon, 1997).

[8] Arnold S. Trebach, *The Great Drug War* (New York: Macmillan, 1987); Erich Goode, *Between Politics and Reason* (New York: St. Martin's Press, 1997).

[9] Sheryl Gay Stolberg, "President Decides against Financing Needle Programs," *NYT*, April 21, 1998.

[10] Neil A. Lewis, "Reno Lifts Barrier to Oregon's Law on Aided Suicide," *NYT*, June 6, 1998.

[11] These products include "Sudafed, Cenafed, Chlor-Trimeton Non-Drowsy Decongestant, Drixoral Non-Drowsy Formula, Efidac/24 and PediaCare Infants' Oral Decongestant Drops": Richard Winton and Nicholas Riccardi, "Meth War Hits Close to Home—at Local Pharmacy," *LAT*, January 31, 1998.

[12] Aldous Huxley, *The Doors of Perception* (London: Penguin, 1959), 53; Siegel is quoted in M. M. Kirsch, *Designer Drugs* (Minneapolis: CompCare Publications, 1986), 96.

Section

II

Linking Drugs and Crime

4

The Drugs-Crime Relationship
An Analytical Framework

Duane C. McBride
Clyde B. McCoy

The relationship between drug using and criminal behavior has been a primary concern of researchers, policymakers and the general public for most of this century (see McBride & McCoy, 1982). Both the scientific and popular media have tended to view the existence of the drugs-crime relationship as the basis of the public concern about drug use, as well as of national and international drug policy and the current infrastructure of drug law enforcement, treatment, and research. Although in the public mind, the relationship between drugs and crime is often seen as fairly straightforward—with drug use being viewed as directly causing criminal behavior—critical research analysis has indicated that the relationship is conceptually and empirically quite complex. Given this, it is the purpose of this article to suggest an organizational paradigm for examining the literature on the drugs-crime relationship, to use that paradigm to review relevant literature, and to examine the policy implications of recent research on the drugs-crime relationship.

An Organizational Paradigm
Although the phrase "drugs-crime relationship" is commonly used, it often masks the variety of substances that are included under the concept of *drugs*, and the specific types of violations of the criminal law that are encompassed by the

term *crime*. In addition, the phrase does not elucidate issues of the etiology of the relationship. It might be helpful if an analysis of the relationship between drug using and criminal behavior were organized within the following framework:

1. the historical underpinnings of current perspectives
2. types of drugs and types of criminal behavior
3. the statistical relationship: the extent and type of criminal behavior among various types of drug users and the extent and type of drug use among various types of criminals
4. the etiological nature of the relationship, including such issues as causality and interaction
5. theoretical interpretations of the relationship
6. the policy implications of research conclusions

Historical Underpinnings of Current Perspectives

THE 19TH-CENTURY NATIONAL DRUG CULTURE

During the late 19th century, American society had a fairly laissez faire attitude toward what were called "patent medicines." These medicines, often containing opium, were touted as cure-alls for whatever ailed a person, from general aches and pains to sexual dysfunctions. They were available through a variety of means, including private physicians, the Sears catalog, and the traveling medicine show. The claims of one patent medicine, Hamlin's Wizard Oil, well illustrate the exaggerated assertions. The advertisement for the Hamlin product claimed that "there is no sore it will not heal, no pain it will not subdue." The oil was "Pleasant to take and magical in its effects" (Inciardi, 1992, p. 4). The makers and distributors of patent medicines were effective entrepreneurs organizing themselves as the Proprietary Medicine Manufacturers Association in 1881. For over two decades they successfully prevented any attempt to limit their enterprise. They effectively marketed their products in most of the mass and professional media and catalogs of the era. The development of the hypodermic needle in the middle of the 19th century and advances in chemistry resulted in the development of more potent drugs that could be delivered in the most efficacious manner. As David Musto (1973) observed, "Opiates and cocaine became popular—if unrecognized—items in the everyday life of Americans" (p. 3). Although exact figures on the consumption of opium during this time period are not available, the U.S. Public Health Service estimated that between 1859 and 1899, 7,000 tons of crude opium and 800 tons of smoking opium were imported in the United States (Kolb & Du Mez, 1924).

The turn of the century seemed to initiate a broad-based social reform movement in a wide variety of areas of American culture. The developing American Medical Association (AMA) began questioning the effectiveness claims of the patent medicines. As a result of the failure to scientifically verify the claims, the AMA removed advertisements for patent medicines from their journals. By this means, the professional physicians began to disassociate themselves from the medicine show. Perhaps as a result of these professional critiques of patent medicines, journalists also began to focus on the industry. One of the most noted series of articles was in the national weekly magazine *Collier's*. For about a four-month period during 1905 and 1906, a *Collier's* reporter, Samuel Adams, chronicled the fraudulent claims of the patent medicine sellers, the toxic ingredients they contained (often high dosages of opium and cocaine), and the consequences of their use. Adams claimed that the use of these medicines made criminals of young men and harlots of young women (see Young, 1967, p. 31).

Although the *Collier's* articles on the patent medicine industry did cause a great deal of discussion in the popular press, it was the impact of Upton Sinclair's *The Jungle* on legal policy that most affected the patent medicine industry. As a result of the documented filthy conditions in the American meat-packing industry, Congress passed the Pure Food and Drug Act in 1906. Although this act did not outlaw patent medicines, it did require that the ingredients and their proportions be listed on each bottle. This, coupled with persistent media focus on the horrors of opium and other drug use, appeared to prepare the public and the Congress for further restrictions on the industry. Within the next few years, many states severely restricted the distribution of narcotics through physicians and pharmacists or over the counter (see Musto, 1973, p. 18). The distribution was further restricted by the Harrison Act of 1914. In spite of what is popularly thought, this act did not make the manufacture, distribution, or use of opium, cocaine, or marijuana illegal. What it did was require that individuals and companies that manufactured or distributed these substances register with the Treasury Department and pay special taxes. The Treasury Department's interpretation of the Harrison Act and subsequent Supreme Court decisions served to make a wide variety of narcotics and other drugs illegal to manufacture, distribute, or even prescribe.

PERCEPTIONS OF DRUGS AND CRIME IN THE EARLY 20TH CENTURY

Some critics have argued that the Harrison Act turned law-abiding users of patent medicines into criminals (King, 1974). Although this is probably an oversimplification, the Harrison Act did culminate and strongly support a popular social reform movement that increasingly defined drug use as criminal and often the cause of violent, bizarre behavior.

The medical literature of the early 20th century, by contrast, viewed the opiate user as lethargic and less likely to engage in violent crime. Whatever criminal behavior resulted from drug use was seen as occurring to obtain money to buy drugs. Shoplifting and other forms of petty theft were seen as the primary types of criminal behavior. Many observers noted that debauchery, laziness, and prostitution were the primary deviant behavioral consequences of opiate use—not violent predatory crime (see Kolb, 1925; Lichtenstein, 1914; Terry & Pellens, 1928). Overall, the medical and psychiatric literature of the early 20th century viewed opiate use as debilitating and a cause of petty property crimes or prostitution, but not as a cause of violent crime.

Some medical practitioners did consider cocaine to be different from opiates in its behavioral consequences (Kolb, 1925). Kolb's observation was that cocaine tended to make individuals more paranoid and that consequently, a cocaine user might strike out violently at an imagined pursuer. Although cocaine was used in many patent medicines and was included in the Harrison Act, the official government position seemed to conclude that cocaine use, although potentially a cause of crime, was relatively small and therefore of insignificant consequence (U.S. Treasury Department, 1939).

Although the medical literature did not see opiate use as a prime cause of violent street crime or crime in general, there were many popular lecturers who did. Perhaps the most prolific and popular antinarcotic lecturer was Richmond P. Hobson. He founded a number of anti-narcotics-use organizations and both published and lectured extensively on the violent crimogenic nature of narcotics use. Throughout the 1920s, Mr. Hobson argued that most property and violent crimes were committed by heroin and other types of drug addicts. He further argued that the continuity of civilization itself depended on the elimination of narcotics use (Hobson, 1928). With his frequent radio broadcasts, he played a significant role in creating a national perception of the direct link between all types of drug use and all types of crime.

Somewhat surprisingly, the primary drugs-crime connection portrayed in popular and government media involved marijuana use. On July 6, 1927, the *New York Times* reported that a family in Mexico City had become hopelessly insane by eating marijuana leaves. The epitome of the marijuana-causes-crime perspective was probably the Hollywood production of the film, *Reefer Madness*. This film was strongly influenced by the Commissioner of the Treasury Department's Bureau of Narcotics, Harry J. Anslinger. *Reefer Madness* portrayed marijuana as the great destroyer of American youth. Marijuana, it was shown in the film, not only caused young people to become sexually promiscuous but also violently criminal and prone to suicide. Marijuana was viewed as the most dangerous substance in America and one that, unless stopped, would lead to the violent downfall of Western civilization. It was not only in the movies that marijuana was portrayed as causing violence. Anslinger and his colleagues at the Bureau of Narcotics published a number of books focusing on the direct violent criminal behavior caused by narcotics, particularly by marijuana use, and on the involvement of criminal gangs in the distribution of illegal drugs (Anslinger & Oursler, 1961; Anslinger & Tompkins, 1953). In all of his work, Anslinger listed cannabis as a narcotic and always described its consequences as the most violent and dangerous. For example, in *The Murderers*, he claimed that "All varieties (of Cannabis) may lead to acts of violence, extremes, madness, homicide" (p. 304). In this book, Anslinger provided many examples of the criminal horrors committed by those who had smoked even one reefer. The most gruesome illustration was the case of a seventeen-month-old white female raped and murdered by a cotton picker who had smoked one marijuana cigarette (Anslinger & Tompkins, 1953, p. 24). The popular book entitled *Dope* argued that "when you have once chosen marijuana, you have selected murder and torture and hideous cruelty to your bosom friends" (Black, 1928, p. 28). Popular periodicals such as *American Magazine* also told in lurid detail about ax-murdering marijuana-intoxicated youths on rampages (Sloman, 1979, p. 63).

A crucial implicit and often explicit aspect of the portrayal of the relationship between drugs and crime was the strong antiforeign feelings and racism of the 1920s and 1930s. Many of the horror stories that focused on the violence and degradation of narcotics users centered on African Americans, Mexicans, and Chinese. All of the illegal drugs were portrayed as foreign imports brought in by dark- or yellow-skinned outsiders wanting to corrupt white youth, seduce white women, and/or overthrow Northern European ascendancy. The drugs-crime relationship was thus an important asset of a popular racial and national isolationist perspective (see Inciardi, 1992; Musto, 1973).

During the 1930s and 1940s, and even into the 1950s, the American government and the popular media seemed to work closely in continuing to create the image of the "dope fiend" as a violent, out-of-control sexual predator who accounted for a large proportion of America's heinous crimes. By the late 1950s, this image had been strongly challenged by a wide variety of academic and other critics. However, these formative images of the bizarre, violent dope fiend continue to provide at least a background schemata that affects cultural perceptions of the drugs-crime relationship.

The Intersection of Typologies

Although the historical and current discussions of the drugs-crime relationship often assume a particular intersection between specific types of drugs and specific types of crime, that intersection is generally not explicit or examined in a logical, sequential manner. As McGlothlin (1979) noted, if the drugs-crime relationship is to be examined logically, it is important to use typologies of both types of behaviors and proceed to review how each type of drug use relates to each type of crime. Drug abuse and crime are complex issues that include a multitude of specific behaviors.

Types of Drugs

At the turn of the century almost all drugs were called narcotics—including opium, marijuana, and cocaine. However, as is apparent, each of these substances has a very different chemical structure and a different psychopharmacological effect. Thus each potentially has a very different relationship to various types of criminal behavior. During the 1960s and 1970s, the term *drug abuse* primarily seemed to mean heroin use and, to a lesser extent, LSD use. Today, the term probably conjures up images of cocaine use. Regardless of what specific drug the term may be most associated with, an analysis of the drugs-crime relationship must conceptually use the major specific categories of drugs.

Generally, it has been recognized that the various types of illegal drugs have different possible relationships to criminal behavior, based on their chemical structure, subculture of use, cost, or differential patterns of control. Over the last decade, major national surveys on illegal drug use have tended to develop a list of drug types that are routinely included in questionnaires (for example, see Clayton et al., 1988; Johnston, O'Malley, & Bachman, 1993; Liska, 1990). These are

1. narcotic analgesics: including heroin, Demoral, Percodan, and Dilaudid
2. stimulants: including cocaine in all of its forms and amphetamines
3. hallucinogens: for example, LSD, PCP and MDA
4. inhalants: including gasoline, paint thinner, glue, other volatile hydrocarbons and amyl/butyl nitrites
5. sedatives: for example, barbiturates and methaqualone
6. major and minor tranquilizers
7. marijuana (although the effects of this drug combine some aspects of sedatives, tranquilizers, and hallucinogens, it is usually placed in its own separate classification)
8. steroids and other types of hormonal substances designed to build muscle or increase aggressiveness.

In some research projects, these categories might need to be expanded to include more specific drugs within each category. However, these are the general categories used in drug research.

Types of Crime

Types of criminal behavior also need to be constructed in drugs-crime research and conceptual understandings. For the last two decades, researchers have explicitly argued that drugs-crime research needs to work within common parameter definitions of categories of criminal behavior (see Inciardi & McBride, 1976). Traditionally, criminologists have had a major focus on the construction of criminal behavior typologies. The aim has been to construct mutually exclusive homogeneous categories (see Hood & Sparks, 1970). Typically, typological constructions in criminology have been based on legal categories, such as the Uniform Crime Reports (UCR) (1993), the public's perception of the severity ranking of specific criminal behaviors (Rossi, Waite, Bose, & Berk, 1974), the social psychology and behavioral characteristics of offenders (Duncan, Ohlin, Reis, & Stanton, 1953), or combinations of all of the preceding (Clinard & Quinney, 1967). Recent criminology and criminal justice texts have tended to use the categorization of the UCR, which includes a sense of public and official views of seriousness plus elements of social psychological characteristics (see Inciardi, 1993). The following categories of crimes are commonly used in criminal justice research:

1. crime against persons: including homicide, manslaughter, rape of all types, aggravated assault, assault and battery, and child molestation

2. armed robbery

3. property crimes: including breaking and entering; larceny; auto theft; arson; forgery; counterfeiting; passing worthless checks; buying, concealing, and receiving stolen property; vandalism

4. income-producing victimless crimes: including prostitution, commercialized vice, and gambling

5. violation of drug laws: including the possession or sale of dangerous drugs or the implements for their use

6. other offenses: for example, disorderly conduct, vagrancy, loitering, and resisting arrest.

Sequentially examining each of the specific intersections between each type of drug and each type of crime could help build a systematic body of knowledge about the totality of the drugs-crime relationship.

The Statistical Overlap

Historically, and currently, one of the major arguments for the existence of a drugs-crime relationship is the high level of drug use among populations of criminals and the frequent involvement in criminal activities of street-drug users. About 40 years ago Anslinger and Tompkins (1953), as a part of their argument that drug use was a component of a criminal culture, claimed that a large proportion of federal prisoners were users of illegal drugs. During the late 1960s and early 1970s, many epidemiologists, and certainly the popular culture, believed that the United States was undergoing a drug epidemic. The evidence for the epidemic was large increases in drug overdosages, drug-related arrests and drug treatment admissions (see O'Donnell, Voss, Clayton, Slatin, & Room, 1976). One of the major perceived consequences of increased drug use was the perception of an associated increase in street crime. This apparent epidemic stimulated the development or reinvigoration of a vast drug treatment, enforcement, and research endeavor culminating in the establishment of the National Institute on Drug Abuse (NIDA) in 1974. In 1971, during an address to Congress on June 17, President Richard M. Nixon called the drug epidemic a national emergency. The Federal Strategy Report of 1975 noted that the crime associated with drug use was a major reason for the national attention focused on drug abuse in that era.

DRUG USE IN POPULATIONS OF CRIMINALS

One of the tasks of the newly created NIDA and the National Institute of Justice was a series of studies and symposiums on the drugs-crime relationship (see Inciardi & McBride, 1976; Gandossy, Williams, Cohen, & Harwood, 1980). As these study groups documented, many research projects conducted in a variety of urban areas during the early 1970s found that somewhere between 15 percent and 40 percent of arrestees and prisoners were users of illegal drugs—mostly marijuana and heroin (see Eckerman, Bates, Rachal, & Poole, 1971; Ford, Hauser, & Jackson, 1975; McBride, 1976). These findings were seen, at the time, as dramatic evidence of the existence of the drug/ crime connection and the need to integrate the criminal justice system with the drug treatment system. One of the outcomes of these types of studies was the establishment of the Treatment Alternatives to Street Crime (TASC) program, which attempted to identify drug users in populations of offenders, assess their treatment needs, and refer them to appropriate treatment facilities (see Inciardi & McBride, 1991).

Recent research has shown an even more extensive use of drugs in a variety of criminally involved populations. In a study of nonincarcerated delinquents in Miami, Florida, Inciardi, Horowitz, and Pottieger (1993) found that some three-fourths of male and female delinquents used cocaine at least weekly. Further, the Drug Use Forecasting (DUF) program collects and analyzes urine from arrestees in 24 major cities across the United States. In most, over 60 percent of the male and female arrestees are positive for illegal drugs. The lowest rates for males were in Omaha and San Antonio, where only 48 percent were positive for an illegal drug. The lowest rate for females was 47 percent in New Orleans. The highest for females was 81 percent in Manhattan, and the highest rate for males was 80 percent in Philadelphia. In almost all of the cities in the study, cocaine was the most common drug found through urinalysis, followed by marijuana and opiates (see DUF, 1993; Wish, 1987).

Surveys of incarcerated populations show a similarly high rate of illegal drug use just prior to incarceration. In 1990, for example, the Bureau of Justice Statistics found that over 40 percent of state prison inmates reported the daily use of illegal drugs in the month prior to the offense that resulted in their incarceration. A comparison of these data to that of criminally involved populations in the 1970s shows a much higher rate of illegal drug use in the current criminal justice population and a dramatic shift from heroin and marijuana to primarily cocaine and marijuana. These data also suggest a virtual saturation of the criminal justice system by illegal drug users who mostly consume cocaine in some form.

There is also a body of research that indicates a high level of drug use among incarcerated individuals. In a study of Delaware prison inmates, Inciardi, Lockwood, and Quinlan (1993) found that 60 percent of the respondents reported the use of drugs, mostly marijuana, while in prison. However, urinalysis found only about a 1 percent positivity rate. A random sample of urine collected in Wisconsin discovered a rate of 25 percent positive, mostly marijuana (Vigdal & Stadler, 1989). There is also some ethnographic evidence that drugs are integrated in the prison culture as a part of control, management, and reward systems (see Hawkins & Alpert, 1989; Inciardi, Horowitz, & Pottieger, 1993). Although there is no evidence that drug use is rampant in jails and prisons, the high use rates in the population prior to incarceration as well as the level of continuing use while in prison have stimulated the development of drug treatment services in prisons throughout the United States (Hayes & Schimmel, 1993).

CRIMINAL BEHAVIOR IN POPULATIONS OF DRUG USERS

Examinations of drug-using populations for the last few decades have found similarly high rates of criminal behavior. Surveys of populations of illegal drug users in the late 1960s and early 1970s generally found that a large majority had extensive criminal histories (see Defleur, Ball, & Snarr, 1969; Voss & Stephens, 1973). Recent local and national research has confirmed these early findings. In a population of over 400 street-injection-drug users in Miami, Florida, for example, McBride and Inciardi (1990) found that over 80 percent had been in jail in the last 5 years and about 45 percent had been incarcerated within the last 6 months. An analysis of over 25,000 street-injection-drug users from 63 cities found that some two-thirds were in jail in the last 5 years, with over one-third currently on probation or parole or awaiting trial (Inciardi, McBride, Platt, & Baxter, 1993). Consistently, examinations of populations of nonincarcerated drug users clearly show a high level of current involvement with criminal behavior and with the criminal justice system.

THE STATISTICAL OVERLAP IN THE GENERAL POPULATION

General-population surveys also show the overlap between drug using and criminal behaviors. In 1991, the National Household Survey of drug use conducted by the NIDA included questions on criminal behavior. Analysis of that data showed a correlation between drug use and engaging in criminal, particularly violent, behavior. Less than 5 percent of those who drank alcohol only or who consumed no substance engaged in a violent or property crime during the last year. About 25 percent of those who had used marijuana and cocaine in addition to alcohol admitted to the commission of a violent and/or property crime in the last year (Harrison & Gfroerer, 1992).

Analyses of data from the National Youth Survey also show a strong correlation between serious drug use and serious delinquent behavior. The National Youth Survey is a longitudinal study initiated in the late 1970s and was designed to survey a variety of behaviors, including substance use and crime (see Huizinga, 1978, for a description of the survey and its methodology). In an analysis of these data, Johnson, Wish, Schmeidler, and Huizinga (1993) found that only 3 percent of nondelinquents used cocaine, whereas 23 percent of those with multiple delinquency index crimes were current cocaine users. Examining the data from the perspective of drug-using behavior, they found that only 2 percent of those who used alcohol only had multiple index offenses compared to 28 percent of the cocaine users. Overall, these researchers found a correlation of .53 between the delinquency and drug use scales.

Although the complexity and causal nature of the drugs-crime relationship is open to considerable debate, there is little contention about the statistical correlation between drug use and crime. For a number of decades, the existence of the empirical relationship has been documented by researchers as well as by criminal justice practitioners and drug treatment professionals. The size of the relationship between using drugs and criminal behavior is a daily reality in criminal justice systems and drug treatment programs throughout the United States. This reality has stimulated a wide variety of critical thinking and research projects designed to sort out the nature of the drugs-crime relationship and policies that could be used to reduce the extent of the relationship.

The Etiological, Nature of the Drugs-Crime Relationship

WHICH CAME FIRST?

The issue of behavioral and causal priority in the drugs-crime relationship has been a primary research focus of numerous investigators. For the past 20 years, researchers have consistently found that individuals who frequently use illegal drugs such as cocaine, heroin, or marijuana have engaged in criminal behavior prior to or concurrent with the initiation of any stable illegal drug use pattern (see Anglin & Speckart, 1988; Huizinga, Menard, & Elliot, 1989; Inciardi, Lockwood, & Quinlan, 1993; O'Donnell et al., 1976; Stephens & McBride, 1976). Rather than innocents seduced or propelled into criminal activity by their drug use, existing data and research indicate that drug abuse and criminal activity are a part of a broader set of integrated deviant behaviors involving crime, drug use, and, often, high-risk sex. Although a variety of empirical data indicate that drug use does not appear to initiate a criminal career, a large volume of research clearly indicates that frequency of drug use has a strong impact on the extent, direction, and duration of that career.

THE IMPACT OF DRUG USE ON FREQUENCY OF CRIMINAL BEHAVIOR

A wide body of research indicates that although criminal behavior may be initiated prior to or concomitant with the genesis of illegal drug use, once illegal drug use is initiated it has a dramatic effect on the amount of criminal activity (Anglin & Hser, 1987; Anglin & Speckart, 1988; Ball, Rosen, Flueck, & Nurco, 1981; Chambers, Cuskey, & Moffett, 1970; Chaiken & Chaiken, 1990; Stephens & McBride, 1976). Particularly the work of Ball and his colleagues (1981), using longitudinal data, and Anglin and his colleagues (Anglin & Hser, 1987; Anglin & Speckart, 1988), using a life history method, clearly indicate the effect of narcotics use on rates of criminal behavior. These researchers found sharp decreases in criminal activity during periods of abstinence from heroin and large increases in criminal activity during periods of increased heroin use (see Anglin & Speckart, 1988; Ball et al., 1981; Ball, Shaffer, & Nurco, 1983).

The expense of cocaine and heroin use and the fact that most frequent users of these drugs are unemployed result in a high level of criminal activity in user populations. Inciardi, McBride, McCoy, and Chitwood describe what they call an amazing amount of criminal activity involving over 100,000 criminal acts (excluding drug law violations) committed by some 700 cocaine users in the 90 days prior to being interviewed. Johnson and his colleagues (1985) reported that over 40 percent of the total income of a population of street-drug users was generated from illegal activity. Using a variety of methodologies, including life histories, surveys, and longitudinal data, the existing research literature suggests that the frequent use of illegal drugs is clearly a part of the motivation for an increase in criminal activities that are designed to obtain funds for drugs or as a part of other activities designed to access, possess, and use drugs. In addition, the available data suggest that, rather than a simple linear relationship between drugs and crime, both may emerge at a similar time period and that the two behaviors may have a recursive element to their relationship. That is, drug use may be involved in increasing criminal behavior, but the initiation of criminal behavior may also result in subcultural participation and individual-risk decision making that involves taking high-risk drugs (see Clayton & Tuchfeld, 1982).

THE IMPACT OF DRUG USE ON SUSTAINED CRIMINAL BEHAVIOR

There is some evidence that frequent hard-drug use may be involved with a sustained criminal career. Longitudinal research indicates that most delinquents cease their illegal activity by late adolescence or early adulthood (e.g., see Kandel, Simcha-Fagan, & Davies, 1986). Traditionally, getting a steady job, getting married, and having children was viewed as a sign of maturation and as increasing an individual's stake in conformity and therefore decreasing rates of illegal behavior. The UCR indicates a sharp drop in arrest rates for populations over 25 years of age. A wide variety of research data indicates that frequent drug use may severely interfere with that maturation process and consequent reduction in crime. National (Elliott & Huizinga, 1985) and local studies (Dembo et al., 1987) have indicated that chronic serious delinquent offenders are more likely to become involved with hard-drug use, which, in turn, relates to continued participation in a criminal subculture and high rates of criminal behavior. Life history research (Faupel & Klockars, 1987) also documents the recursive relationship of using drugs and criminal behavior.

The recursive nature of the drugs-crime relationship appears to act to reinforce continued drug use and crime. Ethnographers have described this as "taking care of business" (Hanson, Beschner, Walters, & Bovelle, 1985). Essentially, the argument is that the subcultural values that emerge in street-drug-using cultures encompass crime as a means to obtain drugs and as a cultural value itself in opposition to the straight world of legitimate low-paying jobs. Using drugs and criminal behavior become well integrated within the cultural/social role of the street-drug user (see Stephens, 1991). From this perspective, drug use does not directly cause crime, but, rather, is an integral part of the street-drug subculture. To focus only on drug-using behavior as a primary means to reduce crime misses the intertwined complexity of the drugs-crime relationship.

DRUG USE AND TYPE OF CRIME

Probably as a result of images created by decades of government and media messages about the violent dope fiend, the public has been concerned about the types of crime in which drug users engage. The particular concern has been that the use of many types of drugs causes extreme violence. As noted earlier in this article, many years ago, Kolb (1925) argued against the prevailing popular view of the crazed dope fiend. From a psychopharmacological perspective, he contended that the biochemical effect of opiate use was to make a user lethargic and less likely to engage in violent crime, at least while under the influence of the drug. This original perspective continued to find empirical support for decades. For example, Finestone (1957) claimed that heroin users were much more likely to engage in petty property crime to support their vice than in noneconomically productive violent crime. In fact, he observed that as street groups initiated and increased heroin use, the rate of violent crime decreased and their rate of property crime increased. These types of research findings continued through most of the next two decades. Basically, heroin users were found to be overrepresented among property criminals and underrepresented among those charged with crimes of violence (see Inciardi & Chambers, 1972; Kozel & DuPont, 1977; McBride, 1976).

In the late 1970s, researchers began to report an increase in violence in the street-heroin-using subculture, particularly among younger cohorts of users (Stephens & Ellis, 1975; Zahn & Bencivengo, 1974). During the 1980s, epidemiological data indicated a rapid increase in cocaine use. As has been noted, DUF (1993) data indicate a virtual saturation of cocaine use in arrested populations. This rapid rise in cocaine use and in rates of violent behavior has stimulated a variety of speculation and research about the impact of cocaine on criminal behavior and on the world of the street-drug user. For most of the last decade, researchers have been reporting that increased cocaine use was related to violent confrontational crime for men and women (Datesman, 1981; Goldstein, 1989; Simonds & Kashani, 1980; Spunt, Goldstein, Bellucci, & Miller, 1990). Research has also indicated that cocaine use may be related not only to being a violent offender but also to being a victim of violent crime. McBride, Burgman-Habermehl, Alpert, and Chitwood (1986), in an analysis of homicides in Miami, Florida, found that after alcohol, cocaine was the most common drug found in the bodies of homicide victims. Almost 10 percent of homicide victims had cocaine in their bodies at the time of death. This was more than 8 times the rate of any other illegal drug. Goldstein, Bellucci, Spunt, and Miller (1993), in a study in New York City, found that increased cocaine use was associated with being a victim of violent crime for women.

Paul Goldstein (1989) has proposed a very useable framework for interpreting the relationship between drugs and violence that seems particularly appropriate to interpreting the relationship between cocaine and violence. He calls this paradigm "a tripartite scheme." Goldstein sees this scheme as involving psychopharmacological, economically compulsive, and systemic aspects. Essentially, a part of the violent behavior of cocaine users may relate to the psychopharmacological consequences of cocaine use. This effect includes a strong stimulant impact, long periods without sleep, and increased paranoia. All of these effects could result in an increased willingness on the part of those using cocaine (and other stimulants, such as amphetamines) to engage in aggressive behavior or to put themselves into situations where aggressive behavior is more likely to occur. The economic demands involve the cost of heavy cocaine or crack use that may result in violent predatory behavior designed to obtain the most money. The systemic aspect of the model involves violent subcultural behavior patterns that are integral to being a street-drug user and those violent behavior patterns that are a part of the street distribution of cocaine. Other researchers (McBride & Swartz, 1990) have suggested that the drugs-violence and cocaine-violence relationship is also occurring within the framework of a rapid increase of heavy armaments in general society. That is, our whole society has undergone an increase in the availability and distribution of powerful automatic weapons. This general availability of weapons has also become a part of the street-drug-using culture. Rather than drug use being a direct cause of violence, it might be important to recognize that the drug culture has adapted the weaponry of the general culture and has used it for its own purposes. Regardless of the exact nature of the relationship, the existing data suggest that, increasingly, drug use, particularly cocaine, has become integrated with a high level of international, national, and local street violence. The extent of cocaine use among felony offenders and the perceived relationship between cocaine and violence has played a major role in the reinvigoration of the debate about national drug policy and the issue of the decriminalization of drug use.

Some Theoretical Perspectives on the Drugs-Crime Relationship

From every conceivable methodological perspective, data consistently show that there is a strong correlation between drug use and criminal behavior and that increases in drug use are related to increases in crime. However, the theoretical analysis of the relationship has not been as extensive. Some perspectives argue that the interpretation of the empirical relationship might be very different from what the data initially suggest.

SUBCULTURAL, ROLE THEORY, AND ECOLOGICAL PERSPECTIVES

Ethnographic and role theory analyses have tended to view the crime and drug relationship as associated with subcultural roles that include what general society would call extreme deviant behavior (Hanson et al., 1985; Stephens, 1991). High frequencies of drug use, high rates of crime, and extensive high-risk sexual behavior are seen from this perspective as "taking care of business" or an integral part of the social role of the street-drug user. This type of conceptual analysis suggests that the drugs/crime relationship may not be directly linear in cause, but, rather, drug use and crime exist as a part of an intertwined mutually reinforcing subculturally contexted set of behaviors.

Ecological theoretical analysis has suggested that the drugs-crime relationship appears to be related because both types of behavior are caused by similar environmental conditions, such as poverty and lack of social control and economic opportunity. In that sense, some observers have concluded that drug use is spuriously related to crime. That is, there is the appearance of a statistical causal relationship, but that relationship may be an artifact of common etiology (Fagan, Weis, & Cheng, 1990; McBride & McCoy, 1981). Drugs and crime occur together because they share a similar set of causal variables and they are a part of the same subcultural value and role system. From these ecological and subcultural theoretical perspectives, the drugs-crime relationship is not so much affected by attempts to stop or reduce drug use but, rather, by attempts to address the common underlying initiating and sustaining causes of both behaviors.

A RADICAL INTERPRETATION OF THE DRUGS-CRIME RELATIONSHIP

Another major theoretical critique of the apparent drugs-crime relationship comes from radical theory. This perspective maintains that the drugs-crime relationship is an artifact of legal policy since 1914. From this viewpoint, the existence of a drugs-crime relationship simply resulted from laws that effectively criminalized a variety of drug-using behaviors. As the result of the Harrison Act and subsequent law, American society created a criminal subculture where none existed; drove up the cost of drugs, thereby providing an economic motivation for drug-related crime; and left the distribution of drugs to organized criminal networks. These, in turn, grew immensely wealthy and powerful through the distribution of the much-in-demand and now-expensive illegal drugs. The current violence, corruption, and civil rights issues associated with drug use and drug law enforcement are seen, from this perspective, as the inevitable result of the social construction of deviance. Radical theorists argue that the drugs-crime relationship can best be disentangled by decriminalizing drugs and treating drug abuse and addiction as mental and public health problems that are best addressed through psychological counseling and social work case management. The drug policy of the Netherlands is often advocated as an example of an enlightened, less criminogenic strategy (see Lindesmith, 1965; Nadelmann, 1989; Trebach & Inciardi, 1993).

There is considerable evidence that much of the crime committed by drug users involves only violations of drug laws involving possession and distribution of illegal drugs. For example, Inciardi et al. found that during the 90 days prior to being interviewed, their sample of some 700 cocaine users had committed over 1.7 million criminal acts with well over 95 percent of them involving violations of drug laws. Further evidence exists in examinations of the current operation of drug courts. Originally, these courts were designed to focus on the increasing number of drug-involved cases coming before the court.

However, these courts may be increasing the focus on drug users who are involved only in drug law violations and not implicated in other types of crime and thereby furthering the appearance of a relationship between drug use and crime, particularly among African Americans in the inner city (Klofas, 1993).

The radical perspective does provide a valuable insight into how society may create by law that which it is attempting to avoid by law, and there may be some applicability to the interpretation of the drugs-crime relationship. The perspective is, however, often built on the notion that somehow the relationship between drug use and crime would virtually disappear if drugs were just decriminalized, that there would be no or minimal increase in drug use, and that any increase would have virtually no impact on violence or crime. Such a view would seem to ignore psychopharmacological aspects of the relationship, the fact that criminal behavior generally precedes drug use, and the findings that both behaviors arise from similar etiological variables and act in a mutually reinforcing manner.

In a recent analysis of the drugs-crime relationship in Amsterdam by Grapendaal, Leuw, and Nelen (1992), it was shown that 53 percent of a sample of 148 polydrug users engaged in acquisitive crime during an average month, and those 79 individuals netted almost $66,000 per month from their property crimes to buy drugs. Further, it was found that property crime accounted for 24 percent of total income in the sample. This was the second highest percentage of total income after welfare payments. During 1991, the city of Zurich, Switzerland experimented with the decriminalization of drugs and experienced an increase in property and violent crimes. Public pressure forced a reversal of Swiss policy (see the *New York Times*, February 11, 1992, A10). Although, as Grapendaal and his colleagues (1992) noted, the extent of drug-related crime in the Netherlands may not be as extensive as in New York or other American cities, there is a significant relationship even in a highly tolerant city. These researchers also noted that the policy of tolerance has created a permanent underclass whose crime may only be lessened by a generous welfare system but not eliminated. Just as the perspective arguing that drug use seduced innocent youth into a life of crime has been shown to be simplistic, so the perspective that drug laws throw otherwise peaceful citizens into a life of criminal violence that can be eliminated if drugs are just decriminalized may also be more simplistic than is warranted by the facts (for perspectives against decriminalization see Inciardi & McBride, 1989; Wilson, 1993).

Policy Implications of the Drugs-Crime Data

Although the drugs-crime data and conceptual understandings may be complex and even contradictory, there appear to be three major common implications from current knowledge.

    1. There is a strong need for treatment services for drug-using, criminally involved populations. This would include both those who are incarcerated as well as those on probation or in a diversion program. Regardless of

the complexity of the data, there is a clear indication that levels of drug use relate to levels of criminal activity. Reducing drug demand through treatment has a strong possibility for reducing levels of crime. Increasing treatment resources at all levels of the criminal justice system to eliminate waiting lists, as well as increasing recruitment outreach in criminal populations, has a significant potential to reduce the level of crime in a community.

2. The ecological and subcultural perspectives remind our society that the drugs-crime relationship is at least in part the result of a history of differential social, political, and economic opportunity. The development of oppositional subcultures in which drug use and crime are an integrated part will be addressed only by major efforts to provide educational and economic development opportunities. Social and economic progress in communities with high rates of drug use and crime must be a local and national priority.

3. The radical perspective reminds us that in any application of drug policy, civil rights must be protected, that there are severe limits to the effectiveness of law enforcement, and enforcement practices can increase the appearance of the drugs-crime relationship well beyond the framework of psychopharmacology, economic demand, and subcultural roles. Drug laws and policy should focus on demand reduction at least equal to supply reduction. Drug law enforcement must never be an excuse for a retreat on hard-won legal and civil rights, and drug law and policy must rest on a strong public support base.

REFERENCES

Anglin, M. D., & Hser, Y. (1987). Addicted women and crime. *Criminology, 25,* 359–397.

Anglin, M. D., & Speckart, F. (1988). Narcotics use and crime: A multi sample, multi method analysis. *Criminology, 26,* 197–233.

Anslinger, H. J., & Ourlser, W. (1961). *The murderers.* New York: Faar, Straus & Cudahy.

Anslinger, H. J., & Tompkins. W. F. (1953). *The traffic in narcotics.* New York: Funk & Wagnall.

Ball, J. C., Rosen, L., Flueck, J. A., & Nurco, D. N. (1981). The criminality of heroin addicts: When addicted and when off opiates. In J. A. Inciardi (Ed.), *The drugs-crime connection* (pp. 39–65). Beverly Hills: Sage.

Ball, J. C., Shaffer, J. W., & Nurco, D. N. (1983). The day-to-day criminality of heroin addicts in Baltimore: A study in the continuity of offense rates. *Drug and Alcohol Dependence, 12,* 119–142.

Black, W. (1928). *Dope: The story of the living dead.* New York: Star & Co.

Bureau of Justice Statistics. (1990). *Drugs and crime facts. 1989.* Washington, DC: Author.

Chaiken, J. M., & Chaiken, M. R. (1990). Drugs and predatory crime. In M. Tonry & J. Q. Wilson (Eds.), *Drugs and crime* (pp. 203–239). Chicago: University of Chicago Press.

Chambers, C. D., Cuskey, W. R., & Moffett, A. D. (1970). Demographic factors associated with opiate addiction among Mexican Americans. *Public Health Reports, 85,* 523–531.

Clayton, R. R., & Tuchfeld, B. S. (1982). The drug-crime debate: Obstacles to understanding the relationship. *Journal of Drug Issues, 12,* 153–166.

Clayton, R. R., Voss, H. L., Loscuito, L., Martin, S. S., Skinner, W. F., Robbins, C., & Santos, R. L. (1988). *National household survey on drug abuse: Main findings, 1985.* Washington DC: U.S. Department of Health & Human Services.

Clinard, M. B., & Quinney, R. (1967). *Criminal behavior systems.* New York: Rinehart & Winston.

Datesman, S. (1981). Women, crime, and drugs. In J. A. Inciardi (Ed.), *The drugs/crime connection* (pp. 85–104). Beverly Hills: Sage.

Defleur, L. B., Ball, J. C., & Snarr, R. W. (1969). The long-term social correlates of opiate abuse. *Social Problems, 17,* 225–234.

Dembo, R., Washburn, M., Wish, E. D., Yeung, H., Getreu, A., Berry, E., & Blount, W. R. (1987). Heavy marijuana use and crime among youths entering a juvenile detention center. *Journal of Psychoactive Drugs, 19,* 47–56.

Drug use forecasting. (1993, May). Washington, DC: National Institute of Justice.

Duncan, O. D., Ohlin, L. E., Reis A. J., & Stanton, H. E. (1953). Formal devises for making selection decisions. *American Journal of Sociology, 58,* 537–584.

Eckerman, W. C., Bates, J. J. D., Rachal, J. V., & Poole, W. K. (1971). *Drug usage and arrest charges.* Washington, DC: Drug Enforcement Administration.

Elliott, D. S., & Huizinga, D. (1985). The relationship between delinquent behavior and ADM problems. *Proceedings of the Prevention Research Conference on Juvenile Offenders with Serious Drug, Alcohol and Mental Health Problems.* Washington, DC: Alcohol, Drug Abuse and Mental Health Administration, Office of Juvenile Justice and Delinquency.

Fagan, J., Weis, J. G., & Cheng, Y. T. (1990). Delinquency and substance use among inner-city students. *Journal of Drug Issues, 20,* 351–402.

Faupel, C. E., & Klockars, C. B. (1987). Drugs-crime connections: Elaborations from the life histories of hard-core heroin addicts. *Social Problems, 34,* 54–68.

Federal strategy for drug abuse and drug traffic prevention. (1975). Washington, DC: U.S. Government Printing Office.

Finestone, H. (1957). Narcotics and criminality. *Law and Contemporary Problems, 9,* 69–85.

Ford, A., Hauser, H., & Jackson, E. (1975). Use of drugs among persons admitted to a county jail. *Public Health Reports, 90,* 504–508.

Gandossy, R. P., Williams, J. R., Cohen, J., & Harwood, H. J. (1980). *Drugs and crime: A survey and analysis of the literature* (National Institute of Justice). Washington, DC: U.S. Government Printing Office.

Goldstein, P. J. (1989). Drugs and violent crime. In N. A. Wiener & M. E. Wolfgang (Eds.), *Pathways to criminal violence* (pp. 16–48). Newbury Park, CA: Sage.

Goldstein, P. J., Bellucci, P. A., Spunt, B. J., & Miller, T. (1993). Volume of cocaine use and violence: A comparison between men and women. In R. Dembo (Ed.), *Drugs and crime* (pp. 141–177). New York: University Press of America.

Grapendaal, M., Leuw, E., & Nelen, H. (1992, Summer). Drugs and crime in an accommodating social context: The situation in Amsterdam. *Contemporary Drug Problems,* pp. 303–326.

Hanson, B., Beschner, G., Walters, J. M., & Bovelle, E. (1985). *Life with heroin: Voices from the inner city.* Lexington, MA. Lexington Books.

Harrison, L., & Gfroerer, J. (1992). The intersection of drug use and criminal behavior: Results from the national household survey on drug abuse. *Crime & Delinquency, 38,* 422–443.

Hawkins, R., & Alpert, G. P. (1989). *American prison systems: Punishment and justice.* Englewood Cliffs, NJ: Prentice-Hall.

Hayes, T. J., & Schimmel, D. J. (1993). Residential drug abuse treatment in the Federal Bureau of Prisons. *Journal of Drug Issues, 28,* 61–73.

Hobson, R. P. (1928). The struggle of mankind against its deadliest foe. *Narcotic Education, 1,* 51–54.

Hood, R., & Sparks, R. (1970). *Key issues in criminology.* New York: McGraw-Hill.

Huizinga, D. H. (1978). *Sample design of the National Youth Survey.* Boulder, CO: Behavioral Research Institute.

Huizinga, D. H., Menard, S., & Elliot, D. S. (1989). Delinquency and drug use: Temporal and developmental patterns. *Justice Quarterly, 6,* 419–455.

Inciardi, J. A. (1992). *The war on drugs II.* Palo Alto, CA: Mayfield.

———. (1993). *Criminal justice.* Fort Worth, TX: Harcourt Brace Jovanovich.

Inciardi, J. A., & Chambers, C. D. (1972). Unreported criminal involvement of narcotic addicts. *Journal of Drug Issues, 2,* 57–64.

Inciardi, J. A., Horowitz, R., & Pottieger, A. E. (1993). *Street kids, street drugs, street crime.* Belmont, CA: Wadsworth.

Inciardi, J. A., Lockwood, D., & Quinlan, J. A. (1993). Drug use in prison: Patterns, processes, and implications for treatment. *Journal of Drug Issues, 23,* 119–129.

Inciardi, J. A., & McBride, D. C. (1976). Considerations in the definition of criminality for the assessment of the relationship between drug use and crime. In Research Triangle Institute (Ed.), *Crime and drugs* (pp. 123–137). Springfield, VA: National Technical Information Service.

———. (1989). Legalization: A high risk alternative in the war on drugs. *American Behavioral Scientist, 32,* 259–289.

———. (1991). *Treatment alternatives to street crime (TASC): History, experiences. and issues.* Rockville, MD: National Institute on Drug Abuse.

Inciardi, J. A., McBride, D. C., Platt, J. J., & Baxter, S. (1993). Injecting drug users, incarceration, and HIV: Some legal and social service delivery issues. In *The national AIDS demonstration research program.* Westport, CT: Greenwood.

Inciardi, J. A., McBride, D. C., McCoy, H. V., & Chitwood, D. D. Recent research on the crack-cocaine/crime connection. *Studies on crime and crime prevention.*

Johnson, B. D., Goldstein, P. J., Preble, E., Schmeidler, J., Lipton, D. S., & Miller, T. (1985). *Taking care of business: The economics of crime by heroin abusers.* Lexington, MA: Lexington Books.

Johnson, B. D., Wish, E. D., Schmeidler, J., & Huizinga, D. (1993). Concentration of delinquent offending: Serious drug involvement and high delinquency rates. In R. Dembo (Ed.), *Drugs and crime* (pp. 1–25). Lanham, MD: University Press of America.

Johnston, L. D., O'Malley, P. M., & Bachman, J. G. (1993). *Drug use among high school seniors, college students and young adults, 1975–1990* (NIH Publication No. 93–3597). Washington, DC: U.S. Department of Health and Human Services.

Kandel, D. B., Simcha-Fagan, O., & Davies, M. (1986). Risk factors for delinquency and illicit drug use from adolescence to young adulthood. *Journal of Drug Issues, 16,* 67–90.

Klofas, J. M. (1993). Drugs and justice: The impact of drugs on criminal justice in a metropolitan community. *Crime & Delinquency, 39,* 204–224.

Kolb, L. (1925, January). Drug addiction in its relation to crime. *Journal of Mental Hygiene,* pp. 74–89.

Kolb, L., & Du Mez, A. G. (1924, May 23). The prevalence and trend of drug addiction in the United States and factors influencing it. *Public Health Reports.*

Kozel, N. J., & Dupont, R. L. (1977). *Criminal charges and drug use patterns of arrestees in the District of Columbia*. Washington, DC: U.S. Government Printing Office.

King, R. (1974). The American system: Legal sanctions to repress drug abuse. In J. A. Inciardi & C. D. Chambers (Eds.), *Drugs and the criminal justice system* (pp. 17–37). Beverly Hills, CA: Sage.

Lichtenstein, P. M. (1914, November 14). Narcotic addiction. *New York Medical Journal*, pp. 962–966.

Lindesmith, A. R. (1965). *The addict and the law*. Bloomington: Indiana University Press.

Liska, K. (1990). *Drugs and the human body*. New York: Macmillan.

McBride, D. C. (1976). The relationship between type of drug use and arrest charge in an arrested population. In Research Triangle Institute (Ed.), *Drug use and crime* (pp. 409–418). Springfield, VA: National Technical Information Service.

McBride D. C., Burgman-Habermehl, C., Alpert, J., & Chitwood, D. D. (1986). Drugs and homicide. *Bulletin of the New York Academy of Medicine, 62*, 497–508.

McBride, D. C., & Inciardi, J. A. (1990). AIDS and the IV drug user in the criminal justice system. *Journal of Drug Issues, 20*, 267–280.

McBride, D. C., & McCoy, C. B. (1981). Crime and drug using behavior: An areal analysis. *Criminology, 19*, 281–302.

———. (1982). Crime and drugs: The issues and literature. *Journal of Drug Issues, 12*, 137–151.

McBride D. C., & Swartz, J. (1990). Drugs and violence in the age of crack cocaine. In R. A. Weisheit (Ed.), *Drugs, crime and the criminal justice system* (American Academy of Criminal Justice Series, pp. 141–169). Cincinnati, OH: Anderson.

McGlothlin, W. (1979). Drugs and crime. In R. L. DuPont, A. Goldstein, & J. A. O'Donnell (Eds.), *Handbook on drug abuse* (pp. 357–364). Washington, DC: National Institute on Drug Abuse, Office of Drug Abuse Policy.

Musto, D. F. (1973). *The American disease*. New Haven, CT: Yale University Press.

Nadelmann, E. A. (1989, September). Drug prohibition in the United States, costs, consequences, and alternatives. *Science*, pp. 939–947.

O'Donnell, J. A., Voss, H. L., Clayton, R. R., Slatin, G. T., & Room, R. G. W. (1976). *Young men and drugs—A national survey* (National Institute on Drug Abuse Research Monograph 5). Washington, DC: U.S. Government Printing Office.

Rossi, P. H., Waite, E., Bose, C. E., & Berk, R. E. (1974). The seriousness of crimes: Normative structure and individual differences. *American Sociological Review, 31*, 324–337.

Simonds, J. F. & Kashani, J. (1980). Specific drug use and violence in delinquent boys. *American Journal of Drug and Alcohol Abuse, 7*, 305–322.

Sloman, L. (1979). *Reefer madness: A history of marijuana in America*. Indianapolis: Bobbs-Merrill.

Spunt B. J., Goldstein, P. J., Bellucci, P. A., & Miller, T. (1990). Race/ethnic and gender differences in the drugs-violence relationship. *Journal of Psychoactive Drugs, 22*, 293–303.

Stephens, R. C. (1991). *The street addict role*. New York: State University of New York Press.

Stephens, R. C., & Ellis, R. D. (1975). Narcotic addicts and crime: An analysis of recent trends. *Criminology, 12*, 474–488.

Stephens, R. C., & McBride, D. C. (1976). Becoming a street addict. *Human Organization, 35*, 87–93.

Terry, C. E., & Pellens, M. (1928). *The opium problem.* New York: Bureau of Social Hygiene.

Trebach, A. S., & Inciardi, J. A. (1993). *Legalize it? Debating American drug policy.* Washington, DC: American University Press.

U.S. Department of Justice, Federal Bureau of Investigation. (1993). *Uniform crime reports.* Washington, DC: U.S. Government Printing Office.

U.S. Treasury Department, Bureau of Narcotics. (1939). *Traffic in opium and other dangerous drugs.* Washington, DC: U.S. Government Printing Office.

Vigdal, G. L., & Stadler, D. W. (1989, June). Controlling inmate drug use: Cut consumption by reducing demand. *Corrections Today,* pp. 96–97.

Voss, H. L., & Stephens, R. C. (1973). Criminal history of narcotic addicts. *Drug Forum, 2,* 191–202.

Young, J. H. (1967). *The medical messiahs: A social history of health quackery in twentieth-century America.* Princeton, NJ: Princeton University Press.

Wilson, J. Q. (1993). Against the legalization of drugs. In R. Goldberg (Ed.), *Taking sides* (p. 25). Guildford, CT: Dushkin.

Wish, E. D. (1987). *Drug use forecasting: New York 1984–1986.* Washington, DC: U.S. Department of Justice.

Zahn, M. A. & Bencivengo, M. (1974). Violent death: A comparison between drug users and non drug users. *Addictive Diseases, 1,* 293–298.

5

Drugs, Alcohol, and Homicide

Kathleen Auerhahn
Robert Nash Parker

There has been a growing interest in the relationship between drugs, alcohol, and violence during the past decade. In addition to what has been mostly misguided attention in mass media and in political circles to the relationship between illegal drugs and violence, a number of empirical studies have examined the relationship between alcohol, drugs, and homicide. Unfortunately, many of these studies are hindered by the lack of coherent theorizing that has characterized a great deal of the examination of the relationship between alcohol, drugs, and homicide.

Although attempting to understand the ways in which drug and alcohol use may contribute to homicide is a useful endeavor, it is also important to consider the manner in which drugs and alcohol relate to human behavior in general. In pursuit of this understanding, advances have been made in the study of psychological expectancies concerning alcohol's effect on behavior (e.g., Brown, 1993; Grube, Ames, & Delaney, 1994), the relationship between alcohol and cognitive functioning (Pihl, Peterson, & Lau, 1993), the impact of alcohol on aggressive behavior (e.g., Leonard & Taylor, 1983), the developmental effects of early exposure to alcohol and violence among young people (e.g., White, Hansell, & Brick, 1993), and the role of alcohol in the lives of women who have been abused as children and as adults (e.g., Mille & Downs, 1993; Widom & Ames, 1994). Despite this progress, there is still a lack of theoretical analysis of the general links between alcohol and other drug use and the impact of their use on human behavior. This contributes to the failure of researchers to develop a specific understanding of the ways in which drugs and alcohol might relate to homicide and its causes.

In addition to the weakness of theory in this area, most of the published studies in the past decade suffer from one or more problems in their research design. For example, most studies of drugs, alcohol, and homicide suffer from selection bias in that research participants have been selected because they committed homicide (e.g., the empirical tests of Goldstein's approach to be discussed below) or have been a victim of homicide (e.g., Welte & Abel, 1989). Such studies typically show that a significant number of persons used alcohol and other drugs prior to the homicide; this information, however, is not particularly helpful in determining the overall risk of homicide among those who drink alcohol or take drugs. One approach to this problem is to generate a comparison group that allows for statistical controls (for case and control model as applied to the study of violence, see Loftin, McDowall, & Wiersema, 1992). This approach, however, is rarely found in this research literature.

Another flaw common to many studies of the linkages between alcohol, drugs, and homicide is the failure to include other factors that are bound to have some impact on the relationship between these phenomena. Kai Pernanen (1981) has observed that any relationship between alcohol/drugs and homicide is difficult to ascertain because both alcohol/drug consumption and homicide are embedded in a complex web of human behavior (see also Pernanen, 1976, 1991). Other social factors such as poverty, family disruption, and racial and ethnic inequality (to name just a few) may contribute moderate the relationship between alcohol, drugs, and homicide. Thus, there remains a need to control for these and other factors to isolate the unique effects that alcohol and drug use contributes to homicide.

Despite these methodological problems, there have been significant advances in the knowledge of how drug and alcohol use may be related to homicide. This article is therefore devoted to a review and critique of the major research efforts that have contributed to the current level of understanding. In organizing this chapter, we acknowledge that an important contextual difference exists between alcohol and drug use. In large part, the research literature inevitably has dealt with *illegal* drug use. The social context of this use is usually distinct from that of alcohol, a commodity that can be legally obtained and legally consumed by adults in a variety of social settings. Although recognizing that there may be some overlap between the social worlds in which drugs and alcohol are used, we approach our discussion by treating separately the two substances and their possible connections to homicide.

Drugs and Homicide

The relationship between drugs and homicide is one that has not been widely investigated. Homicide is a relatively rare occurrence that must necessarily be studied after the fact, making it difficult to assign causality. Attempts to develop theories about illicit drugs and homicide are also hindered by the lack of reliable information about the extent of illicit drug use in the population. For this reason, research in this area tends to be primarily descriptive.

THE GOLDSTEIN TYPOLOGY

Paul J. Goldstein (1985) made an explicit attempt to develop a theoretical framework by which to describe and explain the relationship between drugs and violence, including lethal violence. Goldstein developed a typology of three ways in which drug use and drug trafficking may be causally related to violence.

Psychopharmacological violence is violence that stems from properties of the drug itself. There is some debate on the issue of the psychopharmacological effects of drugs on aggression and violent behavior, but evidence suggests that there may be such effects associated with alcohol, cocaine, and PCP. In Goldstein's framework, this includes violence that is associated with drug ingestion by the victim, the perpetrator, or both. An example of one way in which violence may be associated with victim drug use is provided by a recent study that found that female cocaine users were more likely to be physically attacked by intimate partners in domestic disputes than were nonusers (Goldstein, Bellucci, Spunt, & Miller, 1991).

Economic compulsive violence is violence associated with the high costs of illicit drug use. This type of violence does not stem directly from the physiological effects of drugs but is motivated by the need or desire to obtain drugs to sustain an addiction. On the basis of the capacity to induce physical dependency, the drugs we expect to be most often associated with economic compulsive violence are opiates (particularly heroin) and cocaine in both powder and "rock" form.

Systemic violence is defined by Goldstein (1985) as that type of violence associated with "traditionally aggressive patterns of interaction within the system of drug distribution and use" (p. 497). In essence, systemic violence arises as a direct result of involvement in trafficking. Goldstein maintains that the risks of violence are greater for those involved in distribution than for those who are only users (Goldstein, Brownstein, Ryan, & Bellucci, 1989).

EMPIRICAL EVALUATIONS OF THE GOLDSTEIN TRIPARTITE FRAMEWORK

In recent years, several empirical tests have been undertaken by Goldstein and his associates in an attempt to understand the relationship between drugs and homicide. One such study (Goldstein et al., 1989) was primarily concerned with the effect on homicide of the crack epidemic that took place in the 1980s. Information from 414 homicides in New York City was gathered for the researchers by police officers at the time of the investigation. The researchers then attempted to categorize the homicides according to Goldstein's framework.

Slightly more than half of the sampled homicides were drug related. Of these, the overwhelming majority (74.3%) were classified as systemic. Of drug-related homicides, 65% involved crack cocaine as the primary substance (26% of all sampled homicides in New York); another 22% were related to other forms of cocaine. *All* homicides in which alcohol was the primary substance involved were classified as psychopharmacological, whereas other drug-related homicides were most likely to be classified as systemic.

Comparison of the circumstances of homicides classified as drug related with the circumstances of those that were not yields some interesting findings. The vast majority of drug-related homicides involved victims and perpetrators who were acquaintances, whereas stranger and intimate (domestic) homicides were significantly more likely to be nondrug related.

Nearly half (44%) of all systemic crack-related homicides were found to involve territorial disputes, whereas 18% involved the robbery of a dealer. An additional 11% were related to the collection of drug-related debts. Goldstein et al. (1989) also found that the large number of crack-related homicides did not increase the homicide rate in New York City: "In both nature and number, crack-related homicides largely appear to be replacing other types of homicides rather than just adding to the existing homicide rate" (p. 683).

Another analysis of the New York City homicide data was designed to determine the specific relationship between drug trafficking and homicide in New York City. Brownstein, Baxi, Goldstein, and Ryan (1992) analyzed a subset of offenders and victims from the data set for whom prior criminal histories were available. They found that both victims and perpetrators of drug-related homicides were substantially more likely than their counterparts in nondrug-related homicides to be known to the police as either drug users (67.5% of those involved in drug-related homicides vs. 22.7% of those involved in nondrug-related homicides) or drug traffickers (59.3% vs. 5.1%). From this analysis, Brownstein et al. concluded,

> Almost no innocent bystanders were victims of homicide. This is not to say that citizens not involved in crime or drugs are never the victims of homicide, but only that the extent of the threat to their safety has been exaggerated. (p. 41)

THE DRUG RELATIONSHIPS IN MURDER PROJECT

The Drug Relationships in Murder Project (DREIM) involved extensive interviews with 268 homicide offenders incarcerated in New York State correctional facilities. All offenders in the study committed a homicide in 1984. One of the purposes of this project was to gain a more extensive understanding than that afforded by official police records of the role that drugs and alcohol play in homicide (for a review of these shortcomings, see Brownstein et al., 1992; Goldstein, Brownstein, & Ryan, 1992; Goldstein et al., 1989).

As a result of the DREIM project, it was found that the substance most likely to be used by homicide offenders on a regular basis as well as during the 24 hours directly preceding the crime was, overwhelmingly, alcohol. Marijuana and cocaine, respectively, were the drugs next most implicated in the lives of homicide offenders, as well in the offense itself (Spunt, Brownstein, Goldstein, Fendrich, & Liberty, 1995; Spunt, Goldstein, Brownstein, Fendrich, & Langley, 1994).

Offenders who were experiencing the effects related to the use of any drug at the time of the offense (in most cases, this was intoxication but included "coming down from" and "in need of" a drug) were specifically asked whether they felt that the homicide was related to their drug use. Overall, 86% of those who were experiencing drug effects at the time of the homicide believed that the homicide was related to their drug use.

The interview data obtained for the DREIM finding that the majority of drug- and alcohol-related homicides are psychopharmacological in nature. This conclusion contradicts Goldstein's earlier finding that most homicides related to drugs other than alcohol are systemic in nature. How can one explain these seemingly irreconcilable results? It appears that the method of data collection is significant. Interview data seem to support the conclusion that the preponderance of drug-related homicides are psychopharmacological, as does analysis of official records. The only support for a systemic link between drugs and homicide derives from the data collected at the time of the homicide investigation via the instrument designed by Goldstein and his colleagues. Clearly, more rigorous data collection will be required to truly use Goldstein's tripartite framework as a classificatory tool.

Other problems are inherent in Goldstein's typology. It is often assumed that a great deal of violent crime that would be classified as economic compulsive is associated with illicit drug use. There are problems in untangling these complicated relationships, however. For example, if a homicide is committed in connection with a robbery, the robbery may be motivated by a need for drugs; the police officer collecting the data, however, is likely to consider robbery as the primary motive and not record the incident as drug related.

An additional problem with the Goldstein framework is that the categories are not mutually exclusive. Many of the situations coded as systemic are economic in nature. "Robbery of a drug dealer" seems to be an economically motivated crime but is classified as systemic on the basis of involvement of the victim and/or perpetrator in drug trafficking. Overall, Goldstein's classificatory scheme seems biased toward support of the systemic model of drug-effected violence. If support for the economic compulsive model is to be found, it will be found through the process of interviewing offenders. The available research using in-depth interviews (Brownstein et al., 1992; Spunt et al., 1995; Spunt et al., 1994), however, indicates that most drug-related homicides are psychopharmacological rather than economic compulsive in nature.

Most other research concerning the relationship of drugs to homicide is much more descriptive than explanatory and therefore lacks a coherent theoretical framework. Because intriguing findings have emerged, however, we provide a review of selected studies from this literature.

HOMICIDE, DRUGS, AND WOMEN

Several recent studies have focused on female homicide offenders. Blount, Silverman, Sellers, and Seese (1994) compared two groups of battered women, those who had killed their abusers and those who had not. They found that the murdered partners of abused women were almost twice as likely to engage in daily alcohol use than were the partners of women who did not kill. An analysis of homicide victims in upstate New York yields a similar result; 61% of male homicide victims killed by women had alcohol in their blood at the time of death (Welte & Abel, 1989). These findings provide some support for the observation that homicides committed by females are more likely to be what Wolfgang (1958) called *victim-precipitated* than are homicides committed by male offenders (Daly, 1994).

In the Blount et al. (1994) study described above, it also was found that battered women who killed their partners were more likely than other battered women to be users of alcohol as well as other drugs. An analysis of the general population of incarcerated females, however, has found an inverse relationship between drug and alcohol use and homicide; in essence, female homicide offenders in this sample were significantly *less* likely to use and/or abuse drugs or alcohol than female inmates incarcerated for other crimes (Blount, Danner, Vega, & Silverman, 1991). It thus appears that drugs and alcohol play a more significant role in the causation of female-perpetrated intimate homicide than in other types of homicides committed by women. Other studies, however, indicate that this relationship does not hold for men; working with predominantly male samples, Lindqvist (1991) and Brownstein et al. (1992) have determined that overall, drugs were less implicated in intimate homicides than in other types of homicide.

OTHER STUDIES OF THE DRUGS-HOMICIDE RELATIONSHIP

In a somewhat different approach to the relationship between drugs and homicide, Brumm and Cloninger (1995) used a *rational choice/opportunity cost* framework. Operating from this framework, they hypothesized that if a greater proportion of law enforcement activity is directed at drug enforcement, then the costs of committing violent crime will decrease proportionately. Consequently, the incidence of violent crime may actually increase. Using cross-sectional data from 59 U.S. cities, Brumm and Cloninger developed a mathematical model from which they estimated that a 1% increase in drug enforcement activities resulted in a 0.17% increase in the homicide rate, a finding confirming their hypothesis. Follow-up studies will be necessary to develop confidence in these findings.

Addressing the current concern surrounding street gangs, violence, and drugs, Klein, Maxson, and Cunningham (1991) attempted to determine whether differences existed in the relationship between crack and homicide in Los Angeles if gang members were involved in the homicide. A sample of police records of homicide cases in South Central Los Angeles, an area characterized by high levels of drug activity and gang violence, was examined. Gang-related homicides were more likely than nongang homicides to involve drugs; nearly 70% of gang-related homicides were drug related, whereas slightly more than half of other homicides were. A comparison of drug-involved gang homicides and gang homicides in which drugs were not involved, however, yielded no significant differences in characteristics such as location, number of participants, or firearm involvement. Also, when the same comparison was made for nongang homicides, drug-related nongang homicides resembled gang homicides on these characteristics. This led the researchers to conclude that the involvement of drugs is a more relevant primary characteristic of homicide than is gang involvement.

Klein et al. (1991) also found a difference through time. Although the incidence of drug involvement in gang homicides showed virtually no change from 1984 to 1985, the incidence of drug involvement in nongang homicides nearly doubled in this same period. This is consistent with the finding that cocaine became increasingly implicated in homicides throughout the 1980s (Garriott, 1993; Hanzlick & Gowitt, 1991).

SUMMARY: DRUGS AND HOMICIDE

It is apparent that drugs are often related in some fashion to homicide. Studies consistently report that approximately half of all homicide offenders and victims are intoxicated on drugs and/or alcohol at the time of the crime. The substance most likely to be implicated is alcohol. Cocaine is the substance next most frequently implicated, a relationship that appears to have increased during the 1980s (Hanzlick & Gowitt, 1991).

Limited data are available to compare these figures with the prevalence of illicit drug use in the U.S. population. It appears, however, that both perpetrators and victims of homicide are more drug involved than is the general population. There is substantial evidence that among drug-involved homicide offenders, polydrug use is common (Fendrich, Mackesy-Amiti, Goldstein, Spunt, & Brownstein, 1995; Garriott, 1993; Ray & Simons, 1987; Spunt et al., 1995; Spunt et al., 1994).

Evidence is mixed regarding demographic differences in substance use and the way in which it relates to homicide. Some researchers report greater drug involvement in homicide for Blacks, Hispanics, and Native Americans (Abel, 1987; Bachman, 1991; Garriott, 1993; Goodman et al., 1986; Tardiff et al., 1995; Welte & Abel, 1989), whereas others find significantly lower substance involvement for Black homicide offenders (Wieczorek, Welte, & Abel, 1990). In both the general population and in homicide-offender studies, persons aged 18 to 25—the age group with the greatest overall involvement in crime—show the highest rates of both alcohol and illicit drug use (Fendrich et al., 1995; Meiczkowski, 1996; Tardiff et al., 1995). Thus, there seem to be correlates between socioeconomic status, age, crime rates, and drug/alcohol use. The co-occurrence of high crime rates and high rates of drug and alcohol use for certain groups in the population can only be considered a coincidence in the absence of carefully developed theories.

Findings that link drugs to victim-offender relationships are also inconclusive. There is some evidence that the overall trend is for drugs to be less implicated in intimate homicides than in other types of homicide (Brownstein et al., 1992; Lindqvist, 1991). There is also evidence, however, that among female homicide offenders only, alcohol and drug involvement is disproportionately associated with intimate homicide (Blount et al., 1994).

We have no concise explanations for the patterns of substance use that seem to surround many homicide events as well as the lives of many homicide offenders. Researchers who questioned a national sample of incarcerated felony offenders about their criminal histories determined that "homicide, which is often depicted as a unique sort of crime, appears to be merely one more aspect of a generally violent and criminal life" (Wright & Rossi, 1986, p. 72). If this is true, then it is apparent that drugs are also a part of this lifestyle.

DIRECTIONS FOR FUTURE RESEARCH

If we assume that one of the main reasons that we wish to understand the relationship of drugs to homicide is to prevent or reduce homicide rates, then we clearly need a better understanding of how drugs and homicide are related. For instance, if Goldstein's systemic model is supported by empirical tests, this would indicate dramatically different public policy approaches than would support for a psychopharmacological relationship between drugs and homicide.

Future research also needs to examine the different dimensions of drug involvement by offenders and victims of homicide. Some questions to be addressed include these: How is victim drug use implicated in homicide? Does offender drug use interact with victim drug use? If so, in what ways? Which is more important to the outcome of the homicide event, victim drug use or offender drug use? How can we reconcile these questions with the notion of victim precipitation? Answers to these questions are needed to formulate a coherent theoretical explanation of the relationship between drugs and homicide.

Given the problems inherent in existing studies that use police records, offenders may be the best source we have to determine the ways in which drug use may have contributed to the homicide. Despite the obviously subjective interpretations they provide, in-depth interviews with homicide offenders seem to be a promising direction in which to move for understanding the relationship between drugs and homicide.

Alcohol and Homicide

The study of the relationship between alcohol and homicide has fared somewhat better than that of drugs and homicide. This is due partly to the legality of alcohol, which makes it possible to access more information than is possible with regard to illegal drugs. To date, there have been two major efforts to theorize a link between alcohol and violence. One of these was specifically focused on homicide (Parker, 1993, 1995; Parker & Rebhun, 1995) and will therefore be discussed at length, whereas the other was devoted to intoxication and interpersonal aggression (Fagan, 1990).

SELECTIVE DISINHIBITION: THE PARKER AND REBHUN APPROACH

This approach (Parker, 1993; Parker & Rebhun, 1995) attempts to specifically link alcohol to homicide in a general conceptual model by advancing a theory of *selective disinhibition*. This approach differs from that taken by earlier researchers who advanced a biologically based disinhibition model (see Room & Collins, 1983, for a review and critique of that literature). A central feature of the earlier model was the treatment of alcohol as a biochemical agent that had a universal effect on social behavior. A primary weakness of this approach is that it ignored evidence of the differential impact of alcohol depending on the social and cultural contexts in which consumption took place (see Marshall, 1979, for cross-cultural examples of this point).

In formulating their social disinhibition approach, Parker and Rebhun try to explain why behavior becomes "disinhibited" in relatively few cases of alcohol consumption and, even then, only rarely results in a homicide. According to their framework, alcohol may selectively disinhibit (i.e., contribute to) violence; this effect, however, depends on a number of social factors, including characteristics of the actors involved, the relationships of the actors to one another, and the impact of bystanders. In U.S. society, norms about the appropriateness of violence as a means of solving interpersonal disputes are mixed, arguing both for and against such behavior, depending on the situation. All else being equal, norms that have the least institutional support are more likely to be disinhibited in a particular situation—that is, to lose their effectiveness in discouraging or inhibiting violence (see also Parker, 1993).

To explain how choices are made within these conflicting normative structures regarding violence, Parker and Rebhun introduce the concept of *active* and *passive constraint*. In many interpersonal disputes, including those under the influence of alcohol, even an impaired rationality discourages the use of violence; hence, the recognition that violence may be inappropriate acts as a passive constraint. Still, in some potentially violent situations, it takes active constraint—a proactive and conscious decision not to use violence to "solve" the dispute—to constrain or preclude violence. The effects of alcohol consumption may block the operation of both passive and active constraints by weakening normative structures that usually discourage individuals from engaging in violent behavior. Thus, the selective nature of alcohol-related homicide is dependent on the interaction of an impaired rationality and the nature of the social situation. The interplay of active and passive constraints explains why most alcohol-involved interpersonal disputes do not result in violence; a few situations, however, result in a loss of inhibition that contributes to the occurrence of a homicide.

Parker and Rebhun also formulate a comprehensive theoretical model of the ways in which alcohol consumption and homicide rates might be related at the aggregate level. This model incorporates concepts from the "subculture of violence" literature (both southern and African American varieties), social bonds theory (e.g., Hirschi, 1969; Krohn, 1991), deterrence via capital punishment, routine activities, and relative and absolute economic deprivation in the forms of economic inequality and poverty rates.

Empirical Tests of the Selective Disinhibition Framework

In testing their theory, Parker and Rebhun (1995) used data collected for a study by Wilbanks (1984), who compiled information for all homicides in Miami in 1980 from various sources. Applying the logic of active constraint as a necessary condition for the inhibition of violence to a sample of these case summaries, they found evidence to support the selective disinhibition framework (pp. 38–40).

Parker and Rebhun (1995) provide two additional tests of their approach. First, using data from 256 American cities in a longitudinal design, they found that increases in alcohol availability helped explain why homicide nearly tripled in these cities between 1960 and 1980. They also found some evidence that the presence of other variables in the model intensifies the strength of the relationship between alcohol availability and homicide rates in the cities they studied; these variables include poverty, differences in the patterns of activity, and a lack of social bonds.

Finally, further exploring the general hypothesis that alcohol has a causal impact on homicide, Parker and Rebhun (1995) analyzed the impact of increases in the minimum drinking age on youth homicide at the state level. Using data from all 50 states for 1976 to 1983, they compared the impacts of different minimum drinking ages on two general types of homicide in three age categories. The homicide types were *primary* (offender and victim acquainted) and *nonprimary* (victims and offenders generally unknown to one another prior to the incident), and the three age categories were 15 to 18, 19 to 20, and 21 to 24. Controlling for the presence of other important predictors, the rate of beer consumption is shown to be a significant predictor of homicide rates in five of the six age/homicide-type combinations. Furthermore, increases in the minimum drinking age are associated with a decrease in primary homicides across all age categories.

A different study (Parker, 1995) provides findings that lend considerable support to the disinhibition framework. State-level data on alcohol sales in 1980 were used to test hypotheses derived from various theoretical perspectives concerning the basic relationship between alcohol consumption and homicide. Separate estimates were made for various categories of offender-victim relationships and circumstances of the homicide (e.g., homicide among intimates and robbery-related homicide).

The results of this analysis revealed that alcohol consumption was a significant predictor of homicides between persons who have some personal relationship. This finding suggests that norms prohibiting violence in resolving interpersonal disputes in close or intimate relationships may be weaker than such norms governing other interactions, such as those with strangers. Thus, alcohol consumption appears to contribute to the selective disinhibition of a normative restraint that is already rather weak. This finding may help explain the frequent association between alcohol and spousal violence noted in the family violence literature (e.g., Stets, 1990).

In addition, the impact of poverty on robbery and other felony homicides was stronger in states with above average rates of alcohol consumption (Parker, 1995). Further, the deterrent effect of capital punishment on homicide rates was found to be strongest in states that had below average rates of alcohol consumption. Applying the logic of rational choice, lower alcohol consumption appears to be associated with greater active constraint such that fewer homicides are committed in the face of the ultimate penalty, execution.

Summary of the Selective Disinhibition Approach

The selective disinhibition approach has received significant support in studies that have used different units of analysis as well as different time points. This suggests that homicide research should more carefully consider the role of alcohol in homicide, as well as the ways in which alcohol may influence the effects of other predictors of homicide.

INTOXICATION AND AGGRESSION: FAGAN'S APPROACH

Fagan (1990) has attempted to synthesize information from many disciplines to present a comprehensive approach to the alcohol/drugs and violence relationship. In doing so, he has reviewed research and theoretical arguments from biological and physiological research, psychopharmacological studies, psychological and psychiatric approaches, and social and cultural perspectives.

Having conducted this multidisciplinary review of research literatures, Fagan (1990) proposes an integrated model in which he argues that the most important areas of consensus from these perspectives are (a) that intoxication has a significant impact on cognitive abilities and functioning and (b) that the nature of this impact varies according to the substance used but is moderated by social and cultural meanings of how people function under the influence of alcohol and drugs. Thus, Fagan believes that intoxicated individuals tend to have limited response sets in situations of social interaction; the nature of the setting in which interaction takes place, however, and the absence or presence of formal and informal means of social control, are also important factors in determining how intoxication influences aggression.

To date, no empirical tests of Fagan's (1990) integrated model have been conducted. One of the reasons for this is that Fagan's approach results in a general theoretical model that requires substantial revision to permit empirical analyses. For example, the outcome measure, aggression, is hardly the same as homicide, although there is certainly some relationship between these concepts. Further theoretical explication is needed to establish the transition from aggression to homicide, as well as the linkages between the antecedents of aggression to aggression itself.

ALCOHOL AND HOMICIDE: A SUMMARY

What do we know about the relationship between alcohol and homicide? The state of knowledge here is more advanced than that with regard to drugs and homicide. Fagan's model provides a more general explanation than the selective disinhibition framework, but both approaches argue that situational factors are important in understanding the impact of alcohol on individuals in altering their behavior toward others and their interpretation of the meaning of the behavior of others with whom they interact.

Not known about the alcohol-homicide relationship is whether the theoretical models discussed here help us understand individual cases of homicide and other outcomes of interpersonal disputes, both violent and nonviolent. An emerging literature in criminology has shown that rates of violence vary dramatically across relatively small distances and spaces within communities, with some areas—so-called hot spots—having great concentrations of violence, whereas others do not (e.g., Roncek & Maier, 1991; Sherman, Gartin, & Buerger, 1989). The extent to which this variation is due in part to alcohol and drug availability and use has not been adequately addressed. The data needed to properly assess a comprehensive model of the relationship between alcohol and homicide include a host of social, psychological, economic, cultural, and cognitive factors, as well as extensive measures of both drug and alcohol use and abuse. At present, such a model does not exist, nor do the data necessary for its development and evaluation.

Drugs, Alcohol, and Homicide: Issues in Research and Policy

We have argued in this article that a major shortcoming of the current literature on the relationship between alcohol, drugs, and homicide is the lack of a comprehensive theoretical framework. Discussion of two major approaches, those of Goldstein and Parker and Rebhun, and to a lesser extent, Fagan's model, has demonstrated the various difficulties arising from the general lack of theoretically guided research on which to build more extensive explanatory models.

Our review of empirical studies further demonstrates the need to devote more energy to research design issues in the study of the complex relationship between drugs, alcohol, and violence. These issues include sample selection problems, too little focus on the contexts in which people interact, a lack of attention to control variables, and, most important, a lack of comprehensive theoretical models.

On the other hand, we now have findings that relate changes in homicide rates to alcohol consumption and availability; thus, we can begin to make predictions about the impact of changing policies on outcomes such as homicide and other forms of violence. For example, the well-documented decreases in homicide rates and other forms of violence in large urban areas such as New York City were preceded by a gradual and eventually significant decline in alcohol consumption in the United States that began in the early 1980s. Given some of the findings cited here, some part of this decline in homicide may well be explained by the reduction in alcohol consumption. In addition, a well-documented change in New York City police tactics discouraged public drunkenness and disrupted street-level drug markets. By decreasing alcohol and drug consumption, this tactical change may have indirectly contributed to a drop in homicide rates.

Although advances have been made in the understanding of the relationship between alcohol, drugs, and homicide, a great deal of work remains to be done. We have outlined potentially fruitful directions that such efforts might take. As researchers in this area, we are optimistic about the possibility of reducing the incidence of homicide as we gain a better understanding of the relationship between drugs, alcohol, and homicide.

REFERENCES

Abel, E. L. (1987). Drugs and homicide in Erie County, New York. *International Journal of the Addictions, 22,* 195–200.

Bachman, R. (1991). The social causes of American Indian homicide as revealed by the life experiences of thirty offenders. *American Indian Quarterly, 15,* 468–492.

Blount, W. R., Danner, T. A., Vega, M., & Silverman, I. J. (1991). The influence of substance use among adult female inmates. *Journal of Drug Issues, 21,* 449–467.

Blount, W. R., Silverman, I. J., Sellers, C. S., & Seese, R. A. (1994). Alcohol and drug use among abused women who kill, abused women who don't, and their abusers. *Journal of Drug Issues, 24,* 165–177.

Brown, S. A. (1993). Drug effect expectancies and addictive behavior change. *Experimental and Clinical Psychopharmacology, 1,* 55–67.

Brownstein, H. H., Baxi, H., Goldstein, P., & Ryan, P. (1992). The relationship of drugs, drug trafficking, and drug traffickers to homicide. *Journal of Crime and Justice, 15,* 25–44.

Brumm, H. J., & Cloninger, D. O. (1995). The drug war and the homicide rate: A direct correlation? *Cato Journal, 14,* 509–517.

Daly, K. (1994). *Gender crime, and punishment.* New Haven, CT: Yale University Press.

Fagan, J. (1990). Intoxication and aggression. In M. Tonry & J. Q. Wilson (Eds.), *Crime and justice: A review of research* (Vol. 14, pp. 241–320). Chicago: University of Chicago Press.

Fendrich, M., Mackesy-Amiti, M. E., Goldstein, P., Spunt, B., & Brownstein, H. (1995). Substance involvement among juvenile murderers: Comparisons with older offenders based on interviews with prison inmates. *International Journal of the Addictions, 30,* 1363–1382.

Garriott, J. C. (1993). Drug use among homicide victims: Changing patterns. *American Journal of Forensic Medicine and Pathology, 14,* 234–237.

Goldstein, P. (1985). The drugs-violence nexus: A tripartite conceptual framework. *Journal of Drug Issues, 14,* 493–506.

Goldstein, P., Bellucci, P. A., Spunt, B. J., & Miller, T. (1991). Volume of cocaine use and violence: A comparison between men and women. *Journal of Drug Issues, 21,* 345–367.

Goldstein, P., Brownstein, H. H., & Ryan, P. J. (1992). Drug-related homicide in New York: 1984 and 1988. *Crime & Delinquency, 38,* 459–476.

Goldstein, P., Brownstein, H. H., Ryan, P. J., & Bellucci, P. A. (1989). Crack and homicide in New York City, 1988: A conceptually based event analysis. *Contemporary Drug Problems, 16,* 651–687.

Goodman, R., Mercy, J. A., Loya, F., Rosenberg, M. L., Smith, J. C., Allen, N. N., Vargas, L., & Kolts, R. (1986). Alcohol use and interpersonal violence: Alcohol detected in homicide victims. *American Journal of Public Health, 76,* 144–149.

Grube, J., Ames, G. M., & Delaney, W. (1994). Alcohol expectancies and workplace drinking. *Journal of Applied Social Psychology, 24,* 646–660.

Hanzlick, R., & Gowitt, G. T. (1991). Cocaine metabolite detection in homicide victims. *Journal of the American Medical Association, 265,* 760–761.

Hirschi, T. (1969). *Causes of delinquency.* Berkeley: University of California Press.

Klein, M. W., Maxson, C. L., & Cunningham, L. C. (1991). Crack, street gangs, and violence. *Criminology, 29,* 623–650.

Krohn, M. D. (1991). Control and deterrence theories. In J. Sheley (Ed.), *Criminology: A contemporary handbook* (pp. 295–314). Belmont, CA: Wadsworth.

Leonard, K. E., & Taylor, S. P. (1983). Exposure to pornography, permissive and non-permissive cues, and male aggression toward females. *Motivation and Emotion, 7,* 291–299.

Lindqvist, P. (1991). Homicides committed by abusers of alcohol and illicit drugs. *British Journal of Addiction, 86,* 321–326.

Loftin, C. K., McDowall, D., & Wiersema, B. (1992). A comparative study of the preventive effects of mandatory sentencing laws for gun crimes. *Journal of Criminal Law and Criminology, 83,* 378–394.

Marshall, M. (Ed.). (1979). *Beliefs, behaviors, and alcoholic beverages: A cross-cultural survey.* Ann Arbor: University of Michigan Press.

Meiczkowski, T. M. (1996). The prevalence of drug use in the United States. In M. Tonry (Ed.), *Crime and justice: A review of research* (Vol. 20, pp. 349–414). Chicago: University of Chicago Press.

Miller, B. A., & Downs, W. R. (1993). The impact of family violence on the use of alcohol by women: Research indicates that women with alcohol problems have experienced high rates of violence during their childhoods and as adults. *Alcohol Health and Research World, 17,* 137–142.

Parker, R. N. (1993). Alcohol and theories of homicide. In F. Adler & W. Laufer (Eds.), *Advances in criminological theory* (Vol. 4, pp. 113–142). New Brunswick, NJ: Transaction Publishing.

Parker, R. N. (1995). Bringing "booze" back in: The relationship between alcohol and homicide. *Journal of Research in Crime and Delinquency, 32,* 3–38.

Parker, R. N., & Rebhun, L. (1995). *Alcohol and homicide: A deadly combination of two American traditions.* Albany: State University of New York Press.

Pernanen, K. (1976). Alcohol and crimes of violence. In B. Kissin & H. Beglieter (Eds.), *The biology of alcoholism: Social aspects of alcoholism* (pp. 351–444). New York: Plenum.

Pernanen, K. (1981). Theoretical aspects of the relationship between alcohol use and crime. In J. J. Collins, Jr. (Ed.), *Drinking and crime: Perspectives on the relationship between alcohol consumption and criminal behavior* (pp. 1–69). New York: Guilford.

Pernanen, K. (1991). *Alcohol in human violence.* New York: Guilford.

Pihl, R. O., Peterson, J. B., & Lau, M. A. (1993, September). A biosocial model of the alcohol-aggression relationship. *Journal of Studies on Alcohol* (Suppl. 11), 128–139.

Ray, M. C., & Simons, R. L. (1987). Convicted murderers' accounts of their crimes: A study of homicide in small communities. *Symbolic Interaction, 10,* 57–70.

Roncek, D. W., & Maier, P. A. (1991). Bars, blocks, and crimes revisited: Linking the theory of routine activities to the empiricism of hot spots. *Criminology, 29,* 725–754.

Room, R., & Collins, G. (Eds.). (1983). *Alcohol and disinhibition: Nature and meaning of the link* (Research Monograph No. 12). Washington, DC: National Institute on Alcohol Abuse and Alcoholism.

Sherman, L. W., Gartin, R. P., & Buerger, M. E. (1989). Hot spots of predatory crime: Routine activities and the criminology of place. *Criminology, 27,* 27–56.

Spunt, B., Brownstein, H., Goldstein, P., Fendrich, M., & Liberty, H. J. (1995). Drug use by homicide offenders. *Journal of Psychoactive Drugs, 27,* 125–134.

Spunt, B., Goldstein, P., Brownstein, H., Fendrich, M., & Langley, S. (1994). Alcohol and homicide: Interviews with prison inmates. *Journal of Drug Issues, 24,* 143–163.

Stets, J. E. (1990). Verbal and physical aggression in marriage. *Journal of Marriage and the Family, 43,* 721–732.

Tardiff, K., Marzuk, P. M., Leon, A. C., Hirsch, C. S., Stajik, M., Portera, L., & Hartwell, N. (1995). Cocaine, opiates, and ethanol in homicides in New York City: 1990 and 1991. *Journal of Forensic Sciences, 40,* 387–390.

Welte, J. W., & Abel, E. L. (1989). Homicide: Drinking by the victim. *Journal of Studies on Alcohol, 50,* 197–201.

White, H. R., Hansell, S., & Brick, J. (1993). Alcohol use and aggression among youth. *Alcohol Health and Research World, 17,* 144–150.

Widom, C. S., & Ames, M. A. (1994). Criminal consequences of childhood sexual victimization. *Child Abuse and Neglect, 18,* 303–318.

Wieczorek, W., Welte, J., & Abel, E. (1990). Alcohol, drugs, and murder: A study of convicted homicide offenders. *Journal of Criminal Justice, 18,* 217–227.

Wilbanks, W. (1984). *Murder in Miami.* Lanham, MD: University Press of America.

Wolfgang, M. E. (1958). *Patterns in criminal homicide.* Philadelphia: University of Pennsylvania Press.

Wright, J. D., & Rossi, P. H. (1986). *Armed and considered dangerous: A survey of felons and their firearms.* Hawthorne, NY: Aldine.

6

Prostitutes on Crack Cocaine
Addiction, Utility, and Marketplace Economics

Thomas E. Feucht

Introduction

A small mountain of research has accumulated regarding prostitution and drugs. Some of the earlier research focused on narcotics, especially heroin, as the drug most widely used by prostitutes (e.g., Chambers, Hinsley, and Moldestad 1970; Cushman 1972; Goldstein 1979; James, Gosho, and Wohl 1979; Miller 1986). More recently, attention has turned to the rapid spread of cocaine use—particularly crack cocaine—and its relation to prostitution. The urgency of this research has been heightened by growing concerns about the spread of human immunodeficiency virus (HIV) through heterosexual contact. For instance, the Centers for Disease Control (1987; 1988) report that increases in the incidence of sexually transmitted diseases (STDs) can be linked to prostitution and contact with prostitution. STDs have been identified as important "multiplier" risk factors for HIV infection because they create lesions through which the HIV can more easily enter the body (Kerr 1988; *The Economist* 1989). In addition, prostitutes frequently associate with intravenous drug users (IDUs) or are IDUs themselves. As a result, prostitutes constitute a primary vector of HIV transmission to others who are not themselves IDUs (Friedman, Dozier, et al. 1988).

These two simultaneous developments—the arrival and spread of HIV and the rapid rise in the popularity of crack cocaine—are closely related, and prostitution appears to be the platform on which the crisis is being built. Many have suggested that the widespread use of cocaine—especially crack cocaine—has accelerated the spread of HIV and other STDs through prostitution and heterosexual contact in general (Abramowitz, Guydish, et al. 1989; Fullilove and Fullilove 1989; Aral and Holmes 1990: Fullilove, Fullilove, et al. 1990; Rolfs, Goldberg, et al. 1990). A review of the literature reveals two related characterizations of cocaine that link it to sex and ultimately to prostitution. These characterizations are cocaine as a highly addictive substance and cocaine as an aphrodisiac or sexual stimulant.

Some early research on cocaine focused on the reputation of the drug as an aphrodisiac or sexual stimulant (Grinspoon and Bakalar 1976; Parr 1976). Although most of these reports were from subjects who used cocaine intranasally, similar characterizations have been reported by people who smoke cocaine (Kerr 1988; MacDonald, Waldorf, et al. 1988; Bowser 1989; *The Economist* 1989; Bowser, Fullilove, et al. 1990). There is some psycho-physiological evidence for this purported effect of cocaine. Buffum (1982, 1988) states that increases in the release of dopamines to the brain have been associated clinically with heightened sexual drive. Because cocaine promotes the production of dopamines, it could well act as a sexual stimulant in some users.

Of course, many dispute the characterization of cocaine as a sexual stimulant or aphrodisiac. Some researchers suggest that male users are more likely than female users to describe cocaine as a sex-enhancing drug (Friedman et al. 1988), whereas others have reported that chronic use of crack eventually results in a lessened interest in sex altogether (Cregler 1989; Fullilove and Fullilove 1989; Inciardi 1993).

In any event, a prostitute's libido may be rather irrelevant to her conducting business, and she may have no desire to increase or enhance her feelings of sensuality or her sexual drive. There are, however, other reputed benefits of cocaine for people involved in prostitution. For example, although subjects in Wesson's (1982) study of masseuses in the San Francisco area often dismissed the sex-enhancing effects of cocaine, they did report that using cocaine made their work more enjoyable by heightening their awareness, suppressing negative feelings, and assisting them in staying awake for long nights of work. Furthermore, clients frequently offered cocaine to the masseuses as a supposed sexual stimulant, confirming that cocaine has at least the reputation of being a sex drug. Thus, even if a prostitute were to deny the aphrodisiacal effects of cocaine, allowing clients to associate her with the drug might make her seem sexier to them, thereby enhancing her reputation and increasing her value in the prostitution marketplace.

Finally, although the aphrodisiacal properties of cocaine may be exaggerated, at a minimum, the use of crack may at least lower inhibitions and provide a subcultural context in which greater sexual activity is acceptable or even expected (Kerr 1988; Abromowitz et al., 1989; Leigh 1990).

A second factor in the increased concern about the risk of HIV infection among crack-using women arises from the popular belief regarding the extremely addictive nature of cocaine. Many studies have identified the need to support a crack habit as a primary factor leading to entry into prostitution (Inciardi and Pottieger 1986; Friedman et al. 1988; Bowser 1989; *The Economist* 1989). Further evidence of the addictive nature of crack cocaine is drawn from the increasingly common practice of exchanging sex for drugs directly. This is by no means a new phenomenon (see Goldstein, 1979, for a discussion of heroin-addicted "bag-brides" who frequently exchanged sex for drugs). However, the proportions to which the behavior has expanded among crack-using women seem unprecedented (Cooper 1988; Inciardi 1989; Isikoff 1989; Minerbrook, 1989).

In addition to these two characterizations of cocaine, researchers have noted several significant developments in the prostitution marketplace that may be direct consequences of the increased use of cocaine. Apparently, the steady influx of women into prostitution has created rather competitive conditions for prostitutes and has changed some aspects of the way in which business is conducted. For instance, *The Economist* (1989) reports that the value of sex has dropped precipitously, and in some places, sex can be purchased at unprecedented low prices. Lower prices and increased competition apparently have resulted in some women engaging in extreme and degrading forms of sex (Bowser et al. 1990), and bartering sex for drugs—a relatively uncommon practice among narcotics-using prostitutes—has become increasingly popular, especially with younger crack-using prostitutes (Fullilove and Fullilove, 1989; Inciardi 1989; *The Economist* 1989; Aral and Holmes 1990; Bowser et al. 1990; Fullilove et al. 1990). In addition, Shedlin (1990) suggests that as more women have entered prostitution to support their crack habits, competition for clients has reduced the use of condoms due in part to clients' disfavor for them in spite of their effective protection against the spread of diseases. Shedlin cites the unwillingness of some prostitutes to spend their earnings on condoms. Instead, oral sex has become the modal form of sex because of its perceived greater safety from infection as well as the speed and ease with which it can be performed. Finally, the increasing competition seems to have forced some women out of the profession entirely: Although prostitutes who use crack have become increasingly active, older prostitutes are reportedly retreating from the streets to avoid the dangers associated with the crack trade (Shedlin 1990).

Though some important work has been done on a typology of prostitution (Winick and Kinsie, 1971), including those who exchange sex for drugs (Goldstein 1979), the body of recent research suggests that prostitution is undergoing a dramatic transformation as a result of the widespread use of crack cocaine. This study reports findings from recent research on crack-using prostitutes that describe three aspects of prostitutes' orientations to crack cocaine. A discussion of the findings focuses on how the deviant roles of prostitute and crack addict are related.

Methods

Intensive interviews were conducted by the author with 39 women who used crack and had multiple sex partners within the week preceding the interview.[1] Interviews were conducted in an office affiliated with a local drug education and outreach project and lasted approximately 1–2 hrs. Subjects were paid $25 for their participation.

The subjects' age averaged approximately 32 years, and about half stated that they had less than a 12th-grade education. Thirty-three subjects were black, and six were white. Though only one was legally employed at the time of the interview, subjects averaged a monthly income of nearly $2,000.

Information was obtained regarding the subject's drug history (particularly her introduction to and use of crack cocaine), her experiences as a prostitute, and other related matters. Tape recordings of the interviews were transcribed by a research assistant, and relevant responses were categorized and coded by the author. Inductive techniques were used to classify subjects' statements about their use of crack cocaine and the relation of the drug to their involvement with prostitution.

Results

An analysis of subjects' statements regarding their use of crack cocaine and its relation to their involvement in prostitution led to the identification of three primary characteristic responses: addiction, utility, and marketplace economics. These responses define the ways in which the role of crack user and prostitute are integrated. All three types of integration were evident in the responses of many of the subjects, and most subjects manifested at least two types to some degree. The implications of this overlap are discussed below.

ADDICTION

Of the various expressions given by subjects for describing their use of crack cocaine and its link to prostitution, none was represented so frequently in the responses as the image of crack addiction. This type of response was typically characterized by straightforward statements of the subject's addiction to crack cocaine. Prostitution was viewed simply as a means—a typically reliable and relatively lucrative means—of securing funds needed to purchase the drug.[2] (Other means included other illegal activities, legal employment, public aid, and financial assistance from family and friends.) Like these other activities, prostitution was typically described as merely a means to obtaining and doing crack.

The responses indicative of this form of role integration clearly place drug use or drug addiction near the center of the subject's identity. Prostitution (as well as many other roles) is secondary. For example:

> I smoke every day, all day. . . . It's like that every day. I just got out of the ward, and it's been like that. . . . I've been smokin' ever since I started. Every day, all day. And the only time I miss smoking is when I'm locked

up. [On prostitution:] I'll be anxious to get it over with so I can go get a rock. I'll be like I wish you would hurry up, don't take so long 'cause I got to go. (Respondent #1238)

This woman went on to state that her need for crack cocaine made it likely that she would have sex without using condoms, something she knew she should not do:

The majority of the time I use condoms. I may just find myself sometimes without, you know just to get what I want. . . . Because I'm a coke addict. I just want to get me some cocaine. Just do it, just to go get me some more cocaine so I don't have to look for more money. (#1238)

Others gave similar expressions of their overwhelming desire to obtain the drug:

The rock is the pimp. . . . We go out there, we do all this, we get all this money, first person we run to is to the dope man. The rock is the pimp. . . . So that's why they call us strawberries, 'cause we get the rocks and we will have oral sex, have you, have your brother too, all at the same time to get this cocaine. (#1221)

When you're using these drugs sometimes you'll do just about anything to get it. (#1217)

I really didn't want to be with them, but I wanted to get high, so I just went ahead and had sex with them to get the money and go on and buy my [rock]. [Q: So, why do you have sex?] So I could get high. (#1240)

When asked whether using crack cocaine had increased their sexual activity, 29 (78.4 percent) of the 37 women who answered the question responded affirmatively. Many said the only reason they were hustling dates was in order to obtain crack.

Although addiction is perhaps the most prevalent motivation for continuing to engage in prostitution, it rarely appeared to be the dominant factor in a respondent's initiation into prostitution. Respondent #1226 was representative of many women who began "dating" (soliciting sex) in order to make money for general living expenses. At the time, her use of drugs was limited and only subsequently did her crack cocaine use become her primary expense. Others suggested that as their use or addiction rises and falls so does their prostitution (#1229). Nearly everyone stated flatly that if she was not using crack cocaine she would not be dating.

In light of their addiction to crack cocaine, the distinction between a sex-for-cash exchange and a sex-for-drugs exchange is one that matters little to many women. One woman stated that it did not matter whether she got cash or rocks as payment for sex because "that [crack cocaine] is what I'm gonna get anyway" (#1208).

UTILITARIANISM

For many subjects, the relation between their prostitution activities and their use of crack cocaine cannot be characterized solely in terms of an addiction model. In particular, there are some connections between the two roles that might at first appear rather incidental but on closer examination are shown to be important facilitating links between the two. Consistent with earlier reports from cocaine users (e.g., Grinspoon and Bakalar 1976; Parr 1976), statements from these women suggest that there is still a fairly widespread perception of cocaine as at least an ameliorating, if not sexually stimulating, drug. For many women, cocaine facilitated the business of prostitution, enabling them to cope with difficult work conditions. For instance, some women reported that smoking crack made them feel sexy and reduced their inhibitions about having sex. Many also reported that smoking made the customer more relaxed, though some stated that crack often interfered with the customer's ability to achieve orgasm, thus unduly prolonging the session. Overwhelmingly, women shared the general view that doing cocaine was at least somewhat useful in their particular line of work:

> I don't think I could do it [have sex with a john] if I wasn't high. . . . A lot of the time I'm smoking while I'm having sex. [She stated that she was high approximately 80–85 percent of the time that she had sex.] (#1217)

> [After the initial high] there is something in the drug that gives you that sexual desire. (#1224)

> Approximately 75 percent of the time coke is involved with the date. It's the drug of choice [among johns]. Why, I don't know, but it's the drug of choice. I always go, yeah, that's what you're supposed to do. (#1231)

> [How much of the time are you high when you're having sex?] All the time. [Laughs.] No, mostly all the time I been had some saved and I hit it before I have sex. [Has cocaine ever increased your desire to have sex?] Yeah, it makes you feel sexy. (#1221)

Many women attempted to counter possible criticism of their admitted dependence on cocaine by citing its usefulness. One respondent, acknowledging this two-sidedness of cocaine, stated that her dependence did not interfere with her ability to work:

> When I'm high though, I usually don't let it affect me, so that I can't take care of my business. It just makes me funky and better. (#1238)

Again, this type of facilitating link between crack use and prostitution is independent of the level of addiction experienced by the women. A few of the women were nightclub dancers or had been dancers in the past. The two occupations of dancer and prostitute were clearly related in the minds of these women. Just as in prostitution, cocaine had a use for the role of dancer:

> The girls that get into drugs real heavy, they get up on stage and do what they have to do. (#1230)

Another useful aspect of doing crack is that the prostitute regularly interacts with "dope men" who have a lot of money, although reports of their willingness to part with it vary. These dope men are good, wealthy clients, but their acquaintance is valuable in other ways as well, as discussed in the next section. One subject spoke repeatedly of the significance of this acquaintance during the interview:

> [Describing some of her better dates, one where a couple of johns went in together and paid her well in rocks:] Usually it be like the dealers, and a couple of guys, usually be the dealers you know, and that's how you get more rocks 'cause usually a person that, unless they done got paid, that would be the only person buy you that many rocks, other than that we can get that many rocks from a dealer. (#1221)

MARKETPLACE ECONOMICS

The third characterization of subjects' use of crack and its relation to prostitution is one in which subjects described their procurement of crack and their selling of sex as fundamental marketplace processes. Responses often exhibited the subject's shrewd understanding of how to thrive in a competitive marketplace. Many of these women engaged in prostitution as a livelihood long before they began using crack cocaine. Specific aspects of their marketplace role relations include: prostitutes as drug couriers, common market interest of prostitutes and crack sellers, frequent sales and bartering between prostitutes and crack sellers, and the social and symbolic benefits of the relation.

Prostitutes as Drug Couriers. The first aspect of the role relation evolves from the common practice among drug buyers and sellers of using women (and young boys) as couriers. This is a frequent practice among drug suppliers and users because women are thought to be less likely to arouse the suspicion of the police. Even though they may possess a certain notoriety vis-à-vis the police, prostitutes would be especially well-suited to this task because they already possess a certain intrepid street savvy. As a result, these women would regularly find themselves in possession of significant quantities of crack. Receiving (or taking outright) some of the contraband as payment for their courier services could be expected to occur rather often. For many women, profits from this work are likely to be as important as those derived from their prostitution activities:

> Uh-huh, I be showin' 'em where, you know, like what area to go in. And then I'll be getting my money, you gonna give me $2 or $3 for shown' 'em. . . . Over the weekend I do it every night. (#1240) [She went on to indicate that this was a function of her being out on the street, hustling.]

> Somebody came by and asked me if I had a stem [a pipe for smoking crack] and did I know where to cop. But they knew, you know, where to get it and everything, but they all gave me the money. (#1238)

Thus, although cocaine was often defined as an aid in the performance of the business of prostitution, it was clear from the interviews that a woman's pursuit of cocaine is well served by her role as a prostitute. For instance, although prostitution constitutes a major source of income and enables many addicted women to purchase crack cocaine, it is often the case that prostitution activities merely provide somewhat serendipitous access to crack. In many ways, prostitution is apparently perceived as a central role in the deviant street network, affording the prostitute knowledge of and access to a wide range of profitable and ostensibly exciting activities. Many prostitutes develop a high profile on the street and are often well connected in the deviant community. These characteristics make them popular choices as sources of information and as couriers for others wishing to purchase drugs. Performing these minor services for other drug users will frequently net the prostitute a share in the drugs. Sometimes she is given a portion of the drugs; other times she skims part of it without the buyer's knowledge. As a courier, some women reported establishing a price with the occasional drug buyer for a certain amount of drugs. Subsequently, the prostitute is able to arrange a more desirable deal with the supplier and keeps the difference for herself. Twenty (51 percent) of the women in the sample reported having served as drug couriers or "coppers" in the previous week, often handling hundreds of dollars of crack cocaine in a single deal. For these women, their street role as a prostitute was extremely useful in their ability to locate, obtain, and profit from cocaine to be delivered to others.

In addition, prostitution sometimes brings women into contact with customers who are in possession of large quantities of drugs. These special customers may occasionally bestow special attention on the prostitute, giving her free gifts of crack or bargain rates, and may provide a certain measure of protection or security because she is often viewed as an important link in the drug information and supply network. Women who take advantage of this fortuitous facilitation of crack use that prostitution provides may or may not be heavy users, and thus, this aspect of the interrelation between the two activities is distinct from the addiction model described above.

Common Market Interests of Prostitutes and Crack Sellers. Because prostitution and crack constitute two major commodities in the inner city, crack dealers and prostitutes are likely to have overlapping markets. Like more conventional retailers who form associations to preserve their market interest, these illegal entrepreneurs have common interests in the marketplace that they no doubt wish to protect, including the stability of prices, the encroachment on established territory by outside vendors, the freedom of the marketplace from police interference, and even the credit ratings of various customers. Regular interaction between prostitutes and crack sellers to exchange information and safeguard their areas of enterprise would be a part of the natural course of doing business:

> They call us little ladies of the night, and the little ladies of the night is
> out there, of them they surely takes good care of us 'cause they know we
> gonna go get the money and come back to them 'cause see sometimes
> when you ask them for something and maybe I have time or maybe I
> want to have sex with you then, they will give you some because if you

are spendin' with them all the time, know what I'm saying, and bring customers to them all the time, oh they'll look out for you before they'll look out for anybody. (#1221)

Frequent Sales and Bartering of Goods and Services. As a natural extension of drug dealers' and prostitutes' common market interests, it is likely that members of these two groups frequently engage in direct sales and exchange of goods. Both crack dealers and prostitutes would at times probably find it expedient to exchange one commodity for the other. For instance, during the days and weeks immediately prior to the mailing of government support checks (e.g., Aid to Families with Dependent Children, social security, etc.) there is often a widespread shortage of cash in neighborhoods where this monthly influx of capital is of significant proportions. Given that easy credit may be difficult to secure from prostitutes and drug dealers, goods and services like crack and sex (as well as food and other necessities) may be available during such times only through bartering. Though by no means a recent phenomenon in the drug culture, bartering has reached impressive dimensions in the crack trade. Goods and services of all sorts can be exchanged in this cashless market:

> [Describing how she let a dealer use her apartment for his business:] If I got a lot of money I might buy me like three rocks. I try not to go with three rocks 'cause usually, I hook up with some of the boys and they *give* it to me. See, you know come in my house and cut up dope and some, they leave me some. They do that too, you know. Well, if they want to sell some out of your house for the day and, um, they'll throw you out some like that too, just to use your house for the day. . . . I had one guy stay there for a whole week. And I had to buy nothing. I just got it free all that week. (#1221)

The economics of prostitution and cocaine are probably as complex as any other illegal market. There are relatively simple issues to resolve such as the quality of the drug being sold and the advantage of buying in quantity. Other issues such as procuring cocaine with cash versus exchanging sex for it are not so straightforward. Some respondents stated that it made more sense to them to be paid by their johns in cash and then purchase drugs with the cash:

> I prefer being paid in cash . . . 'cause you can do with it what you want. I may not want to buy $200 worth of rock. I might want to buy [something else] and some rock, you know. Whereas, if you turn a date for drugs and you take drugs you might tell yourself you're gonna sell it but you're not gonna sell it. . . . So I would prefer to be paid with cash. (#1217)

This sentiment was echoed by another who said that all her dates are cash dates, and she buys her rocks. Being paid in cash allows her to "do what I want to do" (#1234). Other women were more willing to accept rocks in payment for sex. Often, this willingness is partly a function of their current need to get high. One respondent who gave considerable evidence of being addicted to cocaine reduced the issue of cash payment versus bartering to a truism: It did not matter, because "that's [crack] what I'm gonna get anyway" (#1208). Even when addiction or immediate need for the drug was apparently not a factor, several women suggested that it was wiser to accept rocks for sex rather than money if the quality of the rocks was certain.

A range of factors impinge on the economic decisions of these women. Some have children to support whereas others cited routine household expenses. The salience of these factors varied. For instance, one woman's children had recently moved in with her mother. This arrangement meant that she required significantly less cash in payment for sex. Other women indicated that the depletion of their public assistance funds by about the middle of each month made for a significant change in the level of their solicitation activities and put a premium on cash dates during the last weeks of the month.

> Well, first of all I really didn't have no place to stay, . . . and I needed somewhere to stay . . . so I walking down the street, in the street rather, and the guy stopped me and said, um, are you dating today? And I thought he was the police so I wouldn't say nothing and kept going. And then he came back around the corner and he said "I got $20," like that, and I said god, I need this $20. I did it with him in the car. And I got the $20, and then I said well, I can get me some more money, you know, like this. . . . . It started becoming a regular thing when I needed a place to stay for good to sleep, something to eat, and clothes and stuff to wear, and just money to get around, you know. (#1221)

Other aspects of this woman's purchasing habits and her sex marketing practices show all the sophistication of a savvy entrepreneur:

> Sometimes I get two rocks, sometimes I don't. Sometimes I may do good they may give me four rocks. The least I ever took was two rocks. They know I ain't going below that. I'll go make me some money, buy my own. (Laughs.) I mean I'm sorry to say that but I will. . . . . They so cheap. [Describing customers who pay in cash, she complained about how little they paid:] About $25, I'll say $20. See they give you more rocks they only gonna give you less money. They give you more rocks you don't get that much money. Sometimes you just get those rocks and you don't get money at all. (#1221)

Social and Symbolic Benefits.   Finally, beyond general economic concern, it is possible that relationships between prostitutes and crack sellers serve other functions as well. For instance, prostitutes willing to exchange sex for crack sometimes seek to establish a fairly stable relationship with a dealer (or several), particularly one who sells "weight" (significant quantities of cocaine) in order to ensure a regular supply of the drug. In lieu of cash payments, crack sellers engaged in such bartering might derive a form of symbolic status by having in their debt women willing to do almost anything for them. The perception of such women as a type of chattel would be consistent with the prevailing low esteem in which "strawberries" are typically held by those inside as well as outside the drug trade.

The issue of surviving in the competitive marketplace (as a supplier in the prostitution market and as a consumer in the cocaine market) underscores the need to establish reliable contacts with others, especially clients, drug users, and drug dealers. Most of the women sought to maintain a regular sex clientele, seeing several customers on a weekly basis. The same reliability was sought in their source of cocaine as well as in opportunities for supplemental income (e.g., by copping drugs for others).

Discussion

Nearly all the women interviewed for this study gave some incidence of being addicted to cocaine. However, the link between prostitution and cocaine is more complex than this. It involves specific utilitarian aspects of the drug (e.g., its stimulant effect) as well as the general symbolic value of cocaine as a "sex drug." In addition, prostitution and consumption of cocaine are parts of larger economic processes that are not unlike those of a more typical worker: occasional changes in expenses and other sources of income, the need to anticipate cash flow needs, the liquidity of assets, and the importance of good credit and reliable marketplace contacts. These economic concerns form the foundation of an important role relationship between prostitutes and others who traffic in cocaine.

Recent reports have suggested that crack sellers frequently target women as a sizable and important market for the drug. Fearful of intravenous use of drugs but desirous of something more potent than marijuana, many women find crack an agreeable alternative (Massing 1989). Even street terminology reflects users' and sellers' sensitization to certain gender implications of the drug, sometimes referring to cocaine as "girl" and heroin as "boy."

The data presented here reveal a multidimensional relation between cocaine and prostitution, but they do not provide a basis for establishing a conclusive priority among the ways in which the relation can be characterized. It seems clear that the effect of cocaine on the libido and acute addiction do not alone explain the high rates of cocaine and crack cocaine use among prostitutes. Rather, the data relating prostitution to the use of cocaine seem to suggest that this use partly reflects specific economic relationships that link prostitutes and crack dealers.

As concern grows regarding the spread of HIV, more attention has been focused on prostitution as a vector of transmission. Increasingly, the examination of prostitution has uncovered how closely related prostitution is to the problem of substance abuse, particularly crack cocaine abuse. As a result, solving the public health problem posed by unsafe sex with prostitutes depends to a great extent on getting a grip on the problems posed by unchecked distribution and consumption of crack cocaine. Traditional substance abuse treatment may remedy the problem of substance addiction, but it does not provide solutions to marketplace processes that, for many, are exploitive and ultimately destructive. These solutions require a more holistic understanding of the cocaine-abusing prostitute and her economic relationships than typically has been the case.

NOTES

[1] Women were recruited for the study by outreach workers of a drug-counseling agency in Cleveland, Ohio. The parameters of the population from which subjects were recruited were women who used cocaine at least three times in the week prior to the interview and had at least three different sex partners during the same week. Because the study was exploratory in nature and because of the lack of shared meaning of labels such as "prostitute" or "strawberry," it was not required that subjects identify themselves *a priori* as either to be included in the study. In response to a question in the interview, all the women in the sample agreed that they would label themselves as either prostitutes or strawberries. (The term "strawberry" is slang for a woman who accepts drugs—especially crack—as payment for sex. One subject informed the interviewer that the term was meant to indicate that such women were "easy pickin's," willing to perform nearly any sort of sexual act for as little as a "bump" or a puff off a crack pipe.)

[2] Of course, for some women, prostitution was a means for obtaining crack directly. Though some have suggested that bartering sex for drugs is an indication of the degree of addiction, it is apparent that other marketplace issues also figure in whether women seek and receive cash in payment for sex or whether they accept drugs in direct exchange. These marketplace issues are discussed later.

REFERENCES

Abramowitz, A., J. Guydish, W. Woods, and W. Clark. 1989. "Increasing Crack Use Among Drug Users in an AIDS Epicenter: San Francisco." *Fifth International Conference on AIDS Abstracts*: 1:764.

Aral, Sevgi O., and King K. Holmes. 1990. "Epidemiology of Sexual Behavior and Sexually Transmitted Diseases," Pp. 19–36 in *Sexually Transmitted Diseases*, edited by King K. Holmes, Willard Cautes, Jr., Stanley Lemon, and Walter E. Stamm. New York: McGraw Hill.

Bowser, Benjamin P. 1989. "Crack and AIDS: An Ethnographic Impression." *Journal of the National Medical Association* 81:538–40.

Bowser, Benjamin P., Mindy Thompson Fullilove, and Robert E. Fullilove. 1990. "African-American Youth and AIDS High-Risk Behavior: The Social Context and Barriers to Prevention." *Youth and Society* 22:54–66.

Buffum, John. 1982. "Pharmacosexology: The Effects of Drugs on Sexual Function—A Review." *Journal of Psychoactive Drugs* 14:5–44.

———. 1988. "Substance Abuse and High-Risk Sexual Behavior: Drugs and Sex—The Dark Side." *Journal of Psychoactive Drugs* 20:165–8.

Centers for Disease Control. 1987. "Antibody for Human Immunodeficiency Virus in Female Prostitutes." *Morbidity and Mortality Weekly Report* 36:157–161.

———. 1988. "Relationship of Syphilis to Drug Use and Prostitution—Connecticut and Philadelphia, Pennsylvania." *Morbidity and Mortality Weekly Report* 37:755–64.

Chambers, Carl D., R. Kent Hinsely, and Mary Moldestad. 1970. "The Female Opiate Addict." Pp. 222–39 in *The Epidemiology of Opiate Addiction in the United States*, edited by John C. Ball and Carl D. Chambers. Springfield, MA: Charles C. Thomas.

Cooper, Mary H. 1988. "The Business of Illicit Drugs." *Congressional Quarterly Editorial Research Reports* May 20:258–71.

Cregler, Louis. 1989. "Adverse Health Consequences of Cocaine Abuse." *Journal of the National Medical Association* 81:27–38.

Cushman, Peter. 1972. "Methadone Maintenance Treatment of Narcotic Addiction: Analysis of Police Records of Arrests Before and During Treatment." *New York State Journal of Medicine* 72:1752–69.

The Economist. 1989. "American Survey: The AIDS Plague Spreads." 312:23–4.

Friedman, S. R., C. Dozier, C. Sterk, T. Williams, J. L. Southeran, D. C. Des Jarlais. 1988. "Crack Use Puts Women at Risk for Heterosexual Transmission of HIV from Intravenous Drug Users." *Fourth International Conference on AIDS Abstracts* 2:396.

Fullilove, Mindy Thompson, and Robert E. Fullilove. 1989. "Intersecting Epidemics: Black Teen Crack Use and Sexually Transmitted Disease." *Journal of the American Medical Women's Association* 44:146–53.

Fullilove, Robert E., Mindy Thompson Fullilove, Benjamin P. Bowser and Shirley A. Gross. 1990. "Risk of Sexually Transmitted Disease Among Black Adolescent Crack Users in Oakland and San Francisco, California." *Journal of the American Medical Association* 263:851–5.

Goldstein, Paul. J. 1979. *Prostitution and Drugs.* Lexington, MA: Lexington Books.

Grinspoon, Lester, and James B. Bakalar. 1976. *Cocaine: A Drug and Its Social Evolution.* New York: Basic Books.

Inciardi, James A. 1989. "Trading Sex for Crack Among Juvenile Drug Users: A Research Note." *Contemporary Drug Problems* 16:689–700.

Inciardi, James A. 1992. "Kingrats, Chicken Heads, Slow Necks, Freaks, and Blood Suckers: A Glimpse at the Miami Sex for Crack Market." Pp. 37–67 in *Crack Pipe as Pimp,* edited by Mitchel Raener. Lexington, MA: Lexington Free Press.

Inciardi, James A., and Anne E. Pottieger. 1986. "Drug Use and Crime Among Two Cohorts of Women Narcotics Users: An Empirical Assessment." *Journal of Drug Issues* 16:91–106.

Isikoff, Michael. 1989. "Crack Holds Many Inner-City Women in Its Grip." Pp. A–18 in *The Washington Post* August 20: Reprinted on the NIJ Conference electronic BBS.

James, Jennifer, Cathleen Gosho, and Robbin Watson Wohl. 1979. "The Relationship Between Female Criminality and Drug Use." *International Journal of the Addictions* 14:215–29.

Kerr, Peter. 1988. "Syphilis Surge with Crack Use Raises Fears on Spread of AIDS." *The New York Times* June 29:B1.

Leigh, Barabara Critchlow. 1990. "The Relationship of Substance Use During Sex to High Risk Behavior." *The Journal of Sex Research* 27:199–213.

MacDonald, Patrick T., Dan Waldorf, Craig Reinarman, and Sheila Murphy. 1988. "Heavy Cocaine Use and Sexual Behavior." *Journal of Drug Issues* 18:437–55.

Massing, Michael. 1989. "Crack's Destructive Sprint Across America." *New York Times Magazine* October 1:38–41 and 58–9.

Miller, Eleanor. 1986. *Street Women.* Philadelphia: Temple University Press.

Minerbrook, Scott. 1989. "A Night in a Crack House." *U.S. News and World Report* April 10:29.

Parr, Denis. 1976. "Sexual Aspects of Drug Abuse in Narcotic Addicts." *British Journal of Psychiatry* 71:261–8.

Rolfs, Robert T., Martin Goldberg, and Robert G. Sharrar. 1990. "Risk Factors for Syphilis: Cocaine Use and Prostitution." *American Journal of Public Health* 80:853–7.

Shedlin, Michele. 1990. "An Ethnographic Approach to Understanding HIV High-Risk Behaviors: Prostitution and Drug Abuse." *National Institute on Drug Abuse Research Monograph Series* 93:134–49.

Wesson, Donald R. 1982. "Cocaine Use by Masseuses." *Journal of Psychoactive Drugs* 14:75–6.

Winick, Charles, and Paul M. Kinsie. 1971. *The Lively Commerce.* Chicago: Quadrangle.

Section
III

THE DRUG INDUSTRY

7

The Youth Gangs, Drugs, and Violence Connection

James C. Howell
Scott H. Decker

The popular image of youth gangs ties them directly to drugs and violent crime (Klein, 1995).[1] How interrelated are youth gangs, drugs, and violent crime? Is drug trafficking a main activity of youth gangs? Is drug trafficking a main cause of violence in youth gangs or only a correlate? Are there other important sources of gang violence? Before this article addresses these questions, a brief historical overview of gang drug use, trafficking, and violent crime is provided. Studies of drug-trafficking operations are then reviewed to provide a better understanding of how illegal drug sales typically are controlled and managed. The article concludes with a detailed review of studies of the gangs, drugs, and violence connection and an examination of other sources of gang violence.

Historical Overview of Gang Drug Use and Trafficking

The predominant image of youth gangs is consistent with a California study of adult (also referred to as criminal) gang members conducted by Skolnick and colleagues (1988) a decade ago. These researchers contended that the two major Los Angeles gangs, the Crips and Bloods, had become entrepre-

From *Juvenile Justice Bulletin*, January 1999, The Office of Juvenile Justice and Delinquency. Washington, DC: U.S. Department of Justice.

neurial and were expanding their drug-trafficking operations to markets in other cities; where drug markets appeared, so did violent crime. Although this research did not address the order of occurrences and the overlap of adult gang violence and street drug sales, youth gangs are still characterized mainly by public perceptions conveyed in the California studies and by popular media images rather than by scientific knowledge (Decker and Kempf, 1991; Hunzeker, 1993; Jackson, 1997; Johnson, 1989; Miller, 1990).

Little mention is made of gang drug use and trafficking in gang studies published before the 1960s and 1970s (Klein, 1971; Short and Strodtbeck, 1965; Spergel, 1964). By all accounts, gang involvement in drug use and trafficking was either very limited or unnoticed before the 1960s (Wilkinson and Fagan, 1996). Moore (1991) described heroin and some barbiturate use among Los Angeles gang members in the 1940s, mostly after they left gangs. In the 1950s and into the 1960s, youth gang members displayed ambivalence about gang member drug use and trafficking (Spergel, 1995). Some gangs of that era used—or at least tolerated—marijuana. Heroin-using cliques were common in East Los Angeles gangs by the middle of the 1950s (Bullington, 1977). Other gang cliques, the partying members of gangs, began to use barbiturates (Moore, 1978). Cloward and Ohlin's (1960) typology of youth gangs put drug users in a "retreatist" subculture of addicts (withdrawing from active involvement in the gang). Even in the 1970s, drug use did not appear to be a dominant form of illegal activity among gang members, either as a proportion of their own arrests or in comparison with arrested non-gang youth (Miller, 1992).

In his historical account of gangs, Spergel (1995) noted that in some instances drug-abusing members, particularly those who used heroin, were forced out of gangs in the 1950s and 1960s (and also in the 1990s) because they could not be relied on in fights with other gangs. Gangs have also been reported to drive drug traffickers out of the neighborhood (Short and Strodtbeck, 1965, Spergel, 1964). A few studies point to marijuana use in the 1960s and 1970s (Klein, 1971; Short and Strodtbeck, 1965) and to the fact that the drug market had "increasingly drawn in gang members as participants in drug distribution networks" (Miller, 1992:144). By the late 1970s, older African-American adult gang members in Chicago were reported to be significantly involved in drug dealing (Spergel, 1995).

Early gang studies do not tie violence to drug trafficking because gangs evidenced little involvement in drug sales. The first major gang study (Thrasher, 1927) described the drug dealing of Chicago's Chinese tongs, but gang violence mainly consisted of fighting. An account of early twentieth century east coast adult gangs linked gang violence to territorial fights among organized crime groups that used teenagers in "numbers running" and as lookouts in gambling and bootlegging operations (Sante, 1991). Except for occasional fighting, violent crime by youth gangs was relatively rare until the latter part of this century (Miller, Geertz, and Cutter, 1962).

Growing Involvement in Drugs and Violent Crime

The early to mid-1980s saw rapid growth in the use of cocaine as crack became the drug of choice in the inner cities (Fagan, 1996; Fagan and Chin, 1990; Klein and Maxson, 1994). Trend data that would indicate whether gang members were responsible for the increased prevalence of cocaine use during this period are not available. However, several studies document considerable youth and adult gang involvement in the drug trade after the cocaine epidemic began around 1985.[2] The Chicago Vice Lords, a large and violent criminal street gang (Dawley, 1992; Keiser, 1969; Spergel, 1995), grew during this era, providing one example that suggests gangs and crack sales emerged concurrently.

Research conducted in the 1980s and 1990s has documented extensive youth and adult gang member involvement in drug use and generally higher levels of use compared with non-gang members.[3]

However, gang members do not all use drugs or do not use them extensively (Chin, 1990; Chin and Fagan, 1990; Fagan, 1989). Studies also show differences in the extent of drug use. For example, Hill, Howell, and Hawkins (1996) found that gang membership was related to increased marijuana use but not crack cocaine use (except among youth who were in the gang for only one year). Huff (1996) reported gangs that used large amounts of all kinds of drugs. Fagan (1989) found variations in drug use among different gangs and several other studies found predominantly drug-trafficking youth gangs.[4]

For the most part, the findings of the studies outlined in the previous paragraph apply only to males. Some cities, such as Detroit (Taylor, 1993) and San Francisco (Lauderback, Hansen, and Waldorf, 1992), found an increasing number of females involved in gang drug trafficking and violent crime, but the consensus is that female involvement in these behaviors has not increased commensurately with the increase among males (Chesney-Lind, 1993; Maxson, 1995; Moore and Hagedorn, 1996).

Why has youth gang involvement in drug trafficking increased in the past decade? Fagan (1993) suggested two reasons: (1) the dramatic expansion of cocaine markets in the 1980s, accompanied by sharp price reductions, and (2) socioeconomic changes in American society that disrupted traditional social controls (Curry and Spergel, 1988).[5]

Fagan (1996; see also Hagedorn, 1988; Wilson, 1996) identified the process by which this disruption of social controls occurred in the employment arena. The decline in manufacturing jobs in the 1970s and the development of technological and service industries led to economic restructuring in many cities. New jobs were created, but they were in the suburbs, leaving unqualified minorities in the inner cities. Dramatic increases in unemployment resulted, especially among minority males, and high unemployment rates were mainly concentrated in specific geographic areas. Drug markets provided "work" for displaced workers, and the growing popularity of crack cocaine opened new opportunities for youth to make money. Traditional pathways from gang life (jobs, marriage, starting a family) were constricted by the changed economy, prolonging gang involvement and making drug trafficking more attractive. The decline of meaningful lifetime employment prospects weakened the stabilizing influences and traditional forms of informal social controls and strengthened gang influence as a dominant informal control and socialization force. Fagan reasoned that these conditions facilitated the transformation of youth groups into loosely structured gangs. As the size and stakes of the cocaine economy grew, violence increasingly came to be used in the regulatory process. "Work and social interactions were now organized around these criminal activities, enforced and regulated increasingly by violence" (Fagan, 1996:64).

The Current Image of Youth Gangs

Because the growth in youth gang violence coincided with the crack cocaine epidemic, the two developments were generally perceived to be interrelated.[6] This same conclusion was reached in assessments conducted at all governmental levels, suggesting that youth gangs were instrumental in the increase in crack cocaine sales and that their involvement in drug trafficking resulted in a growth in youth violence.[7]

Skolnick and his colleagues provided an image of drug trafficking that the media magnified and stereotyped (Klein, 1995). Based on interviews with prison inmates, police, and correctional officials, they described entrepreneurial criminal gangs (Bloods and Crips) that emerged out of African-American "cultural" (neighborhood) youth gangs in Los Angeles and Northern California (Skolnick, 1989, 1990, 1991; Skolnick et al., 1988). Skolnick and his colleagues contended that these new criminal gangs were organized for and actively involved in street drug sales. The Bloods and Crips increasingly looked like criminal gangs designed for the sale of drugs. They enjoyed the benefits of being able to deal cocaine in the neighborhoods they controlled, without intrusion by competitors. They had a territorial monopoly, backed by force. Driven by escalating violence in Los Angeles, declining drug prices, and intensified law enforcement, the California gangs sought out new markets for crack cocaine in other cities.

It was not until the early 1990s that a national study of street gang migration was conducted (Maxson, Woods, and Klein, 1996). In *Gang Members on the Move*, gang migration is defined as the movement of gang members from one city to another, which could include temporary relocation (e.g., visits to relatives, short trips to sell drugs) and longer stays (Maxson, 1998b). The study found street gang migration to be very limited. Nevertheless, in about one-third of the cities that did experience substantial gang migration, drug market expansion and pursuit of other criminal activities were the primary motivations, suggesting that drug gangs may be more involved in migration. Most of the gang migration, however, was regional, within about 100 miles of the city of origin. A number of local studies of individual gangs questioned their ties to larger gangs such as the Crips and Bloods in distant cities (Decker and Van Winkle, 1994).[8]

In the meantime, police and investigatory agencies reported criminal gang drug-trafficking links across the country. A U.S. Congress study (General Accounting Office, 1989) concluded that during the latter part of the 1980s, the Crips and Bloods gained control of 30 percent of the crack cocaine market in the United States. Another Federal agency, the Drug Enforcement Administration (1988), reported links between these Los Angeles street gangs and drug sales in 46 states. Police and Federal Bureau of Investigation (FBI) officials reported that by the late 1980s, the Los Angeles Bloods and Crips had migrated to 45 other cities and set up crack cocaine trafficking operations (Skolnick, 1989).

Shortly after Skolnick's studies were released, the Los Angeles County District Attorney made a comprehensive assessment of Los Angeles youth gangs (Reiner, 1992). His office concluded that "gang members are heavy drug users and even heavier drug sellers [than nongang youth], yet drugs and gangs are not two halves of the same phenomenon. *Though they threaten many of the same neighborhoods, and involve some of the same people, gangs and drugs must be treated as separate evils*" [emphasis added] (Reiner, 1992:5). District Attorney Reiner's office estimated that more than 70 percent of gang members in Los Angeles used drugs and that the incidence of drug sales among gang members was seven times higher than among non-gang youth. The study concluded, however, that most gang members were not drug dealers, in any meaningful sense of the word; only 1 in 7 gang members was estimated to sell drugs as often as 12 times a year. Reiner's office also concluded that "most L.A. gangs are not being transformed into organized drug distribution rings. Many individual gang members (and former members) are involved with drugs, but drugs remain peripheral to the purposes and activities of the gang" (Reiner, 1992:5).

As more information on youth gang activities has become available, investigatory agencies have made more precise assessments of gang drug trafficking. The National Drug Intelligence Centers (NDIC's) Street Gang Symposium, held in Johnstown, PA, November 2–3, 1994, focused on the Bloods and Crips. Symposium participants concluded that some well-organized street gangs are engaged in interstate drug trafficking, but for the most part, a gang's drug-trafficking connections are indirectly expanded when members relocate to different areas. NDIC concluded that most street gangs are involved in drug trafficking to some extent, generally in a street-level distribution network, both individually and in small groups.

Reports of youth gang involvement in drug trafficking stimulated a major debate about the capacity of such gangs to manage drug sales operations. The two main camps in this debate are best represented by Skolnick and his colleagues and Sanchez-Jankowski on the one hand and Klein and his colleagues and Decker and Van Winkle on the other.[9] The former described gangs as formal-rational organizations with an established leadership structure, roles, rules, and control over members, such that gangs are quite capable of organizing and managing top-level drug-trafficking operations. The latter described gangs as loosely confederated groups that generally lack cohesion and would be incapable of organizing and managing drug-trafficking operations.

The California-based image of a close connection among gangs, drugs, and violent crime has been buttressed by a number of studies. Although neither of them appears to be a bona fide youth gang, Williams' (1989) "cocaine kids" and Padilla's (1992) drug-dealing Puerto Rican gang in Chicago (Klein, 1995) epitomize the economic opportunities the new drug markets provided—and the surrounding violence. Venkatesh (1996) reported that the illicit drug economy transformed gang violence in Chicago's Robert Taylor Homes from gang wars to drug wars. Taylor (1990) described how the Detroit economy and the drug market turned "scavenger" gangs of the 1950s to 1970s into "corporate" gangs involved in illegal moneymaking ventures in an interstate network. He interviewed a retired Detroit police official who described the city's gang drug problem this way:

> It's like feudal China, there are pockets of entrenched drug operations all over the city. . . . You have warlords over little areas that control their little fiefdoms. There are young people acting as contractors for the warlords. . . . Kids and adults see the warlords spreading money and fame. They want some of that money. Soon as we put away one bunch, another one takes its place. Then you got professional people, like lawyers, giving these punks their service. Dope has made these characters think they're rich and powerful (Taylor, 1990:114).

Thus, studies have produced conflicting images of youth gang involvement in drug trafficking. In part, these different images stem from the lack of a clear distinction between youth gangs and adult criminal drug-trafficking organizations.

Street Gangs Versus Drug Gangs

Klein (1995) suggested that to provide a better understanding of violence related to drug marketing, a distinction needs to be made between street-level drug distribution and high-level control of drug distribution networks. He distinguished drug gangs from street gangs, which he contended are not the same.

Unfortunately, youth gang studies have not revealed much about management and control of drug-trafficking operations versus street-level distribution systems. Most studies of youth gangs that are involved in drug trafficking describe their involvement in street-level distribution only. A notable exception is Moore's (1978) description of the Happy Valley gang in Los Angeles, which maintained strong connections with Mexican barbiturate manufacturers who created "designer" barbiturates to their order, which the gang sold. The entire Happy Valley gang was involved, not just individual members.[10]

Information on the prevalence of youth drug gangs has only recently become available. In Klein's (1995) interviews with 261 police officers (mostly gang specialists) in U.S. cities (with a population of more than 100,000) in which law enforcement agencies said they had a gang problem, 16 percent reported drug gangs. In another law enforcement survey in 201 cities, Klein and Maxson (1996) found that "specialty drug gangs" comprised only 9 percent of all gangs. Nevertheless, the membership of such gangs may be very large, and thus they may be responsible for a significant proportion of drug sales and violence in some cities.

Huff (1996) assessed the extent to which Cleveland gang members believed that gangs controlled drug-trafficking operations. Only 10 percent believed such control to be the case. About 10 to 14 percent believed gangs had some control over the organization and management of drug sales along with other organizations, such as foreign groups and organized crime. More than two-thirds of the gang members believed other organizations controlled drug trafficking.

What happens to the profits of drug sales is another key indicator of the extent to which gang drug distribution is directly connected to high-level drug organizations. In the gangs Decker and Van Winkle (1996) studied, the profits from drug sales were retained by the gang members and usually were spent on typical teenage purchases. Most studies show that profits are either kept by the individual or accumulated by the gang for parties and other social events (Decker and Van Winkle, 1996; Hagedorn, 1994a; Sanchez-Jankowski, 1991).

To what extent are adult criminal organizations involved in the drug market and violent crime? A few studies and investigative reports of crack cocaine and heroin trafficking provide a thumbnail sketch of the high-level organization of the drug trade. The relationship between drugs and violence is widely accepted in adult criminal organizations such as drug cartels and prison gangs; in some instances, however, it is difficult to distinguish these adult criminal organizations from youth gangs.[11]

The Office of National Drug Control Policy's (ONDCP's) *Pulse Check* Reports (ONDCP, 1995a, 1995b, 1996) describe high-level drug distribution organizations that are not youth gangs. The typical organizational structure uses franchise operators to control an area and delegates street-level sales to others. Only a few of ONDCP's ethnographers report that cocaine sellers are organized in youth gangs.

Moore (1990) contends that many of the adult criminal organizations that control drug trafficking existed before the crack cocaine epidemic. Others were formed in the 1980s to service the growing crack cocaine market (Curtis, 1992; Fagan, 1996; Johnson, Hamid, and Sanabria, 1990; Taylor, 1989, 1990). There is evidence that when crack cocaine was first introduced, a great deal of violence ensued (Taylor, 1989). Violence associated with crack cocaine was linked to organizational competition for market share and profits; protection of drug-trafficking territory; regulation of employees in the new selling organizations; the urge among habitual users for money to buy crack; its liquid value among the poor; and, for a small group, its psychoactive effects (Fagan, 1996).

The Connection between Youth Gangs and Adult Criminal Organizations

A classic issue in gang research concerns a possible connection between youth gangs and adult criminal organizations (Thrasher, 1927). Taylor (1990) illustrated the transformation of a scavenger gang to a territorial gang, then to a corporate criminal gang with the case of the "42 Gang" in Chicago. It was considered the best "farm team" Chicago's Capone mob ever had. Some of the youth in it graduated into the lower ranks of the Capone mob. Spergel (1995) suggested that there is some indication that particular street-gang cliques have been integrated into some criminal organizations, but Fagan (1996) contended that this does not appear to be a predominant pattern. Fagan argued that available evidence suggests that this transition involves individual, talented young gang members, not groups.[12]

The connection between youth gangs and adult criminal organizations appears far more important in the case of adult prison gangs. Prison gang members are more violent than nongang inmates; they account for a disproportionate amount of prison violence and they often control drug trafficking and other criminal enterprises in prisons (Jackson and McBride, 1985; Ralph et al., 1996). Having been confined in a juvenile correctional facility is a strong predictor of adult prison gang membership (Ralph et al., 1996). Prison criminal gang members, in turn, contribute to the growth of youth gangs. Involvement of ex-convicts in youth gangs extends the life of the gangs and increases their level of violent crime, in part because of the ex-convicts' increased proclivity to violence following imprisonment and the visibility and history they contribute to youth gangs (Moore, 1978; Vigil and Long, 1990). In some cities, prison gangs rather than youth gangs dominate local drug markets (Hagedorn, 1998; Moore, 1996; Valdez, 1997).

Studies of the Youth Gangs, Drugs, and Violence Connection

The relationship between drugs, drug trafficking, and violent crime is the subject of much debate and research (see De La Rosa, Lambert, and Gropper, 1990, for an exhaustive review). Goldstein (1985) suggested three possible relationships: (1) the "pharmacological" effects of the drug on the user can induce violent behavior; (2) the high cost of drug use often impels users to commit "economic compulsive" violent crime to support continued drug use (e.g., robbery for the purpose of securing money to buy drugs); and (3) "systemic" violence is a common feature of the drug-distribution system, including protection or expansion of the drug distribution market share, retaliation against market participants who violate the rules that govern transactions, or maintenance of the drug-trafficking organization.

Collins (1990) summarized the research evidence supporting each of the three types of drug violence Goldstein suggested. First, there is virtually no evidence of the pharmacological effects of drugs (excluding, perhaps, alcohol) on violence. Second, there is considerable evidence of a relationship between drug use and economic compulsive violence. Third, although research is scarce on "systemic" (drug distribution) violence, this form appears to be the most predominant. "Drug distribution system violence tends to occur (at least most visibly) in areas that: are socially disorganized, that is, in which formal and informal social control is absent or ineffective; have traditionally high rates of interpersonal violence; and are economically disadvantaged" (Collins, 1990:266). Collins noted that the Goldstein typology has its limitations, mainly because there are other important sources of violence. This is an especially important point with respect to the gang context. A review of these other sources is divided into two parts: gang homicide and the causes and correlates of youth gang violence.

Youth Gang Homicide and Drug Trafficking
Although youth gang homicides are characterized by periodic spurts and declines, they have been increasing nationwide and evidence an overall growth trend in certain cities (Maxson, 1998a). These spurts are explained largely by "turf" disputes between warring gangs (Block and Block, 1993; Block and Christakos, 1995; Block et al., 1996). The spurts are not city-wide—they occur in specific neighborhoods and involve particular youth gangs in escalating incidents of provocation, retaliation, and revenge. The annual number of homicides involving Chicago street gangs increased almost fivefold between 1987 and 1994 (Block et al., 1996). Youth and adult gang-related homicides in Los Angeles County more than doubled from 1987 to 1992, then dropped in 1993 and 1994 (Maxson, 1998a).

To what extent is the large volume of and increase in gang homicides caused by drug trafficking? This popular assumption is tied to the image of youth gangs as entrepreneurial drug-trafficking operations that began to spread across the country during the crack cocaine epidemic.

Klein and his colleagues were the first researchers to test the popular assumption of a strong relationship between youth and adult gang drug trafficking and homicide. In a series of Los Angeles studies, they found that the connection between gang-related homicides and drug trafficking is not strong.[13] This relationship has also been found to be weak in several other studies in Boston, Chicago, Los Angeles, Miami, and St. Louis (see Howell, 1999 [a] for a review of this research).

There are exceptions to this general conclusion. Some ongoing drug market wars account for a significant number of homicides (Block et al., 1996). Block and her colleagues also noted an indirect relationship among homicides, drug trafficking, and street gang activity. Many of the street gang-related homicides might not occur without the existence of drug markets, which routinely bring members of opposing gangs into contact with one another. How can the increase in gang-related homicides over the past decade be explained?

The role of firearms in gang violence. The presence of firearms significantly increases the likelihood of murder. The routine use of guns in gang conflict is a fairly recent development, having occurred in the past decade (Miller, 1992). Recent studies show that firearms are now prevalent in youth gangs (Bjerregaard and Lizotte, 1995; Howell, 1998; Lizotte et al., 1994). There also is evidence that the impact of drug selling on illegal gun carrying is greater than the impact of gang membership and that drug selling increases with age. Thus, "unlike the diminished role of gangs, drug selling grows as the subjects get older and this enhances hidden gun carrying" (Lizotte et al., 1997:388). A strong association is found between illegal gun use and gang membership and between illicit drug sales and illegal gun use (Decker, 1996; Decker, Pennell, and Caldwell, 1997; Sanders, 1994; Sheley and Wright, 1993, 1995).

Using data gathered from interviews in 1995 with arrested juveniles in the Drug Use Forecasting (DUF) study, Decker and colleagues (1997) found that gang members are much more likely than other juveniles to carry guns most or all of the time (31 percent versus 20 percent). Percentages of arrestees who reported using a gun to commit a crime, were higher among adolescents who sold drugs (42 percent) or belonged to a gang (50 percent) than among other juveniles (33 percent). One-third of gang members said it was okay to shoot someone who disrespected them. These findings confirm the importance of gun ownership and use among gang members.

In a 3-year field study of active youth gang members in St. Louis, Decker and Van Winkle (1996) reported that 81 percent owned guns. The mean number of guns owned was more than four. Two-thirds of gang members had used their guns at least once. The most common use was in gang fights; infrequent use was reported in drive-bys, defense against attacks by strangers, and other incidents. Only four members mentioned a drug-related motive. In each of these incidents, the gang members used their guns to prevent a drug customer from robbing them.

Decker (1996) contended that gang interactions, mainly the threat a rival gang presents, help to explain the increasing sophistication of weapons used by gang members. The Blocks showed that most of the increase in Chicago street gang homicides is attributable to an increase in more lethal weapons, not an increase in assaults (Block and Block, 1993; Howell, 1999; Hutson et al., 1995; Zimring, 1996). Rosenfeld and Decker (1996:200) found that the St. Louis youth (under age 24) homicide problem "is largely a gun homicide problem."

Causes and Correlates of Youth Gang Violence

Some studies support the notion that youth and adult gang involvement in drug trafficking has led to more violent crime.[14] Other studies suggest that the connection between youth and adult gang drug sales and violence is indirect or weak.[15] Some of these studies that shed light on the gangs, drugs, and violence connection are reviewed below.

Huff (1996) studied two samples of Cleveland adolescents: currently or formerly active youth gang members and a second group of youth who had not joined gangs but were deemed similarly at risk of delinquency. Major Cleveland gangs were well represented in the sample. Gang youth were significantly more involved in marijuana and cocaine drug sales and in more serious and violent crimes than nongang adolescents. Gang members were far more likely to sell high-profit drugs and to sell drugs more frequently than nongang adolescents. Huff asked both groups about the source of the drugs they sold. Gangs were not the primary source for either group. A majority of both gang and nongang youth said "others" controlled drug supplies. Gang sellers were far more likely than nongang sellers to go out of state for their supply.

In a unique aspect of this study, police gang experts identified 83 gang members who were leaders in 1986. Huff (1996) compiled their arrest histories from 1980 to 1994. The overwhelming majority of arrests (which averaged 10 per leader) began at or near the time of their initial gang involvement. Most of the arrests (37 percent) were for violent crimes, 29 percent for property crimes, 18 percent for drug offenses, and 6 percent for weapons offenses.

In his investigation of possible crime progression, Huff (1996) determined the year in which gang leaders' arrests for property, drug, and violent offenses peaked. Peaks for all three offenses clustered within less than 2 years. His discovery that violent crime arrests peaked about 3 months before drug offenses led Huff (1996:99) to suggest that this might be evidence of "a close connection between drug trafficking and violence that is often associated with conflict over 'turf.'"

Venkatesh's (1996) ethnography of gangs in Chicago's Robert Taylor Homes described one of the worst cases of gang drug trafficking and violence. His study documented the transformation of gangs in this low-income public housing development from turf gangs to drug gangs and the escalation of gang violence with the advent of crack cocaine. In the 1960s and 1970s, these gangs fought over pride or turf in hand-to-hand conflicts, sometimes using zip guns (homemade, single-shot pistols). Their violence was controlled largely by tenant networks. When crack cocaine was introduced in the 1980s, a notable escalation in gang violence occurred. Several gangs controlled drug-trafficking turfs in one or more buildings in the housing development. Previously contained fights then burst into the open, endangering residents in gang-related crossfire. In 1992, several children, all innocent bystanders, were shot and killed. Neither police nor tenant organizations were able to contain the gang violence. Rival gangs continued fighting. Eventually, community leaders, youth workers, and tenants were able to effect a truce that Venkatesh predicted would not last.

Hagedorn (1991, 1998) found that few (mostly adult) Milwaukee gang members were involved in cocaine sales in 1987. But by 1991, 75 percent of them were reported as having been involved in cocaine trafficking. Adult gang members said that one-half or more of the dope houses in gang neighborhoods were run by gangs (Hagedorn, 1994b). He estimated that about one-quarter of all homicides and from one-third to one-half of all adult gang violence in which gang members were involved or which they witnessed were drug related (Hagedorn, 1996).

In one of the most detailed studies of the gangs, drugs, and violence connections, Decker and Van Winkle (1994, 1996) found that the St. Louis gangs to which youth belonged, mostly local Crips and Bloods, were extensively involved in drug trafficking, especially cocaine. Members of these gangs fought often, generally using guns. Ammunition, drugs, and guns were sometimes obtained from gangs in Los Angeles and Detroit. Rival gangs often fought over drug customer turf. Decker and Van Winkle found, however, that gang violence has many other sources related to everyday gang social processes.[16] They saw three main sources of violence among St. Louis gang members (Decker and Van Winkle, 1996). First, violence is a part of everyday life in their neighborhoods and families. Second, conflict differentiates gangs from other delinquent groups. Third, violence is an endemic part of their status as individuals and as gang members. In St. Louis gangs, "members are expected to always be ready to commit violence, to participate in violent acts, and to have engaged in some sort of violence in their initiation" into the gang (Decker and Van Winkle, 1996:173).

Decker (1996) offered a more detailed explanation of the origin and spurt pattern of gang violence that Block (1993) discovered. He used Loftin's (1984) "contagion" concept and the notion that gang cohesion grows in proportion to the perceived threat represented by rival gangs (Klein, 1971). Loftin argued that three conditions must be present if contagion is to occur: a spatial concentration of assaultive violence, a reciprocal nature to assaultive violence (see Miller, 1958), and escalations in assaultive violence. Decker (1996) explained how the threat of attack by another group ignites the gang, increases cohesion, and produces deadly consequences. Most gang violence, he argued, is retaliatory, a response to violence—real or perceived—against the gang. Spurts of gang violence appear to follow predictable patterns, in a sequence that is initially motivated by the perceived threat that another gang poses, then instigated by a precipitating event, followed by escalation of activity, a violent event, rapid deescalation, and finally, retaliation.

Long-Term Studies of Adolescent Samples

Most of the studies reviewed thus far focus on specific gangs or individual gang members, capturing the significance of their experiences. A different view of the connection between gang drug trafficking and violence is obtained by studying large representative samples of adolescents over a long period of time. OJJDP's Program of Research on the Causes and Correlates of Delinquency, which studied large adolescent samples in the emerging gang cities of Denver, CO, and Rochester, NY, has produced a number of important findings on the gangs, drugs, and violence connection. Although these studies were not designed specifically to examine youth gangs, they permit comparisons between gang and nongang members in larger samples.

Each of these studies addresses the extent to which gang membership facilitates drug trafficking. Similar patterns were observed in both cities. In Rochester, Thornberry and his colleagues (1993) found that gang members were involved in three to five times as many drug sales as nongang youth in sequential time periods. In Denver, gang members reported nearly seven times as many drug sales as nongang youth (Huizinga, 1997). In another study, supported by OJJDP and several other agencies and organizations, Seattle gang members reported involvement in 10 times as many drug sales as nongang youth (Hill, Howell, and Hawkins, 1996). In Seattle (Hill et al., 1996) and in Rochester (Bjerregaard and Lizotte, 1995), drug use and trafficking rates still remained high after individuals left the gang, indicating that gang influence on drug trafficking extends beyond the period of gang membership. Gang members in all three study sites reported from three to seven times as many serious and violent delinquent acts as nongang youth (Howell, 1998).

A key question is, Does gang involvement in drug trafficking cause subsequent violent crime? The Seattle gang studies have examined this issue. Despite a high prevalence of Seattle gang member involvement in drug trafficking, accelerated adolescent involvement in drug trafficking after joining a gang, and strong evidence that gang involvement prolongs drug trafficking (Hill, Howell, and Hawkins, 1996; Hill et al., 1996), an analysis shows that gang member involvement in drug trafficking at age 16 does not predict assaultive violence at age 18 but does predict drug trafficking at age 18 (Howell et al., 1996). Surprisingly (given this finding), the study also showed that drug trafficking at age 16 predicts significantly more assaultive violence and handgun possession at age 18 among nongang youth.[17]

In Denver, Esbensen and Huizinga (1993:571) reported that drug sales "were not driving" street offending. Both violent (gang fighting, rape, robbery, and aggravated assault) and nonviolent offenses (burglary, theft, fencing stolen goods) composed the "street offending" measure. Although Rochester analyses showed an association between gang drug trafficking and violent offenses (Thornberry et al., 1993), neither the strength of the relationship nor the temporal order of the two behaviors has yet been examined. Several other studies of either gang or nongang samples have shown an association between adolescent drug trafficking and violence.[18]

These findings make a persuasive case that drug trafficking is strongly associated with other serious and violent crimes but not necessarily that drug trafficking by gang members *causes* more frequent violent offending. In Pittsburgh—the third site in OJJDP's Program of Research on the Causes and Correlates of Delinquency—a study of nongang youth suggested that drug use, serious theft, and violence precede drug selling (Van Kammen, Maguin, and Loeber, 1994). Van Kammen and her colleagues also found that sales of illicit drugs started significantly later in adolescence than the other three behaviors. Initiation of drug selling was strongly related to previous involvement in multiple types of delinquency. The authors concluded that "the present study indicated a temporal sequence between the delinquent behaviors and the onset of drug dealing. This does not mean that the relationship is causal. Instead, it is likely that drug dealing and serious forms of delinquency are expressions of similar antisocial tendencies. Whether the same etiological factors apply to each still remains to be demonstrated" (Van Kammen, Maguin, and Loeber, 1994:240).

Although a causal relationship between gang drug trafficking and violence has not yet been demonstrated in the above studies, it is important to remember that, in the main, the findings this article reviews come from two sources: gang studies in emerging gang cities and nongang samples. A key question is the extent to which gang membership facilitates gun use in drug trafficking—possibly resulting in higher levels of violence—in the same way that the gang facilitates overall violent offending. This may hold true in two cases; gang member drug trafficking may indirectly contribute to more violent encounters with other gangs involving guns when (1) drug trafficking exacerbates the need for guns and (2) the perceived threat of violence from rival groups increases. Resolution of this connection requires further examination.

Summary

Empirical support for the popular image of youth gangs as promulgated by Skolnick and his colleagues in the California studies is limited. There is little evidence of gang migration for the explicit purpose of setting up drug-trafficking operations in distant locations. Youth gangs sometimes obtain guns, drugs, and ammunition from gangs in other cities. Some gangs expand their operations to other markets. These fit the stereotype conveyed by the media and investigatory agencies. Yet there does not appear to be a large number of youth gangs that fit the stereotype. Moreover, interstate drug trafficking appears to be mainly the province of adult criminal organizations.

Youth gang members actively engage in drug use, drug trafficking, and violent crime. In other words, these problems overlap considerably. Gang members are more likely than nongang youth to be involved in drug trafficking and violence. Gang involvement appears to promote individual participation in violence, drug use, and drug trafficking and perhaps prolong gang member involvement in drug sales. Although drug trafficking is strongly associated with other serious and violent crimes, gang member involvement in drug sales does not necessarily result in more frequent violent offenses.

Most gang members have engaged in illegal activities, generally including violence, before they join gangs. Many have guns. Thus, gangs recruit or attract potentially or already violent individuals, and involvement in violent activities increases during periods of gang membership, even among those who enter the gang with a history of violent crime. The evidence to date suggests that gang participation, drug trafficking, and violence occur together.

Some youth gangs are actively involved in street-level drug trafficking. With some notable exceptions, they do not appear to control drug-trafficking operations. Large, adult criminal gangs that traffic in drugs and drug-selling cliques within gangs do exist, and they are responsible for a great deal of violence. Most of their violence may be directly or indirectly related to drug trafficking.

A distinction should be made between youth gangs and adult criminal organizations that existed before the crack cocaine epidemic or were created to profit from crack. Overall, adult criminal organizations appear to be responsible for a large percentage of the violence related to drug trafficking, particularly the most violent crimes such as homicide, assault, and robbery. However, some younger youth gangs may evolve into drug-trafficking operations as they grow older or take on older members. This appears to be more common in cities with a longer tradition of gang activities than in emerging gang problem cities, and this trend may be fueled by deteriorating economic conditions in inner-city areas.

Although common sense suggests a link between gangs, drugs, and violence (Hagedorn, 1998), which is strongly promoted in media representations of youth gangs (Klein, 1995), such a link is questioned in longitudinal data on adolescents that examine the causal connections among these variables. However, these connections may be stronger in adult gangs (see Hagedorn, 1998) and adult criminal organizations, including in a few areas experiencing a chronic youth gang problem.

Most gang violence is endemic to gang life, separate from drug trafficking because of several reasons. Violence is a part of the everyday life of gang members, even when they are apart from the gang; it is in their neighborhoods and within families. Second, conflict differentiates gangs from other law-violating youth groups. Third, violence is an expected part of their individual status and roles as gang members.

For the most part, the growth in youth gang homicides appears to be independent of the increase in gang drug trafficking. Youth gang drug wars represent a notable exception. The absence of a strong causal connection between gang drug trafficking and homicide suggests that gang involvement and drug trafficking are separate risk factors for homicide rather than interrelated factors (Meehan and O'Carroll, 1992). Maxson (1998a) calls for careful analysis of the specific characteristics of gang homicides in different cities and communities so that solutions can be crafted that are appropriate for the local gang homicide problem.

Once communities gain insight into the sources of gang violence, they will see opportunities for intervening in the patterns, or spurts, of gang violence that occur (Decker, 1996). Communities that engage in this process can learn about interventions other communities are using, such as Chicago's "Little Village" Gang Violence Reduction Project and OJJDP's Comprehensive Community-Wide Approach to Gang Prevention, Intervention, and Suppression demonstration model, which is being implemented in five sites: Mesa, AZ; Tucson, AZ; Riverside, CA; Bloomington, IL; and San Antonio, TX (Thornberry and Burch, 1997).

Gang violence has been exacerbated by the ready availability and use of firearms, especially more lethal guns, coupled with frequent use of automobiles in attacks on other gangs. However, the role of firearms in gang-related violence is not well understood. The extent to which gang firearm possession and use is causally related to gang functions versus drug trafficking is unclear.

Policy and Program Implications

As a matter of policy, youth gang drug trafficking needs to be addressed separately from adult criminal drug-trafficking organizations. These distinctly different problems require unique solutions. Youth gang drug trafficking coexists with other gang crimes, mainly intergang turf conflicts and interpersonal violence, that are unrelated or only tangential to drug trafficking. Violence in adult criminal drug-trafficking organizations, cartels, and syndicates appears to be connected much more directly to the drug-trafficking enterprise. Reducing drug trafficking in youth gangs is not likely to have a significant impact on violent youth gang crime (except in the case of particular drug gangs), whereas successful reduction of drug trafficking in adult criminal organizations is likely to produce a significant reduction in violent crime.

BREAKING THE CYCLE

Before communities can begin to craft a response, an assessment of the local gang problem needs to take place. It is important that communities have an accurate understanding of and agree on which types of gang problems they are experiencing. In order to conduct a thorough assessment, communities should look at community perceptions and available data. Data from law enforcement sources such as local gang and general crime data are critical to the assessment. Other data should be collected from probation officers, schools, community-based youth agencies, prosecutors, community residents, and gang and nongang youth. In essence, the nature of the drug and violence problem and its relationship to the gang problem should be determined and special attention should be placed on where—and on whom—prevention, intervention, and suppression efforts should be focused. Although not primarily designed to be an assessment but rather a broad training approach, OJJDP's Gang and Drug POLICY training program brings together community leaders to systematically assess the nature and extent of the community gang and drug problem.

Successfully breaking up youth gang drug operations may require different approaches depending on the type of gang. Because youth gangs generally are involved only in street-level distribution, the proceeds of which typically are used for personal consumption, providing legitimate ways of earning money may prove effective with their members. Suppression approaches may be more effective with drug gangs.

Programs are needed to break the cycle of gang members moving from detention and corrections to prisons to communities. Research and program development are needed in several areas. Better screening and risk classification of gang members in juvenile and adult correctional facilities are imperative. This would help protect the public by giving correctional staff reliable information to classify gang offenders at the appropriate level of risk and to match juvenile offenders with gang treatment programs available in correctional facilities. Effective programs are needed in these facilities to prevent gang formation, membership, and victimization and also to break up drug operations inside prisons. There also needs to be an end to the recycling of adult gang members into gang-infested communities once they leave prison. Ex-convicts need marketable job skills and gainful employment opportunities to avoid the lucrative drug market. Breaking this cycle becomes all the more important as states are imprisoning younger and younger offenders, who will be returning to the streets at a younger age than is the case today. Making effective drug treatment programs available, along with legitimate job opportunities, would also help break the cycle.

Preventing adolescents from joining gangs should be a top priority. One place to begin is preventing youth from dropping out of school. Discouraging children and young adolescents from joining gangs is particularly important because of the lure of the illicit economy and the drug kingpin lifestyle, which the media sensationalizes. Opportunities for success and access to them must be provided. At the same time, a community's social control of pregang and gang groups needs to be increased. Communities' comprehensive, coordinated approaches should include measures to increase social control of youth by strengthening social institutions and emphasizing the roles that residents, parents, youth workers, and community leaders play in supervising adolescents. Community businesses can play a key role by providing legitimate work opportunities. Focused prevention is the best way to ensure adequate resource allocation and to have the greatest impact.

Existing gun interdiction efforts can be enhanced and new ones implemented as part of a coordinated effort to reduce gang violence. A user-reduction strategy buttressed by collaboration between police and probation officers, as in Boston's Youth Violence Strike Force (Kennedy, Piehl, and Braga, 1996), is one way of removing guns from the streets and the possession of gang members.[19] The case for removing illegal firearms from the possession of gang members is unequivocal. Guns are vital tools for resolving gang conflicts. A reduction in gang-related homicides will follow, even without a reduction in drug trafficking.

NOTES

[1] Youth gangs are considered to consist of adolescents and young adults from the ages of 12 to 24. Unfortunately, there is no commonly accepted parameter of either the age range or proportion of individuals below a certain age (i.e., a youth) that can be used to differentiate youth gangs from adult gangs. This makes definitive conclusions from the research difficult and exacerbates the difference between research findings and real world experiences of practitioners concerned with the prevention of gang involvement and the suppression of gang activity. The term "youth gang" is commonly used interchangeably with "street gang," referring to neighborhood or street-based youth groups that are substantially made up of individuals under the age of 24. "Street gangs" may include both youth gangs and adult criminal organizations. Motorcycle gangs, prison gangs, racial supremacists, and other hate groups are excluded. Miller's definition of a youth gang is applicable to this review: "A youth gang is a

self-formed association of peers, united by mutual interests, with identifiable leadership and internal organization, who act collectively or as individuals to achieve specific purposes, including the conduct of illegal activity and control of a particular territory, facility, or enterprise" (Miller, 1992:21). Unless otherwise noted, the term "gangs" refers to youth gangs.

[2] See Anderson, 1990; Block and Block, 1993; Decker and Van Winkle, 1994, 1996; Hagedorn, 1991, 1994a, 1994b; Maxson, Gordon, and Klein, 1985; Padilla, 1992; Perkins, 1987; Reiner, 1992; Sanchez-Jankowski, 1991; Sanders, 1994; Skolnick, 1989; Taylor, 1989, 1990; Venkatesh, 1996; Waldorf, 1993.

[3] These studies include Battin and colleagues (1998), Bjerregaard and Smith (1993), Curry and Spergel (1992), Esbensen and Huizinga (1993), Esbensen and colleagues (1993), Fagan (1989), Hagedorn (1988, 1994a, 1994b), Hill, Howell, and Hawkins (1996), Long (1990), Thornberry and colleagues (1993), Vigil (1988), and Waldorf (1993).

[4] See also Decker and Van Winkle, 1994; Hagedorn, 1994a, 1994b; Sanchez-Jankowski, 1991; Sanders, 1994; Taylor, 1989; Venkatesh, 1996; Waldorf, 1993.

[5] Others agree (Decker and Van Winkle, 1996; Fagan, 1996; Hagedorn, 1988; Klein, 1995; Moore, 1985, 1988; Sanchez-Jankowski, 1991; Spergel, 1995; Vigil, 1988).

[6] See Inciardi, 1986; Inciardi and Pottieger, 1991; Klein, 1995; Decker and Van Winkle, 1996; Klein, Maxson, and Cunningham, 1991; Moore, 1990.

[7] See California Council on Criminal Justice, 1989; Clark, 1991; Drug Enforcement Administration, 1988; General Accounting Office, 1989; Hayeslip, 1989; McKinney, 1988.

[8] See also Hagedorn, 1988; Huff, 1989; Rosenbaum and Grant, 1983; Zevitz and Takata, 1992.

[9] See Skolnick, 1989, 1990; Skolnick et al., 1988; Sanchez-Jankowski, 1991; Klein and Maxson, 1994; Klein, Maxson, and Cunningham, 1991; and Decker and Van Winkle, 1996.

[10] Other examples of drug-trafficking youth gangs are described by Fagan (1989), Hagedorn (1994a, 1994b, 1998), Sanchez-Jankowski (1991), and Sanders (1994).

[11] See Fagan and Chin, 1990; General Accounting Office, 1989, 1996; Jackson and McBride, 1985; Moore, 1990; Reiner, 1992; Sanchez-Jankowski, 1991; Taylor, 1989. Klein (1995) and Spergel (1995) provide excellent discussions of this issue.

[12] Fagan's argument is similar to Hagedorn (1991, 1994a, 1994b), Klein (1995), and Moore (1990, 1992).

[13] See Klein and Maxson, 1985; Klein, Maxson, and Cunningham, 1988, 1991; Maxson, 1995, 1998a.

[14] See Hagedorn, 1996; Padilla, 1992; Sanchez-Jankowski, 1991; Sanders, 1994; Short, 1996; Skolnick 1989, 1990, 1991; Skolnick et al., 1988; Taylor, 1989, 1990; Venkatesh, 1996.

[15] See Block and Block, 1993; Chin, 1990, 1995, 1996; Decker, Pennell, and Caldwell, 1997; Decker and Van Winkle, 1996; Esbensen and Huizinga, 1993; Fagan, 1989; Huff, 1989, 1996; Klein, Maxson, and Cunningham, 1991; MacLeod, 1987; Maxson, 1995; Maxson and Klein, 1996; Moore, 1990, 1991; Waldorf and Lauderback, 1993.

[16] See also Anderson, 1994; Block and Block, 1993; Chin, 1996; Decker and Van Winkle, 1996; Horowitz, 1983; Kennedy, Piehl, and Braga, 1996; Sanchez-Jankowski, 1991.

[17] The researchers selected drug selling at age 16 and violence and other outcomes at age 18 in part because the average ages for joining a gang are 14 to 15 in Seattle. Thus, it was anticipated that gang membership and involvement in gang-related drug trafficking would be very prevalent by age 16. Measuring violence at age 18 would allow time for gang drug trafficking to cause violence—if that were the case.

[18] See Altschuler and Brounstein, 1991; Dembo et al., 1993; Padilla, 1992; Van Kammen and Loeber, 1994; Williams, 1989.

[19] For more information on this and other gang prevention and control approaches, see Howell (2000).

REFERENCES

Altschuler, D., and Brounstein, P. J. 1991. Patterns of drug use, drug trafficking and other delinquency among inner city adolescent males in Washington, D.C. *Criminology* 29:589–622.

Anderson, E. 1990. *Streetwise: Race, Class, and Change in an Urban Community*. Chicago, IL: University of Chicago Press.

Anderson, E. 1994. The code of the streets. *The Atlantic Monthly* (May):81–94.

Battin, S. R., Hill, K. G., Abbott, R. D., Catalano, R. F., and Hawkins, J. D. 1998. The contribution of gang membership to delinquency above and beyond delinquent friends. *Criminology* 36:93–115.

Bjerregaard, B., and Lizotte, A. J. 1995. Gun ownership and gang membership. *The Journal of Criminal Law and Criminology* 86:37–58.

Bjerregaard, B., and Smith, C. 1993. Gender differences in gang participation, delinquency, and substance use. *Journal of Quantitative Criminology* 9:329–355.

Block, C. R. 1993. Lethal violence in the Chicago Latino community. In *Homicide: The Victim/Offender Connection*, edited by A. V. Wilson. Cincinnati, OH: Anderson, pp. 267–342.

Block, C. R., and Christakos, A. 1995. *Major Trends in Chicago Homicide: 1965–1994*. Research Bulletin. Chicago, IL: Illinois Criminal Justice Information Authority.

Block, C. R., Christakos, A., Jacob, A., and Przybylski, R. 1996. *Street Gangs and Crime: Patterns and Trends in Chicago*. Research Bulletin. Chicago: Illinois Criminal Justice Information Authority.

Block, R., and Block, C. R. 1993. *Street Gang Crime in Chicago*. Research in Brief. Washington, DC: U.S. Department of Justice, Office of Justice Programs, National Institute of Justice.

Bullington, B. 1977. *Heroin Use in the Barrio*. Lexington, MA: D. C. Heath.

California Council on Criminal Justice. 1989. *Task Force Report on Gangs and Drugs*. Sacramento, CA: California Council on Criminal Justice.

Chesney-Lind, M. 1993. Girls, gangs and violence: Anatomy of a backlash. *Humanity and Society* 17:321–344.

Chin, K. 1990. *Chinese Subculture and Criminality: Non-Traditional Crime Groups in America*. Westport, CT: Greenwood.

Chin, K. 1995. *Chinatown Gangs*. New York, NY: Oxford University Press.

Chin, K. 1996. Gang violence in Chinatown. In *Gangs in America*, edited by C. R. Huff. Newbury Park, CA: Sage Publications, pp. 157–184.

Chin, K., and Fagan, J. A. 1990 (November). The impact of crack on drug and crime involvement. Unpublished paper presented at the annual meeting of the American Society of Criminology, New Orleans, LA.

Clark, C. S. 1991. Youth gangs. *Congressional Quarterly Research* 22:755–771.

Cloward, R. A., and Ohlin, L. E. 1960. *Delinquency and Opportunity: A Theory of Delinquent Gangs*. New York, NY: The Free Press.

Collins, J. A. 1990. Summary thoughts about drugs and violence. In *Drugs and Violence: Causes, Correlates, and Consequences*, edited by M. De La Rosa, E. Y. Lambert, and B. Gropper. NIDA Research Monograph 103. Rockville, MD: U.S. Department of Health and Human Services, National Institutes of Health, National Institute on Drug Abuse.

Curry, G. D., and Spergel, I. A. 1988. Gang homicide, delinquency, and community. *Criminology* 26:381–405.

Curry, G. D., and Spergel, I. A. 1992. Gang involvement and delinquency among Hispanic and African-American adolescent males. *Journal of Research in Crime and Delinquency* 29:273–291.

Curtis, R. A. 1992. Highly structured crack markets in the southside of Williamsburg, Brooklyn. In *The Ecology of Crime and Drug Use in Inner Cities*, edited by J. Fagan. New York, NY: Social Science Research Council.

Dawley, D. 1992. *A Nation of Lords: The Autobiography of the Vice Lords.* 2d ed. Prospect Heights, IL: Waveland.

Decker, S. H. 1996. Collective and normative features of gang violence. *Justice Quarterly* 13:243–264.

Decker, S. H., and Kempf, K. 1991. Constructing gangs: The social construction of youth activities. *Criminal Justice Policy Review* 5:271–291.

Decker, S. H., Pennell, S., and Caldwell, A. 1997 (January). *Illegal Firearms; Access and Use by Arrestees.* Research in Brief. Washington, DC: U.S. Department of Justice, Office of Justice Programs, National Institute of Justice.

Decker, S. H., and Van Winkle, B. 1994. Slinging dope: The role of gangs and gang members in drug sales. *Justice Quarterly* 11:583–604.

Decker, S. H., and Van Winkle, B. 1996. *Life in the Gang: Family, Friends, and Violence.* New York, NY: Cambridge University Press.

De La Rosa, M., Lambert, E. Y., and Gropper, B., eds. 1990. *Drugs and Violence: Causes, Correlates, and Consequences.* NIDA Research Monograph 103. Rockville, MD: U.S. Department of Health and Human Services, National Institutes of Health, National Institute on Drug Abuse.

Dembo, R., Hughes, P., Jackson, L., and Mieczkowski, T. 1993. Crack cocaine dealing by adolescents in two public housing projects: A pilot study. *Human Organization* 52:89–96.

Drug Enforcement Administration. 1988. *Crack Cocaine Availability and Trafficking in the United States.* Washington, DC: U.S. Department of Justice, Drug Enforcement Administration.

Esbensen, F., and Huizinga, D. 1993. Gangs, drugs, and delinquency in a survey of urban youth. *Criminology* 31:565–589.

Esbensen, F., Huizinga, D., and Weiher, A. W. 1993. Gang and nongang youth: Differences in explanatory variables. *Journal of Contemporary Criminal Justice* 9:94–116.

Fagan, J. E. 1989. The social organization of drug use and drug dealing among urban gangs. *Criminology* 27:633–669.

Fagan, J. E. 1993. The political economy of drug dealing among urban gangs. In *Drugs and Community,* edited by R. Davis, A. Lurgicio, and D. P. Rosenbaum. Springfield, IL: Charles C Thomas, pp. 19–54.

Fagan, J. E. 1996. Gangs, drugs, and neighborhood change. In *Gangs in America,* 2d ed., edited by C. R. Huff. Thousand Oaks, CA: Sage Publications, pp. 39–74.

Fagan, J. E., and Chin, K. 1990. Violence as regulation and social control in the distribution of crack. In *Drugs and Violence: Causes, Correlates, and Consequences,* edited by M. De La Rosa, E. Y. Lambert, and B. Gropper. NIDA Research Monograph 103. Rockville, MD: U.S. Department of Health and Human Services, National Institutes of Health, National Institute on Drug Abuse, pp. 8–43.

General Accounting Office. 1989. *Nontraditional Organized Crime.* Washington, DC: U.S. Government Printing Office.

General Accounting Office. 1996. *Violent Crime: Federal Law Enforcement Assistance in Fighting Los Angeles Gang Violence.* Washington, DC: U.S. Government Printing Office.

Goldstein, P. J. 1985. The drugs/violence nexus: A tripartite conceptual framework. *Journal of Drug Issues* 15:493–506.

Hagedorn, J. M. 1988. *People and Folks: Gangs, Crime and the Underclass in a Rustbelt City.* Chicago, IL: Lakeview Press.

Hagedorn, J. M. 1991. Gangs, neighborhoods and public policy. *Social Problems* 38:529–542.

Hagedorn, J. M. 1994a. Homeboys, dope fiends, legits, and new jacks. *Criminology* 32:197–217.

Hagedorn, J. M. 1994b. Neighborhoods, markets, and gang drug organization. *Journal of Research in Crime and Delinquency* 31:264–294.

Hagedorn, J. M. 1996. Gang violence in Milwaukee. Unpublished paper presented at the conference on Cross-Cultural Perspectives on Youth Radicalism and Violence, Milwaukee, WI.

Hagedorn, J. M. 1998. Gang violence in the postindustrial era. In *Youth Violence, Crime and Justice Series*, Vol. 24, edited by M. Tonry and M. Moore. Chicago, IL: University of Chicago.

Hayeslip, D. W., Jr. 1989. *Local-Level Drug Enforcement: New Strategies.* Research in Action No. 213. Washington, DC: U.S. Department of Justice, Office of Justice Programs, National Institute of Justice.

Hill, K. G., Hawkins, J. D., Catalano, R. F., Kosterman, R., Abbott, R., and Edwards, T. 1996 (November). The longitudinal dynamics of gang membership and problem behavior: A replication and extension of the Denver and Rochester gang studies in Seattle. Unpublished paper presented at the annual meeting of the American Society of Criminology, Chicago, IL.

Hill, K. G., Howell, J. C., and Hawkins, J. D. 1996 (June). Risk factors in childhood for adolescent gang membership. Unpublished paper presented at the 1996 National Youth Gang Symposium, Dallas, TX.

Horowitz, R. 1983. *Honor and the American Dream: Culture and Identity in a Chicano Community.* New Brunswick, NJ: Rutgers University.

Howell, J. C. 1997. Youth gang homicides, drug trafficking and program interventions. In *Juvenile Justice and Youth Violence.* Thousand Oaks, CA: Sage Publications, pp. 115–132.

Howell, J. C. 1998. *Youth Gangs: An Overview.* Bulletin. Washington, DC: U.S. Department of Justice, Office of Justice Programs, Office of Juvenile Justice and Delinquency Prevention.

Howell, J. C. 1999. Youth gangs homicides: A literature review. *Crime and Delinquency,* vol. 45, number 2, pp. 208–241.

Howell, J. C. 2000. *Youth Gang Programs and Strategies.* Bulletin. Washington, DC: U.S. Department of Justice, Office of Justice Programs, Office of Juvenile Justice and Delinquency Prevention.

Howell, J. C., Hill, K. G., Battin, S. R., and Hawkins, J. D. 1996 (November). Youth gang involvement in drug trafficking and violent crime in Seattle. Unpublished paper presented at the annual meeting of the American Society of Criminology, Chicago, IL.

Huff, C. R. 1989. Youth gangs and public policy. *Crime and Delinquency* 35:524–537.

Huff, C. R. 1996. The criminal behavior of gang members and nongang at-risk youth. In *Gangs in America,* 2d ed., edited by C. R. Huff. Thousand Oaks, CA: Sage Publications, pp. 75–102.

Huizinga, D. 1997 (November). The volume of crime by gang and nongang members. Unpublished paper presented at the annual meeting of the American Society of Criminology, San Diego, CA.

Hunzeker, D. 1993. Ganging up against violence. *State Legislatures.* Denver, CO: National Conference of State Legislatures.

Hutson, H. R., Anglin, D., Kyriacou, D. N., Hart, J., and Spears, K. 1995. The epidemic of gang-related homicides in Los Angeles County from 1979 through 1994. The *Journal of the American Medical Association* 274:1031–1036.

Inciardi, J. A. 1986. *The War on Drugs: Heroin, Cocaine, Crime, and Public Policy.* Palo Alto, CA: Mayfield.

Inciardi, J. A., and Pottieger, A. E. 1991. Kids, crack, and crime. *Journal of Drug Issues* 21:257–270.

Jackson, R. L. 1997. Nationwide spread of L.A. gangs is alarming, FBI says. *Los Angeles Times* (May 24):A11.

Jackson, R. K., and McBride, W. 1985. *Understanding Street Gangs.* Plackerville, CA: Custom Publishing.

Johnson, J. 1989. Drug gangs are now operating in rural states, Justice Department says. *New York Times* (August 4):A1.

Johnson, B. D., Hamid, A., and Sanabria, H. 1990. Emerging models of crack distribution. In *Drugs and Crime: A Reader*, edited by T. Mieczkowski. Boston, MA: Allyn & Bacon.

Keiser, R. L. 1969. *The Vice Lords: Warriors of the Street.* New York, NY: Holt, Rinehart and Winston.

Kennedy, D. M., Piehl, A. M., and Braga, A. A. 1996. Youth violence in Boston: Gun markets, serious youth offenders, and a user-education strategy. *Law and Contemporary Problems* 59:147–196. Special Issue.

Klein, M. W. 1971. *Street Gangs and Street Workers.* Englewood Cliffs, NJ: Prentice-Hall.

Klein, M. W. 1995. *The American Street Gang.* New York, NY: Oxford University Press.

Klein, M. W., and Maxson, C. L. 1985. Rock sales in South L.A. *Social Science Research* 69:561–565.

Klein, M. W., and Maxson, C. L. 1994. Gangs and cocaine trafficking. In *Drugs and Crime: Evaluating Public Policy Initiatives*, edited by D. MacKenzie and C. Uchida. Thousand Oaks, CA: Sage Publications, pp. 42–58.

Klein, M. W., and Maxson, C. L. 1996. Gang structures, crime patterns, and police responses. Unpublished report. Los Angeles, CA: Social Science Research Institute, University of Southern California.

Klein, M. W., Maxson, C. L., and Cunningham, L. C. 1988. Gang involvement in cocaine rock trafficking. Unpublished report. Los Angeles, CA: Social Science Research Institute, University of Southern California.

Klein, M. W., Maxson, C. L., and Cunningham, L.C. 1991. Crack, street gangs, and violence. *Criminology* 29:623–650.

Lauderback, D., Hansen, J., and Waldorf, D. 1992. Sisters are doin' it for themselves: A black female gang in San Francisco. *Gang Journal* 1:57–72.

Lizotte, A. J., Howard, G. J., Krohn, M. D., and Thornberry, T. P. 1997. Patterns of illegal gun carrying among young urban males. *Valparaiso University Law Review* 31:375–393.

Lizotte, A. J., Tesoriero, J. M., Thornberry, T. P., and Krohn, M. D. 1994. Patterns of adolescent firearms ownership and use. *Justice Quarterly* 11:51–73.

Loftin, C. 1984. Assaultive violence as a contagious social process. *Bulletin of the New York Academy of Medicine* 62:550–555.

Long, J. 1990. Drug use patterns in two Los Angeles barrio gangs. In *Drugs and Hispanic Communities*, edited by R. Glick and J. Moore. New Brunswick, NJ: Rutgers University Press, pp. 155–165.

MacLeod, J. 1987. *Ain't No Makin' It: Leveled Aspirations in a Low-Income Neighborhood.* Boulder, CO: Westview.

Maxson, C. L. 1995 (September). *Street Gangs and Drug Sales in Two Suburban Cities.* Research in Brief. Washington, DC: U.S. Department of Justice, Office of Justice Programs, National Institute of Justice.

Maxson, C. L. 1998a. Gang homicide: A review and extension of the literature. In *Homicide: A Sourcebook of Social Research*, edited by D. Smith and M. Zahn. Thousand Oaks, CA: Sage Publications.

Maxson, C. L. 1998b. *Gang Members on the Move*. Bulletin. Washington, DC: U.S. Department of Justice, Office of Justice Programs, Office of Juvenile Justice and Delinquency Prevention.

Maxson, C. L., Gordon, M. A., and Klein, M. W. 1985. Differences between gang and nongang homicides. *Criminology* 23:209–222.

Maxson, C. L., and Klein, M. W. 1996. *Defining Gang Homicide: An Updated Look at Member and Motive Approaches*, 2d ed., edited by C. R. Huff. Thousand Oaks, CA: Sage Publications, pp. 3–20.

Maxson, C. L., Woods, K., and Klein, M. W. 1996 (February). Street gang migration: How big a threat? *National Institute of Justice Journal* 230:26–31.

McKinney, K. C. 1988 (September). *Juvenile Gangs: Crime and Drug Trafficking*. Bulletin. Washington, DC: U.S. Department of Justice, Office of Justice Programs, Office of Juvenile Justice and Delinquency Prevention.

Meehan, P. J., and O'Carroll, P. W. 1992. Gangs, drugs, and homicide in Los Angeles. *American Journal of the Disabled Child* 146:683–687.

Miller, W. B. 1958. Lower class culture as a generating milieu of gang delinquency. *Journal of Social Issues* 14:5–19.

Miller, W. B. 1990. Why the United States has failed to solve its youth gang problem. In *Gangs in America*, edited by C. R. Huff. Newbury Park, CA: Sage Publications, pp. 263–87.

Miller, W. B. 1992 (Revised from 1982). *Crime by Youth Gangs and Groups in the United States*. Washington, DC: U.S. Department of Justice, Office of Justice Programs, Office of Juvenile Justice and Delinquency Prevention.

Miller, W. B., Geertz, H., and Cutter, H. S. G. 1962. Aggression in a boys' streetcorner group. *Psychiatry* 24:283–298.

Moore, J. W. 1978. *Homeboys: Gangs, Drugs and Prison in the Barrios of Los Angeles*. Philadelphia, PA: Temple University Press.

Moore, J. W. 1985. Isolation and stigmatization in the development of an underclass: The case of Chicano gangs in East Los Angeles. *Social Problems* 33:1–13.

Moore, J. W. 1988. Introduction: Gangs and the underclass: A comparative perspective. In *People and Folks*, by J. Hagedorn. Chicago, IL: Lake View, pp. 3–17.

Moore, J. W. 1990. Gangs, drugs, and violence. In *Drugs and Violence: Causes, Correlates, and Consequences*, edited by M. De La Rosa, E. Y. Lambert, and B. Gropper. Research Monograph No. 103. Rockville, MD: U.S. Department of Health and Human Services, National Institutes of Health, National Institute on Drug Abuse, pp. 160–176.

Moore, J. W. 1991. *Going Down to the Barrio: Homeboys and Homegirls in Change*. Philadelphia, PA: Temple University Press.

Moore, J. W. 1992. Institutionalized youth gangs: Why White Fence and El Hoyo Maravilla change so slowly. In *The Ecology of Crime and Drug Use in Inner Cities*, edited by J. E. Fagan. New York, NY: Social Science Research Council.

Moore, J. W. 1996. Bearing the burden: How incarceration policies weaken inner-city communities. In *The Unintended Consequences of Incarceration*, edited by K. Fulbright. New York, NY: Vera Institute of Justice.

Moore, J. W., and Hagedorn, J. M. 1996. What happens to girls in the gang? In *Gangs in America*, 2d ed., edited by C. R. Huff. Thousand Oaks, CA: Sage Publications, pp. 205–218.

Office of National Drug Control Policy. 1995a (Summer). *Pulse Check: National Trends in Drug Abuse.* Washington, DC: Executive Office of the President.

Office of National Drug Control Policy. 1995b (Fall). *Pulse Check: National Trends in Drug Abuse.* Washington, DC: Executive Office of the President.

Office of National Drug Control Policy. 1996. *Pulse Check: National Trends in Drug Abuse.* Washington, DC: Executive Office of the President.

Padilla, F. M. 1992. *The Gang as an American Enterprise: Puerto Rican Youth and the American Dream.* New Brunswick, NJ: Rutgers University.

Perkins, U. E. 1987. *Explosion of Chicago's Black Street Gangs: 1900 to the Present.* Chicago, IL: Third World Press.

Ralph, P., Hunter, R. J., Marquart, J. W., Cuvelier, S. J., and Merianos, D. 1996. Exploring the differences between gang and non-gang prisoners. In *Gangs in America*, 2d ed., edited by C. R. Huff. Thousand Oaks, CA: Sage Publications, pp. 241–256.

Reiner, I. 1992. Gangs, crime and violence in Los Angeles. Unpublished manuscript. Office of the District Attorney of the County of Los Angeles.

Rosenbaum, D. P., and Grant, J. A. 1983. *Gangs and Youth Problems in Evanston: Research Findings and Policy Options.* Evanston, IL: Center for Urban Affairs and Policy Research, Northwestern University.

Rosenfeld, R., and Decker, H. 1996 (Winter). Consent to search and seize: Evaluating an innovative youth firearm suppression program. *Law and Contemporary Problems* 59:197–220. Special Issue.

Sanchez-Jankowski, M. S. 1991. *Islands in the Street: Gangs and American Urban Society.* Berkeley, CA: University of California Press.

Sanders, W. 1994. *Gangbangs and Drive-bys: Grounded Culture and Juvenile Gang Violence.* New York, NY: Aldine de Gruyter.

Sante, L. 1991. *Low Life: Lures and Snares of Old New York.* New York, NY: Vintage Books.

Sheley, J. F., and Wright, J. D. 1993. *Gun Acquisition and Possession in Selected Juvenile Samples.* Research in Brief. Washington, DC: U.S. Department of Justice, Office of Justice Programs, National Institute of Justice and Office of Juvenile Justice and Delinquency Prevention.

Sheley, J. F., and Wright, J. D. 1995. *In the Line of Fire: Youth, Guns and Violence in Urban America.* Hawthorne, NY: Aldine De Gruyter.

Short, J. F., Jr., 1996. Foreword: Diversity and change in U.S. gangs. In *Gangs in America*, 2d ed., edited by C. R. Huff. Thousand Oaks, CA: Sage Publications, pp. vii–xviii.

Short, J. F., Jr., and Strodtbeck, F. L. 1965. *Group Process and Gang Delinquency.* Chicago, IL: University of Chicago.

Skolnick, J. H. 1989. Gang organization and migration—drugs, gangs, and law enforcement. Unpublished manuscript. Berkeley, CA: University of California, Berkeley.

Skolnick, J. H. 1990. The social structure of street drug dealing. *American Journal of Police* 9:1–41.

Skolnick, J. H. 1991. Gang organization and migration. Unpublished report. Sacramento, CA: California Department of Justice.

Skolnick, J. H., Correl, T., Navarro, E., and Rabb, R. 1988. The social structure of street drug dealing. Unpublished report to the Office of the Attorney General of the State of California. Berkeley, CA: University of California, Berkeley.

Spergel, I. A. 1964. *Racketville, Slumtown and Haulberg: An Exploratory Study of Delinquent Subcultures.* Chicago, IL: University of Chicago Press.

Spergel, I. A. 1995. *The Youth Gang Problem.* New York, NY: Oxford University Press.

Taylor, C. S. 1989. *Dangerous Society.* East Lansing, MI: Michigan State University Press.

Taylor, C. S. 1990. Gang imperialism. In *Gangs in America*, edited by C. R. Huff. Newbury Park, CA: Sage Publications, pp. 103–115.

Taylor, C. S. 1993. *Girls, Gangs, Women, and Drugs.* East Lansing, MI: Michigan State University Press.

Thornberry, T. P., and Burch, J. H. 1997. *Gang Members and Delinquent Behavior.* Bulletin. Washington, DC: U.S. Department of Justice, Office of Justice Programs, Office of Juvenile Justice and Delinquency Prevention.

Thornberry, T. P., Krohn, M. D., Lizotte, A. J., and Chard-Wierschem, D. 1993. The role of juvenile gangs in facilitating delinquent behavior. *Journal of Research in Crime and Delinquency* 30:55–87.

Thrasher, F. M. 1927. *The Gang.* Chicago, IL: University of Chicago Press.

Valdez, A. 1997 (November). A contemporary assessment of Mexican American youth gangs in South Texas. Unpublished paper presented at the Annual Meeting of the American Society of Criminology, San Diego, CA.

Van Kammen, W. B., and Loeber, R. 1994. Are fluctuations in delinquent activities related to the onset and offset in juvenile illegal drug use and drug dealing? *Journal of Drug Issues* 24:9–24.

Van Kammen, W. B., Maguin, E., and Loeber, R. 1994. Initiation of drug selling and its relationship with illicit drug use and serious delinquency in adolescent boys. In *Cross-National Longitudinal Research on Human Development and Criminal Behavior*, edited by E. G. M. Weitekamp and H. Kerner. Dordrecht, Netherlands: Kluwer, pp. 229–241.

Venkatesh, S. A. 1996. The gang and the community. In *Gangs in America*, 2d ed., edited by C. R. Huff. Thousand Oaks, CA: Sage Publications.

Vigil, J. D. 1988. *Barrio Gangs: Street Life and Identity in Southern California.* Austin, TX: University of Texas Press.

Vigil, J. D., and Long, J. M. 1990. Emic and etic perspectives on gang culture. In *Gangs in America*, edited by C. R. Huff. Newbury Park CA: Sage Publications, pp. 55–70.

Waldorf, D. 1993. Don't be your own best customer—Drug use of San Francisco gang drug sellers. *Crime, Law and Social Change* 19:1–15.

Waldorf, D., and Lauderback, D. 1993. Gang drug sales in San Francisco: Organized or freelance? Unpublished report. Alameda, CA: Institute for Scientific Analysis.

Wilkinson, D. L., and Fagan, J. 1996. The role of firearms and violence "scripts": The dynamics of gun events among adolescent males. *Law and Contemporary Problems* 59:55–89. Special Issue.

Williams, T. 1989. *The Cocaine Kids: The Inside Story of a Teenage Drug Ring.* Reading, MA: Addison-Wesley.

Wilson, W. J. 1996. *When Work Disappears.* New York, NY: Alfred A. Knopf.

Zevitz, R. G., and Takata, S. R. 1992. Metropolitan gang influence and the emergence of group delinquency in a regional community. *Journal of Criminal Justice* 20:93–106.

Zimring, F. E. 1996. Kids, guns, and homicide: Policy notes on an age-specific epidemic. *Law and Contemporary Problems* 59:25–38. Special Issue.

The Distribution of
Illegal Drugs at the Retail Level
The Street Dealers

George F. Rengert

Retailers of illegal drugs face many of the same concerns as retailers of legal commodities. Their objectives are to sell as high a volume as possible at a price as high as the market will allow. These factors are related; as the price of illegal drugs increases, fewer customers will be willing to pay that price. Some will switch to other drugs, including legal alcohol. Others, especially dabblers who have not developed an addiction, will stop purchasing drugs (Kleiman, 1991; Mehay, 1972). There is some evidence that heroin addicts deliberately detoxify themselves when their habits grow too expensive (Kaplan, 1983). If changes in price influence the frequency of initiation of new users and the rate of addicts' detoxification, they may induce a signifi-cant elasticity in aggregate demand for even highly addictive substances (Kle-iman, 1991). As in the case of legal commodities, a supply and demand exist, which are affected by price. At a particular theoretical equilibrium point, sup-ply equals demand at a given price.

Competition also is important. If a dealer can sell drugs at a price and a volume high enough to make a large profit, other potential dealers will have a strong incentive to begin sales in the area to share in the profit. Profits, of course, are due to the illicit drug retailer's ability to attract customers. To attract customers, the new dealer may take advantage of either of two options: he or she may lower the price or increase the quality (purity) in comparison with the competition, or establish sales in a more desirable location than the competition so as to attract more customers. Such a location may be closer to a major transportation artery or a high school, which generates many potential customers (Rengert and Chakravorty, 1995). In these ways, illegal and legal retail sales are similar.

There are two important differences between selling illegal and legal commodities. First, illegal retailers must be concerned about apprehension by the police, so they cannot advertise or be too open about their sales operations. Second, illegal retailers cannot depend on the civil or criminal justice systems to mediate disputes or to protect them from theft or violence. These differences alter the classical location preferences that would result if their merchandise were legal. Rather than maximizing their access to customers, illegal drug dealers also prefer to locate where they can scrutinize approaching customers and where they have many avenues for escape if the police arrive. The greater the control over the exchange of drugs and money that a location gives the dealer, the more desirable that location is because it allows the dealer to control arrest, theft, and violence (Eck, 1994b).

On the other hand, customers of illicit drug dealers have locational concerns that also revolve around the chance of being caught by the police or of being cheated, robbed, or assaulted when buying drugs. Rational buyers would prefer not to visit areas where dealers have a great deal of control because these areas appear to place the customer at the most risk (Eck, 1994b). Customers would prefer to purchase drugs from their cars or in their own neighborhoods, where they feel more secure. Kleiman (1991) observes that relatively small differences in travel time, convenience, and perceived safety are likely to override price differences for the consumer. For more than a decade in Manhattan, the purity-adjusted price of heroin in Central Harlem was roughly twice as great as in "Alphabet City" on the lower East Side. Yet Central Harlem customers continue to purchase heroin in their own neighborhood because they desire the security of familiar surroundings their own neighborhoods provide and wish to minimize the time they spend in a vulnerable drug-purchasing situation. This preference places the customer at odds with the seller of illicit drugs in determining the best location for the sale.

If not too inconvenient, customers may be enticed to a riskier location by lower drug prices or higher-quality drugs (Eck, 1994b). Dealers may take greater risks if they can increase their sales volume or charge higher prices. In other words, customers will pay the highest prices when they take the fewest risks, and dealers will sell drugs for the lowest prices when they take the fewest risks. As on the supply and demand curve, which describes an equilibrium price for legitimate commodities, a trade-off exists between the risks taken by the seller and by the buyer of illicit drugs in a given neighborhood. The equilibrium defines the optimal location for sustained drug dealing. A location that minimizes the risks of theft or violence to a customer may increase these risks to a dealer. For example, if a customer wishes to purchase drugs from his or her car window, the dealer is left in a vulnerable position during the transaction. On the other hand, an abandoned building (turned into crack-house) may be a very secure location for a dealer but a very insecure location for a customer. Equilibrium locations are not the same in each community: The equilibrium location for Central Harlem, for example, may involve a higher price than that for Alphabet City if the overall risks to the seller are higher in this area.

Eck (1994b) uses these contrasting concerns about security on the par of drug dealers and customers to identify four types of drug markets: neighbor-hood, open regional, semi-open regional, and closed regional. In a neighbor-hood drug market, transactions take place in locations where both the cus-tomer and the dealer feel comfortable. These markets are likely to be the site of very small transactions between friends and neighbors. They are not large, important markets that are likely to be known to the police.

Open regional drug markets are located near places that are used rou-tinely by a large number of nonresidents, such as shopping centers, schools, or major transportation thoroughfares. Such locations may attract enough potential customers to support many competing drug dealers. These are large, important markets that are likely to be well known to the police.

Semi-open regional drug markets develop when dealers and customers wish to reduce the risk involved in an open drug market. Dealers sacrifice vol-ume by restricting sales to customers they know or who are referred to them. Customers buy only from known or referred dealers. This type of market differs from the neighborhood market in that dealers and customers do not live in the same neighborhood. They reduce risk by belonging to a network of friends who live in a wide area. This strategy produces dealing locations that are spread out rather than concentrated; there are no agglomeration economies due to locating in a well known drug-dealing area. Customers determine the transaction sites through a social network rather than by an area's reputation as a drug-dealing neighborhood. Police find it difficult to gain knowledge of these locations, and the sites are easily displaced spatially to a new location by police activity. Eck (1994a) reports that methamphetamine is sold in San Diego in this manner.

Finally, the closed regional markets draw customers from a wide area through a closed network of acquaintances. Friends and acquaintances from such an area patronize a dealer whose location is not related to the ability to attract customers. Access to the network is controlled very carefully. High-level wholesale drug transactions, such as wholesale marijuana sales in California (Adler, 1985), belong to this category. Dorn, Murji, and South 1992, p. 3) describe wholesale trade in Great Britain as a closed network operating over a wide area, which they term "trading charities." Law enforce-ment efforts to infiltrate such networks are time-consuming and expensive, with few tangible successes (Gugliotta, 1992).

This classification of drug markets is the result of the interaction of two variables: whether the customers are local or regional, and whether the loca-tion of the drug market attracts customers or whether customers determine the location through a social network. The first variable is closely related to that used by Reuter and MacCoun (1992), who create a typology of drug markets based on whether customers and dealers are mostly residents of the transaction neighborhood or mostly outsiders. They use these criteria to describe whether or not money is flowing into or out of the neighborhoods where drug dealing is taking place.

The money involved in illicit drug transactions is central to the operation. If the dealers are not making a profit, they will not continue to sell drugs. As in any business, illicit drug dealers attempt to maximize their profits and will go out of business if their profits do not at least cover their expenses over the long run. We do not know, however, how great their expenses are and how much profit they must make to remain in business. It is very difficult to conduct careful economic analysis of drug markets because the dealers will not let us examine their sales records. Therefore we have no exact measures of sales volume, the spatial range of customers, the extent of the market area, or the effectiveness of various marketing strategies. We must rely on indirect measures if we are to describe the nature of an illegal drug sales operation.

Rather than studying actual sales figures, we must examine what geographers call "revealed activities," whereby the dealers' and customers' behavior reveals the nature of the sales operation. In the following discussion, I build on Eck's (1994a) and Reuter and MacCoun's (1992) classifications by using measures related to the economic viability of an illicit drug market. I also identify the countermeasures that may be applied most successfully against each type of drug market.

Concepts Which Describe the Types of Drug Distribution

Two central terms—threshold and range—are used in marketing geography to describe the different forms of markets. The threshold is the volume of sales needed to make a certain type of sales operation or organization profitable. The range is the distance customers are willing to travel to shop at a specific retail outlet or combination of outlets, such as a shopping mall. These concepts can be used to classify illegal retail drug markets as well as legal markets if we can identify surrogate measures of each concept. Revealed activities can be used as surrogate measures (Rushton, 1969).

On the basis of revealed activities rather than actual sales figures, we reason that if a sales location is profitable, an illegal drug seller will use it during those times of the day when it is profitable. Furthermore, if profits are realized beyond the threshold required to keep an illegal drug dealer in business at a specific location, studies in marketing geography show that competing sellers will locate as close as possible to the original seller to siphon off these excess profits (King, 1984). I say "as close as possible" because illicit drug dealers may resort to violence if a competing dealer either operates too close to their base of operations or siphons off so much profit that their sales operation is no longer economically viable. If profits are large enough, however, empirical research has demonstrated that more than one dealer may operate in the same block without violence (Cooper, 1990; Eck, 1994a).

Researchers can determine whether competing drug dealers are operating from the same locality. Therefore I have identified two surrogate measures of the threshold of a specific sales location. The first is the length of time a sales site is open for business during the day. The second is the number of competing sellers operating close to one another in a specific neighborhood. For example, Albini quotes Massing (1989), who describes an especially profitable location in Washington Heights (New York) as follows:

> On every block there are four or five different crews or gangs each touting its own brand of the drug . . . Some blocks were hotter than others, depending on the availability of the crack. On the hottest blocks (crack) is available "24/7"; 24 hours a day, seven days a week. (1992, p. 104)

The range of an illegal drug market is also represented by two surrogate measures taken from revealed activities of the drug dealers and their customers. The first measure is whether the dealer moves to the customers' location so that the customers do not have to expend any effort to purchase illegal drugs (as in door-to-door delivery). The second is the mode of transportation used by the customers if they travel to an illegal drug marketplace. The reasoning supporting the second measure is that customers who come by automobile to purchase drugs probably have traveled farther than those who come on foot (Pettiway, 1994; Pettiway, 1995). Therefore, if a sales location caters to customers who arrive by automobile, it is likely to have a much larger spatial range than locations catering predominantly to customers on foot.

Using these surrogate measures of the threshold and range of a drug distribution location, we can classify drug markets by type, and can identify and evaluate enforcement tactics for each. I use unique combinations of the surrogate measures to describe the threshold and range of retail distributors of illegal drugs.

A Typology of Drug Distribution Locations

MUTUAL SOCIETIES

At the earliest stages of diffusion, illegal drugs can be distributed outside the marketplace with no identifiable threshold or range. In this situation, drugs are shared at parties and teenage hangouts. Drug distribution may not be the primary purpose of these gatherings; therefore the availability may not be predictable, and different persons may have the supply of drugs at different times. Dorn, Murji, and South (1992, p. xiii) refer to this form of trafficking as mutual societies, which they describe as "friendship networks . . . who support each other and sell or exchange drugs amongst themselves in a reciprocal fashion." At these social gatherings, drug use is relatively casual and experimental, and the users often are youths.

Several problems are associated with drug exchange among adolescents, which are less severe among adults. First, adolescents are less able than adults to resist the lure of dangerous drugs because they are less able to comprehend the risks. Youths tend to be less safety- and health-conscious than adults; they are more prone to engage in risky behavior because they tend to believe that nothing bad will happen to them, as evidenced by fast driving, rock climbing, whitewater rafting, and high school football. Young people tend to live on the edge.

A second problem associated with drug exchange between youths is that young people are very conscious of fashion and fads. Drug use by a youth whose opinion is valued by other adolescents will tend to increase drug use by his or her peers. Thus the use of illegal drugs may spread through a social group of otherwise wholesome young people. Group members may experiment in drug use in order to remain part of the social circle. If popular individuals are using drugs, others find it more difficult to resist and still remain active, accepted participants in group activities. Weiner and Macklin illustrate this pressure to belong:

> But if you talk to the kids themselves and ask why they . . . dabble . . ., they talk about their siblings, their cousins, and their friends. If they've used, they point to someone they respect, someone whose approval and acceptance they crave, who told them to give it a try . . . Peer pressure is "the number one reason," said a 14 year old West Philadelphia middle school student. "Everybody is doing it, and you think it's cool. They do it because they want to be popular, they want to be cool . . . " (1995, p. H6)

A third problem is that drug use early in life will limit life choices. Educational performance in particular is likely to suffer. Many youths will leave school to enjoy longer uninterrupted social gatherings involving illegal drugs. For those who do not leave school, drug use usually impairs concentration on schoolwork and thus leads to lower grades. As a result, these students are less well prepared for college entrance or technical careers than those who do not use illegal drugs.

Finally, for some youths, early initiation into illegal drug use is associated with early entry into a criminal career. Because they are young, virtually all of their crime-committing years lie ahead of them. Society pays a heavy price for the early onset of a crime-drug lifestyle. Specifically, parents and siblings are profoundly affected by the lifestyle of young drug-abusing family members. The worry and concern are compounded by the financial drain of stolen objects and criminal justice expenses. Whole families' lives can be destroyed.

Several solutions have been suggested. Nancy Reagan, for example, suggests that one should "just say no." Through socialization and education, an attempt is being made to teach our young people to resist the lure of illegal drugs. Law enforcement becomes involved when police officers are detailed to schools to educate the students in the dangers of drug use (Dejong, 1987; Marvin, 1993b). The most commonly recognized program is DARE (Drug

Abuse Resistance Education), which originated in Los Angeles. In this program, police officers spend an hour a week for 13 weeks with students in grades 7 and 8. Rather than focusing entirely on drugs, the officers stress reasons for deciding for or against alternative courses of action, resisting peer pressure and emotional arguments, and saying "no" gracefully (Kleiman and Smith, 1990). They teach these skills through a series of role-playing exercises. In addition, the federal government has devised the McGruff Crime Dog to teach even younger children to "just say no" to drug use and to other crime (Marvin, 1993a).

If this education and socialization mission is not successful, however, a taste for drug use may develop and a local demand may be created. As a result, a second type of drug distribution will be layered onto the first. At this point, a threshold of sales can be identified.

PERIODIC MARKETS

In the second type, the periodic market, the profit at any specific location is small because sales can be made only at limited times during the day. In this case, a dealer may have to travel to the sites of several groups of potential customers to stay in business. In the morning, for example, the dealer may travel to a local high school to sell to students on their way to classes. After school, the same dealer may travel to a local playground or park, again to sell to young buyers. In the evening, the dealer may operate out of a local bar, selling to older customers. This type of market has little or no range because the dealer travels to the customers' location. Each location is unprofitable during certain times of day, so the dealer may make sales only for a short period each day at each location. By exploiting several locations, however, the dealer reaches threshold levels of sales and thus remains in business. Few competitors, if any, are spatially close to this seller.

A subtype of periodic market may develop when demand at a specific time and place is so great that competitors establish themselves close to one another during certain hours of the day. The opening of a rock concert is such an occasion: for example, Grateful Dead fans follow the group from city to city and refer to themselves as "Deadheads." Many dealers may sell drugs in the parking lots before these concerts begin. In another subtype, dealers use beepers to take orders for drugs, which then are delivered to the buyer's location.

Three kinds of enforcement tactics are used to combat this type of sales operation. First, a jurisdiction may set up a "drug-free zone" around all public and private schools. Signs are posted on the perimeter of drug-free school zones, warning people what they are entering such a zone. This arrangement increases the penalties for anyone caught selling within these zones; in turn, the penalties increase the opportunity costs of doing business at such locations. For example, federal law doubles the penalties of anyone convicted of distributing drugs within 1,000 feet of a school, college, or university (Harrington, 1993). It is hoped that threshold sales will not equal or exceed these opportunity costs, so that sales in a drug-free zone will no longer be profitable.

Kleiman and Smith argue that drug-free school zones are not likely to be effective because most final sales to adolescents are made by other adolescents young enough to qualify for lenient juvenile treatment: "Moving middle-level suppliers 1,000 feet from the nearest school is unlikely to substantially decrease the accessibility of drugs to schoolchildren" (1990, p. 94).

Rengert and Chakravorty (1995), using police arrest data, investigated the issue of students selling drugs to students in central Philadelphia. They discovered that on average, those arrested for selling drugs inside drug-free school zones were too old to be students. Furthermore, the average age of those arrested for selling drugs in these zones (27.33 years) was about the same as the age of those arrested for selling outside such zones (27.96 years). Again, there is no evidence that students are more likely than older individuals to sell drugs in a drug-free school zone. In fact, very few students were arrested for street sales within these zones.

Rengert and Chakravorty also found that drug-free school zones were ineffective for deterring drug sales. They discovered that 3.9 arrests for drug sales per million square feet were made inside these zones, and 1.2 arrests per million square feet were made outside. They argue that the zones may be ineffective because they are so large that they exclude very little of the surrounding residential area. Therefore little space is left into which drug dealers can be forced. The effect is simply the same as increasing the penalty for selling drugs nearly everywhere in central Philadelphia's residential community.

Schools, however, are not the only establishments that attract periodic drug dealers. A second type of enforcement tactic focuses on the owners and operators of local bars and restaurants. These persons can be encouraged to control drug sales in their establishments through licensing enforcement by state liquor control boards. Again, an opportunity cost is evident: if bartenders and owners do not control drug dealing by their customers, the liquor control board can rescind their license to operate a bar. Because most bartenders, for reasons of liability, are keenly aware of most of their customers' activities, they can be held accountable for illegal drug sales in their establishments. Third, "buy and bust" operations are especially effective where sales are made predominantly to strangers—for example, at rock concerts or at vacation spots such as beaches, where the clientele changes regularly. These undercover operations are expensive and arrest only the lowest-level drug dealers on the sales hierarchy. In the resort community of Sea Isle City, New Jersey, police conducted a summerlong undercover investigation that resulted in the arrest of 20 suspected low-level drug dealers (Solovitch and Schurman, 1984). In this investigation, known as "Triple Header," Sea Isle City traded police officers with Atlantic City, so the officers would not be known in their local areas. In the summer, two Atlantic City police officers posed as summer residents of Sea Isle City; during the winter, two Sea Isle City officers worked under cover in Atlantic City. The cost of the operation included not only the salaries of two officers who were taken from regular duty, but also the buy money: "the officers posed as buyers . . . and purchased assorted drugs on 48 occasions. The cost of the average purchase was $50.00 . . ." (Solovitch and Schurman, 1984, p. 12B). Therefore the buy money used in this operation was $2,400, not an insignificant amount for a small community to spend on one police operation. When the administrative costs of the operation are added, one might question whether it is worth the effort to arrest 20 low-level drug dealers. The expense may be justified, however, if the operation is focused on a socially sensitive location such as a high school, where there is much at stake.

If the demand for illegal drugs increases markedly in a specific area, a third layer of drug marketing may emerge alongside the first two. In this phase, the drug dealer is not required to journey to the gathering sites of a few potential drug consumers. Therefore a range of drug sales is identifiable.

FIXED-SITE NEIGHBORHOOD SALES

This third phase, termed fixed-site neighborhood sales, emerges when the demand is great enough to reach threshold conditions at a specific site. In this case, the seller remains in one location during the day, with few (if any) competitors nearby. Yet because consumers now must travel to the dealer's location, the range of sales can be identified. In this phase, consumers travel largely by foot and are mostly neighborhood residents in the inner city. These dealers are the "mom and pop" type, operating out of local crack houses or shooting galleries. In the suburbs, these operations may be approached by car.

Enforcement efforts focused on fixed-site neighborhood sales include identifying the site and sealing the establishment. The idea is to make the building unusable by drug dealers by preventing them from entering. This concept, however, presents two problems. First, if a drug dealer wants to enter a property, he or she has plenty of time to reopen an entrance. Once the dealer is inside, the other sealed openings provide added security. . . . When police encounter an especially well-fortified building from which drugs are distributed, they may find it easier to bring in heavy equipment and knock a hole in an outside wall.

The second problem with the concept of sealing buildings used to deal drugs is that the sealed building is an eyesore for the neighborhood. It is an incivility, much like the broken window in Wilson and Kelling's (1982) argument against leaving property unrepaired. Many people would not want to live next to a building in which all the windows and doors are covered by cement blocks. Sealed buildings are the equivalent of a sign saying "This is a drug-dealing neighborhood in which the neighbors cannot control their environment. Therefore the city has had to seal it up."

A second tactic is to confiscate the property rather than sealing it. This is made possible by the Racketeering Influenced and Corrupt Organizations (RICO) law, which includes dealing in narcotics or other dangerous drugs.

This law contains civil forfeiture provisions requiring the violator to forfeit to the government any business or property that he or she has acquired in violation of RICO (Abadinsky, 1990). These assets may be frozen before trial. This tool is very powerful, if used judiciously, in taking the profit out of drug organizations. In fact, the Drug Enforcement Administration (DEA) claims to operate at a profit as a result of this statute. Gugliotta states:

> Law enforcement agencies made a lot of money fighting the cocaine war. For years the DEA boasted that it was the only U.S. government agency outside the IRS that operated at a profit. In 1989 the DEA seized $1.1 billion in cash on a budget of $500 million. (1992, p. 119)

RICO laws can be used to confiscate the drug dealers' property and the location from which they are dealing. If they are dealing from an abandoned property, however, no direct costs accrue to them as a result of confiscation. The dealers simply find another abandoned property in the neighborhood and resume their operations. Because of the dilemma whereby the dealer incurs no direct costs when abandoned properties are confiscated, the problem of housing abandonment in the neighborhood may have to be addressed.

In the suburbs, these houses often have value, and the police or the neighbors of the drug establishment may bring civil cases. The neighbors of an illicit drug establishment can bring civil action under a provision of the RICO statute which allows any person injured in his business or property by reason of a violation of RICO laws to sue in a United States district court; three times the actual damages plus costs and attorneys' fees may be recovered. If successful, the suits may lead to the selling of the property from which drugs are distributed, and the proceeds may be distributed to the complainants.

Civil enforcement procedures are gaining acceptance in the city as well. For example, if a building is being used as a drug-dealing location, city officials notify the owner that the property is being used for illegal drug sales. If the owner fails to take action, the property undergoes civil seizure and may be forfeited or destroyed. Building and fire code enforcement also may be used to pressure owners to clean up drug-infested properties. Green (1993) has determined that when the image of a community is improved, the spillover effects on surrounding neighborhoods are positive. In public housing projects, authorities may evict tenants who distribute drugs. Finally, in some jurisdictions police may seize automobiles of users who purchase drugs from their cars (Hayeslip, 1989). If the public officials fail in this effort, however, the neighborhood may deteriorate into a Type 4 drug market.

DRUG MARTS

Phase 4 occurs when drug dealers and the associated drug-dependent property criminals have made life so difficult in a neighborhood that nearly all of the law-abiding residents either have moved away or have entrenched themselves in their fortified homes, and have left the streets to the criminal element, especially at night (Rengert and Wasilchick, 1989). When this occurs, conditions are ripe for the establishment of a drug mart, in which dealers remain in one location while selling drugs. Profits are so high that competing dealers are attracted to the neighborhood to siphon off some of the excess profits.

Profits are high at these locations because the drug dealers have circumvented a major problem: they cannot advertise their products to the public in the local and regional news media. If drug sales in the neighborhood become notorious, however, the media will send reporters to the scene to describe the situation. Commonly the reporters not only give the dealers' exact location, but also state exactly how drugs are purchased (Sills, 1989). This information allows customers served only by Type 1 or Type 2 distributors to locate a drug source whenever they want to buy drugs. They may travel relatively far to this location by automobile, and purchase drugs through the car window.

Because the range is expanded greatly by this form of advertisement, excess profits will accrue, and competing sellers will establish themselves on the major routes leading into the "advertised" neighborhood. Many consumers travel to the area by automobile: therefore one tactic is to confiscate the cars after a drug purchase has been made. William Bennett champions this approach:

> The suburban man who drives his BMW downtown to buy cocaine is killing himself, of course. But he is killing the city at the same time. And his "casual" use is best deterred not by empty threats of long, hard punishment, but by certain punishment. Compel him, as authorities are doing in Phoenix, to pay a steep fine and spend a weekend in jail. Seize his BMW right after he has bought some dope, and when he is convicted, take the car away from him for good. That is what they do in Philadelphia. (1989, p. 5)

If this tactic were publicized, few consumers would be willing to risk their cars to purchase drugs from this neighborhood. This situation in turn would lower the profit level; if threshold conditions could not be met, some of the competing drug dealers might be driven out of business. Dorn, Murji, and South explain this scenario as follows:

> The suggestion is that police activities could be more effectively targeted at "affluent" buyers who use street markets because they are an anonymous trading place. Such buyers are more likely to feel the deterrent effect (presumably because of their otherwise "respectable" backgrounds) of having criminal records and receiving financial penalties or being imprisoned. If this worked and affluent buyers stop using street markets, this in turn would make those markets less profitable for sellers. (1992, p. 112)

In any case, street sales to buyers in automobiles would be nearly eliminated, and would provide the local government with an income source in the form of confiscated cars (Kennedy, 1993). Ethical problems can be circumvented somewhat by selling cars back to their owners at discounted prices rather than auctioning them to the public. Essentially this method amounts to a fine in which the wealthy would pay more to retrieve their expensive cars than the poor who drive less valuable cars.

If confiscating drug purchasers' cars is not considered desirable, an alternative approach would be to change the street patterns so that drug marts are less accessible to automobile traffic. This may force customers into unfamiliar territory in their approach to a drug market. Eck observes:

> Because they are unlikely to have objective measures of risk, buyers . . . are likely to gauge riskiness by the familiarity of a situation, i.e., the people involved and the setting in which the exchange takes place. The stranger the area and the people are to . . . the customer, the greater the perceived risk. (1994a, p. 143)

We might add that the approach to and exit from a drug market may also create anxiety if they are unfamiliar. One method of forcing an illicit drug customer into unfamiliar territory is by creating a system of one-way streets leading away from the drug mart location onto major traffic arteries (rather than toward the drug mart). The City of Philadelphia, for example, changed a pattern of one-way streets to make a drug mart in north Philadelphia more difficult to approach. Nonresident customers were forced to drive through an unfamiliar, threatening neighborhood to approach the original drug market. Yogi Berra sums up the problem facing the buyers of illegal drugs in these neighborhoods: "You got to be careful if you don't know where you're going, because you might not get there." Our objective is to create a pattern of one-way streets so that the nonresident buyers might not get there.

A second method of causing anxiety in customers is to create dead-end private streets in the neighborhood by blocking off one end of through streets. Beavon (1984), in studying the relationship between crime risk and the physical street pattern, noted the number of turns into each block. For example, an L-shaped pattern has only one turn into a dead-end street, a T-shaped pattern has two, and a cross has three. If the street does not come to a dead end, the same patterns exist as well in the other direction, creating four, five, or six turns into a street. By counting the number of turns into each block, Beavon found a correlation of more than .95 between the number of streets turning into a block and the property crime rate on that block. This very high correlation could exist for drug sales as well. Most drug purchasers want an easy exit from a drug mart. If they are required to drive down a one-way street, stop, and turn around, they will feel much less secure about purchasing drugs in a strange neighborhood. Furthermore, law-abiding residents of the area will find it easier to regain control of a street that is no longer a thoroughfare (Bevis and Nutter, 1977; Newman, 1972). They can observe more closely the people who drive down the street because through traffic will be funneled onto neighboring transportation arteries (Felson, 1994).

A third method of controlling access to a drug marketplace is to block access by nonresidents, either temporarily or permanently. Houston's Link Valley, once a fashionable residential community, had deteriorated into a drive-through drug market just off the highway. Residents formed a coalition and worked with the Houston police to seal up the community for one month. They permitted access only to residents and their guests. In combination with other tactics, this action evidently has been effective (Weingart, 1993).

Finally, "weed and seed" tactics can be initiated to revitalize the neighborhood. In such cases, police sweeps are used to rid a neighborhood of local dealers, and abandoned properties are torn down or rehabilitated. Local residents are provided with information and services to combat the reestablishment of drug markets in the community. Problem-oriented policing tactics especially are fostered so that neighbors and police can form a partnership to combat illegal drug dealers' activities.

If they succeed in combating the activities of illegal drug dealers, residents may take renewed pride in their community and may engage in practices that will discourage the return of drug dealers. Simply keeping a neighborhood neat and clean discourages those who practice incivilities.

There is some concern that drug dealers will simply move from "weed and seed" neighborhoods to set up business in a new community. Eck (1992), however, discounts the likelihood that dealers will be displaced over long distances. He has determined in San Diego that most low-level drug dealers operate from their own neighborhoods, often out of their own homes. Rengert and Chakravorty (1995) also have found that most dealers in central Philadelphia sold drugs from their own neighborhoods, even in drug-free school zones. Therefore drug dealers are not likely to be displaced far from their home communities. As a result, if these dealers are controlled in their own neighborhoods, they may be under control permanently as long as they live at that location. More research is required to substantiate this point.

These four types of drug trafficking can be identified by the threshold and the range associated with each. Table 8.1 illustrates the different combinations of threshold and range associated with each type. This classification has an advantage over Eck's (1994a) and Reuter and MacCoun's (1992) classifications in that it does not require the researcher to establish whether the

TABLE 8.1   Distribution Characteristics of Illicit Drugs

	Threshold		Range	
Market Characteristics	*Hours of Day Open*	*Competitors*	*Dominate Mode of Transportation*	*Location of Dealer*
Drug Mart	Full Time	Many	Car	Permanent
Fixed Site Neighborhood Sales	Full Time	Few	Foot*	Permanent
Periodic Market	Part Time	None	None	Temporary
No Market (Parties)	No Threshold		No Range	

*Applies only to the city; cars are almost always used in the suburbs or rural areas.
  Source: Author

illicit drug customers are regional or local, but only the mode of transportation they use to travel to the drug market. This classification does not depend on police data (which might not detect small local network markets), but on empirical observation and local knowledge by the researcher. Classification of a drug market is important, however, if effective countermeasures are to be developed.

The tactics designed to disrupt the distribution of illegal drugs in one type of market may not be effective in another. It is unlikely, for example, that a habitual drug user will "just say no" to drugs without the help of special treatment programs (Inciardi, 1994). Education and socialization are most effective among young people who are still only considering drug use. At the other extreme, a program to confiscate drug purchasers' cars will be useless in a "mom and pop" marketplace where most of the customers arrive on foot. Also, sealing crack houses will not help if the neighborhood contains many abandoned houses. These abandoned houses can be removed. The City of Philadelphia, for example, has torn down entire blocks of drug-ridden houses. The form of the drug market must be determined before effective tactics to disrupt drug sales can be initiated. In fact, the appropriate mix of tactics may be distinctive for each drug marketplace, especially if a location has developed into a high-level market. This is the case because a neighborhood may contain more than one type of drug distribution; one phase does not end when another begins. Rather, the phases are layered onto one another as new phases develop. Table 8.2 illustrates this process: Phases 1, 2, and 3 may exist in a single neighborhood. Later a Phase 4 may develop as an additional layer. Therefore a combination of tactics must be applied to rid a neighborhood of drug distribution.

Classification of markets also addresses the problem of labeling enforcement tactics as failures when they do not work in all drug-distribution areas. Many of these tactics work well in the types of markets for which they were designed; thus different prescriptions are needed for different types of markets. Firsthand knowledge of a drug marketplace is important if we are to develop a successful mix of countermeasures. It is much more difficult to establish an effective program if one relies only on police data. On the other

TABLE 8.2   Layering of Drug Markets within Neighborhoods

		Neighborhoods			
		1	2	3	4
Drug	Phase 1	X	X	X	X
Market	Phase 2		X	X	X
Type or	Phase 3			X	X
Phase	Phase 4				X

Source: Author

hand, the police often are the public officials who know the most about the neighborhoods and their associated problems. Therefore they are in the best position to initiate remedial action.

LAW ENFORCEMENT AT THE RETAIL LEVEL

Most municipal police departments operate on a tight budget. Their problem is to construct a coherent package from the many tactics available to counteract the particular drug problems facing their jurisdiction. Should they organize a DARE program to teach students in the local schools to resist drugs, or hire Spanish-speaking undercover agents to investigate a local drug-distribution organization? Should they concentrate enforcement efforts in a neighborhood where the drug problems are most serious, or in a neighborhood where they think they might have the greatest success? Or should they spread their drug enforcement resources throughout the city so that all citizens will benefit from their efforts? These are only a few of the issues facing police administrators. Obviously they cannot do everything for everyone; choices must be made.

Kleiman and Smith (1990) argue that there are theoretical as well as practical reasons to focus on the retail rather than the wholesale level of drug distribution. The aim is to make the retail transactions riskier and less convenient. Given limited resources, police must make a tactical decision: whether to focus on those periodic markets which operate discreetly indoors or to concentrate on fixed-site establishments and drug marts that operate less discreetly, often outdoors.

Open-air locations are both more noxious and more susceptible to control than discreet dealing. They are more noxious because they are a visible incivility that operates in the presence of local residents and of innocent visitors who may be passing through the neighborhood (Wilson and Kelling, 1982). Also, the competition for lucrative sites may result in violence, which may involve innocent people who happen to be in the wrong place at the wrong time. Finally, open-air sales are more available to new users, who may have difficulty locating a more discreet dealing site. If open-air drug markets can be closed, the availability of drugs to new users will be reduced.

Open-air locations are more susceptible to control because the deals can be observed by passing police patrols and undercover agents. Where practical, closing such markets should be a top priority. Doing so serves four important goals of drug enforcement: (a) it reduces drug abuse by reducing availability; (b) it reduces user crime by decreasing consumption without increasing the price; (c) it weakens major drug-dealing organizations by reducing the dollar value of the market; and (d) it protects neighborhoods by reducing the flagrancy of illicit drug activity (Kleiman and Smith, 1990).

Cities without large-scale street drug dealing should go to great lengths to avoid developing such markets. In cities with well-developed open-air markets, however, forceful attack may not be a practicable option because it may overwhelm the rest of the criminal justice system. The massive effort may take police resources from other important efforts and leave parts of the city underserved. The flood of arrests may strain prosecutors, courts, and corrections facilities. Prosecutors and judges are likely to react with lenient plea bargains to unclog the court systems; corrections officials are likely to adapt to prison overcrowding with early-release policies. Furthermore, if the open-air markets are large enough, they may be able to absorb many arrests without shrinking or changing form. In any case, a police administrator who contemplates closing open-air markets through massive arrests must anticipate the reactions of other criminal justice administrators, who have their own agendas.

A serious problem in retail-level drug enforcement is the potential abuse of authority by police officers. This includes illegal searches of homes and autos, harassment of citizens, and planting of evidence. Philadelphia presently is facing millions of dollars in legal actions because of the activities of several police officers in the 39th District. These officers have been accused of beating suspects, planting evidence, and falsifying reports. A similar problem occurred earlier in Philadelphia during "Operation Cold Turkey," in which a significant number of innocent residents were arrested because they happened to be on the wrong street corner at the wrong time (Pothier, 1987). Other cities have faced similar problems. These difficulties can be avoided by better training and closer supervision of police patrol officers.

A more common problem is police corruption associated with drug enforcement. Kleiman and Smith point out that corruption is more likely to occur in a specialized narcotics bureau than in everyday patrol because "the more complete the 'protection' from enforcement attention any one police unit can provide to a criminal organization, the greater the feasibility of establishing and maintaining corrupt relationships" (1990, p. 86). Therefore concentrating drug enforcement in a single unit is not likely to lessen corruption but to increase it. To make matters worse, forbidding patrol officers to make drug arrests will lower morale and will convince residents that the police must be corrupt if they do not arrest drug dealers who are selling in plain view. In short, concern about corruption is not a convincing reason to forbid police patrol officers to arrest drug dealers they can identify. A more serious problem is that in most major cities, police patrol officers can arrest more drug dealers than other parts of the criminal justice system can process. In such cases, police administrators may decide to concentrate on specific neighborhoods rather than on the entire city, in what is called a focused crackdown.

A focused crackdown has an advantage over wider-scale operations in that it can be tailored to the characteristics of a specific place. Also, more effort can be exerted in gathering tactical intelligence and ensuring cooperation from neighborhood residents. "Hot line" telephone numbers can be established, giving residents direct access to a command center. Police can establish contact with key neighbors to develop a plan for cooperation. The objective is to produce results so dramatic that residents view the police as an effective tool for neighborhood revitalization; such results might not occur if resources were spread more thinly, with only slight improvements in many places.

Increased neighborhood efforts against drug dealing are essential to long-run control, given limited police resources. Police must rid a neighborhood of most drug dealers, turn the task over to the residents, and move on to another neighborhood. Kleiman and Smith summarize the advantage of focused crackdowns over spreading police resources more widely:

> Virtually eliminating drug dealing in one drug-infested neighborhood—thus creating an area where residents feel safe and parents can let their children roam free—may be more valuable than reducing drug activity by 10 percent in each of ten drug-infested neighborhoods, just as picking up all the litter in one filthy park creates one clean park, while picking up 10 percent of the litter in each of ten parks leaves ten slightly less filthy parks, none of them attractive as places to play or relax . . . The ideal focused crackdown strategy in a big city would move slowly from neighborhood to neighborhood, leaving behind vigilant citizens and residual markets small enough to be controlled with residual enforcement efforts. (1990, p. 89)

An important outcome of focused street-level enforcement is that it can reduce a selected large illicit market to a smaller, less noxious form. For drug dealers, big, active markets have two advantages over smaller ones. First, buyers and sellers can find each other more easily in large markets. Therefore the buyer's search time and effort are reduced. Second, a given number of police officers pose a smaller threat to any one drug transaction if many other transactions are in progress in the same area at the same time (Kleiman and Smith, 1990). As buyers and sellers are forced out of the market, enforcement risks increase for those who remain. In addition, buyers need more time to find the remaining sellers. Therefore a large market that can easily absorb a small increase in enforcement without shrinking or changing form may be altered profoundly by a large, persistent increase in police activity.

Critics of focused enforcement claim that a focused response will only displace a drug market to neighborhoods outside the sphere of police activity; therefore drug dealing will not be reduced but merely will move to a new location. These critics, however, do not understand that location is one determinant of the volume of drug sales. Relatively accessible locations are more convenient and more easily identifiable by potential buyers. Furthermore, the availability of drugs in a local neighborhood affects the rate of use by dabblers and by ex-users trying to remain drug-free. If drugs are not flaunted, these two categories of potential users may avoid drugs. Therefore reducing the number of active drug-dealing locations has the potential to reduce the demand.

According to Kleiman and Smith (1990), both theory and experience demonstrate that neither high-level enforcement nor unfocused retail-level enforcement is likely to contribute much to solving the problem under current conditions in large cities. Yet administrators in these cities commonly choose a mix of these two ineffective strategies.

Crackdowns focused on particular neighborhoods are more likely to be successful. If this strategy is to succeed over the long term, enforcement resources must be moved periodically to a new area, and the process repeated. This approach requires neighborhood residents in the original crackdown area to assume responsibility for resisting the return of drug dealers. They must not continue to rely on the police to protect their community, once most of the dealers have been removed.

REFERENCES

Abadinsky, H. 1990. *Organized Crime.* Chicago: Nelson-Hall.

Adler, P. 1985. *Wheeling and Dealing: An Ethnography of an Upper-Level Drug Dealing and Smuggling Community.* New York: Columbia University Press.

Albini, J. 1992. "The Distribution of Drugs; Models of Criminal Organization and Their Intergration," in T. Mieczkowski, ed., *Drugs, Crime, and Social Policy.* Pp. 79–108. Boston: Allyn and Bacon.

Beavon, D. J. 1984. Crime and the Environmental Opportunity Structure: The Influence of Street Networks on the Patterning of Property Offenses. Master Thesis, Simon Fraser University, British Columbia, Canada.

Bennett, W. 1989. "Restoring Authority." *New Perspective Quarterly* 6: 4–7.

Bevis, C. and J. Nutter. 1977. "Changing Street Layouts to Reduce Residential Burglary." Paper presented to the American Society of Criminology, Atlanta (November).

Cooper, M. 1990. *The Business of Drugs.* Washington, D.C.: Congressional Quarterly.

Dejong, W. 1987. *Arresting the Demand for Drugs: Police and School Partnerships To Prevent Drug Abuse.* Washington, D.C.: National Institute of Justice.

Dorn, N., K. Murji and N. South. 1992. *Traffickers: Drug Markets and Law Enforcement.* New York: Routledge.

Eck, J. 1992. "Drug Trips: Drug Offender Mobility." Paper presented to The American Society of Criminology, New Orleans (November).

Eck, J. 1994a. "Drug Markets and Drug Places: A Case-Control Study of the Spatial Structure of Illicit Drug Dealing." Ph.D. Thesis, The University of Maryland, College Park, Maryland.

Eck, J. 1994b. "The Shadow of the Invisible Hand: A General Model of the Geography of Illicit Retail Market Places." Paper presented to The American Society of Criminology, Miami (November).

Felson, M. 1994. *Crime and Everyday Life: Insights and Implications for Society.* Thousand Oaks, Calif.: Pine Forge Press.

Green, L. 1993. "Treating Deviant Places: A Case Study Examination of the Beat Health Program in Oakland, California." Ph.D. Thesis, Rutgers University, Newark, New Jersey.

Gugliotta, G. 1992. "The Colombian Cartels and How to Stop Them," in P. Smith, ed., *Drug Policy in the Americas.* Pp. 111–128. San Francisco: Westview Press.

Harrington, C. 1993. *Drug Free Workplace Act of 1988.* Philadelphia: Temple University.

Hayeslip, D. Jr. 1989. "Local-level Drug Enforcement: New Strategies." Research in Action. Washington, D.C.: National Institute of Justice.

Inciardi, J. 1994. "Drug Use in America." Seminar presented to the Department of Criminal Justice, Temple University (September).

Kaplan, J. 1983. *The Hardest Drug: Heroin and Public Policy.* Chicago: University of Chicago Press.

Kennedy, D. 1993. *Closing the Market: Controlling the Drug Trade in Tampa, Florida.*

Washington, D.C.: U.S. Department of Justice, National Institute of Justice.

King, L. 1984. *Central Place Theory.* Beverly Hills, California: Sage.

Kleiman, M. 1991. "Economic Models of Drug Markets." Paper presented to The American Society of Criminology, San Francisco (November).

Kleiman, M. and K. Smith. 1990. "State and Local Drug Enforcement: In Search of a Strategy," in M. Tonry and J. Wilson, eds., *Drugs and Crime.* Pp. 69–108. Chicago: The University of Chicago Press.

Marvin, M. 1993a. "Celebrate October, Crime Prevention Month 1993, With McGruff's Educational Products." *Catalyst.* 13: 6.

Marvin, M. 1993b. "P.S. 163: A School, A Safe Haven, A Family." *Catalyst.* 13:1–2.

Massing, M. 1989. "Crack's Destructive Sprint Across America." *New York Times.* October 1: 38.

Mehay, S. 1973. "The Use and Control of Heroin: An Economic Perspective." *Federal Reserve Bank of Philadelphia: Business Review.* December: 14–21.

Newman, O. 1972. *Defensible Space: Crime Prevention Through Urban Design.* New York: Macmillan.

Pettiway, L. 1995. "Copping Crack: The Travel Behavior of Crack Users." *Justice Quarterly.* 12: 499–524.

Pettiway, L. 1994. "Travel Behavior of Crack Users: Implications for Law Enforcement and Drug Control." University of Delaware, Division of Criminal Justice. Unpublished Manuscript.

Pothier, D. 1987. "Department's Reputation Grew Uglier Over the Years." *Philadelphia Inquirer.* March 11.

Rengert, G. and S. Chakravorty. 1995. "Illegal Drug Sales and Drug Free School Zones." Paper presented to The Association of American Geographers, Chicago (March).

Rengert, G. and J. Wasilchick. 1989. "Space, Time, and Crime: Ethnographic Insights into Residential Burglar." Final Report. Washington, D.C.: The National Institute of Justice.

Reuter, P. and R. MacCoun. 1992. "Street Drug Markets in Inner-City Neighborhoods: Matching Policy to Reality," in J. Steinberg, D. Lyon, and M. Vaiana, eds., *Urban America: Policy Choices for Los Angles and the Nation.* Santa Monica: Rand Corporation.

Rushton, G. 1969. "Analysis of Spatial Behavior by Revealed Space Preference." *Annals of the Association of American Geographers.* 59: 391–400.

Sills, J. 1989. "Dealers 'Buy' and 'Rent' Drug Corners: $30,000 the Going Rate." *Philadelphia Daily News.* April 19: 3.

Solovitch, L. and M. Schurman 984. "20 Suspected Drug Dealers Arrested After 3-Month Probe in South Jersey." *The Philadelphia Inquirer.* September 23: 12B.

Weiner, J. and W. Macklin. 1995. "Getting Hooked." *The Philadelphia Inquirer,* November 12: M1 and M6.

Weingart, S. 1993. "A Typology of Community Responses to Drugs," in R. Davis, A. Lurigio and D. Rosenbaum, eds., *Drugs and the Community: Involving Community Residents in Combating the Sale of Illegal Drugs.* Pp. 85–105. Springfield, Ill.: Charles Thomas.

Wilson, J. Q. and G. Kelling. 1982. "Broken Windows: The Police and Neighborhood Safety." *Atlantic Monthly.* March: 29–36.

9

Reefer Madness in Bluegrass County

Community Structure and Roles in the Rural Kentucky Marijuana Industry

Sandra Riggs Hafley
Richard Tewksbury

Marijuana is often viewed as a harmful drug from which the public must be protected. In reality marijuana has been in use for at least 5,000 years and is one of the oldest agricultural crops in existence (Schlosser, 1994a, 1994b). The negative image marijuana now possesses is largely a social construction, created by moral entrepreneurs, not a product of concrete, scientific evidence attesting to the social and medical dangers of the drug. However, marijuana has served many purposes (in addition to being a recreational drug) over the years ranging from the manufacture of cloth and rope to medicinal applications. Despite its value, marijuana continues to maintain a negative image generating controversy whenever potential legalization is discussed in the United States (Szasz, 1992).

Early recreational use of marijuana in the United States had begun by the early 1900s and efforts to ban it soon followed (Himmelstein, 1986; Goldman, 1979). In 1906 the Pure Food and Drug Act banned the use of marijuana for manufacturing, medical and recreational purposes and the importa-

From *Journal of Crime and Justice*, 1996, 19(1): 75–92. Used with permission of Anderson Publishing Co. and the authors.

tion of marijuana (Himmelstein, 1986; McWilliams, 1993). In 1914, the Harrison Narcotics Act was enacted by Congress, ultimately giving the drug a prohibited status (Szasz, 1992). In the 1920s, the Volstead Act was used to control the lower classes and to educate the public about the "evils" of marijuana (Goldman, 1979; Himmelstein, 1986). During the years of 1933–1940 nearly all states adopted the Uniform Drugs Act, typically with a provision against marijuana (Weisheit, 1991). In 1937, Congress passed the Marijuana Tax Act that prohibited the "use and sale" of marijuana. It did not prohibit producing or growing marijuana since most marijuana was imported from Mexico. There was marijuana growing in the United States, but it was of low potency (Himmelstein, 1986).

The federal government has continued to enact new drug laws into the present day. In 1970, the Controlled Substance Act was passed, which changed the focus of federal government regulations from taxation to regulating interstate traffic (McWilliams, 1993). In the 1980s, the Comprehensive Drug Control Act, the Anti-Drug Abuse Act and the Anti-Drug Abuse Amendment Act were also passed. These acts raised the federal penalties for involvement in the cultivation, possession and trafficking of marijuana (Schlosser, 1994a). These were not the only offensives in the 1980s war on drugs, however. This was also the decade of numerous educational campaigns, such as Nancy Reagan's Just Say No, and the establishment of the national "Drug Czar." Accompanying these changes have been modifications to sentencing considerations that focus on "conspiracies" and "attempts" which may now result in severe punishment for those who consider an illegal action but do not carry it to completion. It is no longer necessary to actually commit a drug offense in order to be arrested and convicted; the discussion and/or intent to do so may be sufficient.

Despite the evolution of public disapproval and legal restrictions on the growth, distribution and use of marijuana, the marijuana industry continues unabated in Kentucky. During 1993, 645,232 plants worth perhaps $1 billion were confiscated and destroyed by law enforcement officials, making Kentucky the state with the most marijuana-related arrests, and the second most (behind Hawaii) number of cultivated plants confiscated (Associated Press, 1994; Nohlgren, 1994). It is widely believed that marijuana is the largest cash crop in the state of Kentucky. In 1991 nearly 905,000 marijuana plans were eradicated, worth over $1.3 billion (*Courier Journal*, 1992). In only eight months of 1992 more than $985 million worth of marijuana was seized; the total value of the state's largest legal cash crop, tobacco, was estimated at between $820 million and $959 million (Bartlett, 1992; Kentucky Agricultural Statistics Service, 1993). Marijuana contributes a major portion of Kentucky's economy, yet is illegal. The purpose of this article is to dispel the myth that such "crime" is an activity of a small minority of rural residents. Rather, our argument is that community and social structures, as exemplified by community members' social roles, function to facilitate this alternative (albeit illegal) industry.

Data Collection Strategies

This research is a combined effort of the two authors. The first author is a lifelong resident of rural Kentucky. Her experiences and community membership facilitated entré to the closed cultural institutions of the communities under study. Through personal contacts and kinship network introductions access was obtained to all aspects and all varieties of participants of the marijuana industry.

Several methods of data collection were utilized for this research. First, relying on personal and kinship network contacts, confidential interviews with a cross-section of community residents, including local law enforcement officials, reputed marijuana industry leaders (some of whom were in federal prison) and both current and former marijuana growers were conducted. A total of fifty-five interviews were completed. To ensure confidentiality and protect the identities and welfare of all interviewees, transcripts and all notes were destroyed upon completion of the research. All names and locations in this analysis are pseudonyms. Additionally, a review of the local newspaper for the period of 1984–1993 was conducted to identify individuals and frequencies of arrests for growing and selling marijuana in Bluegrass County.

Numerous copies of this analysis were, and continue to be, distributed within the rural community. This includes circulation among residents and former residents of other Eastern Kentucky communities. Comments were noted where differences were consistently evident. Overall, issues and typologies reported herein were confirmed by residents from numerous communities in rural Central and Eastern Kentucky. Where residents consistently pointed out discrepancies, modifications have been made. . . .

Typology of Marijuana Growers

The typical rural Kentucky marijuana grower is a white male between the ages of 35 and 50, with a high school education (Weisheit, 1991b) who lives in deep or shallow rural areas of Kentucky. He is a member of the "We Poor Folk" social class (Davis, Gardner, and Gardner, 1941). He is almost always married, with at least one child. He is rarely a user of marijuana and is often a respected, church-going, community leader with no previous arrest record (Weisheit, 1991a; Hafley and Tewksbury,1995) The typical marijuana grower, as is the case with nearly all community members, has strong, extensive kinship ties with roots in his community dating back to the first settlers.

Data about individuals involved in the marijuana industry and their culture and communities are relatively scarce in the academic literature. That which is available comes primarily from the work of Weisheit (1990a, 1990b, 1991a, 1991b, 1992, 1993; Weisheit, Falcone, and Wells, 1994; Weisheit, Smith and Johnson, 1991) as well as Potter and Gaines (1992; also Potter, Gaines and Holbrook, 1990) and the present authors (Hafley and Tewksbury, 1995). Weisheit, working in rural Illinois, has described the roles of marijuana industry participants, analyzed how the business of marijuana operates, and discussed the influence of marijuana users and growers on society at large. In his work, Weisheit has described three types of marijuana growers in Illinois: (1) the communal grower (2) the hustler, and (3) the pragmatist. The *communal grower* believes growing marijuana makes a social statement. Some purchase land with the intention of growing marijuana, others drift into marijuana production as a part of their lifestyle. In Kentucky, a similar motivation drives some marijuana growers who desire self-sufficiency and seek to earn additional money as a supplement to low paying jobs. Unlike the young, urban, outsiders who migrated into Kentucky for a short period of time, the rural resident is not retreating from society. He is trying to survive within his society and maintain his way of life.

The hustlers have both used and sold marijuana. They may grow a marijuana crop on land they own or they may purchase or rent land specifically for this purpose. Always adventuresome, the danger is an added appeal to the endeavor and allows the grower opportunities to match wits with law enforcement. When the excitement fades they may retire. These people might well be equally successful in a legitimate business. Many members of the "Country Boys," who dominate the Bluegrass County marijuana industry, fit in this category.

The pragmatist grows marijuana due to economic hardship. These individuals acknowledge that growing marijuana is morally and legally wrong, but feel that due to circumstances they have no better option. Most Kentucky marijuana growers fit into this variety of grower. While Weisheit's typology may appropriately explain the marijuana industry in Illinois, the unique cultural environment of rural Kentucky necessitates an expansion of this typology. In addition to Weisheit's three varieties, we argue that there must be two additional categories of participants in the rural marijuana industry; young punks and entrepreneurs.

The *young punk* is the marijuana wanna-be. These are young men between the ages of eighteen and thirty who are most likely without both older male relatives within the marijuana industry and a kinship network that is significantly tied to the marijuana industry. They do not own land or have the agricultural skills necessary to grow quality marijuana. True marijuana growers may use these young men as mules to transport their marijuana.

The *entrepreneur* most commonly begins as a hustler or pragmatist. In the beginning he grows marijuana out of economic necessity or he may view his actions simply as an alternative business venture. As time passes, he comes to enjoy devising new methods to elude detection. Even when he is financially secure, and no longer has an economic need to grow marijuana, he will continue to grow this crop and/or develop new ways of concealing and growing marijuana. Within this typology lies the primary reason why any attempts to eradicate marijuana growers from the hills of Kentucky have been, and will likely continue to be, next to impossible. The typical rural resident deeply resents interference from outsiders (Caudill, 1962; Montell, 1986; Pearce, 1994). Marijuana growers' attitudes towards outsiders is even more intense.

Rural residents will not discuss illegal activities that occur within the community with outsiders.

It can be extremely difficult for the outsider to identify the marijuana industry participants within a rural Kentucky community. Marijuana growers are perceived as respectable citizens of the community and do not fit the stereotype of a "drug dealer" often portrayed in the media (Hafley and Tewksbury, 1995). The rural Kentucky resident knows who participates in the marijuana industry in the same way everyone in the community knows who is sleeping with whom and other community gossip.

The Marijuana Industry in Kentucky

Historically, illegal activities have been a part of rural Kentucky culture. Many marijuana growers are the descendants of moonshiners and bootleggers. Within rural Kentucky communities, a culture exists that protects and shelters those engaging in illegal activities from the scrutiny of outsiders (Pearce, 1994; Potter and Gaines, 1992; Hafley and Tewksbury, 1995). These norms and values, coupled with the economic crises facing the agricultural industry in recent decades, have pushed rural families to pursue off-farm income sources (Deseran, Falk and Jenkins, 1984; Herbst and Hanson, 1971; Larson, 1976). However, rural Kentucky values encourage independence and self-reliance. One consequence of such values is resistance to outside interference or attempts to control rural activities, including eradication of marijuana. The small rural community and the rural culture provide the necessary structure and stabilizing factors to successfully raise and sell marijuana. These communities provide safety for both small independent growers as well as those involved in the organized aspect of the industry.

The secrecy that surrounds marijuana growers (due to marijuana's illegal status) and the reluctance of the rural resident to discuss such activities with outsiders indicates an element of strong informal social control within the rural community. Such informal social control allows the marijuana industry to exist and flourish. Within the small rural community, many expected social controls that are evident in mainstream society are not present. Thus, participants in illegal activities are allowed to function within the community without censor. Members of crime groups are not shunned, as would be expected if marijuana growers were perceived as deviants. Marijuana growers receive strong community support; the prevailing view in the community is that those involved in growing "alternative crops" have done nothing wrong.

Economic factors play a large part in the introduction of organized crime to rural Kentucky. Rural Americans have been entering off-farm employment in large numbers in the past three decades. By 1983 non-farm income accounted for over 70% of U.S. farm family income (Pulver, 1986:491–2). However, while farmers are increasingly relying on non-farm employment, in rural Kentucky high rates of unemployment lead many residents to the marijuana industry (Potter and Gaines, 1992; Voskull, 1993). In 1989 Kentucky had an unemployment rate of 6.2%; however, Bluegrass County's unemployment rate was more than 30% higher at 8.3% overall and 9.7% for Bluegrass County males (Cabinet for Human Resources, 1990). Lacking plentiful employment opportunities, many rural Kentuckians are forced to migrate to cities. In an effort to retain their community, rural residents often remain silent or protect those involved in the marijuana industry and thereby keep residents in the community. Rural residents do not want their "kin" to migrate; consequently many rural citizens endure a long drive to and from the city rather than moving nearer their urban place of employment. Lacking well paying jobs, many rural males opt to grow marijuana to generate or supplement their incomes.

Reflecting on the perceived limited avenues to economic success, one member of a rural community that supports the marijuana industry argues that it is common for individuals to struggle for economic survival. Joe David is one among many trying to "make do" the Kentucky way. He explains:

> You don't know what it's like to work in that factory. I been shut up in that place for 10 years, day after day. I ain't making no money. Hell, when I retire I won't draw nothin'. I spent my life in that box and will be ready to die when I leave it. Why shouldn't I grow a crop? So what if the law don't like it. A crop or two and I'll be set. At least I'll have something put by.

The marijuana industry in Bluegrass County continues to flourish despite the incarceration of members of the Country Boys. On April 22, 1994, a Bluegrass County resident was arrested in Western Kentucky and thirty pounds of marijuana was discovered in his plane. When this individual was apprehended, "respectable" citizens of Bluegrass County denied the presence of marijuana in their county. They asserted that if marijuana was being grown and distributed, it was only by a small group of "outsiders." In a way, this is true. The arrested individual, despite many years of residence in Bluegrass County, was considered an outsider to the culture. Unless one's family has lived in Bluegrass County for generations, one is initially considered an "outsider." To overcome this status requires acceptance into a kinship network. Only in this way can an individual earn the trust of industry insiders. When trust is not achieved, the rural community will not fully accept an individual. This perspective is clearly seen in the explanation of the situation offered by Donnie Ray, a life long resident of Bluegrass County:

> Did you see where they got that man out at the airport? Everybody knowed he was doing it. We tried to warn him to stay away from that good old boy but he wouldn't listen. We're just ignorant country folk. We don't know more than a big city man like him. Well, we knowed enough to stay away from the one that ratted him out and we tried to tell him. He wouldn't listen.

Similarly, Jimmy Dale, another Bluegrass County industry insider, reflected on this incident: "That fool with the airplane, hell he ditched it because it was loaded with dope. We warned him but you can't tell an outsider nothing. Now he's lost it all and he's going to jail too."

Residents of Bluegrass County regard outsiders with distrust, believing outsiders do not respect them. The example of a Bluegrass County resident being apprehended for trafficking in marijuana is tinged with resentment—not empathy or compassion—towards the resident outsider. Because he refused to heed their warnings, community insiders perceive him as remaining aloof and rejecting Bluegrass County residents as ignorant. However, despite the arrests, many community members continue to grow and sell marijuana. Joe Paul explains the persistence of the marijuana industry in Bluegrass County, saying:

> They's several that was bigger than Buford and them Country Boys ever thought about being. Hell they got him for organized crime. He ain't no big boss but they's others in Bluegrass County that are. The law's ignorant. They nailed Buford but they cover up their own screw-ups.

Roles of Community Members

It would be erroneous to assume that rural Kentucky communities present universally supportive or even knowledgeable fronts regarding the marijuana industry. Rather, individuals in these communities can be identified as occupying one of seven primary roles. It is important to note, however, that these roles are primarily males' roles. (Women's roles will be discussed below.) The primary roles of community members are as ostriches, the fringe group, the in-the-knows, the profiteers, the part-timers, the retirees, and the active participants.

The Ostriches are aware that people in the community grow marijuana but, like myths about the flightless bird, stick their heads in the sand and pretend not to know anything about illegal activities. Consequently, these persons are the least informed about the nature and scope of the marijuana industry. Their constant denial serves to protect the marijuana grower from outside scrutiny. These people portray the marijuana grower as a deviant outsider and not one of "us" even when there is evidence to the contrary. This group attempts to project the image of a community of only good, law-abiding people. The role of the ostriches is to promote this image to outsiders and to reassure themselves of the goodness of the people within the community. For the most part they do not profit from the marijuana grower's enterprise. . . .

The Fringe group is aware that the marijuana industry is a part of their community, but these people have no connection to kinship networks that participate in the marijuana industry. These individuals will acknowledge the industry's existence to others (while ostriches will not). However, they will rarely, if ever, inform law enforcement officials about such activity. The belief is that such knowledge should be contained within the community. They believe only insiders can and should exert social control over community and industry members.

The fringe group persistently asserts that marijuana growers are a small deviant group within the community. This perspective, like that of the ostrich, offers the marijuana grower a degree of protection from outsiders. If organized crime is perceived as small and powerless, its members stand a better chance of avoiding detection and thereby enabling them to continue illegal activities (and presumably maintain community stability). For these reasons, those who disapprove of the marijuana grower facilitate his avoiding detection. Wearing the mantle of respectability, the grower is not recognized or acknowledged as a member of the marijuana industry (or, he is not recognized as a community member). In reality, the fringe group's failure to publicly identify the scope of industry participation facilitates the invisibility enjoyed by many members, thus further entrenching the industry in the community fabric.

The In-The-Knows differ from the fringe group because they have friends and relatives involved in growing and selling marijuana. These persons may be present and witness others' illegal activities or such activities may be discussed in their presence. This group is trusted by marijuana growers, and due to their strong kinship ties to those inside the marijuana industry, they never disclose information regarding illegal activities to law enforcement officials. Furthermore, kinship ties motivate these persons to protect industry participants whenever possible (Pearce, 1994). Most commonly this occurs via warnings of impending raids or investigations known to individuals because of their professional and personal access to such information. By protecting others from detection and apprehension, these individuals promote community cohesion and continuation of current community structures and social/ economic activities.

The Profiteers are those community members who, while not directly participating in the activities of the marijuana industry, indirectly benefit from the economic impact it has on the community. This group is made up of local business people who have knowledge of and often support the marijuana growers. Marijuana is a major part of rural Kentucky communities' economies. Many businesses will accept cash for both large and small purchases. Large purchases, such as new cars, are not questioned when paid in cash (Weisheit, 1990b). The fact that a $20,000 vehicle is paid for in cash by someone whose home lacks indoor plumbing would draw attention from most, but not in a community that supports the rural marijuana industry.

Many members of organized growers, such as the Country Boys, are not full time participants. Some work in the marijuana industry for a short period of time; others move in and out of the group. Still others retire from the group but remain willing to help out when they are needed. All, however, remain fiercely loyal to the group. The Retiree is even more difficult to detect than the part-timer. He is no longer a participant, having retired due to advancing age (which may range from 60–80 years old). While no longer active in growing and selling, he is willing to teach other young men his trade and introduce them to his connections. On occasion retirement may be involuntary, a result of incarceration. Retirees may be extremely difficult for the outsider to identify. They are legitimate sector businessmen and professionals or literally almost anyone in the community. However, most community residents are keenly aware of these men's past activities.

It is rarely discussed, but community members know of these activities in the same way they know of the community's gossip. Wearing an air of respectability, the retiree may aid the active marijuana grower in laundering his money by introducing him to legitimate business opportunities and to those willing to accept cash for goods and services as well as finding markets for his product. The retiree has connections for the sale and safe transportation of marijuana, along with accumulated skills regarding efficient means to grow a crop. He may personally introduce novice growers within his kinship network to others who can provide information and resources. He may also teach the novice how to plant and grow marijuana or simply instruct him verbally about what is needed or how to correct a problem. Retirees serve as an example to younger growers, modeling how to evade detection and achieve financial success. Those whose retirement is a result of imprisonment also serve as models, demonstrating that prison may be a part of doing business within the marijuana industry.

The final role available to community members encompasses all aspects of active, regular, involvement in growing and selling marijuana. These persons often have made the marijuana industry their career, and their primary source of income is generated by their marijuana crops. As noted above, active rural Kentucky marijuana participants are found in five forms: communal growers, hustlers, pragmatists, young punks, and entrepreneurs. Most of the active participants, like Weisheit's (1990b) pragmatist, have never been arrested and function on a limited scale. Others, such as members of the Country Boys, expand their operations and grow marijuana on a much larger scale. Most small growers do so because of perceived financial necessity. When so motivated, business operations are rarely expanded. The hustlers enjoy living on the edge and pursue their goals by increasing the size of their crops (often venturing outside their communities to enlarge their illegal activities). This, of course, also means hustlers increase the likelihood of their detection, therefore putting the image and stability of the community in jeopardy. Young punks may be unable to obtain legitimate employment and so work as mules and tend the crops of the hustlers. As the economic underclass, young punks are cared for by those in the community who employ (exploit?) them.

The most obvious similarity across the varieties of active participants is that those involved are nearly all men. Women, however, do fulfill roles in the rural marijuana industry, but their roles are significantly different from men's roles. . . .

Women's Roles

Women in the male-dominated, rural culture of central and eastern Kentucky are often viewed as weak and passive. Growing up in a patriarchal society, many women outwardly display passivity when relating to men. They have been taught to submit to their fathers and husbands and bend to their will. However, while public displays often fit this mold, many women are in fact very strong and important contributors to their families, kinship network, and communities.

Just as there are certain types of male marijuana growers, there are also differing types of women associated with these men. Each of these varieties of women serves different roles in the business and life of the male marijuana grower. Women's functional roles include assisting in recruiting men into the industry and providing domestic and sexual services for isolated growers and aiding the men in growing, harvesting, transporting, and selling the crop. Females' roles, to an even greater extent than their male counterparts, in the marijuana industry are dependent upon social class membership. Women's degree of involvement ranges from passively assisting their husbands to playing highly active central roles. Theoretically more important, though, is a view of women's cultural statuses in the communities of the rural marijuana industry. There are three distinct roles for women in these communities: Strumpets, Decent Women and the Women-in-Between.

The Strumpet is typically a young, uneducated, and unmarried woman. Strumpets usually have one or more illegitimate children, are often substance abusers, and therefore are perceived as being of loose morals. Additionally, or perhaps consequently, the strumpet rarely attends church, which is an important social function for the rural woman. The roles expected of the strumpet are to provide companionship, sexual services and to perform domestic chores for rural men, including marijuana growers. Unless she is fortunate enough to marry, as the strumpet ages she becomes increasingly expendable to the men in her life. In such a case, due to a lack of education and jobs available to women, the strumpet will live out the rest of her life in poverty, and be looked down upon by other, more respectable women. While marriage will not bring the strumpet the same degree of respectability afforded the decent woman, marriage will bring her relative financial security. These young women often associate with marijuana growers for personal gain. She receives clothing for herself and her children, is taken to restaurants and other places of entertainment, travels with her male associate and may receive additional money for her living expenses.

Strumpets display strong loyalty to the men of the marijuana industry. However, this loyalty does not extend to waiting for a grower after he is imprisoned, leaves the area, or ends their relationship. She is typically a very pragmatic and self-interested person. Despite her avowed love for her man, she realizes that when he is no longer immediately available, it is in her financial best interest to seek out another man. The rural male also recognizes this relationship as a practical arrangement. The strumpet fulfills very specific, and for him important, roles in his life. He does not expect the same loyalty from her that he does from his wife. The strumpet's role is to keep him sexually satisfied and to perform jobs decent women cannot and would not be asked to perform. Because including women in the growing operations would require living with other men, rural Kentucky males would never allow their wives or other female relatives to be involved. Those considered to be decent women would not consent to such an arrangement in any case (Halperin, 1990). When discussing the roles fulfilled by women in his organization, Buford described strumpets saying:

> Most of us had girlfriends that we could trust with our lives even though most of us were married at the time. These girls would go on some deals, more or less to keep us company. Also they kept the guys happy and content. . . . They didn't need to leave the marijuana farm for sex. We all loved women and always will.

Strumpets are not respected in their rural communities. As might be expected, such women receive especially strong disdain from female relatives of the men in the marijuana industry. However, even though any man's female kin will disapprove of a strumpet, because the culture is extremely patriarchal their disapproval need not drive him away from a relationship with a strumpet. The marijuana grower accepts the strumpet as a necessary, and sometimes valuable, part of his business. She is a commodity, valued only by the men with whom she couples.

The second type of female is quite different and much more respected. Decent Women are highly respected and very rarely placed in any jeopardy by rural men. Decent women include the majority of mothers, sisters, grandmothers, daughters, aunts, and wives of the active participants in the marijuana industry (as well as many women with no connection to the industry). Although there are a few exceptions, these women do not generally grow, transport or in any way become involved with the activities of the marijuana industry. They are, for the most part, aware of illegal activities engaged in by the men in their lives, but they themselves rarely participate. Among decent women those most likely to express strong disapproval for marijuana-related activities are the mothers and grandmothers of the men involved. Country men show great respect, both real and ritual, for these women, displaying great deference to them. However, Decent Women's expressed disapproval does not lead the men to curtail their activities, for after all, they are "just women."

Living in a strictly patriarchal culture, the decent woman may be called upon by her male relatives to assist in recruiting new members of the marijuana industry. New participants, for the most part, are introduced into a kinship network involved in the marijuana industry by marriage to a decent woman. For the decent woman's husband to be incorporated into her kinship network of marijuana growers she must "indirectly" indicate her endorsement of her husband's involvement. It is her responsibility to communicate her husband's desire for inclusion. While she may (and probably will) voice her disapproval, in the end she will bow to her male relatives' wishes. Jolene, a decent woman, explains how her husband became involved in the marijuana industry by way of her male relatives:

> My husband and I was married about six years before he got in with the
> family. I kind of had an idea what my uncle was doing. My husband said
> he wanted some good pot. . . . The only way my husband could be
> brought in was if I said the word. . . . Finally, I mentioned it to my uncle
> in an off-hand sort of way. My uncle said for me to tell him to drop by, he
> might be able to help him out. I couldn't have gotten him in sooner. They
> had to see what he was like before inviting him in and then on my say-so.

Women-in-Between are distinct from, yet a combination of qualities
found in, decent women and strumpets. They may be divorced and employed
at the local factory. If unmarried they may frequent the local nightclubs in
search of a new husband. They often meet and form intimate relationships
with marijuana growers. Unlike strumpets, these women may insist upon a
monogamous relationship of either marriage or at least living together. While
more respected than the strumpet, they are still less respected than the decent
woman. The woman-in-between is unique; she often has an active role in
growing and distributing marijuana. Buford described the role of these
women as a relatively recent development in rural culture:

> Until 1983 or so women didn't play hardly any role at all in the growing
> or selling operation. Then things changed and we worked couples that
> were either married or shacking up on some farm. These girls worked
> and got a percentage of the crop just like the guys.

The woman-in-between is a new social category in the world of marijuana growers. It is difficult to ascertain the full extent of her role in this culture partly because of her recent emergence and partly because of their status
as a hidden member of the culture. Few of the women have been arrested and
none has chosen to discuss her role. In this patriarchal society, she is apt to
have been recruited and trained by male relatives, her husband or boyfriend.
Her future in the marijuana industry remains to be seen. It appears women
may be developing more egalitarian roles in the marijuana industry. It can
also be speculated that as male marijuana growers are being imprisoned for
longer periods of time the women are stepping in to replace them. It remains
unclear, then, whether the emergence of women that is presently being seen is
due to feminist politics or simple necessity. All three groups of women play
significant roles in the marijuana industry. Some are respected in their community, others are not. They all reflect the culture in which they have been
raised and have the same distrust of outsiders as their male counterparts.

Conclusion

The marijuana industry is a powerful economic and social force in the
United States, especially in economically depressed, rural regions of the
country. The growth and distribution of marijuana is not a randomly occurring, scattered endeavor, but rather is a structured industry that occupies an
important cultural position in rural communities. Throughout this article, we
have argued that the organization of the rural Kentucky marijuana industry is

composed of various identifiable roles and includes all aspects of rural communities. Even those individuals who are not themselves actively involved in the industry play important roles in facilitating the industry's economic success and continued operation. Furthermore, within the organization of rural Kentucky communities there are structural factors that promote and support the marijuana industry. Due to cultural and economic factors of the region, the roles rural residents occupy in relation to the industry are focused on the maintenance of community and culture, not necessarily making the success of the industry itself the primary focus.

All varieties of male and female marijuana industry participants can be found throughout rural regions of central and eastern Kentucky. Growers' efforts are significantly assisted by the supportive and generally accepting community culture. Community members perform a variety of roles in regards to the marijuana industry, often protecting (sometimes unknowingly) the activities of the growers and distributors. Generally those involved in the industry come from the lower social classes, although this is not a hard and fast rule. However, the rural Kentucky marijuana industry is a near exclusively white and male endeavor. Women's roles are primarily centered on providing for the needs—personal, business and family—of men. Strict patriarchal structures have severely limited women's roles and activities. There does appear to be evidence of change occurring in this regard however.

Across the board, women's roles are predominantly passive, although within the last decade women-in-between have begun to play more active roles. For the male marijuana grower, women fulfill essential, but subservient roles. Women are an intrinsic part of rural men's lives, and largely fulfill similar roles whether their men are or are not involved in the marijuana industry. Women are most valued for their abilities and willingness to provide their men with love, loyalty, and sexual services. The culture of rural Kentucky enables and encourages rural residents to retain their culture, even when survival hinges on illegal activities. Generations of rural Kentuckians have made do in the Kentucky way by bootlegging, moonshine, and the growing of marijuana. Despite arduous efforts of law enforcement officials the industry flourishes, and can be expected to continue to flourish. The rural marijuana industry is a cultural phenomenon, driven by a combination of economic hardship and long-held cultural traditions.

REFERENCES

Associated Press. (1994). "State is No. 1 in Nation in Arrests Involving Pot." *The Courier Journal*, March 16, 1994: 7B.

Cabinet for Human Resources. (1990) *Kentucky Total and Nonwhite Population and Labor Force Data by County*. Frankfort: Cabinet for Human Resources.

Caudill, H. M. (1962). *Night Comes to the Cumberlands*. Boston: Little, Brown.

Courier-Journal. (1992). "900,000 Pot Plants Destroyed." *The Courier-Journal*, November 10, 1992: 7B.

Currie, Elliot. (1993). "Toward a policy on drugs." *Dissent*, Winter 1993: 65–71.

Davis, A., B. G. Gardner, and M. Gardner. (1941). *Deep South*. Los Angeles: University of California, Los Angeles Press.

Deseran, F. A., W. W. Falk, and P. Jenkins. (1984). "Determinants of Earnings of Farm Families in the U.S." *Rural Sociology*, 49: 210–229.

Goldman, A. (1979). *Grassroots: Marijuana in America Today*. New York: Harper and Row.

Hafley, Sandra Riggs, and Richard Tewksbury. (1995). "The Rural Kentucky Marijuana Industry: Organization and Community Involvement." *Deviant Behavior*, 16, (3): NEED PAGE # REF.

Halperin, Rhoda. (1990). *The Livelihood of Kin: Making Ends Meet the Kentucky Way*. Austin: University of Texas Free Press.

Herbst, T. H., and R. J. Hanson. (1971). "Non-farm work as a substitute for farm enterprises." *American Society of Farm Managers and Rural Appraisers*, 35: 63–68.

Hill, B. (1989). "The Cornbread Mafia: How good ol' boys from Kentucky organized the biggest marijuana farming operation in U.S. history." *Louisville Courier Journal Magazine*, October 8, 1989: 1A.

Himmelstein, J. L. (1986). "The continuing career of marijuana backlash within limits." *Contemporary Drug Problems*, 13: 1–21.

Irwin, H. D. (1979). *Women in Kentucky*. Lexington: The University of Kentucky Press.

Kentucky Agricultural Statistics Service. (1993). *1992–1993 Kentucky Agricultural Statistics*. Louisville: Kentucky Department of Agriculture.

Larson, D. K. (1976). "Impact of off-farm income in farm family income levels." *Agricultural Finance Review*, 36: 7–11.

McWilliams, P. (1993). *Ain't Nobody's Business if You Do: The Absurdity of Consensual Crimes in a Free Society*. Los Angeles: Prelude Press.

Montell, William L. (1986). *Killings: Folk Justice in the Upper South*. Lexington: University of Kentucky Press.

Pearce, John E. (1994). *Days of Darkness: The Feuds of Eastern Kentucky*. Lexington: University of Kentucky Press.

Potter, Gary, and Larry Gaines. (1992). "Country Comfort: Vice and Corruption in Rural Settings." *Journal of Contemporary Criminal Justice*, 8, (1): 36–61.

Potter, Gary, Larry Gaines, and B. Holbrook. (1990). "Blowing smoke: An evaluation of Kentucky's marijuana eradication program." *American Journal of Police*, 9.

Pulver, G. (1986). "Economic Growth in Rural America." In *New Dimensions in Rural Policy: Building Upon Our Heritage*. Washington, DC: U.S. Government Printing Office.

Schlosser, E. (1994a). "Reefer Madness." *The Atlantic Monthly*, August: 45–63.

———. (1994b). "Marijuana and the Law." *The Atlantic Monthly*, September: 84–94.

Szasz, Thomas. (1992). *Our Right to Drugs: The Case for a Free Market*. New York: Praeger.

U.S. Department of Justice (1992). *1992 Domestic Cannabis Eradication/Suppression Program*. Washington, DC: Cannabis Investigations Section, Drug Enforcement Administration.

Voskull, J. (1993). "Prison Poverty Has No Bounds." *Louisville Courier-Journal*, December 5, 1993: 1A.

Weisheit, Ralph. (1990a). *Cash crop: A study of illicit marijuana growers*. (Draft of report for grant Cx-0016). Washington, DC: National Institute of Justice.

———. (1990b). "Domestic Marijuana Growers: Mainstreaming Deviance." *Deviant Behavior*, 11, (2): 107–129.

————. (1991a). "Drug use among domestic marijuana growers." *Contemporary Drug Problems*, Summer: 191–217.

————. (1991b). "The Intangible Rewards from Crime: The Case of Domestic Marijuana Cultivation." *Crime and Delinquency*, 37: 506–527.

————. (1992). *Domestic Marijuana: A Neglected Industry.* Westport, CT: Greenwood Press.

————. (1993). "Studying Drugs in Rural Areas: Notes from the Field." *Journal of Research in Crime and Delinquency*, 30: 213–232.

Weisheit, R. A., B. A. Smith, and K. Johnson. (1991). "Does the American experience with alcohol prohibition generalize to marijuana?" *American Journal of Criminal Justice*, 15, (2): 13–55.

Weisheit, R. A., D. Falcone, and L. Wells. (1994). *Rural crime and rural policing.* Washington, DC: National Institute of Justice.

10

Crack to Heroin?
Drug Markets and Transition

Bruce A. Jacobs

Virtually every fad, fashion and innovation that emerges on the social land-scape goes through four identifiable phases. From yo-yos to Nintendo, poodle skirts to bell bottom jeans, Morse code to e-mail, products incubate, expand, plateau and decline. In each case, it comes down to how long a particular phase lasts, the steepness of its rise and fall, the rate at which one phase transitions into another and the triggers responsible for these transitions. Illicit drugs are no exception.

Within five years of crack's emergence in 1984, the United States found itself in the midst of its worst drug epidemic in history. In rock form, cocaine could be sold on the streets for eight to ten times its wholesale powder price (Bourgois 1995). The drug rapidly expanded the opportunity structure for street-level drug selling. Entrepreneurs facilitated access to supplies, offered controlled selling territories and created entry-level roles in drug selling that required only minimal training and start-up capital (Johnson *et al.* 1995: 281). Users in the thousands were lured by a high so penetrating it was said to be unrivalled by any substance known to man (Ohlms 1997). Reports of the extreme lengths consumers would go to get more of the drug rapidly surfaced in the mass media, transfixing viewers by the millions (Chitwood *et al.* 1996). By 1988, crack was the most popular and profitable substance in the street drug market (Johnson 1991). It was a mass-marketing craze that "would have made McDonald's proud" (Witkin 1991: 44).

From *British Journal of Criminology*, 1999, 39(4): 555–574, by permission of Oxford University Press.

As early as 1990, however, the epidemic began to show evidence of remission. New users failed to replace old ones at the rate they were lost. Quantitative indicators have since documented meaningful and significant reductions in rates of crack consumption in major cities across the country— a function of both desistance among previously active users and decreasing rates of initiation among new users (see Golub and Johnson 1997).

Powerful anti-crack conduct norms have arisen in response to the personal and social devastation the drug wrought. To be labelled a crackhead is to be considered the "lowest of the low" in the hierarchy of the streets (Furst et al. 1999). Youths are known to ridicule and beat up such persons as a pastime, claiming they are nuisances, thieves and disgraces to the neighbourhood. Crack is now a dirty word. The epidemic is essentially over; demand for the substance has been siphoned off by stigma.

If history is any indication, however, it is not question of if a new drug will emerge but when and what form it will take. "Every new beginning," as they say, "comes from some other beginning's end" (Semisonic 1998). Indeed, the decline of one drug often signals the incubation of another (Johnson et al. 1997; see also Hunt and Chambers 1976). Recent epidemiological evidence suggests that this drug may be heroin. Nationwide, the number of new heroin users has risen significantly in the past five years (CEWG 1994). Approximately 320,000 occasional users and 810,000 chronic users were reported in 1997 (ONDCP 1997) up from 136,000 (1990) and 692,000 (1992) respectively. Since 1996, a number of US cities have demonstrated marked increases in opiate-positive rates among arrestees (ADAM 1997). Many such persons are aged 18 to 26—the cohort most likely to become long-term adult users (Golub and Johnson 1997; Golub et al.1995). Emergency room mentions and treatment admissions for heroin have grown significantly across the country. Between 1991 and 1995, the annual number of heroin-related ER visits rose from 36,000 to 76,000, while the annual number of heroin-related deaths swelled from 2,300 to 4,000 (NIH 1997). Between 1988 and 1993, the number of ER visits resulting from snorting heroin (a new, higher-purity version) rose 470 percent, from 1,100 to 6,000 (Bowersox 1995). Though the overall incidence of drug-related emergency episodes decreased from a peak of 518,000 (1995) to 487,000 (1996) the decline can be traced primarily to five US cities and heroin-related admissions actually jumped 20 percent in the last two years of the study period (DAWN 1996).

A number of supply-side indicators (DUF 1996) support a post-crack "re-incubation" of heroin as well. In the past ten years, heroin output has tripled (United Nations International Drug Programme 1997). In Afghanistan alone (a major source country) poppy production has risen to 2,800 metric tons. This represents an increase of 25 percent in one year (UNIDP 1997). Opium production also has begun in nations that heretofore have not grown the plant. These include Kenya, Nigeria, Morocco, Ukraine and Tajikistan; several already are demonstrating advanced techniques of cultivation, harvesting and processing (OGD 1991; 1992). A growing number of large-scale seizures of high-purity heroin were reported in the United States in the last six months of 1997 (UPI 1997a) and several from North Texas (a region recently flooded with high quality Mexican and South American heroin). Since 1987, heroin seizures by US Customs have increased nearly 266 percent, from 600 lbs to over 2,200 in 1994 (over 3,000 lbs were seized in 1993; *Sourcebook* 1996). Similarly, DEA reports seizing 1,500 kilos of heroin in 1996, up 80 percent from six years prior (Office of National Drug Control Policy 1998).

Perhaps anticipating crack's inevitable decline, Colombian cocaine cartels branched off into opium poppy planting in the 1980s (National Narcotics Intelligence Consumers Committee 1995; see also Chitwood *et al.* 1998). Since the early 1990s, South American-grown opium has become increasingly available (NNICC 1996) particularly in the Northeast—which many consider a drug market bellwether. Bruce Johnson and his colleagues in New York report kilos of top-grade heroin being offered by South American wholesalers to Brooklyn dealers for the unbelievable bargain of $20,000. "By undercutting the existing wholesale price ($100,000–$120,000) this insurgent group of wholesalers won over many existing heroin retailers and attracted several crack distributors with the lure of exorbitant profits" (Johnson *et al.* 1997: 491).

The high-purity street heroin currently available in New York (Hoffman 1996) and reportedly infiltrating other US cities (Gervitz 1997; Israel and Topolski 1996; UPI 1997a, b, c) is luring users in search of a more tempered, non-stigmatizing, snortable and "safe" high, relative to crack. Innovative marketing tactics—such as small, sniffable bags—are being targeted at new users and are becoming quite popular in many US municipalities (for an overview, see Neaigus *et al.* 1998). Moonrock or "speedball" rock—a crack/heroin amalgam with the addictive potential of cocaine and heroin combined—is reportedly being sold in New York and Chicago (Johnson *et al.* 1997; Oullet *et al.* 1995). This innovation appears to have the concealability and heartiness of crack, the marketing and packaging flexibility found in retail crack units and arguably, the income-generating potential of cocaine and heroin combined. Around the country, urban police and street ethnographers report an increasing number of street-level sellers purveying crack and heroin at the same time (ONDCP 1998; Rhodes *et al.* 1994). This represents a transition in many drug markets, where crack and heroin formerly were close in proximity but sold separately. Moonrock or some similar innovation may not be far off.

The purpose of this article is to assess the extent to which these and other trends converge with reports of active street-level heroin users and dealers operating on the streets of a large midwestern American city (St. Louis, MO). St. Louis is a medium-sized metropolitan area (population: 2.2 million) with a central city population of 360,000. Historically, St. Louis has had one of the largest illicit drug markets in mid-America. In many neighbourhoods, crack, heroin, marijuana and PCP are sold openly and available throughout the day—particularly on the troubled north side. St. Louis arrestees have demonstrated persistently elevated rates of cocaine, opiate and marijuana-positive urine specimens—rates among the highest of the 24 cities measured in the Drug Use Forecasting programme (DUF 1996). Increases and decreases in these rates—though at a different scale—tend to mirror other US cities. This makes St. Louis an ideal laboratory for investigating important correlates of crime such as drug market participation (see also Rosenfeld and Decker 1996).

Active drug market participants provide a vitally important firsthand perspective. They are positioned to triangulate officially reported trends and can also capture emergent processes on the "cutting-edge." Such processes often evolve before emergency room data, police reports and other conventional forms of information become available. This is important given the tendency for indicator data (i.e., health and criminal justice statistics) to lag—particularly when it comes to issues concerning street drug users (a hidden population that is difficult to find and sample; see, e.g., Inciardi and Harrison 1998a). Street heroin users may be especially prone to this problem, since it often takes considerable time for initiates to move from first use to arrest or treatment (much more time than crack users, for example; see Chitwood *et al.* 1998: 68). This can result in gross underestimation of the diffusion of opiate use—a shortfall ethnographic research can help avoid.

METHODS

This research is based on interviews with 27 active drug market participants operating on the streets of St. Louis, MO. Snowball sampling was used to locate these individuals, a strategy borrowed directly from Wright and Decker's (1997) study of active armed robbers. The first study participants were recruited by a trained project fieldworker. An active heroin user/dealer, this person had earned a considerable amount of trust among his fellow offenders. Using his reputation as collateral, he initiated the recruitment process by approaching offenders with whom he was familiar. After explaining the project to them—and stressing that law enforcement was not involved— he asked them to participate in interviews and to provide names of others who were currently active.

Respondents were recruited from a number of different networks and drug sets within the city. One particular district, however, was responsible for a disproportionate amount of heroin sales; several offenders were recruited from there. The vast majority of these respondents were "urban nomads" (Wright and Decker 1997) who moved from set to set in search of the best possible transactional conditions. As such, their mobility helped capture features, patterns and dynamics generic to multiple drug sets. This helps to minimize reliance on one particular geographic frame and also helps guard against having a sample of highly atypical offenders—a problem with snowball samples.

Inclusion criteria were taken from the literature to guide the referral process (see MacCoun and Reuter 1992; for more on eligibility criteria and potential problems researchers may have in respondents meeting them, see Jacobs 1996; Wright and Decker 1994: 23). Every respondent but one was reportedly using heroin at the time of interview; one claimed to have just become clean. On average, respondents reported using between $30 and $100 worth of the substance per day. Seven respondents considered themselves full-time heroin dealers, 11 dealt occasionally or had just recently stopped, nine were no longer actively dealing but used the drug (nearly each of these nine, however, had sold sometime in the recent past). Twenty-four of the 27 respondents were African-American, three were white. Twenty-five respondents were male, two were female. The respondents' mean age was 39. Their age range was 19–58; ten respondents were between 19 and 32, 17 were 40 or older (most of whom had used heroin for over 25 years). This proportion is roughly equivalent to the age-defined population of street heroin market participants known to street ethnographers around the country circa 1998 (see ONDCP 1998; also see Johnson *et al.* 1997). On average, offenders either were unemployed, partially employed, or worked sporadic "odd jobs" (e.g., cutting grass, painting, raking leaves, cleaning out basements).

The focus on heroin market participants necessarily brings certain limitations to this research, but the present study is exploratory. The primary concern here is to explore heroin's evolution and growth among those who are best-positioned to provide information about it: heroin market participants themselves. Targeted sampling is used to capture the perspective of both long-term opiate users and their more recently initiated counterparts. Long-term consumers provide context for heroin's evolution and make possible the documentation of important contemporary shifts in markets. Recent initiates permit the identification of factors central to heroin's exploding popularity among younger users—the central growth population attracted to heroin for the very reasons responsible for crack's fall from grace (e.g., stigma, uncontrolled use, etc.).

Interviews took place in a quiet room, were tape-recorded and transcribed verbatim. The interviews were semi-structured and conducted in an informal manner. They revolved around a basic set of questions that concerned the offenders' experiences with, and knowledge of, street heroin. As with most qualitative research, some issues presented themselves later in the study period that were not anticipated at the study's inception. Attempts were made to pursue these areas, even though this meant that only a minority of offenders would be able to discuss them (see also Wright and Decker 1997). The fact that responses became repetitive suggested topical saturation, though this could have been an artifact of the sampling design. The sample, moreover, was purposive in nature, meaning I cannot claim to have accomplished *theoretical* saturation.[1]

Drug Markets in Transition?

QUALITY AND PRICE

An important operational measure of a drug market in transition is the extent to which the quality of an emerging or re-emerging substance outstrips price (see, e.g., Johnson *et al.* 1997). When this shift is recent, strong, meaningful and perceptibly widespread, drug markets may be on the verge of fundamental change.

Up to the early 1990s, St. Louis retail heroin markets were dominated by the sale of "buttons." Buttons, or "pills" as they sometimes are referred to on the streets, contain a blend of black tar heroin and crushed, over-the-counter Dormin sleeping pills (active ingredient, diphenhydramine hydrochloride). A gram of black tar typically will be mixed with ten to 15 Dormin capsules (25mg each), to yield between 30 and 50 buttons (depending on purity). Buttons are sold on the street for $10 each.[2] Though still popular, buttons appear to have lost at least some ground to prepackaged retail black tar. This reportedly is a rather recent and significant change. Respondents refer to tar as "P" for pure, as it is "uncut" and of much better quality.

> It's way different [now]. It's pure heroin, mud, it's tar. [Used to be] mixed pills, in the buttons, but now can buy pure tar. [Pure tar's] better . . . no mix on that tar. Ain't nothin' on there . . . Everybody wanting that tar cause it's pure. [015 and 016]
>
> I've noticed now, especially real recently like in the last six months, I've gotten hold of some dope that's just, oh man, I thought I was gonna die. Not needing more amount than I usually do, but just the quality . . . much better. [018]

The modal retail unit of street tar is a tenth of a gram:

> Tenths of tar, they just started selling them I would say within the last two years. Basically they still sell buttons but basically I would say the last two years they been selling tenths of P on the streets . . . the buttons they sell, you know, as soon as you put the mix [Dormin] on it's not as potent, not as good as buying a piece of the tar . . . People more ready to spend $20 for a tenth of "P" than $20 for two buttons cause really that's better, you know what I'm saying. [With tenths] you get more for your money and it's gonna be stronger. [04]

Tenths are packaged in cellophane bundles and sold for $20. This price appears to be considerably lower than it has been in recent months. "It's cheaper, yeah it's cheaper," one respondent claimed. "[Before it was] $40 a tenth, $50 a tenth. Now it's down to $20. You can get a tenth for $20, sometimes $15." Larger packages of black tar also are reportedly available but are bought and sold less frequently due to the limited resources of most street-level drug users. Half-grams typically retail for $100–$150, full grams for $200–$300. A number of offenders claimed that the price of these quantities has been declining significantly in recent months as well. "[The price has] just dropped," one insisted.

"Like when I first started getting the stuff it was well over $225 to $250 a gram and now I can find it from anywhere from $150 to $175."

Whether in tar- or button-form, heroin is perceived to be widely available and easy to obtain. "I think they flooding this city with heroin right now," one offender insisted. Another agreed, claiming that "everybody and they momma got it." This reputedly represents a drastic shift from the recent past, as a third offender notes:

> A couple of years ago, I only knew one place to get dope at. It seemed like it was difficult to get dope, it would be a big hassle a lot of times, they would run out, you couldn't find any. Now, I know. . . I can get it . . . It's everywhere. Any part of St. Louis I've been there's dope. [018]

Others agreed:

> Heroin['s] plentiful . . . Plentiful, as small a town as St. Louis is, per capita, this is the most plentiful, per capita, this is the biggest dope area in, I don't know, everybody seem like they got some tar . . . It used to be just pills [buttons] and something that just a few people had. . . . [Now, everybody's got the tenths, it's easy to get]. [015 and 016].
>
> Everybody['s] selling . . . Basically in every place, in every nigger ghetto is heroin . . . Plentiful, area is flooded with heroin. [026]}

Authorities confirm the spirit if not the letter of such reports. St. Louis' DEA Domestic Monitor Program recently purchased equal quantities of heroin on both the north and south sides of the city—a measure of wide market availability (Israel and Topolski 1996; Topolski 1997). The agency also reports a significant increase in the "purity-price ratio". Street-level retail units purchased by agency informants have nearly doubled in purity in one year—from 12.9 percent in 1996 to 22 percent in the first half of 1997—while the price has remained constant (St. Louis DEA 1997). National DEA reports that a good deal of the American midwestern black tar heroin is coming from Mexican sources via the southwestern US border. North Texas (Plano, Dallas), recently designated by policymakers as a High Intensity Drug Trafficking Area (UPI 1997b), is a day's drive from St. Louis. A mere 650-mile trip, interstates 35 and 44 provide an efficient route of transmission.

Across the country, street purity levels reputedly are even higher than authorities report here. In 1995, for example, the average purity of a retail gram was between 56 percent and 64 percent (ONDCP 1996a)—significantly higher than the 7 percent reported ten years ago (NNICC 1996). The quality of increasingly available South American heroin reportedly is even better, nearly 76 percent in New York City and as high as 97 percent in Boston (Gervitz 1997; NNICC 1996). Sixty-two percent of all US heroin seizures since 1995 have involved this South American-grown heroin (UPI 1997c) a seizure source figure that has doubled every year since 1993 (DEA 1996). Widespread reports of high-purity, South American-grown smack reaching St. Louis, however, were noticeably absent. Only a small number of offenders spoke directly of such an infiltration, insisting at it was short-lived.[3]

NEW, YOUNGER USERS?

Drug markets in transition often are characterized by a significant influx of new, younger users. As a cohort ages into its late-teens to twenties, at-risk members experiment with the most popular, cool and least stigmatized phase substance of the day (ONDCP 1997). Crack was this drug in 1988; heroin appears to be becoming it a decade later. Nationwide, the number of heroin addicts has been increasing since the 1970s. Growing numbers of teenagers and young adults report using the drug. New users numbered 141,000 were reported in 1996 alone (up from 40,000 in 1992)—the majority of whom are under 26 years old (Wren 1997). The mean age of initiation has declined from 27.3 in 1988 to 19.3 years old in 1995 (National Household Survey on Drug Abuse 1996). Heroin use among eighth graders doubled in 1996, as did use by teenagers overall between 1991 and 1996—even while the use of other hard drugs declined (National Center on Addiction and Substance Abuse 1997). The number of first-time teenage heroin users recently reached a record high. Just-released numbers suggest that 171,000 teens used heroin for the first time in 1996, up 46 percent from the prior year. Extrapolating from such figures, this translates into a tenfold increase in the rate of potential new (long-term) users per 1,000 persons between 1991 and 1996 (NHSDA 1998).

Eastern Missouri has not gone unaffected by such trends. The number of persons 24 years old and younger admitted to drug treatment programmes for heroin addiction in the St. Louis region increased a remarkable 435 percent between 1993 and 1997 (Missouri Health Department 1998). The percentage of male arrestees who test opiate-positive in St. Louis has risen to over 10 percent, nearly double the number reported five years ago. More troubling, approximately 40 percent of these arrestees are aged 15–35 (ADAM 1997).

A number of long-time users confirmed the influx of new younger users firsthand, at street-level where emergent patterns often are evidenced first:

> A lot of these young people out here that's using. Before it was just a certain age people that using in the past, older people . . . I know a lot of people that's messing with heroin now that normally wasn't. But they basically, like I said, the younger generation . . . Most of them sniffing that I know of. [04]
>
> You could look at people pop out of the woodwork. I would have to say it's a lot of younger ones . . . using it now . . . I would say between 16 and 30, those are the ones that more than likely have access to heroin and using . . . [010]

Relative to crack, heroin is considered a more sophisticated, sedating, safe and controllable experience. As one respondent put it, "That crack affects your nervous system and that's the reason I see that they [younger users turn to heroin] . . . the younger guys are beginning to find out and they . . . try both of them . . . and come up with the answer that heroin is better . . . it's more relaxing you know, you're not as frantic. It doesn't keep you on edge." Young experimenters believe that they can sniff and snort the reputedly higher purity smack in moderation without becoming addicted, while maintaining the ability to lead a "normal" life (see also Neaigus *et al.* 1998). This perception is supported by the proportion of lifetime users nationwide who smoke or snort the drug rather than inject it. In 1994, this figure was 55 percent; by 1996, it had climbed to 82 percent (NHSDA 1997).

Buttons and tenths are inexpensive and widely available, fuelling the drug's allure. The high from heroin, moreover, can last for hours and cost a minimal amount (at least initially). "It's real cheap at first," one young user remarked. "You can buy a $10 button and you get real, real, high when you first start doing it." This compares quite favourably to crack:

> You get a better high out of it [heroin]. A crack high only last like maybe one, two, three, maybe five minutes man and then it's gone. You done spent $300, $400 just like that in 10, 15 minutes, gone you know. [With heroin], you spend $200 or $300 and get high all day, get high for two or three day, you know what I'm saying. [023]
>
> See now when we first started getting high we were doing one pill and were like this is great because we had done coke for years. Coke for two people to get high all night, you're talking $200, $300. Ten dollars for one button when you first start. That's enough to get high. You are going from $300 to $20. Ten dollars to get high . . . it's not like cocaine, "oh my God, I need another blast, oh I need another shot, I need another line," however you do it. It's not like that. You're happy. [024]

There is no post-use crash with heroin as there is with crack, nor are there intense cravings for more immediately following last use. That heroin can be sniffed or snorted means novice users can do it conveniently and easily—avoiding the discomfort and stigma of injection (see Johnson *et al.* 1998). "Safer"-use methods provide a readily deliverable high that lasts longer and allegedly is near in quality to that of injection—at least at first:

> . . . put it in a squeeze bottle, the mud, the tar, they put it in nasal spray [bottles] and [add] hot water on it, shake it up and squeeze it in your nose . . . [Buy] a tenth and put it down there . . . [Add] warm water and shake it up and it melts . . . And that's a better high all the way . . . You don't have to worry about it, snort it, put the bottle back in your pocket and it take you all day [to finish] . . . [015 and 016]

Heroin's attraction involves more than just its convenience, economy, controllability or notorious rush. A number of respondents in their late teens and 20s spoke of an "attitude" the drug gave them, an attitude that complemented the serene nod in a somewhat unexpected way:

> That heroin make you feel like Superman. It gives you an attitude and you feel good you know. It's like raw, it's the diamond you know . . . Young guys . . . they like the attitude, the boost that make them feel like they tough. Especially the gang members, they gonna have that gangster mentality and stuff. [09]
>
> [Author): The heroin, doesn't it mellow you out?

INT 09: Oh yeah, it mellows you out until somebody makes you upset and then you just go off on the deep end, you have an attitude . . . it doesn't matter, you could be laid back and relaxed then somebody say something that you don't like, you'll snap. [09]

[Heroin's] a downer high, it calms your nerves and everything so you just be mellow but it gives you an attitude . . . I mean the attitude is like extremely out of control, you don't want to be messed with. You just want to meditate off your high and when somebody disturbs that mode you snap. . . . [026]

It kind of toughens [you] up. It seems like [people on heroin] don't give a fuck once they get to snorting or whatever, they don't care no more . . . They [young gang members] got that "I don't give a fuck mentality" . . . so they can go do what they want to do. They gonna have no remorse about it . . . Everybody hear other people doing it and they like, "oh man, he doing that heroin when he did this or did that, oh yeah," so they want to do it. [027]

This "heroin attitude" is particularly useful on the streetcorner. The streets are an encapsulated social world enshrouded by conduct norms that "devalue intimacy and label those who express [affect] as weaklings" (Fleisher 1995: 145). A "don't mess with me", "crazy" reputation is absolutely essential in this world, where bad-ass self presentations are necessary to intimidate would-be victimizers (Maher and Daly 1996: 471). To the extent that heroin use produces an attitude that facilitates the projection of a capacity for violence, it may provide inoculation from victimization. This is especially important for younger drug market participants, many of whom dabble in drug dealing to finance their own use (Johnson *et al.* 1992).

In this vein, a number of my respondents reported the existence of young *heroin* users selling *crack* to finance their burgeoning (opiate) habits. This is a bit surprising. Drug dealers almost invariably are users of the drug they sell, whether that drug is marijuana, cocaine powder, heroin or crack (see, e.g., Johnson *et al.* 1992). Indeed, the widely believed stereotype of a drug seller—someone who sells drugs that he seldom uses—is largely unsupported by available evidence (Johnson *et al.* 1985). It also is intriguing given that crack is in decline.

Yet selling a product one does not use—even a product in decline—may be the best way to go about things. As one respondent—a young crack seller/heroin user himself—put it, "If I sell heroin, then I'm gonna be using the same product I sell. I'm not gonna be making no money. So I would always be out there broke and that might have me out there doing things that I don't really supposed to be doing." Another agreed, adding, "You can make more money selling something that you don't use instead of something that you do use . . . [You] sell one product to get another product. That crack was something that you do use . . . [You] sell one product to get another product." That crack was something with which these young offenders were familiar selling increased its attractiveness. As one older respondent reflected, "Crack was the new thing when they generation came up right. This is the drug they know how to make money off of . . . So this is the drug that they sell . . . they make money off this drug but they use the other drug [heroin]." As crack continues its inexorable decline and heroin its rise, it may only a matter of time before such persons switch to selling the latter out of economic necessity. This day may be fast approaching, as factors addressed later in this paper will attest.

CRACK TO HEROIN OR CRACK AND HEROIN?

Another operational measure of a drug market in transition is the speed with which the decline of a formerly popular substance funnels its users to the emergent drug. It is virtually impossible to measure this rate precisely or reliably. And even if crack users were switching to heroin in large numbers, neither ethnographic nor quantitative data are available to prove it. Longitudinal research collected among large numbers of (specific) users is necessary for such documentation (and such data do not exist). Drug Use Forecasting data provide perhaps the only crude proxy and they clearly suggest that heroin's rise has not tracked proportionally with crack's decline (at least among arrestees; DUF 1993–97).

This is not remarkable. Drug market transitions take time. Substance use conduct norms shift gradually. Declines of one drug and incubations of another start slowly and proceed deliberately (see also Valente 1995: 26). This is not true of all products and it may be less true of illicit drugs than other commodities, but a certain degree of lethargy can be expected.

At the same time, given crack's vicious stigma, its costliness and devastating effects, it is plausible that existing rock users might seek out an alternative in heroin. "Motherfucker, you lose your business, you lose your home, everything smoking that crack," one offender commented. "Snort some heroin, you can get high. You might fall off a little bit but it ain't gonna take you down like that crack. That crack will slam you. The heroin will push you down, the crack will slam you." Others agreed, all of whom had either direct or vicarious experience with the drug:

> Crack will make a bum out of you . . . with crack your money leaves you a lot quicker and you might loan out your car or your house or whatever and with the heroin you be more, you know, you have a little bit more finesse than people with crack cause people on crack, they'll do anything. [09]

> Heroin users . . . they use but they still try to keep their self up and everything and it seem like crack users just let their self go. Just they different from night and day. A heroin user is a hustler and a thief. A crack dealer will steal from his mother. [08]

Though heroin also is said to create an overpowering high, it is one that users liken to an all over body rush that calms and satiates rather than excites or makes desperate. The paranoid agitation caused by crack contrasts sharply with the serene tranquility produced by heroin (the opiate "attitude" aside). The heroin high offers a surreally euphoric experience, transporting the user to the best of all possible psychotropic worlds:

> I fell in love with heroin . . . It's wonderful. It's a great feeling . . . you'll get this taste in your throat and then it will kind of come [over] you. It goes to your head and then it goes all through your body. You can feel it. It's like a whole process. First you taste it and it kind of goes up to your head and then it goes all through your body and you are just like ahhh, it's like a wave . . . [024]
>
> I waited for about three minutes, it wasn't even two or three minutes and I felt it man. it felt like I was in heaven somewhere. My eyes rolled back in my head and I was like, man. I sat there for about two or three hours just feeling good. I'll never forget that feeling. [023]

Though one respondent claimed that "it just seems like everybody that used to do cocaine is getting into heroin now" and that he himself "got tired of the coke thing, jonesing, strung out and stressed on it", while another added that "everybody that used to do cocaine is getting into heroin now. . .", widespread reports of crack users quitting to adopt heroin were lacking. Some proportion of crack users, it appears, have added heroin to an existing rock habit, but my transcripts, as well as other available data sources (ADAM 1997; Johnson et al.1998; ONDCP 1998) provide little support for a fundamental or drastic switch. As one respondent put it, "the one thing I found about crack, seems like everybody that uses, it's hard for them to get away [from it]."

This is not surprising. Those who began using crack in the late 1980s and who continue to use crack in the 1990s are highly likely to persist well into the next decade (see Golub and Johnson 1997). At the same time, adding heroin to an existing crack addiction can be quite "functional". A CNS depressant, heroin is an effective complement to the intense stimulation produced by crack (see also Kleber 1991; Oullet et al. 1995). The calming opiate influence can tame the crack high and make its post-use side-effects less fearsome:

> You got one of them that races you and one of them that slows you down. The one that races gets you in the most trouble all the time. Instead of doing something, the other one slow you down. [02]
>
> I don't know too many people that was crack user that have switched to heroin . . . I know some people that use crack and then started using heroin but they was just using both of them now, not just from crack to heroin per se . . . I guess maybe because they get so wired up off of the crack, they want something to mellow out with, come down from it. [04]

It should be noted that long-time opiate users who considered heroin to be their "mainline drug" (forgive the pun) did not necessarily use heroin to the exclusion of cocaine. Some users—including a few of my respondents—began using crack with that drug's emergence in the late 1980s. A number of them had speedballed with cocaine powder for years prior. Cocaine hydrochloride, however, is difficult to obtain in St. Louis circa 1998—thanks to its decade-long displacement by crack. "It's [powder] hard to find now," insisted one respondent. "See most everyone, cocaine dealers, most of them taking cocaine and rocking it up. It's hard to find powder cocaine, especially like powder form for $10 [an ideal amount for injection]."

The problem for most users, then, became one not so much about finding crack to use but of finding crack to transform into cocaine powder to use. Those who wished to speedball were compelled to buy rock cocaine from one source and heroin from another—soaking the alkaloid rocks in vinegar or lemon juice (acetic and citric acid respectively) to transform them back into injectable salts. ". . . Most of the time you buy a rock, a crack rock and dilute, break it down to liquid form," explained one. "Put vinegar and lemon juice on it," expanded another, "and it melts it down where you can put it in the boy [heroin]. You can get a blast that way . . ." Absent here were widespread reports of "double-breasted" dealers (ONDCP 1998)—sellers who purvey crack and heroin at the same time. This compelled respondents who desired both drugs to take an extra step in procurement.

Whether or when double-breasting becomes widely institutionalized in St. Louis is a matter of speculation. Anecdotal reports from the author's field contacts in a related project suggest that it is occurring in some drug sets. Regardless, the fact that the vast majority of speedballers I interviewed reportedly did not smoke the rocks they purchased, but melted them down to inject—out of habit, stigma avoidance or both—is instructive. It highlights a clear division respondents insisted on making between crack and heroin users, a division of status. The former who add the latter are not necessarily less stigmatized because, in some central way, they remain "slaves to the pipe." The latter who add the former, by contrast, are making it appear as if they really are doing nothing different from what they have done for perhaps many years.[4]

It may only be a matter of time before this changes. As crack's stigma continues to grow, as more and more users "burn out" on the substance and as draconian penalties for crack possession continue to make it troublesome to deal with, heroin is poised to emerge as an attractive replacement. Across the country, thousands of rock users may be on the verge of switching (see, e.g., Inciardi and Harrison 1998a). Cheap, high-purity heroin is already being made available by crack sellers to their customers to boost sagging sales and profits (see Rhodes *et al.* 1994). Coupled with heroin's pharmacological complementarity (to rock cocaine, that is) a potentially steady (and additional) stream of initiates into opiate consumption is in the offing (Chitwood *et al.* 1998: 68; Johnson *et al.* 1998). The public health consequences of such a shift are worrying, particularly if and when large numbers of crack users-turned-heroin snorters start injecting (see Inciardi and Harrison 1998b). Though this possibility still is within the realm of speculation, it warrants attention.

THE STREET DEALING SCENE

For some time now, active, street-level crack markets have been saturated and unprofitable. Sellers who remain often compete intensely over a relatively small, largely indigent cadre of street addicts responsible for more than 70 percent of all cocaine consumption (Cesar 1997; DUF 1996). As already noted, their numbers are dwindling, as is the amount of money they have available for purchases. Recent changes in public transfer payments (e.g., welfare, AFDC, disability, social security) magnify this effect by altering the form of payments made and rendering them less liquid. Excepting brief periods of intense activity near the first of the month, the rosy days of yesteryear generally have disappeared for crack sellers. Many have learned that early and rapid success is unlikely. Some inner-city youths are becoming reluctant to sell crack and are faring relatively poorly if they decide to do so (see Golub and Johnson 1997; Johnson *et al.* 1997). Alternatives need to be sought. Heroin may be one of them.

A number of respondents claimed that heroin selling is quite lucrative and compares very favourably to crack.

> . . . the last couple of years heroin have came up so a lot of people make more money off of heroin than they do crack cause a lot of people ain't using the crack like the heroin. Most people using heroin so they just switch from crack to heroin and making more money off that. [027]
>
> Yeah, they [today's street drug user] ask for heroin now, man, because all last night I ran out. So I was getting so sick of all these people steady coming over, boom, boom, boom, I had nothing but some crack. They ain't be wanting that.

Part of the reason for heroin's economic lure can be located in the drug's pharmacology. Sustained or intense use, for even a relatively short time period, can result in increasing tolerance and a fast-developing addiction. Unlike crack (which involves no physical addiction in the clinical sense of the term) heroin quickly becomes a necessity like food or water. Heroin withdrawal is perceived to be acutely painful and something to be avoided at all costs. Getting more becomes a daily necessity (see Rosenbaum 1981).

These factors provide an ideal marketing situation for sellers in an era of apparent reincubation. Increasing numbers of users, growing tolerance among them, coupled with the existing cadre of long-time users can make for robust business. That heroin is less sensitive to the volatile peak-and-valley type use patterns of crack makes conditions only better. Crack sales, for example, are often quite brisk near the first of the month but tail off considerably by the 15th (Jacobs 1999). With heroin, money is perceived to come steadily, reliably, predictably and in rather significant amounts. This is consistent with the daily use patterns heroin addiction foments. One seller claimed to sell 200 units on an "average" day ($2,000 worth) 400 on a good one ($4,000 worth). Another declared selling nearly $1,000 worth a day, every day of the week. A third talked of his participation a 24-hour selling operation, making around $2,000 a night for himself. A fourth insisted that selling 600 (about $6,000 worth) units in a very short time span was not uncommon:

> You could sell them in one day . . . If people come because the dope is good and they been coming and they know you got good dope, you could sell 400, 500, 600 in a couple of days . . . it don't take no time to get rid of it . . . you can have $25,000 in no time [01]

The perception by some respondents that involvement with heroin was a less sanctionable offence seemed to make it even more enticing. A few offenders, for example, noted a distinct difference in the zeal with which law enforcement pursued the two drugs. These offenders implied that the draconian enforcement policies instituted against crack have not caught up with heroin, at least not yet:

> You get caught with one stone they want to give you at least six years, you know what I'm saying? . . . that shit is most definitely Federal. I don't want to be caught with no shit like that.[5]
>
> See the crack scene is real hot cause the police be tough on that crack but them pills they just tell you to go to rehab, like if you get caught with some [heroin]. They . . . lock you up with crack, but the [heroin], . . . they'll take the [heroin] and let me go . . . You take less of a risk [with heroin]. You can better get it off [use/sell it more easily and safely] . . . I don't know what it is about crack man, they come up with the dogs and got trucks . . . they come with the dogs and they on you. With the heroin, you can get off with it. [023]
>
> If I was to get stopped with what I have it wouldn't even be a case, it would be a misdemeanour. [A little heroin] . . . wouldn't matter, you got to have a nice quantity in order for them to give you a case for it. [027]

Given that street dealers typically keep only a small amount of drugs on their person . . . hiding larger inventories in secret stash spots nearby for restocking purposes—their explanation may be valid. Though crack dealers often take similar precautions, the amount of crack required to qualify as a felony is so low (any amount under two grams) that getting caught with one or two rocks—a typical sale amount—can result in a substantial penalty. Given the juridical stakes involved and our knowledge that offenders inevitably seek to maximize rewards and minimize possible punishment, it is not surprising that heroin appears for some as an attractive alternative.

Discussion

This paper has drawn from interviews with active heroin market participants to explore the processes relevant to heroin's reincubation in an era of crack's decline. In St. Louis, heroin is perceived to be widely available and a good value. Its pharmacology appears to compare quite favourably to crack due to its greater "controllability." Apparently, this has attracted new, younger users in search of a less stigmatizing, snortable high. The quality of street-level retail units is said to have escalated, in part a function of newly marketed "uncut" black tar. Selling heroin, finally, is perceived by some offenders to be lucrative and less sensitive to the spikes and dips in demand associated with crack.

Though anecdotal reports abound of heroin's exploding popularity outside the inner city (see, e.g., ONDCP 1998; UPI 1997a) there is little systematic evidence to back them up. In the near term, the drug's expansion hinges first and foremost on rates of initiation among street users in central cities.

An encapsulated social world with entrenched drug markets and established cohorts of hard drug users, the streets provide an ideal context for diffusion (for more on the notion of diffusion, see Hunt and Chambers 1976).

They enmesh participants in an expansive web of diffuse relations. The distance between ties is short. Individuals "know of" one another even if they do not know each other personally. Weak ties allow otherwise unconnected groups and networks to be bridged, accelerating rates of information flow. Kinship relations expedite the rate at which information is shared and acted upon. Given our knowledge that the more members of a network there are, the denser the network is (indicating amount and frequency of information transmitted) and the more "transmittable" a contagion is, the more rapidly new users will adopt it (see Katz 1957) conditions look ripe for heroin's expansion. Members will hear about its chic sooner and be influenced more strongly and in greater numbers to try it (see also Valente 1995).

Conduct norms specific to street culture fuel this hypothesized outcome. The streets place tremendous emphasis on spontaneity and impulsivity (Shover and Honaker 1992: 283). The hedonistic pursuit of sensation-seeking, a lack of future orientation and a global contempt for "regular living" become standards to live by (see Fleisher 1995: 213–4). Street culture participants are prone to getting caught up in fads whose consequences they may not understand, but feel they must adopt lest they be left behind or labelled as losers (cf. Wright and Decker 1994).

"Leading behavior" is of particular importance when it involves pleasure-inducing street drugs like heroin. Absent of stigma, high in quality, hip and trendy, the substance presents few obstacles to would-be initiates. What's more, new initiates are more prone than others to entice similarly positioned associates to try the drug: "they have not begun to suffer the adverse health and legal consequences of long-terms drug use" (Kinlock et al. 1998:21). Given that such persons represent the leading edge of users, heroin's diffusion may be hastened. Coupled with the drug's ease of administration and reinforcement potential, the gap between first use and adoption is likely to be short—not as short as crack's, but short nonetheless.

To be sure, the drug's growth also hinges on the extent to which supply-side factors respond to or amplify demand. Expansionary phases in "freelance" drug markets (the modal organizational form in St. Louis and elsewhere) tend to be associated with high competition. Brand loyalty is of paramount importance and sellers seek to capture the greatest possible market share (Johnson et al. 1992). Cultivation strategies are employed to this end. Free bags, extra quantities, or credit may be offered to hook buyers into particular sellers. Price wars are common and "good deals" abound. Exponentially growing worldwide opium supply facilitates these practices and permits retail vendors to pass their savings on to customers. And cultivation need not be intentional. Novice sellers are known to flood expanding markets in search of profit. Lacking expertise in mixing or packaging the dope, they might give users a better deal without knowing it.

The combination of low prices, high quality and widespread availability has a tendency to generate demand. This is true for virtually any product and heroin is no exception.

Indeed, the extent to which supply-side factors "create" demand is one of the most enduring, and elusive, questions in all economics. We know that demand is highly elastic when it comes to illicit drugs (Stephens 1991): the cheaper, better and easier to get they are, the more of them will be purchased (McEachem 1997). Though the demand elasticity for heroin is clearly lower than that for crack (due to the drugs' different physiological effects) heroin users generally will consume as much as they can afford to buy within the parameters of what they consider to be a safe dose. This is likely to result in increasing tolerance. Presupposing that enough existing users are affected, and assuming that (1) sensation-seeking novices continue to enter the market in pursuit of a cheap, safe and easy-to-get high (particularly those who would have previously been deterred from trying heroin due to the stigmatizing and/or fear-inducing requirement to inject it), (2) crack users who switch to and/or add heroin to their using repertoire begin appearing (Kleber 1991), and (3) former users turned clean re-initiate consumption in the presence of "new," high-quality heroin, demand should grow exponentially.

How long such growth can be sustained is another matter. As in all markets, conditions change. Prices rise, quality declines and the product becomes less available. In the face of increasing tolerance, falling quality and/or dwindling resources relative to what one used to need to get high or well, snorting becomes less and less practical (Kinlock *et al.* 1998). And regardless of price or quality, studies unequivocally demonstrate that snorters and smokers rapidly become injectors (Center for Substance Abuse Research 1996; Oullet *et al.* 1994; Pearson 1987). The switch is more rapid than sniffers would have us believe. Yet in their quest to maximize the "bang for their buck," injection becomes the only viable response (see e.g. Oullet *et al.* 1994).

The public health consequences from such a shift could be devastating. Scores of snorters-turned-injectors have the potential for recreating the AIDS crisis of the late 1980s and early 1990s (see also Grund 1998: 252). What is more, hard drug users are known for engaging in high-risk sexual behaviors and for harbouring perceptions of invincibility (Walters 1990; for an overview, see Chitwood *et al.* 1998). Some may even believe that if they do become HIV-positive, protease inhibitors and combination drug therapy will cure them (see, e.g., UPI 1997d). Lured by the safety of snorting, guided by the perception that their consumption is not a problem and confident that they are, or never will be, "junkies," new users constitute a large (and perhaps unwitting) pool of potential future injectors (Neaigus *et al.* 1998). The fact that snorters-turned-shooters are much less likely than experienced users to engage in safe injecting practices—especially when they first start shooting (Neigus *et al.* 1996; Vlahov *et al.* 1990)—only makes matters worse.

The extent to which heroin's reincarnation could trigger market destabilization is a related matter of considerable interest. It is doubtful that the magnitude of destabilization experienced in the crack era (1984 and 1994) will ever be matched. Increasing community involvement in dispute arbitration, greater job availability in a rapidly growing economy and incapacitation effects from swelling prison populations quell potential volatility (Blumstein and Rosenfeld 1998; Riley 1997). Key psychopharmacological factors (Goldstein 1985) also do not seem to be in place for it to happen. The effects of withdrawal aside, heroin is not nearly as "agitating" or violence-producing a drug as crack. Heroin may "rule" users but only insofar as they need enough of it to keep going. Many opiate users are able to maintain "normal lives" (Faupel 1987). To the extent that quality, price and availability remain within an acceptable range, the forces leading to psychopharmacologically driven crime will be stayed. To the degree that the policing of heroin is lax relative to crack, participants also may be more able to finance their use through dealing (Johnson et al. 1998). This will delay any fundamental shift to economically compulsive, income-generating crime. Less intensive policing can also function to depress rates of drug market violence: when sanction risks are low, offenders may not be as inclined to "rub people out" who snitch on them, for example (Rosenfeld 1998). Less vigorous social control also can make street transactions less furtive, which contributes to fewer rip-offs and greater security.

Predicting the future is not the criminologist's strong suit, but that does not diminish the importance of using current trends to forecast future outcomes. The spectre of heroin's suburban diffusion, for example, warrants further attention. Anecdotal reports suggest that heroin is becoming "hip" among younger white suburban cohorts cued by trends in fashion (i.e., "heroin chic") and depictions in mass media. The extent to which the drug is becoming what cocaine powder was to white middle-class users in the early 1980s is a matter of considerable interest (see Mundell 1994). So is the degree to which young white persons (as well as their older (30s and 40s), more affluent counterparts) will bring the same "noncritical, romantic" view to the drug that inner-city drug market participants seem to have (see Chitwood et al. 1998). To what extent will growth in suburban demand create a more intense or lasting epidemic? Will new suburban markets arise with ties to inner-city suppliers or will such markets be stunted by fear, racism and suspicion? Can autonomous suburban heroin markets develop on their own? These and related issues provide fruitful directions for future inquiry.

NOTES

[1] The sample's purposive nature restricts its generalizability. Nonetheless, exploratory data can be quite effective in expanding our understanding of how offenders think and act in real-life settings and circumstances. The research setting—St. Louis—also would seem to provide findings relevant to a wide array of Midwestern (US) and other cities like it.

[2] Users typically buy two to five at a time but, depending on their financial resources, stage of addiction and time of last use, may base less or more.

[3] Broadly speaking, the offenders' comments about quality speak to perceived trends and patterns. A few offenders reported that quality had not necessarily improved all that drastically in recent months. Others claimed that quality was variable; one day it might be great, the next perhaps not so good. It was clear, however, that most of the recent initiates (one to three years of use) as well as their longer-term counterparts, insisted that there was a decided improvement during their recall period.

[4] To be sure, a few speedballers did admit to smoking crack. Yet the vast majority claimed their use to be episodic, infrequent and opportunistic. Simply put, crack was not their drug of choice.
[5] Note is taken from a respondent participating in a related study on drug markets, but matches the respondents here on drug market participation criteria.

REFERENCES

Akers, R. L. (1992) *Drugs, Alcohol and Society.* Belmont, CA: Wadsworth.

Arrestee Drug Abuse Monitoring Program (ADAM) (1997) *Annual Report.* Washington, DC: National Institute of Justice.

Ball, J. C. (1967) "The Reliability and Validity of Interview Data Obtained from 59 Narcotic Drug Addicts," *American Journal of Sociology* 72: 650–4.

Blumstein, A. and Rosenfeld, R. (1998) "Explaining Recent Trends in US Homicide Rates," *Journal of Criminology and Criminal Law.*

Urgois, P. (1995) *In Search of Respect: Selling Crack in El Barrio.* Cambridge: Cambridge University Press.

Bowersox, J. A. (1995) "Heroin Update: Smoking, Injecting Cause Similar Effects; Usage Patterns May Be Shifting," *NIDA Notes,* July/August.

Center for Substance Abuse Research (1996) "ONDCP Releases Spring 1996 National Pulse Check," *Cesar Fax,* 5: 30.

Cesar (1997) "Marijuana Replacing Cocaine as Drug of Choice Among Adult Arrestees," *Cesar Fax,* 6/25,30 June.

Chaiken, J. M. and Chaiken, R. (1982) *Varieties of Criminal Behavior.* Santa Monica: Rand.

Chitwood, D., Comerford, M. and Weatherby, N. (1998) "The Initiation of the Use of Heroin in the Age of Crack," in J. A. Inciardi and Lana D. Harison, eds., *Heroin in the Age of Crack Cocaine,* 51–76. Thousand Oaks, CA. Sage.

Chitwood, D., Rivers, J. E. and Inciardi, J. A. (1996) *The American Pipe Dream: Crack Cocaine and the Inner City.* New York: Harcourt Brace.

Community Epidemiology Work Group (CEWG) (1994) *Epidemiological Trends in Drug Abuse, Vol. II Proceedings.* Rockville, MD: National Institute on Drug Abuse.

Drug Abuse Warning Network (DAAN) (1996) "Preliminary Estimates of Drug-Related Emergency Department Episodes," Report No. 14. Washington, DC: US Department of Health and Human Services.

Drug Enforcement Administration (DEA) (1996) "The 1995 Heroin Signature Program," *Intelligence Bulletin.*

Drug Use Forecasting (DUF) (1996) *Annual Report.* Washington, DC: National Institute of Justice.

——. (1993–97) *Annual Reports.* Washington, DC: National Institute of Justice.

Faupel, C. E. (1987) "Heroin Use and Criminal Careers," *Qualitative Sociology,* 10: 5–31.

Fleisher, M. S. (1995) *Beggars and Thieves.* Madison: University of Wisconsin Press.

Furst, R. T., Johnson, B. O., Dunlop, E. and Curtis, R. (1999) "The Stigmatized Image of the 'Crackhead': A Sociocultural Exploration of a Barrier to Cocaine Smoking among a Cohort of Youth in New York City," *Deviant Behaviour,* 20: 153–81.

Gervitz, L. (1997). "Purer, Cheaper Snortable Heroin Floods US," *Reuters News Service,* 31 December.

Goldstein, P. J. (1985) "The Drugs/Violence Nexus: A Tripartite Conceptual Framework," *Journal of Drug Issues,* 15: 493–506.

Golub, A. and Johnson, B. D. (1997) "Crack's Decline: Some Surprises across US Cities," Research in Brief. Washington DC: National Institute of Justice.

Golub, A., Hakeem, F. and Johnson, B. D. (1995) "Who's Still Using Crack? What Does it Mean? Age-Period-Cohort Analysis in Six American Cities," presented at the American Criminological Society's Annual Meetings, Boston, MA.

Grund, Jean-Paul, C. (1998) "From the Straw to the Needle? Determinants of Heroin Administration Routes," in J. A. Inciardi and L. D. Harrison, eds., *Heroin in the Age of Crack Cocaine*, 215–58. Thousand Oaks, CA: Sage.

Henslin, J. M. (1972) "Studying Deviance in Four Settings: Research Experiences with Cabbies, Suicides, Drug Users and Abortionees," in J. Douglas, ed., *Research on Deviance*. New York: Random House.

Hindelang, M. J., Hirschi, T. and Weis, J. G. (1981) *Measuring Delinquency*. Beverly Hills: Sage.

Hoffman, C. G. (1996) "Cocaine and Heroin Indicators from the DAWN and STRIDE Data," presented at the Annual DUF Director's Meeting.

Huizinga, D. and Elliott, D. (1986) "Reassessing the Reliability and Validity of Self-Report Delinquency Measures," *Journal of Quantitative Criminology*, 2: 293–327.

Hunt, L. G. and Chambers, C. D. (1976) *The Heroin Epidemics*. New York: Spectrum.

Inciardi, J. A. and Harrison, L. D. (1998a) "The Re-emergence of Heroin in the Age of Crack-Cocaine," in J. A. Inciardi and L. D. Harrison, eds., *Heroin in the Age of Crack Cocaine*, vii–xii. Thousand Oaks, CA: Sage.

———. (eds.) (1998b) *Heroin in the Age of Crack Cocaine*. Thousand Oaks, CA: Sage.

Israel, H. and Topolski, J. (1996) "Drug Trends in St. Louis," St. Louis: Community Epidemiological Work Group.

Jacobs, B. A. (1999) *Dealing Crack: The Social World of Streetcorner Selling*. Boston: Northeastern University Press.

Johnson, B. D. (1991) "The Crack Era in New York City," *Addiction and Recovery*, 24–7, May/June.

Johnson, B. D., Thomas, G. and Golub, A. (1998) "Trends in Heroin. Use among Manhattan Arrestees from the Heroin and Crack Eras," in J. A. Inciardi and L. D. Harrison, eds., *Heroin in the Age of Crack Cocaine*, 109–30. Thousand Oaks, CA: Sage.

Johnson, B. D., Dunlap, E., Boyle, K. and Jacobs, B. (1997) "Natural Transitions in Crack Distribution/Abuse," for NIDA. New York: NDRI.

Johnson, B. D., Golub A. and Fagan, J. (1995) "Careers in Crack, Drug Use, Drug Distribution and Nondrug Criminality," *Crime and Delinquency*, 41: 275–95.

Johnson, B. D., Hamid, A. and Sanabria, H. (1992) "Emerging Models of Crack Distribution," in T. Mieczkowski, ed., *Drugs and Crime: A Reader*, 56–78. Boston: Allyn and Bacon.

Johnson, B. D., Goldstein, P., Preble, E., Schmeidler, J., Lipton, D. S., Spunt, B. and Miller, J. (1985) *Taking Care of Business: The Economics of Crime by Heroin Abusers*. Lexington, MA. Lexington Books.

Katz, E. (1957) "The Two-step Flow of Communication: An Up-to-date Report on a Hypothesis," *Public Opinion Quarterly*, 21: 61–78.

King, L.J. (1984) *Central Place Theory*. Newbury, Park, CA: Sage.

Kinlock, T., Hanlon, T. E. and Nurco, D. N. (1998) "Heroin Use in the United States. History and Present Developments," in J. A. Inciardi and L. D. Harrison, eds., *Heroin in the Age of Crack Cocaine*, 1–30. Thousand Oaks, CA: Sage.

Kleber, H. D. (1991) "Heroin trafficking and abuse: A growing crisis," Hearing before the Select Committee on Narcotic Abuse and Control, House of Representatives, One Hundred First Congress, Second Session, 19 July 1990, 68–74. Washington, DC: Government Printing Office.

MacCoun, R. and Reuter, P. (1992) "Are the Wages of Sin $30 an Hour? Economic Aspects of Street-Level Drug Dealing," *Crime and Delinquency*, 38: 477–91.

McEachern, W. A. (1997) *Microeconomics*, 4th ed. Cincinnati: Southwestern.

Maher, L. (1997) *Sexed Work*. New York: Clarendon.

Maher, L. and Daly, K (1996) "Women in the Street-level Drug Economy: Continuity or Change?" *Criminology*, 34: 465–91.

Missouri Health Department (1998) *Public Health Statistics*. Jefferson City, MO.

Morrill, R., Gayle, G. L. and Thrall, G. I. (1988) *Spatial Diffusion*. Newbury Park, CA: Sage.

Mundell, C. (1994) *Drug Abuse in Washington, DC*. Center for Substance Abuse Research, University of Maryland.

National Center on Addiction and Substance Abuse (1997) Press release, 13 August.

National Household Survey on Drug Abuse (1998) Preliminary results, Office of Applied Studies. Rockville, MD: US Department of Health and Human Services.

———. (1996) Office of Applied Studies. Rockville, MD: US Department of Health and Human Services.

National Institutes of Health (1997) "Effective Medical Treatment of Heroin Addiction," Online Bulletin.

National Narcotics Intelligence Consumers Committee (1996) *The NNICC Report 1995: The Supply of Illicit Drugs to the United States*. Washington, DC.

———. (1995) *The NNICC Report 1995. The Supply of Illicit Drugs to the United States*. Washington, DC.

Neaigus, A., Atillasoy, A., Friedman, S. R. Andrade, X., Miller, M., Indefonso, G. and Des Jarlais, D. C. (1998) "Trends in the Noninjected Use of Heroin and Factors Associated with the Transition to Injecting," in J. A. Inciardi and L. D. Harrison, eds., *Heroin in the Age of Crack Cocaine*, 131–59. Thousand Oaks, CA: Sage.

Neaigus, A., Friedman, S. R., Jose, B., Goldstein, M., Curtis, R., Indefenso, G. and Des Jarlais, D. C. (1996) "High risk personal networks and syringe sharing as risk factors for HIV infection among new drug injectors," *Journal of Acquired Immune Deficiency Syndromes and Human Retrovirology*, 11: 499–509.

Office of National Drug Control Policy (1996a, 1997, 1998) *Pulse Check: National Trends in Abuse*. Washington, DC

———. (1996b) *Drugs and Crime Data*. Washington, DC.

———. (1990) *National Drug Control Strategy*. Washington, DC: The White House.

OGD CORRESPONDENT (1992) "Colombia: From Bekaa to Cauca," *Observatoire Géopolitique des Drogues*, 4.

———. (1991) *Observatoire Géopolitique des Drogues*, 1, 3 and 4.

Ohlms, D. (1997) Former Regional President of the National Council on Drug and Alcohol Abuse, Personal communication.

Oullet, L., Wiebel, W. W. and Jimenez, A. D. (1994) *Heroin Again: New Users of Heroin in Chicago*. Chicago: School of Public Health, University of Illinois at Chicago.

———. (1995) *Team Research Methods for Studying Intranasal Heroin Use and its Risks*. Chicago: School of Public Health, University of Illinois at Chicago.

Parker, H., Newcombe, R. and Bakx, K. (1987) "The New Heroin Users: Prevalence and Characteristics in Wirral, Merseyside," *British Journal of Addiction*, 82: 147–57.

Pearson, G. (1987) *The New Heroin Users*. New York: Basil Blackwell.

Rhodes, W., Hyatt, R. and Scheiman, P. (1994) "The Price of Cocaine, Heroin and Marijuana, 1981–1993," *Journal of Drug Issues*, 24, 383–402.

Riley, K. J. (1997) "Homicide and Drugs: A Tale of Six Cities," *Homicide Studies*, 2: 176–205.

Rosenbaum, M. (1981) *Women on Heroin*. New Brunswick, NJ: Rutgers University Press.

Rosenfeld, R. (1998) Personal communication.

Rosenfeld, K. and Decker, S. H. (1996) "Consent to Search and Seize: Evaluating an Innovative Youth Firearm Suppression Program," *Law and Contemporary Problems*, 59: 197–219.

Semisonic (1998) "Closing Time," MCA Records.

Shover, N. and Honaker, D. (1992) "The Socially-Bounded Decision Making of Persistent Property Offenders," *Howard Journal of Criminal Justice*, 31: 276–93.

Sourcebook (1996) Bureau of Justice Statistics. Washington, DC: Department of Justice.

Stephens, R. C. (1991) *The Street Addict Role*. Albany, NY: State University of New York Press.

St. Louis Drug Enforcement Agency (DEA) (1997) Personal communication (Special Agents Bob Dwyer and Darell Skaggs).

Topolski, J. (1997) Missouri Institute of Mental Health, Associate Director of Policy, Ethics and Evaluation, Personal communication.

United Nations International Drug Programme (1997) *Annual Report*. United Nations: Vienna, Austria.

United Press International (UPIa) (1997) "Heroin Suspected in Teen Death," from Yahoo! Search Engine, 19 April.

———. (UPIb) (1997.) "45 Drug Arrests Made in Texas," from Yahoo! Search Engine, 5 December.

———. (UPIc) (1997.) "Heroin Use on the Rise Nationwide," from Yahoo! Search Engine, 22 July.

———. (UPId) (1997.) "AIDS Treatments Add to Risky Behaviour," from Yahoo! Search Engine, 13 August.

Valente, T. W. (1995) *Network Models of the Diffusion of Innovations*. Cresskill, NJ: Hampton.

Vlahov, D., Munoz, A., Anthony, J. C., Cohn, S., Celentano, D. D. and, Nelson, K. E. (1990) "Association of Drug Injection Patterns with Antibody to Human Immunodeficieficy Virus Type 1 among Intravenous Drug Users in Baltimore, Maryland," *American Journal of Epidemiology*, 17: 39–48.

Waldorf, D. (1973) *Careers in Dope*. Englewood Cliffs, NJ: Simon and Schuster.

Walters, G. B. (1990) *The Criminal Lifestyle*. Newbury Park: Sage.

Witkin, G. (1991) "The Men Who Created Crack," *US News and World Report,* 44–53, August.

Wren, Q. S. (1997) "US Convenes Drug Experts to Grapple with Rise in Heroin Use," *New York Times*, 30 September, A 17.

Wright, R. T. and Decker, S. H. (1994) *Burglars on the Job*. Boston: Northeastern University Press.

———. (1997) *Armed Robbers in Action*. Boston: Northeastern University Press.

Yablonsky, L. (1966) *The Violent Gang*. New York: MacMillan.

11

Citizens and Outlaws
The Private Lives and Public Lifestyles of Women in the Illicit Drug Economy

Patricia Morgan
Karen Ann Joe

Introduction

The historical compulsion to limit the contexts of women's drug use to gendered relationships continues to cling tenaciously to the research literature. For decades, patriarchal worldviews placed women's drug use as a symptom of an underlying moral weakness or sexual deviance. Consequently, research restricted them to passive or victimized roles in social worlds dominated by men. Rationales for use depended on race, class, or type of substance. Women drug users were either good citizens suffering from "addiction" or "bad" ones whose drug use reflected their roles as deviants. This conceptual framework limited the context of women's drug use almost totally to their relationship with men. It was rarely considered that a woman's drug use could be shaped by choices outside the gendered relationship.

Beginning in the 1980s however, growing evidence from research began to reveal broader contexts framing women's use of illicit drugs (Ettorre 1992; Fagan 1994). Ethnographic studies found that women had rationales for use outside the world of men, that women often control their context of use, and that they play a larger role in the illicit drug economy than previously thought (Rosenbaum 1981; Mieczkowski 1992; Maher 1992). However, because most

From *Journal of Drug Issues*, 1996, 26(1): 125–142.

research continues to focus on disenfranchised marginalized women, and on drug use in the context of subordinate power relationships and victimized lifestyles, it is difficult to uncover the full range of the values and motivations which guide behavior. Yet, the only way to move outside traditional patriarchal paradigms is to identify these unexplored and hidden worlds of women's drug use. Consequently, the purpose of this article is to undertake this task by utilizing findings from a comparative study of methamphetamine use. Findings revealed complex systems of normative behavior framing overlapping contexts of drug use careers, personal lifestyles, and involvement in the illicit drug economy among women in the study. Moreover, it provides evidence that women have been especially safe in this hidden world of drug use for decades, overshadowed by the glare of traditional patriarchal interpretations.

Constructing the Image

Until relatively recently, women were largely ignored in the drug and alcohol research field. The few studies which were conducted before the 1980s limited their focus to women on either end of the lifestyle continuum. One body of literature grew out of Alcoholics Anonymous and the "addiction model." These were mostly clinical studies of women alcoholics who were said to suffer more severe forms of pathology than men because their addiction inherently conflicted with their natural role as wives and mothers (Hirsh 1962; Curlee 1967). The other body of literature were criminologic studies of women occupying outlaw social worlds. These focused almost exclusively on women prostitutes suffering from heroin addiction. They were studied as members of "deviant subcultures," who were thought to automatically violate basic gender norms, by neglecting traditional roles as wives and mothers (Woodhouse 1992).

The growth of crack use during the 1980s spurred a renewed emphasis on these disenfranchised women who used illicit drugs. (Anglin and Hser 1987; Hser et al. 1992; Chambers, et al. 1981; Fagan 1994; Inciardi et al. 1993; Bourgois and Dunlap 1993; Sanchez and Johnson 1987). The high risk associated with the use of drugs in pregnancy further stigmatized and reinforced women drug users' deviant status (Colten and Marsh 1984). Moralistic explanations expanded with the growing problem of "crack babies" (Callahan and Knight 1992; Maher 1992; Chavkin 1992; Humphries et al. 1992). A parallel spotlight focused on the links between women's drug use and prostitution (Goldstein 1979) especially the "sex for crack" phenomenon (Ratner 1993; Bourgois and Dunlap 1993). Fears of increasing HIV risk among women and their potential as a vector to a wider population completed the image. The picture was stark; it was static; and its blinding glare cast a powerful hegemonic shadow over the field. The sexual, perinatal, and HIV risk problems related to crack use among women defined the research agenda in the United States during the 1980s. It was a serious issue and a valid research priority. Unfortunately, it became the only one.

After 1990, several studies began showing women unexpectedly inhabiting diverse social worlds of illicit users equally complex as their male counterparts: Dunlap and Johnson (1996); Fagan (1994); Mieczkowski (1994); Granfield and Cloud (1996); and Sterk-Elifson (1996). Much of the information came from ethnographic studies revealing that even among the most marginalized and heaviest users, women were able to exercise a measure of control over many contexts of use (Mieczkowski 1994; Murphy et al. 1990; Dunlap 1992). Moreover, Maher and Curtis (1992) found that even women sex workers expanded their roles in the illicit drug economy after the crack epidemic forced them to adjust to changes in the sex market. They argue: "Rather than one-dimensional characters defined by traditional gender roles, our research reveals that women act within a number of overlapping contextual environments that are socially, culturally, economically and psychologically constructed (249)."

Other evidence reveals the need to systematically examine the possibility that women from a range of backgrounds make conscious choices toward a lifestyle involving drug use along with a career in the illicit drug economy (Waldorf and Murphy 1995). Growing evidence of expanded roles for women in the illicit drug economy provides formidable testimony against traditional gender-role interpretations (Johnson et al. 1991; Mieczkowski 1994; Maher and Curtis 1992; Maher 1996; Waldorf and Murphy 1995).

This article utilizes an exploratory community-based study of methamphetamine in California and Hawaii to disclose hidden worlds of drug use involving independent and active participation among women across diverse lifestyles and experiences.[1] The hidden contexts of their social worlds link women's roles in the illicit drug economy to the rationales and norms guiding their experience. This hidden world also exposes a dynamic relationship between varied lifestyles and shifting patterns of involvement in the methamphetamine drug economy.

Lifestyle Contexts

Women respondents fit a wide array of user lifestyles, both within and across study sites. Four primary lifestyle contexts were identified: outlaw, floater, welfare mom, and citizen (Morgan et al. 1994). We found that most of these women experienced more than one lifestyle change during different periods in their drug-use careers. An examination of these lifestyles enabled us to understand the contexts of experience among our female methamphetamine users. We also found that success in the illicit marketplace was not measured necessarily in terms of dollars, but frequently in terms of a person's ability to control his/her environment. It highlighted the need to examine closely the similarities and differences in the normative values guiding women in various lifestyle and economic contexts.

Outlaw Lifestyle

A definition of an outlaw lifestyle context involved respondents who were significantly immersed in deviant activities and marginal lives. The character of that lifestyle differed significantly depending on whether these women viewed themselves as "victims" or as "survivors." Those women who saw themselves trapped within an outlaw lifestyle were at the lowest level of economic and social status. With histories of chaotic and very unstable lives, many were merely existing, and often homeless. Most were barely surviving as hustlers and/or prostitutes. Some had lost touch with reality and with mainstream society. They generally engaged in the lowest level of dealing—as traders or sellers. Many of these women were heavy users for whom dealing to make a living and to maintain a steady supply has become a way of life. One respondent who has been in and out of jail for prostitution, drugs, and other crimes states, for example: "I do speed to stay up so I can sell speed to make money, but I sold speed to make money so I can buy more speed. I don't make a living at all. I'm existing, I don't call this living now (056)!"

Other women respondents were able to maintain more control, because they saw an outlaw way of life as a chosen lifestyle. They perceived themselves as long-time survivors who have managed to earn respect on the streets as either dealers or hustlers. A 27-year-old white IV user from the Tenderloin has been using drugs and has been a sex worker since coming to San Francisco at age 17. She claims she has a good life, even though she's been busted a few times, is currently on parole, and only makes about $5,000 per year.

> Yes. I'm 27 years old now and I'm told that I look younger now than when I did when I first came here to the city! I don't work the streets, I don't have too many hassles, I have pretty good friends and I support myself pretty well. There's no hassles, I don't have to go out there and do whatever. I don't hurt for nothing 'cause it comes easy. Do that, because it's there. As long as you're not burning nobody, it pays for itself. (018)

In San Francisco, there were over 12 women over 40 who had been using drugs continuously for over 2 decades. The matriarch of this subsample was a 59-year-old survivor of the Beat Generation who has been injecting speed and heroin for over 40 years prior to the interview. She began selling liquid ampules in the 1950s, helped run the first bathtub crank operation, ran a bordello, spent many years in prison, and claimed to have given Lenny Bruce his first hit of speed. Most of this activity happened in and around the Tenderloin were she continued to live and sell methamphetamine. At the time of the interview, although living on about $10,000 per year, she described a life of excitement and adventure. In another example, a 48-year-old woman from Richmond with over 26 years experience, admitted to having held a legitimate job for only 6 months out of the previous 20 years.

Almost all women leading outlaw lifestyles had criminal arrest histories and bad rip-off experiences. Many in this outlaw lifestyle were often former high-level dealers, distributors, or cooks. Some of these women were born into this lifestyle, especially those from second or third generation outlaw biker families. The parents of a 29-year-old respondent had long criminal histories, including murder. She began IV meth use at the age of 12 with the assistance of her mother. Since then, she has been a high-level cook, distributor, and a dealer. At the time of the interview she reported a history of violent crime which resulted in several prison terms. She has been diagnosed with many medical problems, some inherited from her mother's drug use while pregnant, and others a product of her own drug abuse. Nonetheless, she sums up her life and her speed use with fatalistic enthusiasm:

> What do I hope for the future? To live every day like it's my last day, cramming everything in that I possibly can into one. Live happy. . . speed is a part of my life. It always will be. Speed, I don't use it because I need it or because my body craves for it it's a must or I'm just gonna go crazy if I don't get that hit. I couldn't care less if I do have it, I couldn't care less if I don't have it. If I've got it at the time, well, damn, that's sufficient.
>
> But if I don't have it, I'm not gonna stress over it. It's not something that I must have and that I won't live without it. But I sure do fucking like it. [Both laugh] It makes you feel good. It takes things away, makes you not think about things, the inedible things. It makes you kind of surpass all that. And then when you come down, you'll think about it. Sometimes you get depressed when you think about it. But basically, it takes away the edgy feeling that you have, your everyday "Enough, stress," your yesterday's life. It takes away a lot of it. I won't never quit. I'll do it till the day I die and I hope somebody puts about a 60 unit hit in my IV bag when I'm sitting in the hospital. (092)

CITIZEN LIFESTYLE

Those in our sample leading citizen lifestyles were women living totally within mainstream society regardless of the amount of drug used or level of drug dealing. Able to retain, or return to, a measure of stability and respectability, they were found living in good neighborhoods. They had money, often a husband and family, and sometimes a legitimate job. They were either high-level dealers with methamphetamine as a major source of income or part-time sellers to limited selected friends and clientele while maintaining regular employment.

The most successful women dealers led citizen lifestyles, and actively participated in mainstream society. For example, in control of a successful high-level illicit business for a number of years, one women "citizen" from San Diego began dealing as a way to get off welfare after her marriage failed. She started 6 years prior to the interview with a quarter ounce and now earns over $50,000 per year working only 1 hour a day.

> I stayed within my goals, basically. . . . I control the people that I sell to. They get it for other people and I never see the people they sell it to. [In a typical week] . . . if it's been flowing real good, $1500 to $2000. With my kids I have to sneak around and do what I'm doing without me taking too much time. So I have to do a little each day . . . I try to put what's important first. Kids eat and do homework first. But this runs a real close second. I deal an hour each evening. (297)

Another woman from San Diego was able to maintain a professional job while dealing in partnership with her husband. Increasing level of use led to her husband's arrest, and the loss of her job. She began to supplement her unemployment benefits by continuing the dealing business that she now controls completely. She now believes this has enabled her to control her use as well.

It was common to find that a citizen lifestyle was not automatically a successful or middle-class one. Many working-class women in all sites began dealing in order to pay for use so that they could maintain at least the appearance of normalcy. For example, since losing her job as an accountant, one woman of mixed-Hawaiian ethnicity described the current level of dealing with her husband: "It's just to break even. Most of the time we don't. You break down your product and put aside what you're gonna smoke and what part to make your money back (415)."

Many of the women in our study fell in between these two extremes. One we defined as a floater lifestyle where their drug use led in and out of mainstream life. Although able to escape full long-term participation in deviant careers, women in this lifestyle seem unable to establish stable lives, relationships, or responsibilities. Another was labeled welfare-mom lifestyle category. These women were full-time participants in a subculture found in impoverished suburban communities where methamphetamine had been part of daily life, often for generations (Morgan et al. 1994). A welfare-mom lifestyle encompassed women's experiences as residents of public housing complexes often selling methamphetamine to pay for personal use and to provide a little extra income.

Economic Contexts

The type of economic activity involving illicit drug dealing varied considerably, from small-time hustling to large-scale distribution. This activity, in turn, was linked to fluid contexts of user lifestyles. They combine to help shape a complex environment connecting patterns and consequences of use to shifts and variations for women's experience in the illicit drug economy. Analysis from our qualitative interview transcripts identified over 100 female methamphetamine users who reported a wide range of experiences as active participants in the illicit drug economy. These ranged from trading favors to large-scale manufacture on a continuum encompassing diverse economic contexts. Importantly, these were rarely static roles, as many women moved from one role to another throughout their drug-use careers.

Although a number of women reported trading favors in exchange for the drug, few stated that these were sexual favors. This is particularly significant in light of the popular belief, especially from studies of female crack users, that sexual favors characterize a woman's role in the trade and barter system involving illicit drugs. More often, women acted as runners, or performed various other chores for dealers. Several women traded items they had stolen, or sold other drugs to obtain methamphetamine. A middle-aged black woman with 30 years experience using methamphetamine found that changing preferences forced her to sell crack; although she strongly dislikes the drug, it's the best way for her to earn money to buy methamphetamine.

Many women limited illicit drug activity to partnerships with their boyfriends or husbands. This was most common among female users in Honolulu and found least among women in San Francisco. In order to be successful, however, women either took over the partnership, or left the relationship to become independent entrepreneurs. For example, a San Diego woman was unable to control her methamphetamine use until she took over the business after her husband went to jail. She is now controlling the business, her own use as well as his:

> I probably have more trouble keeping D. to a daily ration, cause he's not handling it, he's not realizing how much of it he's doing. So I just dole him a certain amount and say "hey man, that's it, after that you start paying for it." Cause I'm not going to end up owing him money out of my pocket, that's not why I'm doing this. D. understands where I'm coming from. (345)

Most women dealers in the study sold methamphetamine on a part-time basis. The two major rationales were to supplement their legitimate income, and/or to pay for their personal use or at least keep the cost down. Among outlaw users in the inner-city, dealing was often episodic and more accurately described a service linking buyer and seller. The description from a sex worker in the Tenderloin is typical:

> I have a request and someone calls and says they want a certain quantity. I call someone and find out if they have it at the price and amount the buyer wanted. The person with the money comes to my house with the money. The person with the product could come over and they'd do their deal without me. They would try it out, if it was fine, the person would buy it and leave. Not more than one person at a time. (014)

Almost a fourth of female respondents in California, especially in San Francisco, reported receiving their main source of income from the illicit drug economy. They ranged from highly successful tightly organized enterprises that included, but were not always limited to, methamphetamine sales. There were a surprising number of women in our sample who had experience with large-scale manufacture and/or distribution. One woman from the Bay Area who dealt both heroin and speed with former boyfriends and her husband averaged about $2,000 per week for almost a decade. Women had a variety of roles at this level of economic activity, which ranged from directing the international importation of cocaine to assisting in the manufacture of methamphetamine. Many involved in manufacturing methamphetamine were involved in a partnership with their husband or boyfriend. For example, a female respondent from eastern San Diego County was the cook and her boyfriend the lookout. She described a high level of weekly production:

> About 5 lbs. per week. We'd distribute to certain people and they'd sell at their levels. We had people who bought one or 2 lbs. at a time! What was the factor was how fast did we want to run out! We moved as much as we made! There was certain people we'd give pure stuff to, but, the majority of the time, we cut at least 25% to half, 50% cut. (255)

Most manufacturers lasted only for limited periods, sometimes less than a year. Some women, however, managed to maintain this level of activity for a number of years. For most, the stressful lifestyle, the violence, gang rivalries, and arrests, marked the experience for these women.

Hidden Contexts

ECONOMIC AND LIFESTYLE MOBILITY

It is important to note that the majority of female respondents engaging in drug sales did not limit their economic activity to trading or bartering for drugs. Those who did were most often in Honolulu where women tended to be more attached to traditional relationships with men and into close family and kinship networks. Most commonly, this level tended to represent an early stage in what became a multifaceted drug-selling career. In each study site, women often began by dealing from a subordinate role in these relationships, only to eventually control or even take over the enterprise even in Honolulu, where dealing involves the entire family. One woman reported how she was introduced to Ice through her stepson, began buying from his dealer, and ended up being his supplier (424). These women stated they felt they needed to take on a more active role with both their and their partner's increasing use, which often led to an increasing inability of the males to handle the responsibility connected to their business enterprise. Many women began in partnership with their husbands, and took over the business after the husband's business or using habits threatened to shut it down. One Bay Area female dealer stated that after she took over the business from her husband,

> It boomed, it just exploded! F. knew everybody but just never had it together enough because he wasn't a business type person. He was Mr. Charisma, party-party, happy-happy. I'm more grounded and business like. That's all he needed and we really clicked. (059)

Similarly, we found that many of these social lifestyles were not static. Women reported life histories that usually included experiences in two or more user-type categories. Some females, for example, began using when they were prostitutes or on welfare, and eventually began leading citizen lifestyles with increasing success. Many others reported moving in the opposite direction, from citizens or successful outlaws to welfare moms or to very marginalized existences.

Examination of these active participants uncovered a complex web connecting drug use and drug dealing experiences over the course of their drug use career. Many women lived a number of user lifestyles while they moved among several different levels of economic activity throughout various stages in their involvement with methamphetamine. One respondent, for example, ran away from home and began shooting heroin at age 13. She eventually married a dentist (who was also a large-scale drug distributor), became a housewife and mother, and also helped with the drug business. Six years later she ended up divorced, homeless, and steadily abused, living in the city's worst neighborhood. Now, however, she has become one of the toughest, most assertive and respected women in this subculture, running a successful small-scale drug dealing enterprise. So, at various times in her life, she has been an outlaw, a citizen, and a floater user type; she has also engaged in large-scale drug distribution and in low-level drug dealing.

We found the contextual relationship integrating patterns and consequences of use with activity in the illicit drug enterprise to involve several interrelated issues, which often shift during different stages in their methamphetamine using careers, with various combinations. Importantly, women were more likely than male dealers in our study to experience upward mobility in the illicit drug economy. Two possible reasons are revealed in major findings from the study. One involved the issue of self-control, and the other the concept of professional pride and ethics. They are interwoven.

Self-Control

One of the most important findings to emerge from this study concerned beliefs and attitudes toward addiction and loss of control. More specifically, this research revealed divergent and specific definitions for the concepts of "control" and "addiction" among our respondents. Although 60% of our sample reported "ever" feeling addicted to methamphetamine, only 48% stated they had lost control over their use. Women were more likely to report feeling addicted than men (63% compared to 60%). And, they were less likely to report losing control over their use (45%) than men (50%). The major exception is in Honolulu, where a higher percentage of male respondents reported an addiction to methamphetamine (58%) than loss of control over their use of the drug (57%).

Analysis from the qualitative data suggests a significant number of our respondents considered themselves to be "controlled addicts." These definitions were particular to the specific context of their drug experience (cf. Morgan and Beck n.d.). Although all respondents had very strong feelings about being either in control, or out of control, over their use, women were much more likely to describe having control over their use and of their lives while using methamphetamine. A woman in Honolulu feels men tend to lose control much easier than women:

> Sometimes they get like that because of being high. They do things that they really normally wouldn't do. It can get your mind screwed up. It's a good high, but you gotta know how to handle it. A lot of my friends say it's strong enough for a man, but it's made for a woman! A lot of guys get

really crazy. Even my boyfriend, he gets crazy off it. Real scary. I don't really want to smoke with him, cause he scares me. He thinks I'm hiding things! I get high all my life, nobody ever bummed my trip! That's bullshit. (459)

Our findings suggest that there were differences in the way male and female respondents talked about self-control. Women were more likely to stress the ways they managed to stay in control. Men, on the other hand, were more likely to discuss ways they had lost control, and were far less likely than women to talk about how to manage to stay in control. For women users the ability to maintain control was a very important issue:

> I have this phobia of something controlling me! Don't get me wrong, this controls me but, I have some kind of hold on it and I refuse to give in. If I have been up two or three days and I feel like I'm getting detached, I don't want to let myself get to the point where it could get any further. You hear these horror stories all the time and I refuse to let myself get to that point. So, if there's any warning signs of any kind, I listen to them and I'll go lay down and go to sleep. If I need to eat then I'll eat . . . I don't want to hallucinate, I don't want to be in la-la land where I have no control over what I'm seeing . . . I know when I get these little signs that it's time to go to bed, then I don't let it overpower me. I never let it come before my rent or food! Ever since I started doing it, I made money on it so I can have my own personal stash, without it coming out of money that is already spent. (297)

Professional Pride and Ethics

Another major finding is the degree to which women dealers discussed the concept of pride in their accomplishments as dealers. The most frequently mentioned reasons centered on their achievements in operating and maintaining a competent business enterprise. Many referred to the bias and difficulties in dealing with men suppliers and customers in particular. One woman, for example, articulated the reasons behind a strong degree of pride in her profession and in her ability to run a successful business enterprise:

> I'm a good dealer. I don't cut my drugs. I have high quality drugs in so far as it's possible to get high quality drugs. I want to be known as somebody who sells good drugs, but doesn't always have them, opposed to someone who always has them and sometimes the drugs are good. (075)

Another female respondent who was formerly a high level dealer provides another example:

> Successful people will always succeed and I don't care if they do drugs or not! There are successful people and they will always succeed. I feel I'm one of those. I turned a real bad situation around, like getting fired from my government job of 15 and a half years invested! I turned that around from a very negative thing. . . . I turned that around to be a positive. That was to take my money out and buy a business, re-vamp it and have a

really fine, workable, collectable antique store that is respected and people desire to shop there. (322)

Importantly, all female dealers tended to have an ability to articulate an ethic that structures both their enterprise and which also speaks to their lives overall. One woman provided an eloquent example:

> It all depends on what your ethics and morality is. Mine is that I don't burn people, I don't fuck with the drugs. The drugs I sell are the drugs I do. If I see that somebody is not handling their drugs, I will not sell to them! I may not tell them that I think they're not handling their drugs because if they aren't, they aren't going to listen to me anyway! But, it's easy for me to disappear from their venue for a while. More ethics and morality is that you don't talk about who you buy from, you don't talk about who you sell to. You do an honest and clean business. You don't fuck people up. You never sell people their first line! I expect the people that I buy from to be as honest as I am! (075)

Incorporating Control As a Dealing Strategy

The issues of self-control and control over others are dynamically interconnected in the lives of these women. We found a notable difference related to the issue of control over one's life framing the context of methamphetamine dealing. For many women dealers, the illicit drug business gave them the power to leave and/or control their husbands/boyfriends. It allowed them to choose their friends, to control their lifestyle, and to maximize their talents relative to their resources. Most of them considered themselves satisfied realists. One woman dealer who prides herself on her ability to have control over her life stated:

> It's my business, my rules! And don't argue with me about it! I get to choose who knows I sell speed. I'm healthier now than I was when I started. I think it's because I don't have any moral dilemma over my drug use. I do drugs for a reason which I have rationalized to myself . . . they are now part and parcel with the whole thing. (075)

A basic rule mentioned by many serious dealers concern protection of their home environment.

> . . . never sold to people from within my home. I would have to go out of my home environment to give it to them or to sell to them. I can't bring people that are using a drug that causes such instability in their life into my home and expect my own lifestyle to stay stable. That would be a paradox within itself! (293)

A major reason for protecting the home, was to separate family life and business, especially women dealers with small children. Faced with living on welfare after her divorce, one woman returned to dealing . . .

> I make money from sales, I never do what I need to sell. I won't take it from my kids or my rent or my food or bills, I wanted off welfare, so

began to sell again. I'm not a stupid person. I don't go around doing stupid things. I don't walk around telling people I have drugs for sale, I don't have people sitting out in front of my house, I don't have traffic in and out of my house. (297)

A San Diego woman who dealt in pounds, did do business from home, but established a long list of rules to guide her customers:

> They had to call first and tell me how much they wanted. They'd come by themselves. I had to know beforehand that they was bringing somebody new or I had to know the person they was bringing. Nobody ever sit out in cars in front of the house. They had to come in. Nobody could hang out in front of my house. Once the deal was made, there was no hanging around, partying. You had to leave. I wasn't a party person with business, this was a business! I gave you time to try the product out if you wanted to. If you liked it, you put your money down and left my house! I couldn't take the chance of being busted with all that stuff there. (281)

A woman of mixed Hawaiian ethnicity dealt in the heart of one of Honolulu's ice communities. Even though ice dealing was common, and use open, in her neighborhood, she set up rules to assure her participation was discreet.

> I was so low profile, not even my own home had traffic. I had good rules and regulations that everyone had to abide by or they didn't get none! . . . no calls after 10:00 at night. No dealings after 10:00 at night. Call my house before you come over, don't just show up. If you see me out in the streets and I'm not expecting you, don't expect to score, you won't get shit! And I'd cut their line! If I say "No more nothing" they know why. They disobeyed my rules. (542)

For some dealers the best method of avoiding an out-of-control use pattern, increasing their use, and thus decreasing profits, was to establish a business ethics involving customers. Other people only did business with people they knew, or who had been introduced by people they knew.

> Even now, my business is largely a matter of acquiring, despite the fact that I can move a lot if I want to, both in quality and in quantity of small amounts or big amounts, my business is a matter of me getting drugs and supplying a selection of a few people. I change the list of people I'm willing to supply regularly. (075)

Other dealers limited their sales to a higher-class customer. One woman learned the hard way after a police raid based on a customer-turned-informant. After that she changed her habits and her buyers.

> I wasn't selling to anybody on the street. I was only selling and made only deliveries. Or, the people came during business hours. They were all professional people, they had money to spend on drugs, they were all employed or their husbands or spouses were employed and they did it together. That is who my clients were. People that maintained control, only! People that are able to get up and go to work every single day and

still do drugs every day, I feel, can have a sense of control and maintain control. I charged them top dollar for the drug because I only had quality drugs. I wasn't that greedy. If I'm gonna sell a drug, it better be the best. These were professionals who didn't mind paying for the best. (322)

Although we found this sample of women to be motivated by three normative guidelines: pride, ethics, and self-control, none were, in themselves, linked to gender relations.

Summary—Citizens and Outlaws

Among the varied and rich discoveries about women found in this study, several emerge as crucial building blocks toward establishing a realistic portrayal of women and illicit drugs. They strip away the primary rationales used as the basis for much of the misconceptions now found in the literature. These include the contention that women have less self-control over their drug use than men; that women suffer more from guilt and low self-esteem than men, and that women use and sell drugs in a subordinate relationship to men. Fundamentally, this study revealed that women's lives in the illicit drug economy are as varied as men, and that they are much more hidden. For example, we found women could simultaneously experience lives as "citizens"—that is, good wives and mothers—as well as "outlaws"—users and sellers of illicit drugs. The experience was almost always dynamic and fluid.

Taken together, these findings clearly underscore the need to move beyond the overwhelming urge of the past decade to focus exclusively on cocaine use (predominantly crack cocaine). It is equally imperative to move beyond the traditional hidden populations of disenfranchised minority women in large concentrated urban environments (cf. Maher and Curtis 1992; Dunlap and Johnson 1996). Our knowledge of the role of women in the illicit drug economy has, been limited to existing structural relationships and conditions most common in these environments. Consequently, much available information on women in the illicit drug economy, by the nature of these limitations, is restricted to street-level low-status involvement often centered around sex workers (Ratner 1993; Maher 1996; Fagan 1994).

In reality, both the use and selling of drugs takes place within social worlds that are much broader and more complex. Most illicit drug users, male or female, do not live in large inner-city environments (Substance Abuse and Mental Health Services Administration 1995). They are not members of impoverished minority populations, and are not primarily crack cocaine users (Substance Abuse and Mental Health Services Administration 1995). Most illicit drug users are not outlaws living on the extreme marginal edge of society.

Furthermore, we found that women's involvement with the illicit drug economy was governed by logical and coherent motives. The research also provided evidence that women who use—and sell—illicit drugs represent a widely diverse population. And finally, the life histories of these women users revealed drug-dealing careers spanning several decades rather than being a recent phenomenon. This demonstrates our need to uncover a previously unknown population of women dealers, to locate and then chart the boundaries of this unknown hidden population.

NOTES

[1] Research findings are drawn from a qualitative study of 450 moderate-to-heavy methamphetamine users in San Francisco, San Diego, and Honolulu, funded by the National Institute of Drug Abuse between 1991 and 1994. It compared gender, race, environmental, and cultural differences, to rationales, patterns, and problems of methamphetamine use. These three geographical areas were selected because the incidence of methamphetamine use and problems was substantially high in each site and because evidence from existing data revealed that the modes of methamphetamine use differed significantly in each locale. In San Diego most methamphetamine use was intranasal; the San Francisco Bay Area represented the highest proportion of IV methamphetamine use, and Honolulu was the major area experiencing widespread use of a smokable form of methamphetamine called ice (or "batu") (Morgan et al. 1994). The Study Design and Methodology and Site and Sample Characteristics sections have been omitted from this article (pp. 127–129 in original).

REFERENCES

Anglin, D.M., and Y. Hser
1987   Addicted women and crime. *Criminology* 25:359–397.
Biernacki, P., and D. Waldorf
1981   Snowball sampling: Problems, techniques and chain referral sampling. *Sociological Methods and Research* 10(2):141–163.
Bourgois, P., and E. Dunlap
1993   Exorcising sex-for-crack: An ethnographic perspective from Harlem. In *Crack as pimp: An ethnographic investigation of sex-for-crack exchanges,* ed. M. S. Ratner, 97–132. New York: Lexington Books.
Callahan, J., and J. Knight
1992   Prenatal harm as child abuse? *Women and Criminal Justice.* 3:5–34.
Chambers, C. D., S. W. Dean, and M. Fletcher
1981   Criminal involvement of minority group addicts. In *The drugs-crime connection,* ed. J. Inciardi, 125–154. Beverly Hills, CA: Sage.
Chavkin, W.
1992   Women and fetus: The social construction of conflict. *Women and Criminal Justice* 3:71–80.
Colten, M., and J. Marsh
1984   A sex roles perspective on drug and alcohol use by women. In *Sex roles and psychopathology,* ed. C. Widom. New York: Plenum Press.
Curlee, J.
1967   Alcoholic women. *Bulletin of the Menninger Clinic* 31:154–163.
Dunlap, E.
1992   The impact of drug on family life and kin networks in the inner-city African-American single-parent household. In *Drugs, crime and social isolation: Barriers to urban opportunity,* eds. A. V. Harrell and G. E. Peterson.
Dunlap, E., and B. D. Johnson
1996   Family and human resources in the development of a female crack seller career: Case study of a hidden population. *Journal of Drug Issues* 26(1):175–198.

Ettorre, E.
1992 *Women and substance use.* New Brunswick, N.J.: Rutgers University Press.
Fagan, J.
1994 Women and drugs revisited: Female participation in the cocaine economy. *Journal of Drug Issues.* 24:179–225.
Geertz, C.
1973 *The interpretation of cultures.* New York: Basic Books.
Goldstein, P.
1979 *Prostitution and drugs.* Lexington, Mass.: Lexington.
Granfield, R., and W. Cloud
1996 The elephant that no one sees: Natural recovery among middle-class addicts. *Journal of Drug Issues* 26(1):45–61.
Hirsh, J.
1962 Women and alcoholism. In *Problems in addiction,* ed. W.C. Bier. New York: Fordham University Press.
Hser, Y., M. D. Anglin, and C. Chih-Ping
1992 Narcotics use and crime among addicted women: Longitudinal patterns and effects of social interventions. In *Drugs, crime and social policy,* ed. T. Mieczkowski. Boston: Allyn and Bacon.
Humphries, D., J. Dawson, V. Cronin, P. Keating, C. Wisniewki, and J. Eichfeld
1992 Mothers and children, drugs and crack: Reactions to maternal drug dependency. *Women and Criminal Justice* 3:81–99.
Inciardi, J., D. Lockwood, and A. E. Pottieger
1993 Women and crack cocaine. New York: MacMillan.
Johnson, B. D., A. Hamid, and H. Sanabria
1991 Emerging models of crack distribution. In *Drugs and crime: A reader,* ed. T. ieczkowski, 56–8. Boston: Allyn and Bacon
Maher, L.
1992 Puishment and welfare: Crack cocaine and the regulation of mothering. *Women and Criminal Justice.* 3:35–70.
Maher, L.
1996 Hidden in the light: Occupational norms among crack-using street-level sex workers. *Journal of Drug Issues* 26(1):143–173.
Maher, L., and R. Curtis
1992 Women on the edge of crime: Crack cocaine and the changing contexts of street-level sex work in New York City. *Crime, Law and Social Change* 18:221–258.
Mieczkowski, T.
1992 *Drugs, crime and social policy.* Boston: Allyn and Bacon.
Mieczkowski, T.
1994 The experiences of women who sell crack: Some descriptive data from the Detroit Crack Ethnography Project. *Journal of Drug Issues.* 24:227–248.
Morgan, P., and J. Beck
n. d. Legacy and paradox: Hidden contexts of methamphetamine use in the United States. In *Current trends in amphetamine abuse: An international perspective,* ed. H. Klee. Forthcoming.
Morgan, P., J. Beck, K. Joe, D. McDonnell, and R. Guiterrez
1994 Ice and other methamphetamine use. *Final report to the National Institute on Drug Abuse, National Institute of Health.* Washington, D.C.: U.S. Government Printing Office.

Morgan, P., and Joe, K.

n. d. Uncharted terrain: Contexts of experience among women in the illicit drug economy. *Women and Criminal Justice*. Forthcoming.

Murphy, S., D. Waldorf, and C. Reinarman

1990 Drifting into dealing: Becoming a cocaine seller. *Qualitative Sociology* 13:321–343.

Ratner, M. S.

1993 Sex, drugs and public policy: Studying and understanding the sex-for-crack phenomenon. In *Crack pipe as pimp: An ethnographic investigation of sex-for-crack exchanges*, ed. M. S. Ratner, 1–36. New York: Lexington Books.

Rosenbaum, M.

1981 *Women on heroin*. New Brunswick, N.J.: Rutgers University Press.

Sanchez, J., and Johnson B.

1987 Women and the drugs-crime connection: Crime rates among drug abusing women at Rikers Island. *Journal of Psychoactive Drugs* 19(2):200–216.

Sterk-Elifson, C.

1996 Just for fun? Cocaine use among middle-class women. *Journal of Drug Issues* 26(1):63–76.

Substance Abuse and Mental Health Services Administration (SAMSA)

1995 *National household survey on drug abuse: Main findings 1992*. United States Department of Health and Human Services. Washington D.C.: Government Printing Office.

Waldorf, D., and S. Murphy

1995 Perceived risks and criminal justice pressures on middle class cocaine sellers. *Journal of Drug Issues* 25(1):11–32.

Waiters, J. K., and P. Biernacki

1989 Targeted sampling: Options for the study of hidden populations. *Social Problems* 36(4).

Woodhouse, L.

1992 Women with jagged edges: Voices from a culture of substance abuse. *Qualitative Health Research*. 2:262–281.

Section
IV

POLICING DRUGS

12

The Police and Drugs

Mark H. Moore
Mark A. R. Kleiman

Many urban communities are now besieged by illegal drugs. Fears of gang violence and muggings keep frightened residents at home. Even at home, citizens feel insecure, for drug-related break-ins and burglaries threaten. Open dealing on the street stirs the community's fears for its children.

The police sometimes seem overwhelmed. Occasionally they are outgunned. More often, they are simply overmatched by the resilience of the drug commerce. Furthermore, their potential impact is neutralized by the incapacity of the courts and penal system to mete out deserved punishments.

Urgent problems and limited resources demand managerial thought for their resolution. Thus, police executives facing the drug problem might usefully consider four strategic questions:

- What goals might reasonably be set for drug enforcement?
- What parts of the police department engage the drug problem and to what effect?
- What role can citizens and community groups usefully (and properly) play in coping with the problem?
- What basic strategies might the police department consider as alterative attacks on the problem?

Perspectives on Policing, No. 11, September 1989. National Institute of Justice, U.S. Dept. of Justice, Office of Justice Programs.

The Goals of Drug Enforcement

From a police chief's perspective, the drug problem presents distinguishable threats to community security. Most pressing is the violence associated with street-level drug dealing—particularly crack cocaine.[1] Much of this violence involves youth gangs.[2] Often the violence spills over into the general population, leaving innocent victims in its wake. There is also the worry that the practice in armed, organized violence is spawning the next generation of organized crime.[3]

Also salient is the close link between drug use and street crime.[4] Criminal activity is known to vary directly with levels of heroin consumption.[5] Many of those arrested for robberies and burglaries, use cocaine during the commission of their crimes or steal to support drug habits.[6] Among the small group of the most active and dangerous offenders, drug users are overrepresented.[7] Thus, controlling drug use (and drug users) opens an avenue for reducing the robberies, burglaries, and petty thefts that have long been the focus of the police.

A third problem is that drug use undermines the health, economic well-being, and social responsibility of drug users. It is hard to stay in school, hold onto a job, or care for a child when one is spending all one's money and attention on getting stoned.[8] The families and friends of drug users are also undermined as their resources are strained by obligations to care for the drug user or to assume responsibilities that the drug user has abandoned.

Fourth, drug trafficking threatens the civility of city life and undermines parenting. While parents can set rules for conduct in their own homes, the rules are hard to extend to city streets and urban classrooms where drug trafficking has become a way of life. Although these threats affect all city neighborhoods, they are perhaps worst for those in the most deprived areas. There, the capacity of the community for self-defense and the ability of parents to guide their children are not only the weakest, but also the most in need of public support and assistance.[9]

Fifth, the police executive knows, even before he commits his troops, that the police can accomplish little by themselves. Drug arrests and prosecutions are exceedingly difficult, owing to the absence of complaining victims and witnesses.[10] Even with these limitations, the police can make many more arrests than prosecutors can prosecute, courts can adjudicate, and prisons can hold.[11] Furthermore, drug distribution systems, held together by the prospect of drug profits, will adapt quickly rather than collapse in the face of police action.

Finally, the police executive knows from bitter experience that in committing his force to attack drug trafficking and drug use, he risks corruption and abuses of authority.[12] Informants and undercover operations—so essential to effective drug enforcement—inevitably draw police officers into close, potentially corrupting relationships with the offenders they are pledged to control. The frustrations of the task lead some officers to cynicism or desperate anger. As the police become more cynical or more angry, the dealers will be standing there with cash in their pockets, ready to make a deal. Or they will mock the police with apparent invulnerability and provoke indignant officers to plant evidence or pursue justice through other illegal means.

These threats define the goals of police action against drug trafficking and use. The goals are:

(1) reduce the gang violence associated with drug trafficking and prevent the emergence of powerful organized criminal groups;

(2) control the street crimes committed by drug users;

(3) improve the health and economic and social well-being of drug users;

(4) restore the quality of life in urban communities by ending street-level drug dealing;

(5) help to prevent children from experimenting with drugs; and

(6) protect the integrity of criminal justice institutions.

The operational question, of course, is how best to accomplish these goals. Or put somewhat differently, the question is how best to deploy police resources to produce the maximum contribution to the achievement of these goals.

Police Organization and Deployment

The narcotics bureau is generally considered the center of the police response to drug trafficking and use. That operational unit aims directly at the source of the problem and mounts the most sophisticated investigations against drug traffickers. It also accumulates the greatest substantive knowledge about drugs in general and in the local community.

Although the narcotics bureau is at the center of the attack, police strategists must recognize that other operating elements of the police department also confront drug trafficking and use. For example, many police departments have established specialized units to attack organized crime or criminal gangs. These units deal with narcotics trafficking because (1) the organized crime groups or gangs that are their central targets are involved in drug dealing; or (2) they have access to informants who can usefully guide narcotics investigations; or (3) they have specialized equipment that can be used in sophisticated drug investigations.

Regular patrol and investigative units also inevitably attack drug trafficking, use, and related violence. Insofar as their efforts are focused generally on street crime, and insofar as drug users commit a large portion of these crimes, patrol units and detectives wind up arresting a great many drug users. Regular patrol and investigative units also end up arresting some drug users for narcotics offenses such as illegal possession and use of drugs.[13] In most cases, the person arrested will not be on probation or parole and must be tried to be punished. In other cases, however, the drug offenses will constitute probation or parole violations that could result in immediate incarceration if the local court system took such offenses seriously.

The patrol bureau will also be engaged in the fight against drugs as a result of calls from citizens complaining about drug dealing in specific locations. Often, in response to citizen complaints or at the initiative of the chief, special drug task forces will be formed to deal with a particularly threatening or flagrant drug market.[14] These operations draw on patrol forces as well as detective units. Typically, they last for a while and then go out of existence.

Somewhat more specialized are those units committed to drug education. Although drug education seems like a significant departure from the usual objectives and methods of policing, increasingly police departments are establishing such programs to fill a perceived void in this important demand-reducing function.[15]

The point of reviewing these different lines of attack is not only to remind enforcement strategists that a police department's overall strategy against drugs includes far more than the activities of the narcotics bureau, but also to raise an important managerial question: who in the police department will be responsible for designing, executing, and evaluating the department-wide drug control strategy? In some cases, the department will make the head of the narcotics bureau responsible for the broad strategy as well as the narrower operational tasks of the narcotics bureau itself. That has the advantage of aligning responsibility for the strategy with substantive expertise. It has the potential disadvantage of focusing too much of the organization's actions against drugs in the narcotics bureau itself, and of limiting the department's imagination about how it can and should engage the problem.

In other cases, a special staff officer might be assigned the responsibility of coordinating department-wide efforts without necessarily being given any line responsibility over the activities. This has the advantage of drawing more widely on the department's operational capabilities. It has the disadvantages of failing to establish clear operational responsibility and of requiring the collection of additional information throughout the department.

In still other cases, the chief might assume that responsibility. That has the advantages of elevating concern for the problem throughout the organization, of giving the department a powerful representative in dealing with other city departments and community groups, and of aligning operational responsibility with authority. It has the disadvantages of focusing the attention of the chief on only one aspect of the organization's fight against crime and disorder and of moving command further from operations.

The Community's Resources

Police strategists must also consider that the assets available to attack the drug problem are not limited to the money and legal powers channelled through the police department. The community itself has resources to deploy against drug trafficking and use. Indeed, without the community's own efforts at self-defense, it is hard to see how the police can possibly succeed.

The importance of community self-defense is evident in a review of the spatial distribution of drug dealing across a city. In some areas, drug dealers cannot gain a foothold. There are too few users to make dealing profitable and too many vigilant people ready to expose and resist the enterprise. Other parts of a city seem to have yielded to the drug trade. Drug users are plentiful. Drug dealers are an influential social and economic force. Local residents and merchants have lost heart.

Often, these conditions bear no relationship to the distribution of police resources. The areas that are safe rarely hear a police siren. Those that have yielded to the drug trade are criss-crossed by racing patrol cars with sirens blaring. The reason that little policing sometimes produces safe communities while heavy policing sometimes fails to do so is simply that success in confronting drug trafficking depends as much (or perhaps more) on the community's self-defense than on official police effort. Where community will and capacity for self-defense are strong, a little official policing goes a long way to keep the neighborhood free of drugs. Where it is weak, even heavy doses of official policing will not get the job done.

Exactly what communities do to defend themselves varies greatly according to their character and resources.[16] Most communities start trying to control the drug problem by calling the police to complain about drug dealing. Such calls, if they come through the regular 911 dispatch system rather than a dedicated hotline, are very difficult for the police, as currently organized, to handle. They cannot be handled like robberies and burglaries, for those directly involved in the offense (and therefore able to give useful testimony) are reluctant to do so. Moreover, by the time the police arrive, the activity has ceased or moved to a new location. Because a response to these calls rarely produces a successful case, the calls tend to get shifted back and forth between the patrol division and the narcotics unit.

When citizens cannot command police attention through telephone calls, they do what they can to defend themselves individually. They stay in their houses, buy locks and shutters, and fret about their children. This, of course, makes their neighborhoods more vulnerable to the drug users and dealers.

Sometimes citizens take more aggressive action against drug dealers. They harass drug users and sellers at some risk to themselves. They demonstrate against drug dealing in their neighborhoods to rally others to their cause. They invite groups such as the Guardian Angels or the Nation of Islam to help them regain the upper hand against the dealers.[17] On some occasions, they burn down crack houses.[18]

From the perspective of effectively controlling drug trafficking and use, the police must be enthusiastic about direct citizen action against drug dealing. Such efforts extend the reach of social control over more terrain and longer periods of time than the police could sustain by themselves.

On the other hand, direct citizen action poses new problems for the police. Citizens who directly confront drug dealers and users might be attacked and injured. If this occurs, the failure of the police to protect the community becomes manifest. Fearful of this result and solicitous of the welfare of citizens, the police often advise citizens not to take direct action against dealers and, instead, to leave enforcement to the police.

Another risk is that sharp conflict between drug dealers and citizens escalates into large-scale violence. Part of this risk is that the rights of citizens who are suspected by the community of being drug dealers and users will be abused; that is, they will be beaten, their property taken, their freedom of movement and expression limited. Although such threats are rarely taken as seriously as the physical threats to citizen activists, there comes a point when direct citizen action becomes vigilantism, and when the police, as officers of the law and defenders of the Constitution, must defend the rights of suspected drug dealers against mob hostility.

Finally, the police have an interest in maintaining their position as independent experts in controlling crime problems and as the principal suppliers of security services to the communities they police. To a degree, this can be understood as nothing more than an expression of professional pride and bureaucratic self-interest. But, insofar as the community prefers the restraint, expertise, and professionalism of policing to the risks of direct citizen action, the desire of the police to retain most of the responsibility and initiative for crime control is consistent with the public interest as well as their parochial interests.

While such concerns about the consequences of community action against drugs are entirely appropriate, they cannot lead to the simple conclusion that the police should suppress all such action. They particularly cannot justify this conclusion in a situation where the police have nothing else to provide to the communities that feel outraged and frightened. Instead, the police must find a way of accommodating, regulating, and using citizen indignation to help them manage the drug problem.

A crucial first step in managing the potential partnership with the community is to learn how to diagnose the community's capacity for self-defense. This diagnosis begins with a community's own attitudes and practices regarding drug use.

Although it is discouraging, an enforcement strategist must recognize that parts of communities are interested in continuing and facilitating drug use.[19] They include at least the users and the dealers. They may also include people who make accommodations with drug dealing, such as those who run shooting galleries, landlords who milk the economic value of deteriorating properties by renting to drug users who are indifferent to their living arrangements, and local merchants or police who earn money from drug dealers to provide safe havens for drug dealing.

Others in the community do not profit from drug dealing, but nonetheless have stopped fighting it. This group includes ordinary people who no longer use local parks and streets because they are intimidated by drug dealers and users. It could also include local police officers who conclude that dealing with the local drug trade is like shovelling sand against the tide and turn their attention to less frustrating problems.

Nevertheless, however widespread support for drug use seems to be, every community also contains some significant elements opposed to at least some aspects of drug use. This is particularly hard to keep in mind when the public face of the community—what is occurring on its streets and public places of business—seems openly tolerant. The reality is, however, that behind the shuttered windows of local merchants and in the apartments off the streets, many citizens are outraged and afraid of the drug use in the community. What outrages them may not be the same things that outrage the police or violate the laws, but there is some level of opposition to drug use. That opposition is the asset that needs to be assessed and mobilized.

In thinking about how the police and citizens might reclaim territory from drug trafficking and use, police strategists must anticipate a special problem in helping neighborhoods make transitions from one condition to another. A community that has had a long tradition of being clean may find it relatively easy to maintain its tradition.[20] Such a community is likely to discover a drug problem early because the community is vigilant and the drug problem sticks out. It is likely to respond quickly and aggressively because the problem is both outrageous and small. Drug dealers and users, confirming their prior expectation that the community is inhospitable, will go somewhere else. The probe will be quickly routed.

A community that has had a long tradition of being tolerant of drug dealing has the opposite problem. It may have difficulty in changing its image and condition to one of intolerance. Changes in the level of drug dealing may be difficult to notice because it is so commonplace. The response to a campaign against drugs may be ambivalent because of active opposition by some elements of the community and a sense of despair and futility among the others. Even if an attack is successfully mounted, the dealers and users may view it as a temporary state of affairs. Thus, sustained efforts will not necessarily discourage the dealers and the users.

In confronting drug trafficking and use, then, the task of a police department is often to find a way to prime the community's own capacities for self-defense so that police efforts may be effectively leveraged through community self-help. This involves learning enough about the community to know the sources of support for drug dealing and use in the neighborhoods and the potential opposition. It also means finding ways to reach out to those people in the community who are hostile to drug dealing and to strengthen their hand in dealing with the problem. For example, it may be as important to organize community meetings as to make it easier for individuals to call the police over the phone. It may be more effective to organize and support citizen patrols than to chase the drug dealers from one block to another. It may be more effective to organize groups of parents, educators, and youth leaders to resist drug dealing in and around schools than to increase arrests of drug dealers by 20 percent. In short, drug enforcement may be as much a political struggle to get neighborhoods to oppose drug use in small, informal ways every day as it is a technical law enforcement problem that can be solved by more resources or more sophisticated investigations.

Alternative Strategies

Police departments rely on many different activities to deal with the drug problem. They conduct sophisticated investigations of trafficking networks. They mount buy and bust operations to suppress open drug dealing. They arrest robbers and burglars who also happen to be drug users. They arrest drug users for illegal possession. They conduct drug education programs in schools.

Most departments do all of these things to some degree. In this sense, departments generally have "comprehensive" approaches to the problem. Departments differ, however, in the overall level of activities they sustain and in the relative emphasis they give to each. Some place greater emphasis on sophisticated investigations, while others stress "user accountability." Departments may also differ in terms of how much thought they have given to deciding on their most important objectives, and in terms of the relationship between the overall objectives and the distribution of the activities.

To help police executives think about how to confront the narcotics problem, we describe seven alternative strategies. The strategies are different from activities not only because they typically involve bundles of activities, but also because each strategy is built upon its own assumption of why the effort is appropriate and valuable to pursue.

EXPRESSIVE LAW ENFORCEMENT: MAXIMUM ARRESTS FOR NARCOTICS OFFENSES

The most common narcotics enforcement strategy could be described as "expressive law enforcement." This differs from other strategies in that it takes all the activities in which the department is engaged and increases them by a factor of two or three. If a city's drug problem is getting worse, the response is simply to increase the resources devoted to the problem. The operational task is to increase the total number of narcotics arrests. The narcotics bureau is expanded and driven to higher levels of productivity. Special task forces are created to deal with brazen street dealing. The patrol force is equipped and encouraged to make more drug arrests. There is much to commend this strategy. First, it is a straightforward approach that citizens, politicians, and police officers understand. It relies on common sense for its justification. It avoids the trap of being too cute, subtle, or sophisticated.

Second, it is what police departments know how to do—namely, enforce the law. It does not make them responsible for outcomes that they cannot control or for activities that they do not do well.

Third, to the extent that the courts and corrections system do their part, the strategy may succeed in bringing drug trafficking and use under control through the mechanisms of incapacitation and deterrence.

Fourth, the all-out, direct attack on the problem sustains and animates a general social norm hostile to drug use. That emboldens and strengthens the hand of those within the community opposed to drug use.

This strategy also has weaknesses. First, it does not admit that police resources, even when multiplied, may not control the problem. It ignores whether the rest of the system can deliver deserved punishments; disregards the scale and resilience of the drug markets; and fails to establish any benchmarks for success other than the promise of a valiant effort to increase arrests.

Second, this strategy rarely examines its impact on the community's own capacities for self-defense. There is a plausible argument that a strong police commitment to aggressive narcotics law enforcement will strengthen the community's resolve to deal with the problem. Under the expressive enforcement strategy, however, no organizational means are created to build community opposition to drugs. Without such efforts, there is the risk that the police action will weaken rather than strengthen community efforts by suggesting that the community has no role to play. Even worse, unilaterally designed and executed drug enforcement efforts may alienate communities from the police rather than build effective partnerships to control drugs.[21] In short, there is the risk that the expressive law enforcement strategy, effective as it may be in its own terms, will fail to develop, and may even inhibit, the development of the self-defense capacities of the communities that must, in the long run, be the route to success.

Mr. Big: Emphasis on High-Level Distributors

A second common strategy to deal with drug trafficking and use is the "Mr. Big" strategy. Its principal operational objective is to reach high levels of the drug distribution systems. The primary tactics are sophisticated investigative procedures using wiretaps, informants, and undercover activities. Often these investigations also depend on "loose" money to purchase evidence and information. The "story" that makes this a plausibly effective attack on the problem is that the immobilization of high-level traffickers will produce larger and more permanent results on the drug-trafficking networks than arrests of lower-level, easily replaced figures.

Again, there is much to commend this strategy. It is common sense that the impact of drug enforcement would be greater if it could reach the source of the problem, the criminal entrepreneur whose energy, intelligence, greed, and ruthlessness animate and sustain the drug trade. This seems particularly true if enforcement and punishment capacity is limited, and must therefore be focused on high-priority targets.

It also seems more just to focus society's efforts on those who are becoming rich and powerful through the trade rather than on those lower-level figures. While lower-level dealers are hardly blameless, they are arguably less culpable and less deserving of punishment than the high-level traffickers who are the focus of the Mr. Big strategy.

Finally, the Mr. Big strategy is consistent with the development of professionalism within police departments. The strategy challenges the departments to develop their investigative and intelligence capabilities.

There are reasons to worry about the overall effectiveness of the Mr. Big strategy, however. First, it is not clear that current investigative techniques are powerful enough to reach Mr. Big. The time, resources, and luck needed to arrest him are much greater than those needed to reach intermediate targets; therefore, the admittedly greater impact of arresting Mr. Big may turn out not to be worth the special effort.

A related point concerns overestimating the significance of Mr. Big. There may be almost as many potential Mr. Bigs as there are street-level dealers. There may also be a great deal of turnover in the ranks of drug entrepreneurs. The implication is that the value associated with arresting any given Mr. Big in terms of supply reduction impact may be much less than is usually considered. A further implication is that no one may know who Mr. Big is. Or, if we knew who he was six months ago, the situation may now be different. Thus, the greater difficulty of arresting Mr. Big may not be offset by any larger, long-term impact.

The final point is organizational. While it is true that the Mr. Big strategy will challenge the police to develop professionalism in dealing with drug traffickers and thus increase the overall capabilities of the narcotics bureau, it is also true that this particular focus may lead to the atrophy of narcotics enforcement efforts in other parts of the agency. Other units may decide to leave drug enforcement to the narcotics bureau.

GANG STRATEGIES

Among the most urgent and oppressive aspects of the current drug problem is the violence of gangs engaged in street-level drug distribution. Some of these groups, like the various "Crip" and "Blood" factions now spreading out from Los Angeles, are formed from traditional youth gangs of the type once romanticized in "West Side Story."[22] Others, like the "posses" of New York's Jamaican neighborhoods, simply began gang life as drug-dealing organizations.[23]

Although violence has always been a feature of drug trafficking, to many observers the current level of violence seems unprecedented. As *The New York Times* reported:

> Older drug rings, wary of drawing police attention, generally avoided conspicuous violence. New York's new gangs, like similar groups in Los Angeles and Washington, are composed mainly of undisciplined teenagers and youths in their early twenties. They engage in gun battles on the street and have been known to execute customers for not leaving a crack den quickly enough.[24]

Indeed, these gangs are held responsible for significant increases in homicide rates in the cities in which they operate.[25] They use violence not only to discipline their own employees and to intimidate and rob their competitors but also to intimidate individual citizens and groups of citizens who resist their intrusion.[26]

Exactly how the police can best deal with this aspect of the drug problem remains uncertain. One approach is to view drug gangs as similar to the youth gangs of the past and to use the same strategies that proved effective in the past.[27] That older strategy was designed primarily to reduce intergang violence, to prevent the extortion of neighborhood citizens and merchants by the gangs and to minimize the seriousness of the crimes committed by gang members. It was not designed to eliminate the gangs, although some efforts were made to turn them to legitimate and constructive activities. It depended for its success on such activities as establishing liaison with the gangs to communicate police expectations and aggressive police action against gang members, their clubhouses, and their activities when the gangs stepped out of line.

Such a strategy does not seem suitable for dealing with the new drug gangs, however. After all, the old gangs were viewed as threatening to society principally through their violence towards one another. Thus, it was possible for the police to make an accommodation: the gangs could remain intact so long as they refrained from violence. No such accommodation seems appropriate with the drug gangs—particularly not with those that are making places for drug distribution through intimidation of local citizens and merchants. Such conduct requires a sterner response.

A second approach is to view the drug gangs as organized criminal enterprises and to use all of the techniques that have been developed to deal with more traditional organized crime. These include: (1) the development of informants through criminal prosecutions, payments, and witness protection programs; (2) heavy reliance on electronic surveillance and long-term undercover investigations; and (3) the use of special statutes that create criminal liabilities for conspiracy, extortion, or engaging in criminal enterprises.

Such tactics work. They can, if executed consistently, destroy the capacities of organized criminal enterprises.[28] However, such efforts are also time-consuming and expensive. Perhaps these elaborate efforts are not required to deal with the relatively unsophisticated street-level drug gangs. Indeed, in the past, relatively superficial undercover approaches seem to have been successful,[29] as were large-scale sweeps targeted on gang members. What seems to be needed to make police efforts succeed once the gangs have been wounded is the willingness of citizens to resist gang intimidation after the police return to ordinary operations.

CITYWIDE STREET-LEVEL DRUG ENFORCEMENT

A fourth narcotics enforcement strategy, now widely discussed, can be described as "citywide, street-level drug enforcement." The principal objective is to disrupt open drug dealing by driving it back indoors, or by forcing the markets to move so frequently that buyers and sellers have difficulty finding one another. The primary tactics include buy-and-bust operations, observation sale arrests, and arrests of users who appear in the market to buy drugs.[30] The major reasons to engage in such activities include: (1) enhancing the quality of life in the communities for residents who are discomfited by the presence of drug dealers; and (2) discouraging young, experimental users from continuing to use drugs by making it harder for them to score.[31]

At first glance, the limitations and hazards of this strategy seem more apparent than its strengths. To many law enforcement professionals and commentators, the idea that one would invest the enormous amount of time and effort that continuing street-level enforcement requires for nothing more than increased inconvenience to buyers and sellers of drugs seems absurd. It hardly seems worthwhile to send the police out daily to battle street-level drug dealers to achieve nothing other than market disruptions.[32]

Second, the police know that they have nowhere near enough manpower to work at street levels across the city. Moreover, they are reluctant to begin doing this job in any particular place because they know that once they have committed police to a given area, it will be hard to withdraw them.

Third, police executives know from much prior experience that street-level narcotics enforcement is extremely vulnerable to various forms of corruption. Bribery, perjured testimony, faked evidence, and abused rights in the past have accompanied street-level narcotics enforcement. Indeed, it was partly to avoid such abuses that many police departments began concentrating on higher-level traffickers and restricted drug enforcement efforts to special units.

Fourth, the police know that they can arrest many more drug traffickers and users than the rest of the criminal justice system can process.If the practical value and moral vindication of arrests for drug offenses only come with successful prosecutions and suitable punishment, then street-level enforcement is undermined from the beginning, for there is no reasonable prospect for such results. The likely outcome of most street-level arrests is several weeks in jail prior to trial, a bargained guilty plea, a sentence to time served, and a long period of inadequately supervised probation.[33]

Knowing this, the police can take one of two stances: (1) they can recognize that, for narcotics offenses, the process is the only punishment that offenders are likely to receive and choose to load into the process what they consider a reasonable level of punishment; or (2) they can grow cynical and refuse to make street-level arrests. In either case, a kind of corruption sets in. The least likely response is the only proper one: namely, to continue to maintain discipline and poise in making narcotics arrests on the street.

Against these disadvantages, the advantages of street-level enforcement seem small and speculative. The most certain and concrete is that street-level enforcement can succeed in restoring the quality of life in a community and bring a feeling of hope to the residents. It can regain, for those citizens, merchants, and parents who disapprove of drug use, a measure of control over their immediate environment. It can reassure them that they have not been abandoned in their struggles against drug dealers. It can provide a shield that protects them from the intimidating tactics of aggressive drug dealers. That is no small effect, though it might be hard to quantify.[34]

A second benefit, somewhat more speculative, is that the strategy might well succeed in discouraging experimental drug use, particularly among those teenagers who are not yet deeply involved in drugs.[35] Merely increasing the inconvenience to drug buyers may be little deterrent to experienced and committed drug users. They will have enough connections in the drug trade and enough determination to find alternative sources. This same effect may be a significant deterrent for young, experimental users, however. They have less experience with drugs, hence fewer alternative sources of supply and less motivation to keep searching when open drug markets are no longer available. It is also possible that with open drug bazaars effectively closed, parents and neighbors may feel sufficiently emboldened to exercise greater efforts at home and on the street.

A third benefit is that street-level drug enforcement has, on occasion, been effective in controlling street crimes such as robbery and burglary.[36] A crackdown on heroin markets in Lynn, Massachusetts, seems to have substantially reduced levels of robbery and burglary. Operation Pressure Point directed at drug markets on New York's Lower East Side also seems to have reduced robbery and burglary. A similar effort in Lawrence, Massachusetts, however, failed to produce the expected effects. This benefit must be treated as uncertain partly because of measurement problems in identifying the effect, and partly because it seems that the tactic produces this effect only under some special circumstances.[37] On the other hand, it does provide an additional reason for considering the potential value of street-level drug enforcement.

NEIGHBORHOOD CRACKDOWNS

A fifth strategy that the police might consider could be called "neighborhood crackdowns." Instead of committing themselves to citywide street-level enforcement, the police might decide to leverage their resources by cracking down on drug offenses in those neighborhoods that are willing to join the police in resisting drug use. Some of these neighborhoods might be those that are just beginning to be invaded by drug dealers. Others might be those that have long been occupied, but have finally reached a stage where they are now determined to rid their area of drugs. Police resources would be attracted to these areas precisely because there is some prospect that the impact of police crackdowns would be prolonged and widened by determined citizens.

News media coverage of the drug problem, particularly the violence associated with drug dealing, suggests that society is handicapped in dealing with the drug problem by a breakdown in the police-community partnership. Wherever there is an opening in a community's self-defense, aggressive young drug dealers seem to find a niche to develop the demand for crack. Sometimes it is a park that the police do not patrol frequently enough and from which other citizens can be driven. Other times it is an abandoned house that can be turned into a shelter for both dealing and using drugs. Still other times it is an all-but-abandoned building whose owner is willing to have anyone pay the rent, and who does not notice that the new tenants arrive with no furniture or clothes, but lots of guns.

Once established, drug dealers send a message that draws customers and other dealers. Many citizens, finding the company no longer to their liking, begin avoiding crack-dealing locales. Citizens who resist are intimidated. Citizens' groups that complain are also threatened. Occasionally violence breaks out among customers, between dealers and customers, or between competing dealers. The violence accelerates the process of intimidation. Eventually, the drug dealers operate alone.[38]

Citizens cannot deal with these situations by themselves. They need laws and law enforcement to oppose the actions of the drug dealers and consumers and to take action against the landlords (both public and private) who allow the drug dealers to operate in their buildings. They need the police to respond to their calls for assistance—including crackdowns designed to break the backs of the drug dealers and reclaim the territory for those not using drugs. They need the police to offer assurances that citizens who resist the drug dealers will be protected from attacks.

It is also clear, however, that the police cannot do this job alone. They have only a certain number of officers and many other duties. Drug cases are hard to make and vulnerable to legal challenges. Police can conduct special operations, but eventually they must leave neighborhoods in the hands of citizens. At that time, whether the drug dealers return or not depends a great deal on what citizens do.

If this analysis is correct, a strategy that uses police crackdowns to break the hold of drug dealing in communities that are prepared to assume some responsibility for holding onto the gains might make sense. The police could conserve resources by focusing on only a limited number of areas for relatively short periods of time. The community, working with the police, could shape a police intervention that would be most effective in helping them reclaim their streets. Each would know what would be expected of the other. The results would be the same as those anticipated in a citywide, street-level drug enforcement strategy: namely, an improved quality of life in the city, reduced experimentation with drugs among young people, and conceivably even reduced street crime in those neighborhoods that succeeded in keeping drugs out.

Just such efforts seem to lie behind the most successful cases of drug enforcement. In one particular case in Brooklyn, a neighborhood invaded by drugs managed to drive out the drug dealing by enlisting police efforts to close the buildings that were used for drug dealing, and then mounting patrols through a local branch of the Nation of Islam.[39] The police were willing to put resources on the line to go after the problem with an aggressive approach that was discussed in advance with the community. The community was prepared to try to hold onto the gains by taking disciplined action on their own that stopped well short of vigilantism. The police promised to back up the citizen groups in the future if their vigilance, now refined by prior experience, revealed a major new incursion of drug dealers.

The nature of the strategy is captured well by the testimony of two participants. The local police commander commented:

> I think the patrols are going well. We now have almost nonexistent drug activity in the locations that had been hard-core drug areas. This is a good example of what the police and the community can do together.[40]

One of the patrolling citizens also gave grudging support to the concept:

> We still believe there are problems with the police, with racism and cor-
> ruption within the department. But we feel we can solve the problems
> together. We learned a lot of lessons during this. The price you have to
> pay to fight against drugs is ongoing struggle. We had to pay the price by
> standing in the cold and rain without pay. But the most interesting thing,
> I think, is that this has given people hope. Apparently, partnerships are
> hard and chancy enterprises, but when they succeed, they are worth a
> great deal.[41]

Controlling Drug-Using Dangerous Offenders

The drug strategies that have been discussed so far have been primarily
focused on drug trafficking and use. They are designed to produce arrests for
narcotics offenses rather than for street crimes such as robbery, burglary, and
assault. This is not to say that drug enforcement strategies have no effect on
these crimes. Relationships between drug use and crime are so strong that
when the police affect drug trafficking and use, they probably affect street
crimes as well. The effect is indirect rather than direct, however.

This suggests a drug enforcement strategy designed to achieve *crime control* rather than *drug control* objectives. Such a strategy would focus enforcement attention on those drug users who are committing large numbers of robberies and burglaries.[42] Studies show that drug users account for a large
proportion of those arrested for these crimes and that they are among the
most active and dangerous offenders.[43] Further, levels of criminal activity
among heroin users are known to be higher when they are using heroin than
when they are not.[44] It stands to reason, then, that the police might affect a
significant portion of the crime problem by controlling the drug use of those
active offenders who are heavily involved with drugs.

The principal operational objectives of this strategy would be: (1) to
arrest and convict drug-using criminal offenders for either narcotics offenses
or street crimes such as robbery and burglary; (2) to identify such offenders
after arrest through a combination of criminal record searches, physical
examination for needle marks, urinalysis in the jails, and interviews; and (3)
to sentence these offenders to dispositions that work directly on their drug
consumption such as intensive probation with mandatory regular urinalysis
or compulsory drug treatment.

The primary activities of the police department would be to continue
making arrests for narcotics and street offenses, improve the records that
would allow them to identify the dangerous offenders among the arrested
population, and lobby for the development of urinalysis, intensive probation,
and mandatory treatment capabilities. The important claim that can be made
for this strategy is that it would address the primary reason that citizens
worry about drugs, namely drug-related crime, and would do so more effectively, cheaply, and humanely than approaches that rely only on repeated
arrests and costly jails to produce the same effects.

There is a reasonable amount of evidence indicating that this approach would work. In California, mandatory treatment programs for drug users are effective in controlling both crime and drug use, both while the person remains under supervision and afterwards.[45] There are also some reasons to believe that coerced abstinence, imposed as a condition of probation and parole and enforced through a system of mandatory urinalysis, can be effective in reducing street crime.[46]

The strategy would also have benefits for organizational development. It would challenge police departments to reach outside their own boundaries, and outside the boundaries of the criminal justice system, to produce the desired effects. Prosecutors, judges, and corrections officials would have to be persuaded of the merits of the strategy.[47] The drug treatment community would also have to be mobilized, their capacity expanded, and their attention focused on the objective of crime control as well as improving the health of users. Perhaps the most challenging aspect of this strategy, however, is that it would require the police to consider the possibility that their primary interest in controlling drug-related street crime could be achieved more directly, surely, and inexpensively by close supervision on the street rather than by the enormously expensive process of repeated arrests, jail, and imprisonment.

The limitations of this strategy are the opposite sides of its strengths. It does little by itself to suppress drug trafficking or to discourage the spread of drug use, except insofar as it succeeds in suppressing the demand for drugs among those users brought into the network of coerced treatment. Moreover, it seems to reduce police control over the problem by forcing them to rely on cooperation with others to produce the desired effects. Finally, it does not seem like a suitable law enforcement approach to the problem. There is not enough punishment and jail to satisfy those who think that effective law enforcement by itself will be enough to deal with the problem. For these reasons, the police have generally neither adopted nor supported such strategies.

PROTECT AND INSULATE THE YOUTH

A final police strategy for dealing with drugs could be built around the objective of drug abuse prevention. Instead of generally attacking drug trafficking, a police department might concentrate on trying to halt the spread of drug abuse to the next cohort of 16-year-olds. Part of this effort would consist of enforcement operations to suppress drug trafficking around and within schools. Another part might consist of police-sponsored drug education designed not only to impart information about drugs and discourage drug use, but also to create a favorable climate for police efforts to suppress drug trafficking. A third part might consist of police-sponsored efforts to create partnerships among parents, schools, and the police to define the outer limits of acceptable drug use and to establish a predictable community response to drugs.

The country now has operating experience with each of these elements. New Jersey has made a concerted effort to mount enforcement operations in and around schools to disrupt the trafficking networks that serve high school students.[48] The Los Angeles Police Department's DARE program has shown the potential of involving police in drug education programs in the schools and has been widely emulated throughout the country.[49] Massachusetts has experimented with establishing community partnerships to confront children with a consistent set of messages about drug use. None of these approaches has been systematically evaluated, however. Nor do we have any documented experience with combining the different approaches in a concerted strategy to prevent new drug use. Thus, the potential of this strategy remains uncertain.

Conclusion

Drug trafficking, use, and associated violence challenge today's police executives to find ways of using the limited resources and capabilities of their departments to reduce the violence, halt the spread of drug use, and control drug-related crime. Moreover, they must do so while protecting the integrity of their own organizations and the legal system.

Past approaches that have relied only on police resources seem to be limited in their ability to achieve any of society's important goals in this domain. To reclaim neighborhoods now yielding to drug use, police must find ways to mobilize and use community opposition to drugs. That the opposition to drugs exists is evident in the willingness of many citizens to take direct action against drug dealers. This adds urgency to the task of thinking through a strategy that builds effective partnerships, for it suggests not only that a resource is available to the police, but also that failing to harness it effectively may compound the problem by inciting vigilantism.

It also seems clear that successful approaches to the problem will rely on enlisting the assistance of other public agencies. For dealing with drug-related crime, the urinalysis and supervisory capacities of out-patient drug treatment programs might turn out to be valuable. To prevent the spread of drugs to new cohorts of teenagers, cooperation with schools and parents is essential.

Thus, to a degree, the drug problem requires first-rate professional law enforcement. Quality arrests for drug offenses are an important part of all police strategies. Great investigative sophistication, and no small amount of force, are required to deal with the traditional organized crime groups and the emergent gangs that now dominate the trade.

Yet it is also true that drug trafficking and use represent a problem that must be addressed through remedies other than arrests and through agencies other than police. The police can play an important role in strengthening neighborhood self-defense capacities by cooperating with local demands rather than suppressing or ignoring them. They can play an important role in mobilizing parents and schools. And they might even succeed in focusing the attention of drug treatment programs on their great opportunity to reduce crime as well as achieve other purposes.

In this domain, as well as in dealing with crime and fear, the methods of problem-solving and community policing combine with the methods of professional law enforcement to produce a perspective and a set of results that neither can produce by itself.

NOTES

[1] William G. Blair, "Study urges new measures to combat drugs," *The New York Times*, March 8, 1987. Jeffrey Yorke, "Pr. George's homicides soar," *The Washington Post*, November 16, 1987. Matt Lait, "The battle to control 50,000 gang members on the streets of Los Angeles," *The Washington Post*, March 12, 1988. George James, "Crime totals confirm fears in Queens," *The New York Times*, April 21, 1988.

[2] "Juvenile gangs: Crime and drug trafficking," *Juvenile Justice Bulletin*, Washington, D.C., Office of Juvenile Justice and Delinquency Prevention, September 1988. Cheryl Carpenter, Barry Glassner, Bruce D. Johnson, and Julia Loughlin, *Kids, Drugs, and Crime*, Lexington, Massachusetts, D.C. Heath, 1988. Robert Reinhold, "Gangs selling crack give rise to new wild west," *The New York Times*, June 21, 1988. Sam Roberts, "Ask not for whom the beeper tolls," *The New York Times*, June 2, 1988.

[3] "Juvenile gangs: Crime and drug trafficking," n. 2 above.

[4] Douglas M. Anglin and George Stenkert, "Narcotics use and crime: a multi-sample multi-method analysis," *Criminology*, Spring 1988. John A. Carver, "Drugs and crime: controlling use and reducing risk through testing," *Research in Action*, Washington, D.C., National Institute of Justice, 1986. Mark A. R. Kleiman, "Crackdowns: the effects of intensive enforcement on retail heroin dealing," in *Street-Level Drug Enforcement: Examining the Issues*, ed. Marcia R. Chaiken, Washington, D.C., National Institute of Justice, August 1988. David N. Nurco, John C. Ball, John W. Schaffer, and Thomas E. Hanlon, "The criminality of narcotic addicts," *Journal of Nervous and Mental Disease* 173, 2 (1985): 94–102. Mary A. Toborg and Michael P. Kirby, "Drug Use and Pretrial Crime in the District of Columbia," *Research in Brief*, Washington, D.C., National Institute of Justice, October 1984. Eric D. Wish, "Drug use in arrestees in Manhattan: the dramatic increase in cocaine from 1984 to 1986," New York, Narcotic and Drug Research, Inc., 1987.

[5] John C. Ball, Lawrence Rosen, John A. Flueck, and David N. Nurco, "The criminality of heroin addicts when addicted and when off opiates," in *The Drug-Crime Connection*, ed. James A. Inciardi, Sage Annual Reviews of Drug and Alcohol Abuse 5, 1981.

[6] National Institute of Justice, *Drug Use Forecasting (DUF)*, May 1988.

[7] Jan Chaiken and Marcia Chaiken, *Varieties of Criminal Behavior*, Santa Monica, RAND Corporation, 1982.

[8] Peter Kerr, "Addiction's hidden toll: poor families in turmoil," *The New York Times*, June 23, 1988. Felicia R. Lee, "Breaking up families, crack besieges a court," *The New York Times*, February 9, 1989.

[9] Ronald F. Ferguson, "The drug problem in black communities," Report to the Ford Foundation, working paper #87-01-01, Program in Criminal Justice Policy and Management, John F. Kennedy School of Government, Harvard University, Cambridge, October 1987.

[10] Peter Manning, *The Narc's Game*, Cambridge, Massachusetts, MIT Press, 1980. James J. Collins and Jay R. Williams, "Police narcotics control: patterns and strategies," Research Triangle Park, North Carolina, Research Triangle Institute, RTI Project No. RTI/1302/00- 01F, May 1978.

[11] Lynn Zimmer, "Operation Pressure Point: the disruption of street-level drug trade on New York's Lower East Side," Occasional Papers from the Center for Research in Crime and Justice, New York University School of Law, 1987.

[12] Gary T. Marx, *Undercover: Police Surveillance in America*, Berkeley and Los Angeles, University of California Press, 1988. Lawrence W. Sherman, ed., *Police Corruption: A Sociological Perspective*, Garden City, New York, Anchor Press, 1974.

[13] For 1986, there was a national total of 691,882 reported arrests for drug abuse violations. See Bureau of Justice Statistics, *Sourcebook of Criminal Justice Statistics 1987*, ed. Timothy J. Flanagan and Katherine M. Jamieson, Washington, D.C., U.S. Government Printing Office, 1988.

[14] Mark A. R. Kleiman, "Crackdowns," n. 4 above.

[15] Daryl F. Gates, "Project DARE—a challenge to arm our youth," *The Police Chief* 54, 10 (October 1987). Evaluation and Training Institute (ETI), "DARE longitudinal evaluation annual report 1987–88," Los Angeles, July 1988.

[16] Wesley G. Skogan and Michael G. Maxfield, *Coping with Crime: Individual and Neighborhood Reactions*, v. 124, Beverly Hills, California, Sage Publications, 1981. Wesley G. Skogan, "Fear of crime and neighborhood change," in *Communities and Crime*, ed. Albert J. Reiss, Jr., and Michael Tonry, *Crime and Justice* 8, Chicago, University of Chicago Press, 1986.

[17] William K. Stevens, "Muslim patrols fight Capital drug trade," *The New York Times*, April 24, 1988. Sari Horwitz and James Rupert, "Calm returns as police, Muslims patrol in NE," *The Washington Post*, April 29, 1988. Peter Kerr, "Citizen anti-crack drive: vigilance or vigilantism," *The New York Times*, May 23, 1988. Steven Erlanger, "The new show off Broadway: 46th Street," *The New York Times*, June 15, 1988.

[18] Isabel Wilkerson, "Crack house fire: justice or vigilantism," *The New York Times*, October 22, 1988.

[19] Ronald F. Ferguson, "The drug problem in black communities," n. 9 above.

[20] James Q. Wilson and George L. Kelling, "Broken windows," *The Atlantic*, March 1982.

[21] See Philadelphia example cited in Mark A. R. Kleiman, "Crackdowns," n. 4 above.

[22] *Juvenile Justice Bulletin*. "Juvenile gangs . . .," n. 2 above.

[23] Linda Wheeler and Keith Harriston, "Jamaican gangs wage war over drugs, area police say," *The Washington Post*, November 19, 1987.

[24] Selwyn Raab, "The ruthless young crack dealers," *The New York Times*, March 20, 1988.

[25] Blair, Yorke, Lait, and James, newspaper stories cited n. 1 above.

[26] Eric Schmitt, "On a corner in North Amityville, a reign of crack and violence," *The New York Times*, October 13, 1987. Peter Kerr, "Crushing the drug dealers of Washington Square," *The New York Times*, November 9, 1987. Jane Gross, "Weathering the crack storms in Queens," *The New York Times*, March 21, 1988.

[27] For discussion of older gang strategy, see Richard A. Cloward and Lloyd E. Ohlin, *Delinquency and Opportunity—A Theory of Delinquent Gangs*, Glencoe, Illinois, Free Press, 1960.

[28] For full account of successful FBI attacks on organized crime (the Cosa Nostra case), see *Organized Crime 25 Years After Valachi: Hearings Before the Permanent Subcommittee on Investigations*, Senate Hearing 100–906, Washington, D.C., U.S. Government Printing Office, April 1988.

[29] For accounts of undercover and plainclothes successes, see Peter Kerr, "Drug dealers of Washington Square," n. 26, and Michael Wines, "Against drug tide, only a holding action," *The New York Times*, June 24, 1988.

[30] Mark H. Moore, *Buy and Bust: The Effective Regulation of an Illicit Market in Heroin*, Lexington, Massachusetts, D.C. Heath, 1976.

[31] Mark A. R. Kleiman, "Crackdowns," n. 4 above.

[32] Anthony V. Bouza, "Evaluating street-level drug enforcement," in *Street-Level Drug Enforcement*, ed. Marcia R. Chaiken, n. 4 above.

[33] Lynn Zimmer, "Operation Pressure Point . . .," n. 11 above.

[34] Benjamin Ward, comments at the fourth meeting of the Executive Session on Community Policing, Program in Criminal Justice Policy and Management, John F. Kennedy School of Government, Harvard University, Cambridge, November 21, 1986.

[35] Mark H. Moore, "Policies to achieve discrimination in the effective price of heroin," *American Economic Review*, May 1973.

[36] Mark A. R. Kleiman, "Crackdowns," n. 4 above.

[37] Kleiman, above, and see Arnold Barnett, "Drug crackdowns and crime rates: a comment on the Kleiman report," also in *Street-Level Drug Enforcement*, ed. Marcia Chaiken.

[38] See Schmitt and Gross, both n. 26 above; also, Reinhold, n. 2 above.

[39] Patrice Gaines-Carter and John Mintz, "Muslims nurture legacy of power," *The Washington Post*, April 20, 1988; also Kerr, "Citizen anti-crack drive," n. 17 above.

[40] Thomas Morgan, "Muslim patrol helps cut crime in Brooklyn," *The New York Times*, February 25, 1988.

[41] Morgan, n. 40 above.

[42] International Association of Chiefs of Police and Bureau of Justice Assistance, *Reducing Crime by Reducing Drug Abuse: A Manual for Police Chiefs and Sheriffs*, Washington, D.C., Bureau of Justice Assistance and U.S. Drug Enforcement Administration, June 1988.

[43] National Institute of Justice, *Drug Use Forecasting* (DUF). Jan Chaiken and Marcia Chaiken, *Varieties of Criminal Behavior*, n. 7 above.

[44] Ball et al., "Criminality of heroin addicts . . .," n. 5 above.

[45] Carl Lukefield and Frank Tims, eds., *Compulsory Treatment of Drug Abuse: Research and Clinical Practice*, NIDA Research Monograph #86, Washington, D.C., National Institute on Drug Abuse, 1988.

[46] For discussions of experiences and problems with implementing drug testing, see: John A. Carver, "Drugs and crime," *Research in Action*, n. 4; Mark A. R. Kleiman, "Heroin crackdowns in two Massachusetts cities: executive summary," Working Paper #89-01-15, Program in Criminal Justice Policy and Management, John F. Kennedy School of Government, Harvard University, Cambridge, March 1989. For a proposal to control crime through the use of intensively supervised probation and urine testing, see: Mark A. R. Kleiman, Mary Ellen Lawrence, and Aaron Saiger, "A drug enforcement program for Santa Cruz County," Working Paper #88-01-13, Program in Criminal Justice Policy and Management, John F. Kennedy School of Government, August 1987.

[47] IACP/BJA, *Manual for Police Chiefs and Sheriffs*, n. 42 above.

[48] Joseph F. Sullivan, "Jersey takes drug effort into schools," *The New York Times*, January 3, 1988.

[49] Gates, "Project DARE"; Evaluation and Training Institute, "DARE longitudinal evaluation," both n. 15.

13

Civil Asset Forfeiture
Past, Present, and Future

John Worrall

Civil asset forfeiture is a tool available to law enforcement officials to strike at the economic foundations of the illicit drug trade. Forfeiture is also an enforcement option for dealing with other varieties of criminal activity, but it is generally tied to the enforcement of drug laws (Department of Justice 1994a). According to the President's Commission on Model State Drug Laws (1993:A-29), civil asset forfeiture serves three remedial goals: it "(1) removes financial incentive to engage in illegal activity; (2) restores economic integrity in the marketplace; and (3) compensates society for economic damages suffered due to illegal activity by rededicating forfeited property to socially beneficial uses."

Hundreds of statutes at the federal and local levels provide for forfeiture of the "fruits" and "facilitators" of certain crimes (President's Commission on Model State Drug Laws 1993). Despite its appeal, however, civil asset forfeiture continues to be a very controversial method for addressing the crime problem, particularly the illegal drug trade (e.g., Morganthau and Katel 1990; Pratt and Peterson 1991; Wisotsky 1991).

A primary reason for the controversy surrounding civil asset forfeiture concerns the disposition of the assets. Unlike the proceeds from fines and criminal forfeiture actions, the proceeds from civil asset forfeiture can be returned to law enforcement agencies (Department of Justice 1994b). Because law enforcement agencies can receive a "cut" of the proceeds from successful forfeiture actions, a number of objections to the practice have been

Written for *Drugs, Crime, and Justice*, 2/E.

raised on conflict-of-interest grounds. Some critics (e.g., Miller and Selva 1994) have argued that civil asset forfeiture laws encourage the seizure of assets instead of the suppression of crime. Other critics have claimed that "policing for profit" (Blumenson and Nilsen 1998) has begun to take precedence over policing to reduce crime.

State and federal laws differ considerably in the extent to which forfeiture proceeds go back to law enforcement agencies. For example, Washington State permits 100 percent of the forfeiture proceeds to go back to participating law enforcement agencies, whereas New Mexico permits (as of 1999) *none* to go back to law enforcement agencies. If state and local agencies work together jointly with federal officials, federal law permits as much as 80 percent to go back to the state or local agency (leaving 20 percent for federal officials). These "adoptive" forfeitures have led to concerns that state and local agencies occasionally avoid state requirements by joining federal investigations to gain a large percentage of the proceeds from forfeiture. Some critics have even argued that this action contributes to an expanded role of the federal government in local crime control efforts (Blumenson and Nilsen 1998). Whether forfeiture action is commenced at the federal or state level, the potential for the proceeds to be returned to law enforcement agencies is a contentious subject in the criminal justice and legal literature.

The conflict-of-interest argument would be less convincing if the proceeds from civil asset forfeiture were inconsequential. However, the proceeds from forfeitures run into the hundreds of millions, if not billions of dollars per year. In just one year, for example, the U.S. Justice Department's Asset Forfeiture Program controlled $338.1 million in U.S. currency as well as tens of thousands of pieces of real property (Department of Justice 1995). According to Hyde (1995), that number was actually down from a high of nearly half-a-billion dollars annually during the height of the drug war in the 1980s. In the *local* law enforcement arena, for example, one researcher recently found that select counties and municipalities receive tens of millions of dollars in forfeiture revenue per year (Worrall 2001a).

Civil asset forfeiture is also controversial because of the procedures that lead up to and follow the forfeiture of assets. Recently, Congress passed the Civil Asset Forfeiture Reform Act of 2000 (CAFRA), which changed forfeiture procedures in a number of ways, but certain aspects of the forfeiture process, including the laws that provide for civil asset forfeiture, remain a source of significant controversy.

This article comments on the past, present, and future of civil asset forfeiture. First, it provides a background for readers who are unfamiliar with civil asset forfeiture. Second, it introduces the competing views on the value of civil asset forfeiture as a law enforcement tool. Next, it discusses the procedural controversies associated with civil asset forfeiture, including the oft-debated practice of equitable sharing. Then the article introduces civil asset forfeiture's legislative progression throughout the 1980s and 1990s and earlier. Special attention is given to *federal* legislation for two reasons: (1) there is too much variation in state laws to give them meaningful attention in this limited space and (2) federal forfeiture law has received a great deal more scrutiny (and criticism) than state laws. Finally, the article concludes with a brief examination and critique of CAFRA by arguing that while CAFRA is a step in the right direction, much remains to be accomplished before civil asset forfeiture critics are satisfied or silenced.

Forfeiture Fundamentals

First and foremost, civil asset forfeiture needs to be distinguished from criminal forfeiture and fines. In legal parlance, *criminal forfeiture* proceedings are *in personam*, which means that they target persons, particularly criminal defendants. According to Warchol, Payne, and Johnson (1996:53–4), criminal forfeiture proceedings "are implemented in conjunction with the criminal prosecution of a defendant." Criminal forfeiture can only follow a criminal conviction. The standard in a criminal conviction is, of course, proof beyond a reasonable doubt, and the prosecution bears the burden of proving guilt.

Fines are similar to criminal forfeiture inasmuch as they require a person to "give up" a certain amount of money because of a crime or violation. A traffic ticket, while not criminal, is still a violation for which a fine is the typical means of enforcement. Even though traffic tickets need not be issued with proof beyond a reasonable doubt, the burden of establishing the violator's guilt falls on the law enforcement officer who writes the ticket.

Civil asset forfeiture, contrary to fines and criminal forfeiture, is *in rem*, meaning it targets *property*. Civil asset forfeiture does not require a criminal proceeding; it can be pursued independently of a criminal proceeding, much like a wrongful death lawsuit can be pursued independently (or in lieu) of a trial for homicide. Significantly, because formal criminal proceedings need not be initiated, the property owner's guilt is basically irrelevant. The fact that the property owner's guilt or innocence is irrelevant in civil forfeiture proceedings is part of what makes the practice controversial; because property is targeted—as opposed to an actual defendant—forfeiture laws conveniently circumvent (or appear to circumvent) some important constitutional protections.

The *in rem* nature of civil asset forfeiture procedure is mostly responsible for the criticism it has received. When property is targeted instead of property owners, the legal and constitutional protections generally are not the same as the protections associated with criminal proceedings. Also, because forfeiture proceedings are *civil* as opposed to criminal, the law treats property owners a great deal differently than if they were criminal defendants. This is precisely why *criminal* forfeiture is not very controversial; it is intimately tied to criminal proceedings where the burden of proof falls on the state. The burden of proof in civil actions does not necessarily fall on the state.

Forfeiture needs to be distinguished from *seizure*. Simply put, the police can seize property (e.g., cash), but forfeiture is a separate action. When something is forfeited, ownership is relinquished. A seizure, on the other hand, implies a temporary action, an action where ownership is not relinquished.

Civil forfeiture can be pursued without an actual seizure, or a seizure can be followed by forfeiture. In the former instance, the government may bring an action against a house. Since a house cannot be "seized" in the literal sense of the term, the only option is forfeiture. However, when property can be picked up, carried, or towed, seizure will often precede forfeiture, but not always. Regardless of how the civil asset forfeiture process plays out, forfeitures never precede seizures.

TYPES OF FORFEITURE PROCEEDINGS

It is important to distinguish between three varieties of civil asset forfeiture proceedings. The term *proceedings* is used with caution because the first form is not really a proceeding at all. The first form of forfeiture proceeding is a *summary forfeiture*. This is where law enforcement officials summarily (on the spot) seize property. Property to which no one can claim ownership—typically contraband—is subject to summary forfeiture. No legal proceeding is necessary and "ownership" of the contraband immediately vests with the police because no one can claim legal ownership of property that is not legal. Of course, certain forms of contraband are introduced into criminal proceedings, usually to establish guilt, but, unless the property is something that the defendant legally owns, it will not be returned. Summary forfeiture, then, is the least controversial of the three proceedings introduced here because it is not designed to exact a financial toll on the person targeted with forfeiture.

The second type of forfeiture proceeding is called *administrative forfeiture*. Administrative forfeiture differs from summary forfeiture in that it requires a formal court proceeding. The process usually unfolds as follows: the property is seized, the property owner is given a certain amount of time in which to challenge the seizure, then a court date is set if, in fact, the property owner wishes to contest the seizure. Consider the case of a drug dealer who is arrested and has a roll of hundred dollar bills in his pocket. The police may— and almost certainly will—seize the money on the theory that it was obtained from the sale of drugs (why else would someone have a wad of hundreds in a pocket?). Then, in accordance with the appropriate law, the "owner" of the cash should be notified of the requirements to go about challenging the seizure. If the drug dealer opts to contest the seizure, then a court date will be set. If, alternatively, the drug dealer decides *not* to challenge the seizure, the money will be forfeited.

A decision not to contest the forfeiture is an attractive one to many criminal defendants, particularly since some jurisdictions around the country use civil asset forfeiture as a plea bargaining mechanism; in exchange for the cash, some prosecutors will reduce the charges and/or forgo prosecution altogether. In fact, some scholars have argued that nearly 80 percent of the property owners whose property is forfeited are never prosecuted (Hyde 1995).

Administrative forfeitures are controversial to the extent that they permit summary seizure of property. Administrative forfeitures are justified by the so-called "relation-back" doctrine (Jankowski 1990). The relation-back doctrine is embodied in 21 U.S.C. sec. 881(h) and provides that "all right, title, and interest in property [subject to forfeiture] shall vest in the United States upon commission of the act given rise to forfeiture" (e.g., *United States v. 92 Buena Vista Ave., Rumson* 1993). Thus, anything that can be carried or towed away can be seized, and it is then up to the property owner to contest the seizure in court. This may be an expensive option, too, because most property owners are not versed in the nuances of civil asset forfeiture legislation, nor are they usually able to defend themselves in court. Even if a property owner is well within his/her right to contest the seizure—and even if he/she is all but guaranteed a decision in his/her favor—a cost benefit decision may have to be made. The costs of attorneys fees vis-à-vis the cost of the property may be such that a court challenge is too costly. Fortunately, however, federal law has changed in this regard, providing for reasonable attorney's fees to property owners whose property is wrongfully seized. The specific changes in the law are reviewed at length below.

The third variety of forfeiture proceeding is known as a *civil judicial proceeding*. A civil judicial proceeding is the least controversial of the three because it is not preceded by a seizure. Usually, civil judicial proceedings are reserved for expensive property or property, such as real estate, that cannot be moved. In either case, the prosecutor will bring a civil action against the property, which, like an administrative proceeding, should give the property owner a reasonable amount of time in which to prepare a defense. If the property owner fails to appear in court in order to contest the proposed forfeiture, ownership will vest with the government, and the proceeds can be returned to the law enforcement agency that was first responsible for the initiation of the proceedings. For example, if a local police department began an investigation of a person who was selling drugs out of her house, then (provided that the law permits it) that agency would receive a "cut" of the proceeds of the forfeited house. The same applies in the case of administrative forfeitures; the money can be returned to the agency or agencies that initiated the proceedings.

In an empirical analysis of civil asset forfeiture, Warchol and Johnson (1996) studied the outcomes of 146 civil judicial asset-seizure cases (in the Northern District of Illinois) from 1985 to 1991. They investigated the types of property seized for forfeiture; the estimated and appraised values of the property forfeited; the type of investigation that precipitated the forfeiture (proactive/reactive); the legal theory used to support/prosecute the seizure, namely whether the property was forfeited because it "facilitated" a drug transaction or because it represented the "proceeds" of a drug transaction; the time in days to prosecute the civil case; and the outcome, specifically whether the case was settled or dismissed or whether the property was forfeited. Warchol and Johnson's (1996) focus on civil judicial asset-seizure cases excluded some 90 percent of seizures that go uncontested, and their analysis, by design, excluded asset forfeiture activities at the state level. Nevertheless, in the cases they investigated, Warchol and Johnson (1996) found that the majority (48.6 percent) of the assets sought in civil judicial proceedings were real property.

More specifically, of the cases where investigations were proactive, the assets were primarily real property. Of the cases where reactive strategies were employed, most assets were monetary instruments. With respect to the legal theory used to justify the forfeiture, facilitation was cited in real property cases; cases that involved currency cited the "proceeds" justification.

ORIGINS OF MODERN-DAY FORFEITURE

Civil forfeiture is based on an "archaic and curious legal fiction that personifies property" (Hyde 1995:17). The personification of property traces its origins to a verse in the Bible (Exodus 21:28), which reads: "When an ox gores a man or woman to death the ox must be stoned; the flesh may not be eaten. The owner of the ox, however, shall go unpunished." This verse implies that an ox, an animate piece of property in essence, can manifest the will to inflict harm.

Furthermore, civil forfeiture traces its origins to the medieval law of "deodand" (from the Latin phrase *Deo dandum*, or "to be given to God") (see *Calero-Toledo v. Pearson Yacht Leasing Co.* 1974). If a vicious dog, for example, killed a child, the animal would be forfeited to the crown as a deodand. What made deodands different from the ox in Exodus 21:28 was that there was usually a person who benefited from the forfeiture. As Hyde (1995:18) pointed out, "the deodand rapidly took on the double purpose of religious expiation and forfeiture, or 'amercement,' similar to other exactions of the Crown aimed at raising revenues rather than at saving souls." Thus, if an *inanimate* object was responsible in some way for a person's death, it was held in forfeit on the belief that the victim's soul could not rest until the object was accused and atoned. According to the Supreme Court:

> Traditionally, forfeiture actions have proceeded upon the fiction that the inanimate objects themselves can be guilty of wrongdoing. Simply put, the theory has been that if the object is "guilty," it should be held in forfeit. In the words of a medieval English writer, "Where a man killeth another with the sword of john at Stile, the sword shall be forfeit as deodand, and yet no default is in the owner." The modern forfeiture statutes are direct descendants of this heritage. (*United States v. United States Coin and Currency* 1971)

Interestingly, the U.S. government in *United States v. One 6.5 mm. Mannlicher-Carcano Military Rifle* (1969) actually sued the rifle that was used to assassinate President John F. Kennedy, on the theory that it was a "species of Deodands."

To see how property is perceived to be "animate" nowadays, one need only look at a sample of civil forfeiture cases. The government essentially sues property, as in *United States v. One Mercedes 560 SEL* (1990) and *United States v. One Parcel of Land at 508 Depot Street* (1992). In every *modern* civil asset forfeiture case the defendant is a piece of inanimate property, anything from a conveyance to currency or real property. The only limitation is that the target of the civil forfeiture action was used to facilitate or was derived from a crime.

If, for example, a woman runs a "meth lab" from her house, the house will most likely be subject to forfeiture. Alternatively, if a person buys an expensive yacht from drug proceeds, it too probably will be subject to forfeiture.

Modern-day civil asset forfeiture also traces its origins to the concept of "outlawry." This was the practice of letting anyone kill a fleeing felon, the reward being the right to take possession of the felon's property. "During the Middle Ages, the concept of outlawry was broadened by the English Crown and used to crush political opponents, revoking a person's civil and property rights at the royal whim" (Hyde 1995:19). Similar to this was the Crown's practice of "attainder," where any person convicted of treason against the English Crown could have his/her civil rights revoked and all his/her property forfeited. "Outlawry" and "attainder," therefore, began to pave the way for contemporary forfeiture insofar as certain parties—usually the government—began to benefit financially from the seizure and forfeiture of property.

English admiralty law is another wellspring of modern forfeiture. Throughout American history forfeiture was a highly unpopular concept, particularly because of the abuses the colonists suffered at the hands of the English Crown. Nevertheless, the first Congress adopted a number of forfeiture laws in an attempt to impose sanctions against ship owners who did not pay customs duties. Despite the resemblance of those used by the British to target people accused of tax or customs evasion, Congress resorted to forfeiture because of the need for money. Well before income taxes were collected in this country, the government survived on customs duties. In fact, customs duties amounted to some 80 percent of the federal budget (Piety 1991).

There were also "practical" reasons for the seizure of ships found guilty of customs evasion. Justice Oliver Wendell Holmes made the interesting—even humorous—observation that "a ship is the most living of inanimate things. . . . Everyone gives a gender to vessels. . . . It is only by supposing the ship to have been treated as if endowed with personality, that the arbitrary seeming peculiarities of the maritime law can be made intelligible" (Holmes 1881).

History also illustrates liberal reliance on civil asset forfeiture in both the Civil War and the Prohibition era. During the Civil War the U.S. Government routinely confiscated the property of Southern rebels. Congress even passed the Confiscation Act on July 17, 1862, which authorized *in rem* proceedings against rebel property. According to the Supreme Court (*Miller v. United States* 1870, p. 305): "The power to declare war involves the power to prosecute it by all means and in any manner in which war may be legitimately prosecuted. It therefore includes the right to seize and confiscate all property of the enemy and dispose of it at the will of the captor."

During Prohibition Congress extended civil asset forfeiture laws to include violations of the Volstead Act. Forfeiture generally was limited to the real property used for the sale of illegal alcoholic beverages. The sale of alcohol from 1919 to 1933 was similar in a sense to the sale of other controlled substances today. Not surprisingly, civil forfeiture became extremely popular during the war on drugs beginning in 1970.

Two Competing Perspectives on Civil Asset Forfeiture

It is risky to speak in simple dichotomies, but most of the literature concerning civil asset forfeiture is either supportive or critical. Those in support of civil asset forfeiture are, not surprisingly, those who have the most to gain from it. This includes nearly everyone affiliated in any way with the law enforcement profession (police officers, prosecutors, etc.). Those against civil asset forfeiture tend to be legal scholars, members of the press, and civil rights organizations. Critics argue that forfeiture practices violate due process (Jensen and Gerber 1996) and help encourage outrageous law enforcement conduct (Hyde 1995). The following incident vividly illustrates this point.

On October 2, 1992, the Los Angeles County Sheriff's Department and agents shot Malibu, California, millionaire Donald Scott to death in his own home during a raid from five federal law enforcement agencies. Officials had obtained a warrant to search for marijuana cultivation on the property, but many believe the search was motivated by a desire to seize the expensive ranch on which Scott and his wife resided. A report of the Ventura County District Attorney concluded that the police lied to obtain the warrant. When they served it in the middle of the night, Scott's wife ran downstairs to hear what the commotion was about, and when Scott appeared at the top of the stairs brandishing a gun, he was shot. The details as to why Scott was shot were not made clear, but this was a clear-cut (and celebrated) case of forfeiture gone awry.

Still other critics believe civil asset forfeiture tramples the Bill of Rights, threatens the freedom of law-abiding citizens, and encourages a conflict of interest between law enforcement and fiscal management (e.g., Rosenburg 1988). They are quick to point to "perverted procedures" (Hyde 1995) and what they perceive to be the insidious side of equitable sharing (the potential for participating agencies to share in the proceeds obtained from successful forfeiture), both of which are addressed in turn.

Articles in the law reviews have been the most critical of civil asset forfeiture. For example, Durkin (1990) and Petrou (1984) examined the shifting burden of proof requirement in civil proceedings. Yoskowitz (1992) studied the effects of forfeiture on poor families in federally assisted housing, and others have researched the rights of third-party, innocent owners (see also Enders 1993; Goldsmith and Linderman 1989; O'Brien 1991; Saltzburg 1992; Stahl 1992; Zeldin and Weiner 1991). Indeed, Canavan (1990) has argued that "the government's weapon against drug traffickers injures innocent owners." Others have questioned the "relation-back doctrine" (Jankowski 1990) and have made suggestions for reforms (e.g., Hyde 1995; Speta 1990). Still others have criticized forfeiture on Fourth Amendment grounds. For example, Nelson (1992:1336) lamented that "the fear that evidence may not be admissible at trial is too remote a concern to compel law enforcement agents to respect the boundaries of the Fourth Amendment."

To further illustrate the concerns surrounding civil asset forfeiture, Pratt and Peterson (1991:653) observed that "Perhaps no area of the law embodies more legal fictions—and better illustrates their use and misuse—than does civil forfeiture." Questioning the war on drugs itself, Steven Wisotsky (1991:658) argued that courts have adopted "the operative premise . . . that 'drugs are bad,' so bad that almost any law or law enforcement measure is validated." Indeed, the title of Blumenson and Nilsen's (1998) recent law review article, "Policing for Profit: The Drug War's Hidden Economic Agenda," summarizes many legal sentiments regarding civil asset forfeiture.

Like legal scholars, the press has questioned the constitutional, legal, and ethical issues involved in civil asset forfeiture (e.g., Morganthau and Katel 1990). For example, Joseph McNamara (1999:5) has claimed that, "in a free society, the police should never be compelled to, or allowed to, view their law enforcement duties as a means of raising revenue for government." As Thomas (1999) observed, civil forfeiture ". . . is a great scam for the government, which knows few people will hire a lawyer to try to prove a negative." Zalman (1997), writing for the *Detroit News*, claimed that "drug asset forfeiture is uncomfortably close to something like a 'legal' shakedown racket."

Perhaps most damning to the practice of civil forfeiture was Schneider and Flaherty's (1991) "Presumed Guilty" series appearing in the *Pittsburgh Press*. So harsh were their allegations that the Department of Justice responded, refuting Schneider and Flaherty's claims of abuses and threats to innocent property owners (Department of Justice 1991; see also Bauman 1995; Burnham 1996; Chapman 1993; Enders 1993; Greenburg 1995).

Other groups also have been critical of civil asset forfeiture. The National Association of Criminal Defense Lawyers (NACDL) has been perhaps the most critical of civil asset forfeiture, as evidenced by their reports before Congress (e.g., NACDL 1996). The American Bar Association's RICO, Forfeiture, and Civil Remedies Committee in the Criminal Justice Section (which is actually being formed as of this writing) appears to be rather critical of forfeiture as well (e.g., Rudnick 1992).

Lobbyists and practitioners have also made it their raison d'être to see forfeiture laws reformed. For example, F.E.A.R, an acronym for Forfeiture Endangers American Rights, is a lobbying organization based in Washington, D.C., whose objective is to change forfeiture law. The American Civil Liberties Union, another critic of civil forfeiture, published a one-page advertisement in a Sunday edition of the *New York Times* to promote awareness about civil asset forfeiture laws and abuses. The Asset Forfeiture Network and the Center for Forfeiture Law are but a few of the other organizations that have campaigned extensively for forfeiture reform.

On the supportive side, the American Prosecutors Research Institute (a.k.a. the National Defense Attorneys Association) sponsors a serial publication, *Beyond Convictions*, that views civil asset forfeiture favorably. There are also numerous government publications and sources of government information concerning civil asset forfeiture. For example, the Office of National

Drug Control Policy and the Drug Enforcement Administration (Drug Enforcement Administration, Strategic Intelligence Division 1993, 1994) have produced several forfeiture related manuals and reports.

The Asset Forfeiture Office, also known as the Executive Office for Asset Forfeiture or the Asset Forfeiture Section of the Justice Department's Criminal Division, publishes various forfeiture-related reports, audits, and policy manuals (Asset Forfeiture Office 1994; Executive Office for Asset Forfeiture 1994a, 1994b). The General Accounting Office is another source of pro-forfeiture literature (e.g., General Accounting Office 1990, 1991, 1992). Finally, the Office of the Attorney General publishes annual forfeiture reports, oversees the equitable sharing program, and otherwise publishes much pro-forfeiture literature (Department of Justice 1990, 1994b, 1995).

Procedural Controversies

Civil asset forfeiture was particularly controversial throughout the height of the drug war during the 1980s and 1990s. Recently, new federal legislation has changed the procedural aspects of civil asset forfeiture in favor of property owners. However, it is worthwhile considering "past" civil asset forfeiture procedure because many state laws remain unchanged. The procedural controversies stem not from the way in which property is seized and then forfeited, but from procedures for the handling of property and the procedures available to property owners for contesting questionable seizures.

By way of introduction, the Civil Asset Forfeiture Reform Act of 2000 changed the burden of proof to a preponderance of evidence standard (see further discussion concerning CAFRA below), but the legislation is federal and thus not binding on the states. As Yoskowitz (1992:575) observed, "as a practical matter, the government usually meets the initial burden of proof of probable cause simply by filing a verified complaint." Courts have allowed the use of hearsay, circumstantial evidence, tips from anonymous informants, and even information obtained *after* an initially illegal seizure to meet the probable cause burden (e.g., *United States v. All Funds on Deposit or Any Accounts Maintained at Merrill Lynch* 1992; *United States v. One 56-Foot Yacht Named Tahuna* 1983; *United States v. One 1977 Mercedes-Benz 450 SEL* 1983; Yoskowitz 1992).

Critics of civil asset forfeiture have also been concerned about what currency and property is subject to forfeiture. The law provides for the forfeiture of property that is derived from or used to "facilitate" certain crimes. Just as it can be difficult to prove that something was derived from illegal activity, it is often difficult to ascertain what constitutes facilitation (e.g., *U.S. v. Real Property Located at 6625 Zumirez Drive* 1994; Heilbroner 1994). Forfeiture legislation has continued to expand over the past two decades. There are many more laws on the books for which forfeiture is an option than there were 20 years ago. Laws have evolved from a focus on property to money and, more recently, to all real property (Hyde 1995; see also Kessler 1993).

Returning to the earlier example of a drug dealer arrested with a roll of cash, the connection between the drugs and the money is understandable.

However, if the same drug dealer lived in a nice house, is the house also subject to forfeiture? This is considerably more difficult to determine, which is why the proliferation of legislation has led to some difficulties determining when property, particularly real property, is derived from or used to facilitate criminal activity.

Civil forfeiture is also controversial because of the remedial options available (or, more aptly, *not* available) to property owners. The odds are typically stacked against property owners, although federal law has begun to change this. In particular, the defenses available to innocent owners have been less than desirable (Goldsmith and Linderman 1989; Kasten 1991). Consider the following hypothetical: A man lends his friend his car. The man's friend is pulled over for speeding and consents to a search of the car. It turns out the man's friend has drugs in the car. He is arrested, the car is impounded, and the prosecutor brings a civil forfeiture action against the car, serving the car's owner with notice that he has a certain number of days to respond to this proposed action. Assuming the car's owner did not consent to or know of his friend's illegal activity, should he be able to get his car back? Most people would argue that, yes, he should, but the law does not necessarily permit this. The *in rem* nature of civil asset forfeiture is again at fault; because the car is targeted and not the car's owner, the car owner's guilt or innocence is largely irrelevant. The effect of forfeiture on innocent owners is one of the more contentious aspects of civil asset forfeiture practice.

While CAFRA has provided for a clearly innocent owner's defense, many state civil asset forfeiture laws have not changed. In the case *Bennis v. Michigan* (1996), for example, the innocent owner problem was manifested clearly. In that case a husband and wife both shared ownership of a car. The police caught the husband in the car with a prostitute. Under a Michigan law that declared the car a "public nuisance" (because it was used in the act of prostitution), the car was seized. The wife contested the forfeiture action on the grounds that she neither consented nor knew of her husband's infidelity. Nevertheless, the court ruled that the forfeiture was legal. As disturbing as the verdict sounds, there was no innocent owner law on the books in Michigan at the time. The U.S. Supreme Court affirmed the decision, holding that Michigan's lack of an innocent owner defense did not violate the Fourteenth Amendment's due process clause or other constitutional provisions.

Finally, although the law (primarily at the federal level) has changed in favor of property owners, there are procedural aspects of civil asset forfeiture that have received a great deal of scrutiny. For a time, federal law required property owners to post a 10 percent cash bond to contest proposed forfeitures. Much like some criminal defendants are allowed to post bond as surety that they will appear in court, federal law once required that a 10 percent bond be posted (based on the value of the property) so as to discourage frivolous challenges. While this may have seemed eminently sensible, it would be difficult to post a 10 percent bond on an expensive piece of real property. Also, the law provided only a limited period of time in which to contest the forfeiture (many state laws still do this), and the government was not always liable for the care of property in dispute.

Equitable Sharing

Sewell's (1999) *Controversial Issues in Policing* pitted two seasoned practitioners against each other in a debate over whether forfeiture is an "effective tool" or "cash register justice." Carl W. Hawkins (Hawkins and Payne 1999), one of the authors, argued that civil forfeiture is particularly advantageous because it deters criminal activity, saves taxpayers money in the war on drugs, and increases officer morale. However, Thomas Payne (Hawkins and Payne 1999:30), taking a critical perspective on civil forfeiture, claimed that "the living frame of our democracy and the Constitution on which it is nourished are being devoured by a 'slow creeping fire'. . . a fever that has invaded our criminal justice system and spread across our nation's courts and law enforcement agencies."

In a creative study, Miller and Selva (1994) observed asset forfeiture activities. One of the authors established a relationship with drug enforcement officials and worked as an informant. "This position provided a rare opportunity to examine, through covert participant observation, the clandestine work of narcotics operations units and to observe undercover narcotics agents, typically an inaccessible subject group" (Miller and Selva 1994:321). Over the course of one year, the researcher observed some 28 narcotics transactions that culminated in arrest and/or civil forfeiture.

The results of the study were startling, and they confirmed what many asset forfeiture critics have long feared: Agents were selective in their enforcement efforts, and the goal of seizing assets took precedence over the goal of taking narcotics out of circulation. Referring to one case where a drug dealer received a large quantity of cocaine, Miller and Selva (1994) reported the following:

> The researcher . . . was surprised when he was instructed to observe the suspect's transactions to determine the rate at which the cocaine was being resold. Less drugs meant more cash, and the agent's objective was to seize currency rather than cocaine. The case was successful as to proceeds, but perhaps not in view of the quantity of cocaine that officers knowingly permitted to reach consumers. (328)

Most critics of asset forfeiture have made reference to botched forfeitures where the police seized the property of innocent owners. Miller and Selva (1994) helped to quell critics' concerns when they found that narcotics agents targeted *criminals*; however, profit was a major incentive. When narcotics agents were confronted with two possible drug transactions, Miller and Selva (1994) made this observation:

> The first case involved five times as much marijuana as the second. . . . The seller was a full-time drug dealer with two prior drug-related convictions, and was on probation at the time of this case. The suspect in the second deal had no arrest record and appeared to be a relatively small-time user who hoped to make a modest profit by selling quarter-ounce bags of

marijuana. Although the first deal seemed more serious, the second would guarantee seizure of at least $700 when the suspect purchased drugs from the agent. In addition, the latter suspect owned a truck, whereas the professional dealer had only a little equity in a late-model sports car. The officer explained that the first deal simply was not profitable. . . . (324)

In a recent empirical study Worrall (2001b) found that a large number of law enforcement organizations are coming to depend on the revenues generated from civil asset forfeiture activities. He conducted a survey of 1,400 law enforcement agencies around the country and asked police chiefs and county sheriffs to respond to the following statement: "Civil asset forfeiture is necessary as a budgetary supplement for my agency." Nearly 40 percent of the respondents reported that civil forfeiture was necessary as a budgetary supplement. Also, the findings suggested that fiscal expenditures were inversely related to dependence on civil asset forfeiture, that is, the smaller an agency's budget (measured in dollars per sworn officer), the more likely it would be to depend on civil asset forfeiture.

Worrall (2001b) concluded with a controversial observation: "the notion that law enforcement is coming to depend on civil asset forfeiture lends support to perspectives such as Reiman's . . . pyrrhic defeat theory, namely that the criminal justice system is designed to fail. It could be that law enforcement has a vested interest in there being a drug problem because of the money and resources that stand to be earned." Worrall also pointed out, however, that such an eventuality is unlikely. More reasonable is the argument that forfeiture proceeds are desirable, even necessary, but they are reserved for continuing the war on drugs and other forms of illicit activity.

Despite legislative changes regarding civil asset forfeiture, equitable sharing remains largely unchanged. Even though the money returned to law enforcement is supposed to go to "law enforcement purposes," and even though most of it does, the "kickback" law enforcement agencies can receive from civil asset forfeiture programs is a benefit not enjoyed by any other public agency. Because forfeiture proceeds need not go through appropriation channels (like the budgets for all other public agencies, including the police) many observers have argued that law enforcement is destined to be "in it for the money" so long as the equitable sharing feature of civil asset forfeiture legislation continues to operate as it does.

Forfeiture Law and the War on Drugs

The Comprehensive Drug Abuse and Prevention and Control Act of 1970 contained the first and most basic forfeiture provision associated with the current war on drugs. It provided for civil forfeiture of the following:

[a]ll controlled substances which have been manufactured, distributed, dispensed, or acquired . . . [a]ll raw materials, products, and equipment . . . which are used, or intended for use, in manufacturing . . . delivering, importing, or exporting any controlled substance[s] . . . property which is

used, or intended for use, as a container for [forfeitable controlled substances] . . . [a]ll conveyances, including aircraft, vehicles, or vessels, which are used, or intended for use, to transport, or in any manner to facilitate the transportation, sale, receipt, possession or concealment [of such controlled substances]. (21 U.S.C. sec. 881[a])

In 1978, the act was amended to provide for the forfeiture of:

[a]ll moneys . . . or other things of value furnished or intended to be furnished by any person in exchange for a controlled substance . . . all proceeds traceable to such an exchange . . . (Psychotropic Substances Act of 1978 [21 U.S.C. sec. 881(a)(6)])

In 1984 the act was again amended to provide for the forfeiture of:

[a]ll real property . . . which is used, or intended to be used, in any manner or part, to commit, or to facilitate the commission of a violation. (Comprehensive Crime Control Act of 1984 [21 U.S.C. sec. 881(a)(7)])

There is an important progression of events here that needs to be highlighted. The 1970 Comprehensive Drug Abuse Prevention and Control Act provided for the forfeiture of property used in connection with controlled substances. The "connection" language was then changed to include money or other things of value used or furnished in exchange for drugs, or the proceeds traceable to such exchanges. Finally, the 1984 Comprehensive Crime Control Act added all real property used (or even intended to be used) to commit or facilitate a drug crime.

Not surprisingly, the legislative progression did not end in 1984. The 1986 Anti-Drug Abuse Act expanded the number of offenses for which forfeiture was available to include money-laundering activities (18 U.S.C. sec. 981[a][1][A]). Further amendments to the 1986 Anti-Drug Abuse Act, made in 1990, included forfeiture for proceeds traceable to counterfeiting and other offenses connected to financial institutions (18 U.S.C. sec. 981[a][1][C]). The law was again amended in 1992 to increase the offenses for which forfeiture was an option, including the proceeds traceable to motor vehicle theft (18 U.S.C. sec. 981[a][1][C]; 18 U.S.C. sec. 981[a][1][F]. One of the more controversial amendments, 18 U.S.C. sec. 984(b)(1), provides for further forfeiture of assets, including: ". . . subject property is cash, monetary instruments in bearer form, funds deposited in an account in a financial institution . . . or other fungible property."

According to Hyde (1995:25), ". . . this recent statutory expansion means not only a dramatic increase in the number of crimes covered by civil asset forfeiture but also a significant lessening of any relationship between an owner's guilty act or offense, if any, and the property that is subjected to forfeiture." Furthermore:

Prompted largely by the war on drugs, this distinctly American forfeiture policy, wisely or unwisely, is now far removed from the ancient notion of "arresting" "guilty" or "tainted" property "accused" of causing a wrong.

And yet for the most part, the original ancient judicial procedures used for forfeitures govern this whole new federal apparatus, often much to the detriment of individual constitutional rights, and the delight of those in and out of government who benefit from wholesale confiscation of billions of dollars worth of private property. (Hyde 1995:25–6)

THE CIVIL ASSET FORFEITURE REFORM ACT OF 2000

The Civil Asset Forfeiture Reform Act (CAFRA) of 2000 marked the culmination of a seven-year effort by Henry Hyde and others to reform the nation's civil asset forfeiture laws. Hyde has long been a champion of forfeiture reform. Time and again he introduced resolutions in the House of Representatives, only to have them defeated or drastically amended. Hyde eventually amassed enough support for asset forfeiture reform to pass HR 1658 by a landslide vote of 375–48. The Senate then passed HR 1658, but their version was significantly watered down. The amended version of HR 1658 then went back to the House where it was accepted as amended. President Clinton signed the bill in 2000.

CAFRA makes eight fundamental changes to federal forfeiture law. First, it requires the government to prove by a preponderance of evidence that the property in question is subject to forfeiture. This stands in stark contrast to the old law, which required that when a property owner goes to federal court to challenge a seizure of property, the government need only make an initial showing of probable cause that the property was subject to forfeiture. It was then up to the property owner to prove that the property was "innocent." Not only has the burden of proof changed, but the burden now falls on the government, not the property owner, to prove that property is subject to forfeiture.

Second, CAFRA provides that the government must show that there was a substantial connection between the property and the commission of a crime. In the past the definition of "facilitation," for example, was construed liberally, providing for the seizure of property that was only minimally connected to the crime. Under the new law, for example, if a drug dealer owns an expensive house and 10 percent of the house was paid for with drug proceeds, the government will probably not succeed in a forfeiture action against the house.

Next, the new legislation provides that property can be released by a federal court pending final disposition of a civil forfeiture case if continued possession by the government would cause the property owner substantial hardship. For example, if a property seizure prevents the functioning of a business or leaves an individual homeless, and if the likely hardship outweighs the risks that the property will be destroyed, damaged, lost, or concealed, then it will be returned (if only temporarily) to the owner so as to minimize hardship.

Fourth, CAFRA provides that property owners who substantially prevail in court proceedings challenging the seizure of their property will receive reasonable attorney's fees. Moreover, the new legislation provides counsel for indigents if appointed counsel in related criminal cases represents them. Under the old law, property owners who successfully challenged the seizure of money or property were rarely, if ever, awarded attorney's fees. Often, in fact, they would have to strike "deals" with the government, agreeing to give up a certain amount of money in exchange for return of their property (see, e.g., Levy 1996). Providing counsel for indigent property owners is also a significant change.

Fifth, the new legislation eliminates the cost bond requirement, which required that property owners post a bond of 10 percent of the value of the seized property merely for the right to contest the seizure in court. CAFRA does provide, however, that if a court finds that a claimant's assertion of an interest in the property under question is frivolous, the court may impose an appropriate fine.

Sixth, CAFRA provides a uniform innocent owner defense for all federal forfeiture statutes. Of particular interest is the change that protects property owners who have given timely notice to the police of the illegal use of their property and have in a timely fashion revoked or made a good faith attempt to revoke permission to use the property from those engaging in illegal conduct. The burden of proving an innocent owner defense, however, falls on the property owner. The claimant must show his or her innocence by a preponderance of evidence.

Seventh, the new legislation allows property owners to sue the federal government for compensation for damage to their property when they prevail in court. In the past the federal government was exempt from liability for damage caused during the handling or storage of property being detained by law enforcement officers. Hyde (1995:12–13) recounted an attempt at forfeiture by Coast Guard officials that almost certainly would not occur under CAFRA:

> On April 9, 1989, Jacksonville, Florida, university professor Craig Klein's new $24,000 sailboat was "inspected" in what turned out to be a fruitless drug search by U.S. Customs Service agents. In the seven hour rampage, the boat was damaged beyond repair. Using axes, power drills, and crowbars, agents dismantled the engine, ruptured the fuel tank, and drilled more than 30 holes in the hull, half of them below the waterline. Yet the Customs Service refused to compensate Klein, who was forced to sell the boat for scrap.

Finally, CAFRA provides a uniform definition of the forfeitable proceeds of criminal acts. In cases involving illegal goods or services, unlawful activities, and telemarketing and health care fraud schemes, proceeds are properties obtained directly or indirectly as a result of the commission of the offenses giving rise to forfeiture, and any properties traceable thereto, and are not limited to the net gain or profit realized from the offenses. In cases involving lawful goods or services that are sold or provided in an illegal manner, proceeds are money acquired through the illegal transactions less the direct costs incurred in providing the goods or services.

CAFRA does include some provisions that benefit the Justice Department and other law enforcement agencies. The law enforcement lobby was vehemently opposed to CAFRA, which is why a degree of compromise between pro- and antiforfeiture advocates had to be reached. These provisions include increased availability of criminal and civil forfeiture for the proceeds of crime, a relaxed statute of limitations for pursuing forfeiture actions, and allowing federal courts to issue civil restraining orders against property where there is a substantial probability that the government will prevail in civil forfeiture actions.

CAFRA: A SHEEP IN WOLF'S CLOTHING?

CAFRA represents a substantial step in the evolution of forfeiture law; notably, the law has changed in favor of property owners. Many of the procedural controversies associated with forfeiture during the height of the drug war will be minimized or eliminated under the new law. However, despite the changes, problems remain. Indeed, it can be argued that CAFRA is akin to a sheep in wolf's clothing (as opposed to a wolf in sheep's clothing). Stated differently, the law sounds "tough" on the government, but may not be, for a number of reasons.

First, CAFRA is binding only on the federal government. States are exempt from CAFRA's provisions. Some states may elect (or already may have elected) to change their laws governing civil asset forfeiture, but there are no requirements or incentives to do so. This is significant to the extent that many states provide no innocent owner defense and attorney's fees. Since the overwhelming majority of forfeiture actions, like any other law enforcement activities, are commenced at the local level, this is a significant limitation.

Second, while CAFRA changed the procedures for federal forfeitures, it did nothing to restrict the numbers of offenses for which forfeiture is an option. In fact, the compromise bill expanded the law to include additional offenses. As new laws are passed, many include forfeiture provisions. This may not be a problem in light of the new procedures, but it is difficult to concede that the motivation for expanded forfeiture laws is crime control. There is a great deal of "money to be had," as a result of successful forfeitures. It is important, therefore, not to lose sight of the pecuniary dimension of civil asset forfeiture.

Finally, CAFRA leaves no mention of equitable sharing. The potential for law enforcement agencies to receive a "kickback" for forfeiture actions is a significant concern. Although CAFRA changes procedures in favor of property owners and minimizes the potential for forfeiture-related abuses, law enforcement agencies can still receive forfeiture proceeds. This a significant source of funding available to no other public agency. Equitable sharing is no doubt desirable (and necessary) insofar as it compensates law enforcement agencies for the expenses incurred during the war on drugs (and crime in general), but equitable sharing has been at the heart of several of the conflict-of-interest critiques of civil asset forfeiture.

Despite CAFRA's limitations, it is arguably a step in the right direction. Most critics of civil asset forfeiture have cited the lack of due process for property owners in forfeiture actions. The new legislation has finally corrected some of the "wrongs" of the past. Critics would argue, however, that much remains to be accomplished. Regardless of any changes, civil asset forfeiture is here to stay. The enormous costs it imposes on crime as well as the resources it provides all but guarantee that it will be a law enforcement mechanism of choice well into the twenty-first century.

REFERENCES

Asset Forfeiture Office. (1994). *Asset Forfeiture Manual: Law and Practice.* Washington, DC: United States Department of Justice.

Bauman, R. (1995). Take it away. *National Review* February 20, 34–38.

Blumenson, E. and Nilsen, E. (1997). Policing for profit: The drug war's hidden economic agenda. *University of Chicago Law Review* 65, 35–114.

Burnham, D. (1996). *Above the Law.* New York: Scribner.

Canavan, P. M. (1990). Civil forfeiture of real property: The government's weapon against drug traffickers injures innocent owners. *Pace Law Review* 10, 485–517.

Chapman, S. (1993). Seizing property: Law enforcement's dangerous weapon. *Chicago Tribune* March 7, sect. 4, 3.

Department of Justice. (1990). *Annual Report of the Department of Justice Asset Forfeiture Program.* Washington, DC: Office of the Attorney General.

Department of Justice. (1991). *Points in Response to Presumed Guilty Series.* Washington, DC: Office of the Attorney General.

Department of Justice. (1994a). *Annual Report of the Attorney General of the United States.* Washington, DC: Office of the Attorney General.

Department of Justice. (1994b). *Guide to Equitable Sharing of Federally Forfeited Property for State and Local Law Enforcement Agencies.* Washington, DC: Office of the Attorney General, Executive Office for Asset Forfeiture.

Department of Justice. (1995). *Audit Report: Asset Forfeiture Program.* Washington, DC: Office of the Inspector General.

Drug Enforcement Administration, Strategic Intelligence Division. (1993). *Illegal Drug Price / Purity Report—United States: January 1990–March 1993.* Washington, DC: United States Department of Justice.

Drug Enforcement Administration, Strategic Intelligence Division. (1994). *Illegal Drug Price / Purity Report—United States: January 1991–June 1994.* Washington, DC: United States Department of Justice.

Durkin, C. (1990). Civil forfeitures under federal narcotics law: the impact of the shifting burden of proof upon the fifth amendment privilege against self-incrimination. *Suffolk University Law Review* 24, 678–709.

Enders, J. (1993). Opposition growing to nation's drug forfeiture laws. *Chicago Daily Law Bulletin* February 11, 2.

Executive Office for Asset Forfeiture. (1994a). *Guide to Equitable Sharing of Federally Forfeited Property for State and Local Law Enforcement Agencies.* Washington, DC: United States Department of Justice.

Executive Office for Asset Forfeiture. (1994b). *Annual Report of the Department of Justice Asset Forfeiture Program.* Washington, DC: United States Department of Justice.

General Accounting Office. (1990, June). *Asset Forfeiture: Legislation Needed to Improve Cash Processing and Financial Reporting* (GAO/GGD-90-94). Washington, DC: Government Printing Office.

General Accounting Office. (1991, September). *Asset Management: Government-wide Asset Disposition Activities* (GAO/GGD-91-139FS). Washington, D.C: Government Printing Office.

General Accounting Office. (1992, September). *Real Property Dispositions: Flexibility Afforded Agencies to Meet Disposition Objectives Varies* (GAO/GGD-92-144FS). Washington, DC: Government Printing Office.

Goldsmith, M. and Linderman, M. J. (1989). Asset forfeiture and third party rights: The need for further law reform. *Duke Law Journal* 39, 1253–1301.

Greenburg, J. C. (1995). Hyde: Easy recovery of seized property. *Chicago Tribune* June 22, 14.

Hawkins, C. W., Jr. and Payne, T. E. (1999). Civil forfeiture in law enforcement: An effective tool or cash register justice? Pp. 23–34 in *Controversial Issues in Policing*, edited by J. D. Sewell. Boston, MA: Allyn and Bacon.

Heilbroner, D. (1994). The law goes on a treasure hunt. *New York Times* Dec. 11, sect. 6, 70.

Holmes, O. W., Jr. (1881). *The Common Law.*

Hyde, H. (1995). *Forfeiting Our Property Rights: Is* Your *Property Safe from Seizure?* Washington, DC: Cato Institute.

Jankowski, M. A. (1990). Tempering the relation-back doctrine: A more reasonable approach to civil forfeiture in drug cases. *Virginia Law Review* 76, 165–195.

Jensen, E. L. and Gerber, J. (1996). The civil forfeiture of assets and the war on drugs: Expanding criminal sanctions while reducing due process protections." *Crime and Delinquency* 42, 421–434.

Kasten, L. (1991). Extending constitutional protection to civil forfeiture that exceeds rough remedial compensation. *George Washington Law Review* 60, 194–244.

Kessler, S. F. (1993). *Civil and Criminal Forfeiture: Federal and State Practice.* St. Paul, MN: West.

Levy, L. W. (1996). *A License to Steal: The Forfeiture of Property.* Chapel Hill: The University of North Carolina Press.

McNamara, J. (1999). When the police take property, who do you call? *Orange County Register* June 6, Commentary, 5.

Miller, J. M. and Selva, L. H. (1994). Drug enforcement's double edged sword: An assessment of asset forfeiture programs. *Justice Quarterly* 11, 313–335.

Morganthau, T. and Katel, P. (1990). Uncivil liberties? Debating whether drug war tactics are eroding constitutional rights. *Newsweek*, April, 29, 18–21.

National Association of Criminal Defense Lawyers. (1996). H.R. 1916 (Civil Asset Forfeiture Reform Act) and the current federal asset seizure and forfeiture program. (Oral testimony presented before the United States House Committee on the Judiciary, July 22, 1996). Washington, D.C: National Association of Criminal Defense Lawyers.

Nelson, W. P. (1992). Should the ranch go free because the constable blundered? Gaining compliance with search and seizure standards in the age of asset forfeiture. *California Law Review* 80, 1309–1359.

O'Brien, A. M. (1991). Caught in the crossfire: Protecting the innocent owner of real property from civil forfeiture under 21 U.S.C. Section 881(a)(7). *St. John's Law Review* 65, 521–551.

Petrou, P. (1984). Due process implications of shifting the burden of proof in forfeiture proceedings arising out of illegal drug transactions. *Duke Law Journal* Sept., 822–843.

Piety, T. R. (1991). Scorched earth: How the expansion of civil forfeiture doctrine has laid waste to Due process. *University of Miami Law Review* 45, 911–978.

Pratt, G. C. and Petersen, W. B. (1991). Civil forfeiture in the second circuit. *St. John's Law Review* 65, 653–700.

President's Commission on Model State Drug Laws. (1993). *Volume 1: Economic Remedies.* Washington, DC: The White House.

Rosenburg, J. A. (1988). Constitutional rights and civil forfeiture actions. *Columbia Law Review* 88, 390–406.

Rudnick, A. G. (1992). Cleaning up money laundering prosecutions: Guidelines for prosecution and asset forfeiture. *Criminal Justice* 7, 2.

Saltzburg, D. G. (1992). Real property forfeitures as a weapon in the government's war on drugs: A failure to protect innocent ownership rights. *Boston University Law Review* 72, 217–242.

Schneider, A. and Flaherty, M. P. (1991, August–December). Presumed guilty. *Pittsburgh Press.* Available at http://www.fear.org/pittpres.html

Sewell, J. D. (1999). *Controversial Issues in Policing.* Boston, MA: Allyn and Bacon.

Speta, J. B. (1990). Narrowing the scope of civil drug forfeiture: Section 881, substantial connection and the eighth amendment. *Michigan Law Review* 89, 165–210.

Stahl, M. (1992). Asset forfeiture, burdens of proof, and the war on drugs. *Journal of Criminal Law and Criminology* 83, 274–337.

Thomas, C. (1999). Civil forfeiture laws in desperate need of change. *The Arizona Republic* May 8, B6.

Warchol, G. L. and Johnson, B. R. (1996). Guilty property: A quantitative analysis of civil asset forfeiture. *American Journal of Criminal Justice* 21, 61–81.

Warchol, G. L., Payne, D. M., and Johnson, B. R. (1996). Criminal forfeiture: An effective alternative to civil and administrative proceedings. *Police Studies* 19, 51–66.

Wisotsky, S. (1991). Not thinking like a lawyer: The case of drugs in the courts. *Notre Dame Journal of Legal Ethics and Public Policy* 5, 651–700.

Worrall, J. L. (2001a). *Civil Lawsuits, Citizen Complaints, and Policing Innovations.* New York: LFB Scholarly Press.

Worrall, J. L. (2001b). Addicted to the drug war: The role of civil asset forfeiture as budgetary supplement in contemporary law enforcement. *Journal of Criminal Justice,* Forthcoming.

Yoskowitz, Jack. (1992). The war on the poor: Civil forfeiture of public housing. *Columbia Journal of Law and Social Problems* 25, 567–600.

Zalman, M. (1997). The insidious side of drug forfeiture laws. *The Detroit News* May 9, A11.

Zeldin, M. F. and Weiner, R. G. (1991). Innocent third parties and their rights in forfeiture proceedings. *American Criminal Law Review* 28, 843–861.

CASES CITED

Bennis v. Michigan, 116 S.Ct. 994 (1996).

Calero-Toledo v. Pearson Yacht Leasing Co., 416 U.S. 663 (1974).

Miller v. United States, 78 U.S. 268 (1870).

United States v. All Funds on Deposit . . . at Merrill Lynch, 801 F. Supp. 984 (E.D. N.Y. 1992).

United States v. One 6.5 mm. Mannlicher-Carcano Military Rifle, 406 F.2d 1170 (1969)

United States v. One Mercedes 560 SEL, 919 F.2d 327 (5th Cir. 1990).

United States v. One 1977 Mercedes-Benz 450 SEL, 708 F.2d 444 (9th Cir. 1983).

United States v. One Parcel of Land at 508 Depot Street, 964 F.2d 814 (8th Cir. 1992).

United States v. One Yacht Named Tahuna, 702 F.2d 1276 (9th Cir. 1983).

United States v. Real Property Located at 6625 Zumirez Drive, 845 F. Supp. 725 (1994).

United States v. United States Coin and Currency, 401 U.S. 715 (1971).

United States v. 92 Buena Vista Ave., Rumson, 507 U.S. 111 (1993).

The Military as Drug Police
Exercising the Ideology of War

Peter B. Kraska

Metaphorically Speaking

Metaphors help us make sense of confusing and complex phenomena by associating those phenomena with something we can easily relate to and comprehend. The "war on drugs" metaphor furnishes society with an appealing association that simplifies our thoughts and actions related to controlling substance abuse. The consequences of thinking about the substance abuse problem and what we should do about it as *war* should not be underestimated. Metaphors provide the framework for constructing and perceiving reality. "Metaphor has a formative impact on language, on the construction and embellishment of meaning, and on the development of theory and knowledge of all kinds" (Morgan, 1993:277). The drug-war metaphor provides the theoretical/ideological backdrop that shapes our approach to drug control.

Nowhere is this connection more evident than in the "militarization" of drug control activities. It seems that where the war metaphor was once intended to be interpreted and used figuratively, current drug-war trends demonstrate a literal application—literal to the point that Congress assigned the Department of Defense a key role in administering all drug-related interdiction efforts. The military currently conducts drug control operations in foreign countries, on the high seas, at our borders, and—with increasing regularity—within the United States. Violating a long-standing principle of demo-

This is a revised version of a chapter titled "Militarizing the Drug War: A Sign of the Times," in P. B. Kraska (ed.), *Altered States of Mind: Critical Observations of the Drug War* (1993). New York: Garland Publishing.

cratic governance, military soldiers and civilian police often collaborate in these operations, blurring their traditionally distinct roles. The Pentagon, in struggling to legitimate itself in the post–cold war environment, has made clear their long-term commitment to the "drug war."

The purpose of this article is to explore the evolution of using the military as drug law enforcers and to uncover this phenomenon's ideological underpinnings. After reviewing the terms "militarization" and "militarism," I present a historical accounting of the military's involvement, followed by an analysis of the strategies used to establish and to legitimate the use of the armed forces. The conclusion explores this phenomenon's significance for trends in drug control efforts—particularly the emerging relationship between the military, the police, and the criminal justice system.

Militarization and Militarism

In order to examine the trend of using the military as drug police we must first understand the concepts of *militarization* and *militarism*. Most analyses begin with Woodrow Wilson, who first popularized the term "militarism" when lecturing at West Point.

> Militarism does not consist of any army, nor even of the existence of a very great army. Militarism is a spirit. It is a point of view. It is a purpose. The purpose of militarism is to use armies for aggression. (Donovan 1970:25)

Wilson's traditional view of militarism, what Janowitz (1964) terms "designed militarism," emphasizes the military's political, economic, and ideological preeminence within the state and society. Nazi Germany is often cited as an example (Vagts 1959). Berghahn (1982) noted a more subtle but just as powerful form of militarism with the advent of nuclear weapons. The possibility of military action resulting in widespread nuclear destruction has created a logical reluctance to embrace outward indications of military force. However, the nuclear war threat provides justification for the continual build-up of an enormous military apparatus. Dwight D. Eisenhower in his farewell speech warned the United States of an "immense military establishment" that fuels itself through the arms industry (Lang 1972). He termed this disturbing development the "Military Industrial Complex" (M.I.C.). The following is a list of dominant features of what we might call *contemporary militarism* (Snow 1991; Glossop 1987; Nisbet 1988; Zinn 1990; Klare 1980; Eide and Thee 1980; Kothari et al. 1987). Each of these is relevant to the militarization of drug control efforts.

- An immense and influential arms industry controlled by national and transnational corporations dependent on the military establishment's well-being.
- A military with an active hand in shaping foreign policy.
- A subtle, yet pervasive, militaristic ideology that stresses aggressiveness and the use of force as an effective problem-solving tool, and the glorification of military power and technology as the means to supremacy.

• An increasing tendency to influence internal and civilian affairs, including the military's involvement in what were traditionally seen as civilian functions (e.g., drug law enforcement).

• A perception by society that the military is a desirable evil, which forces the difficult-to-hide M.I.C. to eschew overt displays of force, weaponry, or publicity, except in times of publicly supported military conflict.

Contemporary militarism represents a set of ideological beliefs that are the guiding force, or in Wilson's terms, the "spirit," behind the process of "militarization." Militarizing the drug war, thus, is the actual application of contemporary militarism to drug control efforts, including the armed forces' involvement and the civilian forces' adoption of militaristic practices, hardware, technology, values, language, and ideology.

In order to examine the extent and significance of the military's involvement, several data-collection strategies were employed. The secrecy surrounding military activity required a mixture of traditional and unorthodox research strategies. Admiral George Gee reported to Congress that the Pentagon is "purposefully" keeping the military's visibility in the drug war as low as possible (C-Span, 1992). "Low visibility" translates into a tight lid on data and information. This research includes data collected through an analysis of over a hundred government documents and congressional hearings; in-depth interviews with military personnel (n=31); interviews with investigative reporters (N=4); observations from the field; and a collection of media accounts, including military periodicals.

The Politics of Drug Wars: Enlisting the Military

Since the criminalization of drugs in the early 1900s, the control of elicit drugs has always contained an element of militaristic thinking and practice. Defining certain types of drug use or distribution as "criminal behavior" automatically invokes the quasi-military institutions of the criminal justice system. Only since the U.S. government's escalation of drug control efforts, however, has ameliorating our substance abuse problem been seen as an appropriate role for the armed forces.

The military, in an uncoordinated fashion, began its involvement in drug control efforts in the late 1970s. Probably the first use of active duty troops was in 1977 when the Governor of Hawaii activated the National Guard to launch Operation Green Harvest (Temple 1989). Like most early programs using the military, this massive marijuana eradication effort was designed to put the marijuana industry out of business. The Coast Guard operates both as a law enforcement agency and a military unit under the Department of Transportation during peacetime. Responsible for maritime law enforcement, it expanded its drug interdiction efforts beginning in the mid-1970s (Walter 1988). The Department of Defense has been lending equipment to the Coast Guard and the U.S. Customs department to aid interdiction efforts since 1971 (Bagley 1988).

Except for these occasional incidents, it was not until 1978, when Congress became aware of the seemingly enormous amount of illicit drugs entering the United States through the maritime borders of Florida, that serious discussions of involving the military on a broader level were considered. On June 9 and 10 of that year, the entire House Select Committee on Narcotic Abuse and Control traveled to Florida to hear and see firsthand the "drug disaster." The committee reported being "shocked" at what they found.

> Almost daily, tons of marijuana and kilos of cocaine were interdicted, yet it is clear from testimony given to the committee that these seizures represent only the tip of the iceberg. . . .The committee estimates that less than 5 percent of the total contraband coming into South Florida was seized prior to the committee's hearing. . . .Illegal drug trafficking had, within the last 2 years, become the largest single commercial activity in the Florida area. (Select Committee on Narcotics, 1978:1)

The investigation focused on the economic impact this problem would have on Southern Florida and the safety of its borders—not the substance abuse problem itself. The members justified military-style measures to combat the problem by claiming that the unchecked smuggling of any contraband leads to the smuggling of "terrorist paraphernalia," which threatens national security. With the Coast Guard and U.S. Customs being plagued by outdated equipment and limited resources, the committee recommended that the military supply law enforcement officials with aircraft, boats, and electronic surveillance equipment. The members voiced their frustration at not being able to more actively involve the military by recommending to the White House a revision of the *Posse Comitatus* legislation of 1878, which prohibited the military from engaging in almost all civilian law enforcement activity. By 1981, the proposed revisions of the *Posse Comitatus* law were passed, allowing the military to loan equipment to the civilian police, train law enforcement personnel, and directly assist in some aspects of interdiction efforts (Moore 1987). The revisions stopped short of giving military personnel arrest or search-and-seizure powers. Funding for this operation came primarily from diversion of $709 million from treatment and education programs to law enforcement (Kraska 1990).

Early appraisals of these military-style operations were naively optimistic. One media report claimed that a single five-month operation raised the price of a kilo of cocaine from $5,000 to $60,000. Military hardware played a critical role:

> The customs service also is benefiting from the addition of three Army Cobra helicopters, formerly used in Vietnam. The Cobras are speedy and highly maneuverable, capable of overtaking slow-moving drug planes, landing next to them and blocking the smugglers' escape. (Penn 1982)

There were several joint efforts between civilian police and the armed forces between 1982 and 1985. In 1983, the National Narcotics Border Interdiction System was designed to link all the military branches—Air Force,

Navy, Army, and Marines—with both local and federal law enforcement agencies (Korb 1985; Moore 1987). This same year, the military began providing "training assistance" to police and military forces in several Latin American Countries (Trebach 1987; Committee on Foreign Affairs 1986). Within the United States, several states began activating the National Guard to help with marijuana eradication programs (Temple 1989). The largest domestic marijuana destruction effort during this period was titled Operation Delta-9. The Attorney General justified this 50-state effort and its expected result:

> We are sending a strong message, both to domestic producers of marijuana and to the source countries outside our borders, that the U.S. government takes very seriously the need to attack the production of this drug. . . . The chief law enforcement officer of the nation promised that no observed marijuana plant would survive on the land of the United States. (Trebach, 1987:149)

These early beginnings of the militarization of drug control efforts, even though unprecedented, were relatively modest. The military was reluctantly involved and only provided technical and training assistance to federal police agencies and the Coast Guard. By 1985–86, however, a groundswell of support for more drastic drug control measures was growing in Congress. Concomitantly, the media began constructing an enticing theme on the cocaine and crack "crisis." The dormant "drug war" was resurrected. A Congressman captured the mood of the media and politicians during a Congressional meeting on the further repeal of the *Posse Comitatus* law:

> . . . this is a war that requires the increased use of our military to protect our nation from being destroyed by the deadly menace of drugs that have inundated every city, town and school in all of our Congressional Districts. (Subcommittee on Crime 1985:44)

Another Congressman focused on a military solution to this rediscovered "deadly menace," claiming that ". . . it would be well if the original Comitatus legislation were repealed, outright and entirely" (Subcommittee on Crime 1985:3). His initial proposal resulted in a toned-down bill known as the Bennet Amendment. It gave the military full law enforcement powers outside the United States and would put them at the forefront of interdiction efforts. The Department of Defense (DoD) protested the amendment, arguing that further military involvement in the drug war violated the sacred separation between the police and military was a detriment to military preparedness, and was not cost-effective (Weinberger 1988). The Pentagon's resistance helped to modify the proposed legislation, but involvement in drug control activities still increased. By late 1986, the cost of U.S. *military* interdiction activities had risen to nearly $400 million, as compared to only $4.9 million in 1982 (Moore 1987).

The "drug war" fever in 1985–86 also led to the Joint Chiefs of Staff recommending in 1985 that the military take on the task of eradicating the production and distribution of cocaine and marijuana in Latin American countries (Wilson 1985). In April 1986 President Reagan signed a National Decision Security Directive declaring drugs an official threat to our national security (Committee on Foreign Affairs 1986). Both of these extraordinary developments were precursors of the first (publicized) U.S. military coordinated strike within an Andean nation—Operation Blast Furnace, conducted in July and August of the same year. The Bolivian government, under the threat of economic sanctions and possibly even being "decertified" by the United States, solicited help from the U.S. military for assistance in destroying coca production labs. The operation was deemed a short-term success—it curtailed the processing of coca for months—but a long-term failure, since it almost toppled the government and coca production rose to an all-time high within only a few months (Marby 1988; Committee on Foreign Affairs 1986).

In May 1988, Congress held hearings on the role of the military in drug interdiction, resulting in the FY 1989 Defense Authorization Act (Committee on Armed Services 1988a). The act designated the Pentagon to serve as the single lead agency for the detection and monitoring of air and marine drug smugglers and to integrate the national command, control, communications, and intelligence assets for drug interdiction. Throughout these hearings Congress demonstrated its preoccupation with "calling out the troops" and having the military completely take over "drug war" operations—including suggestions for the military to set up "detention camps" (Committee on Armed Services 1988b:109).

Military officials once again exhibited some reluctance to fight the drug war, but the resistance was regarded as "bureaucratic footdragging." Several political changes combined to force the military's cooperation. The DoD under the Reagan administration wielded considerable influence. They were the focal point of Reagan's conservative administration, which nearly doubled defense spending in only a few years. Reagan was a laissez-faire manager, who allowed the Secretary of Defense to minimize the military's involvement in drug control activities (Weinberger 1988). The next administration dramatically changed the political landscape. The new Defense Secretary, Richard Cheney, did not question the push to enlist the military (Select Committee on Narcotics 1991b:87). The Pentagon recognized that the "Soviet war threat" was evaporating as a rationale for maintaining the military budget. Ensuring only modest cuts in a nearly $300-billion-a-year budget would require a cooperative relationship with Congress and a willingness to adopt new roles (Abel 1990; Irwin 1988; Kenney 1989). Consequently, only four months after the passage of the Defense Authorization Act (September 18, 1988) Cheney granted the drug war "high priority" status and directed all branches of the military to draw up plans for their increased involvement (Cheney 1989).

The DoD's new "lead agency" role went a long way toward giving President George H. Bush direct oversight of drug control efforts. He further strengthened his administrative control with the passage of a drug bill in October of 1988, creating the Office of National Drug Control Policy (ONDCP). William Bennett became the country's first self-proclaimed "drug czar."

A czar, of course, is an emperor or person having unlimited power over others. The term's martial connotations certainly fit well with the "drug war" rhetoric. Bennett immediately did his title justice by strengthening interdiction efforts while de-emphasizing education and treatment. He released plans in 1989 to spend an extra $270 million, in addition to the approximately $100 million already being spent, on military and some economic aid for the Andean nations—Colombia, Peru, and Bolivia—to fight drug production (Select Committee on Narcotics 1988a; Shannon 1989). Bennett extended the approach taken in Operation Blast Furnace by putting more funds into an ongoing project titled Operation Snowcap. This operation officially began in April of 1987 and was designed to provide "full-time operational capability as a follow-up to Operation Blast Furnace" (Select Committee on Narcotics 1991a:80).

Snowcap's mode of operation was and still is to suppress the cocaine supply by funding, training, and assisting the Andean nations' police and military forces in destroying cocaine production. U.S. support for these efforts came in the form of military economic aid and military hardware; Green Beret, Navy Seal, and other military advisors ostensibly used for training and transportation purposes; and U.S. law enforcement assistance (Select Committee on Narcotics 1991a; Conniff 1992; Kirk 1991; Reynolds 1990). Bennett's plan, first disclosed by *Time* magazine in August of 1989, was to double what was already an unprecedented level of military involvement. He switched from the original plans that emphasized crop eradication and substitution to an approach that relied on paramilitary search-and-destroy missions of processing labs, airstrips, and storehouses (Shannon 1989).

The Bush administration remained sensitive to the negative consequences of appearing to "militarize the drug war" abroad. By threatening economic sanctions and dangling the carrot of increased military aid, the United States was able to persuade the Andean nations to militarize drug control activities (Klare 1990; Kawell 1991; Reynolds 1990; Kirk 1991). The overall strategy, thus, was to minimize actual U.S. troop involvement by using them in an "advisory" capacity. However, in late 1989 the United States shocked the Andean nations by taking overt military steps.

In November, two seemingly unrelated bits of information were revealed. First, the Justice Department ruled that *Posse Comitatus* revisions allowed U.S. military soldiers to legally arrest drug traffickers within their own countries (Anderson 1990). Second, it was disclosed that President Bush, under executive order, planned to send the USS *John F. Kennedy* (a carrier) and a nuclear powered cruiser to Colombia. Bush also planned to send additional ships soon thereafter in order to intensify drug interdiction efforts. The White House refused to respond to requests from the press in the Andean nations for full disclosure of U.S. plans and intentions.

The actual reason for the Justice Department's ruling on military soldiers making arrests soon became clear. On December 20, 1989, the U.S. military invaded Panama, and U.S. soldiers arrested Manuel Noriega for violating federal drug trafficking laws. The government of a sovereign nation had been toppled using military force under the auspices of enforcing U.S. drug laws. On December 28, Press Secretary Marlin Fitzwater admitted for the first time that the United States was planning to send Navy warships to Colombia for drug interdiction purposes. The Panamanian invasion, however, had incited such criticism from Latin American countries that President Bush decided to terminate the operation (Kamen 1990; Isikoff 1990).

These incidents forced the Bush administration, the ONDCP, and Congress to avoid policies that appear to directly involve the U.S. military. In an extreme example of this approach, Bush ordered General Maxwell Thurman, the director of operations in the Panamanian invasion, to draft similar plans for a simultaneous "hemispheric drug raid" of all the Andean countries. By using these countries' police and military forces, one Defense Department analyst said, "We wouldn't pull the trigger, but we'd point the gun" (Waller et al. 1990: 16).

Bennett (the "drug czar") soon recognized, however, that successfully exporting the military model would require the United States to prove its willingness to use its military domestically. U.S. domestic marijuana production doubled between 1985 and 1990. To avoid being labelled the "Yankee Hypocrites to the North" (Isikoff, 1990), Bennett persuaded Bush to order nearly 200 army and special forces troops to invade the King Range Conservation area in Northern California (Stein 1990). Operation Green Harvest was the first of increased domestic interdiction efforts by the military. Although the bulk of National Guard activity involved marijuana eradication and border patrol missions, Bush seriously considered calling them into the streets of Washington D.C. in order to "fight drug violence" (Weinraub 1989; Sanchez 1990). The Department of Defense, in 1990, allocated over $70 million for National Guard units to conduct over 5,000 interdiction missions in all 50 states (Duncan 1991). Many financially strapped National Guard units suddenly found lucrative new roles (Kraska 1991). Antidrug funds provided to California's National Guard, for instance, went from $1.75 million in 1989 to more than $17 million in 1991 (National Guard 1992).

CURRENT STATE OF AFFAIRS

The preceding chronology of events documents the progression of the U.S. military's involvement in the "drug war" from the 1970s to about 1990. The current state of affairs demonstrates an acceleration of this trend. By late 1990 the military fully recognized their precarious standing in the post–cold war era (the Berlin Wall came down in November, 1990). One military observer notes how the Navy views their involvement in the drug war.

> The Navy must find itself a new reason to justify spending. While the Iraqi invasion of Kuwait may have postponed the day of reckoning for the military budgets, the world of tomorrow is certain to be different. . . . The conclusion of the cold war took a reluctant bit player [in the drug war] and made it a star. This transformation was all about money; the drug war is a source of new funds. The Navy has followed a wide trail of

dollars to the one "war" in town. . . . The Navy could quickly become the
top cop on the maritime beat. (Abel 1990: 58–59)

Even by 1990, then, the previously mentioned hesitation of military officials to get involved had dissipated. The military even began to talk of their
long-term involvement. By 1992 the military claimed that the drug war was a
long-term, high-priority mission and that "we have a substantial commitment, we're in it for the long haul" (C-Span 1992; see also, Select Committee
on Narcotics 1991b).

Although President Clinton de-emphasized the use of the military in the
drug war during his first two years in office, he appointed a military general
as the country's new drug czar in 1996. The military is still conducting interdiction efforts in several different "theaters"—namely, within the United
States, at or near the U.S. land/maritime borders both within and outside the
United States, and within foreign countries (including at or near foreign sea
borders). All branches of the armed forces are involved.

Joint Task Force Six (JTF-6), a nationwide anti-narcotics force based at
Fort Bliss in southwest Texas, provides 500 training missions to 2700 local law
enforcement officers each year (Scarborough, 1999). It has a permanent staff
of 170 and the authority to summon active-duty and reserve personnel. The
task force suspended its patrol of the Southwest border after a JTF-6 marine
shot and killed an 18-year-old goat-herder, Esequiel Hernandez, Jr., near Red-
ford, Texas. In 1996–97, the Pentagon issued more than a million pieces of
equipment to police departments. The budget for drug spending by the
Department of Defense in 2000 was 1,273 million dollars (ONDCP, 2001).

Excavating Ideology:
Examining Construction and Legitimation Strategies

These developments clearly demonstrate an unprecedented use of our military.
The U.S. government reacts to the abuse of mind-altering substances as a
problem of criminality—so threatening that it must mobilize our armed forces
to combat it. The United States has a long tradition of temporarily using
military troops to quell what it defines as collective criminality during prison
riots, civilian demonstrations and riots, labor strikes, or to control looting after
a natural disaster (Houseman, 1986). What we have here, however, is a significant departure from a guiding tenet of democratic governance—the clear
separation of a military designed to engage in war, and the civilian police who
enforce the law. Even more noteworthy is how this phenomenon has silently
expanded with minimal public recognition, debate, or resistance.

What is the underlying ideological context driving this phenomenon?
Specifically, what strategies were used in successfully constructing and legiti-
mating the need for and the use of the military in policing the drug problem
(Deetz and Kersten, 1983; Spector and Kitsuse, 1987). The myriad rationalizations and claims-making activities mentioned earlier are consolidated into
three broad strategies: (1) demonizing the enemy; (2) sanitizing the enforcers;

and (3) embracing the opposition. The objective here is to analyze the taken-for-granted aspects of militarizing the drug war and to decode the outward actions, policies, and interests of those involved in the construction and legitimation process (Deetz and Kersten 1983).

DEMONIZING THE ENEMY

The construction of social problems occurs not in a vacuum but within a social and political context. This latest drug war exemplifies the reciprocal process of the political system reacting to society's outcry while at the same time orchestrating, with the aid of the media, the volume and nature of the outcry itself (Spector and Kitsuse 1987). Whether based on hysteria or fact, this process has created an image of the drug problem as "endangering" society itself.

A similar construction process occurs when gaining support for waging "real" wars. Whether it is Manuel Noriega or Saddam Hussein, "demonizing the enemy" helps to justify what would normally be unacceptable means. It does this by magnifying the differences between foe and friend so that the conflict becomes a morally righteous one, "between total good and total evil" (Zinn, 1990:71). In the drug war, mind-altering substances are defined as having seductive intentions and sinister motives, the distributors are perceived as ruthless peddlers of death and destruction, and the users are seen as criminogenic co-conspirators deserving harsh punishment.

For many claims makers, as the following passage from Congressional hearings demonstrates:

> There is no greater threat to the survival of our society than drugs. If the present condition continues, we will no longer be free independent citizens but people entwined and imprisoned by drugs. The military forces of this country must become more involved. (Committee on Armed Services, 1988b:112)

Demonizing the drug problem thus creates an environment whereby almost any policy on behalf of victory becomes morally acceptable. As mentioned earlier, this demonization process so intensified in 1986 that President Reagan declared illegal drugs a "national security threat" justifying the military Operation Blast Furnace and the further involvement of all the armed forces. This strategy, then, has legitimated the broadening of the definition of what constitutes a threat to national security and the situations where military intervention is appropriate.

The military itself, however, has made it clear during the formative years of their involvement that they rejected outright this expanding definition of their role. They philosophically disagreed with using the military as cops and feared being a scapegoat for what they repeatedly described as a futile approach (Committee on Armed Services 1988a; Weinberger 1988). They even commissioned a research study by the Rand Corporation to document what many already knew—interdiction, even with the military's resources, would have little impact (Reuter et al. 1988). So while the demonization tactic helped establish the importance of militarizing the drug war for others, the military did not and still has not succumbed to the tactic.

Why, then, do they now accept what they once passionately rejected? The answer is simple yet has disturbing implications—the Department of Defense now realizes the necessity in the post–cold war era of developing a *socially useful* military. William Taylor used this concept when testifying to Congress on the appropriateness of military involvement in policing narcotics (Committee on Armed Services 1988a). Taylor chastised the military officials' myopia in not seeing the greater utility of fighting the drug war. The following passage discloses what he meant by the military becoming "socially useful."

> Now I think there is one more thing that the Department of Defense leadership ought to start thinking about. Defense spending has not only declined recently, it will decline because there is a declining perception of military threat in the Congress and among the American public. . . . If the DoD leadership were smart about the coming environment, they would approach the Congress with a military "social utility" argument which says that military manpower should not be further reduced because the Congress is mandating increased military involvement in the "war on drugs." They should, in fact, argue further that new funds should be appropriated for these expanded missions which are *socially useful*. (Committee on Armed Service 1988a:12–13)

In other words, Taylor recommended that the military get involved not because of the urgency of the substance abuse problem, but because it would help rebuild the military's eroding legitimacy. Fears of communism would be replaced by fears of social problems to maintain public support. During these same hearings the military sternly opposed Taylor's position, contending that the drug problem did not threaten national security and that their efforts would only fail. Taylor's views were obviously the more prescient. As one observer put it, "the military sneered at drug interdiction—until they saw the budget crunch coming" (Magnulson 1990:23).

As will be discussed later, militarizing the drug war can be viewed as only part of an even larger trend associated with the military industrial complex: broadening the definition of national security and widening the military's range of legitimate activity, including that of "law enforcement" (Kothari et al. 1988; Eide and Thee 1980; Snow 1991). It is important, from the military's point of view, to maintain that they are only capitalizing on what Congress and two presidential administrations forced upon them. The next strategy, sanitizing the enforcers, operates to maximize the palatability of militarizing drug law enforcement.

SANITIZING THE ENFORCERS

Visualize for a moment National Guard soldiers, armed to the hilt, breaking into a U.S. citizen's home, searching for evidence of crack cocaine and arresting the occupants. Or picture an elite force of Green Berets and Navy Seals conducting a clandestine raid on a drug lab in Bolivia, where they destroy buildings, engage in a firefight, and capture the surviving drug insurgents. And lastly, imagine a Navy ship bearing down on a recreational yacht off the coast of Florida, firing warning shots across its bow, and detaining it while armed Navy soldiers search the entire vessel and arrest the occupants.

Each of these scenarios is of course fictitious. Except for hard-core drug war militarists, these scenes are offensive to our sense of what constitutes proper military action. Interestingly, however, the central point of debate in the last ten years about involving the military in the drug war has been whether military soldiers could make arrests, search and seize evidence, and use force to accomplish their mission. The battle has centered around the repeal of the *Posse Comitatus* Act, originally designed to prohibit the use of the military in civilian law enforcement (Moore 1987). As of this date, despite efforts by members of Congress, the Council of Governors, and the League of Mayors, the *Posse Comitatus* Act has been revised significantly but not repealed. Military soldiers, therefore, except under some circumstances in foreign countries, do not technically have full law enforcement powers. How, then, do we explain their high level of involvement in the drug war?

By making only minor modifications to the above scenarios we can produce more realistic scenarios, routinely occurring in the drug war. In the first scenario using the National Guard, for instance, we would still have heavily armed soldiers, and they would still be involved in law enforcement activities. Instead of military uniforms, however, the soldiers might wear t-shirts (over their flack jackets) and would stand behind law enforcement personnel in a "support" or "backup" role. They would not actually collect evidence or put on handcuffs, but they could use force to "aid" in detaining someone. Bocklet (1990:75) explains how in Portland,

> the traditional separation between military and police operations walks a thinner line. Portland became the first municipality to deploy Guardsmen to assist local police in drug raid operations in crack-plagued neighborhoods.

As has occurred in Washington D.C., a military helicopter and crew could chase suspected drug violators through the city if they decided to flee, but they could only provide surveillance and/or transportation for the civilian police (Kraska 1991; Bocklet 1990). As mentioned earlier, the National Guard has taken an even more overt law enforcement role during marijuana eradication exercises, but always with the support of civilian police.

During the Waco debacle in 1993, the U.S. military provided intelligence, weaponry, armory, and special operations advisors. Some evidence indicated that actual military personnel assisted in the final raid of the Waco complex. This high level of involvement was justified on an unsubstantiated claim that the Branch Davidians might have been manufacturing illegal drugs, thereby circumventing Posse Comitatus restrictions (Kraska 2001).

These practices should shed light on the original question: how is it that a military prohibited by law from engaging in civilian law enforcement is so highly involved in the drug war? The answer lies in a powerful construction and legitimation tactic herein termed *sanitizing the enforcers*. The "enforcers" are the military themselves, and "sanitization" refers to freeing these enforcers from association with anything that might be considered undesirable or damaging. A host of innovative means are employed in order to make more palatable the government's exercise, both domestically and abroad, of its earliest and most crude assertion of its legal authority—military force (Turk 1982; Bittner 1980).

This sanitization strategy might seem constructive to the casual observer. It does restrain the military's full involvement; it maintains at least a symbolic separation between the military and civilian police activity; and, for those immersed in the militarization process, *Posse Comitatus* is viewed as substantively separating police from military activity. The concern here lies in the deceptive nature of this strategy. As evidenced in the scenarios, the sanitization techniques manage to uphold the integrity of the autonomous legal order by sustaining only the outward signs of a clear separation between military and civilian police functions. In drug-war practice, however, the demarcation between civilian police and military activity disappears almost completely.

Outside the United States, specifically within the Andean nations, these types of sanitization tactics take on a unique importance. Recall how a Defense Department analyst earlier characterized the U.S. role in Operation Snowcap: "We wouldn't pull the trigger, but we'd point the gun" (Waller et al. 1990:16). Apparently the U.S. government exports to other countries that which it considers unacceptable for itself: a fully militarized drug war with nothing distinguishing civilian police from the military. "Pointing the gun" means that the United States supplies the money, weapons, expertise, transportation, and assistance both to the actual military forces of a country and to its civilian police forces. The Department of Defense's involvement has been sanctioned only because of these sanitization tactics that allow the United States to "vicariously" militarize the Andean-nation drug war. As illustrated by the uproar discussed earlier over a military carrier being sent to Colombia, whenever the United States has tried to shift from vicarious militarization to direct participation, the presence of U.S. military force becomes too conspicuous (Farah 1990; Duzan 1990; Smith 1990). In short, vicarious militarization still allows the DoD to assume a rather active role, yielding the same end result.

Sanitizing the enforcers is a deceptive yet effective strategy that contributes to the construction and legitimation of militarizing the drug war. It institutes a "win-win" situation for those with a vested interest. It maintains the technical separation between the military and civilian police when fighting the drug war, allowing both not to fully implicate each other in their mutual activities. The military wins by becoming more socially useful while artificially sanitizing itself from the enforcement of the law. As one member of the Joint Chiefs of Staff put it, "We are only in the business of putting trophies in the law enforcement showcase" (C-Span 1992). The civilian police win by receiving military hardware, training, and assistance. Indeed, the sanitization strategy enables the civilian police to communicate, act, and think militarily, while still technically retaining their civilian status.

EMBRACING THE OPPOSITION

A strategy related to sanitizing the enforcers, because it enhances the palatability of militarizing the drug war, deals with how those promoting and implementing an interdiction-oriented approach to the substance abuse problem embrace its opposition's approach—demand reduction—as a means to further perpetuate the interdiction enterprise.

The interdiction approach to rectify the substance abuse problem is the theoretical/ideological underpinning of the militarization trend. The term *interdiction* means to forbid with force or state authority. When applied to drug control efforts, it refers to law enforcement activities that attempt to reduce the availability of illicit drugs through state force. It assumes that a sustained effort at targeting the source of drugs (e.g., crop eradication, lab destruction), the distribution system (e.g., maritime law enforcement, border security), and the sale of drugs (e.g., undercover buy-bust operations) will chip away at supply and eventually diminish the problem. The military has an abundance of tools to implement supply policies: military hardware/technology plus use-of-force capabilities (or, hardware/technology + force = control). This equation underlies the push for the armed forces' involvement and the militarization of law enforcement agencies as well. Hartlyn (1988:184) terms this approach the "containment model."

Critics see drug interdiction efforts as only displacing and transforming the substance abuse problem. Interdiction efforts to contain the marijuana supply, for example, have proved counterproductive by generating an enormous domestic marijuana industry (displacement) and marijuana with four times the psychoactive potency of the original, imported marijuana (transformation) (Gaines and Potter, 1993). Hartlyn (1988) terms this approach the "balloon model."

With the bulk of drug-war dollars going toward interdiction efforts (with the help of the military), one would assume that at least some evidence exists to support the containment model's efficacy. Without discussing the voluminous literature in this area, the "overall" consensus of evidence and opinion—even according to the General Accounting Office and many drug control bureaucrats—is that the containment approach has failed and will continue to fail (Barnett 1987; Hamowy 1987; Reuter et al. 1988; Slaughter 1988; Nadelman 1988; Wistosky 1986; Trebach 1987; Kenny, 1989; Duca 1987; Committee on Armed Services 1988b; Blair 1990).

How do interdiction advocates and practitioners negate this condemnatory evidence and criticism? One would assume that they would quell the opposition with strong, critical rhetoric and an ardent defense of the militarization of the drug war (Henry and Milovanovic 1991). Instead, they initially embrace the opposition's position, admit the limitations of containment, and then capitalize on the opposition's terminology to further the interdiction enterprise.

On the first account, those involved in militarizing the drug war have been able to define and react to the substance abuse problem as one of supply yet also claim that the best solution is to address demand. After listing the many problems plaguing the military's drug control efforts, a commander of one of two major drug task forces stated:

> But I am optimistic. It is going to take time, and we will never solve it all. And like everyone in the interdiction business will say, the ultimate solution is education. But we haven't made the required effort yet in education. (Irwin 1989:64)

The foremost legislative expert on military affairs, Senator Sam Nunn, at a hearing on drug a interdiction with the Joint Chiefs of Staff, criticized interdiction efforts by maintaining that demand reduction is the "only way" to curb the problem and interdiction strategies will have only a minimal impact. He never voiced any opposition, however, to the Navy's, Marines', Army's, or National Guard's aggressive interdiction activities (C-Span 1992). Similarly, the drug czar after a visit to the Andean nations, admitted that the only solution to cocaine production and distribution is through "economic reorientation," not further militarizing the drug war. What came out of his visit, however, were stepped-up interdiction activities by the D.E.A., the U.S. military, and the host country's military and police forces (Select Committee on Narcotics 1991).

How do the military and other interdiction players justify their activities and budgets while waiting for demand reduction to take place? Fortunately for them, the illicit drug industry is able to "donate" an impressive amount of drugs and assets. These seizures are displayed as an indication of performance, even though they have little bearing on the efficacy of interdiction efforts. Reuter terms this the "quantity illusion" (Reuter 1988; Fuss 1989). The "evidence" of immediate results ("we're accomplishing something"), bides time and provides support, while the more substantive solution—demand reduction—is being sought.

This reverence for demand reduction brings up the second strategy which is related to embracing the opposition and helps to sustain militaristic interdiction activities: the military is beginning to develop their own variety of demand-reduction strategies based on interdiction ideology. While most people associate education and treatment with demand-reduction tactics, drug-control militarists define demand in martial ways, such as mandatory drug testing; zero-tolerance policies designed to bring pain to casual users; and boot camps, detention camps, and antidrug youth camps all run by military soldiers (Federal Bureau of Prisons 1992; The White House 1991; C-Span 1992; Kraska 1991).

In short, these are all interdiction-oriented strategies to reduce demand. "Embracing the opposition" thus perpetuates what underlies the militarization of the drug war—an emphasis on interdiction—not by opposing but by extolling the demand-reduction virtues of its opposition.

Streamlining the Police and Military in the Post-Cold War Era

The interdiction enterprise is further advanced by its use of martial tactics in demand-reduction efforts. What accounts for what we could term the "interdiction addiction" in the government's drug control efforts? The answer lies in recognizing the government response to other forms of behavior it defines as criminal. The dominant "crime control ideology" rests on the same interdiction equation as do militarized drug control efforts—use of force plus hardware/technology equals control. In sum, both embrace the metaphor of war and the ideology of militarism. Given these ideological leanings it seems both consistent and logical, when determining policy on the drug/crime problem, to steer toward the militarization of the police and, more importantly, the "police-ization" of the military.

Earlier we discussed how the *war* metaphor, more than just a cliché, reflects the ideological underpinnings of drug control efforts. Lakoff and Johnson (1980) note that the metaphors we use to organize our thoughts and actions mirror the values we harbor. The value-rich concept discussed earlier, contemporary militarism, may constitute the most important factor driving the militarization of the drug war. The tendency of a society to adopt the use of force as a viable problem-solving tool signals the degree to which the tenets of militarism are institutionalized in its civilian affairs, its government, and its ideological structures. Contemporary militarism emanates an ideology that stresses the use of force and domination as an appropriate means to solve problems and to gain political power, while glorifying the tools used to accomplish this—military power, hardware, and technology. Militarizing drug control efforts, therefore, can be viewed as evidence of the encroachment of the military and its ideology into the thinking, discourse, and actions of those who construct, carry out, and support policies for society's problems. The legitimation strategy of embracing the opposition demonstrates the myopic focus on militaristic remedies.

Klare (1980:37) warns that the military industrial complex has an important influence on civilian affairs, including the nature of domestic order maintenance. He calls this the *national security syndrome*: "the tendency to expand the definition of 'national security' to require ever-greater control over national life." As noted earlier, the construction strategy of demonizing the enemy defined illicit drugs as posing such a serious social threat that it endangers our society's very existence. Consequently, the Reagan administration in 1986, with the blessing of Congress, took the drastic step of declaring the substance abuse problem an official threat to national security, justifying the escalation of the military's involvement in the Andean nations and within the United States itself.

It is critical to recognize that broadening the definition of "national security" to include the policing of the drug problem preceded the demise of the cold war. It would be misguided, thus, to attribute the militarization of the drug war solely as a result of the M.I.C. grasping for new threats in a post–cold war environment. The influence of contemporary militarism, therefore, stands alone as a critical sociological factor fostering this trend.

The M.I.C.'s precarious standing in the post–cold war world, though, has accelerated and deepened the trend toward militarizing drug control efforts. The United States now has a Department of Defense and its political supporters intent on making the military more "socially useful" by expanding its roles into domestic and international law enforcement. Resistance to this expansion seems minimal, partly because it is a logical extension of the nature of civilian law enforcement, and partly due to the neutralizing effects of the sanitization tactics discussed earlier.

The significance of this departure from the traditional roles of the military, police, and criminal justice system cannot be overstated. During the war on crime in the 1970s criminologists witnessed a similar, unprecedented development with the state expending large sums of money on the criminal justice system in order to wage a more technologically advanced fight against crime (McLauchlan, 1975). Quinney (1975) recognized this shift as signaling the development of an enormous, self-perpetuating crime control industry with militaristic undertones; he referred to it as the "criminal justice-industrial complex." Militarizing the drug war transcends what was once only an ideological link between criminal justice and militarism, and takes a small yet significant and possibly prophetic step toward incorporating the military industrial complex with the criminal justice-industrial complex. This step toward militarizing drug policies requires close scrutiny, considering that it was generated in an atmosphere of drug-war fever, has little chance of working, and violates the most basic tenets of democratic governance.

REFERENCES

Abel, A. (1989). "When Johnny Comes Marching Home." *Proceedings* 115(10): 40–45.
———. (1990). "Hunker Down Now!" *Proceedings* 116:58–64.
Allen, S. (1990). "Hot on Their Trail: Navy, Law Enforcement Agencies Team Up to Stop Drug Smugglers." *All Hands* (June): 18–30.
America's Defense Monitor (1992). "How Much Is Enough." Washington, DC: Center for Defense Information.
Anderson, C. (1990). "Uncle Sam Gets Serious: A Report From the Front Line." *The ABA Journal* (February): 60–63.
Ault, F. (1990). "We Must Be On Drugs!" *Proceedings* 116:46–51.
Bagley, B. (1988). "The New Hundred Years War? US National Security and the War on Drugs in Latin America." *Journal of InterAmerican Studies and World Affairs* 30 (2, 3): 161–81.
Bak, D., and R. Fournier (1989). "New Weapons in the War Against Drugs." *Design News* (September 4): 117–21.
Barnett, R. (1987). "Curing the Drug-Law Addiction: The Harmful Side Effects of Legal Prohibition." In R. Hamowy (ed.), *Dealing With Drugs: Consequences of Governmental Control*. San Francisco: Pacific Research Institute for Public Policy.
Berghahn, V. (1982). *Militarism: 1861–1979*. New York: St. Martin's Press.

Bittner, E. (1980). *The Functions of Police in Modern Society.* Cambridge: Olegeschlager, Gunn, and Hain.

Blair, D. (1990). "Drug War Delusions." *The Humanist* 50(5): 7–9.

Bocklet, R. (1990). "National Guard Drug Mission Help to Law Enforcement." *Law and Order* 38(2): 71–77.

C-Span (March 26, 1992). Televised Coverage of the Senate Armed Forces Hearing on the Military's Drug-Interdiction Efforts.

Cheney, R. (1989). "Department of Defense Guidance for Implementation of the President's National Drug Control Strategy." Speech delivered to the Senate on September 18.

Coast Guard Pacific Area Public Affairs Office (1988). *Zero-Tolerance: Facts from the Coast Guard.* U.S. Coast Guard, U.S. Department of Transportation.

Committee on Armed Services (1988a). *Narcotics Interdiction and the Use of the Military: Issues for Congress.* Washington, DC: U.S. Government Printing Office.

———. (1988b). *The Role of the Military in Drug Interdiction.* Washington, DC: U.S. Government Printing Office.

Committee on Foreign Affairs (1986). *The Role of the U.S. Military in Narcotics Control Overseas.* Washington, DC: U.S. Government Printing Office.

Conniff, R. (1992). "Colombia's Dirty War, Washington's Dirty Hands." *The Progressive* (May): 20–27.

Deetz, S., and A. Kersten (1983). "Critical Models of Interpretive Research." In L. Putman and M. Pacanowsky (eds.), *Communication and Organizations: An Interpretive Approach.* Beverly Hills: Sage.

Diaz, C. (1990). "DoD Plays in the Drug War." *Proceedings* Annual Review: 76–86.

Donovan, J. (1970). *Militarism, U.S.A.* New York: Scribner.

Duca, S. (1987). "The Ad Hoc Drug War." *Proceedings* 113 (12): 86–91.

Duzan, M. (1990). "Leave the Army Out of Colombian Anti-Drug Operations." *Wall Street Journal* (May 18): A1.

Eide, A., and M. Thee (1980). *Problems of Contemporary Militarism.* New York: St. Martin's Press.

Farah, D. (1990). "Troops' Drug War Role Questioned: Critics Wary of U.S. Push to Expand Colombian Military's Duties." *Washington Post* (July 24): A16.

Federal Bureau of Prisons (1992). *State of the Bureau 1991.* Washington, DC: U.S. Department of Justice.

Feldman, P. (1988). "Zero-Tolerance." *Los Angeles Times* (May 15): 5.

Fuss, C. (1989). "Lies, Damn Lies, Statistics, and the Drug War." *Proceedings* (December): 65–69.

Gerstenzang, J., and R. Ostrow (1985). "U.S. Launches Massive Caribbean Drug Drive." *New York Times* (November 2): 1, 3.

Glossop, R. (1987). *Confronting War: An Examination of Humanity's Most Pressing Problem.* Jefferson: McFarland and Company.

Hamowy, R. (1987). *Dealing With Drugs: Consequences of Government Control.* San Francisco: Pacific Research Institute for Public Policy.

Hartlyn, J. (1988). "Commentary on Bagley's 'The New Hundred Years War? National Security and The War On Drugs in Latin America'." *Journal of Inter-American Studies and World Affairs* 30 (2, 3): 183–86.

Henry, S., and D. Milovanovic (1991). "Constitutive Criminology: The Maturation of Critical Theory." *Criminology: An Interdisciplinary Journal* 29 (2): 293–316.

Houseman, G. (1986). *State and Local Government: The New Battleground.* Englewood Cliffs, NJ: Prentice Hall.

Ingrwerson, M. (1990). "US Andean Plan Seen as Risky to Democracies." *Christian Science Monitor* (May 9): 1–2.

Irwin, J. (1989). "Interview: Vice Admiral James C. Irwin, Commander Joint Task Force Four." *Proceedings* 115(10): 60–64.

Isikoff, M. (1990). "U.S. Defers Antidrug Naval Plan." *Washington Post* (January 9): A6.

Janowitz, M. (1964). *The Military in the Political Development of New Nations: An Essay in Comparative Analysis.* Chicago: University of Chicago Press.

Kamen, A. (1990). "Colombian Assent to Drug-Monitoring Flotilla Seen." *Washington Post* (January 8): A8.

Kawell, J. (1991). "Troops, Not Talks in Bolivia." *The Progressive* 55(7): 27–29.

Kenny, J. (1989). "Brace Yourself, DoD, Here Comes Another Mission." *Proceedings* 115 (10): 76–77.

Kirk, R. (1991). "Oh! What a Lovely Drug War in Peru." *The Nation* (September 30): 372–76.

Klare, M. (1980). "Militarism: the Issues Today." In A. Eide and M. Thee (eds.), *Problems of Contemporary Militarism.* New York: St. Martin's Press.

———. (1990). "Fighting Drugs With The Military." *The Nation* (January 1): 8–11.

Korb, L. (1985). "DoD Assistance in the War On Drugs." *Police Chief* (October): 57–62.

Kothari, R., R. Falk, M. Kaldor, L. Ghee, G. Deshingkar, J. Omo-Fadaka, T. Szentes, J. Silva-Michelena, I. Sabri-Abdalla, and Y. Sakamoto (1988). *Towards a Liberating Peace.* New York: New Horizons Press.

Kraska, P. (1990). "The Unmentionable Alternative: The Need For and The Argument Against the Decriminalization of Drug Laws." In R. Weisheit (ed.), *Drugs, Crime, and the Criminal Justice System.* Cincinnati: Anderson Publishing.

———. (1991). From field interviews with members of the armed forces and police agencies.

———. (2001). *Militarizing the American Criminal Justice System: Changing Roles of the Armed Forces and the Police.* Boston: Northeastern University Press.

Kufus, M. (1992). "Drug Wars." *Command: Military History, Strategy and Analysis* 18 (September-October): 18–49.

Lahneman, W. (1990). "Interdicting Drugs in the Big Pond." *Proceedings* (July): 56–63.

Lakoff, G., and M. Johnson (1980). *Metaphors We Live By.* Chicago: University of Chicago Press.

Lang, K. (1972). *Military Institutions and the Sociology of War.* Beverly Hills: Sage.

Lens, S. (1987). *Permanent War: The Militarization of America.* New York: Schocken Books.

McLauchlan, G. (1975). "LEAA: A Case Study in the Development of the Social Industrial Complex." *Crime and Social Justice* 4 (Fall-Winter): 15–23.

Mann, M. (1987). "The Roots and Contradiction of Modern Militarism." *The New Left Review* 162: 35–50.

Matthews, W. (1991a). "Military Produces Results in Drug War." *Army Times* 41 (May 13): 17.

———. (1991b). "Lawmaker Shoots for Higher Stakes in Drug War." *Army Times* 49 (July 8): 12.

Magnulson, E. (1990). "More and More, a Real War." *Time*, January 22.

Marby, D. (1988). "The U.S. Military and the War on Drugs in Latin America." *Journal of InterAmerican Studies and World Affairs* 30 (2, 3): 53–76.

Marx, G. (1988). *Undercover Policing: Police Surveillance in America.* Berkeley: University of California Press.

Melman, S. (1991). "The Juggernaut: Military State Capitalism." *The Nation* (May 20): 649, 664.

Moore, R. (1987). "Posse Comitatus Revisited: The Use of Military in Civilian Law Enforcement." *Journal of Criminal Justice* 15:375–86.

Moore, W. (1987). "No Quick Fix." *National Journal* (November 21): 2954–59.

Nadelman, E. (1988). "The Case for Legalization." *The Public Interest* 2 (92): 3–31.

National Guard Bureau (1992). *National Guard Drug Interdiction and Counter Drug Activities.* Departments of the Army and Air Force.

Nisbet, R. (1988). *The Present Age: Progress and Anarchy in Modern America.* New York: Harper and Row.

ONDCP budget 2001. Scarborough, Rowan. 1999 (Sept. 9, p. A-1, A15). "Congress has paved way with legislation," The *Washington Times.*

Penn, S. (1982). "Joint Agency Effort Is Curbing Smuggling of Drugs Into Florida: Army, Navy, Planes, Help Out On Patrols." *Wall Street Journal* (August 5): 1.

Quinney, R. (1975). *Criminology.* Boston: Little Brown.

Reiss, M. (1991). "Pushing the Pentagon." *Mother Jones* 16 (4): 40.

Reuter, P., G. Crawford, and J. Cave (1988). *Sealing the Borders: The Effects of Increased Military Participation in Drug Interdiction.* Santa Monica: The Rand Corporation.

Reuter, P. (1988). "Quantity Illusions and Paradoxes of Drug Interdiction: Federal Intervention Into Vice Policy." *Law and Contemporary Problems* 51 (1): 233–52.

Reynolds, D. (1990). "The Golden Lie." *The Humanist* 50 (5): 10–14.

Sanchez, R. (1990). "D.C. Curfew Is Proposed by Barry." *Washington Post* (October 18): A4.

Shannon, E. (1989). "Attacking the Source: Bennet's Plans to Send Military Advisers to Aid Anti-Narcotics Campaigns in Peru and Bolivia Arouses Serious Worries." *Time* 134 (9): 10–12.

Select Committee on Narcotics Abuse and Control (1978). *Problems of Law Enforcement and Its Efforts to Reduce the Level of Drug Trafficking in South Florida.* Washington, DC: U.S. Government Printing Office.

Select Committee on Narcotics Abuse and Control (1991a). *Andean Strategy.* Washington, DC: U.S. Government Printing Office.

———. (1991b). *Federal Drug Interdiction Efforts.* Washington, DC: U.S. Government Printing Office.

Sinoway, R. (1990). "Peaceful Countryside Turns Into Battlefield." *The Drug Policy Letter* 2(4): 4–6.

Skinner, J. (1990). "Narco-Guerilla Warfare: Is the U.S. Prepared?" *Defense and Diplomacy* 4: 48–53.

Slaughter, J. (1988). "Marijuana Prohibition in the United States: History and Analysis of a Failed Policy." *Columbia Journal of Law and Social Change* 21 (4): 417–74.

Smith, P. (1990). "High Political Price Exacted for Any Potential Benefits." *Los Angeles Times* (March 16): 16.

Snow, D. (1991). *The Shape of the Future: The Post-Cold War World.* New York: M.E. Sharpe.

Sommer, M. (1990). "Perils of the Drug War." *The Christian Science Monitor* (September 21): 22–23.

Spector, M., and J. Kitsuse (1987). *Constructing Social Problems.* New York: Aldine DeGruyter.

Stafford, T. (1990). "Snuffing Cocaine at its Source." *Proceedings* Annual Review: 90–91.

Stein, M. (1990). "Army Troops Join Marijuana Raids." *Los Angeles Times* (July 31): A3.

Subcommittee on Crime (1985). *Military Cooperation with Civilian Law Enforcement.* Washington, DC: U.S. Government Printing Office.

Temple, H. (1989). "The Nation's War on Drugs." *Vital Speeches of the Day* (April): 516–19.

Trebach, A. (1987). *The Great Drug War: And Radical Proposals That Could Make America Safe Again.* New York: Macmillan.

Turk, A. (1982). *Political Criminality: The Defiance and Defense of Authority.* Beverly Hills: Sage Publications.

Vagts, A. (1959). *A History of Militarism: Civilian and Military.* New York: Free Press.

Walter, C. (1988). "The Death of the Coast Guard." *Proceedings* (June): 29–33.

Waller, D., M. Miller, J. Barry, and S. Reiss (1990). "Risky Business." *Newsweek* (July 16): 16–19.

Weeks, S. (1992). "Crafting a New Marine Strategy." *Proceedings* (January): 34–38.

Weinberger, C. (1988). "Our Troops Shouldn't Be Drug Cops: Don't Draft the Military to Solve a Law Enforcement Problem." *Washington Post* (May 22): C2.

Weinner, E. (1991). "Drug 'War' Rhetoric Said to be Linked to Police Misconduct." *Drug Enforcement Report* (April 23): 8.

Weinraub, B. (1989). "Bush Considers Calling in Guard to Fight Drug Violence in Capital." *New York Times* (March 21): A1.

Weisheit, R. (1990). *Drugs, Crime, and the Criminal Justice System.* Cincinnati: Anderson Publishing.

White House (1991). *National Drug Control Strategy.* Washington, DC: U.S. Government Printing Office.

Wilson, G. (1985). "Military Urges Wider Drug War: Training Central American Teams, Blocking Transport Envisioned." *Washington Post* (June 20): A22.

Wisotosky, S. (1986). *Breaking the Impasse in the War on Drugs.* New York: Greenwood Press.

Zamichow, N. (1990). "Marines Fight Drug Smugglers in Texas With Flying Drones." *Los Angeles Times* (March 8): A28–A29.

Zinn, H. (1990). *Declarations of Independence: Cross-Examining American Ideology.* New York: Harper-Collins.

Section
V

TREATING THE
DRUG OFFENDER

15

The Failure of Drug Education

D. M. Gorman

The role of the federal government in preventing adolescent drug use was a central issue of the 1996 presidential campaign. Bob Dole criticized the Clinton administration for slashing the staff of the Office of National Drug Control Policy (ONDCP) while Clinton criticized attempts by the Republican majority in Congress to cut federal support of drug-prevention programs—the most dramatic being a proposal to rescind the entire $482 million prevention budget of the Department of Education. It seemed as though everyone, Democrats and Republicans, liberals and conservatives, wanted to be seen as favoring federal spending on drug prevention and, in particular, drug education.

Indeed, 65 percent of congressional candidates polled in 1996 by the Community Anti-Drug Coalitions of America ranked prevention programs as the number one priority in reducing the country's drug problem, compared to just 9 percent for both interdiction and treatment. By the close of 1996, Republicans had abandoned their attempts to reduce the federal prevention budget and Clinton had secured extra funds for drug-education programs within the Department of Health and Human Services and the Department of Education.

There is no mystery in the bi-partisan popularity of such education programs. Recently completed large-scale surveys have shown that illicit drug use among young people (primarily in the form of marijuana smoking) increased in the past three years, following more than a decade of steady decline. In the National Household Survey, conducted by the Department of Health and Human Services, monthly marijuana use among children between 12 and 17 increased from 4 percent in 1992 to more than 7 percent in 1994 while the per-

Reprinted with permission of *The Public Interest*, No. 129, pp. 50–61. © 1997 by National Affairs, Inc.

ceived risks of use declined. The National Institute on Drug Abuse's Monitoring the Future Study showed that this trend was evident among eighth, tenth, and twelfth graders. Among the latter, reported use of any illicit drug during the previous 30 days rose from 14.4 percent in 1992 to 23.8 percent in 1995.

Advocates of drug education, from Health and Human Services Secretary Donna Shalala to former drug czar William Bennett, argue that federally funded initiatives of the past 10 years contributed, at least in part, to the decline in adolescent drug taking and that cuts in federal spending led to the recent increased use. However, unlike other aspects of drug control policy, prevention or education hardly has been analyzed. Law enforcement and interdiction efforts have been the subject of debate in both the popular press and academic circles, as have treatments such as needle exchange and methadone maintenance. In contrast, prevention is simply assumed to be a laudable enterprise, and, as will be discussed later, the claims of its proponents are uncritically accepted by the press and policy makers. But is it really the case that such programs succeed? And, more particularly, did federal spending on drug-prevention activities play a role in reducing adolescent drug use over the past 10 years?

The Rise of Drug Prevention

Prior to the mid-1980s, the federal drug-prevention budget was $200 million a year or less and was concentrated in just three agencies—the Department of Defense, the Department of Labor, and the Alcohol, Drug, and Mental Health Administration, later renamed the Substance Abuse and Mental Health Services Administration (SAMHSA). By today's standards, the budgets of these agencies were modest. For example, in 1986, the Department of Defense received $85 million,[1] and the other two agencies $45 million each. Only five other federal agencies had drug-prevention budgets prior to 1986— the Corporation for National Service, the Agency for International Development, the Department of Education, the Drug Enforcement Administration, and the Federal Aviation Administration—and were generally below $10 million per annum.

The federal drug-prevention budget increased almost threefold in real terms in the final years of the Reagan administration (rising from $196 million in 1986 to $582 million in 1988).[2] Much of this was accounted for by the growth in the Department of Education budget, which rose by more than $200 million between 1986 and 1987. Over the next three years, the federal drug-prevention budget almost tripled again. Entirely new initiatives were established in the Department of Health and Human Services through the creation of the Office of Substance Abuse Prevention (OSAP) and in the Department of Housing and Urban Development (HUD). The federal drug-prevention budget peaked at just over $1.6 billion in 1992, after which it leveled off in real terms. It is this leveling off that drug-education advocates maintain helps to explain the recent reversal in the decline of reported drug use among American youth.

What Federal Dollars Buy

Data contained in the National Institute on Drug Abuse's Monitoring the Future Study—the main source for tracking adolescent drug use—and ONDCP's National Drug Control Strategy—the primary source for identifying federal expenditures across agencies and functions—enable one to assess the relationship between annual federal expenditures on drug-use prevention and the prevalence of illicit drug use among adolescents. The latter document lists agency drug-control budgets starting in 1981 for a number of broad functions, including interdiction, prosecution, and treatment. Just over 30 agencies are listed in the 1996 Strategy as having performed the function entitled "drug abuse prevention" during one or more years between 1981 and 1995, with three—the Department of Education, HUD and SAMHSA—as primary beneficiaries. Together they received more than $1.1 billion of the total $1.5 billion prevention budget in 1995.

The Monitoring the Future Study reports data on adolescent drug use from 1975 onwards. I will discuss only the twelfth-grade data, as the reports for eighth and tenth graders do not extend back to 1981 (the first year for which ONDCP data on federal expenditures are available). Specifically, I will focus on 30-day "prevalence of use" of any illicit drug among twelfth graders. Throughout the 1980s and 1990s, marijuana has been the most widely used illicit drug among this age group (about 85 percent of those reporting any drug use specify marijuana).

Examination of data contained in the two documents reveals drug use was falling steadily among young people prior to the increase in government spending that occurred in the late 1980s. By 1987, when federal spending really began to accelerate, the proportion of twelfth graders reporting use of any illicit substance had already fallen to 25 percent, from its high of 39 percent in 1979. The figure was down to 17 percent when the federal drug-prevention budget crossed the billion-dollar threshold in 1990. Between 1981 and 1992, 30-day prevalence of illicit drug use fell by three-fifths (from 36.9 percent to 14.4 percent). The rate of decline was virtually the same during years of modest federal spending (1981–1986), as during years of accelerated federal spending (1987–1991). During the former period, the average yearly growth in the drug-prevention budget was $11.5 million, with a corresponding average yearly decline in drug use of 1.7 percent. During the latter period, there was close to a 25-fold increase in the size of the average yearly growth of the prevention budget ($281 million per annum), while the average decline in drug use rose by just one-half of 1 percent per year (to 2.2 percent).

Federal budgets, of course, represent less than half of what the nation spends on policies to reduce illicit drug use, even following the huge post-1986 increase. And the level of drug use is influenced by numerous factors other than federally funded initiatives. However, the above statistics are sufficient to address the fundamental issue raised by advocates of current drug-prevention policies and programs—namely, whether a sustained level of federal funding is necessary to reduce drug use among young people. Clearly the impact is negligible. Indeed, federal spending on drug-education programs and activities might have made things worse.

At first glance, this admittedly seems unlikely. The federal budget began to increase five years before the rise in reported drug use. However, it is important to note that the agency budgets listed in the National Drug Control Strategy refer to federal appropriations, not actual spending on programmatic activity. These appropriations typically take time to filter down to the state and local level—for example, most of the Drug-Free Schools and Community funds authorized by the 1986 Anti-Drug Abuse Act were not available to local education agencies until early 1988. These agencies had then to recruit staff and to select curricula, before actually implementing their programs. Moreover, the effects of these activities on recipients' drug use would not be evident for some time, perhaps a year or two. Given this, it seems reasonable to assume that there is a lag of three to five years between the appropriation of moneys for drug-prevention programs and the manifestation of their effects on rates of adolescent drug use. Accordingly, the period of rapid federal spending, which commenced in 1987, coincides—closely in the case of a three-year lag, or exactly in the case of a five-year lag—to the period of increased drug use (1992 to 1995).

Testing the New Programs

How might federal spending on drug prevention have encouraged drug use? This is a difficult question to answer, as details on exactly how the money is spent are sparse and controlled studies of programs rare. However, an examination of school-based prevention programs—the mainstay of drug prevention in the United States—suggests why drug-prevention activities might have unintended consequences.

Prior to the mid-1980s, there existed little or no research indicating that school-based prevention was an effective means of reducing drug use among young people. Indeed, many researchers believed that such education could do as much harm as good. Writing in the *Journal of Drug Education* in 1980, Michael Goodstadt, a prevention researcher at the Addiction Research Foundation in Toronto, concluded that available evidence indicated "that 'negative' program effects were not an isolated phenomen[on], but occur frequently enough and affect self-reported behavior often enough to require more careful scrutiny." Nor was this opinion exclusively held by academics. The Second Report of the National Commission on Marihuana and Drug Abuse, published in 1973, recommended that policy makers should "seriously consider declaring a moratorium on all drug education programs in schools, at least until programs already in operation have been evaluated and a coherent approach with realistic objectives has been developed."

Opinions differed regarding why prevention efforts could produce increased drug use. Some blamed the content of the programs: Knowledge-based programs of the 1960s and 1970s simply piqued students' *interest* while the values-clarification methods of the mid-1970s confused students in that they failed to condemn drug use unambiguously. But others argued that it was the "zero tolerance" message that was at fault, insofar as it inspired incredulity and skepticism among many young people.

Despite these doubts, by the end of the 1980s, the prevailing wisdom among researchers, educators, and policy makers was that school-based programs could prevent adolescents from using drugs, providing the right type of program was used. And a growing body of empirical evidence, it was argued, demonstrated the effectiveness of a new type of curriculum, based on the principles of social-learning theory, the so-called "social-influence" approach.

Social-influence programs retained the zero-tolerance message of their predecessors—all drug use was considered harmful and wrong. In addition, however, students were now taught the social skills that were supposedly necessary to remain drug free: In some cases, the programs employed a narrowly focused approach primarily concerned with teaching drug-resistance skills; in others, a broad-based approach was used to enhance a wide range of "life skills." The former type of program, called "resistance-skills training," could be delivered in eight to 10 classroom sessions. The latter, called "social-skills training," took 15 to 20 sessions to deliver. The latter are now more popular, at least among academics and policy makers. (The technique has been applied to problem behaviors other than drug use, for example violence and teen sex.)

The programs attempt to teach "affective techniques," such as assertiveness training, self-esteem enhancement, and improved decision making. A person who possesses these skills, it is argued, is better able to cope with life and, hence, has no reason to experiment with drugs. In short, the underlying assumption is that young people who use drugs are socially incompetent. But there is little empirical evidence to support this idea. A study by Jonathan Shedler and Jack Block, researchers from the University of California at Berkeley, in the 1990 *American Psychologist*, for example, found that adolescents who engaged in experimental drug use were psychologically better adjusted than either heavy users or abstainers. Needless to say, this study is seldom cited by prevention advocates.

Moreover, at the time that it was decided to shift to the social-influence approach, there was little evidence to indicate that it was effective. In 1985, Robert Battjes of the National Institute on Drug Abuse published a paper in the *International Journal of the Addictions* which summarized the disappointing findings from evaluations of drug-prevention efforts of the 1970s and also discussed more recent evaluations of social-influence programs and their application to drug abuse in general. Gilbert Botvin, a prevention researcher at Cornell University Medical College, covered similar ground in a review published a year later in the *Journal of School Health*.

Each of these influential reviews discussed the same two studies. The first study, published in the *American Journal of Public Health* in 1979, assessed the effects of a resistance-skills training program (which lasted for eight sessions) on seventh-grade students. Students who participated in the program were compared to students (from a different school) who did not. Some 20 months after the intervention, about 8 percent of students in the intervention school reported smoking marijuana in the past week or day compared to 15 percent of the comparison group. However, since there was no baseline assessment of drug use, it is entirely possible that students from the two schools differed before the intervention was delivered. In the second study, published in *Addictive Behaviors* in 1984, seventh-grade students from four schools were randomly assigned to receive a 20-session social-skills training program delivered by classroom teachers; students from four other schools received the same program delivered by "peer leaders"; and those from two additional schools acted as controls. The results: There were significantly fewer students using marijuana in the peer-led group than in the control group, but no differences between the teacher-led group and controls.

Such findings could hardly be called compelling. The social-influence model, which was soon to be heralded as the way forward, had been tested almost exclusively on cigarette smoking, with only two published accounts describing its effects on use of illicit drugs. Yet, by 1986, the federal government would commit more than $200 million to school-based drug-prevention programs through the 1986 Drug-Free Schools and Communities Act (part of the broader 1986 Anti-Drug Abuse Act).

Limitations of Life Skills Training

Some researchers will now admit that drug-education programs do not work. They are especially willing to criticize the widely adopted DARE program. But they are quick to add that the problem is not drug education but the type of program adopted. What is needed is more federal money on "state-of-the-art" programs.

The state-of-the-art program most frequently mentioned in the popular press, as well as in academic journals is the Life Skills Training (LST) program of Gilbert Botvin. Both the *New York Times* and *Time* recently carried pieces that contrasted the research records of DARE and LST. The largest longitudinal evaluation of the LST program, the *New York Times* noted, showed that behavioral changes initiated by the program lasted the entire six years of the study. The use of cigarettes, alcohol and marijuana among teenagers who had had the program was half that of similar teenagers who had not had the program.

Both the *New York Times* and *Time* concluded that what was needed was for the LST program to be marketed and disseminated with the skill and aggression used for DARE.

The study referred to in both of these articles is a six-year follow-up of about 3,500 adolescents reported in the *Journal of the American Medical Association* in 1995. Once again, however, careful examination shows that the claims being made on behalf of the program are largely unsupported by the data presented in the article. Among all subjects for whom follow-up data were available, there were no statistically significant differences in illicit drug use between those who received the program and those who did not. Thirteen percent of LST subjects reported monthly marijuana use compared to 14 percent of control subjects; weekly use was 6 percent and 9 percent, respectively. How then does the *New York Times* report reductions of 50 percent in marijuana use?

The answer lies in the fact that the study presents an additional set of analyses based on a so-called "high fidelity" sample. To be included in this group, an individual had to receive at least 60 percent of the intervention over the three-year period during which it was delivered. As a result of this procedure, one-third of the LST group (including students from six entire schools) was removed from the study. A comparison of this refined sample of program recipients with the control subjects produced statistically significant differences. Most noticeably, the proportion reporting weekly use of marijuana was lower in the LST than in the control group—5 percent versus 9 percent. This, presumably, is the 50 percent host reduction referred to in the *New York Times* article.

As far as one can determine from the published data, the high-fidelity group represents less than half of those recruited into the intervention at the start of the project. It is a self-selected sub-sample that is no longer comparable to subjects in the control group. There are probably many drug-control activities that would appear to be effective under conditions where those who did not receive some ideal "dosage" of intervention are discounted. Moreover, the limited audience penetration obtained by the LST program—and within the context of a research project—does not bode well for its use in the "real world." In the absence of formal monitoring of program implementation and the expenditure of time and money to recruit subjects, participant retention and program fidelity would presumably be even lower.

Thus the findings from the study are hardly what the popular press and the professionals would have us believe. And unfortunately, the weaknesses of the LST programs are common in the field of drug prevention. Another key issue here is the almost total absence of independent evaluation: With very few exceptions, programs are developed, implemented, evaluated, marketed by the same group of people. Much of the research in this area has a decidedly inductive quality—its goal being to prove that the program under study is effective.

Trust but Verify

Despite claims to the contrary, available data do not support the view that the decline in adolescent drug use that occurred between the early 1980s and early 1990s was influenced by the level of federal spending on drug-education activities. Indeed, if one takes into account the fact that the effects of spending do not manifest themselves in actual behavior for at least three years, then increased spending coincided with increased drug use.

The massive increase in federal spending that occurred in the mid-1980s drew a lot of people and programs into the drug-prevention arena in an indiscriminate manner. Politicians apparently believed that there existed sufficient latent skills and expertise to put these moneys to good use—that there were school superintendents, principals, teachers, community activists, local government officials, and others who knew what effective drug prevention was and how to deliver it efficiently to those most in need. They appear to have been mistaken. A good deal of this money went to people with limited experience and expertise in drug prevention. It is thus hardly surprising that we often get more, not less, drug use as a result of these activities.

Moreover, nobody really knows what an effective drug-education program would look like. In the mid-1980s, when the federal government began to embrace the social-influence model, there was little evidence that it could reduce drug use. Recent evaluations show that programs that purport to be effective in reducing adolescent experimentation with drugs do so only when highly self-selected sub-samples are used in data analysis. Contrary to what is now being said in the popular press, these programs are unlikely to have any significant effect on adolescent drug use. There never was, and nor is there now, strong empirical evidence to show that social-influence programs can succeed where previous forms of drug-prevention activities failed.

Where does this leave us? First of all, it is imperative that we avoid the temptation to make lavish claims about other ways of dealing with teenage drug use (e.g., law enforcement, interdiction, or "decriminalization"), simply because the evidence concerning drug prevention is so weak. We need to be guided by evidence concerning the effects of a particular approach on drug use, not by what we hope its effects will be or by the assumed good intentions of those who develop and implement programmatic activities.

With regard to education, the available evidence indicates that we have yet to develop strategies that can significantly reduce illicit drug use among young people. We could almost certainly stop funding certain activities, such as school-based-prevention programs, with no adverse consequences. However, given the bi-partisan popularity of drug education, dramatic reductions in federal drug-prevention funding are unlikely to occur, at least in the near future. In the meantime, local agencies such as school boards and city councils need to establish exactly what their drug-prevention dollars are buying. They should cease funding activities that have the potential to do harm and ensure that claims concerning new, more effective programs are subject to assessment by independent observers. Until that is done no one will know whether education efforts are doing more harm than good.

NOTES

[1] Budget figures have been converted to constant 1994 dollars.

[2] Federal spending on all categories of drug-control policies increased substantially during this period as a result of two pieces of legislation—the Anti-Drug Abuse Act of 1986 and the Anti-Drug Abuse Act of 1988. The total drug-control budget rose from $3.9 billion in 1986 to $11 billion in 1990. Although the primary focus of each piece of legislation was on "supply-side" strategies (for example, domestic law enforcement and international drug control or interdiction), "demand-side" strategies focusing on treatment and prevention also expanded from this intensified federal effort.

16

Drug Courts
What Is Their Future?

Dale K. Sechrest

Introduction

The concept of the drug court is a fairly new approach to the management of substance abuse offenders in the criminal justice system. Several have been established around the county, and a First National Drug Court Conference was held in Miami in 1993 (see Travis, 1997). At the conference more than 400 judges, prosecutors, defense lawyers, and drug treatment specialists identified core elements of successful drug courts; rehabilitation was one. Drug courts, in essence, represent a coordinated response that ties drug treatment with control and possible correctional sanctions.

Burden, Roll, Prendergast and Rawson (2001) note that drug courts are an effort at all levels of government to carry out the "war on drugs." Similar to the heroin epidemic of the 1970s, the expanding crack cocaine epidemic of the 1980s and 1990s and the public's perception of it appeared to drive the drug court movement. Increases in drug usage were coupled with mandatory sentencing laws that substantially reduced judicial discretion when sentencing defendants convicted of drug-related offenses. This subsequently overloaded court dockets with drug offenders and overloaded prisons and jails. According to the Bureau of Justice Statistics (BJS), the number of adults arrested for drug-related violations increased 273 percent between 1980 and 1995, from 471,200 to 1,285,700 (BJS, 1997b). During that same period, the percentage of prisoners in the custody of state correctional authorities for

Written for *Drugs, Crime, and Justice*, 2/E.

drug offenses increased from 6.4 percent to 22.7 percent (BJS, 1997a). It seemed clear that incarceration alone did not stop substance abuse and that something else had to be done. Drug courts were seen as a panacea that not only would rehabilitate drug addicts but also would reduce costs for the criminal justice system.

The 1997 National Household Survey on Drug Abuse of the Office of National Drug Control Policy found that "77 million (35.6 percent of) Americans aged 12 and older reported some use of an illicit drug at least once during their lifetime, 11.2 percent reported use during the past year, and 6.4 percent . . . in the month before the survey was conducted" (McCaffrey, 1999, p. 1). The 1999 National Institute of Justice report on illegal drug abuse by arrestees in 27 of 34 sites found that "more than 60 percent of the adult male arrestees tested positive for the presence of at least one illegal drug, ranging from 50 percent in San Antonio to 77 percent in Atlanta" (Reno, 2000). The median rate of use for females was 67 percent, up from 64 percent from 1998 to 1999; for males the rate was 64 percent for both years. These statistics point to a substantial workload for the criminal justice system and make it abundantly clear that correctional sanctions alone have not solved the drug problem. Drug rehabilitation must be an integral part of our response to the drug problem if we are to be successful.

History of Drug Treatment Efforts

In the late 1960s, the public had become increasingly alarmed by the burgeoning drug problem in the United States. In the early 1970s, federal law enforcement agencies and the National Institute of Drug Abuse (NIDA) began developing the concept of linking treatment and the judicial process for the specific purpose of interrupting the relationship between addictive behavior and criminal activity. The result was an initiative named Treatment Alternatives to Street Crime (TASC). Program guidelines were issued, and the first TASC program opened in Wilmington, Delaware, in 1972. By 2002, there were over 130 TASC programs in 28 states. With its emphasis on diversion and strict accountability, the TASC approach began the movement toward drug courts.

An outgrowth of the movement toward treatment was the use of methadone to manage heroin addiction in the 1970s and '80s, which had some success (Sechrest, 1975, 1979). However, methadone maintenance was criticized for trying to cure drug abuse with another drug. It is still used today in several jurisdictions, especially for detoxification. The introduction of crack cocaine and methamphetamine resulted in more substance abusers and a new urgency for sound interventions. Most participants in drug courts have been polydrug users (using multiple kinds of drugs) for a significant length of time. To treat such addiction requires time, often from one to two years of close supervision and drug testing. Drug courts were seen as a means to meet the need for long-term treatment of addicts in the community, with the additional feature of close accountability through monitoring by treatment specialists.

Early attempts to manage the growing use of illicit drugs met with mixed success but did not truly address the underlying problem of substance abuse. One of the early responses was the harsh prosecution of narcotics offenders, which began in New York State with the passage of the "Rockefeller Drug Laws" of the early 1970s. The Rockefeller drug laws increased criminal penalties and changed the classification of many drug offenses to higher-level felonies. They moved drug cases from regular criminal courts to newly developed drug courts, also called narcotics courts or "N Parts," created to administer the new, harsher laws. Since these courts were designed primarily for case management, later known as "differentiated case management" (DCM), they had no treatment component (Hoffman, 2000, p. 1461). Although the overall number of offenders was not reduced, the new courts did relieve some of the overcrowding in the regular court system. Later, treatment-based drug courts also adopted the case management model to deal with the increasing numbers of cases.

A "DCM-based" treatment court began operations in Miami in 1989 (Hoffman, 2000, p. 1461) to address the impact substance abuse was having on local courts. This drug court provided a unique approach that included some key factors characteristic of modern drug courts. The court identified drug-abusing offenders early in the adjudication process and offered them immediate access to treatment under the direct and close supervision of the judge, with the assistance of drug treatment specialists, as an alternative to jail or prison (see Goldkamp, 1994). The nonadversarial nature of the court, which brought judges, prosecutors, defense attorneys, probation, and community-based treatment providers into a collaborative effort to reduce illicit drug use and related criminal behavior, helped to decrease the burden on the courts and the correctional system.

Due largely to early (primarily anecdotal) indications of success, the approach adopted by the Miami drug court became the model, with local variations, for similar drug courts established around the country. Greater numbers of participants seemed to be completing these programs more successfully than those in other diversion programs or under other forms of supervision; rates of recidivism (rearrests and new convictions) were lower, coupled with longer time periods until rearrest (Terry, 1999).

Cumulative experience and initial positive outcomes led to a surge of interest in drug courts throughout the nation; the National Association of Drug Court Professionals was formed in 1994. There are now over 500 drug courts, up from 20 in 1994; an estimated 200,000 individuals have been enrolled in various programs (Satel, 2000, p. 29). Current terminology often defines their function as delivering "restorative justice" and "therapeutic jurisprudence." Support for the growth of drug courts through federal funds for planning, development, and implementation fueled the growth (Burden et al., 2001; Belenko, 1998). "The Drug Courts Program Office . . . awarded in excess of $47 million in grants to approximately 270 different jurisdictions from 1995 to 1997" (p. ii). Proponents of the movement are staunch defenders of the ability of the programs to "reduce recidivism, respond to relapse, and reunite families, with a high degree of cost effectiveness" (Dodge, 2001, p. ii).

The primary components of the drug court model are early identification and referral of drug-involved defendants to community-based treatment (i.e., at the arrest, pretrial, or presentencing phase of the adjudication process); close integration of judicial supervision and treatment; frequent monitoring by a judge for compliance with treatment; and frequent drug testing. The drug-court model is behaviorally oriented, based on clear rules and expectations, with specific punishments imposed by the judge, using graduated sanctions for repeated noncompliance. As such, most drug courts can be characterized as contingency-management programs (see Burden et al., 2001) that rely heavily on punishment for inappropriate behavior (in contrast to the treatment procedures of behavioral psychology that place the emphasis on reinforcement for appropriate behavior).

National studies report that recidivism has been "significantly reduced" for drug-court program participants—as many as 89 percent were not rearrested in Miami after one year (Compendium Research Report, 1996, p. 1). Significant drops in drug use during program participation are also reported. Of 20 drug-court programs studied, retention rates were 60 percent, and successes were attributed to better supervision where little or none existed before (see *Court News*, 1996). Costs are in the $900 to $1,600 per participant range, which is considerably lower than detention costs and prosecution costs (discussed in the section on research).

How Drug Courts Operate

Sechrest and Shichor (2001) describe the typical sequence of events in a California drug court. Defense attorneys, probation officers, or prosecutors refer potential candidates to the drug court. Admission is limited to offenders charged with a felony drug offense, judged (using a screening instrument) to be serious drug abusers, and lawfully residing in the United States. They cannot be on parole, cannot be evaluated (using a risk-assessment screening form) as a violent gang member, and cannot have a prior serious or violent felony conviction. These criteria were developed to identify those with the highest probability of success and to relieve overcrowding.

Candidates are screened by probation officers for initial eligibility for the drug court, advised in writing of their "preliminary" eligibility, and asked if they wish to be considered for admission. If so, these "eligibles" are referred to drug-court staff for further determination of eligibility. The drug-court district attorney and public defender then review the candidate's legal and social file and upon agreement present the case to the court for a final determination of eligibility. The drug-court probation officer joins in the review to determine if the offender is, in fact, "institution bound" without program intervention.

Legal provisions require offenders charged with drug offenses to waive served time and their right to a jury trial, stipulate to drug tests, and voluntarily enter an agreement to participate in the drug-court program for a year. In the Recovery Opportunity Center (ROC) program, which is operated by Riverside County Probation Department, potential participants sign a contract that the court reviews with them in detail at arraignment. They are then ordered to undergo a 14-day initial review (screening) prior to implementing the contract for voluntary participation for one year. The California program is divided into three phases, which can vary by jurisdiction:

1. *Initial phase, 14-day review period.* Applicants are evaluated for level and scope of substance abuse, overall health, personal history (education, employment, family, social and criminal background), and financial status. During this "dropout" period either the offender or program staff may terminate participation. If termination occurs, the offender's case goes back to trial for adjudication, and a court other than a drug court hears the case.

2. *Evaluation Phase, 4 to 6 months.* Recovery Opportunity Center (ROC) team members assess participants and develop a case plan. Participants report to the ROC building (located in the City of Riverside) daily and attend drug education classes, individual and group counseling, and NA/AA meetings (Narcotics Anonymous and Alcoholics Anonymous). Program counselors use diagnostic instruments to determine participants' needs and then develop a program plan that best meets these needs. Participants submit to drug testing and attend G.E.D and adult literacy programs as well as vocational training, if appropriate. Education and treatment are the focus of these plans. Successful completion of this phase leads to regular probation supervision. Most programs use contract services on an outpatient basis for similar periods of time.

3. *Supervision Phase, 4 to 12 months.* Participants continue attendance at ROC to complete individualized case plans. (In many jurisdictions, this phase is contracted to private treatment providers.) They report to probation officers weekly, continue to submit to drug testing as well as attend NA/AA meetings, and go to drug-court review hearings that can occur as often as monthly. These hearings are conducted to determine if participants have progressed to the point that they no longer require supervision to remain drug free. Successful completion of this phase leads to graduation.

At the conclusion of phase three, participants (in most programs) are assessed to determine their suitability for graduation. Those who are ready at this stage will participate in a formal graduation ceremony, which family members and significant others are encouraged to attend.

Judicial reviews are scheduled regularly. The judge can decide to remove a participant at any time. Criteria for removal include new arrests, absconding from supervision (resulting in a bench warrant), and failure to comply with program rules specific to conduct during the program (e.g., fighting, intimidation, threats). As with most programs, it is possible for participants who commit a removal violation to get a second chance to continue in the program. At ROC, program administrators require participants to spend up to 90 days at the county's correctional facility before returning to the program.

At all times, program participants receive judicially monitored probation supervision and frequent urinalysis to guarantee abstinence; supervision ensures that participants adhere to program rules. These programs recognize that drug abuse is a serious, debilitating disorder that is not created overnight and cannot be cured without the adequate intervention of specialists. Oftentimes, drug usage is a symptom of only one of several life-skills problems. Specialist or rehabilitation practitioners recognize that some of the people they encounter are in this situation because of life circumstances. Drug addiction interdiction may very well fail if these other problems are not adequately addressed. Specifically designed programs provide training and education to help with some of the life circumstance problems.

One of the strengths of all drug courts lies in the "hands-on" approach that practitioners deliver to their clients. This "hands-on" approach sometimes goes beyond support and assistance given as part of the program. For example, the San Bernardino drug-court program staff devote volunteer hours every month in order to raise additional monies for drug-court participants. The money raised goes directly into a fund that is used to meet participants' needs. These needs may be as diverse as a form of transportation or clothes for a new infant.

Teaching participants how to be accountable for their own actions is yet another strength of drug-court programs. Participants have the flexibility within a structured program to set up their own goals and aim for their achievement. Being exposed to new and diverse opportunities, they become empowered as managers and directors of their own lives. This requires a substantial amount of counseling and support since many drug offenders do not possess the life skills to manage their daily lives. Some of the programs offered as a part of drug court include money management, anger management, and parenting skills.

The Riverside drug court described here is very similar to other drug courts across the country. For example, Miami's drug court consists of three components: (1) detoxification, (2) stabilization, and (3) aftercare. As with Riverside, the Miami state's attorney must agree to diversion to drug court. In Miami, defendants must be charged with drug possession or purchasing drugs in order to qualify. This differs from Riverside where some offenders who were arrested for trafficking can enter the program. Miami, like Riverside, has other program entry requirements including not having a conviction for a violent felony or not having more than two previous nondrug felony convictions.

Although most drug courts operate using essentially the same format, there are differences in terms of the levels and types of treatment and sanctions. Since some drug courts are expanding their selection criteria, allowing a wider range of offenders to participate, there is a need to investigate the blend of treatment and sanctions that works best for various types of clients. Goldkamp, White, and Robinson (2001) advise that we must research various treatment modalities and how they interact with or have an impact on various types of drug offenders. In other words, we should depart from any assembly-line approach and strive to match participants to programs based on projected outcomes.

Burden and his associates (2001) emphasize the importance of positive rewards or incentives. They say that many drug-court programs rely too heavily on negative reinforcement. Positive behavioral rewards, especially early in the program, may contribute to longer commitments to the program by clients and to more successful outcomes. Positive inducements certainly would give drug courts additional tools to effect change in their clients. However, the need for accountability leads inevitably to a coercive approach.

The Coercion-Accountability Argument

One of the major components of drug court treatment is the accountability required of the offender by the judge and the staff of the drug court. Sechrest and Shichor (2001) point this out, noting that cooperation between the courts and the treatment staff is the unique feature of the drug courts that may account for their success. In a very real sense, the drug court links offender accountability with the application of known techniques for treating substance abusers.

Drug court programs combine the best features of the classical approach in criminology with the positivist approach. In the classical approach, the offense is the key determining factor. The court strives to make the offender accountable for the crime (see Sechrest & Shichor, 2001). In contrast, the positivist approach strives to find the cause of the crime within the individual offender and remedy it using behavioral approaches. The drug-court structure and its representatives exercise the most control over the individual, allowing program staff to work within the limits provided.[1] When treatment staff or the courts sense that individual failure is imminent, which may be based on experience that is to some degree intuitive, public safety becomes the primary consideration, and the withheld sanction may be imposed. Due to stringent court review requirements, removal and sentencing are swift and sure.[2]

S. L. Satel (2000), a practicing psychiatrist at a Washington, D.C., clinic, has directly addressed the coercive value of the drug court. After placing the drug problem in perspective between the "drug warriors" (who seek to stamp out drugs), and the "drug legalizers" (who seek relaxed controls and some regulation), Satel addresses the problem of drug treatment within the context of accountability. He makes the case for "coerced" or "compulsory" treatment, indicating that it is more effective in terminating substance abuse and criminal careers and that it increases the likelihood of success for these individuals. Satel bases this notion on the success of other types of coerced treatment modalities, such as the federally sponsored Treatment Alternatives to Street Crime (TASC).

According to Satel, the evidence shows that treatment mandated by the courts or employers is as beneficial as programs that addicts enter voluntarily. The length of time a patient spends in treatment is a reliable predictor of his or her posttreatment performance. This performance was based on "almost any kind of treatment" beyond a 90-day threshold, after which "treatment outcomes improved in direct relationship to the length of time spent in treatment, with one year generally found to be the minimum effective duration of treatment" (p. 5). She notes also that coerced patients, such as those in TASC programs, tended to stay in treatment longer. This finding is supported by recent evidence from drug courts, which shows that between 60 and 70 percent of the participants stay in treatment for at least one year. Voluntary participants in drug programs often drop out within three months (Langenbucher et al., 1993).

It appears that coerced treatment is effective, even though research indicates that clients do not like the coerced treatment in drug courts, often preferring something less intrusive such as probation (Cresswell & Deschenes, 2001). In short, the more treatment the better, although the National Center for Drug Control Policy estimates that only half of the country's 3.5 million addicts can be accommodated by present treatment programs, thus calling into question the ability to provide more treatment. Regardless, it appears that drug courts have the ability to improve clients' performance.

Criticism of Drug Courts

There are critics of drug courts. Judge Morris Hoffman of Colorado notes that the "scandal of America's drug courts is that we have rushed headlong into them—driven by politics, judicial pop-psychopharmacology, fuzzy-headed notions about 'restorative justice' and 'therapeutic jurisprudence,' and by the bureaucrats' universal fear of being the last on the block to have the latest administrative gimmick" (Hoffman, 2000, p. 1440).

Some jurisdictions perceive drug courts as too liberal. For example, in California's San Bernardino County, there has been open hostility between the district attorney and the drug-court judge. The district attorney's office viewed the judge's placement of a substance abuser in the drug court as circumventing California's "three strikes" law, which requires 25 years to life for a third serious felony (Brooks, 1999). The judge defended his position by arguing that the offense was drug possession, and the offender had never undergone intensive long-term treatment. The judge viewed the offender as "one who only partially is within the spirit of the three strikes law" because he appeared "on the verge of overcoming drugs and crime" (p. A4). California judges are allowed to "strike a strike" or not count an offense as a strike. Prosecutors have retaliated by "papering the judge," a practice that allows them automatically to disqualify one judge in each case. In San Bernardino County, the district attorney's office is attempting to restrict judicial discretion and to undermine the drug court.

Judge Hoffman asks several important questions regarding the purpose of drug courts, their costs in relation to benefits achieved, and whether the sentencing philosophy of a single drug-court judge or group of judges should be institutionalized. The latter question relates to his concern about "judges making drug policy simply because elected officials lack the political will to do so" (Hoffman, 2000, p. 1441). He is concerned with extending the jurisdiction of drug courts from individuals involved in low-level drug possession or sales to individuals who are less likely to achieve a successful outcome, and he questions the use of limited judicial resources to have drug-court judges serving as "glorified probation officers" (p. 1439).

Saum, Scarpitti, and Robbins (2001) found that a number of drug courts are accepting clients whose criminal offenses are more severe than those recommended by the original selection criteria. They note that as drug courts accept participants with more substantial criminal records, they run the risk of not only increasing the failure rate but also adversely affecting clients who normally succeed. It is difficult and important for drug courts to identify the right "mix" of clients.

Voicing another concern, Judge Hoffman notes that the existence of the drug court in Denver has increased filings, especially for cases that would not have been filed earlier, in what he calls the "popcorn effect," defined as "net-widening" in the criminal justice system (p. 1504). Cases that previously would have been disposed of through plea bargaining, probation, or charge reduction are making their way to the drug courts. Are drug courts "creaming" participants and selecting only those cases that have a greater chance of success? If this occurs, it means that drug courts likely are focusing on those who are "minor problems" and may be treated or rehabilitated at the same success rate with conventional criminal justice sanctions.

One way to resolve these problems is for drug courts to initiate careful research on who succeeds. Historically, the decision to allow someone to enter a drug court has been more intuitive rather than scientific, where the judge, prosecutor, or probation officer use their "feelings or impressions" beyond baseline entry requirements when approving a participant. Such an intuitive process may be wrought with problems and inaccuracies. Few drug-court administrators have attempted to validate their decisions by collecting data on successes and failures.

Drug-Court Research

Drug courts are sometimes criticized as "boutique courts" that are unnecessarily specialized. Moreover, their advocates have sometimes produced success rates that seem too good to be true. Part of the problem emanated from the fact that many evaluations of drug courts were not true evaluations. Anecdotal information and case studies have been used to support drug courts. While useful in examining how drug courts operate, anecdotes and case studies seldom provide hard evidence about overall effectiveness. Comprehensive evaluation studies are required to determine the potential of drug courts for the long-term treatment of addicted offenders.

There are two criteria for measuring drug treatment program success: program retention (or graduation from the program) and recidivism. Relapse can occur but is not necessarily a cause for removal from most programs. A complicating factor is that recidivism rates are sometimes based only on program graduates and not on all admissions, which inflates the success of the drug courts.

The Drug Courts Program Office reported a general recidivism rate of 45 percent within two to three years of defendants convicted of drug possession (Roberts & Cooper, 1998). They report that recidivism for drug-court participants has ranged between 5 and 28 percent. Recidivism for graduates, however, has been as low as 4 percent and generally is substantially lower than for those who drop out of the program. Program retention rates average 70 percent (graduates and active participants). This suggests, of course, that individuals must be retained in the program to gain the higher recidivism rates.

Roberts and Cooper also found that about 90 percent of program participants had produced "dirty urines" (positive urine tests), indicating substance abuse. Urine tests revealed that both successful and unsuccessful drug-court participants had lapses and sometimes used drugs. When a participant had a dirty urine, programs sometimes used counseling, others had mandatory jail time, and still others dismissed the participant. Evidence of dirty urine is not always a cause for rejection, but it certainly must result in some program action.

The Riverside County program had an evaluation that showed a 56 percent retention rate for graduates after one year of probation (Sechrest, Shichor, Artist, & Briceno, 1998). For program graduates, 57.9 percent had no positive urine tests, somewhat below the average cited by Roberts and Cooper. However, only 25 percent of program removals had no positive urine tests. Recidivism for the Riverside County program was in the 5 to 28 percent range. Based on available Riverside County probation data and program records, 85.3 percent (87) of the 102 program admissions committed no new crime. Graduates were in the community an average of 22.3 months and were under probation supervision after graduation for 10 to 12 months. Graduates clearly engaged in less criminal activity postprogram. The two graduates who reoffended did so at 14 and 18 months, respectively.

To understand postprogram performance adequately, a study compared the 102 Riverside drug-court admissions and a group of 243 potential admissions for 1995. The comparison group consisted of arrested substance abusers who might have been candidates for a drug court, had it existed in 1995. Females and African Americans were overrepresented in the drug court; Hispanics were underrepresented . For both groups, the number of new offenses pre- and postprogram showed that offenses leading to drug court were comparable and there were no differences in the number of priors by gender, with an average of about one each. Caucasians were slightly more likely to have priors than other groups.

Fifteen drug court participants reoffended, which was 14.7 percent of all 102 admissions. In the comparison group, 25.5 percent reoffended over a period of 2.5 years. Bearing in mind that the follow-up period was more than six months longer for comparison group members, all drug-court participants showed a 20.2 percent improvement in recidivism rates over the comparison group, and graduates showed a 30.3 percent improvement over the comparison group. Moreover, those who were removed from the drug-court program fared better than the comparison group, with a recidivism rate that was 8.1 percent lower. Most important, the two graduates who did recidivate were not involved in drug crimes or violent crimes. Removals from the program were involved in possession and possession for sale (10), with two property offenders and one probation violator. These data show that drug courts can substantially reduce recidivism, even for those who drop out of the program.

Current Developments

Drug courts have shown a reasonable degree of success with a very difficult population. Other approaches may impact on the work of the drug courts. Arizona voters passed Proposition 200, the Drug Medicalization, Prevention, and Control Act of 1996, which required probation and treatment instead of incarceration for first- and second-time drug offenders. It was financed by a liquor tax. A report issued in April (1999) by the Arizona Supreme Court said that the new law had saved $2.5 million in its first year of operation. This was the difference between $16 per day for the program and $50 per day for custody. However, these results are for a smaller population than planned and require more documentation.

In California, the passage of Proposition 36, the Substance Abuse and Crime Prevention Act, has raised significant issues for the continuing existence of drug courts. The proposition, similar to the one passed and implemented in Arizona, says that nonviolent drug offenders convicted for the first or second time after July 1, 2001, will get mandatory, court-supervised treatment instead of jail (Jones, 2000). The focus is on nonviolent individuals guilty of drug possession, the very same population now managed by drug courts. The law may force prosecutors to allow more individuals into drug courts, thus changing the type of population served. Moreover, a major criticism of the law is that it will take the accountability factor away from the drug-court judge because the jail or prison sanction cannot be used unless a continuing probation violation or new crimes occur. Also, a past record of violent behavior may not be considered—only the current drug offense.

While the program is going into effect, critics in California and nationwide worry about the success of such an approach and its impact on existing drug courts. Dean Schultheiss cites Proposition 36 as a "poison pill" for drug courts. He criticizes the proposition for omitting the critical elements of supervision and drug testing. Drug offenders must be held accountable for their behavior. The California Association of Drug Court Professionals took a strong stand against the act. A major criticism is that the act eliminates the power to use short periods of jail to motivate the drug-using offender toward sobriety and sets up an adversarial relationship that defeats the "team-based, non-adversarial approach" now used by drug courts. Since passage, it also has been found that many of California's counties are ill-prepared to implement the act (Gronke & Krikorian, 2001).

Conclusions

Drug courts have been idolized and criticized. Are they as successful as they claim to be, or are they extravagant "boutique" courts that are too costly? If drug courts rely on more intensive evaluation, programming, and supervision, how can they not cost more? Do savings in "social costs" (e.g., reduced crime, welfare, and unemployment costs) balance out as gains for society? Do they widen the net of individuals brought into court? There is limited evidence in these areas. Judge Morris Hoffman ponders the implications of this major policy shift, absent the approval of elected officials, especially in the use of limited judicial resources. He laments our rush into drug courts, which he sees as being driven by unsubstantiated notions of treatment and bureaucratic fears of not using the latest administrative gimmick. He expresses the view that the most basic questions are unanswered: the purpose of drug courts, whether they work, whether their costs are worth their benefits, and whether the philosophy of a single judge should be institutionalized.

From another perspective, the issue of cost savings, mentioned by Hoffman and others, raises some interesting questions because much of the savings in incarceration costs are state prison costs, not local (county jail or probation) savings. Moreover, due to the size of the populations involved, reductions in costs to state or local correctional facilities by a small number of offenders produces marginal reductions, if any, in the costs of operating these facilities. Many proponents of drug legalization parrot such savings in corrections as a primary reason for legalization. It may be that costs are not an issue, but can drug courts ultimately reduce crime?

It is difficult to draw conclusions about the effectiveness of drug courts and to make generalizations about their future. This is due to their sheer numbers and to variations in programs, their management practices, screening policies, types of participants, staffing, local criminal justice practices, and many other characteristics of various jurisdictions. Nevertheless, the basic idea of a criminal justice alternative to traditional punishment, involving some degree of treatment under supervision for certain types of substance abusers, remains a general characteristic of these programs. The concept appears to be gaining acceptance in the broader use of drug diversion programs, even extending to the area of "DUI/Drug Courts," which is already being pioneered (Tauber & Huddleston, 1999). The degree to which the combination of punishment and treatment provided by the drug courts or similar types of courts will succeed requires further program refinements and rigorous, ongoing evaluation.

ENDNOTES

[1] This model is very close to the goals and purposes of the original juvenile court, which combined "benevolent" judges with caring treatment staff in the interests of the child.

[2] In fact, the emphasis on "public safety" may endanger the future of programs such as drug courts by restricting admissions unduly.

REFERENCES

Belenko, S. (1998). Research on drug courts: A critical review. *National Drug Court Institute Review I* (Summer,1):1–42. Alexandria, VA: National Drug Court Institute.

Brooks, R. (1999). Drug-court judge's leniency raises ire among prosecutors. *San Bernardino County Sun* 9-27-99, p. A1.

Burden, W., Roll, J. M., Prendergast, M. L., & Rawson, R. A. (2001). Drug courts and contingency management. *Journal of Drug Issues 31*(1) Winter 2001, 73–90.

Bureau of Justice Statistics. (1997a). *Correctional populations in the United States—1995* (NCJ-156241). Washington, DC: Bureau of Justice Statistics, U. S. Department of Justice.

Bureau of Justice Statistics. (1997b). *Sourcebook of criminal justice statistics 1997.* Washington, DC: Bureau of Justice Statistics, U.S. Department of Justice.

Compendium Research Report (1996). Drug courts: What's the verdict? *Corrections Compendium.* Lincoln, NE.

Court News (1996). Judges take to heart their challenging drug-court role. San Francisco, CA: Judicial Council of California, Administrative Office of the Courts.

Cresswell, L. & Deschenes, E. (2001). Minority and non-minority perceptions of drug court program severity and effectiveness. *Journal of Drug Issues 31*(1) Winter 2001, 259–292.

Dodge, M. (2001). Preface. *Journal of Drug Issues 31*(1) Winter 2001, i–iv.

Goldkamp, J. S. (1994). *Justice and treatment innovation: The drug court movement.* Washington, DC: Office of Justice Programs, U.S. Department of Justice.

Goldkamp, J. S., White, M.D., & Robinson, J. (2001). Do drug courts work? Getting inside the drug court black box. *Journal of Drug Issues 31*(1) Winter 2001, 27–72.

Gronke, A., & Krikorian, G. (2001). Study criticizes readiness for diversion law. *L.A. Times* 6-28-01, p. B1.

Hoffman, M. B. (2000). Commentary: The drug court scandal. *North Carolina Law Review 78*, 1437–1615.

Jones, Bill (2000). California Official Voter Information Guide. Sacramento: Secretary of State, 8/14/2000.

Langenbucher, J., McCrady, B.S., Brick, J. & Esterly, R. (1993). Socioeconomic evaluations of addictions treatment. NCJRS Publication No. NCJ 150474. Washington, DC: White House Printing Office.

McCaffrey, B.R. (1999, April). ONDCP Drug Policy Information Clearinghouse Fact Sheet. Washington, DC: Office of National Drug Control Policy.

Reno, J. (2000). *1999 Annual Report on Drug Use among Adult and Juvenile Arrestees.* Washington, DC: U.S. Department of Justice, National Institute of Justice.

Roberts, M., & Cooper, C. (1998). Looking at a decade of drug courts. Washington, DC: U.S. Department of Justice, Drug Courts Program Office.

Satel, S.L. (2000) Drug treatment: The case for coercion. *National Drug Court Institute Review III* (Winter,1). Alexandria, VA: National Drug Court Institute.

Saum, C.A., Scarpitti, F.R., & Robbins, C.A. (2001). Violent offenders in drug court. *Journal of Drug Issues 31*(1) Winter 2001, 107–128.

Sechrest, D. K. (1975). Criminal activity, wages earned and drug use after two years of methadone treatment. *Addictive Diseases: An International Journal* 1(4): 491–512.

Sechrest, D.K. (1979). Methadone programs and crime reduction: A comparison of New York and California addicts. *The International Journal of the Addictions 14*(3):377–400.

Sechrest, D.K., Shichor, D., Artist, K., & Briceno, G. (1998). Final research report for the Riverside County Probation Department. Technical Report.

Sechrest, D.K., & Shichor, D. (2001). Determinants of graduation from a drug court in California: A Preliminary Study. *Journal of Drug Issues 31*(1) Winter 2001, 129–149.

Terry, W.C. (1999). *The early drug courts: Case studies in judicial innovation.* Thousand Oaks, CA: Sage Publications.

Travis, J. (1997). Drug court evaluation I. *Solicitation.* Washington, DC: National Institute of Justice.

17

Correctional Alternatives for Drug Offenders in an Era of Overcrowding

Todd R. Clear
Val B. Clear
Anthony A. Braga

The antidrug movement in the United States is running on a collision course with the problem of overcrowded prisons and jails. Regardless of the sincerity with which political leadership seeks to reduce certain types of drug use, the realities of the justice system are seriously strained resources at all levels of law enforcement, prosecution and adjudication, and correctional supervision and treatment. If there is hope for the so-called war on drugs, it must be based on a realistic assessment of affordable costs.

In corrections, this means that extensive use of alternatives to traditional corrections must occur. Stated bluntly, most corrections systems in the United States are so seriously overburdened in their traditional resources of jails, prisons, and probation, that small increases in demand will constitute major management problems.

Because of strained resources, many corrections systems have experimented with new types of alternatives to the traditional forms of corrections. The purpose of this article is to explore how the "new generation" alternatives to traditional corrections are relevant for the drug offender. The article

From *The Prison Journal* 73(2): 178–198, copyright © 1993 by Sage Publications. Reprinted by permission of Sage Publications.

begins with a description of the major types of correctional alternatives currently being used around the country, followed by a description of types of drug offenders and their suitability for different forms of alternatives. Drawing from research on alternatives, a set of principles in their application to offenders is then developed. The article concludes with suggested strategies for using alternative correctional forms for drug offenders.

Major Forms of Alternatives to Traditional Corrections

Nearly every jurisdiction has experimented with one form or another of corrections alternatives in recent years. This has resulted in a rich variety of programs for offenders falling between the prison and traditional probation. A description of prototypical programs is provided below, but the reader should be aware that many versions of each of these prototypes exist, and each extant program has unique characteristics that help it fit its jurisdiction.

SHOCK INCARCERATION

One of the newest forms of correctional alternatives involves a sentence to a "boot camp" type experience (Parent, 1989). Normally, the term is short (30 to 90 days), but the experience is intentionally harsh. Offenders are put through a regimen of long days of intense physical effort under strict discipline. In some respects, the new shock programs are a throwback to early forms of imprisonment that extolled the virtues of hard work and daily discipline. The idea of these programs is to "shock" offenders in two ways: first, by removing them from the community and, second, by subjecting them to harsh, unrelenting conditions of work.

Most shock programs target first offenders—many require no prior felony convictions—and most exclude violent or previously incarcerated offenders. In addition, most programs are limited to persons under a certain age, no older than early 20s, to have young, impressionable inmates in the programs.

RESIDENTIAL CENTERS

Because prisons are so expensive to build, many urban areas have renovated existing buildings, turning them into part-time or full-time residential facilities. In many ways, these programs resemble the traditional work release center or halfway house. Part-time programs are the most common, and they allow the offender to be away during work hours and for some social time, returning to sleep at night. Full-time programs usually restrict the offender's ability to be away from the facility to only special occasions.

Residential centers normally incorporate a treatment regime into their programs. Commonly, they use group-based approaches such as "guided group interaction" to help offenders confront their lifestyles. They also commonly restrict their populations to specific target groups: probation failures, substance abusers, persons owing restitution, and so forth. This enables the treatment programs to concentrate on a more homogeneous population. With drug-involved offenders, residential centers have often used "therapeutic community" methods (DeLeon, 1987).

FINANCIAL PENALTIES

Financial penalties such as fines, restitution, and forfeitures have recently been advanced as an alternative approach to punishment. Advocates of financial penalties argue that they are particularly well suited to a capitalist society that places importance on monetary incentives and the accumulation of wealth. Not only can the fruits of crime be eliminated through monetary sanctions, but also substantial punishment can be inflicted on offenders by imposition of a financial penalty, all without the severe costs of incarceration (Hillsman & Greene, 1992).

The aim of fines and forfeitures is essentially punitive and deterrent, not reformative. The severity of a fine can even be adjusted to the seriousness of the offense and to the offender's financial circumstances taking into consideration the amount of the offender's income and assets (called the "day fine"). Some observers have argued that, potentially, fines are very different—and much fairer—than forfeitures, which can be arbitrary and disproportionate in impact.

COMMUNITY SERVICE

Community service—labor performed by the offender, generally for a public agency or nonprofit organization—has many attractive features: The person "pays back" to the offended community, all offenders are charged equally (in hours) regardless of their circumstances, and the cost is much less than prison (McDonald, 1992). Community service sanctioning programs have been successfully run in numerous jurisdictions around the United States.

One advantage of community service approaches has been that they provide a relatively efficient way to sanction repetitive minor offenders, such as misdemeanants. The cost of law enforcement for these offenders often outweighs the seriousness of their crimes, and community service can provide a vehicle for appropriate, inexpensive consequences for minor illegal activity.

CONVENTIONAL PROBATION

With caseloads often ranging from 100 to 300 offenders, most conventional probation systems do little more than monitor compliance and react to misbehavior of clients. Recently developed classification systems have allowed conventional probation supervision to focus attention on the most risky and needy clients within a caseload (Clear & Gallagher, 1983), and some research suggests that this approach can be promising with serious offenders (Markley & Eisenberg, 1987).

In many areas of the country, however, conventional probation remains a highly criticized form of correctional treatment. Some studies have shown that probationers exhibit high rates of rearrest while under supervision (Petersilia,

Turner, Kahan, & Peterson, 1985), although this appears to be less true in some parts of the country than in others (Ficher, Hirschberg, & McGaha, 1987).

INTENSIVE SUPERVISION PROGRAMS (ISPS)

One of the most popular new approaches is to intensify the level of probation (or parole) supervision given to offenders. Instead of the common practice of one or two face-to-face contacts each month, these ISPs require a minimum of two or three per week, including unannounced evening visits to the home. They also typically employ "back-up" controls of electronic monitoring and/or urine testing (described below) to augment the level of surveillance (Byrne, 1990).

ISPs differ in their offender eligibility criteria and program philosophy. Many are designed to divert offenders from incarceration, and these typically will not consider offenders convicted of violent offenses. Other ISPs target the most difficult offenders already on probation or parole caseloads, and these ISPs normally do not use exclusionary criteria (Byrne, Lurigio, & Baird, 1989). Unlike their predecessors in the 1960s, most modern ISPs are unabashedly "tough" in their stance with offenders, although a handful advertise a treatment orientation.

ELECTRONIC MONITORING

The "hottest" of the new alternatives is not a program per se but, instead, a technique applied within a program. Made possible by recent technical advances in computers and telephones, electronic monitors are devices that emit a coded signal to a receiver. When these devices are attached to the body (usually the wrist or ankle) the signal can be used to indicate the offender's whereabouts—and especially to certify that the offender is home in accordance with a curfew or court order (Schmidt, 1989).

The use of monitors is in its technical and experiential infancy, and although the early results of these programs are intriguing, there is as yet no basis to say whether they succeed. Early experiments reported considerable technical problems, although many of these problems appear to have been eradicated in revised units. They are, however, expensive, running as much as $300 per month (although most units are considerably cheaper). Many programs therefore restrict themselves to offenders who are able to pay for the equipment, those who have telephones, and those whose offenses are nonviolent.

URINE TESTING

Like electronic monitoring, urine testing is not a program but a surveillance component that can be used in conjunction with any correctional program, even incarceration. These tests not only indicate whether a person has been using a substance, but they also indicate which substances. When urine testing is done with any population, a high proportion of "hits" (indicators of substance use) is found—but this is especially true for offender groups (Wish & Gropper, 1990).

Questions have been raised about the accuracy of urine tests, but research consistently shows that when recommended procedures are followed, the test results are highly reliable. For this reason, the high level of drug use in arrested offenders (ranging across the country from 50 percent to over 80 percent) is remarkable evidence about the extensiveness of drug involvement in this population.

ANTIDOTE DRUGS

A variety of drug use suppressants exist that either reduce the desire for drugs or counteract their effects. The oldest versions are methadone, a drug that replaces the heroin urge, and Antabuse, which causes unpleasant side effects when mixed with alcohol. Both drugs have been available for decades. More recently, new drugs have been used experimentally to combat the effects of cocaine and other sources of the "high" (Anglin & Hser, 1990).

Drug use suppression is controversial. All tests of the technique find that there are limits to the success experienced in eradication of substance use—often offenders under one drug suppression regimen simply change drugs of preference (Rosenbaum & Murphy, 1984). There is also a nagging conceptual problem with using drugs to fight drugs. Nonetheless, this approach is a frequently used tool in the arsenal of drug treatment agencies, once offenders have shown a motivation to quit.

TREATMENT

Although technically, all forms of intervention with drug offenders are *treatment*, the term usually denotes mental health approaches with the aim to change the offender's lifestyle. Treatment programs for drug offenders focus on the rationalizations, dependencies, and delusional thinking that feed the addictive lifestyle. They attempt, through therapeutic interaction with others, to convince the offender of the value of the wholesale lifestyle change needed to overcome drug abuse.

Treatment Alternatives to Street Crime (TASC) is a nationwide program that specializes in working with drug-abusing offenders. The program is eclectic, using numerous techniques, from direct, random urine testing to job training, counseling, and referral. Programs vary their approaches to fit local environments, but all serve as adjuncts to probation and parole operations, using specially trained staff to work with drug users.

Narcotics Anonymous (NA) and Alcoholics Anonymous (AA) are well-established self-help programs that rely on reformed users (called *recovering*) to provide support for others interested in ending their drug use. Because the program is based on the desire of the clients to change, it is entirely voluntary (although courts will often violate this by ordering attendance). Members are aware of the games that drug users play, see through their manipulations, and challenge their co-users to sustain recovery.

In-patient drug treatment programs have become more common in recent years. These programs usually have highly structured environments in which the patient proceeds through a series of stages of treatment requiring 30 to 90 days to complete. Most programs accept nonoffenders, and all are expensive. Experts believe that follow-up treatment and support are necessary if drug abusers are to stay clean after release (Wexler & Lipton, 1985).

JAIL AND PRISON

Although these are not truly *alternatives* as the term is commonly used, short-term prison and jail stays are an important approach to be considered in lieu of longer penalties. When incapacitation is not a consideration, short prison stays are thought to provide an incentive for the offender to avoid repeat crimes. Although evidence for the usefulness of short-term prison sentences is inconclusive, many people argue that short prison sentences are as effective as long ones for most offenders, even drug offenders (Wexler & Williams, 1986).

Jail terms, by contrast, can play an important role in reinforcing compliance with alternative programs. Nearly all alternative programs have strict rules, and when these are broken, it is often inadvisable to revoke the offender and impose the full, original sentence. Short stays in the local jail of 24 to 72 hours in length can serve to confirm the importance of the program's rules for offenders who are otherwise doing well in the community.

A Drug-Crime Behavior Typology

The phrase "drug offender," when used to refer to all people who both use drugs and commit crimes, can be a misleading oversimplification. The high proportion of arrestees who have used drugs prior to their crimes is evidence that not all drug-crime relationships are the same (Fagan, 1990). The optimal use of correctional alternatives requires an understanding of the nature of drug-crime behaviors and their suitability for different types of programs. This suggests the need for a typology of offenders' drug-crime relationships. A typology would allow differential assignment of offenders to correctional programs, based on the nature of the program and the offender's crime-related drug problems.

In developing such a typology, an implicit assumption is made that the purpose of correctional intervention is to prevent or control the risk of criminal recidivism. Correctional programs are interested in the drug use of offenders only insofar as drug use relates to the potential for new criminal behavior. A typology is helpful if it identifies the different ways that drugs and crime can be related and classifies offenders according to those patterns.

Using such a typology requires caution, however. Although any correctional typology has the ultimate aim of informing action about offenders, the following typology is not about *people*, but about *events*. It posits that for drug-using offenders, their criminal events vary in the way they relate to drug use. Rather than classifying people, then, this typology attempts to classify drug use and criminal events into a logical framework.

The resulting behavior types are, in actuality, stereotypes—they fit more or less well to certain offenders. Although offenders vary in their drug-crime behavior pattern, the implication is that many offenders will exhibit a high concentration of one pattern. Stereotypes are not used merely to classify offenders but are developed to decide the kind of correctional programs that might be effective for an offender and why (Chaiken & Chaiken, 1984).

It is also important to note that a behavior will sometimes change; especially, their drug-crime behavior may evolve. Correctional strategies should be designed to inhibit the continuation of this process. Interventions should aim to prevent the habituation of illicit drug involvement for the offender's current behavioral type.

TYPES OF DRUG-CRIME BEHAVIORS

The typology recognizes that drug use and criminal behavior are two different forms of deviance, and an offender might be more, or less, committed to either. Figure 1 shows the model.

Figure 1:
A Model for Identifying Correctional Programs for Drug Offenders

		Commitment to Crime	
		High	Low
Commitment to Drugs	High	Predator	Addict
	Low	Seller	User

For linguistic ease, the stereotypes will be described for persons whose drug-crime behavior is exclusively of that type. The reader should remember our caveats stated above. There are offenders for whom a "pure type" model is simplistic, and many (perhaps most) offenders will experience a change in the drug-crime pattern of their behavior over their lifetimes. Four types of drug-crime relationships are identified. *Users* are those who have little commitment to either drugs or crime. *Addicts* are committed to drugs but not to crime. *Sellers* are committed to crime but not to drugs. *Predators* are committed to both crime and drugs. A description of the four types follows.

Addicts. The Addict has become so attached to drug use that his or her lifestyle is built around the acquisition and consumption of drugs (Ball, Shaffer, & Nurco, 1983; Hanson, Beschner, Walters, & Bovelle, 1985). Because Addicts are physically and/or psychologically dependent on the drug, their problem is to break the addiction and learn a substance-free lifestyle.

Because many drugs are expensive, many Addicts must engage in criminal activity to obtain money to support their drug use. Studies show that criminal behavior remains high during periods of drug use (Speckart & Anglin, 1986). Common forms of such criminality are burglary, small item theft, and drug sales, although middle-class Addicts will choose other types of crime and alcoholics commit crimes by driving (Goldstein, 1981). For Addicts, however, the criminal activity is not an end but a means (Mieczkowski, 1986).

Addicts need correctional approaches that force them (or enable them) to confront the circumstances of their abuse of drugs. Many treatment programs are based on this model. They use various techniques to demonstrate to the offender the consequences of drug use, including direct education, confrontive counseling, drug therapy, and interventions from friends and family (Platt, 1986). When treatment is successful with this person, the results are significant: A drug user is reformed and criminal activity is prevented (Ball, Rosen, Flueck, & Nurco, 1982).

Sellers. The essential cog in the illicit drug machine is the Seller of drugs. Among Sellers there is a hierarchy, of course, with the street salespersons occupying the lowest rung and representing the most commonly arrested type. The drug-crime connection of many of those engaged in street sales is, in fact, the Addict variety (Chaiken & Johnson, 1988).

True Sellers are involved with drugs solely (or primarily) as a way to make large amounts of money. Studies show that a small percentage of offenders arrested for drug sales or possession test negatively for drug use— these are economically motivated drug offenders engaging in business (Goldkamp, 1989). Although the business risks are high—especially in terms of the violence inherent to the drug market—the potential reward is considerable (Reuter, Macoun, & Murphy, 1990). A street Seller can make hundreds of dollars in a day; a higher-level person even more. Frequently, juveniles are used in this role to avoid processing by the adult criminal justice system.

Because the Seller has no personal commitment to drugs but has accepted the risk of crime, little drug treatment is needed. Moreover, punishment is not likely to do much good, at least for crime control. A person who is willing to risk death is probably willing to risk prison—and while he or she is incarcerated, someone else will sell in his or her place.

Users. Unlike Addicts, Users have little commitment to drugs, and unlike Sellers, they are basically noncriminal in lifestyle. These offenders use drugs periodically because they like the high. Their lives are otherwise more or less normal, but they come to the attention of the criminal justice system as a result of an instance of their occasional drug use (Zinberg, 1984).

The Users' main problem is that they are now identified offenders. Treatment may help forestall movement toward greater drug abuse, and it may provide the offender with information, but it can do little to prevent crime, because there is little crime to prevent. For most Users, the issue is to avoid creating problems through correctional programming.

Predators. Some drug-using offenders are committed to a criminal lifestyle, a lifestyle of risk and excitement, and a part of that lifestyle is extensive use of drugs (Ball, 1986). Patterns of criminal behavior will include serious, violent crimes such as rape, armed robbery, assault, and burglary—drugs are often used to generate the "courage" to commit the offense (Chaiken & Chaiken, 1990; Johnson & Wish, 1987).

For the Predator, crime and drugs are linked (as they are for the addict), but crime is not just a means, it is also an end. These criminals enjoy the thrill and fruits of criminal acts as well as the thrill of drug use.

Correctional treatment can be useful for Predators but must be undertaken with the recognition that their drug use behavior is not the central cause of criminal behavior; instead, there is a criminal orientation that needs to be overcome. Treatment will need to address both the mood-changing aspects of drugs and the criminal thought patterns and desires of the offender (Andrews, Kessling, Robinson, & Mickus, 1986).

Principles of the Use of Correctional Alternatives

Before concluding with a discussion of the strategies for using alternatives with drug offenders, it is important to summarize prior experiences with these alternatives when used on the larger body of offenders. These experiences form a framework for developing drug offender strategies.

ALTERNATIVES ARE SUSCEPTIBLE TO NET-WIDENING

The most pernicious aspect of alternatives to traditional corrections is that they frequently end up costing more tax dollars and interfering more with offenders than the programs they were designed to replace. Called *net-widening*, this means that the ultimate result of these programs is greater social control rather than reduced state involvement in cases (Austin & Krisberg, 1980). This is especially unfortunate, because these programs are normally based on the premise that they are less intrusive than traditional prison and more effective than traditional probation. Often sold as cost-effective alternatives to crowded prison systems, when these programs prove to be more expensive than the traditional system, serious questions are raised about their overall value.

There are two ways that programs widen the net. First, they may advertise that they are alternatives to prison, but instead they serve as alternatives to probation. In the typical case, judges are given authority to sentence directly to the program. Net-widening occurs when judges place borderline cases into the new programs, when most of the borderline cases otherwise would have gone to probation. The consequence is that the program is used to augment probation supervision, not to reduce reliance on incarceration. Because "new generation" programs are always more expensive than traditional probation, this means the programs fail to save tax dollars.

This problem happens in new programs when eligibility criteria are too conservative. For example, to restrict a program to nonviolent nonrecidivists, as so many of the new boot camps have done, is to invite net widening because these offenders seldom go to prison or jail anyway. To attain a diversion population, programs must be willing to accept offenders whose profiles and prior record make them likely prison candidates.

The second way that these programs can widen the net is by increasing the rate of imprisoned failures. Often, people who fail under a new program are charged an added "premium" for their failure. They receive a prison sentence of several years to make a point about the toughness of the alternative, even though their original sentence would have been much less had they not been given the alternative.

These two problems are particularly acute for drug offenders. Users seldom receive incarcerative terms. Admitting them to the alternatives is almost always going to widen the net. Addicts, on the other hand, go to prison or jail when their accompanying crimes are serious. They make good candidates for diversion, but their prognosis in these programs is problematic, although somewhat better than their prognosis in prison. Admitting them to these programs can accomplish goals of diversion and crime control, but it will guarantee a client group experiencing high levels of difficulty—dirty urines, unemployment, and so forth. Sellers and Predators are normally excluded from alternative programs by virtue of their criminal history. In short, trying to reduce prison population through diverting drug offenders requires making difficult choices.

In addition, the experience of the alternative can actually be more intrusive than prison. Intensive supervision for 18 months, with surprise home visits, urine monitoring, a 7:00 P.M. curfew, electronic bracelets, and 120 hours of community service—many offenders might consider this worse than 6 months in jail. And there is the very real question that such close control might draw a user into further difficulty with the system, even though adjustment is otherwise adequate.

The main point is that correctional alternatives are not a fail-safe way to reduce the pressure of prisons. If they are to work as true alternatives, they must be carefully designed, with eligibility criteria that are tightly drawn to guarantee true diversion from incarceration.

IT IS EASIER TO CONTAIN COSTS THAN TO REDUCE THEM

Much is made of the fact that alternatives are cheaper than traditional prison. When offenders assigned to alternatives are truly diverted from prison, they generally receive a less costly sentence. But this may not necessarily translate into cost savings. For one thing, the very best alternatives can approach the cost of prison. In-residence treatment and shock incarceration can be more expensive per day than traditional prison—they cost less only when the terms are shorter. ISPs, when truly intensive, can involve costs nearly half that of prison, and may be imposed for twice as long (McDonald, 1989).

A more difficult problem is that the total cost of running a prison is about the same when the prison is 90 percent full as when it is at capacity. The housing costs of a given prison (food and clothing) contribute insignificantly to the daily prison budget, but security needs, mostly in the form of personnel requirements, stay relatively stable within a range of capacity. (Conditions of extreme crowding will aggravate security costs, whereas closing unused units can eliminate some personnel needs.) No matter how extensively systems use their new alternatives, almost no states find they have vacant cells as a result.

Rather than reducing total systems costs, it is better to think in terms of cost containment, whereby expenditures on new facilities are avoided (or delayed) through the extensive use of less expensive alternatives. This strategy seems especially applicable to those drug offenders, in particular, addicts, who experience the system serially over their lifetimes (Ball et al., 1982). Costs of managing these offenders can be contained through careful use of layered alternatives, in which short treatment experiences are augmented by community control approaches (such as ISP). The long-term goal is desistance, which may require several years to achieve and may be accomplished through repeated use of alternatives that seem to fail in the short run. In this approach, program failure is accompanied by short-term consequences, including even short jail stays, followed by renewed attempts at treatment/ control. If this seems an unappealing strategy, it is more desirable than longer prison stays, which cost much more and have little impact on desistance.

For Predators and Users, the concept of cost containment may not be so relevant. With Predators, their procriminal lifestyle is precisely the type on which correctional costs should be concentrated. For Users, the benefits of any system expenditures should be questioned. Sellers, on the other hand, pose a dilemma. In today's atmosphere of toughness with "pushers," it is not easy to argue for cost containment. Yet research shows, first, that these offenders are quickly replaced by other sellers after their incarceration, and, second, that they have low failure rates after release. In other words, few crimes are prevented by their incarceration.

THE COSTS OF TOUGH ENFORCEMENT CAN BE CONSIDERABLE

All research on the new alternatives finds that they enforce program requirements stringently and thus have high program failure rates (Petersilia, Peterson, & Turner, 1992). This result should not surprise anyone. Offenders are not a compliant group to begin with. When they are made accountable for a large number of strict rules and then are closely monitored for compliance, they often fail. On the face of it, this seems both obvious and desirable. Closer analysis raises questions about the wisdom of a strategy of unrelenting enforcement.

The process of tough enforcement in these programs involves the imposition of costly consequences for behavior that is either noncriminal (failure to comply with curfew or failure to complete community service work) or of minor seriousness (marijuana in the urine). Imposition of an original prison term for such behavior may satisfy program directors that their requirements "have teeth," but it seems to miss the point that the program's ultimate responsibility is to prevent crime and change the offender's behavior patterns, not simply to run a tight ship. When program requirements are so strict that offenders are returned to prison for rules violations despite the absence of evidence of new criminality or impending criminal conduct, both the offender and the system lose.

This is especially likely to happen with drug offenders. Addicts will fail, and they will fail frequently. Any program built on a foundation of zero tolerance for failure will find the fully successful Addict to be in a small minority. By the same token, professionals who work with Addicts know that misbehavior must be met with consequences. The strategy is normally to impose sanctions of slowly ascending seriousness in the face of "slips" for persons thought otherwise to be noncriminal. Addicts can move up and down through phases of increased urine testing, curfews, loss of privileges (such as driving), and even short jail stays several times before they finally establish a period of sobriety that can form the foundation for recovery.

When prison is thought of as a last resort, programs take the approach of working with Addicts who exhibit motivation to stay clean, even in the face of occasional slips. The idea is to decrease the incidence and frequency of the slips and reward the offender in the process. But when reincarceration is thought of as the only consequence for misbehavior, none of this sequencing is possible, and addicts fail at very high rates.

This program is all the more difficult for Users, whose involvement in the criminal justice system is essentially a result of drug laws. To enforce packages of requirements on them in a nonnegotiable fashion is to invite failure where there would otherwise be success. For Predators and Sellers, the story is quite different. Misbehavior on the part of these offenders can be interpreted as predictive of a resumption of criminal activity. In these cases, rapid and serious consequences for noncompliance with program rules may prevent crime.

ALL ALTERNATIVES IMPOSE OPPORTUNITY COSTS

The popularity of alternatives to traditional corrections should not obscure the fact that the decision to invest in these programs ties up public dollars. It is the same for prisons—the decision to construct a prison means that dollars dedicated to that task cannot be spent on public health, schools, transportation, or other worthy public causes. The decision to develop alternatives may contain costs of traditional corrections, but that still means the devotion of tax dollars to that alternative.

From a broad perspective, the decision to expand alternatives for drug offenders may mean, for example, that noncorrectional treatment approaches receive less support. This certainly appears to have been the case since 1980, at least at the federal level of government. The appropriate public policy question is whether dollars put into correctional forms of treatment, traditional or nontraditional, pay off to the public more than dollars in noncustodial treatment or prevention. Insufficient information exists to answer this question, but it is certainly a question worth asking: If investing in prisons and special correctional programs means the decimation of mental health alternatives, is that a wise trade-off?

More narrowly, the problem of opportunity costs applies to the assignment of "spaces" to persons in alternatives programs. An ISP caseload, for example, has a capacity of 20 to 25 cases. It is better to place a burglar or a drug offender under such close scrutiny? The question is not merely rhetorical, for as the system begins to devote more attention to the problem of drugs, other types of offenders take a backseat in its priorities.

The question of the wisdom of focusing alternatives on drug offenders instead of other offenders is probably dependent on the type of offender being considered. It would appear unwise, for example, to use up the scarce resources of an ISP program on mere Users when the traditional probation caseload contains burglars, assaulters, and others representing a much more significant risk to the general public. Regardless of the public relations value of zero tolerance, there may be serious detriment to focusing such resources on relatively minor problems (and problem makers). By contrast, when Predators are released from prison, it would seem wise to give them the closest control available (ISP with electronic and urine monitoring, for example) instead of traditional parole. Yet many of the alternative programs specifically exclude the latter and seek the former, advertising themselves as "fighting drugs." When this occurs, there are substantial opportunity costs in the misapplication of risk management resources in correction.

Four Strategies for Effective Use of Alternatives with Drug Offenders

A clearer understanding of the types of alternative programs available and the types of offenders to be assigned to them helps put the usefulness of alternatives into perspective. The following discussion should not be taken as a recommendation for prison in cases where no other program seems to make sense. With the exception of some Predators, no consistent evidence can be found that prison is a preferable program placement to lesser alternatives for any drug offenders. Failure rates of drug offenders in most programs are high, but failure rates after prison are just as high and may be higher. Instead, the aim should be to put the use of alternatives into a perspective that both reflects evidence about their suitability and resists overreliance on them and unrealistic expectations of them.

DRUG OFFENDERS SHOULD BE ASSIGNED TO PROGRAMS THAT FIT THEIR DRUG-CRIME BEHAVIOR

Alternatives are not equally suitable for all drug offenders. Drug offenders vary in their manageability, their risk to the community, and their compunction to commit crimes. Using the typology described earlier, program recommendations can be made reflecting the fit between the program's ordinary capacity and the drug offender's needs. A summary of such suitability is presented in Table 1.

Predatory offenders appear well suited for several of these programs, especially intensive supervision and the close control inherent in residential programs and urine monitoring (Anglin & Hser, 1990). For the most part however, Predators are not suitable subjects for diversion into these programs, for they are strong candidates for incarceration in the first place. After incarceration, Predators benefit (and the community can be protected) by the close supervision in these alternatives programs (Wexler, Lipton & Johnson, 1988).

Addicts also fit intensive alternatives well, especially when control-oriented approaches are closely coupled with treatment interventions (Anglin, 1988). Conventional probation is seldom useful for long-term Addicts. Shock approaches also appear inadvisable, because the addict's drug use is not easily susceptible to deterrence through threats. The main aim of programs for Addicts is to lengthen the periods of drug-free street time. Total abstinence is usually seen as an unreasonable goal (Wexler & Lipton, 1985).

Table 1: Fitting Drug Offenders to Appropriate Correctional Alternatives

Type of Correctional Alternative	Type of Offender			
	Seller	*Addict*	*Predator*	*User*
Shock incarceration	−	−	−	0
Residential programs	0	+	+	0
Intensive supervision	+	+	+	0
Electronic monitoring	0	0	+	−
Urine testing	−	+	+	−
Drug suppression	−	+		0
Treatment programs	−	+	+	+

+ = Suggested as appropriate by research and theory.
0 = No research or theory to support this option.
− = Research or theory suggests this option is inappropriate.

Users, by contrast, might benefit from treatment approaches, but the heavy control approaches are liable to be counterproductive by forcing the User deeper into the criminal justice system, should there be noncompliance with program rules (Petersilia, 1987; Petersilia & Turner, 1990). For many Users, fines, community service, and conventional probation are enough to deter.

Sellers can be managed in the context of intensive supervision but are not likely to do well in other strategies. Residential programs provide an audience of potential consumers; shock approaches are unlikely to deter, given the financial incentives of the drug business. Some have argued that fines and forfeiture help to remove the financial incentives for the drug business and thus are relevant to the Seller (Cole, Mahoney, Thornton, & Hanson, 1987).

These general strategies are suggested with caution. The research on program effectiveness with drug offenders is scanty at best, and few of the studies attempt to isolate the interaction effects proposed here. The type of research needed in this area is illustrated by a RAND study that attempted to classify offenders in an ISP experiment according to the model we have proposed. Overall, offenders did no better on ISP than on regular probation (in fact, evidence suggested they may have done worse under the ISP option). However, Users had a 50 percent higher (nonsignificant) arrest rate under ISP as compared to regular probation, consistent with the model (Deschenes, Turner, & Petersilia, 1992). (There was no difference for the other three types—a result perhaps due to small sample size, the pure control nature of the program, and the limited ability to classify offenders, post hoc.)

EXPECT HIGH RATES OF FAILURE; PREPARE PROGRAMMING OPTIONS

With the exception of users, drug offenders fail at high rates in any program placement, including prison (Wish & Johnson, 1986). Working with these offenders requires a large number of options and schedules of reinforcement, with the ability to intensify or reduce controls in small increments as justified by the offender's behavior.

One implication of this caution is that if these programs are working well, they will have lots of action in relation to offenders' conduct. Programs with low failure rates are probably either lax in enforcement or are drawing too heavily from user populations that would produce high success rates.

Because alternative programs have high levels of enforcement action, they require a special type of staff and unusually consistent support from the courts. Staff need to be professionally trained and well experienced with drug users' special problems. Their expectations should be realistic, and their patience (grounded in firmness) should enable them to have credibility with the offenders they see. Courts need to encourage latitude in working with offenders, supporting approaches that maintain consistent programs of consequences. There is always a temptation to "do treatment" from the bench, but courts should resist the desire to innovate on an ad hoc basis because this usually undercuts the logic of a program.

The larger the number of alternatives, the better. It makes good public relations to present programs as "tough last stops before prison," but if this is the way the programs operate, they will be irrelevant to many drug users. Prison is a necessary option in the enforcement spectrum, especially for criminally active addicts, sellers, and predators, but its benefits are often overstated. Eventually, offenders are released, and drug programs have to begin with the progress made earlier on the street.

One way to view this system of approaches is to see traditional probation and prison as the "bookends" of a spectrum of available interventions. Strict enforcement requires that misbehaving drug users be moved off traditional probation relatively easily into nontraditional approaches but should encounter prison only as a last resort (except for Predators), and perhaps only for short periods. Offenders moving out of the courts (at sentencing) and out of prison (onto parole) should be placed initially in the approach that best fits their circumstances, not the one that has available space or is currently popular.

THERE ARE NO "PURE" TYPES AND NO "PERFECT" PROGRAMS

It goes without saying that complexity underlies any system of dealing with drug offenders, and so no perfect solution exists. In fact, many sellers are involved in other predatory crime (Spunt et al., 1987); many users stand on the brink of addiction and sell drugs to a small circle of friends (Biernacki, 1986). The drug offender types provide a heuristic device to analyze the problem, the program prototypes display general programs, but there is much overlap among them in practice (Chaiken & Johnson, 1988).

In the real world, the best program fit for an offender will not always be obvious, and all programs will have idiosyncratic strengths and weaknesses, often due to unique staff configurations. Predators will sometimes do quite well in response to an electronic monitoring program; users will occasionally fail miserably on traditional probation.

The term used to describe this situation is *technical uncertainty*—it means that the technologies for working with drug offenders are unpredictable in their outcomes. Because technical uncertainty produces frustrations for staff and system decision makers, there is a constant temptation to perceive alternatives to traditional corrections as ineffectual. The usual choice in the face of frustration is incarceration. Imprisonment has the advantage for decision makers of disengaging the decision from the feedback about its effectiveness. When drug offenders recidivate after imprisonment, it is unusual for the judge or the prosecutor to admit it was the wrong choice, even though they will be quick to do so after a similar failure under an alternative program.

If there is a secret in dealing with drug offenders, it is creative persistence with individually scripted strategies. Imprisonment has a role, but it will ultimately prove frustratingly ineffectual unless it is used appropriately in response to the right offenders and in the right situation.

FOCUS ON THE GOAL OF REDUCING THE PAINS OF DRUGS

In recent years, the American public has become increasingly sensitized to the harmful effects of drugs. There are many: Criminal networks, criminal acts, physical side effects, unsafe streets and lost lives are among them. These problems have fueled the war on drugs (Inciardi, 1992).

There are also harmful effects, just of the war itself. Sending people to prison seldom improves their life chances and is almost never intended to do so. When youngsters enter the criminal justice system, they face long odds of overcoming the negative impact of a record and the affiliations produced in processing their case. Removing men and women from their families can be permanently damaging to children and to their family units. Whole neighborhoods become dominated by definitions of deviance, lawbreaking, and avoiding "the man"—this changes the meaning of "growing up." In the pressure to respond to the problem of drugs, families are uprooted from public housing, draconian penalties are handed out, and irretrievable resources are committed to the problem. Almost no proposal is seen as too excessive. It is hard, sometimes, to know if the cure is more painful than the disease.

It is time to admit that a drug-free society is not now and never was a realistic aim. Whether or not it is good rhetoric, the desire for zero tolerance has fed a zealousness that overwhelms the realities of modern, urban America. A much more realistic and realizable goal must replace this unrealistic vision. The purpose of correctional intervention is to prevent crimes where possible, reduce harms to families and communities where feasible, and take reasonable steps to encourage and assist offenders to forgo drug use and related criminal activity. The aim is to reduce, in small measures, the pain experienced by all citizens, offenders and others alike, resulting from drugs in America.

REFERENCES

Andrews, D., Kessling, J., Robinson, D., & Mickus, S. (1986). The risk principle of case classification: An outcome evaluation with adult probationers. *Canadian Journal of Criminology, 28*, 377–396.

Anglin, D. (1988). The efficacy of civil commitment in treating narcotic addiction. In C. Leukefeld & F. M. Tims (Eds.), *Compulsory treatment of drug abuse.* Rockville, MD: National Institute on Drug Abuse.

Anglin, D., & Hser, Y. (1990). Treatment of drug abuse. In M. Tonry & J. Q. Wilson (Eds.), *Drugs and crime.* Chicago: University of Chicago Press.

Austin, J., & Krisberg, B. (1980). *The unmet promise of alternatives to corrections.* San Francisco: National Council on Crime and Delinquency.

Ball, J. C. (1986). The hyper-criminal opiate addict. In B. D. Johnson & E. Wish (Eds.), *Crime rates among drug abusing offenders* (Final Report to the National Institute of Justice). New York: Narcotic and Drug Research, Inc.

Ball, J. C., Rosen, L., Flueck, J., & Nurco, D. (1982). Lifetime criminality of heroin addicts in the United States. *Journal of Drug Issues, 3*, 225–239.

Ball, J. C., Shaffer, J., & Nurco, D. (1983). The day-to-day criminality of heroin addicts in Baltimore: A study in the continuity of offense rates. *Drug and Alcohol Dependence, 12*, 119–142.

Biernacki, P. (1986). *Pathways to addiction.* Philadelphia: Temple University Press.

Byrne, J. (1990). The future of intensive probation supervision and the new intermediate sanctions. *Crime & Delinquency, 36*, 6–41.

Byrne, J., Lurigio, A., & Baird, C. S. (1989). *The effectiveness of the new intensive supervision programs* (Research in Corrections, No. 5). Washington, DC: National Institute of Corrections.

Chaiken, M., & Chaiken, J. (1984). Offender types and public policy. *Crime & Delinquency, 30*, 195–226.

Chaiken, J., & Chaiken, M. (1990). Drugs and predatory crime. In M. Tonry & J. Q. Wilson (Eds.), *Drugs and crime.* Chicago: University of Chicago Press.

Chaiken, M., & Johnson, B. (1988). *Characteristics of different types of drug involved offenders.* Washington, DC: National Institute of Justice.

Clear, T., & Gallagher, K. (1983). Screening devices in probation and parole: Management problems. *Evaluation Review, 7*, 217–234.

Cole, G. F., Mahoney, B., Thornton, M., & Hanson, R. (1987). *Attitudes and practices of trial court judges toward the use of fines.* Denver: Institute for Court Management.

DeLeon, G. (1987). Alcohol use among drug abusers: Treatment outcomes in a therapeutic community. *Alcoholism Clinical and Experimental Research, 11*, 430–436.

Deschenes, E., Turner, S., & Petersilia, J. (1992). *The effectiveness and costs of intensive supervision for drug offenders* (Working paper). Santa Monica, CA: RAND.

Fagan, J. (1990). Intoxication and aggression. In M. Tonry & J. Q. Wilson (Eds.), *Drugs and crime.* Chicago: University of Chicago Press.

Ficher, M., Hirschberg, P., & McGaha, J. (1987). Felony probation: A comparative analysis of public risk in two states. *Perspectives, 11*, 6–11.

Goldkamp, J. (1989, March). *The effectiveness of drug testing in the courts.* Paper presented to the Conference on Drugs and the Courts, Denver, CO.

Goldstein, P. (1981). Getting over: Economic alternatives to predatory crime among street drug users. In J. Inciardi (Ed.), *The drugs/crime connection.* Beverly Hills: Sage.

Hanson, B., Beschner, G., Walters, J., & Bovelle, E. (1985). *Life with heroin: Voices from the inner city.* Lexington, MA: Lexington Books.

Hillsman, S., & Greene, J. (1992). The use of fines as an intermediate sanction. In J. Byrne, A. Lurigio, & J. Petersilia (Eds.), *Smart sentencing: The emergence of intermediate sanctions.* Newbury Park, CA: Sage.

Inciardi, J. (1992). *The war on drugs II.* Palo Alto, CA: Mayfield.

Johnson, B., & Wish, E. (1987). *Criminal events among seriously criminal drug abusers* (Final Report to the National Institute of Justice). New York: Narcotic and Drug Research, Inc.

Markley, G., & Eisenberg, M. (1987). *Evaluation of the Texas parole classification and case management system.* Austin: Texas Board of Pardons and Paroles.

McDonald, D. (1989). *The cost of corrections* (Research in Corrections, No. 4). Washington, DC: National Institute of Corrections.

McDonald, D. (1992). Punishing labor: Unpaid community service as a criminal sentence. In J. Byrne, A. Lurigio, & J. Petersilia (Eds.), *Smart sentencing: The emergence of intermediate sanctions.* Newbury Park, CA: Sage.

Mieczkowski, T. (1986). Geeking up and throwing down: Heroin street life in Detroit. *Criminology, 24*, 645–666.

Parent, D. (1989). *Shock incarceration: An overview of existing programs.* Washington, DC: National Institute of Justice.

Petersilia, J. (1987). *Expanding options for criminal sentencing.* Santa Monica, CA: RAND.

Petersilia, J., Peterson, J., & Turner, S. (1992). *Intensive probation and parole: Research findings and policy implications* (Working paper). Santa Monica, CA: RAND.

Petersilia, J., & Turner, S. (1990). Comparing intensive and regular supervision for high-risk probationers: Early results from an experiment in California. *Crime & Delinquency, 36*, 87–111.

Petersilia, J., Turner, S., Kahan, J., & Peterson, J. (1985). *Granting felons probation: Public risks and alternatives.* Santa Monica, CA: RAND.

Platt, J. (1986). *Heroin Addiction: Theory, research and treatment* (2nd ed.). Malabar, FL: Krieger.

Reuter, P., Macoun, R., & Murphy, P. (1990). *Money from crime.* Santa Monica, CA: RAND.

Rosenbaum, M., & Murphy, S. (1984). Always a junkie? The arduous task of getting off methadone maintenance. *Journal of Drug Issues, 3,* 527–552.

Speckart, G., & Anglin, D. (1986). Narcotics use and crime: A causal modeling approach. *Journal of Quantitative Criminology, 2,* 3–28.

Schmidt, A. (1989). Electronic monitoring of offenders increases. *NIJ Reports,* 212, 2–5.

Spunt, B., Goldstein, P., Lipton, D., Belluci, P., Miller, T., Cortez, N., Kahn, M., & Kale, A. (1987, November). *Systemic violence among street drug distributors.* Paper presented at the annual meetings of American Society of Criminology, Montreal, Canada.

Wexler, H., & Lipton, D. (1985, November). *Prison drug treatment: The critical ninety days of re-entry.* Paper presented at the annual meetings of the American Society of Criminology, San Diego, CA.

Wexler, H., Lipton, D., & Johnson, B. (1988). *A criminal justice strategy for treating drug offenders in custody.* Washington, DC: National Institute of Justice.

Wexler, H., & Williams, R. (1986). The Stay N' Out therapeutic community: Prison treatment for substance abusers. *Journal of Psychoactive Drugs, 18,* 221–230.

Wish, E., & Gropper, B. (1990). Drug testing by the criminal justice system: Methods, research, and applications. In M. Tonry & J. Q. Wilson (Eds.), *Drugs and crime.* Chicago: University of Chicago Press.

Wish, E., & Johnson, B. (1986). The impact of substance abuse on criminal career. In A. Blumstein, J. Cohen, J. A. Roth, & C. Visher (Eds.), *Criminal careers and "career criminals"* (Vol. 2). Washington, DC: National Academy Press.

Zinberg, N. (1984). *Drug, set, and setting.* New Haven, CT: Yale University Press.

Section
VI

PERSPECTIVES ON
THE DRUG PROBLEM

18

Drugs in Schools
Myths and Realities

Peter J. Venturelli

Drugs? Yeah, I do drugs a lot. My friends, we chill out together a lot and every time we share what we have [referring to licit and illicit drugs]. Sometimes, Joe shares his weed with us; other friends of mine bring some liquor from home; and some of us have cigarettes that we share. On other nights, mostly right after school and before going home for dinner ([for] those of us that even go home for dinner) or even after dinner for a few hours before curfew, we just get high and drive around cruising. We try to pick up chicks and party with them. A lot of my friends go to school high in the morning or during lunchtime, then the rest of the day just goes real fine. (From an interview with a male high school junior, aged 16, in a smaller midwestern city, 12 June 1998)[1]

Given that a drug is "any substance that modifies body functions," when commentators talk about drug use or abuse, they are really referring to the more restrictive pharmacological definition that identifies substances that modify the central nervous system by altering consciousness and/or perceptions (Hanson and Venturelli 1998, 5).[2] Moreover, when talking about drugs in schools, they are likely talking about the distribution, availability, and use of illegal forms of such mind-altering substances. In terms of use rates, the most frequently used drugs ("ever used") by eighth through twelfth graders are listed in Table 1. Excluding legal drugs that are illegal for youths, the

From *Annals of the American Academy of Political and Social Science* 567:72–78, copyright © 2000 by Sage Publications. Reprinted by permission of Sage Publications.

mind-altering effects of the first five of the drugs listed are used basically to create euphoria, to relax, and to alter perceptions—that is, to feel good and to escape.

Table 1
Ranking of Drugs Most Frequently Used

Drug Type	Slang Name	Percentage Who Ever Used			Effect
		Eighth Graders	Tenth Graders	Twelfth Graders	
1. Alcohol	Booze, juice, brew	55	71	81	Relaxation, impaired coordination
2. Tobacco	Cigarettes, smokes	46	58	64	Relaxation
3. Marijuana	Dope, weed, hash, gold, joint, buds	20	34	42	Relaxation, euphoria
4. Inhalants	Huff, rush, poppers	22	19	17	Relaxation, euphoria, violence
5. Stimulants	Uppers, bennies, speed, crystal meth	13	17	15	Excitation, restlessness, anxiety
6. Hallucinogens	Mushrooms, shrooms, buttons	5	9	13	Altered senses, distorted perception, reduced inhibitions, euphoria, relaxation
7. LSD	Acid, trip, tab, blotters, gel, microdots, purple haze, white lightning	4	8	12	Altered senses, distorted perception, reduced inhibitions, euphoria, relaxation
8. Tranquilizers	Downers, barbies, tanks, goofballs	5	6	7	Relaxation, stress relief, sleep
9. Cocaine	Snow, coke, crack, stardust, Big C	4	5	6	Euphoria, exhilaration, restlessness, excitation
10. Steroids	Droids	2	2	2	Stimulated tissue mass
11. Heroin	Horse, sugar, junk, smack, China white	1	2	2	Euphoria, relaxation, insensibility, stupor, decreased coordination

SOURCES: Adapted from Hanson and Venturelli 1998, 9, 449; U.S. Department of Justice 1998b, 239.

Extent and Trends of Drug Use

The long-term data show that drug use consistently declined from 1980 to 1992. The data on recent illicit drug use (for the drugs mentioned in Table 1 excluding alcohol and tobacco) show that between 1988 and 1995, for all age groups, "use in the past year" declined annually. "Use in the past month" declined through 1992 and increased slightly in 1994 and again in 1995, although still not to its 1988 levels (Hanson and Venturelli 1998, 11). However, the data also indicate that, for youths aged 12 to 17, overall drug use in the preceding year increased from a low of 11.7 percent in 1992 to 18.0 percent in 1995, higher than it had been at any time in the previous seven years; whether drugs had "ever [been] used" and "use in the past month" by this same group showed the same trends. Overall, drug use—along with alcohol and cigarette use—is occurring among an increasingly younger population of children (Drug Strategies 1996, 2–3).

This pattern continued between 1995 and 1998. Indeed, "the number of current illicit drug users did not change significantly from 1995 (12.8 million) to 1996 (13 million)" (U.S. Department of Health and Human Services, NIDA 1999). However, "between 1996 and 1997, current illicit drug use increased significantly for youth age 12 to 13, rising from 2.2 to 3.8 percent" (U.S. Department of Health and Human Services, SAMHSA 1998b). The trend was true in general and for particular drugs such as cocaine, marijuana, and LSD. For cocaine, "the rate of new use among youth age 12–17 increased from 4.0 in 1991 to 11.3 in 1996. The age-specific rate of first use of cocaine among youth was at its highest level in 30 years" (U.S. Department of Health and Human Services, NIDA 1998). Marijuana use, which declined every year from 1978 to 1991 among young people, has doubled over the past few years. There was a similar growth in hallucinogen use: "In 1996, there were an estimated 1.1 million new hallucinogen users, approximately twice the annual average observed during the 1980s. The rate of initiation among youth age 12–19 increased between 1991 and 1996 from 11.7 to 25.8 per thousand potential new users" (U.S. Department of Health and Human Services, NIDA 1998). A large proportion of recent heroin initiates are young and are smoking, sniffing, or snorting heroin. Ninety percent were under the age of 26, and only 46 percent had never injected heroin (U.S. Department of Health and Human Services, SAMHSA 1998b, 27). As an indication of the recent pattern of increase in drug use, Figure 1 shows the trends in marijuana and LSD use by eighth, tenth, and twelfth graders.

"In 1997, 11 million current drinkers were age 12 to 19. Of this group, 4.8 million, or more than 40 percent, engaged in binge drinking, including 2.0 million heavy drinkers" (U.S. Department of Health and Human Services, SAMHSA 1998b). Indeed, a lifetime prevalence of alcohol use alone was 81.7 percent for twelfth graders in 1997 (U.S. Department of Health and Human Services, SAMHSA 1998b, 21). Importantly, as was seen in Table 1, alcohol and cigarettes are the main psychotropic substances used by youths. Consumption of them has increased in recent years: "For youth age 12 to 13, there was a significant increase in the rate of current use of cigarettes from 7.3 percent in 1996 to 9.7 percent in 1997" (U.S. Department of Health and Human Services, SAMHSA 1998b, 23).

With regard to gender differences, the percentages of male and female drug use are approximately equivalent from the ages of 12 through 17 in the "ever used," "used in the past year," and "used in the past month" time periods. However, from ages 18 through 25, males significantly outnumber female drug users. More males have ever used illicit drugs (50.3 percent) than have females (40.4 percent). If these percentages reflected alcohol, tobacco (including smokeless tobacco), and steroids, they would be much higher (see Table 2).

Figure 1
Drug Use Trends for Eighth, Tenth, and Twelfth Graders, 1991–97: Marijuana and LSD

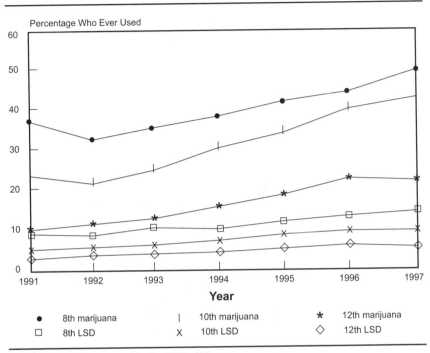

SOURCE: U.S. Department of Justice 1998b, 239.

Table 2
Illicit Drug Use by Gender, Ages 12–17 and 18–25, 1997

	Percentages (Estimated) Who Used Drugs		
Age and Gender	Ever used	Used in the past year	Used in the past month
12–17			
All	23.7	18.8	11.4
Male	24.3	18.9	12.3
Female	23.2	18.6	10.6
18–25			
All	45.4	25.3	14.7
Male	50.3	30.8	19.6
Female	40.4	19.7	9.6

SOURCE: Adapted from U.S. Department of Health and Human Servics, SAMHSA 1998b, 73, 82, 88, and 89.

For specific ages, illicit drug use has increased from 1996 to 1997. Rates of drug use show substantial variation by age. Among youths 12 to 13 years of age, 3.8 percent were current illicit drug users. The highest rates were found among young people 16 to 17 years of age (19.2 percent) and 18 to 20 years of age (17.3 percent) (U.S. Department of Health and Human Services, SAMHSA 1998b, 11). In Figure 2, we see that for both time periods (past year and past month) for 1996 and 1997 and in all age categories, those using illicit drugs increased their usage of those drugs.

In summary, we can see that, since 1992 and particularly since 1996, use of illegal substances by American youths has increased. Interestingly, however, victimization data from students' reports of drug availability in the schools in 1995 showed little increase over the 1989 data (see Figure 3).

Figure 2
Youths Reporting Illicit Drug Use During the
Past Month or the Past Year, 1996–97

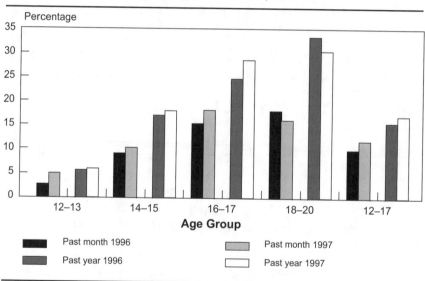

SOURCE: U.S. Department of Justice 1998a.

Myths and Realities

Given the criminalization of the drug problem in the United States, and the related hysteria that surrounds the idea that youths are imbibing substances that change their minds and bodies, it is not surprising that information becomes distorted. While there are numerous debates about the harmful effects of long-term, habitual substance abuse (see Hanson and Venturelli 1998; Venturelli 1994), there are also several myths that have arisen about drug use, drug users, and the legal response to the putative drug problem in the United States. These myths generally tend to be exaggerations based upon fear of what might happen. As Pfuhl and Henry (1993) say,

Figure 3
Drug Availability in Schools, 1989 and 1995,
Students Aged 12–19

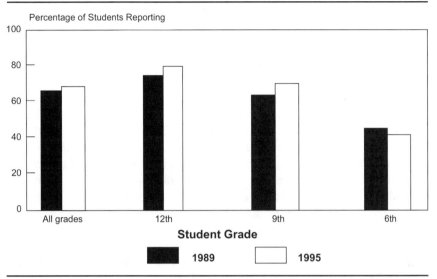

SOURCE: U.S. Department of Justice 1998a.

The concepts of *myth* and *legend* refer to the usually apocryphal, but believable tales, stories, and accounts that help people make sense of (i.e., explain, interpret, justify) the stuff of everyday life. . . . They also deal with "evildoers" whom they portray as opposed to the legitimate values embraced by the community, and persons who intentionally or otherwise undermine the vitality of fundamental moral precepts and institutions. (98)

Here I draw on social science research literature in order to place some of the myths about drug use in perspective. I will first look at myths surrounding the effects of drug use on behavior and then at myths about the impact of antidrug campaigns.

MYTHS ABOUT DRUGS AND BEHAVIOR

Lindesmith (1940) termed the folklore that surrounded drug users the "'dope fiend' mythology." This mythology portrays users of illegal mind-altering substances as discreditable individuals who are prone to violence, as in the terms "dope-crazed killer" and "dope-fiend rapist" (Brunvand 1984, 62–69). Cohen (1980) described the phenomenon in which specific groups of people are designated as "folk devils" and are held accountable for a particular problem in society, such as a "moral panic." As Goode (1999) says, "We often 'panic' about how widespread the use of a given drug is or what its effects are. Sociologists refer to a 'panic' or 'scare' when fear of and concern about the use of a given drug [are] far greater than what a systemic, empirical scrutiny of the situation could sustain" (20). Drug legislation, such as the 1914 Harrison Act and the anti-marijuana legislation of the 1930s, was fed by the fear of immigrant groups and the myths that surrounded their use of drugs. Thus the perceived harm that drugs cause becomes exaggerated and politicized by legislators, the media, and law enforcement.

Myth 1: Drug use causes violence. While there is ample evidence that drug use is associated with higher rates of illegal activity, this fact alone does not establish a causal relationship between the two (Osgood 1985, 1). Individuals predisposed toward drug use may be the same individuals who are predisposed toward any illegal behavior—including violence—quite apart from any consequences of drug use itself (Osgood 1985, 2; Webb and Delone 1995). Indeed, hundreds of thousands of people routinely use drugs without ever committing a single property crime, much less an act of violence. In his analysis of the drug-crime connection, Osgood (1985, 5) found no evidence of any influence of the specific features of one behavior on another behavior, such as an influence of current drug use on later illegal behavior.

The recent spate of suburban school violence is even less likely than street crime to be related to drug use by the perpetrators. As for schools in large urban areas, the violence associated with drugs stems more from turf battles between police and drug dealers, and between drug dealers battling to control lucrative markets, than from the chemical effects of drugs themselves (Donziger 1996, 119).

Overall, our current criminal justice policy that declares a "war on drugs" has only increased the violence associated with drug markets. America's disastrous lesson with Prohibition should remind us that the use of alcohol and drugs is an important part of our culture. Efforts to reduce addiction by prohibiting the use of either are destined to fail and tend to compound the problem. In fact, the continuing failure of drug prohibition could be described as worse than the failures of earlier attempts to use the criminal law to control alcohol use, gambling, and abortion (Martin 1997, 107). The "war on drugs" as currently pursued is analogous to putting out a fire with gasoline; it has been seen by some as the real violence associated with drugs (Johns 1992).

Myth 2: Most drug users graduate from soft to hard drugs. A second myth surrounding drug users' behavior concerns the fear of contagion, namely, that drug users have a mania to convert others into users and, relatedly, that drug use is insidious: "even using mild drugs allegedly results in an inevitable progression to the use of stronger drugs" (Pfuhl and Henry 1993, 99). This progression in the use of drugs is known as the gateway concept.

Research using participant observation, interviews, and ethnographic techniques reveals consistently that most drug users set limits on which type of drugs (marijuana as opposed to prescription drugs, for example) they will use regularly; most avoid certain drugs altogether; and only a minority gravitate to stronger or more addictive drugs.[3]

Myth 3: Drinking alcoholic beverages leads to alcoholism. Findings show that "approximately 111 million persons or 52 percent of all Americans aged 12 or older drank in the last month" (Hanson and Venturelli 1998, 200). Yet only 10 percent became alcoholic. Obviously, while 10 percent of 111 million Americans does produce a sizable number of alcoholics, 90 percent are neither alcoholic nor violent.

MYTHS ABOUT ANTIDRUG MEDIA CAMPAIGNS

America's "war on drugs" and its tough zero-tolerance policies have been claimed to be the right approach to dealing with the use and abuse of drugs. Particularly significant in this war is the claimed value of media antidrug campaigns.

Myth 4: Media campaigns and drug education programs have the potential to reduce adolescent drug use. Unfortunately, after considerable effort on antidrug media campaigns, available statistics regarding the extent of drug use clearly show that, for many drugs of abuse, the percentage using has not been significantly altered. In fact, as we saw earlier, for most drugs abused by youths, the percentage of drug users has been increasing. Researchers find that drug education and media campaigns have very little effect on habitual users of illicit-type drugs (Lenson 1995; Goode 1999). This is reflected in the comments of one interviewee:

> Yes, I have watched commercials against drug use, especially the one where an egg is frying in a pan and someone says, "This is your brain on drugs." My reaction to this commercial? . . . I have been on drugs many times, a couple of times very high on drugs, and I don't think my brain was frying away. Sure, I was very high, but it was more of a daze than anything else and most of the times, it feels good to be high. The next morning, my brain is still there and everything is OK. So those commercials and even the high school classes I have on the dangers of drug use are interesting, but I still don't think it really changes my view on my drug use. I think most of my friends feel the same about this. When you are learning the dangers of drug use, that's one thing, but when you are chilling out with friends, or especially at a party, who gives a f--- about the dangers of drug use? I use drugs and never had a bad or dangerous experience. Now driving a car while high can be another thing for some people who are not too good at driving. I think alcohol is the worst thing to be on while driving. But, when it comes to weed or even coke, I drive better. If you are not good at driving, then I don't think you should do drugs [while driving]. But, if you are a pretty good driver, certain drugs like weed and especially coke, can make you a better driver if you are used to driving while high. (From an interview with a male, aged 17, residing in a midsized midwestern town, 3 May 1999)

Nor does it seem, at least from the following comments of another interviewee, that these campaigns are effective over the longer term:

> Yeah, I started having drug education classes in junior high school. It was often every year that we heard about and studied the effects of drugs. Today, I still enjoy smoking cigarettes and weed on weekends with my

fiancée, and drinking alcohol. I remember that in college we used to watch media campaigns against drug use on TV and many of my fraternity brothers were high while watching these warnings. During station breaks, we were smoking joints, drinking beer, and some of my roommates were smoking cigarettes and we found them amusing. I know that if someone likes to get high on whatever drug of choice, he or she will do it against whoever or whatever is saying not to use drugs. Even law enforcement against drug use hardly ever forces people to stop their drug use. Now, if you have court-ordered drug education classes, that may be a different story. But, soon as I finished those classes, which [were] a bunch of bullshit, I went back to my drugs. In order to stop using drugs, it has to come from within, not from the outside. Does anyone realize that, for many people, drugs are as natural as breathing? (From an interview with a male accountant, aged 24, Chicago, 9 May 1999)

It is interesting to note that youths have very different perceptions, beliefs, and understandings about drug use and, equally important, about why drug use is undesirable. Rather than media campaigns, the effective inhibitions seem to come from the individual's own negative experience, or what Pfuhl and Henry (1993) call "turning off." For example, for a non-drug-using high school student, experience was the greater teacher:

No, I would never ride in a car with someone who is high on drugs. My mom and dad drink very little, and I don't like the feeling of getting high. I tried it with alcohol once and I got very sick. Maybe it's because of my mom and dad or even my friends. You see, most of my friends—actually, all of my real friends—are like me; they like getting high on life, not on drugs. Also, another influence is that my older brother nearly died in a car accident coming home from a wedding, and the car that hit him, the driver, was drunk. (From an interview with a female high school student, aged 16, Chicago, 6 May 1999)

Myth 5: Media campaigns against drug use have been successful in changing the attitudes of high school students toward drug use. The evidence on attitudes toward drugs suggests that media campaigns have not been successful in changing the attitudes of youths. Consider the following:

1. The most important difference is observed for the regular smoking of cigarettes. Unfortunately, perceived risk is lowest at the ages when initiation is most likely to occur; while two-thirds of high school seniors (69 percent) see great risk in smoking a pack a day or more, fewer tenth graders (60 percent) and only one-half (53 percent) of eighth graders see similar risk. Despite all that is known today about the health consequences of cigarette smoking, about one-third (31 percent) of twelfth-grade students still do not believe that there is a great risk in smoking a pack or more of cigarettes per day. With regard to regular use of smokeless tobacco, very few high school seniors report perceiving much risk. From 1993 to 1995, such concerns decreased a little, declining to 33 percent in 1995, but then rose back to 39 percent by 1997 (U.S. Department of Health and Human Services, SAMHSA 1998a, 219).

2. Only 15 percent of high school seniors see experimenting with marijuana as entailing great risk. For eighth graders, the percentage perceiving risk in trying marijuana dropped from 40 in 1991 to 25 in 1997. For tenth graders, this measure dropped from 32 percent in 1992 to 19 percent in 1997. The decline in perceived risk for marijuana use has been decelerating (U.S. Department of Health and Human Services, SAMHSA 1998a, 219).

3. Just 7 percent of senior high school students believe there is much risk involved in trying an alcoholic beverage once or twice. Disapproval of weekend binge drinking declined among eighth graders between 1991 and 1994 and among tenth and twelfth graders between 1992 and 1994. In 1995, there was no change in eighth and tenth graders' disapproval of binge drinking (U.S. Department of Health and Human Services, SAMHSA 1998a, 219).

4. A relatively low percentage of eighth-grade students (40 percent) and high school sophomores (48 percent) see experimentation with inhalants as dangerous, which may explain the rather widespread use of such substances (U.S. Department of Health and Human Services, SAMHSA 1998a, 219).

5. The perceived risk of LSD use also had been declining among eighth, tenth, and twelfth graders since it was first measured in 1993; however, the decline leveled off in 1996. Actual use of LSD—which had been increasing steadily for several years—leveled off in 1997. Recent self-report studies of LSD use, however, indicate that it is once again on the increase (U.S. Department of Health and Human Services, SAMHSA 1998a, 219).

6. From 1992 through 1996, the use of cocaine powder and crack drugs was up in all grades, some times significantly (U.S. Department of Health and Human Services, SAMHSA 1998a, 219).

7. Regarding heroin use, there was a decline in perceived risk among seniors from 1990 through 1995. Often, as the perceived risk declined, use by seniors rose, with the annual prevalence increasing from 0.4 percent in 1991 to 1.1 percent in 1995 (U.S. Department of Health and Human Services, SAMHSA 1998a, 219).

8. Finally, for all drugs included in the National Household Survey on Drug Use from the Monitoring the Future Study, 1975–1997 (U.S. Department of Health and Human Services, SAMHSA 1998a), fewer seniors believe that use in private settings should be illegal. This is particularly true for alcohol and marijuana (U.S. Department of Health and Human Services, SAMHSA 1998a, 219).

It is important to emphasize, however, that when antidrug attitudes decline, use tends to increase appreciably a year or two later, according to survey data (U.S. Department of Health and Human Services, SAMHSA 1998a).

In looking at the myths and evidence of drug use by students in junior high school, high school, and college, then, we find that these students are a difficult group to convince not to use drugs. The latest percentage increases in drug use are a reality that needs to be heeded.

Drug Use in Schools: A Constructionist Perspective

If popular culture and the media promote various myths about drug use and desistance, what is the reality and is there more than one reality? Part of the reality of the drug issue in contemporary society is that produced by parents, school officials, and even the federal, state, and local government, each of whom believes in pressing forward with zero tolerance. Schools' adoption of zero tolerance of drugs has led to the use of drug-sniffing dogs and random drug tests for students involved in extracurricular activities. Part of the reason for these policies has to do with the construction of the meaning of the negative effects of drug use by various interests groups, such as the Parents' Resources Institute for Drug Education. The meaning constructed is based on the view that improper use of nonprescribed drugs results in students who are not consciously normal. Further, it is believed that learning in school is diminished, that the teaching and learning environment is compromised, and that using drugs not only poses a danger to the user's health but also affects his or her thinking, which in turn can result in harm to others. However, social constructionist theory informs us that social meanings, and, in particular, moral meanings, are multiple and variable, as are the different "social worlds" (Schutz 1966) that youths inhabit. Indeed,

> for most children any sense of certainty and universality of truth is short-lived, surviving only until they move beyond the home . . . and into the morally heterogeneous neighborhood, street and school subcultures and other progressively larger, more complex social situations. Induced to a variety of different and often contradictory social realities and sub-universes of meaning reflecting the diverse biographies of people differing in race, ethnicity, age, gender, sexual orientation, religion, social class, and occupation. . . . Social reality is multiple rather than singular, and the several realities both coalesce and contradict one another. Consistent moral meanings may be said to exist only in the abstract. As applied to concrete events, these definitions are highly variable and fluctuate from one setting or context to another even though they may be treated as though they are the same. (Pfuhl and Henry 1993, 20–22)

In order to consider the social reality of drug use, it is necessary, therefore, to explore and understand the meaning that drug use has for youths, not all of whom share the same moral meaning about the issue. In looking at the viewpoints of drug users versus non-drug-users, we find that different realities are operating. From a more phenomenological perspective, drug users and non-drug-users live in separate worlds and construct their realities differently. Interviews with drug users and non-drug-users underscore the differences in attitudes and definitions. Consider the remarks of one drug user about his social world:

> I have been using drugs since I was 12 years old. Nearly all of my best friends are like me [in using drugs]. We just don't hang around with people who are against or afraid to use drugs. We are just different in almost

everything we believe in. People say that you can't learn or study while on drugs. For me, I do everything when I am high on weed. If I have homework to do, I probably do waste more time when I am high, but I still get the work done. I don't have any problems with drugs unless I get too high, then I can't concentrate on doing any work. After a few years of first using drugs, most normal people learn how to live their life around drug use. You learn when it's too much and learn how to not overdo a particular drug. I know there are many drug users who don't learn very well, but that's an individual thing. Actually, I know more people who use drugs wisely (most of the time) and really don't have a problem. On the other hand, they may have a problem for a while, but learn from their mistakes. (From an interview with a male college student, aged 21, 16 April 1999)

It's funny, but I was nearly always at least a little high in high school. It's been that way since I was 16. I had a B average in high school, and now in college, I have a B+ to an A– average in all the courses I am taking. I did nearly flunk out of college my first year, but that was not because of drugs, but because I was in the wrong major. Engineering was my dad's idea, not mine. Now, I am a psychology major and doing pretty good. I usually stay away from people who are against drugs and somehow they stay away from me. (From an interview with a male college student, aged 22, 16 April 1999)

Now consider this contrasting view from another social world:

Drugs? I feel uncomfortable around drug users. They waste a lot of time being high, and you can tell they are lost people. Especially drug users who cannot go a day without using drugs. They have a problem with wanting to get high all the time. You know, I think it's a biological thing with drug users. The few times I tried marijuana, I just did not like the feelings. I became very paranoid and just felt out of kilter, so to say. Alcohol is OK, but even that makes me tired and not in touch with life. Living life makes me high sometimes; drugs are for those needing medicine from doctors. Why do I have to use any type of drug, if I just don't feel right when it starts reacting in my body? (From an interview with a female college student, aged 22, residing in a midsized midwestern city, 12 May 1999).

Countless other interviews reveal similar differences. Drug users construct their social worlds from their perceptions of the meaning of social reality, and similarly non-drug-users do the same. In order to understand drug use in schools, it is necessary to probe the meaning that drugs have for the users; herein lies the reality of high school drug use. When we do that, we find that the meaning of drug use is shaped by the social context of human development and particularly by the meaning of adolescence at century's end. In the next section of this article, I will explore this particular construction of meaning by pubescent adolescents.

Drug Use and Youth

From age 13 through 18, most adolescents experience an increase in psychological, social, and biological changes. Most often, a disruption of the body's harmony (homeostasis) occurs. This period of "storm and stress" results in distancing from parental authority and increasing intimacy with peers. Further, the adolescent's body is stretching, growing, and changing due to hormonal changes. When all this is occurring, adolescents are uncertain and confused about not knowing who or what they are becoming. They are often confused about their worth in their families, among peers, within society, and even to themselves.

Adding to this frustration of growing up, the cultural status of adolescents is poorly defined. They find themselves trapped in a no-person's-land between two polar opposites: the acceptance, simplicity, and security of childhood, and the stress, complexities, expectations, independence, and responsibilities of adulthood:

> Yeah, sometimes I think that I am still "Johnny," but I am getting hair all over my body, even hair around the pubic areas. I am actually taller than both my grandparents now. One day, my grandfather came to the airport to pick me up with my aunt. [It had been a year since I'd seen him, and] as soon as I got off the plane, he kept talking about all the hair on my legs. I was so embarrassed when he said, "Look at my grandson. He is now a man. He is becoming more and more like a man." What can you say when someone embarrasses you like that? (From an interview with a male high school student, aged 16, residing in a smaller midwestern city, 16 April 1999)

During this period of development, the following issues appear to be prevalent among adolescents: discovering and understanding their distinctive identities; forming more intimate and caring relationships with others; establishing a sense of autonomy; coming to terms with the feelings of puberty and expressing their sexuality; and learning to become dependable and productive members of society (Elmen and Offer 1993). Because of such developmental issues, well-adjusted behavior is often difficult to establish. Experts generally agree that persistent low self-esteem, depression, and other severe emotional disturbances can be troublesome for teenagers. Although many adolescents experience such adjustment problems, most are relatively well adjusted and able to cope with the social, psychological, and biological changes of this time in their lives. Adolescents who experience problems are often unable or unwilling to ask for help. As a result, many turn to hazardous coping methods, one of which is the use or abuse of drugs.

Social, psychological, and biological problems of adjustment to society and its expectations carry over into school—a place where adolescents spend approximately 40 hours per week, much like full-time employment. Although delinquency, drug use, and other forms of deviance can be exacerbated by poor school performance (Hirschi 1971), it is not the schools that are responsible for drug abuse. Drug abuse is merely a problem that appears serious in school because, in the social environment of the school, students are the majority of the population, and a noticeable percentage of students are often using drugs or under the influence of drugs on school premises.

The reason why students elect to use drugs has to do more with the meaninglessness of school, and of life in general, at a time when they are going through large biological and social transformations. In this context, drugs provide the means to cope or even to gain some control over life's problems. Consider the following observations of an interviewee who clearly used drugs just to cope:

> The world is all messed up. . . . Nobody gives a damn anymore about anyone else. It seems like life just seems to go on and on. . . . I know that when I am under the influence, life is more mellow. I feel great! When I'm high, I can take things better. Before I came to . . . college, I felt home life was one great big mess; now that I'm here, this college is also a big pile of crap. I guess that is why I like smoking dope. When I'm high, I can forget my problems. My surroundings are friendlier; I'm even more pleasant! (From an interview with a male college student, aged 19, attending a private liberal arts college in the Southeast, 12 February 1984)

Indeed, for many teenagers, the motivation for using drugs is to help cope with and escape from problems. Violence is neither the motivation nor the effect of their quest for tranquillity and transcendence from the boredom of day-to-day existence.

Conclusion

With regard to drug use or abuse by school-age students, this discussion and the findings are not advocating that drug use or abuse is acceptable. It may not be as harmful as much of the debate on the topic projects; it is not the most constructive way to respond to problems, but it is a way. Constructionist theory suggests that drug education, efforts by law enforcement, and the current drug prevention strategies remain very limited in their success. The evidence discussed in this article suggests that drug prohibition has failed in the past; the most recent statistics available indicate that drug use is increasing; and our legal system continues to fail in eradicating drug use. With such dismal results in lessening illicit drug use, it could be maintained that, until individual drug users begin to perceive the personal need to stop using drugs, familial, social, institutional, medical, legal, and governmental efforts against drug use will not convince individual users or drug-using cliques. Is it time to reconsider that "the practice of getting high has existed from the dawn of time, and all efforts to eradicate it are based on an incomplete understanding of human nature" (Lenson 1995, 190)? Further, Lenson (1995, 190) is very insightful in arguing that, since the 1960s, our society has begun to establish a trend toward accepting racial, ethnic, sexual, religious, and physical differences. As we continue to progress in this new century, would it be too early to include diversity of consciousness as another right that citizens should have in our democracy? In this new century, should we begin discussions and debates about allowing some form of diversity of consciousness as an inalienable right of U.S. citizens? More precisely, should we at least begin national, local, and even international forums of information, discussion, and debate centered on the issue of responsible diversity of consciousness (Venturelli 1997, 12–14), an allowable diversity of consciousness without legal sanctions and criminalization of youth but perhaps with medical interventions? Here it appears that some form of harm reduction strategy[4] could be the overarching perspective from which to begin.

NOTES

[1] In this and other quotations from interviews, all names used are pseudonyms.

[2] Drugs are defined as any compound or mixture that affects the functioning of both mind and body. They include both licit- and illicit-type drugs, such as alcohol, tobacco, marijuana, cocaine, hallucinogenic drugs, stimulants, and depressants (see Hanson and Venturelli 1998).

[3] Ironically, many drug users, who by definition are breaking the law, are reluctant to seek treatment if it exposes them to the risk of apprehension by law enforcement officials.

[4] Harm reduction is a drug policy originally implemented in the Netherlands. The focus of this model is on eliminating the strong punishment measures for cannabis use previously advocated by the punitive model of drug control and minimizing the financial costs of drug enforcement for tax-paying citizens. Overall, the goal is to reduce personal harm, such as stiff jail sentences for drug use, while simultaneously increasing educational programs and treatment and prevention facilities for chronic drug users. Another way of thinking about harm reduction is to view it as a midpoint between prohibition and full legalization.

REFERENCES

Brunvand, Jan H. 1984. *The Choking Doberman and Other "New" Urban Legends*. New York: Norton.

Cohen, Stanley. 1980. *Folk Devils and Moral Panics*. New York: St. Martin's Press.

Donziger, Steven R., ed. 1996. *The Real War on Crime: The Report of the National Criminal Justice Commission*. New York: Harper Perennial.

Drug Strategies. 1996. *Keeping Score: What Are We Getting for Our Federal Drug Control Dollars, 1996*. Washington, DC: Drug Strategies. Available at http://res/colleges/bss/depts/cesar/drugs/ks.

Elmen, J. and D. Offer. 1993. Normality Turmoil and Adolescence. In *Handbook of Clinical Research and Practice with Adolescents*, ed. P. Tolan and B. Cohler. New York: John Wiley.

Goode, Eric. 1999. *Drugs in American Society*. 5th ed. New York: McGraw Hill College.

Hanson, Glenn and Peter J. Venturelli. 1998. *Drugs and Society*. 5th ed. Sudbury, MA: Jones & Bartlett.

Hirschi, Travis. 1971. *Causes of Delinquency*. 2d ed. Los Angeles: University of California Press.

Johns, Christina. 1992. *The War on Drugs*. Westport, CT: Praeger.

Lenson, David. 1995. *On Drugs*. Minneapolis: University of Minnesota Press.

Lindesmith, Alfred. 1940. The "Dope Fiend" Mythology. *Journal of Criminal Law and Criminology* 31:199–208.

Martin, Susan E. 1997. Alcohol and Homicide: A Deadly Combination of Two American Traditions. *Journal of Studies on Alcohol* 58:107.

Osgood, D. Wayne. 1985. The Drug-Crime Connection and the Generality and Stability of Deviance. Paper presented at the annual meeting of the American Society of Criminology, Nov., San Diego, CA.

Parker, Robert Nash. 1995. *Alcohol and Homicide: A Deadly Combination of Two American Traditions*. Albany: State University of New York Press.

Pfuhl, Erdwin H. and Stuart Henry. 1993. *The Deviance Process.* 3d ed. New York: Aldine de Gruyter.

Schutz, Alfred. 1966. *Collected Papers III: Studies in Phenomenological Philosophy*, ed. I. Schutz. The Hague: Martins Nijhoff.

U.S. Department of Health and Human Services. NIDA (National Institute on Drug Abuse). 1998. 1997 National Household Survey on Drug Abuse. Preliminary Results: Highlights. Rockville, MD: Department of Health and Human Services, National Institutes of Health. Available at http://www.health.org/pubs.

———. 1999. *Nationwide Trends.* Rockville, MD: Department of Health and Human Services, National Institutes of Health. Available at http://www.nida.nih.gov.

———. SAMHSA (Substance Abuse and Mental Health Services Administration). 1998a. *National Survey Results on Drug Use from the Monitoring the Future Study, 1975–1997.* Vol. 1, *Secondary School Students.* Rockville, MD: Department of Health and Human Services, National Institutes of Health, National Institute on Drug Abuse.

———. 1998b. Preliminary Results from the 1997 National Household Survey on Drug Abuse. Rockville, MD: Department of Health and Human Services, National Institutes of Health, National Institute on Drug Abuse. Available at http://www.health.org/pubs.

U.S. Department of Justice. Office of Justice Programs. Bureau of Justice Statistics. 1998a. *School Crime Supplement to the National Crime Victimization Survey, 1989 and 1995.* Washington, DC: Department of Justice, Office of Justice Programs.

———. 1998b. *Sourcebook of Criminal Justice Statistics 1997.* Washington, DC: Department of Justice, Office of Justice Programs.

Venturelli, Peter J., ed. 1994. *Drug Use in America: Social, Cultural and Political Perspectives.* Boston: Jones & Bartlett.

———. 1997. Drinking and Drugs [Our Division's Vision]. In *Working Toward a Just World: Visions, Experiences and Challenges*, ed. Pamela Roby. Knoxville, TN: Society for the Study of Social Problems.

Webb, Vincent J. and Miriam A. Delone. 1995. Drug Use Among a Misdemeanant Population: Exploration of a Legal Syllogism of the "Drug War." *Crime, Law and Social Change* 24:241–55.

19

The Wrong Race, Committing Crime, Doing Drugs, and Maladjusted for Motherhood
The Nation's Fury over "Crack Babies"

Enid Logan

Introduction

During the 1990s, women who use illicit drugs during pregnancy became the subject of intense public attention and social stigmatization. They are regarded as incapable of responsible decision-making, morally deviant, and increasingly, unfit for motherhood. In recent years, the civil courts have terminated the parental rights of thousands of women whose infants tested positive for drug exposure at birth (Beckett, 1995). Women have also faced criminal prosecution for prenatal drug use, under statutes including criminal child abuse, neglect, manslaughter, and delivering substances to a minor. For the most part, the women targeted by the courts and the media have been black, poor, and addicted to crack cocaine (Roberts, 1991; Krauss, 1991; Beckett, 1995; Neuspiel et al., 1994; Greene, 1991).

I argue here that the phenomenon of the "crack-baby" is not produced simply by a tragic interaction between illicit substances and a growing fetus. The "crack-baby," rather, has resulted from a broader conjunction of practices and ideologies associated with race, gender, and class oppression, including the war on drugs and the discourse of fetal rights. In the late 1980s

From *Social Justice*, 1999, 26(1): 115–127. Reprinted with permission.

and early 1990s, the image of trembling, helpless infants irrevocably damaged by their mothers' irresponsible actions became a potent symbol of all that was wrong with the poor, the black, and the new mothers in the post-women's movement, post-civil rights era. Crack-babies provided society with a powerful iconography of multiple social deviance (nonmarital sexuality, criminality, drug addiction, aberrant maternal behavior)' perpetrated upon the most innocent, by the least innocent: women who are in fact "shameless" and "scandalous" (Irwin, 1995).

Below I will discuss the issue of prenatal substance abuse, focusing on women addicted to crack and their children. As I will illustrate, the social, legal, and political trends that comprise the nation's response to this problem have been largely inspired by racial, gendered, and socioeconomic imperatives, rather than by the blind hand of justice.

The Media and the Crack-Baby in the Popular Imagination

In the 1990s, a crack cocaine epidemic exploded in the U.S., sweeping through low-income black communities with a vengeance (Roberts, 1991). Perceiving a dramatic rise in the number of boarder babies and children born to women abusing drugs, the media began to present the public with reports on a drug like no other, crack, and on appearance of a "different" kind of child—the crack-baby. The narrative of the crack-baby interwove specific messages about crack, pregnant addicts, and crack-exposed children. Crack cocaine, journalists wrote, was a drug like no other previously on the streets. Crack was more potent, more addictive, and more likely to lead its users to acts of violence, crime, and desperation.

Among its most desperate and debased users were pregnant women. One of the most harmful effects of crack was said to be that it literally *destroyed* the maternal instinct in the women who used it (Irwin, 1995; Hopkins, 1990; Appel, 1992; Elshtain, 1990; Debettencourt, 1990). Utterly irresponsible and incompetent addicted mothers were seen as "inhumane threats to the social order" who willingly tortured their helpless fetuses (Irwin, 1995: 635). One California doctor was quoted as saying, "with every hit the mother plays Russian roulette with the baby's brain" (Hopkins, 1990: 108). Only concerned with feeding their addictions, mothers on crack were said to be incapable of taking care of their children or even caring about the irreparable harm that smoking crack would do to their unborn fetuses. A *Rolling Stone* article reported that the crack epidemic had left s social service workers "nostalgic" for the heroin mothers who "could buy groceries occasionally and give the kid a bath." "Crack," on the other hand, "leaves nothing to chance. It makes babies that only a mother could love, and wipes out that love as well" (*Ibid.*: 71).

The press often spoke of the frustration or anger that many health care workers felt toward pregnant addicts. The *Economist*, for example, reported

> Heartbreaking as it is for the doctors and nurses who care for the babies
> [to see them suffer] . . . they find it even more distressing to return the
> babies to mothers for whom drugs remain the dominant feature of life.
> (*Economist*, April 1, 1989: 28)

In a 1990 *People* magazine interview, Katherine Jorgensen, head nurse in the
neonatal intensive care unit at Boston City Hospital, explained that the hardest
part of her job "is when new mothers come to look in on their children." Seeing
women come to visit their babies "with their pimps" or "while they are high,"
she said, made her "want to slug them" (Plummer and Brown, 1990: 85).

In the eyes of the media, the inhumane actions of addicted mothers
often produced children who were almost beyond the pale of humanity.
Crack-exposed babies were "supposedly doomed to a life of suboptimal
intelligence, uncontrollable behavior, and criminal tendencies" (Neuspiel et
al., 1994: 47). According to *People*, some crack-babies "shake so badly they
rub their limbs raw" (Plummer and Brown, 1990: 85). In *Rolling Stone* we
read, "During a crying jag their rigid little arms flap about, which makes
them even more frantic: They seem to believe their arms belong to someone
else, a vicious someone who relentlessly flogs them" (Hopkins, 1990: 71).
Pictures of children who tested positive for exposure to drugs at birth most
often showed them crying, "shrieking like cats" or staring, bug eyed into
space for hours. According to the logic of the crack-baby narrative, the variety of physical and emotional problems faced by these children could be
attributed to a single cause: prenatal exposure to crack cocaine (Greider,
1995; Griffith, 1992).

Children exposed to crack in the womb, it was reported, were likely to
suffer from any number of serious medical conditions. Among the most frequently cited were hemorrhaging and intracranial lesions, prematurity, birth
defects, genito-urinary and cardiac abnormalities, prenatal strokes, heart
attacks or death, fine motor disorders, low birth weight, and neonatal growth
retardation (Hopkins, 1990; Sexton, 1993; Hoffman, 1990; Plummer and
Brown, 1990; Langone, 1988, Zitella, 1996). Fetal exposure to cocaine was
also said to greatly increase the risk of postnatal neurological complications,
such as extreme sensitivity to external stimuli, unpredictable mood swings,
high-pitched "cat-like" crying, tremulousness, and difficulty interacting with
others (Appel, 1992; Sexton, 1993; Hopkins, 1990; *Economist*, April 1989).
Even in the mildest cases, crack-exposed children would likely suffer grave
emotional and cognitive abnormalities. Crack-babies, we read, were generally
unable to concentrate, prone toward violence and destructive behavior, and
were averse to light, touch, and affection (Zitella, 1996; Hopkins, 1990).

From the inner cities, a new breed of child was being produced, one that
was loveless, tortured, and demented. In the words of one pediatric
researcher, "You can't tell what makes these children happy or sad. *They are
like automatons* (Hopkins, 1990: 72; emphasis added). Even in the "best case"
scenario" crack-exposed children were somehow fundamentally "different"
from the rest of us—less *human*. As Doctor Judy Howard told *Newsweek*, "in

crack-babies the part of the brains that makes us a human being, capable of discussion or reflection, has been wiped out" (Greider, 1995: 54). Similarly, another piece asserted that crack cocaine "robbed [exposed] children of 'the central core of what it is to be human'" (Irwin, 1995: 633).

Worst of all, the damage done to these children by their crack-smoking mothers was believed to be permanent and irreparable. In the chilling words of one journalist, "crack damages fetuses like no other drug . . . [and] the damage the drug causes . . . doesn't go away" (Hopkins, 1990: 68). Though the press was generally sympathetic to the plight of crack-exposed children, it typically portrayed them as damaged goods, largely beyond hope or salvation, and damned by the actions of their irresponsible mothers. One article read "for [some] people this is truly a lost generation, and neither love nor money is ever going to change that. . . . Love can't make a damaged brain whole" (*Ibid.*: 68–69).

State Response to Prenatal Cocaine Use: Prosecute and Terminate

The moral indignation, shock, and pity that such media imagery aroused in the American public were accompanied by an aggressive state response. Policy initiatives addressing the crack-baby phenomenon have been concentrated in the legal and social service arenas.

LEGAL PROSECUTION OF PREGNANT ADDICTS

In the later part of the 1980s, the country witnessed the emergence of a new and unprecedented legal strategy: the criminal prosecution of pregnant drug addicts. Due to the successful lobbying of the ACLU and medical, health, and women's organizations, no state has passed laws that make prenatal substance abuse an independent crime (Beckett, 1995; Lieb and Sterk-Elifson, 1995; Neil, 1992). Therefore, prosecutors have used "innovative" applications of existing laws to bring cases against pregnant addicts. Women have been charged under statutes for child abuse, neglect, vehicular homicide, encouraging the delinquency of a minor, involuntary manslaughter, drug trafficking, failure to provide child support, and assault with a deadly weapon (Mariner, Glantz, and Annas, 1990; Beckett, 1995; Sexton, 1993; Paltrow, 1990; Roberts, 1991; Greene, 1991).

In July 1989, Jennifer Johnson, a poor, 23-year-old African-American woman, became the first person convicted in the U.S. for giving birth to a drug-exposed infant. She was charged and found guilty of delivery of a controlled substance to a minor. Florida prosecutor Jeff Deen argued that this had taken place in the 30 to 90 seconds after the birth of the infant and before the cutting of the umbilical chord (Dobson and Eby, 1992).

Johnson received a 15-year sentence, including 14 years of probation, strict supervision during the first year, mandatory drug treatment, random drug testing, and mandatory educational and vocational training (Sexton,

1993; Logli, 1990; Neil, 1992). Johnson was further prohibited from "consuming alcohol, socializing with anyone who possessed drugs, and going to a bar without first receiving consent from her probation officer" (Sexton, 1993: 413). The court also ruled that if Johnson ever intended to again become pregnant, she must inform her probation officer and enroll in an intensive "judicially approved" prenatal care program (Logli, 1990; Sexton, 1993). Under Florida state law, she could have received a 30-year prison sentence (Curriden, 1990). Prosecutor Deen believed that prosecution "was the only way to stop her from using cocaine" and that Johnson "had used up all her chances" (*Ibid.*: 51). The case, Deen claimed, served to send the message "that this community cannot afford to have two or three cocaine babies from the same person."

Another highly publicized case was that of Kimberly Ann Hardy, also a poor, single young black woman addicted to crack cocaine. Hardy's case first came to the attention of the Department of Social Services in Muskegon County, Michigan, when the local hospital reported that her newborn had tested positive for cocaine at birth. Hardy's urine was tested for drugs because she had been identified as a "high-risk pregnancy" upon admission to the hospital: she had received no prenatal care and delivered six to eight weeks early (Hoffman, 1990).

Eleven days after she left the hospital, county prosecutor Tony Tague ordered Hardy arrested on the charge of delivering drugs in the amount of less than 50 grams—one generally used in prosecuting drug dealers (*Ibid.*). Though Hardy's case did not result in a conviction, district attorney Tague felt that the prosecution served to fulfill several important goals: it got Hardy into treatment and gave other pregnant crack addicts a strong warning to get clean or face jail and the loss of their children. Muskegon County Sergeant Van Hemert stated that adopting the hard line in prosecuting mothers is "a form of caring." Speaking with anger that many seem to hold toward pregnant addicts, he adds: "If the mother wants to smoke crack and kill herself I don't care. *Let her die, but don't take that poor baby with her*" (*Ibid.*: 34, emphasis added).

These two cases are fairly typical. The prosecutors are white males, the defendants are young black women, the drug is crack, and the rationale is safeguarding the health of babies. By 1992, 24 states had brought criminal charges against women for use of illicit drugs while pregnant. All of the defendants in these cases were poor and most were nonwhite (Beckett, 1995; Lieb and Sterk-Elifson, 1995). Nearly all of the convictions obtained in criminal prosecutions for perinatal substance abuse have been overturned (including Jennifer Johnson's), on the grounds that the charges against the defendants were not congruent with legislative intent (Beckett, 1995; Logli, 1990). Despite this fact, district attorneys continue to bring pregnant women up on criminal charges for substance abuse. As Beckett (1995: 603) has stated, "the continuation of these efforts reflects their political utility in our cultural climate."

Polls taken in the last few years have found that a large and growing proportion of the American public (71% in one survey) believes that women who use drugs while pregnant should be held criminally liable (Curriden, 1990; Sexton, 1993; Hoffman, 1990). The prosecutions of Johnson, Hardy, and others have boosted the careers of the attorneys who put them on trial, who some have heralded as "crusaders" in the war against drugs.

"PROTECTIVE INCARCERATION"

Protective incarceration is another legal tactic that is becoming increasingly popular (Appel, 1992). In these cases, judges send pregnant women convicted of charges unrelated to their drug use to jail to "protect" their fetuses. At the 1988 sentencing of a pregnant addict convicted of writing bad checks, the judge stated:

> I'm going to keep her locked up until that baby is born because she's tested positive for cocaine. . . . She's apparently an addictive personality, and I'll be darned if I'm going to have a baby born that way (Roberts, 1991: 1431, *fn.* 55).

Other addicts have been sent to jail for violations of their probation, in lieu of a probationary sentence, or for longer periods than is standard (Lieb and Sterk-Elifson, 1995; Schroedel, Reith, and Peretz, 1995; Appel, 1992).

HOSPITAL POLICY

Currently, at least 13 states require that public hospitals test women "suspected" of drug abuse and that they report those who test positive to social services or the police (Sexton, 1993). As in the Hardy case, mandatory reporting is often what triggers prosecution. Yet, drug screening conducted at public hospitals regularly takes place without women's consent or their being informed of possible legal ramifications.

In South Carolina, one hospital's testing and reporting policy (which stipulated that the police be notified of positive prenatal drug toxicologies) landed it a three million dollar lawsuit on the grounds that it violated patients' civil rights and discriminated on the basis of class and color. At the Medical University of South Carolina in Charleston, six lower-income women (five black and one white) who tested positive for drug use were "taken out of their hospital beds, handcuffed, and sent to jail without their babies" within days or hours after delivery (Furio, 1994: 93). At least one of the women "arrived at the jail still bleeding from the delivery; she was told to sit on a towel" (Paltrow, 1990: 41). The white woman was "detained for three weeks, put into a choke hold, and shackled by police during her eighth month of pregnancy . . . then placed against her will in a psychiatric hospital" (Furio, 1994:93).

In September 1994, the case ended with a settlement and the requirement that the hospital abandon its practices. By that time, however, several hundred women had faced criminal prosecution under the reporting policy. Further, many other states continue to bring criminal or civil charges against women on the basis of drug tests performed without their consent.

SOCIAL SERVICES—UNFIT FOR MOTHERHOOD

The most frequent penalty for a mother's prenatal drug use is permanent or temporary removal of the newborn and/or other children. Based upon the results of drug screening, infants may be removed from their mothers right after birth, often without trial or hearing (Young, 1995). In today's political climate "positive neonatal toxicologies raise strong presumption of parental unfitness" (Roberts, 1991: 1431). Increasingly, civil courts agree that prenatal use of drugs constitutes neglect and is sufficient evidence for termination of parental rights (Beckett, 1995). In the last decade, literally thousands of women have permanently lost custody of their children as a result of their addiction. Upon appeal, the lower and appellate family courts have generally upheld these decisions (*Ibid.*).

Representative Kerry Patrick of Kansas introduced legislation that would require female addicts to have Noroplant capsules inserted in their arms or else go to jail. Patrick says of his plan: "I've gotten a lot of support from nurses who deal with crack-babies. Once you see one, you don't care about the rights of the mother" (Willwerth, 1991: 62). Others echo his anger. One employee of the Los Angeles County Department of Health says: "Damn it, babies are dying out there! . . . You get someone with a terrible family history, stoned, no parenting skills—and we keep giving back her babies because we don't want to look racist or sexist" (*Ibid.*: 62).

Assumptions Behind the Crack-Baby Narrative and Punitive Treatment of Addicted Women

The intensity of legal, civil, and journalistic activity centering on babies born addicted to crack cocaine has been undergirded by three main sets of assumptions: about the effects of crack cocaine on fetal and child development, about the pregnant addicts targeted by the courts and the press, and about the efficacy of prosecution and punishment. The following section explores each of these assumptions and shows that despite their power, they are not substantiated by empirical evidence. Their tenacity comes not from their basis in fact, but from their ideological resonance with popular beliefs about drugs, crime, race, and motherhood.

THE MEDICAL EFFECTS OF CRACK COCAINE ON FETAL HEALTH

The first assumption fueling the crack-baby scare is that crack is far more dangerous to fetal health than any other drug. As new evidence has emerged in the last five to six years, it has become apparent that early reports as to the impact of crack cocaine on fetal development were grossly exaggerated, and that what was painted as the norm is most likely the worst-case scenario. Perhaps the primary shortcoming of the early research was that it failed to disentangle the effects of cocaine from the effects of other chemical and environmental factors (Appel, 1992; Greider, 1995; *Science News*, November 19,

1991; Gittler and McPherson, 1990; Neuspiel, Markowitz, and Drucker, 1994). This was a particularly serious flaw given the population of drug users under study. Women who use crack are more likely to smoke cigarettes, drink alcohol, use other drugs, and to be malnourished; they are also less likely to obtain adequate prenatal care (Greider, 1995; Feldman et al., 1992; Griffith, 1992; Appel, 1992; Debettencourt, 1990;. Neuspiel, Markowitz and Drucker, 1994). Each of these factors has been documented to seriously impair fetal development—in the *absence* of cocaine (Appel, 1992; Neuspiel, Markowitz, and Drucker, 1994; *Science News*, November 19, 1991; *American Journal of Nursing*, May 1995).

Moreover, the presence of post-natal risk factors has also confounded the results of many studies. Cocaine-exposed children, like many poor black American children, are exposed to a higher-than-average level of violence, neglect, and abuse in their daily environments. Some scientists claim that "the social context of crack cocaine use, or more commonly polydrug use, is *more likely* to be related to the poor medical and developmental outcomes than to the actual drug exposure of the fetus" (Lieb and Sterk-Elifson, 1995: 690; emphasis added).

Despite these and other shortcomings, it was fairly easy for researchers to get this type of research published; conversely, it has been difficult to publicize findings that crack's effects on fetal development were minimal or nil (Greider, 1995; Pollitt, 1990; Beckett, 1995). Scientists whose work refuted the alarmist findings of the earliest published reports on crack cocaine and fetal development were often confronted with the disbelief, censure, and anger of their colleagues. In the words of one researcher, "I'd never experienced anything like this. . . . I've never had people accuse me of making up data or being an incompetent scientist or believing in drug abuse" (Greider, 1995: 54).

Dr. Ira Chasnoff has been a leading scientist in the field of prenatal cocaine exposure research since 1985. When Dr. Chasnoff recognized that his research was primarily being used to stigmatize and punish the women and children for whom he considered himself an advocate, however, he was appalled. In 1992, he stated that on average, crack-exposed children "are no different from other children growing up." Indicating his disgust with the popular rhetoric on "crack-babies," Dr. Chasnoff added, "they are not the retarded imbeciles people talk about. . . . As I study the problem more and more, I think the placenta does a better job protecting the child than we do as a society" (Sullum, 1992: 14).

Developmental psychologist Dan Griffith (formerly a member of Chasnoff's research group) has also sought to rectify the misimpressions concerning "crack-babies" so prevalent in the public imagination. Griffith notes that the most common assumptions about crack-kids—"(1) that all cocaine-exposed children are severely affected, (2) that little can be done for them, and (3) that all the medical, behavioral, and learning problems exhibited by these children are caused directly by their exposure to cocaine"—are false. Dr. Griffith cautions that far too little research has been conducted to allow scientists "to make any firm statement about the long-term prognosis" for cocaine-exposed children (Griffith, 1992: 30). However, his own research indicates that with early intervention and the reduction of other risk factors, most coke-exposed children "seem completely normal with regard to intellectual, social, emotional, and behavioral development though age three" (*Ibid.*: 31).[1]

Recent studies, which attempt to "smoke out" crack's unique impact on fetal development, tend to agree that cocaine increases the risk of low birth weight and prematurity in infants (Greider, 1995; Feldman et al., 1992; Barone, 1994; Beckett, 1995). Scientists have also found that receiving adequate prenatal care and curtailing drug usage significantly improves developmental outcomes for cocaine-exposed infants (Appel, 1992; Griffith, 1992). The extent to which cocaine alone causes neurobehavioral and other abnormalities is still up for debate. However, the consensus is that the average harm posed to infants by cocaine is far less than previously feared. Prematurity and low birth weight are indeed dangerous conditions for an infant and each significantly contributes to the high rates of infant mortality and morbidity among African-Americans.[2] Yet these two primary effects are a far cry from the cranial hemorrhages, severe retardation, and lack of "human" qualities said to be typical of children born exposed to crack cocaine.

Current evidence also suggests that the effects of crack are *not* so different from those of tobacco or some other common street drugs. Comparison of scientific data on the effects of several chemical factors on fetal development demonstrates that the selection of pregnant crack-addicts in particular for censure and prosecution "has a discriminatory impact that cannot be medically justified" (Roberts, 1991: 1435). It may make no more sense, then, to speak about "crack-babies" than it does to speak of "cigarette-babies," "pot-babies," or "speed-babies." Most crack-exposed children will not suffer permanent pharmacologically induced brain damage and are not, medically speaking, beyond "hope." Whatever developmental delays or antisocial behavior they appear to express in later life may have more to do with poisons in their postnatal environment than in the fetal one.

PREGNANT ADDICTS TARGETED BY COURTS

The crack-baby mythology is also powerfully buttressed by a set of assumptions and stereotypes concerning the pregnant addicts who have been targeted by the courts and the media. Despite popular mythology to the contrary, empirical evidence shows that rates of prenatal drug use are consistent across race and class fines (Neuspiel et al., 1994; Lieb and Sterk-Elifson, 1995; Beckett, 1995; Appel, 1992). Stated otherwise, white middle-class women are no less likely to abstain from the use of illicit substances during pregnancy than are poor minority women. Ira Chasnoff's 1989 study of patterns of prenatal drug use and reporting policies in Pinellas County, Florida, clearly documented this trend.

In a toxicological screen for evidence of alcohol, marijuana, cocaine, and/or opiate use, 14.8% of women in the study tested positive overall. Chasnoff found that "there was little difference in the percentage of drug detection between women seen in public clinics (16.3) and those seen in private offices (13.1), or between blacks (14.1) and whites (15.4)" (Neuspiel, 1996: 48). There were, however, significant racial differences in the drug of choice. A higher percentage of pregnant black women (7.8) used cocaine than did pregnant white women (1.8); and pregnant white women (14.4) evidenced significantly higher usage of marijuana than their black counterparts (6.0). A more striking finding of the study concerned the discrepancy in the rates of reporting. In the state of Florida, health care providers are required by law to report both marijuana and cocaine use to authorities. Chasnoff discovered that "despite similar levels of use, black women were reported at *10 times* the rate for white women" and that poorer women were reported more often than middle-class women were (*Ibid.*: 48, emphasis added).

If not substance abuse rates themselves, then what explains the overwhelming race/class discrepancy in reporting and prosecution of prenatal drug use? This discrepancy has its roots in the fact that "the process in which pregnant women are suspected of substance abuse, diagnosed, and prosecuted is suffused with enormous discretion" (Lieb and Sterk-Elifson, 1995: 691). As the data indicate, this discretion quite often translates into pernicious discrimination along lines of race and class.

THE HEALTH CARE PROFESSION: SHOULD WE TEST? SHOULD WE REPORT?

There are many loci where discretion is exercised and discrimination occurs. It begins with the decision whether to test a woman for substance use. State guidelines for mandatory reporting and testing are often vague and underspecified, leaving the implementation of policies up to individual doctors, clinics, or hospitals. The criteria for determining likelihood of prenatal drug use vary tremendously, but most "risk factors" are associated with socioeconomic status (Beckett, 1995) and race. Physicians often decide whether to order a newborn urine screen based upon whether the mother received timely and adequate prenatal care. Since black women as a group "are twice as likely as white women to begin prenatal care late or not at all" (Krauss, 1991: 528), and poor women are often unable to afford adequate prenatal care, this testing criterion tends to discriminate both by race and by class.

Health care providers also may act upon the basis of straightforward prejudice. As Krauss (*Ibid.*: 527) writes,

> suspicions of substance abuse may be informed by stereotyped assumptions about the identities of drug addicts. . . . [These stereotypes are] reinforced by studies in medical journals which list, with questionable accuracy, the characteristics of those presumed to be at risk.

Florida's reporting policy "does not require documentation of maternal drug use, but only a 'reasonable cause to suspect it . . .'" (*Ibid.*: 527). Therefore, regardless of actual drug history, all women who appear to "fit the profile" are at risk of being subjected to particular scrutiny by social services and the police.

The fact that most testing is conducted at public hospitals that service low-income communities also means that poor women of color are more likely to face drug screening than are women protected by race and class privilege. In private hospitals, pregnant women are usually *not* tested for drug use, even if drug use is suspected (Beckett, 1995). Furthermore, even if they present a positive drug toxicology or admit drug use to their physicians, most women seen in private facilities are not reported to the authorities. Prenatal drug use by women who are affluent and/or white may often be viewed by private and *public* physicians as an exception, a lapse in judgment, or as incidental. Prenatal drug use by poor black women, however, is often viewed as endemic, typical, and evidence of their unfitness for motherhood.

PROSECUTORIAL DISCRETION

Once prenatal drug use is reported, the authorities must then decide what, if any, course of action to take. Dwight Green argues that the unchecked discretion of prosecutors, who are overwhelmingly white and male, means that prenatal drug cases are often based not upon "unbiased law enforcement," but on "pluralistic ignorance" and race, gender, and class discrimination (Greene, 1991). Prosecutors must first decide what statutes, if any, apply to the offense at hand. As mentioned, prosecutors brought prenatal drug abuse trials into existence by stretching the interpretations of existing laws.

Having found an appropriate statute under which to press charges, prosecutors then decide whether to take a given case to trial. There are many intervening factors that go into this decision, often colored by considerations of race and class. Women who drink alcohol or ingest marijuana are quite unlikely to face criminal sanctions for prenatal drug use, even when they are reported to the police (Hoffman, 1990). Greene (1991: 745, *fn.* 28) writes,

> If long-term harm to children was the triggering event, this would present the unlikely image of affluent pregnant white women being subject to arrest at their country clubs or in the suburban home of a friend for having a drink.

The relative influence of a potential defendant may also influence the decision whether to press charges. Suspects in "white collar" crimes, for example, are often able to:

> hire well-paid criminal defense lawyers with social, political, and professional access to the prosecutor's office to argue at case screening conferences against instituting criminal charges or to lessen the seriousness of the crimes to be charged (*Ibid.*: 755).

Even after initiating a criminal case, the prosecutor still has the option to discontinue prosecution. Although prosecuting a poor black crack-addict can boost a district attorney's reelection chances, taking an expectant socialite to trial for popping a handful of barbiturates with a glass of wine may only bring him embarrassment or ridicule.

THE EFFICACY OF CRIMINAL PUNISHMENT

The oft-repeated rationales for taking punitive action against pregnant substance abusers are to force them to enter drug treatment and to safeguard the health of their fetuses. The reality is that taking such action does not ensure, and may often be counterproductive to, the realization of these goals.

Threatening women with jail time in no way ensures that treatment services appropriate for pregnant addicts will be available (Beckett, 1995). One of the ironies of the criminalization of prenatal drug use is that as a "general rule," substance abuse programs do not accept pregnant women (Sexton, 1993). A 1989 study of 78 treatment programs in New York City found that 54% refused all pregnant women, 67% refused pregnant women on Medicaid, and 87% would not accept pregnant women on Medicaid who were addicted to crack (Appel, 1992; Hoffman, 1990; Roberts, 1991). Few addiction programs provide prenatal or obstetrical care and therefore most turn women away rather than risk treatment without these services (Lieb and Sterk-Elifson, 1995; Roberts, 1991).

Drug treatment programs designed primarily to serve men can also be alienating and ineffective for women. Appel (1992: 141) writes, "most treatment approaches are based on the characteristics and dynamics among male populations and comparatively little has been done to define the unique nature of addiction to women." Many female addicts, for example, "turned to drugs, because they were sexually abused or raped as children, and they need help repairing the damage" (Willwerth, 1991: 63). According to one estimate, *80 to 90%* of female alcoholics and drug addicts have been victims of rape or incest (Paltrow, 1990). A program that does not address the special issues facing pregnant addicts will doubtlessly have high rates of withdrawal and relapse. Yet the focus on punishment has generally *not* been accompanied by a correspondingly intense drive to increase the availability of services geared toward the needs of pregnant addicts.[3]

Instituting criminal sanctions for perinatal substance abuse is also counterproductive to the goal of helping women and children because it serves to deter pregnant addicts from seeking medical attention. Medical evidence (cited above) indicates that receiving adequate prenatal care and/or curtailing drug consumption can significantly improve developmental outcomes for cocaine-exposed infants. Yet many women will avoid seeking the information and treatment they need if they realize that a positive urine screen could result in their children being placed in foster care or land them in jail (Krauss, 1991).[4]

Putting women in jail for evidence of drug use upon delivery will not undo whatever harm was done to their newborns in utero. Sending women to prison while pregnant is unlikely to ensure the health of their fetuses either. While incarcerated, pregnant women "face conditions hazardous to fetal health, including overcrowding, poor nutrition, and exposure to contagious disease' (*Ibid.*: 537). Prison health facilities generally provide little or no pre-natal care and are ill-equipped to handle the medical needs of pregnant women, especially those with drug histories. Like other inmates, pregnant addicts may also be able to obtain while imprisoned (Paltrow, 1990; Schroedel and Peretz, 1995). Moreover, if the supply of drugs is suddenly cut off, the physiological changes that immediate withdrawal brings about in the mother and the fetus can be dangerous to both (Schroedel and Peretz, 1995; Appel, 1992).

Criminalizing prenatal substance abuse punishes women for failing to obtain treatment that is generally unavailable and may prevent them from seeking prenatal care. Because of the harm that it is likely to cause, prominent sectors of the medical community have taken a stand against this policy. In a paper published in 1988, the American Medical Association stated that:

> the current policy of prosecuting women who use drugs during preg-nancy is irrational because it does not further the state's purpose of pre-venting harm to infants. . . . [D]rug addiction is an illness, which like any illness, is not due simply to a failure of individual willpower (Lieb and Sterk-Elifson, 1995: 693).

NOTES

[1] All mothers in the study used cocaine and most also used other drugs during their pregnan-cies. Griffith's recent research was conducted with a study population in which several prena-tal risk factors had been eliminated: while pregnant, expectant mothers received prenatal care, nutritional counseling, and therapy for chemical dependency.

[2] Infants born prematurely have increased risk of breathing difficulties, brain hemorrhage, and mental defects. Babies born underweight are 40 times more likely to die than are nor-mal-weight babies and 10 times more likely to have cerebral palsy (Appel, 1992). The black infant mortality rate in 1987 was 17.9 deaths out of 1,000, compared to a white infant mortal-ity rate of 8.6 per 1,000 (Roberts, 1991).

[3] As of 1993, the states of Georgia and New York had instituted mandatory reporting require-ments, yet had allocated no funding for treatment of perinatal addiction (Sexton, 1993).

[4] In 1988, Minnesota became the first state to include perinatal drug use in its legal definition of child abuse. Since that time, observers have claimed that despite the fact that the revised law does not call for criminal sanctions against prenatal drug abusers, it has deterred pregnant addicts from seeking drug treatment and from disclosing their drug use to their doctors (Sex-ton, 1993; Paltrow, 1990).

REFERENCES

Appel, Deborah. 1992. "Drug Use During Pregnancy: State Strategies to Reduce the Prevalence of Prenatal Drug Exposure." *University of Florida Journal of Law and Public Policy* 5 (Fall): 103–148.

Barone, Diane. 1994. "Myths About 'Crack Babies.'" *Educational Leadership* 52 (Octo-ber): 67–68.

Beckett, Katherine. 1995. "Fetal Rights and 'Crack Moms': Pregnant Women in the War on Drugs." *Contemporary Drug Problems* 22 (Winter): 587–612.

Curriden, Mark. 1990. "Holding Mom Accountable." *ABA Journal* (March): 50–53.

Debettencourt, Kathleen B. 1990. "The Wisdom of Solomon: Cutting the Chord That Harms." *Children Today* 19 (August): 17–20.

Dobson, Tracy and Kimberly K. Eby. 1992. "Criminal Liability for Substance Abuse During Pregnancy: The Controversy of Maternal v. Fetal Rights." *Saint Louis University Law Journal* 36,3 (Spring): 655–694.

Elshtain, Jean Bethke. 1990. "Pregnancy Police: If You're an Addict It's Now a Crime to Give Birth." *The Progressive* 54 (December): 26–28.

Feldman, Joseph G., Howard L. Minkoff, Sandra McCalla, and Martin Salwen. 1992. "A Cohort Study of the Impact of Perinatal Drug Use on Prematurity in an Inner-City Population." *American Journal of Public Health* 82 (May): 726–728.

Furio, Joanne. 1994. "Women Fight Civil Rights Abuse in South Carolina." *Ms.* 5 (November/December): 93.

Gittler, Josephine and Dr. Merle McPherson. 1990. "Prenatal Substance Abuse." *Children Today* 19 (July/August): 3–7.

Greene, Dwight L. 1991. "Abusive Prosecutors: Gender, Race, and Class Discretion and the Prosecution of Drug-Addicted Mothers." *Buffalo Law Review* 39,3 (Fall): 737.

Greider, Katherine. 1995. "Crackpot Ideas." *Mother Jones* 20 (July/August): 52–56.

Griffith, Dan R. 1992. "Prenatal Exposure to Cocaine and Other Drugs: Developmental and Educational Prognoses." *Phi Delta Kappan* 74 (September): 30–34.

Hoffman, Jan. 1990. "Pregnant, Addicted—and Guilty?" The *New York Times Magazine* (August 19): 32–35.

Hopkins, Ellen. 1990. "Childhood's End." *Rolling Stone* (October 18): 66–69; 71–72; 108–110.

Irwin, Katherine. 1995. "Ideology, Pregnancy, and Drugs: Differences Between Crack-Cocaine, Heroin, and Methamphetamine Users." *Contemporary Drug Problems* 22 (Winter): 613–637.

Krauss, Deborah K. 1991. "Regulating Women's Bodies: The Adverse Effect of Fetal Rights Theory on Childbirth Decisions and Women of Color." *Harvard Civil Rights Civil Liberties Law Review* 26,4 (Summer): 523–548.

Langone, John. 1995. "Crack Comes to the Nursery: More and More Cocaine-Using Mothers Are Bearing Afflicted Infants." *Time* 132 (September 19): 85.

Lieb, John J., and Claire Sterk-Elifson. 1995. "Crack in the Cradle: Social Policy and Reproductive Rights Among Crack-Using Females." *Contemporary Drug Problems* 22 (Winter): 687–705.

Logli, Paul A. 1990. "Drugs in the Womb: The Newest Battlefield in the War on Drugs." *Criminal Justice Ethics* (Winter/Spring): 23–29.

Manner, Wendy K., Leonard H. Glantz, and George J. Annas 1990. "Pregnancy, Drugs, and the Perils of Prosecution." *Criminal Justice Ethics* (Winter/Spring): 30–41.

Neil, Benjamin A. 1992. "Prenatal Drug Abuse: Is the Mother Criminally Liable?" *Trial Diplomacy Journal* 15:129–135.

Neuspiel, Daniel R., Morri Markowitz, and Ernest Drucker. 1994. "Intrauterine Cocaine, Lead, and Nicotine Exposure and Fetal Growth." *American Journal of Public Health* 84 (September): 1492–1495.

Paltrow, Lynn M. 1990. "When Becoming Pregnant Is a Crime." *Criminal Justice Ethics* (Winter/ Spring): 42–47.

Plummer, William, and S. Avery Brown. 1990. "Children in Peril." *People Weekly* 33 (April 16): 82–91.

Pollitt, Kathy. 1990. "'Fetal Rights': A New Assault on Feminism." *The Nation* 250 (March 26): 409–411; 414–416.

Roberts, Dorothy E. 1991. "Punishing Drug Addicts Who Have Babies: Women of Color, Equality, and the Right of Privacy." *Harvard Law Review* 104,7 (May): 1419–1482.

Schroedel, Jean Reith, and Paul Peretz. 1995. "A Gender Analysis of Policy Formation: The Case of Fetal Abuse." Patricia Boling (ed.), *Expecting Trouble: Surrogacy, Fetal Abuse, and New Reproductive Technologies.* Boulder: Westview Press.

Sexton, Patricia A. 1993. "Imposing Criminal Sanctions on Pregnant Drug Users: Throwing the Baby out with the Bath Water." *Washburn Law Journal* 32 (Spring): 410–430.

Sullum, Jacob. 1992. "The Cocaine Kids." *Reason* 24 (August/September): 14.

Willwerth, James. 1991. "Should We Take Away Their Kids?" *Time* 137 (May 13):62–63.

Young, Iris Marion. 1995. "Punishment, Treatment, Empowerment: Three Approaches to Policy for Pregnant Addicts." Patricia Boling (ed.), *Expecting Trouble: Surrogacy, Fetal Abuse, and New Reproductive Technologies.* Boulder: Westview Press.

Zitella, Julia J. 1996. "Protecting Our Children: A Call to Reform State Policies to Hold Pregnant Drug Addicts Accountable." *John Marshall Law Review* 29,3 (Spring): 768–798.

20

Alcohol and Tobacco
The Real Dangerous Drugs?

Erich Goode

James Q. Wilson (1990a) asks us to perform a mental experiment. Imagine, he says, that in the 1920s, alcohol had been criminalized, and cocaine and heroin remained legal. Would the criminalization of alcohol have produced a criminal underworld of users and addicts? In contrast, would the two currently illegal drugs have become socially acceptable and widely used? If so, would the legalizers now be claiming that it is *cocaine* and *heroin* that are the more dangerous drugs, and that *alcohol*, being safer, should be legalized? In short, are the legalizers being duped into thinking that legal drugs are the more dangerous, not because of their intrinsic qualities, but simply because they are more widely used? Shouldn't we be worried about what will happen when cocaine and heroin are legalized and, hence, much more widely used? There's a lesson to be learned from this mental experiment, Wilson warns.

Legalizers claim that the legal drugs, alcohol and tobacco, are more dangerous than has been acknowledged and, in fact, more dangerous than the illegal drugs—heroin, cocaine, marijuana, LSD, methedrine ("ice"), PCP (Sernyl, or "angel dust"), and the prescription drugs (when used for the purpose of intoxication rather than medication). Consequently, they say, the law and its enforcement are targeting the wrong drugs. As a result, prohibition is both discriminatory and ineffective. Why waste tens of billions of dollars, ruining hundreds of thousands of lives in the process, by criminalizing the

From *Between Politics and Reason: The Drug Legalization Debate*, 135–149. © 1997 St. Martins Press. Used with the permission of Worth Publishers.

users of comparatively safe drugs while the use and sale of *more* dangerous drugs are tolerated, even encouraged?

Let's . . . separate two entirely different issues here: the *moral/ideological* and the *empirical* issues. The moral or ideological issue says, arresting illegal drug users but permitting consumers of alcohol and tobacco to go their merry way is *unfair* and *discriminatory*. The *empirical* issue says, alcohol and tobacco are medically more harmful than cocaine, heroin, and the other illegal drugs. The first issue, that of fairness, is essentially resolvable; it has its roots in philosophy and even theology. It is a non sequitur, a "So what?" argument. To say that it is unfair to arrest drug users and sellers but tolerate drinkers and smokers and that, *therefore*, the former substances should be legalized, does not logically follow. There may be a variety of reasons why a given activity or substance is banned while another is permitted; their relative dangerousness is only one of them. For instance, penalizing one activity may result in far more negative consequences than the other; the total damage may tip the balance in favor of cracking down on one and tolerating the other. Consequently, let's concentrate on the second issue, the *consequentialist* or *empirical* question, and ignore the first, the moral issue. More specifically, let's examine the evidence on the relative harm of the substances in question.

What is the scorecard on harm? There is no doubt whatsoever that the legal drugs are a great deal more dangerous than most of us believe, while it's possible that the illegal drugs are less so. It's hard to imagine any public health expert questioning this point. But what about the harm of the illegal relative to the legal drugs? The legalizers argue: Let's compare the number of deaths from legal drugs with the number of deaths from illegal drugs. Pile up the bodies, and which source wins? It's legal drugs, hands down. But they also make a second empirical point as well; they argue that *if* the currently illegal drugs were to be legalized, their medical harm would decline, just as with crime and violence. Legalized, heroin and cocaine would cause less disease and fewer deaths than they do now.

As to the first point, let's look at the medical record, they say. We've already seen that the two legal drugs cause or significantly contribute to the loss of well over half a million American lives per year—430,000 for tobacco and between 100,000 and 150,000 for alcohol. The methods by which these estimates were reached are complex and technical, and widely accepted; they need not detain us here. The important point is that our legal drugs kill hundreds of thousands of users—and nonusers as well, counting victims of homicide, accidents, and passive smoke. In contrast, the legalizers say, the total number of deaths from illegal drugs adds up to a mere 3,500 in a recent year, according to one advocate (Nadelmann, 1989, p.943). Are legal drugs almost 150 times more dangerous than illegal drugs? Are alcohol and tobacco far more dangerous than heroin and cocaine? Is this possible? Are the legal drugs more dangerous than the illegal drugs?

The legalizers make a second and even stronger point: It is *criminalization* that makes the currently illegal drugs *as harmful as they are*. Legalize them, and they would be *even less* harmful. Here's what legalization would do, they say: regulate the production and sale of the now-illegal drugs, standardize the dose, make certain that they contain no impurities, distribute clean needles and condoms, make sure that treatment and maintenance programs are available to addicts and abusers on a walk-in basis. All these changes would result in a dramatic reduction in drug-related deaths (Nadelmann, 1989, p.942).

Legal or illegal drugs: Which category is more dangerous? While legal drugs do cause more deaths, there are at least four problems with the legalizers' comparison between legal and illegal drugs as sources of death. First, the comparisons that are most often made are between apples and oranges. For the *legal* drugs, deaths from *all* sources, as well as for the *entire country*, are tallied; for the *illegal* drugs, deaths from only *certain* sources and only in certain *areas* of the country are tabulated. Second, the figures on drug-related deaths are meaningless until they are connected to the *extent* and *frequency* of use. Third . . . we don't know whether or how these figures will change under legalization. The legalizers are placing their money on no increases in the use of heroin and cocaine under legalization; the rest of us aren't so sure about this. What if use skyrockets? And fourth, the legalization tally makes no mention of an absolutely crucial measure in the field of public health: *number of years of life lost*. But the legalizers do insist on a crucial point, one that is in their favor: A distinction must be made between *primary* (or direct) and *secondary* (or indirect) drug harms.

Apples and Oranges

Let's start with the "apples and oranges" issue; for the illegal drugs, we need to estimate roughly the overall total deaths they cause. . . . DAWN estimates that 430,000 drug-related emergency room episodes took place in the coterminous United States. During the same period, 8,500 drug abuse-related deaths were tallied by DAWN, but only 43 metropolitan areas were included in the program (HHS, 1994b, 1994d, 1995b). If we use the same formula DAWN used to extrapolate from the emergency rooms they studied to the country as a whole, we come up with a total of 16,500 acute drug-related deaths. Some of these deaths entailed the use of alcohol in combination with illegal drugs, and some entailed the recreational use of, or suicides by taking, prescription drugs, that is, the illegal use of legal prescription drugs. A few are the result of taking overdoses of over-the-counter drugs like aspirin and Tylenol. Even so, 16,500 deaths is a very long way from the tally racked up by the legal drugs— 430,000 for cigarettes and roughly 100,000 to 150,000 for alcohol.

Of course, these medical examiners' reports on drug-related and drug-caused deaths only entail *acute* reactions, as well as deaths from fairly *direct* medical causes. We know nothing from the DAWN data about deaths from *chronic* illegal drug-related causes. We know that most of the deaths that legal drugs cause are from *chronic*, not acute, causes—for instance, lung cancer as a result of cigarette smoking and cirrhosis of the liver from excessive drinking. Yes, the major slice of the deaths that the illegal drugs cause is acute in origin. This is partly because most drug addicts, unlike drinkers and smokers, do not live long enough to become victims of many chronic drug-related illnesses. But at least two additional sources of death are worth mentioning; one is nonacute in nature and the other is not, strictly speaking, medical in origin: the first, contracting the AIDS/HIV virus, and the second, drug-related violence.

Half the roughly half a million to a million needle-using heroin addicts in the country are infected with the HIV virus. It is not unlikely that almost all of them (that is, a quarter to half a million) will die within a decade or two. And a very high proportion, perhaps as many as 10 percent, of the heaviest chronic cocaine and crack-dependent abusers are similarly infected, some through the use of needles and some as a result of engaging in unprotected sex (McCoy and Inciardi, 1995); hence, they share the same medical fate as the infected heroin addicts. Clearly, then, drug abuse is a prodigious—and growing—source of AIDS-related death. It is possible that, as a result of their use of heroin and cocaine, 25,000 to as many as 50,000 Americans *a year* will die of AIDS in the early years of the twenty-first century. The legalizers argue that these deaths are largely or entirely due to the current ban on needle exchange programs; their numbers would drastically decline under the plan legalizers propose. And AIDS is a secondary consequence of drug use, but that's a separate issue. And violence? Here, we're relying on a bit more speculation than for AIDS-related deaths. Roughly 25,000 Americans are murdered each year. How many are drug-related? A common estimate is that half of all large-city criminal homicides, or perhaps a quarter of the total, some 6,000 to 8,000, are causally related to the use of illegal drugs. This is a lot of people, but the total is unlikely to exceed the deaths racked up for alcohol. . . .

Suffice it to say that, if the total sources of yearly death from illegal drugs are tallied for the country as a whole, we'd come up with a total many times higher than Nadelmann's 3,500 figure. Illegal drug use is a great deal more dangerous than the legalizers claim.

Extent and Frequency of Use

Second point. To me, the key question here relates to the extent and frequency of use: Under legalization, would the use of heroin and cocaine rise and, with it, the damage their use causes? Many observers say yes. I agree. As John Kaplan says, denying that it would simply ignores one of the most basic generalizations in the field of pharmacology (1988, p.33). Statistics on harm must be considered with reference to total use, or prevalence. . . . Not only are there more *users* of legal than illegal drugs, but their continuance rates, likewise, are considerably higher. Suffice it to say that *legal* drugs are used *vastly* more often than the *illegal* drugs are, on an episode-for-episode basis. Roughly 60 to 70 billion "doses" of alcohol (that is, drinks containing one ounce) and something like 500 billion "doses" of nicotine (that is, individual cigarettes) are consumed in the United States each year. The point is, when discussing the dangers of these two legal drugs, we must keep in mind their total number of users and the total number of *episodes* of their use. In contrast, there are between half a million and a million heroin addicts or more-or-less daily abusers, and between two and three million Americans taking cocaine weekly or more (Goldstein, 1994, p.241; Kleiman, 1992b, p.288), which add up to vastly smaller use figures for the illegal drugs than for alcohol and cigarettes. Estimating the total number of times addicts as well as the more casual users of these two drugs take heroin and cocaine is likely to be tricky; still, it is unlikely to be more than a tenth the number of doses of alcohol and one one-hundredth that of cigarettes.

On an episode-for-episode basis, which is more dangerous: using legal or illegal drugs? We may not come up with a clearly more dangerous category. Different drugs kill in different ways, and our evidence is quite messy and inexact. In the absence of more precise measures, it should be sufficient to say that, while, *descriptively*, the legal drugs kill many more Americans than the illegal drugs do, *relative to the extent of their use*, we may have something of a tie. To answer the question definitively, we'd need more data. Both categories certainly kill a lot of people; both categories include very dangerous drugs. Consider the fact that heroin appears almost as often in DAWN's lethal "overdose" statistics as cocaine—and the fact that, in the United States, cocaine is used something like 10 times as often as heroin. It seems almost certain that there is something *intrinsic* about heroin itself, not the mere fact that it is illegal, that is related to its capacity to kill.

Years of Life Lost

Another point concerning the legalizers' flawed argument: ignoring years of life lost. Legal and illegal drugs do not kill their victims at the same age in the life span. The legal drugs kill *older* victims, and, hence, there are fewer years of life lost per victim; the average victim of the illegal drugs tends to be younger, and, hence, for each death, far more years of life are lost. Tobacco and alcohol are most likely to kill persons in their fifties, sixties, and seventies—tobacco kills those a bit older, alcohol those a bit younger; but taken as a whole and on average, they kill the middle-aged to the elderly. In contrast, heroin and cocaine are most likely to kill victims in their twenties and thirties. The fact that AIDS, almost entirely contracted from drug-addicted mothers, is the number one killer of children age one to four in New York City is dramatic evidence that age cannot be ignored in any evaluation of harm. Thus, on a death-by-death basis, far more years of life are lost as a consequence of the use of the illegal drugs than of the legal drugs. This point cannot be ignored in any public health tabulation of the relative harm of these two categories of drugs. Even factoring this into the equation, we're still a long way from parity for the two drug categories as a source of death, but it does tip the scales a bit.

Primary Versus Secondary Harm

One problem with any exercise which equates sources of death as a result of the use of different drugs is that it is difficult to separate the contribution that drug use per se makes to drug-related medical problems, death, accidents, violence, and other measures of harm and dangerousness from the legal status of these drugs. That is, are the correlations between drug use and harm a *primary* effect of the drug itself or a *secondary* product of the circumstances of use, including the drug's legal status? Says Mark Kleiman: "The failure to distinguish between the bad effects of drug abuse and the bad effects of drug abuse control sometimes reduces public discourse about drugs to gibberish" (1992b, p.17). At the same time, in some cases, this distinction is not always easy to make. "Some aspects of the drug problem defy division into results of pharmacology and results of legislation" (p. 17). We know that, by itself, heroin does not make the user sick, and that moderate and controlled doses do not cause the user to die. On the other hand, heroin addicts are taking a drug that can kill them; it is *heroin* that causes addicts to overdose if they take too much. It is not legal policy by itself that causes the medical problem addicts experience, nor is it the pharmacology of narcotics alone. We must free ourselves from the clutches of either-or-thinking; we must stop imagining that drugs, by themselves, are magical substances that have harmful effects—*and* that law enforcement alone is responsible for the medical harm we see in addicts and abusers. It is a combination of the two.

Nonetheless, if the currently illegal drugs were legalized, would they inflict less—or more—harm on the American public? Would as many users die of drug overdoses? Of drug-related disease? The legalizers claim that, in comparison with the legal drugs, not only are the currently illegal drugs relatively safe but they also would be a great deal *safer* if they were to be legalized (Nadelmann, 1989, pp. 941–942). In opposition, the prohibitionists argue that the statistics measuring the relative harm of legal versus illegal drugs is an artifact of their legal status. Legalize the currently illegal drugs, and they will become a great deal *more* dangerous, not less. It is only because of their illegality that heroin and cocaine are expensive, difficult to obtain, and therefore relatively infrequently used; legalize them, and more people will use them—and more will become sick and die as a result (Wilson, 1990a).

As I've already argued, here I agree with the criminalizers far more than with the legalizers. The evidence is extremely strong that more people would use the currently illegal drugs if the drugs were legalized and made more readily accessible. More important, the current addicts and abusers of heroin and cocaine would use a great deal *more frequently*—and more abusively—if they found that they could obtain these drugs with less cost and less hassle than is true now. It is difficult to imagine that anyone would discount the role of opportunity in use; regardless of the restrictions that legalization might place in the path of cocaine and heroin users, the restrictions would inevitably be less binding than is true under criminalization. To the extent that restrictions would apply, addicts and abusers would simply seek out the illicit market for their needs. No amount of good intentions will alter that fact.

Still, the legalizers do make several good points. First, state-distributed drugs will be purer and more dosage-controlled than are the illicit drugs currently sold on the street. Contamination is not *the*, or even *a*, major problem for drugs sold on the street; a certain proportion of the batches of illicit drugs are contaminated, of course, but dealers who sell such goods are not likely to stay in business very long. (Marijuana sprayed with Paraquat, once a serious problem, hardly ever shows up any more.) Potency and purity vary greatly from one batch to another and can pose a serious problem for any user, but users tend to be foolhardy about the number of doses they take at one time as well as taking several different drugs at the same time. Variations in potency and purity simply add another problem on top of several others that will still prevail, whether legalization is instituted or not. Keep in mind the fact that the rate of death among heroin addicts in the United Kingdom and the United States (mostly drug overdoses in both places) is the same, about 2 percent a year (Goldstein, 1994, p. 241). Although Great Britain is a long way from legalization—some of its jurisdictions, such as Liverpool, are a great deal closer to it than others—it is also a system that is far more liberal and flexible, and less punitive, than is true of the United States. The fact that Great Britain has a somewhat different system but practically identical rates of drug-related death among addicts does not speak strongly for the legalizers' argument on harm.

Their point on expanding drug treatment programs (along with a reduction in law enforcement directed at drug violators) is well taken. The problem is, hardly any drug expert questions it. It has become almost a truism that our priorities are misplaced; instead of a budget that allocates 25 percent to treatment (and education) and 75 percent to law enforcement, including interdiction and incarceration, we should have one where this ratio is reversed. Methadone maintenance programs should be expanded; so should therapeutic communities. Needle exchange and condom distribution programs promise to keep the rate of HIV and AIDS among addicts and drug abusers from rising (Lee, 1994). Clinics in mobile vans can search out addicts who are unwilling to come into an established program and can distribute methadone, needles, condoms, medical care, and information. There are many ways that the harmful consequences of drug abuse can be kept in check short of outright legalization, and many experts support a number of them. If nothing *aside from the factors that legalizers discuss* were to change, of course, legalization would produce less disease and fewer deaths among addicts and abusers. The problem is, drug use is a dynamic and volatile proposition; many observers believe that many of the changes that legalization would bring about would result in more medical harm, not less.

The Scorecard

After all the possible sources of death are considered—and we have considered only a few—what does our scorecard look like? Which is the more dangerous category of drugs: legal or illegal? Are alcohol and tobacco more capable of causing harm—or heroin and cocaine? Focusing narrowly on *acute* medical effects, there is absolutely no doubt that heroin and cocaine—especially heroin—are far more likely to cause a medical emergency and lead to death by overdose on *an episode-by-episode basis.* Their contribution to DAWN's lethal medical examiners' reports is truly prodigious. (Alcohol causes many overdoses, most not counted by DAWN, but it is a far, far more widely used drug.) In contrast, focusing narrowly on direct, *chronic* medical effects, heroin and the narcotics do not cause the medical pathologies that alcohol and tobacco cigarettes do. (Incredibly, overdosing aside, narcotics cause no life-threatening medical pathologies of any kind.) It would be difficult for any drug to match alcohol's ravaging impact on the liver or tobacco's carcinogenic impact on the lungs. (The exact nature of the long-term impact of cocaine—and amphetamine—on the brain remains to be seen; we already know that in large doses over a long period of time, alcohol does damage the brain.) In addition, the illegal drugs are *indirectly* implicated in death in at least two major ways: the transmission of the HIV virus, through contaminated needles and unprotected sex, and murder resulting from dealing-related conflicts.

All in all, the sources of drug-related death from both legal and illegal substances are considerable. It is difficult to select one category over the other as incontestably safer or more dangerous. Certainly criminalization contributes to some sources of illegal drug-related death (violence and AIDS), but it may inhibit others (acute and chronic medical pathologies). In the process of weighing the relative dangers of these two drug categories, it is difficult to come away with anything other than a mixed scorecard. Legalization is extremely unlikely to result in all the medical benefits legalizers argue for it. Addicts and drug abusers lead extremely unsafe lives; a surprisingly high proportion of them drink heavily—a substantial minority of methadone maintenance patients drink at alcoholic levels—take a variety of drugs simultaneously, use wildly different quantities and potencies of heroin and cocaine from one day to the next, use unsterile needles, are oblivious to nutrition, engage in dangerous illegal activities (such as robbery), are often arrested, and so on. While some of these factors will probably change under legalization, the total picture is not likely to change very much, for the one burning factor the legalizers are unable to dismiss is a rise in drug use following legalization. This renders their argument shaky if not specious.

Controls on Alcohol and Tobacco

As I said at the beginning of this chapter, the question of whether it is fair or just to criminalize the possession and sale of heroin and cocaine while keeping alcohol and tobacco legal is essentially unanswerable; it is a moral and ideological, not a sociological, issue. However, there is no contradiction between advocating legal reform for the currently illegal drugs—even legalization—*and* tighter restrictions on the legal drugs. In fact, following the "harm reduction" line of reasoning, it is likely that more lives will be saved by making tobacco and alcohol less accessible than by instituting any conceivable drug legalization or decriminalization program. In fact, Ethan Nadelmann, a major legalization spokesperson, has argued for control strategies aimed at tobacco and cigarettes (1989, p.945), and Mark Kleiman, a drug reformer who advocates limited legalization of marijuana, supports a variety of controls on the legal drugs (1992b, 203ff., 317ff.). The logic? Again, consider the numbers: Alcohol and tobacco kill many more people than the illegal drugs do because they are much more widely used; in the case of tobacco, roughly 50 million addicts use it dozens of times each day. The legal drugs are harmful because too many people use them far too frequently. Said another way, the legal drugs are far too readily available; too many people are finding it far too easy to get their hands on them. There is practically no "hassle factor" involved in obtaining and using them. (It is only after many episodes of use—in the case of tobacco, after literally decades of use—that the debt for use must be paid.) Hence, the question becomes, how do we lower the use of alcohol and tobacco? If we are serious about rewriting legal policy to reduce harm, this is an extremely important question.

Please note that the following discussion of harm reduction strategies aimed at the legal drugs is not a display of my ideological or moral biases. I am not endorsing them as strategies so much as proposing that *if* they are adopted, fewer people will get sick and die as a result of use-related ailments. This is an empirically defensible exercise. Also note that, for tobacco at least, *almost all* smokers began the habit by age 19. Hence, any strategy that delays the onset of smoking will prolong life. This means that the most meaningful and most viable harm reduction strategies should be aimed at teenagers. The earlier in their lives that potential smokers are targeted, the greater the possible impact such a strategy is likely to have.

Can we control tobacco and alcohol abuse through the vehicle of taxation? In fact, why not kill two birds with one stone? We could increase taxes to reduce use and, at the same time, offset the costs that smokers and drinkers impose on the rest of us by charging them more for using those substances. We already know that the cost of a psychoactive substance is correlated with its use—the higher the cost, the lower the use. What increases the cost of legal drugs? Why, an increase in taxation, of course; increase the taxes on tobacco and alcohol products, and use will decline (Goldstein, 1994, p.278; Goldstein and Kalant, 1990). The data supporting our ability to kill (or at least wound) the bird of high-volume use is fairly clear-cut and unambiguous. Of course, with higher taxation comes its inevitable by-product: a certain volume of clandestine, illegal, or underground sales of the product that is taxed. But once again, choosing a total package—lower use and a larger black market versus higher use and a smaller black market—is a political and ideological not an empirical question.

The other bird isn't so easy to kill or wound, in part because the figures are more difficult to come by. Weighing the economic cost that smoking and drinking impose on the society versus the tax revenue that these products generate is an exceedingly complicated exercise. Tracing out all the economic costs, direct and indirect, of indulgence in these two legal drugs is not an easy matter; as soon as we alter one factor, the entire picture changes. Moreover, what do we include in the picture? In the case of alcohol, do we include the increased cost of an already-substantial criminal justice system? How do we measure the decline in productivity that takes place when the drinker can't show up for work? Or a decline in efficiency on the job the morning after an alcoholic binge? Another consideration: Often, observers fail to distinguish between costs that public facilities or nonsmokers incur ("external" costs) and those costs that are paid for directly by the smoker ("internal" costs). And do we calculate the costs incurred by a smoker's or a drinker's family as "external" or "internal" costs? Likewise, consider the following: Smokers get sick more often than nonsmokers and, hence, cost the rest of us far higher medical bills. However, they also tend to die at a significantly younger age; thus, they are less likely to need medical care and collect Social Security and retirement benefits when they become aged—because they more rarely *live* to be aged. Hence, ironically (at least in this one respect), the smoking habit actually *saves* the society a great deal of money! And, while heavy drinking is also related to an earlier demise, this is offset by the fact that alcoholics are more likely to *retire* significantly earlier than nondrinkers and moderate drinkers and, hence, are likely to draw public benefits for a longer period of time. Again, it should be clear that calculating the strictly economic costs of the use of the legal drugs is an exceedingly tricky proposition.

Alcoholic beverages are taxed about 25 cents per ounce of absolute alcohol; this has actually declined, relative to inflation, over the past half century. For cigarettes, the current total for local, state, and federal taxes—averaged out nationwide—is about 53 cents per pack. To put a very long and complex equation into extremely simple terms, economic experts who have studied the question say that alcohol taxes do not pay for the costs they impose, while taxes on cigarettes *do* pay their own way. Taxes on alcohol would have to be approximately *doubled* to reach a breakeven point (let's say to 50 cents per ounce of absolute alcohol); in contrast, all things considered, each pack of cigarettes sold only costs the society 33 cents in economic cost, for a net saving of 20 cents (Gravelle and Zimmerman, 1994; Kotata, 1989; Manning et al., 1989; Viscusi, 1995; Warner et al., 1995). One major difference between smokers and heavy drinkers is the fact that drinkers are more likely to harm other parties in addition to themselves (accident and crime victims, for instance), while smokers are more likely to harm only themselves.

Whether we are killing one bird or two, taxation can be used as a policy both to discourage use and to pay for the costs legal drug users impose on the rest of us. To reduce the harm inflicted on society *and* reduce use, one expert has tentatively proposed a tax of $1 per alcoholic drink and $5 per pack of cigarettes (Kleiman, 1992b, pp.248, 352). Of course, the tax rate would have to be standardized—or at least the differences minimized—for all states to keep the level of smuggling to a minimum. For tobacco at least, increasing taxation "offers the single greatest opportunity for reducing the toll drug taking takes on American life. There is no comparable opportunity for improving health through policy regarding any of the currently illicit drugs" (1992b, p.354). Another consideration: The likelihood that a proposal entailing hugely increased taxes on cigarettes and alcohol will be enacted within the next two decades is very nearly zero, however much sense it makes from a public health standpoint; too many powerful vested interests would oppose the measure and, chances are, would also convince the public that it is in their interest to oppose it as well. Still, restrictions on both alcohol and cigarette consumption are taking hold nationwide on a piecemeal basis; perhaps, eventually, the wisdom of control through taxation, likewise, will begin to occur to harm reduction reformers. Keep in mind that younger users and potential users, who have the least amount of money, will be most likely to be affected by tax increases. And keep in mind, too, that the further down the income ladder we look, taxes on alcohol and cigarettes will take up a greater proportion of the user's total income.

Harm reduction control strategies need not remain the exclusive domain of federal, state, and local government; private citizens, too, could explore ways to reduce the harm that the legal drugs cause. Aside from increasing taxes, some possible strategies might include:

Ban all cigarette vending machines. This not only would reduce availability and possibly use overall but also would almost certainly reduce use among underage smokers. Although only one pack of cigarettes in 20 purchased by a teenager is obtained from a vending machine, roughly 10 times as many 14-year-olds as 18-year-olds obtain cigarettes from a vending machine. Harm reduction strategy dictates that vending machines dispensing cigarettes be banned altogether—or, at the very least, that they be banned in areas that are accessible to minors.

Enforce the law against cigarette sales to minors. Some 90 percent of teenagers say they purchase their own cigarettes (Kleiman, 1992b, p.343). Unlike establishments that sell liquor, vendors selling cigarettes do not have a license to lose; hence, violations are common. Knowing that selling to minors is illegal, nearly three-quarters of vendors questioned said that they would be willing to sell cigarettes to an 11-year-old girl (DiFranza et al., 1987). A 1993 study commissioned by the New York City Department of Consumer Affairs found that 48 of 60 stores sold *loose* cigarettes (for 15 to 20 cents apiece) to 12-to-14-year-old undercover agents; *all* the rest sold *packs* of cigarettes to these same teenagers (Messenger, 1995). Perhaps licensing for the sale of cigarettes could be explored: If vendors violate the law by selling to a minor, they lose the right to sell cigarettes. One study of 6,000 teenagers found that nearly half (45 percent) were *never* asked for proof of age (Feder, 1996).

Increase negative advertising. The alcohol and tobacco industry could be taxed to support a vigorous and effective campaign designed to reduce heavy drinking and smoking. In addition, cigarette ads blatantly aimed at children could be banned altogether. The misleading and false disinformation distributed by the tobacco industry—the alcoholic beverage industry has not launched comparable campaigns—could be offset by counter-advertising and valid information that have a concrete impact on use. The distribution of free samples of cigarettes could be outlawed. The effectiveness of banning *all* cigarette and alcohol advertising could be explored. Would a ban it be effective? If evidence says yes, outlaw it.

Ban the export of American cigarette products abroad. As the number of cigarettes sold domestically declines, tobacco companies are targeting sales to other countries. All too often this means sales to developing Third World countries, which can least bear the burden of crushing medical expenses and the premature death of substantial segments of their populations. Should the American tobacco industry have the legal right to export death abroad? Jesse Helms, [former] senator from the tobacco-growing state of North Carolina, put strong pressure on some countries that import U.S. tobacco to lift any and all tobacco restrictions. (Recall that Helms urged that federal support for AIDS be reduced because its victims brought the disease on themselves.) Such complicity with death might be exposed, publicized, and counteracted (Goldstein, 1994, p.279; Kleiman, 1992b, p.348).

Enact legislation outlawing the use of tobacco by minors. The fact is, purchasing a pack of cigarettes takes a few seconds, while smoking a cigarette takes a number of minutes—and, hence, the latter is much more vulnerable to detection. Such laws should *not* fall in the realm of the criminal law—entailing, as they could, arrest, jail, prison, and an arrest record—but should be regarded as minor offenses, somewhere in between a speeding ticket and a citation for driving while intoxicated. Fines, community service, or meaningful reeducation programs would be appropriate penalties (Kleiman, 1992b, pp.344–345).

Enact legislation further restricting public smoking. This has begun to take place in some locales—for instance, in restaurants in San Francisco, in restaurants above a certain size in New York City, on most airline flights, and in many work sites nationwide. Citizens could urge legislation further restricting where smokers are allowed to blow smoke in the faces of nonsmokers. The nonsmoking majority should make it clear to legislators that they endorse their right to breathe uncontaminated air.

Enforce the drunk driving laws. At present, penalties for drunk driving are ludicrously light and only fitfully applied. In Scandinavia, a loss of one's license is the penalty for first offenses, and jail sentences are imposed for second offenses; the impact of such penalties is not clear, with some observers arguing that the policy is effective and others claiming that it has no effect. An experiment in Oklahoma (Grasmick, Bursik, and Arneklev, 1993) showed that, when legal sanctions and the threat of public embarrassment and shame for drunk driving are combined, drunk driving declines. A variety of possible sanctions should be explored; what counts is what works. For the most part, however, alcohol-related auto fatalities have declined in the United States over the past two decades, from half to a third. Even among teenagers, the decline has been significant and striking. We must be doing something right.

Restrict the sale of alcoholic beverages. Should beer and wine be sold in supermarkets? In fact, perhaps the sale of all alcoholic beverages could be restricted to a small number of state-run Alcoholic Beverage Control or "package" stores. Abolish all "happy hours" and all other special occasions in bars during which large discounts are offered to customers. Abolish all sale and use of alcoholic beverages at sporting events, on college and university campuses, on public transportation, and at all government functions (Goldstein, 1994, p.280). While none of these, by themselves, is likely to have a measurable impact on drinking, they send a message and set a climate that may signal a move to greater moderation in drinking.

Four additional points. First, the goal of such proposals is not to catch offenders but to reduce drinking and smoking and therefore harm; enforcement should be flexible and pragmatic, not vindictive. Second, policy should always maximize citizen-based initiative and minimize government intervention; the latter becomes necessary only when it becomes clear either that private citizens do not have certain powers or that they are unwilling to exercise them. Third, to repeat a point worth repeating, my speculation that these proposals will reduce harm to the society are empirical in nature, not moral or ideological. They may sound Puritanical and anti-hedonistic. Personally, I am very much in favor of pleasure; I indulge in it myself. But pleasure should not be purchased at the cost of far greater pain. Worldwide, in the twentieth century, tens of millions of human beings have died as a result of indulgence in the *legal* drugs. Does not such a tragic loss of life deserve—demand—effective intervention? How many will die in the twenty-first century? If we do nothing, the figure could be far greater than the number of bodies that have piled up already. And fourth, again, to repeat an important point, very few of these proposals have any hope of implementation in the near future, at least in the form in which I've stated them. Right now, they are in the realm of utopianism. But consider, as Trebach does (1993, pp.81–82), the fact that before 1990, hardly anyone would have given the peaceful collapse of the Soviet Union much of a chance. He feels that this indicates that the very long shot of some form of legalization might be possible in the United States. I disagree, but my guess is, some of the preceding controls over alcohol and tobacco are a great deal more likely. In 1995, the American Medical Association recommended some of these reforms (Maier and Yu, 1995). And beginning in 1996, several former employees of the tobacco industry, a scientist and an executive, presented documentation that high-level managers were aware of tobacco's addicting properties and lied about this fact under oath. Perhaps these revelations will yield valuable resources for future lawsuits against the industry and will cripple its capacity to sell a dangerous drug to the public. Some of the proposals outlined above may be adopted here and there in the near future, and perhaps many of them will be implemented during the twenty-first century. If not, it is our loss.

REFERENCES

DiFranza, Joseph, et al. 1987. "Legislative Efforts to Protect Children from Tobacco." *Journal of the American Medical Association*, 257 (24 June): 3387–3389.

Feder, Barnaby J. 1996. "A Study Finds Minors Buying More Cigarettes." *The New York Times*, February 16, p. A24.

Goldstein, Avram. 1994. *Addiction: From Biology to Drug Policy.* New York: W. H. Freeman.

Goldstein, Avram, and Harold Kalant. 1990. "Drug Policy: Striking the Right Balance." *Science*, vol. 249 (28 September): 1513–1521.

Grasmick, Harold G., Robert J. Bursik, Jr., and Bruce J. Arneklev. 1993. "Reductions in Drunk Driving as a Response to Increased Threats of Shame, Embarrassment, and Legal Sanctions." *Criminology*, 31 (February): 41–67.

Gravelle, Jane, and Dennis Zimmerman. 1994. "The Marlboro Math." *Washington Post*, June 5, pp. C1, C4.

HHS (U.S. Department of Health and Human Services). 1994b. *Annual Medical Examiner Data, 1992: Data from the Drug Abuse Warning Network (DAWN).* Rockville, Md.: Substance Abuse and Mental Health Services Administration, Office of Applied Studies.

HHS (U.S. Department of Health and Human Services). 1994d. *Preliminary Estimates from the Drug Abuse Warning Network: 1993 Preliminary Estimates of Drug-Related Emergency Department Episodes.* Rockville, Md.: Substance Abuse and Mental Health Services Administration, Office of Applied Studies.

HHS (U.S. Department of Health and Human Services). 1995b. *Annual Medical Examiner Data, 1993: Data from the Drug Abuse Warning Network (DAWN).* Rockville, Md.: Substance Abuse and Mental Health Services Administration, Office of Applied Studies.

Kaplan, John. 1988. "Taking Drugs Seriously." *The Public Interest*, no. 92, Summer, pp. 32–50.

Kleiman, Mark A. R. 1992b. *Against Excess: Drug Policy for Results.* New York: Basic Books.

Kolata, Gina. 1989. "Taxes Fail to Cover Drinking's Costs, Study Finds." *The New York Times*, March 17, p. A13.

Lee, Felicia R. 1994. "Data Show Needle Exchange Curbs H.I.V. Among Addicts." *The New York Times*, November 26, pp. 1, 26.

Maier, Thomas, and Timothy Yu. 1995. "AMA Demanding Tobacco Controls." *Newsday*, July 14, pp. A6, A30.

Manning, Willard G., et al. 1989. "The Taxes of Sin: Do Smokers and Drinkers Pay Their Way?" *Journal of the American Medical Association*, 261 (March 17): 1604–1609.

McCoy, Clyde B., and James A. Inciardi. 1995. *Sex, Drugs, and the Continuing Spread of AIDS.* Los Angeles: Roxbury.

Messenger, Ruth W. 1995. "New York Needs to Enforce the Tobacco Act." *The New York Times*, August 10, p. A18.

Nadelmann, Ethan A. 1989. "Drug Prohibition in the United States: Costs, Consequences, and Alternatives." *Science*, 245 (1 September): 939–947.

Trebach, Arnold S. 1993. "For Legalization of Drugs." In Arnold S. Trebach and James A. Inciardi, *Legalize It? Debating American Drug Policy.* Washington, D.C.: American University Press, pp. 7–138.

Viscusi, W. Kip. 1995. "Cigarette Taxation and the Social Consequences of Smoking." In James M. Poterba (ed.), *Tax Policy and the Economy.* Cambridge, Mass.: MIT Press, pp. 51–101.

Wilson, James Q. 1990a. "Against the Legalization of Drugs." *Commentary,* February, pp. 21–28.

Index